ANDREAS BODENSTEIN
VON KARLSTADT

# STUDIES
# IN MEDIEVAL AND
# REFORMATION THOUGHT

EDITED BY

HEIKO A. OBERMAN, Tübingen

IN COOPERATION WITH

E. JANE DEMPSEY DOUGLASS, Claremont, California
LEIF GRANE, Copenhagen
GUILLAUME H. M. POSTHUMES MEYJES, Leiden
ANTON G. WEILER, Nijmegen

VOLUME XI

**RONALD J. SIDER**

ANDREAS BODENSTEIN
VON KARLSTADT

LEIDEN
E. J. BRILL
1974

# ANDREAS BODENSTEIN VON KARLSTADT

## THE DEVELOPMENT OF HIS THOUGHT
### 1517-1525

BY

RONALD J. SIDER

LEIDEN
E. J. BRILL
1974

ISBN 90 04 03896 5

*To Arbutus*

# TABLE OF CONTENTS

# PREFACE

One of the important trends in more recent Reformation scholarship has been the extensive attention given the major "secondary" Reformers who aided and abetted—and sometimes challenged and infuriated—Luther, Zwingli, and Calvin. This book, which began as a doctoral dissertation at Yale University, is an attempt to elucidate the thought of one of the most important of these "Reformers in the Wings."

I am indebted to many people. Professor Roland H. Bainton first suggested that the Karlstadt material should be reexamined. Professor Jaroslav J. Pelikan directed the dissertation. Professors Hans J. Hillerbrand, Ernst Kähler, Steven Ozment, and Walter Klaassen answered epistolary queries at various times. Dr. Friedel Kriechbaum kindly sent a microfilm of her then unpublished dissertation. To Dr. Ulrich Bubenheimer who added precision to my translations from the German, I owe a special debt of gratitude. A stimulating week spent in Professor Heiko Oberman's seminar on "Luther and Karlstadt" at the Fourth International Congress on Luther Research in 1971 added to my understanding of Karlstadt. Professor Arthur Carl Piepkorn transcribed a handwritten letter.

An almost equally difficult and exceedingly more extensive task of transcription was done by the only typist capable of deciphering my original handwritten text, my wife Arbutus, to whom this dissertation is affectionately dedicated. To her and to Ted (whose introduction to academic pursuits came at the tender age of 5 months as he sat on my desk daily and watched me turn the pages of Professor Barge's learned tomes) and Michael (whose charming smile can revive even the most weary scholar), I owe a debt of gratitude which cannot be repaid in scholarly prefaces.

Messiah College Campus                               RONALD J. SIDER
at Temple University

# ABBREVIATIONS *

| | |
|---|---|
| *ARG* | *Archiv für Reformationsgeschichte* |
| *CH* | *Church History* |
| *De sp.*, Kähler | Kähler, Ernst. *Karlstadt und Augustin: Der Kommentar des Andreas Bodenstein von Karlstadt zu Augustins Schrift De Spiritu et Litera.* Halle: Max Niemeyer, 1952. |
| *FG* | Barge, Hermann. *Frühprotestantisches Gemeindechristentum in Wittenberg und Orlamünde.* Leipzig: M. Heinsius Nachfolger, 1909. |
| Gerdes | Gerdes, Daniel, ed. *Scrinium Antiquarium sive Miscellanea Groningana Nova.* . . . 8 vols. Groningen and Bremen: Hajo Spandaw and G. W. Rump, n.d. [c. 1750]-1765. |
| *GGA* | A review article by Walther Köhler in *Göttingische gelehrte Anzeigen*, CLXXIV (1912), 505-550. |
| Greving | Greving, Joseph, ed. *Johannes Eck: Defensio Contra Amarulentas D. Andreae Bodenstein Carolstatini Invectiones* (1518). Münster: Aschendorffsche Verlagsbuchhandlung, 1919. |
| Hase | Hase, E. "Karlstadt in Orlamünda," *Mitteilungen der Geschichts- und Altertumsforschende Gesellschaft des Osterlandes*, IV (1858), 42-125. |
| Hertzsch I, II | Hertzsch, Erich, ed. *Karlstadts Schriften aus den Jahren 1523-1525.* 2 vols. Halle (Saale): Max Niemeyer, 1956-1957. |
| *JTS* | *Journal of Theological Studies* |
| *LuK* | Müller, Karl. *Luther und Karlstadt.* Tübingen: J. C. B. Mohr, 1907. |
| *LW* | Luther, Martin. *Luther's Works.* Ed. H. T. Lehmann and J. J. Pelikan. 55 vols. Philadelphia: Muhlenberg Press, 1955 ff. |
| *MQR* | *Mennonite Quarterly Review* |
| Verzeichnis | Barge, H. and E. Freys. "Verzeichnis der gedruckten Schriften des Andreas Bodenstein von Karlstadt," *Zentralblatt für Bibliothekswesen*, XXI (1904), 153-179, 209-243, 305-323. |
| *WA* | Luther, Martin. *D. Martin Luthers Werke.* Weimar: Hermann Böhlau, 1883 ff. |
| *WABr* | *Weimarer Ausgabe, Briefe.* |
| *WB* | Müller, Nikolaus. *Die Wittenberger Bewegung 1521 und 1522.* 2nd ed. Leipzig: M. Heinsius Nachfolger, 1911. |
| *ZKG* | *Zeitschrift für Kirchengeschichte* |
| *ZST* | *Zeitschrift für systematische Theologie* |
| *ZTK* | *Zeitschrift für Theologie und Kirche* |

---

*For the abbreviations of Karlstadt's writings see the first part of the bibliography.

# INTRODUCTION

Andreas Bodenstein von Karlstadt (c. 1480-1541) was a friend and ally—and then a bitter enemy—of the great reformer of Wittenberg. In 1512 he promoted Luther to the doctorate. Five years later at Luther's prodding, he abandoned his attachment to scholasticism and became an effective and leading polemicist for Luther during the next four years. It was Karlstadt whom Eck first challenged to the Leipzig debate. His leading role in the occasionally violent Wittenberg Movement of late 1521 and early 1522, however, led to his disgrace. Unhappy with Luther's demand for gradual implementation of proposed ecclesiastical changes, Karlstadt moved to the important Saxon town of Orlamünde where he was able to introduce his more radical program of reform in 1523 and 1524. In 1524, by attacking Luther's doctrine of the Real Presence, Karlstadt initiated the important sacramentarian controversy of the 1520's and thus contributed to the division of Protestantism. The later years of his life he spent with the Swiss Reformers, teaching at the University of Basle and engaging in occasional controversy.

## 1. The State of Scholarship on Karlstadt

Not until the end of the nineteenth century did anyone seriously challenge Luther's depiction of Karlstadt as a legalistic, spiritualistic revolutionary.[1] In 1904 E. Freys and Hermann Barge published a list of all known printed editions of Karlstadt's works.[2] The following year Barge published a massive two volume biography,[3] the controversial thesis of which provoked an extended scholarly debate. Barge was concerned to prove that in new insights and innovations, originality and priority often lay with Karlstadt rather than with his more illustrious Wittenberg colleague. A Lutheran historian, Karl Müller, attacked Barge's book and defended Luther's originality.[4] Barge, in turn, attempted to defend his position in succeeding books and

---

[1] C. F. Jäger, *Andreas Bodenstein von Carlstadt* (Stuttgart, 1856) is perhaps the best of the older, "Lutheran" works on Karlstadt.

[2] "Verzeichnis der gedruckten Schriften des Andreas Bodenstein von Karlstadt," *Zentralblatt für Bibliothekswesen*, XXI (1904), 153-79, 209-43, 305-23. This work has recently been reprinted: Nieuwkoop, 1965.

[3] *Andreas Bodenstein von Karlstadt* (2 vols.; Leipzig, 1905).

[4] *Luther und Karlstadt : Stücke aus ihrem gegenseitigen Verhältnis* (Tübingen, 1907).

articles.[5] In 1912 Walter Köhler wrote a lengthy article on the Barge-Müller debate and concluded that Müller was usually correct in defending the priority of Luther and the traditional critique of Karlstadt. Barge had been so blinded by love for his hero that he had idealized Karlstadt and belittled Luther.[6]

Erich Hertzsch produced the next important work on Karlstadt in 1932.[7] He deplored the fact that Luther and then Lutherans had misunderstood and rejected Karlstadt's commendable theology which would have been an excellent corrective to Luther's allegedly one-sided emphasis on *sola fide*. Even Barge had accepted Luther's picture of Karlstadt. Barge had merely said that Karlstadt, as depicted by Luther, was more interesting than Luther.[8] Hertzsch then proceeded to deny that Karlstadt was a mystic, a legalist, or a *Schwärmer*. In 1952 Ernst Kähler published an introduction and notes to Karlstadt's commentary on Augustine's *De spiritu et litera*. Kähler thought this commentary, which shows Karlstadt's great debt to Augustine, was a key to the understanding of his later development. He showed that Barge not only used this commentary very little, but also misunderstood it because he was not certain what represented Karlstadt's and what Augustine's views.[9] Gerhard Fuchs published a suggestive Marxist interpretation of Karlstadt in an article in the early fifties.[10]

Recently, widespread interest in Karlstadt has developed. A number of articles have appeared.[11] Friedel Kriechbaum has published a

---

[5] "Die älteste evangelische Armenordnung," *Historische Vierteljahrsschrift*, XI (1908), 193-225; *Frühprotestantisches Gemeindechristentum in Wittenberg und Orlamünde: Zugleich eine Abwehr gegen Karl Müllers "Luther und Karlstadt"* (Leipzig, 1909); "Der Streit über die Grundlagen der religiösen Erneuerung in der Kontroverse zwischen Luther und Karlstadt," *Studium Lipsiense*, 1909, 192-213; *Aktenstücke zur Wittenberger Bewegung Anfang 1522* (Leipzig, 1912).

[6] *Göttingische gelehrte Anzeigen*, CLXXIV (1912), 505-50.

[7] *Karlstadt und seine Bedeutung für das Luthertum* (Gotha, 1932).

[8] *Ibid.*, p. 20. Twenty years later, Hertzsch published an article on Karlstadt: "Luther und Karlstadt," *Luther in Thüringen*, ed. Reinhold Jauernig (Berlin, 1952), pp. 87-107. Subsequently he also edited a collection of Karlstadt's works: *Karlstadts Schriften aus den Jahren 1523-25* ("Neudrucke deutscher Literaturwerke des 16. und 17. Jahrhunderts," No. 325); 2 vols.; Halle, 1956-57.

[9] Ernst Kähler, *Karlstadt und Augustin* (Halle, 1952), p. 2*. The same year, Kähler published a short article: "Karlstadts Protest gegen die theologische Wissenschaft," *450 Jahre Martin-Luther-Universität Halle-Wittenberg*, Volume I: *Wittenberg 1502-1817* (Halle-Wittenberg, 1952), pp. 299-312.

[10] "Karlstadts radikal-reformatorisches Wirken und seine Stellung zwischen Müntzer und Luther," *Wissenschaftliche Zeitschrift der Martin-Luther-Universität Halle-Wittenberg*, III (1953-54), 523-551.

[11] Gordon Rupp, "Andrew Karlstadt and Reformation Puritanism," *JTS*, X (1959), 308-26. A more recent, revised and considerably expanded version of this

monograph in which she sets out to interpret Karlstadt independently of Luther. The author herself states, however, that this approach will not involve a weakening of the traditional evaluation of Karlstadt.[12] Clearly, present Reformation scholarship is concerned with Karlstadt.[13]

Unfortunately at least as much contradiction as consensus has resulted from the seventy years of scholarship just surveyed. In 1932 Hertzsch noted that in spite of Barge's fundamental work, the thought world of Karlstadt was still confused and unclear.[14] Kähler began his introduction with a similar admission: "For some time it has been a more or less open secret among Reformation historians that, in spite of the work of the last decades on Karlstadt's history and theology, . . . the real key to the understanding of his theology and also his activity had not been found." [15] Kähler thought he had discovered the key in Karlstadt's relation to Augustine. But there seems to be no consensus yet about any such master key. Indeed a survey of the literature

article has recently appeared in Gordon Rupp, *Patterns of Reformation* (Philadelphia, 1969), pp. 49-153. Robert Stupperich, ed., "Karlstadts Sabbat-Traktat von 1524," *NZST*, I (1959), 349-75. Hans J. Hillerbrand, "Andreas Bodenstein of Carlstadt," *CH*, XXXV (1966), 379-98. Heiko A. Oberman, "Wittenbergs Zweifrontenkrieg gegen Prierias und Eck: Hintergrund und Entscheidungen des Jahres 1518," *ZKG*, LXXX (1969), 331-358. Ernst Kähler, "Nicht Luther, sondern Karlstadt," *ZKG*, LXXXII (1971), 351-360.

[12] "Diese verschiedenen Urteile wecken das Interesse, nach dem wahren Gehalt der Theologie Karlstadts zu fragen und dabei nicht mit den Augen Luthers an sie heranzugehen . . . . Die Ausführungen werden zeigen, dass dies nicht einer Erweichung der Fronten gleichkommt." Friedel Kriechbaum, *Grundzüge der Theologie Karlstadts* (Hamburg-Bergstedt, 1967), pp. 9-10. Unfortunately, Kriechbaum frequently draws her interpretative categories from Luther rather than Karlstadt. Her systematic approach also tends to obscure the development of Karlstadt's thought.

[13] Two doctoral dissertations should also be mentioned. In his "Consonantia Theologiae et Jurisprudentiae: Andreas Bodenstein von Karlstadt als Theologe und Jurist auf dem Weg von der Scholastik zur Reformation 1515-1522" (unpublished doctoral dissertation, Eberhard-Karls-Universität, Tübingen, 1971), Ulrich Bubenheimer makes a major contribution to our understanding of Karlstadt by examining the influence of the medieval legal tradition upon Karlstadt. Another strand of Karlstadt's thought is examined by Alden Lorne Thompson, "*Tertius Usus Legis* in the Theology of Andreas Bodenstein von Karlstadt" (unpublished Ph. D. dissertation, University of Southern California, 1969).

[14] "Die Gedankenwelt Karlstadts erscheint auch heute noch trotz Barges grundlegender Arbeit vielen als verworren und unklar." *Bedeutung*, p. 19.

[15] "Es war unter den Reformationsgeschichtlern seit geraumer Zeit ein mehr oder weniger offenes Geheimnis, dass trotz der Bemühungen um die Erkenntnis der Geschichte und Theologie Karlstadts, die die letzten Jahrzehnte gebracht hatten, und die vor allem mit der grossen Biographie Hermann Barges verbunden sind, der eigentliche Schlüssel zum Verständnis seiner Theologie, aber auch seines Handelns, noch nicht gefunden war." Kähler, *Karlstadt und Augustin*, p. 1*.

on Karlstadt reveals an amazing array of contradictory views apropos Karlstadt's alleged mysticism, legalism, spiritualism, and revolutionary inclinations.

Walter Köhler and Gordon Rupp were among those who found a strong mystical strain in Karlstadt. Indeed Köhler thought Karlstadt's whole originality lay in his combination of mystical ideas with views obtained from Luther.[16] Contra Barge, Rupp believed that mysticism had a great influence on Karlstadt.[17] Barge had tried to show that although Karlstadt used a number of mystical terms, he nevertheless was not deeply influenced by them.[18] Stupperich charged that Barge belittled the mystics' influence in order to assert Karlstadt's independence and originality.[19] Hertzsch, however, also denied that the mystics deeply affected Karlstadt's thinking.[20] Thus the extent and nature of Karlstadt's mysticism is problematic.

Equally contradictory are the views about Karlstadt's "legalism." Köhler perceived an obvious "legalism" which Barge missed only because of his idealization of his hero. Karlstadt's "legalism" was so strong that Luther's charge that Karlstadt had fallen back into medieval works-righteousness was justified.[21] According to Hertzsch's definition of "legalism," on the other hand, Karlstadt was by no means a "legalist." He believed *sola fide* as much as Luther, but had less fear that ethical encouragement would endanger justification by faith alone.[22] Clearly great care will need to be exercised in the definition and use of this epithet.

In his elaborate classification of the Radical Reformation, George H. Williams called Karlstadt a "revolutionary spiritualist," [23] which

---

[16] "Das Alles ist ganz klar; die Schwierigkeit hebt erst an bei der eigenartigen Verbindung der mystischen Gedankengänge mit den reformatorisch-Lutherschen. Denn K.s. *ganze Originalität beruht auf der Verbindung von Lutherscher und mystischer Religionsauffassung . . .*" (Köhler's italics). *GGA*, p. 546.

[17] "*Karlstadt*," p. 312.

[18] E.g. *Karlstadt*, II, 25, 75.

[19] "Karlstadts Sabbat-Traktat," p. 370.

[20] Hertzsch I, XVI.

[21] "Es war darum nicht unrichtig empfunden, wenn Luther das Wesen der K.schen Theologie in einem Rückfall in alttestamentliche mittelalterliche Werkgerechtigkeit setzte." *GGA*, pp. 547-9. Rupp, "Karlstadt," p. 511 also speaks of "legalism."

[22] Hertzsch, *Bedeutung*, pp. 21-4, 45.

[23] *Spiritual and Anabaptist Writers* (Philadelphia, 1957), p. 32. Williams reaffirmed the validity of this label more recently. George H. Williams, "Sanctification in the Testimony of Several So-Called Schwärmer," *Kirche, Mystik, Heiligung und das Natürliche bei Luther*, ed. Ivar Asheim (Göttingen, 1967), p. 195.

certainly captures part of the meaning of Luther's term, "Schwärmer."
Rupp agreed that Karlstadt was a spiritualist, but denied that he was a
revolutionary.[24] Hertzsch denied both accusations.[25] It seems reasonable to conclude from this summary of the literature on Karlstadt that
our understanding of his thought and work is still somewhat unclear.

Research and documents published since Barge wrote will greatly
facilitate a reassessment of Karlstadt. One reason for Barge's exaggeration of Karlstadt's theological originality was the fact that Luther's
Romans lectures were still not available in 1904. The recent work on
late medieval thought and theology will facilitate the tracing of
Karlstadt's theological development in his earlier publications. Similarly, the Luther research of the past several decades will contribute to
a more accurate picture of Luther's influence on Karlstadt. When
Barge wrote, scholarly study of the German mystics was just beginning. The past half-century of work on German mysticism will enable
one to determine more accurately the nature and extent of Karlstadt's
mysticism. Subsequently published collections of documents and a few
as yet unused documents will contribute to the solution of a few
biographical problems.

Both Gordon Rupp and Hans J. Hillerbrand have called for further
study of Karlstadt's theology. Rupp suggests that Karlstadt's importance has been obscured not only by the more virulent originality of
Müntzer, but also by the "lack of any real theological interpretation in
monograph form of his theology." [26] Hillerbrand refers to the same
deficiency:

> It is regrettable that no definitive study of Carlstadt's thought is
> available. Reformation scholarship has by and large ignored Carlstadt.
> . . . Particularly in connection with the rise of the Radical Reformation,
> Carlstadt's role is a significant one which has hitherto been consider-
> ably underestimated.[27]

This study hopes to meet this need by tracing the development of
Karlstadt's theological thought.

It is not true as Jäger has said that every writing of Karlstadt was
different and consequently Karlstadt had no systematic theology.[28]

---

[24] Rupp, "Karlstadt," pp. 311, 323.
[25] *Bedeutung*, pp. 25-34, 60-6.
[26] Rupp, "Word and Spirit in the First Years of the Reformation," *ARG*,
XLIX (1958), 18-9.
[27] Hans J. Hillerbrand, "The Origins of Sixteenth-Century Anabaptism:
Another Look," *ARG*, LIII (1962), 162.
[28] Jäger, *Carlstadt*, p. v.

Chapters one, four and seven below are a sufficient refutation. Therefore, rather than describe Karlstadt's theology publication by publication, as to a large degree Barge did, a systematic outline of Karlstadt's theology will be provided. It is true, however, that Karlstadt's theological outlook developed rapidly, especially in the period from 1517 to 1521. One of the weaknesses of some treatments of Karlstadt's theology has been the tendency to treat the period from 1517 to 1521 as a unit. In order to do justice both to the development and the systematic character of Karlstadt's thought, his theology will be outlined systematically at three different significant periods of his theological development. Hopefully both the continuity and the change will become evident.

Since Karlstadt's thought was shaped both by the intellectual influences which played upon him and also by the experiences of his life, both will need to be examined, although the focus will be upon the former. Kähler's suggestion, which he did not elaborate in detail, that Augustine is the key to Karlstadt's theological development must be tested.[29] Without being unduly preoccupied with Luther,[30] Luther's influence must also be traced, and, *pace* Barge, acknowledged. A third important influence to be examined is German mysticism. It has been noted recently that "the relation between medieval mysticism and the theology of the Reformation has not yet been clarified in present-day research." [31] This study will help illuminate one aspect of this relationship by examining the extent to which Karlstadt borrowed not only language, but also important ideas from the German mystics. The examination of the interplay of Augustininan, Lutheran, and mystical theological concepts will constitute the major focus of this work. It is hoped that the tracing of these and other influences against the backdrop of events in Saxony through 1524 will make Karlstadt's life and thought less puzzling to Reformation scholars.

## 2. The Early Years (c. 1480-1516)

As his most commonly used name indicates, Andreas Bodenstein was born in Karlstadt, a small town on the Main River not too far from Würzburg. His family, apparently, had a respected position in

---

[29]  Kähler, *Karlstadt und Augustin*, p. 45*.

[30]  Jaroslav J. Pelikan suggested in his review of Ernst Kähler's *Karlstadt und Augustin* that Kähler's book still suffered from this tendency. *ARG*, XLV (1954), 268.

[31]  Bengt Hägglund, "The Background of Luther's Doctrine of Justification in Late Medieval Theology," *Lutheran World*, VIII (1961), 25.

the town. A certain Peter Bodenstein, who quite possibly was his father, was burgomaster in 1481 and the head of the brotherhood of St. Urban in the parish church in 1485.[32] The date of his birth is uncertain. Since he entered the University of Erfurt in the winter semester of 1499-1500,[33] whereas Martin Luther entered in May, 1501,[34] it is quite possible that he was slightly older than Luther who was very probably born in 1483.

Karlstadt's studies in the liberal arts took place at three universities: Erfurt, Cologne, and Wittenberg. At Erfurt Karlstadt must have followed the traditional scholastic course of studies, for humanism had penetrated the university only superficially and sporadically.[35] Very probably he listened to the lectures on logic of Dr. Judocus Trutvetter, a leader of the *via moderna*, whom he was to replace at Wittenberg a decade later. Sometime after obtaining his bachelor of arts degree in 1502 at Erfurt, Karlstadt moved to Cologne where he registered in the University on June 17, 1503.[36] At Cologne Karlstadt probably lived at a center of Thomistic studies (the *Bursa montis*) reorganized while he was there by Valentin Engelhart; in his second publication Karlstadt spoke of "the many distinguished Thomists of the *Bursa montis*, my Cologne teachers, among whom is the extraordinary Valentinus Engelhart de Geltershaym." [37] Apparently this representative of rigid Thomistic orthodoxy impressed Karlstadt temporarily, although by the time of the Reuchlin affair when Engelhart was satirized in *Letters of Obscure Men*,[38] Karlstadt, as will be seen, sided with the humanists. Karlstadt became a Thomist at Cologne, but he did not stay to take his master's degree. Instead, he transferred to Frederick the Wise's new university at Wittenberg and received the degree there on August 12, 1505.[39]

---

[32] J. Hoernes, *Kurze historisch-topographische Beschreibung der Karlsburg und der Stadt Karlstadt* (Karlstadt a. M., 1898), pp. 74, 163.

[33] J. C. Hermann Weissenborn, ed., *Acten der Erfurter Universität* (3 vols.; Halle, 1881-1899), II, 212.

[34] *Ibid.*, p. 219.

[35] Robert H. Fife, *The Revolt of Martin Luther* (New York, 1957), pp. 39-65, especially p. 52.

[36] Gustav Bauch, "Andreas Carlstadt als Scholastiker," *ZKG*, XVIII (1897), 37.

[37] *Distinctiones Thomistarum*, N (Verzeichnis, No. 2): "Circa illam materiam dicunt multi egregii Thomiste de Bursa montis preceptores mei Colonienses, inter quos non modicus extat Valentinus Engelhart de Geltershaym."

[38] Letter No. 7; Francis G. Stokes, trans., *On the Eve of the Reformation : "Letters of Obscure Men"* (New York, 1964), p. 17.

[39] J. Köstlin, *Die Baccalaurei und Magistri der Wittenberger philos. Fakultät*, p. 12; *Karlstadt*, I, 8, n. 29.

Karlstadt quickly attracted attention as a young professor in the
arts faculty. Less than two years after completing his second degree, he
published a tolerably competent popularization of Thomist logic
called *De intentionibus*.[40] The importance of the book consists chiefly
in the fact that it was the first original work published by any professor
at the new university of Wittenberg.[41] The work's mediocrity,
however, did not preclude appreciation and reward from the young
university. Karlstadt was chosen dean of the arts faculty for the
winter semester, 1507-1508.[42] In December, 1507 Karlstadt finished
a second work on logical problems called *Distinctiones Thomistarum*.
Exaggerated praise followed quickly. In a public speech at All Saints
on November 15, 1508, Christoph Scheurl, a professor of law at
Wittenberg, lauded Karlstadt most highly for his two writings.
Karlstadt is great as a philosopher, greater as a theologian and greatest
as a Thomist. "If we had a lot of Karlstadts, I think we could easily
engage and be a match for the Parisians." [43] Although one must
partially discount these words as official praise, they indicate nonetheless that the young professor's publications on logic had given him a
position of honor at Wittenberg.

Philosophy, however, was not Karlstadt's sole concern. By the
winter semester of 1507-1508 already, he had obtained his bachelor's
in theology. In 1508-1509 he was granted the intermediate theological
degrees and then on November 13, 1510, he obtained a doctorate in
theology.[44] The medieval love of pomp and circumstance received full
rein at doctoral promotions. After witty speeches, lively debates and
long solemn oaths, the new doctor of theology was presented with
a Bible and the silver doctor's ring. At the end of the proceedings,
Karlstadt gave a splendid party.

Perhaps the granting of Karlstadt's doctorate was accelerated in

---

[40] It was completed on August 10, 1507; see Verzeichnis, No. 1.
[41] Bauch, "Carlstadt als Scholastiker," p. 45, n. 2.
[42] Köstlin, *Baccalaurei und Magistri*, p. 8. Karlstadt was already "sacrae theologiae baccalaureus."
[43] "Qualem etiam nominavimus Andream Bodenstenum Carolstatinum, virum
latine, graece et hebraice vehementer eruditum, magnum philosophum, maiorem
theologum, maximum Thomistam, quod facile ostendunt monumenta sua, quae in
laudem gymnasii nostri de intentionibus et formalitatibus thomisticis edidit. . . .
Quod si multos Carolstadios haberemus, facile, puto, nos cum Parisiensibus
manum posse conserere atque pedem conferre." Quoted in Bauch, "Carlstadt als
Scholastiker," p. 49.
[44] Karl E. Förstemann, ed., *Liber decanorum facultatis theologicae academiae
Vitebergensis* (Leipzig, 1838), pp. 3, 4, 8, 9.

order to make him eligible for the position vacated by Trutvetter
whose nominalism had been unwelcome since he moved to Wittenberg about the beginning of 1507.[45] Fortunately for Karlstadt,
Martin Polich von Mellerstadt, one of the most influential professors
at Wittenberg and a zealous adherent of Aquinas moved quickly to
have his young Thomist supporter, Karlstadt, installed in Trutvetter's place as archdeacon of All Saints, a position which involved
responsibilities in both the university and the church of All Saints.[46]

As archdeacon of All Saints, the church where the Elector's
precious relics were stored, Karlstadt acquired both new duties and
new influence. His tasks in the church included responsibility for the
preaching at All Saints, the celebration of mass on certain feast days
and the reading of at least two other masses per week.[47] Both his
frequent public sermons and his style of living made possible by the
fact that he possessed the second highest income among the sixty-
four clerics at All Saints must have made him a well-known citizen of
the town. In the university, too, Karlstadt's prominence increased.
In the theological faculty where he now lectured, he served as dean for
eight terms beginning in 1512.[48] As a leading member of the theological faculty he was Martin Luther's "promotor," and gave him his
doctorate.[49]

That Karlstadt was a professor of some stature at Wittenberg can
be seen from the report of a young humanist who visited several
universities in 1514 and described the persons at Leipzig, Frankfurt
and Wittenberg whom he considered noteworthy. There is not a word
about Luther. But Karlstadt receives flowery praise. He is experienced in holy scripture and very learned in both canon law and Aristo-

---

[45] Although Trutvetter left Wittenberg in 1510, he did not formally resign
until 1511. See Ulrich Bubenheimer's correction of Barge's dating, "Consonantia
Theologiae et Jurisprudentiae," p. 15, n. 1.

[46] Walter Friedensburg, *Geschichte der Universität Wittenberg*, pp. 10-14, 46,
52-53.

[47] In *Karlstadt*, II, 525-529 Barge has printed a document giving the regulations
of the foundation. For Karlstadt's income see *ibid*, p. 530.

[48] The summer semesters of 1512, 1514, 1516, 1518, 1520, 1521, and the winter
semester of 1522-3. Förstemann, ed., *Liber decanorum*, pp. 11, 15, 18-9, 21, 23, 25,
27, 28. He also filled in as dean for part of the winter semester of 1516-7 (p. 20).

[49] Historians have confused Karlstadt's exact role in the ceremonies. Some have
linked his role in the proceedings with the fact that he was dean in 1512. Actually
Karlstadt probably surrendered the insignia of the deanship a few hours before
he initiated the doctoral ceremonies as Luther's "promotor." See my article,
"Karlstadt and Luther's Doctorate," *Journal of Theological Studies*," N. S., XXII
(1971), 168-9.

telian philosophy. Indeed, he is "a very famous philosopher, orator, poet and theologian." Learned in the biblical languages, a keen debater, and "a particularly alert disciple of Thomas as well as Scotus," "he has written many works through which he has made his memory almost immortal among us." The young humanist also indicated that Karlstadt had a keen interest in both canon and secular law.[50] Although one must discount the typical humanist superlatives, there is little reason to doubt the assertion that Karlstadt was a prominent member of the Wittenberg faculty.

The wandering humanist may have been attracted by Karlstadt's superficial bows to the intellectual fashion of the day. Both his writings on problems of scholastic logic had contained humanistic references. On the title page of his first work, *De intentionibus*, he referred to the goddess of wisdom by her Greek and Latin names and declared that what his book offered had been given by "Thomas and the heavenly Apollo." He concluded his second book with a poem in Sapphic verse in honor of the Elector.[51] In a letter of 1514 Karlstadt turned his back on his conservative Cologne teachers and strongly supported Reuchlin in the great *cause célèbre* of the humanists. Reuchlin may prove to have made occasional mistakes, but the famous Phoebus of Germany certainly is not to be condemned as a heretic.[52] These

---

[50] *Scriptorum insignium qui in celeberrimis praesertim Lipsiensi, Wittenbergensi, Francofordiana ad Oderam academiis a fundatione ipsarum usque ad annum Christi 1515 floruerunt centuria...*, ed. Joach. Joh. Mader (Helmstedt, 1660), fol G3af; see also J. F. L. Th. Merzdorf's edition (Leipzig, 1839), pp. 82-3. "Andreas Bodenstein ... vir in divinis scripturis eruditus, et tam in iure Canonico quam in Philosophia Aristotelica valde doctus: Philosophus, Orator, Poeta nec non Theologus plurimum famigeratus. Ingenio subtilis ac vehemens, clarusque eloquio, Hebraicarum, Graecarum, Latinarumque literarum non ignarus, Dialecticus disputator acerrimus, Thomae pariter et Scoti sectator vigilantissimus. ... Scripsit multa insignia opuscula, quibus memoriam nobis sui (ut ita dicam) reddidit immortalem. ... Comportavit insuper novas concordantias seu convenientias ad forum contentiosum pertinentes, iuris tam Canonici quam civilis et Doctorum Scholasticorum S. Thomae et subtilissimi Scoti." An increasing Scotist influence is certain for Karlstadt was lecturing regularly on Scotus: "... exposuit quotidie una hora in conventu Minorum legens Doctorem subtilissimum per eundem Doctorem, i.e. Scotum per Scotum." *Ibid.* See further Karlstadt's comment in n. 66 below.

[51] Barge (*Karlstadt*, I, 28) thinks his mastery of classical latin was about as good as that of the average humanist.

[52] Karlstadt to Spalatin, February 13 (not 23 as in *Karlstadt*, I, 47) 1514 printed in Johann Friedrich Heckel, *Manipulus primus epistolarum singularium, ab heroibus inclutis ac viris illustribus* (1695), pp. 17-20. "Quod tua eruditio, *dulcissime Magister*, petierit, ut una tam Librum praeclarissimi Germaniae Phoebi, et totius reipublicae litterariae adjutoris, Dn. Joannis Reuchlins, viri egregii et eximii et nostri amici maximi ... quam meam vilissimam sententiam remitterem, utrumque mihi facile

incidents, of course, by no means prove that humanism had exercised more than a superficial influence upon our Thomist scholastic. What they do suggest, however, is that he liked to think of himself as a follower not only of the angelic doctor but also of the celestial Apollo.[53]

Karlstadt's humanism was not sufficient to prevent his requesting permission from the university to make a pilgrimage to Rome in 1515. His ostensible purpose was to fulfil a vow made some five years earlier when thieves had mugged and robbed him.[54] Apparently it was common knowledge, however, that he hoped to secure a quick doctorate of both laws in Italy, for the rector of the university recommended to the Elector that he be allowed to go only on condition that he arrange for a substitute, stay only four months, and not attend lectures on civil law. The Elector agreed to these provisions.[55] Dismayed with these stipulations, Karlstadt went to talk with the Elector. He apparently obtained Frederick's permission to stay longer and study law. But he disobeyed instructions both by failing to get a replacement and by omitting to secure the approval of the university and chapter.[56] Consequently, when he returned sporting a doctorate

---

est explere cum Liber ille majoris virtutis quam quantitatis, praesto sit, et in eo nihil non magnum, non eruditum, si modo lector tam verborum quam sententiarum ἐνέργειαν justo libraverit examine, reperiendum, quod, quantum intelligo, sacris obsit oraculis, et quod sanctorum decretis a Sacro-Sancta Romana Ecclesia approbatis adversetur. . . . Esto, illum communia aliqua futuris per Ecclesiae disterminationem temporibus rejicienda conscripsisse; attamen catholica sua protestatio salvabit eum, et omnis criminis reddet immunem."

[53] This conclusion corresponds with Karl Bauer's evaluation of the general situation at Wittenberg in the early years: "Die vorherrschende Richtung war in der ersten Zeit durchaus die Scholastik, neben der der Humanismus zunächst einen ziemlich bescheidenen Platz einnahm." *Die Wittenberger Universitätstheologie und die Anfänge der Deutschen Reformation* (Tübingen, 1928), p. 4.

[54] Karlstadt's formal request to the University for permission to make the pilgrimage is printed in J. J. Müller, *Entdecktes Staatscabinet darinnen so wohl das jus publicum, feudale, und ecclesiasticum . . . illustriret wird*, zweite Eröffnung (Jena, 1714), pp. 318-319. "Clarissimi Patres et Dom. Preceptores, annus iam agitur quintus, cum in Vigilia sancti Marci Evangeliste premitias Dei ope celebraturus patriam versus proficiscebar, prope villam . . . ex latere cuiusdam montis illic siti, quo itinere ducente equitabam, tres equites armatis impositis hastis et quartus balista, omnes quidem bellicis instructi munimentis, incurrentibus equis, me hostiliter aggressi sunt, et nec quidem interrogatu, ex sella et equo excussum in terram seminortuum deiectarunt. . . . Ideoque Deum, omnium adiutorem, in sanctis Petro et Paulo apostolis invocavi, votumque feci, quod si eorum ope ob illatis angustiis eximerer, et irrogatis infirmitatibus restituerer, commoditate data, me ipsum velle eis sacrificium offerre in urbe Romana."

[55] The rector's letter to the Elector and the latter's reply are in *ibid.*, pp. 323-326.

[56] See the letter of the Chapter of All Saints to the Elector (no date, but probably late in 1515): "Erleubt Im die Universität vier Monden, also dass er

in both laws from Rome,[57] the chapter refused to allow him to collect
the income which had accrued during his absence.[58] While Karlstadt
fumed and appealed to the Elector, the provost at All Saints threatened to imprison him.[59] Unfortunately we do not know how a settle-
ment was reached, except that a year later Provost Göde informed the
Elector that he had never had anything against Karlstadt's person.
In the dispute with his archdeacon he had merely wanted to maintain
the rights of the chapter.[60]

Another otherwise minor dispute is equally illustrative of our
canon's exasperating and volatile personality.[61] In 1515 when the

darinnen seine Wahlfahrt volbrechte, und sich wieder allher in die Residenz
fügte.... Darauf ist Carlstadt hinweg und nach Torgau geritten, so ist gesagt
worden, er habe von Ew. Churf. G. Orlaub erlangt lenger, wan er gebeten habe,
derhalben wir geschwiegen und E. G. nichts davon geschrieben haben.... Er hat
aber alhie in der Kirchen den Predig-Stuel, noch sein Priesterlich Ampt, das ihne
auffgelegt ist auffn hohen Altar, nit bestalt, dorumb wir dem Prediger und auch
seinem Capellan ihren Soldt zu geben haben zusagen müssen, solten anders die
Göttlichen Ambt nit fallen..., so hat er auch in der Universität sein Lection in
der Theologia nit bestelt, anders dann, dass er den Augustiner Doct. Hergott nach
seinem Abziehen geschrieben hat, dass er vor In lesen wolte, welches er abge-
schlagen...." *Ibid.*, pp. 331-333. Contrary to George H. Williams, *The Radical
Reformation* (Philadelphia, 1962), p. 39, the Elector did not encourage Karlstadt's
studies and Karlstadt did not become provost after returning from Italy.

[57] Barge (*Karlstadt*, I, 52, n. 54) argued that Karlstadt took his degree in Siena,
but Bubenheimer has shown that he received the doctorate in Rome ("Consonantia Theologiae et Jurisprudentiae," 41ff). Bubenheimer's important work shows
how significant was Karlstadt's early interest in jurisprudence.

[58] Weimarer Archiv Reg. N No. 624, cited in *Karlstadt*, I, 54, n. 58.

[59] Karlstadt to the Elector, no date, but certainly the summer of 1516: "Gnedigster Churfürst und Her. Ich bin verstendigt und wais eigentlich, das der Probst
zcu Wittenbergk, der mir die andern abgunstig gemacht und mit ynen meyn
pension zcu Orlamünde zcu inen genommen und sich trewlicher wordt hat lassen
vernehmen, mich gefengklich zcu seczen....

'So E.C.G.... dem Capittel schrieben, alsso das E.C.G. die irrunge und
sperre, sso sich czwischen dem Capittel ader Probst eynes, und mir anders teyls
hielten, zcu erkennen vorbehalten." E. Hase, "Karlstadt in Orlamünda," *Mitteilungen der Geschichts-und Altertumsforschende Gesellschaft des Osterlandes*, IV (1858),
86-7.

[60] Göde to the Elector, May 16, 1517, Weimarer Archiv Reg. O No. 209 f. 92,
cited in *Karlstadt*, I, 64. Barge is wrong, however, in arguing that the theological
faculty's selection of Karlstadt immediately after his return as dean for the summer
of 1516 "war eine ostentative Vertrauenskundgebung, durch welche die theologischen Kollegen Karlstadts an der Universität für ihn und gegen das Kapitel
Partei ergriffen" (*ibid.*, p. 55). In fact, the office rotated (Friedensburg, *Universität
Wittenberg*, p. 36), and it was Karlstadt's turn. As the references in n. 48 show,
Karlstadt was dean every other summer from 1512 to 1520.

[61] The Chapter at All Saints to the Elector, no date (almost certainly late 1515):
"Erstlich E. G. Schösser alhie genanten Doctor vor Probst und Capitel umb
zwelff Gülden vor Hauss-Zinss angeklaget, und als der Doctor In wiederum vorm

Wittenberg tax collector charged Karlstadt with failure to pay twelve gulden in taxes, Karlstadt agreed, but insisted that the official also owed him three gulden for a load of hay which the official had wrongly sold. It was agreed that the chapter would estimate the value of Karlstadt's hay. But when the chapter decided the official owed only two-and-a-half gulden for the hay, Karlstadt appealed to the Pope!

What kind of man would appeal to the Pope for half a gulden? Unfortunately most of the evidence necessary for an examination of Karlstadt's psyche is lacking. Hence speculation must remain very tentative. Two brief descriptions of his physical appearance, however, may provide a clue. A few months after the Leipzig debate, the humanist Peter Mosellanus jotted down his impression of the three combatants. Luther had obviously impressed him greatly. "He plays the man at all seasons." Karlstadt by contrast was not attractive: "He is shorter, his face dark and burned, his voice thick and unpleasant, his memory weaker and his anger more prompt." [62] Another contemporary spoke of Karlstadt's "repulsive, unbearded face." [63] Hertzsch has suggested that one might legitimately infer that Karlstadt suffered from an inferiority complex.[64]

Although the thought of categorizing a personality on the basis of two brief descriptions might give pause even to Erik Erikson,[65] it is nonetheless interesting to see how many of the more unpleasant aspects of Karlstadt's personality and action seem more understandable when viewed as compensation for an inner sense of inferiority.

---

Dechant und Capittel umb ein Fuder Haus angesprochen, so er Im verkaufft, und das Hau auf drey Gülden angeschlagen, dem Schösser auch die 12 fl. vor Haus-Miede bekant und wiederum den Schösser Im das Fuder Haues, und die Wiederung aufs Capittel gestelt, haben wir auf solch beeder Teil Bekentnüs erkant, dass der Doctor dem Schösser solche 12 fl. als er Im bekentlich gewesen, solt geben, also dass ihme doran drittehalb Gülden vor das Hau abginge, davon hat Karlstadt appellirt an Päbstliche Heiligkeit . . . ." Müller, *Entdecktes Staatscabinet*, p. 330.

[62] "Haec pleraque omnia in Carolostadio paulo minora deprehendas; Nisi quod huic statura est brevior, facies autem nigricans et adusta: Vox obscura et inamoena, memoria infirmior et ad iracundiam promtior." Mosellanus to J. Pflug, December 7, 1519; V. E. Löscher, *Vollständige Reformations - Acta und Documenta* (3 vols.; Leipzig, 1720-1729), III, 248. See the translation of Preserved Smith, ed., *Luther's Correspondence and Other Contemporary Letters* (2 vols.; Philadelphia, 1913-18), I, 261.

[63] Cochläus, *Ein christl. Vermahnung an Deutschland*, Fib; quoted in *Karlstadt*, I, 153, n. 67.

[64] "Luther und Karlstadt," *Luther in Thüringen*, ed. Jauernig, p. 90.

[65] See the review of Erik H. Erikson's *Young Man Luther* (New York, 1962) by Roland H. Bainton: "Psychiatry and History: An Examination of Erikson's "Young Man Luther," *Religion in Life*, XL (1971), 1-29.

If he was aware of the fact that others found him unattractive, he may very well have attempted to compensate by searching for tangible signs of status and acceptance. As a young teacher at Wittenberg he certainly was quick to seize the opportunity to receive recognition by publishing two scholastic treatises in rapid succession. Later, he confessed that his initial reluctance to follow Luther's rejection of scholasticism was due to the fact that he was proud of the still unpublished scholastic "commentariola" which other scholastic doctors had already praised.[66] The dean's book took special note of Karlstadt's doctoral celebration. Karlstadt took the opportunity to display his largesse by throwing a singularly expensive party.[67] Apparently he was not at all above seeking to impress people with his splendid clothes for when he was negotiating with the Elector apropos a return to Denmark in 1521, he demanded a loan for a damask (an expensive garment originally of Damascan silk). He also claimed he needed a coat which had to be either a black English one or crimson.[68] Nor, as has been noted, was he above scheming and defying the university

---

[66] "Disperiam [Kähler suggests dispeream] si amicus mihi quidem alioqui integerrimus non sepicule bilem moverat, cum me Sophistam nuncuparet, emoriar si non excandui; veruntamen inficias ire nequibam, quia sectam et Capreolinam et Scotisticam manifesta interpretatione successive profitebar. Accedebant mea commentariola non parvo congesta labore, tametsi nondum ediderim. Sed et erant testimonio scholasticorum doctorum libri, quos mihi clariores atque cumulaciores fecisse videbar. Veruntamen ut mihi et mundo stulticiam atque confusionem, deo autem sapientiam et justiciam deputem, ingenue fatear, ut Christiano decorum est, illa me vanitate invaluisse. . . . Cum itaque in huiuscemodi tenebris potius durescerem ac rigerem et delicias sub sentibus collocassem quam transversariis gressibus superbis affectibus atque lutulentis ambulaverim pedibus, potissime dum meo Marte recte vivere conabar, deus amplius me scit." *De sp., Kähler*, 3.17-4.13. Apropos the "commentariola," see above, n. 50.

[67] "Insuper doctor novellus de speciali benevolentia et liberalitate splendidum instituit et dedit prandium omnibus doctoribus superiorum facultatum una cum decano artium et aliquibus civibus ad hoc vocatis." Förstemann, *Liber decanorum*, p. 9. Cf. his comments in 1523 (below chapter VI, n. 17).

[68] "Weyl ich auch an geld und anderen beschätiget und got weiss, das ich nit so vermugen bin, das ich erlich zu konig. wirden magk komen, ist mein bith und will darauff ruhen.

"Das mir von dem capitel oder sunst von ymants eyn damastk mit eynem zimlichen futer aussgenumen und von dem geld, so mir von Michaelis kunfftig, dass negst volgende zustendig wurt, bezalt werd.

"Auch will ich einen schwartzen engelischen oder purpuranischen rock haben. . . ." Karlstadt to Spalatin (probably), c. June, 1521; Otto Waltz, "Epistolae Reformatorum I," *ZKG*, II (1878), 129. Much later, in 1525 he confessed that love of expensive clothes formerly caused him to sin: "Nu soll D. Luther dartzu wissen, das ich, Gott lob, einen grawen hab, gegen dem schmuck, der mich zeytten fast belusten thet, und zu sünden bracht." *Anzeig*, Hertzsch, II, 94.38-95.1. See further chapter VI, n. 19.

to secure the additional stature and benefit of an Italian doctorate of both laws.

A sense of inferiority and insecurity would also help explain Karlstadt's fiery temper. His first reaction was anger when young Martin presumed to challenge the authority and validity of the scholastics to whom he had devoted ten years of his life.[69] In his replies to Eck's post-Leipzig attack and mocking, he descended to such angry vituperation that he was ashamed to send his last book to Spalatin.[70] When his status or fame was threatened, he fought back desperately.

As will be seen in chapter one, anger and a challenge to do verbal battle were his first response to his younger colleague when Brother Martin began offering a new interpretation of St. Augustine. Fortunately for our professor's weak ego, he was oblivious at this time of the fact that his fellow theologian's fame would soon largely eclipse his own.

---

[69] See above, n. 66. The entire biographical section in *De sp.*, Kähler, pp. 3-5 reflects Karlstadt's initial frustration and anger.

[70] Karlstadt to Spalatin, about March, 1520. Daniel Gerdes, ed., *Scrinium Antiquarium sive Miscellanea Groningana Nova.* . . . (8 vols.; Groningen and Bremen, [c. 1750] - 1765), VII, 344-45. For the date, see Barge's comments (*Karlstadt*, I, 180 and 466-67).

# CHAPTER ONE

# THE ADOPTION OF AN AUGUSTINIAN THEOLOGY
## (1517-1518)

### 1. LUTHER AND STAUPITZ AND THE INNER STRUGGLE

There was spirited controversy in the theological faculty at Wittenberg in 1516. A year later Karlstadt confessed that while he had still been preoccupied solely with scholastic theologians, his younger colleague, Father Martin had arrived at a thorough understanding of scripture. When Luther presumed to declare that the scholastics misunderstood both scripture and Augustine, acrimonious debate resulted during theological disputations.[1] Luther himself reported that in the disputation of September 25, 1516, Karlstadt in particular became highly incensed when Luther rejected the generally accepted ascription of *De vera et falsa poenitentia* to Augustine.[2] When Karlstadt insisted with annoyance that the scholastic doctors had also read Augustine, Luther challenged Karlstadt to check the fathers' writings himself. With confidence he accepted.[3]

Lacking any writings of the fathers, Karlstadt purchased an edition of Augustine at the famous Leipzig fair on January 13, 1517 and proceeded to excerpt texts for use in debate against his colleague.[4] As he read further, however, it seemed that the entire scholastic edifice began to totter. "I was amazed, speechless and angry." Although he grasped desperately for even a sophistical defense of the scholastics, the

---

[1] "Exurrexit dei ope quidam de nostris Venerandus Pater Martinus Luther et arcium acutissimus et theologiae doctor acerrimus atque eorundem fratrum per Saxoniam Vicarius, qui meraciores sanctae scripturae litteras perdidicit et earum succum ultra fidem epotavit asserebatque scholasticos doctores et a Christi non solum documentis sed et intelligentia tam Augustini (cuius documenta frequentius citat) tam aliorum similium esse alienissimos. Verumtamen ego de mea intelligentia atque scholasticorum dexteritate confidebam intra me sicut phariseus ille, qui et mussitare et clamore in disputationibus (more solito), quod deficiente veritate non valui, affirmare cepi." *De sp.*, Kähler, p. 4. 13-22. See all of pp. 3-10 for Karlstadt's fascinating dexcription of his theological "conversion."

[2] Luther to Lang, October, 1516; *WABr*, I, 65.24-66.30.

[3] "Credite mihi, dicebam, quod illi doctores scholastici etiam legerunt et intellexerunt et sacras literas et Augustinum similesque. . . . Sed mihi ita inclamanti prisceque moriae meae laudes profundenti pius Pater respondebat pie: Ego te, ait, arbitrum diligenter monumenta ecclesiasticorum rimantem seligo constituoque." *De sp.*, Kähler, p. 4. 22-28.

[4] *Ibid.*, p. 5. 4-7.

awareness spread that he had been "deceived by a thousand scholastic opinions." [5]

Karlstadt reported that in the midst of this turmoil, repeated perusal of a writing of Johann von Staupitz, a former professor of theology at Wittenberg, helped him make up his mind.[6] The cause of Karlstadt's struggle was probably two-fold. Karlstadt was a scholastic academician. Hence Luther's position involved a frontal attack on precisely that which had given his colleague fame and honor. In addition to his well-received books on scholastic logic, he had invested a great deal of labor in still unpublished scholastic "commentariola." Karlstadt was honest enough to admit that he was proud of his scholastic achievements.[7] To accept Luther, therefore, was to reject ten years of academic activity. In addition Karlstadt probably rebelled against the strong statement of *sola gratia* which he found in the African *doctor gratiae*. Later in the commentary he confessed that the doctrine of the will's inability to do anything but sin apart from grace "once was vinegar to my teeth and smoke to my eyes." [8] Undoubtedly Staupitz helped him accept Augustine on this point for he was quite correct in thinking of Staupitz as a "most ample and distinguished preacher of the grace of Christ." [9] By the end of March, Karlstadt had

---

[5] "Obstupui, obmutui, succensui. . . . cognovi enim me in scholasticis mille sententiis deceptum." *Ibid.*, p. 5.9-12.

[6] "Et tu, Reverende Pater, non multo post tempore stimulos adiecisti et spinam impegisti. Dumque configerer spina, sum versus in erumnam, hortatorium tuum lectitavi epistolium, quo Christi dulcedinem, quam hii, qui puro corde in sacris literis Christum videntes, non qui eas velo obductas iudaice extrospicientes pregustant, egregie extulisti atque ultra meam de tua elegantia existimationem purpurato et elegantissimo sermone suasisti, immo persuasisti. Tunc cepi diligentiam, operam et curam in scholasticis doctoribus navatam detrahere ac pariter ecclesiasticis Christianisque doctoribus incumbere omni cura, diligentia, studio, admotis oculatis luminibus." *Ibid.*, p. 5.15-24. The work of Staupitz which helped Karlstadt was probably *Libellus de executione aeternae praedestinationis* which appeared on February 2, 1517. See Kähler, pp. 4*-7* and Oberman, "Wittenbergs Zweifrontenkrieg," pp. 350-51, n. 64.

[7] See his candid statement quoted in the Introduction, n. 66. In *De impii justificatione* (1519), Karlstadt again referred to the great labor and unfortunate result ("magna quidem opera, sed infoelici, quemadmodum nunc experior, eventu") of his scholastic period (Aii).

[8] "Hanc collige regulam et eam tene, quod liberum arbitrium sine gratia non valet quicquam nisi ad peccandum. Haec regula fuit dentibus meis quandoque acetum et oculis fumus." *De sp.*, Kähler, p. 30. 7-10. Earlier, in the preface, he had acknowledged that formerly he was trying to live rightly in his own strength ("meo Marte recte vivere conabar"). *Ibid.*, p. 4.12-13.

[9] "Verumtamen cum Tu, Reverende Pater, multis beneficiis me devinxeris, Et illius sincerioris theologiae promotor sis amplissimus atque eximius Christi

decided in favor of Augustine and the fathers. Luther could report that Karlstadt was ready to oppose all sophists and canonists with joy.[10]

Karlstadt's new stance found public expression very quickly. On April 26, 1517 he published 151 theses which showed that he had read Augustine's anti-Pelagian treatises carefully.[11] The big debate which he asked Spalatin to arrange failed to materialize, but the theses improved relations with Luther.[12] About the same time a student's inability to comprehend Augustine's *De spiritu et litera* led to lectures and a printed commentary on the book in 1517 and 1518.[13] One can hardly exaggerate the importance to Karlstadt of Augustine's treatise. He declared that he had "found the book to be a handle and entrance to all theology." [14]

One reason the Augustine commentary took so long was that Karlstadt became embroiled in the indulgence controversy in 1518. After reading Luther's "Ninety-Five Theses," John Eck in February, 1518 had written a short refutation which Luther christened *Obelisci*.[15] While Luther was at Heidelberg in April and May, Karlstadt decided to defend Luther and Wittenberg University's good name by publishing *370 apologeticae conclusiones*.[16] Since Karlstadt directed some of his

---

gratiae predicator. . . ." *Ibid.*, p. 6. 6-9. Kähler suggests that the doctrine of predestination was the problem (*ibid.*, pp. 5*-6*).

[10] "Paratus est vel unus Carolstadius etiam cum gaudio cunctis eius modi sophistis et iuristis contraire." A fragment of a letter of Luther to Lang, March 28, 1517, *WABr*, I, 33; see Kähler, p. 4*, n. 6 and "Ein übersehenes Lutherfragment," *Theologische Literaturzeitung*, LXXV (1950), 170-1 for the date.

[11] For the date of the theses, cf. Karlstadt to Spalatin, April 28, 1517 in Daniel Gerdes, *Scrinium antiquarium* (8 vols.; Groningen and Bremen, n.d.-1765), VII, 296. Kähler, pp. 11*-36* has reprinted the theses. It should be noted that Barge's attempt (*Karlstadt*, I, 81, 85) to argue that in these theses Karlstadt's thought had developed further than Luther's is no longer acceptable in light of Luther's Romans lectures discovered after Barge wrote.

[12] Luther praised them highly in a letter to Christoph Scheurl, May 6, 1517, *WABr*, I, 94. 15-25.

[13] The commentary was printed in four installments, the first of which appeared in Jan. 1518 and the last in early 1519, although the text was finished by October, 1518. Kähler, pp. 46*-52* has assembled all the data on the history of the text.

[14] "Inveni illum librum ansam et limen ad totam prestare theologiam." *De sp.*, Kähler, p. 5. 34. In a letter to Spalatin on January 17, 1518 he repeated this idea and urged Spalatin to read and reread this "most learned book." "Ego profecto librum *de Spiritu et litera* Augustini doctissimum comperi ansam ad secretiora theologiae latibula praestantem. Hunc legas atque relegas, consulo." Gerdes, VII, 297.

[15] Joseph Greving, ed., *Johannes Eck : Defensio* (Münster, 1919), pp. 7-11.

[16] See Verzeichnis, No. 3. They were finished on May 9, 1518, and there are really 405 theses. They are reprinted in V. E. Löscher, *Vollständige Reformations-Acta und Documenta* (3 vols.; Leipzig, 1720-23), II, 79-104. Theses 102-213 (against Eck) will be cited from Greving who reprinted them along with Eck's *Defensio*.

statements directly at Eck's theses, the latter felt obliged to publish a *Defensio* in August. Karlstadt finished his reply, also called *Defensio*, on September 14, 1518.[17] Thus in the eighteen months following his abandonment of the scholastic theologians, Karlstadt wrote two sets of theses, a polemic and a large commentary.

Before turning to an examination of the theology of these writings, one should briefly note another issue which must be kept in mind. Was Staupitz or Luther the more important factor in Karlstadt's move toward Augustine and in the kind of Augustinianism he exhibited in 1517 and 1518? Kähler asserts that Karlstadt's brand of Augustinian theology was more nearly like that of Staupitz than that of Luther.[18] There has been a good deal of discussion recently about an alleged late-medieval Augustinian school which may have influenced the young Luther.[19] To what extent was Karlstadt's Augustinianism due to some late medieval Augustinian sentiment and to what extent was it the result of his (and Luther's) independent rediscovery of the African bishop? If a late medieval Augustinian movement or tendency did influence Karlstadt, one of the most obvious channels for such influence would have been the Augustinian theology of Staupitz.[20] As Karlstadt's theology of 1517 and 1518 is examined, therefore, it will be important to try to detect instances of Staupitz's influence as well as differences from Staupitz. In light of his explicit preoccupation with and constant citation of Augustine, however, one cannot overlook the possibility that Karlstadt frequently derived his Augustinian themes directly from the master himself rather than via some late medieval intermediary.[21]

---

[17] Verzeichnis, Nos. 10-11; reprinted in Löscher, *Reformations-Acta*, II, 108-170.

[18] "... kennzeichnend [ist] fur die Theologie K.s, dass er bei seiner Wendung zu Augustin nicht eigentlich den Gedankengängen Luthers nachgab, sondern der Autorität und dem Vorgang Staupitzens folgte." Kähler, p. 7*. Cf. Rupp, "Karlstadt," p. 312: "From the first Karlstadt stood nearer to Staupitz than to Luther."

[19] See Bernard Lohse, "Die Bedeutung Augustins für den jungen Luther," *Kerygma und Dogma*, XI (1965), 117, n. 4 and 118, n.6 for an extensive bibliography related to this discussion. See also David C. Steinmetz, *Misericordia Dei*: The *Theology of Johannes von Staupitz in its Late Medieval Setting* ("Studies in Medieval and Reformation Thought," No. IV; Leiden, 1968), pp. 30-34. Steinmetz prefers to speak of "a late medieval Augustinian sentiment in theology." *Ibid.*, p. 30.

[20] See Wolf's *Staupitz und Luther* and Steinmetz's *Misericordia Dei*. Steinmetz shows that although Staupitz's theology was nominalist on some issues, it is correct to think of him as more genuinely Augustinian than Aquinas and Bonaventure.

[21] Lohse thinks this is true of Luther; "Bedeutung Augustins," *KuD*, XI, 118-119.

## 2. KARLSTADT'S AUGUSTINIAN THEOLOGY OF GRACE

Although it is correct to describe medieval theology as a series of footnotes to Augustine,[22] it is also true many medieval theologians weakened or abandoned Augustine's fundamental emphases at crucial junctures. The task of this section, accordingly, will be to examine the degree and nature of Karlstadt's dependence on Augustine in the basic doctrines of sin, the bondage of the will, law and grace, *justificatio* and *justitia Dei*, salvation as the reward of divinely bestowed merits, and predestination.[23]

### (a) *Sin*

How Augustinian was Karlstadt's conception of man's sinful state after the fall? As originally created by God, man's will was upright. Furthermore, it possessed that "prima gratia" by means of which man could have willed to be obedient.[24] His failure to do so, however, resulted in both guilt and a deformed heart for all men.[25] The fundamental fact about man after the fall in Karlstadt as in Augustine is the

---

[22] "All medieval theologians are, in some measure at least, Augustinian theologians. The question is not whether a theologian is indebted to Augustine but rather what is the degree and nature of his indebtedness." Steinmetz, *Misericordia Dei*, p. 33.

[23] In *Karlstadt und Augustin*, Ernst Kähler has made a significant contribution to this discussion, by reprinting and examining the 151 theses and the commentary on *De spiritu et litera*. One measure of Kähler's contribution can be seen if one notes that some statements (from the commentary) ascribed by Barge to Karlstadt are really Karlstadt's quotations from Augustine. Eg., cf. *Karlstadt*, I, 103 and n. 110 with *De sp.*, Kähler, pp. 74.27-75.4; and *Karlstadt*, I, 104 with *De sp.*, Kähler, p. 96. 19ff. A minor weakness of his work, however, is that he limits his analysis primarily to these two writings. But one would expect Karlstadt to be Augustinian in a commentary the explicit purpose of which was to explain Augustine's ideas. (As the introduction shows, he began the lectures on *De spiritu* at the request of a student who could not understand Augustine's theology; *De sp.*, Kähler, p. 5. 26-34.) And many of the 151 theses are direct quotations of the bishop of Hippo. Accordingly in discussing Karlstadt's theology in 1517-1518 it will be necessary to examine the *370 Conclusiones*, the *Defensio*, a 1518 sermon and his correspondence as well as the two writings on which Kähler focused his attention.

[24] "Numquid legis, fecit Deus hominem rectum? Idcirco scripturam debes intelligere cum effectu ut scias quale initium homo habuerit, videlicet quod rectum. Si rectum? ergo cum prima gratia, qua primus homo stare potuisset, si voluisset. . . ." *Defensio*, Löscher, *Reformations-Acta*, II, 154; for "prima gratia" in Augustine cf. *De correp. et grat.*, xi (31).

[25] "Exemplum de infantibus, qui in originali decedentes, aeterno tenebuntur igne, quod si est verum, prout est verissimum, consequens est eos qualitatibus ignis, hoc est cruciatibus affici ignis, et aeternis, si est aeternus." Thesis 84, *370 Concl.*, Löscher, *Reformations-Acta* II, 85. Cf. also theses 266-7 (*ibid.*, p. 92) where Karlstadt refers explicitly to Augustine. "Pravum est cor hominis et sibi ipsi inperscrutabile. . . ." Thesis 230, *ibid.*, p. 90.

existence of the radically depraved heart or disordered will which is
completely captive to wrong desire. "When the free will is led
captive under sin and suffers the domination of sin, then it is compelled to endure temptations, to consent to them and constantly to
sin." [26] Man's real problem is a weak corrupted will which needs to be
healed.[27] Man's will has become so twisted that, in Augustines'
phrase, man cannot but sin (*non posse non peccare*). In the commentary on
Augustine, Karlstadt declared: "To live according to the free will is
to live badly, to perish, to lie, to sin and to do nothing good." [28] As
will be seen presently, Karlstadt was more interested in grace than in
sin. However, in spite of the relative paucity of references to man's
condition after the fall, one may safely conclude that his conception
was genuinely Augustinian.[29]

### (b) Law and grace

Karlstadt also accurately reflected the thought of his African
mentor in his discussion of the relationship of law and grace. Ignorance of the law and its function is disgraceful for a theologian. The
proper role of the law is to reveal how God wants man to live,
show man his sinful helplessness, and thereby prompt him to seek

---

[26] "Liberum arbitrium, cum sub peccato captivum ducatur peccati dominium
patiens, tentationes pati, eis consentire, et sem[per] peccare cogitur." Thesis 314,
*ibid.*, p. 96.

[27] *De sp.*, Kähler, p. 72.17-20.

[28] "Tene igitur, quod vivere secundum liberum arbitrium est male vivere, est
perire, est mentiri, peccare, nihil boni facere." *Ibid.*, p. 39. 15-16. Earlier (see
above, n. 8) he had underlined Augustine's declaration in iii (5) that the will apart
from grace can only sin: "Nam neque liberum arbitrium quicquam nisi ad peccandum valet." *Ibid.*, p. 26. 24-25.

[29] One exception should be noted. In theses 181ff (of the *370 Concl.*), he defined
sin in a way which, while not untrue to Augustine, nevertheless was not characteristic of him. Sin is egocentrism. "As long as 'I,' 'we,' 'our own', 'one's own,'
'my,' and 'our' something are pleasing to men, so long there is in man that which
displeases God." ("Quam diu placent homini 'ego', 'nos', 'nostra', 'propria' et
'meum' [et] 'nostrum' aliquid, tam diu vicissim in homine est, quod Deo displicet.") Thesis 184, Greving, p. 60. The reference is to [Pseudo-] Ambrose, *De
vocatione gentium*, I, ii. In chap. vi, the author does say: "Quamdiu ergo homini
ea placent, quae Deo displicent, voluntas eius animalis est" (*PL*, LI, 652C).
However, although this work speaks of sin as egocentrism, it does not use the
peculiar terminology of 'I,' 'me,' etc. Such language is a peculiarity of the mystics
(cf. *Theologia Deutsch*, Mandel, p. 9.8-14 and pp. 10.14-11.7). Since Luther had published part of the *Theologia Deutsch* in 1516 (*WA*, I, 153) and Karlstadt had
purchased a copy of Tauler in 1517 (*Karlstadt*, I, 147), it is probable that this is one
of the very first reflections of mystical influence on Karlstadt.

grace.[30] It is the holy law which points out how man should live and act'
but precisely in so doing, it also reveals his inability and sinfulness.
"Thus, however much the weak will attempts to conform itself to the
holy law, it cannot perform that righteousness which is revealed
through the law." [31] The law can do no more than show man his
radical weakness and total inability to obey the divine commands
apart from grace. Ultimately, therefore, the law drives man to grace.[32]

Karlstadt affirmed most clearly the sharp Augustinian dichotomy
between the external demands of the law and the internal activity of
the Holy Spirit which is grace. The external, written law is a "killing
letter" because man foolishly tries to obey it in his own strength.
Mere knowledge of sin via the external law actually injures one because it gives understanding without also providing the ability to
live accordingly.[33] Man requires not only knowledge but assistance.
What is needed is grace which Karlstadt conceived of in terms of the
internal activity of the Spirit which transforms the disordered will
and creates good deeds.[34] Very frequently Karlstadt borrowed
Augustine's phrase and defined grace as "charity shed abroad in our
hearts through the Holy Spirit." [35] God (or grace or the Holy Spirit)
creates a new will in the sinner.[36] When grace has effected an inner

---

[30] "Nec lex sancta (quae facienda et devitanda demonstrat) et liberum arbitrium
cum ea ad faciendum salutis opera sufficiunt." Thesis 205 of *370 Concl.*, Greving,
p. 74. "Docet nos quoque sancta lex, quod gratia deserente nequaquam mandata
dei implere possumus." *De sp.*, Kähler, p. 78. 28-29. " . . . [lex] docet nos scire
nostram infirmitatem et que facere debemus." *Ibid.*, p. 71.4-5.

[31] "Ideoque quantumcumque infirmum arbitrium se legi conformare sancte
conabitur, non faciet illam iusticiam, que per legem ostensa est." *De sp.*, Kähler,
p. 69. 22-24.

[32] "Lex incutit nobis dolorem quem non sanat, sed admonet ut medicum quera-
mus (67). Lex demonstrat vicia (68). Lex ostendit nobis nostram infirmitatem
(69), ut supplicemus reformatori ne in illa remaneamus foeditate (70)." Theses
67-70, "151 Theses," Kähler, p. 23*. So Aug. in *De grat. et lib. arb.*, xiv (30), xviii
(37) and *De corr. et grat.*, i(2), ii(3).

[33] Theses 202-3 of *370 Concl.*, Greving, p. 74 (see below, n. 58).

[34] "Tu es factor meus, tu creas hominem in bonis operibus. . . . Sola tua gratia
mihi sufficit. . . . Tibi fateor infirmitates meas, ut virtus Spiritus tui inhabitet
me." Karlstadt to Spalatin, Feb. 5, 1518; E. L. Enders, *Dr. Martin Luther's
Briefwechsel* (19 vols.; Frankfurt am Main, 1884-1932), I, 146.85-147.99.

[35] "Lex fidei in tabulis cordis carnalibus scripta est ipsa charitas diffusa in
cordibus nostris per spiritum sanctum (105)." Thesis 105 of "151 Theses,"
Kähler, p. 28*. Also, *De sp.*, Kähler, p. 23.34-36 (see below, n. 65). So too Aug.,
*De sp. et lit.*, iii(5) and xxix(51).

[36] " 'Deus operatur in nobis,' — et quomodo in nobis? — 'in bona voluntate'
dicit. Sed unde bona voluntas? 'Ipsius, ait, sumus figmentum, creati in bonis
operibus' [cf. Eph. 2:10 and Phil. 2:13]. Bona voluntas a deo creatur." *De sp.*,

transformation, then the purified will can bear fruit and do good deeds.[37] Thus, whereas the external law written in ink brings only death and damnation, the internal writing on the heart by the finger of God results in a liberated will.[38] For Karlstadt as for Augustine the basic antithesis is that of law versus grace.[39]

*Sola gratia* became Karlstadt's favorite theme after he turned to Augustine. He proclaimed his firm conviction that our human infirmity can be aided by absolutely nothing at all except the grace of God.[40] He emphasized the prevenience of grace most clearly in his discussion of the will vis à vis grace. As noted above, the sinful will can only sin. Accordingly, it cannot contribute anything of its own in the reception of grace. Grace makes the will consent.[41] " ' The will does not attain grace by free choice, but rather the contrary' . . . for it is solely of God that we will well." [42] Thus the external law can demonstrate the will's weakness, but only grace can heal it. In his conception of law and grace, Karlstadt was genuinely Augustinian.

---

Kähler, p. 18.12-15. "Therefore a good will is a plant planted by the Heavenly Gardener" (see below, n. 52). *Defensio*, Löscher, *Reformations-Acta*, II, 150.

[37] *Ibid.* (see below, n. 52). Also, *ibid.*, p. 139.

[38] "Omnis lex atramento scripta est 'ministracio mortis' 'et dampnacionis.' Contra Sanctum Thomam (103). Scripta autem digito dei est ministracio libertatis Spiritus et gratiae (104)." Theses 103-4 of "151 Theses," Kähler, p. 28*.

[39] Thus when Barge uses Karlstadt's *De sp.* commentary to argue that "es kann kein Zweifel darüber bestehen, dass Karlstadt früher und folgerichtiger als Luther das Verhältnis zwischen Gesetz und Evangelium erkannt" (*Karlstadt*, I, 102), he is wrong not only on the question of Karlstadt's priority but also in his inference that the antithesis of law and Gospel was important for Karlstadt at this time. It was not.

[40] "Ubi maxime dei benignitas commendatur et e regione alia ex regula firmiter tenemus, humanae huic nostrae infirmitati nullo modo, nulla re, nullo robore subveniri posse, nisi dei gratia—ad quid? ad implenda dei precepta." *De sp.*, Kähler, p. 91.17-20. Karlstadt's letter to Spalatin on Feb. 5, 1518 is a ringing popularization of this theme (Enders, I, 144-46).

[41] ". . . manifestum est frustra nos velle, nisi Deus misereatur; Deum vero non frustra misereri. Si enim Deus miseretur, volumus. Porro bona voluntas non praecedit vocationem, sed vocatio bonam voluntatem praecedit." *Defensio*, Löscher, *Reformations-Acta*, II, 161. In *De sp. et lit.*, xxx(52)ff (412 A.D.), Augustine appears to want to find a very small place for the free consent of the will to grace. But in *De gratia et lib. arbitrio* (c. 427) he asserts unequivocally: "Faith is given to us, even when it is not sought;" xiv (28).

[42] " 'Voluntas' 'non libertate consequitur gratiam sed' econtra (Contra communem). Ut bene velimus solius dei est (Contra communem)." Theses 21-22 of "151 Theses," Kähler, p. 16*. The first clause is taken from Augustine's *De corr. et grat.*, viii (17) written in c. 427. Karlstadt indicated his agreement by his addition. So, too, in *Defensio* (Löscher, *Reformations-Acta*, II, 163): "Deus non eget praeparatorio assensu. Nam si facit conversionem, facit assensum."

## (c) *The external word and the mediation of grace*

Was he equally faithful to Augustine in his conception of the role of the external word in the mediation of grace? Since Kähler has argued that he separated the inner working of the Spirit further from the external word than did Augustine,[43] it is necessary first to examine Augustine's position and then to compare it with Karlstadt's statements.

The external word was so essential for salvation in Augustine's thought that he could argue that the absence of the proclamation of the Gospel at a given time or place was a clear sign that God foreknew there would be no elect there.[44] However, if the external word is necessary, it is by no means sufficient. This is true for two reasons.

> It was also a purely philosophical preconception that made Augustine take a very modest view of the effectiveness of his words. His theory of knowledge made it impossible for him to believe that one man could really instruct another. ... Whatever is known by a man is known by reason of the divine light which shines from above.... What, then, can a preacher do? He can point towards true knowledge, but he cannot bestow it.[45]

The second reason for Augustine's separation of the external word from the internal divine activity was the historical fact that the Pelagians identified grace with the external word (i.e. the law).

> But we must refuse the argument that we cannot be righteous without the operation of God's grace *merely* because God gave the law, instituted the teaching, delivered good precepts. For all this, apart from the Spirit's aid, is undubitably the letter that killeth: only when the life-giving Spirit is present, does he cause to be written within, and loved, that which when it was written externally the law caused to be feared.[46]

---

[43] Kähler, pp. 40*-42*. Steinmetz follows Kähler and relates Karlstadt's "spiritualism" to Staupitz: "In interpreting Augustine, Karlstadt demonstrates in a more extreme form a spiritualism which one also finds in the theology of Staupitz." *Misericordia Dei*, p. 172.

[44] "Those to whom the faith was not announced at all were foreknown as those who would not believe." *De praed. sanct.*, ix(17).

[45] F. van der Meer, *Augustine the Bishop* (London, 1961), p. 450. "In everything we learn we have but one master, namely the inner truth which presides over the soul, i.e. Christ." E. Gilson, *The Christian Philosophy of Saint Augustine* (New York, 1960), p. 74. Cf. *In ep. Jo. tractatus decem*, III, 13: "The sound of our words strikes the ears, the Master is within. Do not suppose that any man learns ought from man. We can admonish by the sound of our voice; if there be not one within that shall teach, vain is the noise we make."

[46] *De sp. et lit.*, xix(32); my italics.

If Augustine usually mentioned the law rather than the entire scripture or the written and preached Gospel when he spoke of the killing external letter, that was not because he thought the external word of the Gospel had any effect apart from grace.

> Brethren, . . . receive what is spoken [by me]. But perhaps you will say that I am more present to you than God. Far be such a thought from you! . . . I appear to your eyes, He presides over your consciences. Give me then your ears, Him your hearts. . . . Behold, your eyes, and those your bodily senses, you lift up to us; and yet not to us, for we are not of those mountains [the authors of scripture], but rather to the gospel itself, to the evangelist himself: your hearts, however, to the Lord to be filled.[47]

Even the external hearing of the Gospel is of no avail unless grace internally transforms the corrupted heart.

Both of the above considerations affected Karlstadt in his longest discussion of the power of the external word.[48] Since he introduced the section by stating the Pelagian identification of grace with free will and the law, one can assume that the point he had in mind was

---

[47] *In Jo. evang. tractatus* I, 7. See too the similar statement of Staupitz in n. 50 below.

[48] *De sp.*, Kähler, pp. 26-28. "Et dicunt pelagiani: probe dicitur, Sine dei adiutorio iusticiam dei attingere nos non posse; hoc et nos profitemur, nam adiutoria ista sunt liberum arbitrium et lex dei demonstrans quid vitandum quidve faciendum sit. potest enim ratio naturalis ex lege dei intellectum capere et dictamina concipere ac liberum arbitrium illis dictaminibus per nolitiones et volitiones atque electiones sese conformare, itaque a malo ad bonum declinare. ut hoc appareat manifestius, audi scripturam qua legitur: 'Levavi oculos meos in montes, unde venit auxilium mihi' [Ps. 120(121):1], hoc est, a predicatoribus vel hominibus illuminatis venit, vel quod proposito vicinius est: Levavi oculos 'ad scripturas' sacras (Augustino interprete super Ioannem tract. 1 c.d.), unde mihi promissum aderit auxilium. Nam deo dicitur: 'illuminans tu mirabiliter a montibus aeternis' [Ps. 75:5 (76:4)]. Quo testimonio rursus patet et homines predicatores atque sancta documenta legis, non ieiunum auxilium, sed pingue et tale quod animum illuminat, conferre posse. Sed illi intellectui repugnat, quod Ioannes scripsit: 'Erat lux vera que illuminat omnem hominem venientem in hunc mundum' [John 1:9], hoc est interiorem hominem in exteriorem corporeum venientem illuminat. Sic sol exterior carneos oculos, Christus vero spiritales oculos illustrat. Augustinus, de pecc. meritis, lib. 1. cap. xxv. Nec obstat versiculus primus adductus. Nam cum dixisset: 'Levavi oculos meos in montes, unde venit auxilium mihi,' continuo supposuit, 'auxilium meum a domino, qui fecit caelum et terram' [Ps. 120(121):2], non dicit primus versiculus 'a montibus' sicut secundus 'a domino,' sed 'de montibus.' August. psal. xxxv k.l. Levamus itaque ad predicatores aures opplendas, ad litteras oculos informandos, sed cor ad solum deum caeli et terrae creatorem, qui intrinsecus 'verax verbum' 'omnia opera' precedens inspirat et cor tangit." *Ibid.*, p. 27.5-31,

Augustine's denial that the external law of itself can help man. Grace
is needed. Then he quoted Psalm 121:1: "I will lift up my eyes to the
mountains whence cometh my help." Since according to Augustine
the mountains are preachers and scripture, the Psalmist must mean
that we should lift our eyes to scripture. "From that text it is clear that
human preachers and the sacred documents of the law can confer, not
weak, but rather strong assistance, namely the kind which illuminates
the soul." Such a view, however, needs qualification for it contra-
dicts—according to Augustine's epistemology and exegesis—St.
John's statement: "He was the true light which lighteth every man"
(1:9).[49] Only Christ and not the preacher can affect the inner man or
the soul. Actually, however, this view does not really contradict the
Psalmist who went on to say: "My help comes from the Lord who
made heaven and earth." Our help (*auxilium*) which Augustine and
Karlstadt certainly understood to be grace, is not of the mountains
(*de montibus*), i.e. the preachers, in the same way it is "of the Lord"
(*a domino*). Hence Karlstadt concluded: "Therefore we lift our ears to
the preachers to be filled and our eyes to the letters to be informed,
but we raise our heart to God alone, the Creator of heaven and earth,
who internally breathes in the true word which precedes all works
and internally touches the heart." [50] The external word is necessary
but insufficient. This passage then would seem to be thoroughly
Augustinian.

Kähler guessed that when Karlstadt spoke of the inner inspiration
which precedes "omnia opera," "opera" referred to the external reading and hearing of the word.[51] If he were correct, then of course Karl-

---

[49] With reference to John 1:9, Augustine said: "The inner... man ... is
enlightened only by Him who is the true Light." *De pecc. meritis*, I, xxv(38).

[50] See above, n. 48. The passage contains an allusion to Ecclesiasticus 37:20.
The following statement of Staupitz is very similar: "Des gleichen ist auch der
buchstab in dem newen testament ein morder der selen, und grosser den der
buechstaben des altenn, darumb das ehr den got vil lieblicher antzeiget, als den der
uns erlost hat, umb unser willen mensch worden, gelitten, gekreutzigt, gestorben,
begraben ist. . . . Dis und der gleichenn bringt der buchstab des newen testaments, unnd todtet. Unnd ob ehr schon Christum in die augenn bringt, unnd sein
lere in die ornn, weil er doch den geist Christi nit vermag in das hertz zubringen,
dient ehr allein zu schwererm todt. Die iuden hetten Christum inn augen, in den
orn, unnd inn henden, sy hetten aber denn geist Christi nit ym hertzen, darumb
waren sy verdamlicher den die heidenn." J. K. F. Knaake, ed., *Johann von Staupitzens sämmtliche Werke*, I: *Deutsche Schriften* (Potsdam, 1867), pp. 97-98. Since *De
amore Dei libellus* was published in 1518 (see *ibid.*, p. 90), Karlstadt could not have
seen this passage. The similarity of thought is striking nonetheless.

[51] "Nun ist zwar auch darüber, was in diesem Satz unter den opera zu verstehen
ist, nichts Genaues auszumachen, doch liegt es angesichts des anderweitig fest-

stadt would have separated the inner activity of grace further from the external word than did Augustine. A reference to Ecclesiasticus 37:20 in *Defensio*, however, proves that Kähler is wrong. In this passage it is perfectly clear that "omnia opera" refer to good deeds which can occur only after grace has transformed the will.[52]

Frequently Karlstadt made strong statements about the inability of the external written word. "Right living is from charity infused in the hearts, not from the written law." [53] "Remember this: God makes good wills in hearts not by the law, not by an externally sounding teaching, but by an internal and hidden, marvelous and ineffable power." [54] "All scripture" is a killing letter if man tries to follow it in his own strength.[55] Salvation is not in the scriptures.[56] Even the written

---

stellbaren Verständnisses von opus und opera nahe, auch hier das Werk des äusseren Lesens und Hörens darunter zu verstehen und nicht das Werk als Erfüllung des Gesetzes." Kähler, p. 42*. See also Kriechbaum's slightly different suggestion (*Grundzüge*, p. 28, n. 6). Karlstadt's statement quoted in n. 52 shows that both suggestions are very unlikely.

[52] "At ego nullam poenitentiam modo salubrem a voluntate elicitam, sed Dei donum esse, et mulierculam, ideo plus aliis fecisse [cf. Mark 12: 41-44] contendo, quod pater coelestis ei ardentem inspirarit amorem. . . . Omnis plantatio quam non plantaverat pater meus eradicabitur, bona ergo voluntas superni agricolae est plantatio, bona etiam voluntas est primum germen omnium bonorum operum, hoc germen praecedit alia secundum quod scriptum est: Ante omnia opera verbum verax praecedet te, et ante omnem actum consilium stabile" [Eccles. 37:20]. *Defensio*, Löscher, *Reformations-Acta*, II, 150. This passage also suggests that no significance should be attached to "verbum verax;" these words are simply part of the text Karlstadt wanted to use here and in *De sp.*, Kähler, p. 27 (see above, n. 48), because he read the text to mean that divine grace precedes all human works.

[53] ". . . bene vivere est ex charitate diffusa in cordibus, non ex lege scripta, non ex arbitrio libero, sed ex deo in voluntate, quia non fit bene vivere nisi in voluntate." *De sp.*, Kähler, p. 40. 6-9.

[54] "Vos autem modo tradiciunculam servate, quod non lege, non doctrina forinsecus insonante, sed interna atque occulta, mirabili ac ineffabili deum potestate operari in cordibus bonas voluntates." *Ibid.*, p. 84.31-34. Cf. Staupitz's similar comment: "Multi namque sunt vocati . . . per legem, per prophetas, per dona, per tribulationes, per apostolos et praedicatores fidei sed non fuerunt omnes electi. Verum hi, quos praedestinavit libere, sunt necessaria consequentia in tempore ad fidem efficaci voluntate vocati, et quidem non per Moysen, prophetas aut apostolos, sed per ipsummet deum, qui loquitur ad cor." *Libellus de executione aeternae praedestinationis* (1517), chapter 4, para. 24.

[55] "In textu: 'ecce quid est: littera occidit' pulcherrima est connexio [margin: 'Littera occidit' de omni scriptura dicitur.]. . . . Nam peccatum per sanctum mandatum vel concupiscentia fallit, et ne minus sit, addidit 'et per illud' secundum mandatum 'occidit.' Vides ergo, quod illa littera 'non concupisces' et omnis littera quae erat ad vitam, illa inventa est esse ad mortem. Ideo per legem peccatum occidit, ideo et littera occidit." *De sp.*, Kähler, p. 34.11-19.

[56] "Si Eckius salutem in scripturis collocari putat, ipsum in Iudeis Christus reprehendit ibi: 'Scrutamini scripturas, quia vos putatis in ipsis' etc. Et ei adver-

Gospel is "old," i.e. powerless.[57] It would be hasty, however, to conclude either that Karlstadt saw no connection between the external word and grace or that he had gone beyond Augustine.

> It is *not sufficient* to preach the Word of God or understand it by reading, for one ought to pray that assent [which grace produces] be added to it. Those who *without grace* perceive the divine, even the evangelical, law by hearing or reading become worse. Knowledge of sin without grace injures, for it makes us understand what we cannot practice in life.[58]

It was not the necessity of the external word, but its sufficiency by itself which both Karlstadt and Augustine denied.[59]

Kähler has also argued that Karlstadt slightly but significantly modified Augustine's notion of the "killing letter." Karlstadt moved in a spiritualistic direction by locating the detrimental characteristic of the law solely in the fact that it is written.[60] Karlstadt did refer to the

---

satur Apostolus, qui dicit, gratiam lege testificari, non conferri." Thesis 206 of *370 Concl.*, Greving, p. 74.

[57] "Lex evangelii scripta est vetus. Indigemus 'deo' 'doctore' et 'adiutore' 'ne dominetur' in nobis 'omnis iniquitas' " [cf. Aug., *De sp. et lit.*, vi (9)]. Theses 109-110 of "151 Theses," Kähler, p. 28*. For similar statements in Staupitz, see above, n. 50. Also: "Dura est lex naturae, durior Moysi, Christi durissima." *Libellus de executione aeternae praedestinationis*, chap. 16, para. 123. Also: "Lex quoque Christi ad literam durissima est. . . . Ista profecto sunt durissima, donec dilectus mittat manum suam secreto per foramen et tangat ventrem sponsae, ad cuius tactum anima repente alteratur" [cf. Cant. 5:4]. *Ibid.*, paragraphs 126, 128. In both Karlstadt and Staupitz, it is because man tries to obey the law in his own strength without the power of the Spirit that even the law of Christ is most hard and killing. See Steinmetz, *Misericordia Dei*, p. 178.

[58] "Cum autem is error, qui in atramento seu litteris eo factis aliud auxilium, quam demonstrationis et manifestationis, ut puta salutem, ponit, in Palestino iudicio sit subversus ac condemnatus: metuendum est, Eckium haeresim in pulmone habere. Non sufficit praedicare verbum Dei aut illud legendo intelligere, sed oportet orare, ut assensus ei accomodetur. Peiores efficiuntur, qui divinam, etiam evangelicam legem sine gratia audiendo vel legendo intelligunt. Cognitio peccati sine gratia nocet; facit enim nos scire, quod vitare non possumus." Theses 200-203 of *370 Concl.*, Greving, p. 74 (my italics). This statement and also the comment quoted above in n. 48 ("homines predicatores atque sancta documenta legis, non ieiunum auxilium, sed pingue et tale quod animum illuminat, conferre posse") show that it is simply incorrect to say apropos Karlstadt that "the external word of preaching or teaching provides no help to man in gaining faith." Steinmetz, *Misericordia Dei.*, p. 173. The external word is necessary even though it is insufficient without grace.

[59] Thus one must also reject Kriechbaum's attempt to find in Karlstadt's early theology a communication of grace without an external word (*Grundzüge*, p. 28).

[60] Kähler, p. 29*. He points to thesis 106 ("Opera charitatis in chartis scripta lex est operum et littera occidens") and thesis 109 ("Lex evangelii scripta est vetus") which he says have a "radical spiritualist character." Against Kähler it should be said that Augustine also said that even the Gospel was insufficient without the activity of grace (*In Jo. ev. tract.*, I, 7) which is almost certainly all Karlstadt meant.

killing letter written in ink, but in so doing he merely echoed Augustine's frequent reference to II Corinthians 3:3.[61] Both theologians referred to the written character of the law merely to underline the argument that the external word, apart from the internal transformation of the will by grace, is insufficient.[62] One can conclude, then, that in his conception of the role of the external word in the communication of grace, Karlstadt followed Augustine very closely.

### (d) *Justitia and justificatio*

For Augustine justification was not a forensic non-imputation of sins, but rather a progressive divine activity by which God transforms the corrupted will and produces actual righteousness in the Christian. "The word 'justified' is equivalent to 'made righteous'—made righteous by him who justifies the ungodly, so that he who was ungodly becomes righteous." [63] And the righteousness of God accordingly, is that actual righteousness with which God "clothes man when he justifies the ungodly." [64]

An identical conception appears in Karlstadt's early theological writings. "The help of God . . . is justifying grace; it is that help by means of which we do works of righteousness. That righteousness is the love of God shed abroad in our hearts through the Holy Spirit." [65] Similarly, "no one does works of righteousness in order to become righteous, but because one has been justified one therefore performs works of righteousness. Accordingly, one performs righteous deeds because God worked righteousness in him." [66] An early

---

[61] "You are a letter from Christ . . . written not with ink but with the Spirit of the living God, not on tablets of stone but on tablets of human hearts." Cf. Aug., *De sp. et lit.*, xvii(30) and *De grat. et lib. arb*, xiv(29).

[62] So Karlstadt in theses 103-4 of "151 Theses," Kähler, p. 28* (see above, n. 38) and theses 200-203 of *370 Concl*. Greving, p. 74 (see above, n. 58).

[63] *De sp. et lit.*, xxvi(45). As John Burnaby says in *Amor Dei* (London, 1960), p. 220: "By justification, Augustine means the progressive restoration of the rule of spirit over flesh."

[64] *De sp. et lit.*, ix(15).

[65] ". . . claret autem per textum nostrum et capitulum sequens, quod adiutorium dei, de quo in textu, est gratia iustificans, est illud auxilium, quo opera iusticiae facimus, Quae est charitas dei diffusa in cordibus nostris per spiritum sanctum." *De sp.*, Kähler, p. 23.33-36. See Obermans's interesting comments on the relationship between Staupitz's peculiar understanding of "gratia gratum faciens" and the Augustinian conception of "charitas dei diffusa in cordibus" ("Wittenbergs Zweifrontenkrieg," pp. 350-51, n. 64).

[66] "Ita nullus facit iusticiae opera, ut fiat iustus, sed quia iustificatus est, ideo iusta agit. Opera igitur iusta facit, quia deus in eo iusticiam operatur in bona voluntate." *De sp.*, Kähler, pp. 55.32-56. 2. A little later he again defined *justitia*:

sermon of 1518 also presupposed this concept of righteousness as something in man.[67] Since the text for the day (the Purification of Mary) included Simeon's words, "Lord, lettest now thy servant depart in peace" (Luke 3:29), Karlstadt discussed the peace which Christ gives. This peace comes from Christ, but it is not an alien peace imputed to man. The peace Karlstadt had in mind is "within us;" in fact it is precisely our divinely bestowed righteousness. Unfortunately this righteousness or peace is imperfect because the righteous man sins frequently. But "to the extent that we have those things which God through Christ works in us, we are called blessed and righteous." [68]

Karlstadt's Augustinian conception of justification led to an interesting interpretation of Paul's words, "by the deeds of the law, no flesh is justified, but by faith in Jesus Christ" (Galatians 2:16). Karlstadt argued that the will by itself can only sin, but when restored and liberated by the Spirit, it lives righteously. And then he added: "Nor does this disagree with 'by the deeds of the law, no one is justified, but by faith in Jesus Christ.' " [69] Justification by faith means that through faith the Spirit actually produces righteousness in man. Accordingly, the verse means not that faith is reckoned as righteousness, but rather that the Spirit and not the unaided will produces righteousness in and thus justifies man.[70]

---

"Non est sensus, quod illa iusticia dei sit per legem testificata, qua deus in se iustus est, sed illa, qua iustificat impium, qua induit hominem, qua instaurat imaginem dei in homine; de hac iusticia, qua deus suos electos iustos et pios efficit, tractamus." *Ibid.*, p. 69. 27-31.

[67] This sermon has been reprinted in *Unschuldige Nachrichten von alten und neuen theologischen Sachen*, 1703, pp. 119-25.

[68] "Meta itaque est, quod Christus est pax nostra, per quem habemus accessum ad Patrem in ejus Spiritu. Simeon venit ad templum et amplectebatur ipsam pacem suis ulnis. . . . Sed advertendus est Christi sermo, qui dicit: Pacem relinquo vobis, pacem meam do vobis. Relinquit pacem inter adversantes, inter inimicitias. . . . Sed illa pax non est plena, quia video aliam legem in membris meis repugnantem legi mentis meae. Habemus carnem repugnantem Spiritui: Itaque in pace nostra intra nos est assidua pugna. . . . Non est homo, qui non peccabit. . . . In quantum igitur ea habemus, quae Deus per Christum in nobis operatur, beati et justi vocamur." *Ibid.*, pp. 121-24.

[69] "Vivit ideo arbitrio bene, si restauratum, si restitutum, si liberatum fuerit per eum, de quo scribitur: 'si vos filius liberaverit, tunc vere estis liberi.' Si autem liberum arbitrium non habuerit dei charitatem, nihil valet nisi ad peccandum. . . . Utrumque iam te docuit Apostolus, videlicet, quod spiritu dei vivit arbitrium bene, at spiritu hominis vel seipso deperit male, cui nec dissonat illud: 'Ex operibus legis non iustificatur omnis caro, sed per fidem Iesu Christi.' Igitur absque fide iniustus manes." *De sp.*, Kähler, p. 39.1-14.

[70] Augustine understood the almost identical verse, Romans 3:28, in the same

Although the bishop of Hippo's understanding of justification was to influence our canon at All Saints for some time, hints of a new conception appeared fairly early.[71] In the summer of 1518 Karlstadt somewhat hesitantly accepted a bold statement the precise implication of which, he confessed, he rather guessed at than thoroughly understood: "The righteous man can sin mortally while righteousness remains." [72] Can *justitia* mean actual righteousness if it is present while the person sins mortally? In the same section he suggested that "he who accuses himself of sins is righteous." [73] In this statement Karlstadt appeared to be defining the righteous man not in terms of actual goodness possessed, but rather in terms of a right relation with God based on self-accusation.[74] It may be significant that both these statements which seem to involve a slight shift away from the Augustinian conception of *justitia* occur in a long section devoted to stressing the presence of sin in believers. In order to explain this point fully,

fashion; e.g., *De gratia et lib. arb.*, vii(18)-viii(20), and *Epistola* 186, iii(8). Seeberg says of Augustine: "Even this great disciple of Paul . . . misunderstood him at the crucial point" (*History of Doctrine*, I, 350). Karlstadt also quoted Romans 4:5 ("To one who does not work but trusts him who justifies the ungodly, his faith is reckoned as righteousness") twice without any indication that he grasped the forensic concept of Paul (*De sp.*, Kähler, pp. 46.11-14, 93.14-34).

[71] At one point in *De sp.* where he is commenting on Augustine's "justitia dei per fidem," Karlstadt actually said that "justitia est fides" (Kähler, p. 71.20). One is tempted to understand that in the forensic sense of Romans 4:5. However, this seems unlikely in light of the preceding section where he said that "man is justified only by the aid of the Spirit." "Grace alone aids us *through* Jesus Christ." (". . . lex . . . neminem iustificando indicat, non seipsa, non libero arbitrio iustificari hominem, sed adiutorio spiritus donaque dei." *Ibid.*, p. 70. 23-27. "Sola igitur gratia dei per Iesum Christum dominum nostrum nos adiuvat." *Ibid.*, p. 71. 14-15). Faith in Jesus Christ is not our righteousness; rather, through faith in him we are made righteous by the assistance of grace. But that still leaves it puzzling why he changed Augustine's "justitia *per* fidem" to "justitia *est* fides."

[72] "Hanc doctrinam, si ad rem propositam dedisti, videlicet, quod super fidem Christi iusti aedificant mortalia peccata, non illibenter contra te retorquendam accepto, quoniam animosa est, neque ego ausus fui ex dialogo citato Hieron. illud dicere, quamvis coniecerim magis quam recte intellexerim iustos peccare posse mortaliter, manente iustitia, hoc tamen scio, . . . iustis esse difficillimum discernere an culpae eorum vel veniales vel mortales sint." *Defensnsio*, Löscher, *Reformations-Acta*, II, 138-39.

[73] "Nam qui peccata accusat iustus est, benefacit qui ad lucem venit, ut manifestentur opera eius, et fidelis est Deus qui confitenti peccata remittit." *Ibid.*, p. 139. See below, chap. II, n. 72 for a discussion of "accusator sui" in Karlstadt, Luther and Staupitz.

[74] For the parallels to, and possible influence from Luther, see below in chapter II ("Justitia and justificatio"), where Karlstadt's further development in 1519 in the direction of Luther's *Demutsgerechtigkeit* is discussed at length.

however, it will be necessary first to discuss Karlstadt's adoption of Augustine's notion of the believer as both partly righteous and partly sinful.

### (e) *Partim justus et partim peccator*

Augustine's concept of the partly righteous, partly sinful Christian is an appropriate counterpart of his doctrine of justification as the progressive establishment of righteousness in man. Although baptism removes the guilt of concupiscence, concupiscence in the sense of a "certain affection of an evil quality" or an inner urge to do evil still remains.[75] Grace overcomes this tinder of sin only slowly. Whenever man permits it to activate itself in the form of illicit works, he sins.[76] On the other hand, "man lives righteously to the extent that he does not yield to evil desires and to the extent that the delight in righteousness conquers." [77] Hence man is partly sinful and partly righteous, both in the sense that his old corrupted nature is only partly renewed and also in the sense that, therefore, he sometimes commits sinful acts and sometimes does not.[78]

Since Karlstadt adopted Augustine's doctrine of justification, he also accepted his view that the Christian is partly righteous and partly sinful. Baptism removes the guilt of original sin, but concupiscence in the sense of the law of sin remains. If man consents to it, sin results.[79] Although the process of renewal has begun in man, it is not yet complete; hence he sins daily. "To the extent that man acts righteously, he is good; but to the extent that he sins, he is evil." [80]

---

[75] *De nuptiis et concupiscentia*, I, xxv (28).

[76] *Ibid.*, I, xxiii(25).

[77] *Enchiridion*, 118; also *De pecc. meritis*, II, viii(10).

[78] So Anders Nygren, "Simul justus et peccator bei Augustin und Luther," *ZST*, XVI (1939), 364, 374. On p. 367, n. 1, he quotes Aug., *Enn. in. ps.* CXL, 15: "ex quadam parte justus, ex quadam parte peccator."

[79] "Per sacramentum regenerationis solvitur reatus sed manet lex peccati (13). Speciale est in peccato hereditario, quod reatu soluto concupiscentia manet (14).... Manet tamen peccatum in membris tanquam superatum et peremptum (16). ... Reviviscit per illicitas consensiones et in regnum proprium dominacionemque revocatur (19)." Theses 13-14, 16, 19 of "151 Theses," Kähler, p. 14*. Also: "Habere peccatum in corpore non est peccare (145). Illud peccatum concipit partus et parit peccata (146)." Theses 145-46. *ibid.*, p. 35*.

[80] "In quantum recte agit, in tantum bonus est, in quantum autem peccat malus." *Defensio*, Löscher, *Reformations-Acta*, II, 148. See also *ibid.*, p. 140. Also: "Inquantum implet [illud mandatum: non concupisces], in tantum non peccat, inquantum autem deficit et minus implet, peccat." *De sp.*, Kähler, p. 36.4-5.

Thus, since the righteous man is only partially renewed and, therefore, sins repeatedly, he is *simul justus et peccator*.[81]

Karlstadt, however, departed slightly from Augustine at one important point. Against the Pelagians the African *doctor gratiae* had been most insistent that the righteous man sins very frequently.[82] However, his basic conception was that, although it occurred very often, the baptized person actually sinned only when he consented to illicit desires.[83] Karlstadt, on the other hand, insisted most vehemently from his earliest theses on, that good deeds themselves contained sin. "There is not a righteous man in the earth who does not sin through the righteous act by which he does well." [84] He interpreted his omnipresent proof-text, Ecclesiastes 7:21 ("Non est enim homo justus in terra, qui faciat bonum et non peccet"), to mean that every good deed is vitiated by sin.[85] "Let us say therefore that there is sin in every good deed." [86]

It is quite probable that Karlstadt owed his interpretation of Ecclesiastes 7:21 to his younger colleague at Wittenberg. Augustine cited this passage sometimes, but never with Karlstadt's interpretation.[87] Luther, however, as early as the lectures on Romans had stated that "we sin even if we do good, unless God ... does not

---

[81] In a response to Eck, Karlstadt said: "Putas enim Ecclesiam fateri iustos a peccatis praeservari, non autem et simul iustos et peccatores." *Defensio*, Löscher, *Reformations-Acta*, II, 137. Karlstadt of course disagreed. Also: "Iustus ergo simul est bonus et malus," thesis 138 of "151 Theses," Kähler, p. 32*.

[82] E.g. *De sp. et lit.*, xxxvi(65).

[83] See above, nn. 75-77. See also chapter II, nn. 57-58. Staupitz's position seems to have been identical with that of Augustine. See Georg Buchwald and E. Wolf, eds., *Staupitz Tübinger Predigten* (Leipzig, 1927), p. 247.4-20. Apropos Staupitz, Steinmetz comments: "The *culpa* of original sin is forgiven in baptism, but concupiscence itself remains as a subterranean power, not sinful in itself, but prompting to sin." *Misericordia Dei*, p. 113.

[84] "Non est iustus in terra qui per iustum actum quo bene facit non peccet." Thesis 136 of "151 Theses," Kähler, p. 32*.

[85] "Exempli causa, cum hac literali et aperta Eccles. auctoritate, non est iustus in terra, qui benefaciat et non peccet, quae aperte, in bono opere, peccatum ponit." Thesis 48 of *370 Concl.*, Löscher, *Reformations-Acta*, II, 82. See also *Defensio*, *ibid.*, p. 146 (see below, n. 92), and the sermon of Feb. 2, 1518 in *Unschuldige Nachrichten*, 1703, p. 124.

[86] "Dicamus ergo cum probatioribus in omni opere bono peccatum esse." *Defensio*, Löscher, *Reformations-Acta*, II, 148.

[87] In *De natura et gratia*, vii(8) and *De perfectione justitiae hominis*, xvii(38) it was mentioned only in passing as a text often cited against the Pelagians. Usually, e.g. in *Ep.* 165, 15 and *De sp. et lit.*, xxxvi(65) Augustine adduced it to prove that no Christian attains perfection in this life. But in no instance did he conclude that good deeds contain sin. Nor—to my knowledge—did Staupitz use Eccles. 7:21 in this way.

impute it to us." [88] Several times in this commentary Luther cited Ecclesiastes 7:20 (21) in connection with his argument that even when the righteous man does good, sinful egocentric inclinations are present.[89] Later, of course, he often stated explicitly that the Ecclesiastes text means that good deeds contain sin.[90]

More significant than the seemingly slight divergence from Augustine was the result of Karlstadt's exegesis of the Ecclesiastes text. After noting that "while the righteous man does well, he sins," Karlstadt went on, in *370 Conclusiones*, to argue that to the righteous, God "does not impute their sins because they recognize their own sins and strike their breasts and forgive their debtors." [91] Emphasis on sin in good deeds also led to the thought of non-imputation of guilt in the *Defensio*. "I hold . . . that the sin of a good act and a righteous deed

---

[88] After citing several texts (including Eccles 7:21) to show that the believer always has sin, Luther stated: "Idcirco enim bene operando peccamus, nisi Deus per Christum nobis hoc imperfectum tegeret et non imputaret." *WA*, LVI, 289. 18-20. Also: "Opera ipsa bona iniusta sint et peccatum" (*ibid.*, p. 289.29).

[89] "Ideo qui iusti sunt vere . . . credunt semper se esse peccatores. . . . semper peccamus." *Ibid.*, p. 235.31-38. Luther then proceeded to cite several texts including Eccles. 7:21 (*ibid.*, p. 236.7). In a later section, he again cited similar texts including Eccles. 7:21 (*ibid.*, p. 260.14-15) and then continued: "Nemo enim vivens iustificatur coram Deo, quod cor eius semper sit infirmum ad bonum et pronum ad malum." *Ibid.*, p. 260. 18-20.

[90] "Quod iustus etiam inter bene operandum peccet, patet: Primo per illud Eccle. 7. Non est iustus in terra, qui faciat bene et non peccet." *Disputatio Heidelbergae habita* (1518), *WA*, I, 367.2-4. Also *ibid.*, p. 366.30-36 and p. 357.28-38. During the Leipzig debate Eck sarcastically suggested that Karlstadt would not be able to adduce any scholastic or church father who thought that good deeds contained sin—except, of course, the Wittenberg father! Otto Seitz, *Der authentische Text der Leipziger Disputation* (Berlin, 1903), p. 233.

[91] "Quod boni et mali, filii Dei, habent; semper enim, dum bene facit iustus, peccat, et bonus et malus est (134). . . . Adde, quod septies in die iustus cadit, sed non colliditur, quia Dominus supponit manum [cf. Prov. 24:16 and Ps. 36:24]; secundum Cassianum patet, quod fideles iusti cadunt (136). Quibus iustis Dominus manum supponit, et ideo non imputat peccata, quod peccata sua agnoscunt ac femur percutiunt et debitoribus remittunt debita (137)." Theses 134, 136-7 of *370 Concl.*, Greving, pp. 44-5. The obscure but very intriguing thesis which follows underlines the importance of thesis 137. "Mordaces illi, qui sub titulo M et A verbum 'imputat' tanquam indecens seu non congruens notant, litteras sacras rident et ecclesiasticos adlatrant, sed cur? quia legere et intelligere, ut bene loquantur, nolunt (138)." *Ibid.*, p. 45. Do M and A stand for Martin and Andreas who were being mocked for some new understanding of the word "imputat"? In his reply (thesis 43, *ibid.*, p. 52) Eck confessed that this thesis was more obscure than the numbers of Plato! Eck did say that he referred to Luther with the letter M, but neither Luther's "95 Theses" nor Eck's "Obelisci" contain the word "impute". However, in the passage cited above from Luther's Romans lectures, Father Martin did connect sin in a good deed with non-imputation (see above, n. 88).

leads to damnation if God imputes it." In the case of the righteous
man, of course, God does not impute the sin because scripture says,
"blessed is the man to whom the Lord does not impute sin" (Psalm
32:2). Accordingly, he to whom the Lord does not impute sin is
blessed. But God's non-imputation of the sin should not obscure the
fact that "sin in a good deed or act is genuinely sin, because scripture
calls it sin." And then he quoted Ecclesiastes 7:21.[92] This passage is
significant because it shows how Karlstadt's slight modification of the
Augustinian conception of *partim justus partim peccator* via a new
exegesis of Ecclesiastes 7:21 prompted a discussion of the non-
imputation of sins. In the process, albeit only in passing, the righteous
man (*beatus*) was defined not in terms of actual righteousness but in
terms of the non-imputation of sins. Such a definition, of course,
could very easily lead to a new understanding of justification. The full
implication of this development will be seen in his subsequent writings.

### (f) *Salvation as the reward of good deeds*

On what basis does man attain eternal life in Augustinian theology?
Since grace has actually produced righteousness in man, he can now
do meritorious deeds and merit salvation.

> Let us then, as many as have a view to reach eternal life, love God with
> all the heart.... For eternal life contains the whole reward in the
> promise of which we rejoice; nor can the reward precede the desert,
> nor be given to a man before he is worthy of it.[93]

The only faith of any avail for salvation is that "faith which works by
love in such wise that God recompenses it according to its works
with eternal life." [94] It is entirely of grace that man can act righteous-

---

[92] "Ad rem non legit D. Eck, nec legere in Conclusionibus meis homo integri
iudicii potest, eodem actu quem mereri aeternam vitam et aeternam damnationem.
... Teneo autem, ... quod iusti operis vel boni actus peccatum, si Deus imputaret, regnet ad damnationem.... Cyprianus subscripsit: At cum bonum opus
sit opus iusti et beati hominis, Deus peccatum in illo opere non imputat secundum
scripturam. Beatus vir, cui Dominus non imputavit peccatum, fatentur ergo
beatum esse eum, cui Dominus non imputat peccatum seu iniquitatem. Idcirco
invenitur in beato peccatum, sed non imputabitur, ait Bern.... Peccatum in bono
opere vel actu, est proprie peccatum, quia scriptura vocat peccatum. Porro sic
scribitur: Non est iustus in terra, qui facit bonum et non peccat [Eccles. 7:21],
idcirco iustus benefaciendo peccat proprie et nisi fateretur se peccare, dolum in
spiritu haberet et non esset beatus." *Defensio*, Löscher, *Reformations-Acta*, II, 146.
[93] *De moribus ecclesiae catholicae*, xxv(47).
[94] *De gratia et lib. arb.*, vii(18).

ly; hence "when God crowns our merits, he crowns nothing but his own gifts." [95] Eternal life, therefore, is both reward for good works and "grace given for grace." [96]

Karlstadt said similar things in his early theological writings.

> But he [Augustine] says that that righteousness, although it does not happen without man's will must nevertheless be referred to the operation of God. Therefore it does not happen without the will since it happens in the will since [the will] is a workshop in which God fashions, creates, forms, makes and performs his own deeds which deserve a crown. [97]

Since man's will is genuinely righteous, it performs meritorious works. However, "God loves, commends and crowns only those works which He Himself inspires." [98] God "crowns his own deeds, not ours." [99] Thus Karlstadt knew and accepted the Augustinian doctrine, although he certainly did not emphasize it. And when he did, he sometimes stressed the element of God's mercy: "Life eternal is grace given for grace out of mercy and compassion." [100]

It is interesting to note that in his *Defensio* against Karlstadt, Eck raised an obvious problem. It is insane, he charged, to say that one sins by the very act with which one merits eternal life.[101] Karlstadt's

---

[95] *Ep.* 194, 19.

[96] *Enchiridion*, 107 ("gratia data pro gratia").

[97] "Sed dicit eam iusticiam, quamvis non fiat sine hominis voluntate, tamen dei operationi acceptam referendam esse. Igitur autem non fit sine voluntate, quoniam in voluntate fit, quoniam ipsa est officina, in qua deus sua coronabilia opera fingit, creat, format, facit et operatur." *De sp.*, Kähler, p. 42.23-27. So to Staupitz: "Converto autem me ad ea, quae operamur in Christo per gratiam innovati, quae incipiunt ab amore dei et in eundem tendunt. . . . Sine talibus operibus nunquam moritur praedestinatus adultus, quia a deo exeunt et ad deum vadunt, placent altissimo et acceptantur gratiose ad praemium aeternum." *Libellus de executione aeternae praedestinationis*, chapter 8, para. 50. See the translation in Heiko A. Oberman, ed., *Forerunners of the Reformation* (New York, 1966), p. 186.

[98] "Summatim deus ea sola diligit et commendat et coronat opera, que ipse inspiravit." *Ibid.*, p. 93.14-15. Also *ibid.*, pp. 94.37-95.3.

[99] "Innumera alia sunt exempla, ex quibus addiscere deberes, deum hoc praestare, quod nos facere iussit, nec alia sibi placere [opera], quam quae ipse largitus est, nec aliquas prosequi actiones, quam quas ipse inspiravit; suas prosequitur, suas adiuvat actiones; sua opera, non nostra coronat." Thesis 174 of *370 Concl.*, Greving, p. 59. So too Staupitz: "Colligunt sapientes . . . deum non praemiare nisi sua opera scientes, quod ipse gratiam et gloriam dat." *Libellus*, chap. 7, para. 38; Oberman, ed., *Forerunners*, p. 183.

[100] "Vita eterna est gratia data pro gratia ex misericordia et miseratione." Thesis 133 of "151 Theses," Kähler, p. 32*.

[101] "At nullus, nisi desipiat, dabit eodem actu quem mereri vitam aeternam, quo proprie peccare dicitur." *Defensio*, Löscher, *Reformations-Acta*, II, 145.

response is intriguing in that he came very close to a new non-Augustinian solution, and yet still failed to see it. First he denied that he said the same act merits eternal life and damnation; but he continued to insist that good deeds would damn one if God imputed the sin. God, however, does not, because scripture says "blessed is the man to whom the Lord does not impute his sin." It is that kind of man who is blessed (*beatus*).[102] The reader almost expects him to take the next step and deny the Augustinian scheme of eternal life as the reward of good deeds. But he does not. Instead he borrowed an unimportant argument from Augustine.[103] Karlstadt apparently was not yet ready to abandon the Augustinian formula of divinely bestowed grace meriting eternal life.

*(g) Predestination*

Karlstadt also accepted Augustine's doctrine of predestination. God mercifully forgives some men and justly condemns others.[104] Both the grace to begin to do good works and also the grace of perseverance result from predestination.[105] Works result from predestination and not vice versa for in predestination God did not take into account any future deeds of man.[106] Some people never receive grace. Only in the

---

[102] See above, n. 92.

[103] "Si bonum opus, cur irascitur Deus? quia culpa inest. . . . Irascitur ait Aug. sicut pater corrigens, non sicut iudex damnans, est ergo in actu bono, quod est corrigendum, est quod flagella meretur. . . . Aug. vide in allegato Ps. et de pecc. me. lib. II C. XVII. XVI. Adsentire igitur in bono actu proprie esse peccatum." *Ibid.*, p. 146. In *De pecc. meritis*, II, xvi(25), Augustine argued that although the righteous often sin, their sins deserve a different kind of punishment than do the sins of the wicked. The sins of the elect receive the punishment of a merciful father whereas the sins of the non-elect receive the punishment of an angry judge (damnation). Presumably, then, Karlstadt still thought it possible for good deeds (whose sin deserves not eternal damnation, but only fatherly chastisement) to merit eternal life.

[104] "Voluntati dei nemo resistit. Deus ex misericordia quibusdam donat penam peccati, a quibusdam iuste exigit penam." Thesis 111 of "151 Theses," Kähler, p. 29*.

[105] "Vocacio est principium bonorum operum (114). . . . Perseverancia in dilectione pertinet ad gratiam dei (119). Et ideo oratio Christi pro petro non erat inanis ne sua fides deficeret" (120). Theses 114, 119, 120 of "151 Theses," Kähler, pp. 29*-30*. See also Defensio, Löscher, *Reformations-Acta*, II, 128. So Aug., *De corr. et grat.*, vii(17).

[106] "Idcirco opera secundum gratiam et praedestinationem, sed non contra, praedestinatio secundum opera defendi potest." "Licet Deus non respiciat opera futura, attamen figmentum hujusmodi duplicis voluntatis Scholastici excogitarunt." Theses 295, 310 of *370 Concl.*, Löscher, *Reformations-Acta.*, II, 94-95. So too Staupitz: "Haec est prima gratia praeveniens et naturam et opus, quam certe nemo petiit, nemo meruit neque praescitis meritis seu praeviso bono usu rationis

case of certain people did God determine that they would not fail to receive grace.[107] It is true that some sons of perdition actually receive grace and begin to live righteously; however, God never permits them to die until they have fallen into sin again.[108] By falling away they prove that they were not of the elect. On the other hand, although the "elect according to God's intention" sometimes stumble,[109] they never perish.[110] All those whose names are written in the book of life will be justified and saved.[111]

Karlstadt seems to have come as close as did Augustine to a doctrine of double predestination. On the one hand Karlstadt could quote the following statement with approval: "He does not predestine all that he foreknows, for He foreknows evils but does not predestine them; but He foreknows and predestines the good." [112] On the other hand Karlstadt quoted with approval Augustine's assertion that if the church knew who those were who "were predestinated to go with the

---

futuro neque exhibitis debetur, sed sola benignissima liberrimaque dei voluntate processit." *Libellus*, chap. 4, para. 21; Oberman, ed., *Forerunners*, p. 179.

[107] "Auxilium gratiae eciam specialis mocionis, ut aiunt quidam, multis deest (Contra Capreolum). Solum illis non deest quibus deesse noluerit deus." Theses 117-118 of "151 Theses," Kähler, p. 30*.

[108] "Filij perdicionum licet incipiant aliquando bene vivere ac iuste ambulare, de hac vita tamen non auferentur nisi ceciderint." Thesis 121 of "151 Theses," Kähler, p. 30*. Also *De sp.*, Kähler, p. 58.9-11. So Aug., *De corr. et grat.*, ix(20)ff. It should be noted that Karlstadt sometimes cited the pseudo-Augustinian *De praedestinatione et gratia* (e.g. *De sp.*, Kähler, pp. 40.33-41.1 and theses 114-115 and 131 of the "151 Theses," Kähler, pp. 29*, 32*). As Kähler points out (p. 32*), however, he understood even this somewhat semi-Pelagian treatise in an Augustinian fashion.

[109] "Electi secundum propositum interdum labuntur." Thesis 123 of "151 Theses," Kälher, p. 31*.

[110] "Non nego fideles et electos dici quos baptizatos et recte vivere novimus, multi tamen illorum in parte fatuarum sunt virginum. . . . At ego de illis loquor fidelibus, qui re et nomine fideles sunt, . . . qui Dei electi sunt, quorum nullus perit." *Defensio*, Löscher, *Reformations-Acta*, II, 133. So Aug., *De correp. et grat.*, vii (11)-ix(20). Augustine distinguished between the *vocati secundum propositum* and those merely *vocati*. Only the latter could perish.

[111] "Omnes qui in libro vitae sunt scripti justificabuntur et fiunt salvi, per illud Hierem. perpetua charitate dilexi te, ideo miserans in misericordia attraxi te." Thesis 291 of *370 Concl.*, Löscher, *Reformations-Acta*, II, 94.

[112] "Aug. hypo. li. vi. a ad finem: 'Non omne, quod prestit, deus predestinat, mala enim prestit, sed non predestinat, bona vero et prescit et predestinat.' " *De sp.*, Kähler, p. 40.18-20. The passage quoted is actually from the Ps. Aug. *Liber hypognost.* VI, i, but Karlstadt also referred to Augustine's *De praed. sanct.* x(19) where in fact Augustine said: "Predestination cannot exist without foreknowledge, although foreknowledge may exist without predestination. . . . He is able to foreknow even those things which he does not himself do—as all sins whatever."

devil into eternal fire," she would not pray for them.[113] Similarly, in rejecting the non-Augustinian interpretation of I Timothy 2:4 ("God wants all men to be saved"), he declared that Romans 9:18 was conclusive: "He had mercy on whom he would and hardened whom he would." [114] Karlstadt could even explain the disaster of a sinful contemporary by adducing the doctrine of predestination.[115] In light of the fact that Staupitz would not adopt the Augustinian doctrine of double predestination,[116] Karlstadt's position here would seem to be one instance where one can assert with certainty that Karlstadt owed his position directly to Augustine.

### 3. SOLA GRATIA AND THE NEW PELAGIANS

Karlstadt discovered that the theology of the *doctor gratiae* was most useful in attacking the "present idea" that man without grace can prepare for grace. Proponents of such a view are "friends of God's enemies" and "most proud new Pelagians." [117] In keeping with his

---

[113] "Quapropter optime Aug. de civi dei ... docuit, dum ait: 'Si' de 'illis ecclesia' esset certa, qui etiam 'adhuc in hac vita constituti' ad 'aeternum ignem ire cum diabolo' essent predestinati, 'tam pro eis non oraret quam nec pro ipso. sed quia de nullo certa est, orat pro omnibus.' " *De sp.*, Kähler, p. 116.17-21; from *De civ. dei*, XXI, 24.

[114] "Ista authoritas deus vult omnes salvos fieri, minus bene exponitur de voluntate antecedente (Contra Scotisticos Theologos). Putamus nec in deo nec in homine antecedentem voluntatem esse (Contra eosdem). ... Conclusive 'cuius vult miseretur, et quem vult indurat' (Rom. 9, 18)." Theses 125-26, 130 of "151 Theses," Kähler, p. 31*. Cf. also theses 315-16 of *370 Concl.* where he added hastily that this does not contradict the fact that all sin is voluntary (Löscher, *Reformations-Acta*, II, 96). The desire to avoid making God responsible for evil was the reason Augustine and Karlstadt sometimes said God foreknows but does not predestine evil acts. It is somewhat difficult, however, to reconcile the two kinds of statements.

[115] "Homo erat mitis et eis permultis dotibus clarus. ... Sed, quid non facit auri sacra fames? quid gloriae cupiditas? hostes nobiscum portamus fortissimos, insidiatores vafros, quam carnem, quam Cacodaemonem, sunt etiam immissiones per malos Angelos, et de nostro etiam corde, ejusque desideria atque facinora nascuntur ac prodeunt, accedit et praesinitio Dei, cui nemo potest resistere." Karlstadt to Spalatin, Feb. 23, 1520, Gerdes, VII, 333.

[116] "Verum cum etiam scriptura dicat, perditionem nostram ex nobis, salutem ex deo dumtaxat...." Staupitz, *Libellus*, chap. 7, para. 38; Oberman, ed., *Forerunners*, p. 183. Cf. also *Libellus*, chap. 13, para. 88. So Steinmetz: "Staupitz cannot bring himself in this instance to embrace the full Augustinian tradition of double predestination." *Misericordia Dei*, p. 81. See also Wolf, *Staupitz und Luther*, p. 70.

[117] "Patet ex hoc, communicationem eorum esse periculosam, qui hodie non modo non putant sed aperto rictu stentoream efflant vocem, dicentes et docentes, hominem sine dei gratia posse se parare ad gratiam ..., quoniam qui illorum est amicus, quid aliud audire a deo debet nisi: mihi adversaris, amicus es inimicorum meorum." *De sp.*, Kähler, p. 23.2-8. Later, he referred to "illis superbissimis

emphasis on *sola gratia*, Karlstadt located the essence of the "new Pelagianism" in the doctrine that man by himself can dispose himself properly for the reception of grace.

It was an established dogma in nominalist theology that the unaided will could by doing its best (*facere quod in se est*) love God above all things and thereby obtain *meritum de congruo*. Gabriel Biel, for instance, taught that man needed nothing other than general grace, which Professor Oberman says was "barely distinguishable from man's natural endowments," in order to dispose himself for and merit the reception of justifying grace (*se disponere de congruo ad gratiam*).[118]

Karlstadt vigorously condemned the entire doctrine. "Dispositions *de congruo* on man's part should be laughed at rather than produced." [119] "He who does his best does what displeases God." [120] Indeed, if we attempt to do "quod in nobis est," we are damned.[121] The unaided will certainly cannot love God above all things. "Notice that to love God is not a human work, as if everything depended on man as some today dream who try to add that men can by nature love God above all things apart from the working of the Holy Spirit." [122] Karlstadt would not tolerate the concept of merit *de con-*

---

novis pelagianis" who "per semetipsos ad Christum accedere presumunt." *Ibid.*, p. 89.2-3.

[118] Heiko A. Oberman, *The Harvest of Medieval Theology* (Cambridge, 1963), p. 138. See also pp. 132-140 and 463.

[119] "Disposiciones de congruo ex parte hominis magis sunt ridende quam ponende. Contra omnes quasi scholasticos." Thesis 46 of "151 Theses," Kähler, p. 19*.

[120] "Qui facit, quod in se est, facit, quod Deo displicet, mentitur, obloquitur ac sibi officit." Thesis 190 of *370 Concl.*, Greving, p. 61. So too *Defensio*, Löscher, *Reformations-Acta*, II, 168. Staupitz, on the other hand, retained the category of the *facere quod in se est*. Eg.: "Sed quia deus omni facienti, quod in se est, iuxta S. Tho. documenta graciam confert, manent simul vera, quod sola gracia resurgendi potestatem tribuit et quod omnis, qui vult, resurgit." *Tübinger Predigten*, pp. 168. 41-169.1. See also *ibid.*, p. 30.15-19. Staupitz of course certainly did not think that man could by means of general grace merit justifying grace (see *ibid.*, p. 135. 30-33). It is only when God gives special grace that the sinner can do *quod in se est* (see Steinmetz, *Misericordia Dei*, pp. 93-97). Thus Karlstadt's and Staupitz's attitudes on this point were *substantially* the same. It is interesting however that whereas Staupitz merely rejected the substance of the nominalist concept of *facere quod in se est*, Karlstadt rejected the entire doctrine.

[121] "Nam si secundum optimum atque supremum hominis, hoc est secundum mentem et rationem vivimus, secundum hominem, non secundum deum vivimus. . . . Si facimus, quod in nobis est, hoc est, 'si est in nobis, quod ipsi fecimus, inde damnamur.' " *De sp.*, Kähler, p. 79.25-28. The quotation is from Ps. Aug., *De vera innoc.* (see *ibid.*, p. 79, n. 10).

[122] "Adverte quod deum diligere non est ita opus humanum, ut ex homine

*gruo*: "I cannot exempt from the Pelagian error those who make grace a servant of the will by asserting that grace is given according to *merita de congruo*." [123]

Equally untenable to him was the use made of the distinction between general and justifying grace. Karlstadt aptly applied Augustine's condemnation of "those who want to praise God because they are men, but themselves because they are righteous" to

> those who say that . . . they can do nothing without the influx of God, but in fact do something else by asserting that free will and general grace, by which they try to dispose themselves for grace, are sufficient for them. And they do not reckon that general grace to justifying grace. [124]

Only justifying grace can enable man to overcome sin: "The grace of God alone—and that justifying grace and no other—destroys the reign of death." [125] Thus Karlstadt rejected the whole concept of a natural disposition for grace. [126]

Karlstadt also thought he detected Pelagianism in a distinguished contemporary, John Eck of Ingolstadt. He selected for attack Eck's thesis against the third of Luther's "Ninety-Five Theses" because Eck ended his statement with the assertion that "the will is in the soul

---

pendeat totum, quemadmodum nonnulli hodie hallucinantur, qui astruere conantur, quod homo deum ex solis naturalibus absque spiritu sancto operante diligere super omnia potest." *De sp.*, Kähler, p. 29.14-17.

[123] "Non possum a Pelagiano errore excusare eos, qui ita voluntati pedissequam faciunt gratiam, quam secundum merita de congruo dari fantur." Thesis 250, *370 Concl.*, Löscher, *Reformations-Acta*, II, 91.

[124] "In textu: Sunt qui laudare deum volunt quod homines sunt, se autem quod iusti sunt [Aug., *De sp. et lit.*, viii (13)]. . . . Quid faciunt aliud qui asseverant generalem gratiam, qua sese ad gratiam disponere conantur, eis sufficere cum libero arbitrio, et tandem eandem gratiam generalem non computant iustificanti gratiae, quam quod laudant deum, quod homines sunt, . . . quod autem se ad gratiam disponere valent, quod bene operari possunt, sibi suisque viribus deputant." *De sp.*, Kähler, pp. 63.29-64.4. Similarly, in theses 388ff of *370 Concl.*, he condemned the view that man can "se disponere . . . ut filius Dei fiat" by "auxilium generale" (Löscher, *Reformations-Acta*, II, 103). See also Karlstadt's lengthy, very important comments on the distinction between *gratia generalis* and *gratia justificans* in *De sp.*, Kähler, pp. 23.1-24.8.

[125] ". . . regnum mortis sola dei gratia, et justificans et aliud nihil destruit." *De sp.*, Kähler, p. 46.24-25. Likewise: "Auxilium dei praevenientis non est distinctum a dono iustificante." Thesis 100 of "151 Theses," Kähler, p. 28*.

[126] "Peccatores non sunt monendi ad faciendum bona opera in genere (contra quasi omnes scholasticos), nec ad opera ut disposiciones de congruo ad gratiam (contra eosdem. mirabile sed verum)." Theses 50-51 of "151 Theses," Kähler, p. 19*.

as a queen in her kingdom." [127] Such a statement was anathema to the new convert to Augustinianism. "The will is mistress and queen of its own acts—i.e., all its evil ones! " Unless God becomes king in the soul, the will only sins.[128] The will is in bondage from which grace alone can free it. Eck is a heretic if he supposes that the will of itself can do any good.[129]

### 4. The Nature of the Augustinian Influence

The foregoing discussion has shown that in a relatively short period of time, Karlstadt acquired a thoroughgoing Augustinian theology. He followed Augustine's teaching on the extreme, sinful depravity of the will, the total uselessness of the law apart from grace, the necessity and insufficiency of the external word, salvation as the reward of divinely bestowed good deeds and predestination. Further, except for a few seemingly slight—albeit potentially significant—exceptions, his understanding of justification and the partly righteous, partly sinful existence of the Christian was also faithful to the thought of the African bishop.

If one asks whether Karlstadt's Augustinianism was more Lutheran or Staupitzian, it is significant that in the areas where Karlstadt did modify Augustine, Luther's influence often seems to be present. Luther had espoused the notion of sin in good deeds and, probably, Ecclesiastes 7:21 as an exegetical support, before Karlstadt adopted this non-Augustinian conception.[130] There were also hints—but only that—of a more forensic conception of justification.

Karlstadt of course owed a great debt to Staupitz who, as he explicitly acknowledged, had helped him decide to exchange the scholastics for St. Augustine.[131] Karlstadt's new Augustinian theology was certainly similar at many points to the theology of the man whose

---

[127] "Est enim voluntas in anima sicut regina in regno." Greving, p. 53.5. For the implication of Eck's "Pelagianism," see theses 196-200 of *370 Concl.*, *ibid.*, pp. 73-4.

[128] "Voluntas est domina et regina suorum actuum, suorum omnium scilicet malorum. . . . Universaliter loquendo: Deus est dominus et rex in anima nostra. Omnia nostra, quae Deus non fecit nostra, mala sunt et peccata." Theses 149, 156-7 of *ibid*,. pp. 54-5.

[129] Since Eck and Karlstadt discussed the problem of "free will" at greatest length at Leipzig, detailed examination of the issue will be left until chapter two.

[130] See above, nn. 88-90. Staupitz, on the other hand was more strictly Augustinian at this point (see above, n. 87).

[131] See above, nn. 5-6.

influence probably enabled him to overcome his initial resistance to the strong Augustinian emphasis on *sola gratia*.[132] On the other hand, there were several places where Karlstadt differed from Staupitz. Karlstadt, unlike Staupitz, totally rejected the conception of a proper disposition for grace.[133] Karlstadt also found Augustine's doctrine of double predestination more palatable than did the head of the German Augustinians.[134] Although not discussed above, it is significant that Karlstadt's theology of grace was not nearly as Christologically orientated as was that of Staupitz.[135] These differences with Staupitz suggest that one should be careful not to exaggerate Staupitz's influence on Karlstadt's theology. As the vast number of quotations from Augustine themselves suggest, the most important factor shaping Karlstadt's new Augustinian theology was his own (and Luther's) direct study of the bishop of Hippo.

---

[132] See above, nn. 8-9. For similarities in theology between Karlstadt and Staupitz, see above, nn. 50, 54, 57, 97, 99, 106.

[133] See above, n. 120.

[134] See above, n. 116.

[135] Kähler (p. 43*) and Kriechbaum (*Grundzüge*, pp. 42-45) both note that Karlstadt's theology in 1517 and 1518 emphasized divine grace, but said little about Christ. One of the most fundamental characteristics of Staupitz's theology, on the other hand, was its profound Christological emphasis. Steinmetz notes that "at the center of Staupitz's kerygma is a message about Jesus Christ, the God-man." *Misericordia Dei*, p. 151.

CHAPTER TWO

# HESITATION, TRANSITION AND DEBATE
## (mid 1518-1519)

## 1. HESITATION

The period following Luther's publication of the "Ninety-Five Theses" was not a time for the faint-hearted. The theses' instant popularity was matched with prompt official hostility. Archbishop Albert of Mainz dispatched them to Rome, and by March, 1518 Luther learned that official action against him was afoot there. In March stories circulated that Luther would burn within the month.[1] The Elector was so concerned about his safety that he gave Luther a safe-conduct for the April-May journey to Heidelberg. Thus when in Luther's absence, Karlstadt penned a long series of theses[2] for debate, he had to take into account the fact that Luther, and presumably anyone who supported him, might have to risk the most dire consequences. A summons to appear in Rome within sixty days reached Luther on August 7. In October it was learned in Wittenberg that a papal breve of August 23 had authorized Cajetan to excommunicate Luther and his followers if the monk would not appear before him.[3] The situation was dangerous and Karlstadt also felt threatened. He suspected Eck of arousing the Pope against him too.[4] With the burning of Hus still a horrid memory, caution seemed advisable. It was quite safe, of course, for Karlstadt to attack current theology as long as he could use as a weapon the unassailably orthodox theology of St. Augustine. But to venture beyond this safe terrain was danger-

---

[1] Luther to Lang, March 21, 1518, *WABr*, I, 154.11-14.

[2] *CCCLXX et apologeticae conclusiones pro sacris literis.* . . . (Wittenberg, 1518). Karlstadt finished the first 380 theses by May 9, 1518. There are actually 405 theses, and they are reprinted in V. E. Löscher, *Vollständige Reformations-Acta und Documenta* . . . (3 vols.; Leipzig, 1720-1729), II 79-104. Theses 102-213 (against Eck) are also reprinted in Joseph Greving, ed., *Johannes Eck: Defensio Contra Amarulentas D. Andreae Bodenstein Carolstatini Invectiones (1518)* ("Corpus Catholicorum," No. 1; Münster, 1919).

[3] See the detailed account in Robert H. Fife, *The Revolt of Martin Luther* (New York, 1957), pp. 256-308.

[4] "Apost. Sedem clandestinis advorsum me blanditiis sollicitat." *Defensio Andreae Carolostadii adversus eximii D. Joannis Eckii theologiae . . . monomachiam . . .*; Löscher, *Reformations-Acta*, II, 170. The work was finished on Sept. 14, 1518.

ous. Thus, in light of both existing circumstances and Karlstadt's extensive study of canon law, it is hardly surprising that he proceeded with considerable care as he penned theses on the important problem of the relationship between scriptural and ecclesiastical authority, and on the related issue of indulgences.

## (a)    The problem of authority

Historians have not usually spoken of hesitation with reference to Karlstadt's early position on the question of authority. Robert Fife expresses what perhaps has been a consensus since Barge, viz. that in his *370 Conclusiones* Karlstadt "took a position well in advance of Martin's in respect to the authority of the scriptures . . . going so far as to state that the declaration of a scholar backed by canonical authority is weightier than a declaration by the pope." [5] Fife's reference is to Barge who cited thesis 12 ("The text of the Bible is to be preferred not only to one or several doctors of the church but even to the authority of the whole church") and thesis 14 ("The foregoing leads to the point that the saying of a doctor supported by canonical authority must be believed rather than the declaration of the pope") to support his assertion that "Karlstadt established with unshakeable firmness the authority of Holy Scripture as the highest source of religious knowledge." [6]

Karlstadt's later refusal to agree with Luther's rejection of papal primacy, however, leads one to question Barge's interpretation of these theses. The last words of a work of January 1519 were: "We submit all things to the holy Roman church." [7] On February 24, he expressed great esteem for the Pope, "whom I will greet with servile

---

[5] Fife, *Revolt*, p. 273.

[6] "Die Autorität der Heiligen Schrift als der obersten religiösen Erkenntnisquelle steht jetzt Karlstadt unerschütterlich fest. *In gleicher Unbedingtheit ist das Schriftprinzip niemals vorher ausgesprochen worden.*" Barge, *Karlstadt* I, 118-19 (Barge's italics). In *Zur Geschichte der evangelischen Beichte* (2 vols: Leipzig, 1902-03), I, 123, n. 1, E. Fischer also cited thesis 12 to the same effect: "Carlstadt habe zuerst die alleinige Autorität der Schrift als Grundsatz ausgesprochen, in seinen Thesen vom Mai 1518 . . .: Textus bibliae non modo uni pluribusve ecclesiae doctoribus, sed etiam totius ecclesiae autoritati praefertur." Even Jäger, *Carlstadt*, p. 12, considered thesis 12 a strong statement of scriptural authority. Recently Gordon Rupp has said: "It may be that he appealed to the supreme authority of Scripture before Luther." "Luther: The Contemporary Image," *Kirche, Mystik, Heiligung und das Natürliche bei Luther: Vorträge des Dritten Internationalen Kongresses für Lutherforschung*, ed. Ivar Asheim (Gottingen, 1967), p. 16.

[7] "Sacrosanctae Ro. Ecclesiae omnia subiicimus." *Epitome Andree Carolostadii de impii justificatione* . . . (Leipzig, 1519), Div.

prostrations." He told Spalatin that he would have advised Luther not to publish his twelfth thesis[8] against Eck. And he assured Spalatin that in private discussion he had informed Luther that the Greeks also granted the primacy to St. Peter.[9] Two months later he reminded Eck that he, too, venerated the Pope and was an obedient member of the body of Christ.[10] He noted that Eck had recently become a self-appointed defender of the Pope. In reply, he insisted that he had never had and could never have anything against the apostolic see.[11] Luther found Karlstadt's hesitation most annoying. In a letter to John Lang he complained that Karlstadt would not debate about indulgences and the papacy at Leipzig because he was afraid to offend the Pope.[12] In light of these statements in 1519, it would seem that a

---

[8] Luther issued the theses against Eck twice. In thesis 12, which became thesis 13 in the May issue, Luther denied that the Roman Church was superior to all others: "Romanam Ecclesiam esse omnibus aliis superiorem, probatur ex frigidissimis Romanorum Pontificum decretis intra CCCC annos natis, contra quae sunt historiae approbatae MC annorum, textus scripturae divinae et decretum Niceni Concilii omnium sacratissimi." *WA*, II, 161.35-38.

[9] "Nisi tu arceas, rursum Eccium remordebo, cum gloria Romani Pontificis, cui cum veritate blandus adulabor. Caeterum Rever. Patri Martino Luthero consuluerim abstinuisse a XII. conclusione, jam vero post editam evidentissimis rationibus loricandum; clam tum, et domi suasi, quod sciam, Graecos scriptores S. Petro apicem et fastigium apostolatus concessisse. Putas autem fieri posse, ut crassulus acutissimo suadere queat?" Karlstadt to Spalatin, February 24, 1519. Daniel Gerdes, ed., *Scrinium Antiquarium sive Miscellanea Groningana Nova ad Historiam Reformationis Ecclesiasticam Praecipue Spectantia* . . . (8 vols.; Groningen and Bremen, [c. 1750] - 1765), VII, 319. It is interesting that Barge noted this letter's contents (*Karlstadt*, I, 142-3) and then simply reasserted his interpretation of the *370 Conclusiones* without implying that there was any contradiction.

[10] "Nisi Sanctissimum in Christo patrem et D. D. Leonem divina providentia Papam X. ac Christi sanctam Ecclesiam amarem, venerarer, suspicerem, crassulam et rusticam tuam impudentiam, invictissime disputator, hac responsione non dignarer. Quo circa eatenus tibi respondisse velim, quatenus pernoscas me Pontificii nominis studiosissimum simul atque dominici corporis, sanguine Iesu pretiosissimo redempti, obsequibile membrum, ut spero." Karlstadt to Eck, April 26, 1519, Löscher, *Reformations-Acta*, III, 284.

[11] "Novissime scribit aculeatus crabrose pro tuitione Sedis Ap. certaturum: Ex quo percunctare, mi lector, quam mihi adversus Sedem Apostolis causave unquam fuit? aut esse potuit? . . . Ego quidem Rom. Pont. cui peculiariter sum obstrictus, Sanctamque Ecclesiam et verbo et re venerabor." *Ibid.*, pp. 288-9. Karlstadt apparently was a papal Vicecomes (see Bubenheimer, "Consonantia," pp. 59-63).

[12] "Disputationem nostram futuram signavit Eccius 27. Junii; erit autem inter me et ipsum, ut videbis in hac schedula. Nam Carolstadius non congredietur illi in istis positionibus, tum quod meae sint, tum quod subdolus sophista eas res movit de Papa etc, quibus illum vel in periculum traheret offensi Papae (quod praebendatis malum intolerabile est [Karlstadt was an archdeacon]), vel periculo eiusmodi absterritum traduceret sine bello sineque victoria. Congredietur tamen

thorough re-examination of Karlstadt's position on the question of authority in 1518 and 1519 is necessary.[13] Such an investigation is especially important since it is now clear that at this time we must think of a Wittenberg theological circle in which Karlstadt was the most prominent after Luther.[14]

What is the proper interpretation of Karlstadt's statements on the problem of authority in the *370 Conclusiones*? The first nine theses clearly differentiated the authority of scripture from that of the statements of the fathers. "A text of the Bible quoted by an ecclesiastical doctor is stronger and proves more than the saying of the one quoting it." [15] Theses 12-15 are most important:

> XII. The text of the Bible is to be preferred not only to one or several doctors of the church but even to the authority of the whole church, . . . XIII. if one understands the church as the congregation or assembly of all believers. XIV. The foregoing leads to the point that the saying of a doctor supported by canonical authority must be believed rather than the declaration of the Pope. . . . XV. But I *do not believe that is true*, unless the Roman Pontiff is deposed and devoid of all authority.[16]

Barge completely ignored thesis fifteen in his analysis! Thesis fifteen limited the applicability of thesis fourteen to the very unusual situation

---

illis rebus, quae de potestate Papae vel indulgentiis silent." Luther to Lang, April 13, 1519. *WABr*, I, 368.18-24.

[13] Upon sharing our respective dissertations with each other, Ulrich Bubenheimer and I were pleasantly surprised to learn that quite independently of each other we had both arrived at the conclusion that Barge and subsequent scholarship had seriously misinterpreted Karlstadt's position on authority in these years. His far more extensive examination of this entire issue should be consulted. "Consonantia Theologiae et Jurisprudentiae," pp. 74-164.

[14] So Heiko A. Oberman, "Wittenbergs Zweifrontenkrieg gegen Prierias und Eck: Hintergrund und Entscheidungen des Jahres 1518," *ZKG*, LXXX (1969), 334.

[15] "I. Textus Bibliae per ecclesiasticum doctorem allegatus, plus valet, ac vehementius urget, quam dictum allegantis." Löscher, *Reformations-Acta*, II, 79.

[16] My italics. "XII. Textus Bibliae non modo uni, pluribusve ecclesiae doctoribus, sed etiam tocius ecclesiae auctoritati, prefertur, Per dict. Aug. de bap. con. Dona: Lib. II. c. III. transumptum ad C. quis nesciat: dis. IX. arg. C. sunt quidam et C. violatores XXV. q. i. et per dict. Aug. epis. XLVIII, quod ponitur in C. noli frater IX. dis. et illud quidem scripsit in epistola. XIX. per Graci: transumptum ad C. ego solis e. q. per Gers. de exa. doc. con. V. XIII. Capiendo ecclesiam pro fidelium omnium congregatione seu contione, XIV. Praemissa in tantum procedit, quod dicto doctoris auctoritate canonica communito, plusquam declarationi papae, credendum est. Gers. de exami. doct. part. I. Cons. V. XV. Quod non credo verum, nisi Ro. Pon. omni auctoritate destitutus et vacuus esset." *Ibid.*, p. 80. The references to Augustine, canon law, and Gerson will be discussed below.

in which a Pope might be deposed because of blatant heresy.[17] Karlstadt's statements from 1519 already noted above show that he by no means thought that that kind of extremely unusual situation existed in 1518 or 1519. Thus Karlstadt did not want to state categorically that a single teacher armed with scripture was to be believed rather than the Roman Pontiff.[18]

Theses 345ff confirm this conclusion. Although they were directed against Tetzel's strong statement of papal power in his fifty theses written in late April or May 1518,[19] they were certainly not a rejection of papal authority. "We do not deny that the Roman pontiff has the authority to establish new laws, likewise to dispense and to interpret fully." [20] This does not mean, of course, that new papal laws can contradict scripture.

> Where the Lord or his apostles have clearly defined things, there the Roman pontiff must not give a new law but rather defend it even with his life.... If the Roman pontiff were inclined to destroy what the apostles and prophets taught, he would be clearly shown not to be giving a judgment, but rather to be erring.[21]

---

[17] As Bubenheimer has demonstrated, Karlstadt was following the medieval canonist tradition. Even Prierias allowed for such a possibility. See Bubenheimer, "Consonantia," pp. 110-113.

[18] Thus it is very misleading simply to quote thesis 14 as Karlstadt's view. The reference in thesis 14 is to Gerson, *De examinatione doctrinarum*, part I, consideration 5 where Gerson in fact said that "in casu doctrinali" someone learned in scripture must be believed more than the Pope because "plus esse credendum Evangelio quam Papae." Gerson, *Opera omnia*, ed. L. E. du Pin (5 vols.; Antwerp, 1706), I, col. 11B. Gerson, however, did not mean exactly what Karlstadt said and then rejected. It will be seen that Karlstadt seems to have overlooked Gerson's fundamental distinction between theological definition "per modum doctrinae" (the exegesis of scripture by those learned in scripture) and "per modum auctoritatis" (dogmatic authoritative definition by a general council or Pope on the basis primarily of scripture, but also non-written revelation). Cf. Oberman, *The Harvest of Medieval Theology*, pp. 385-6 (and pp. 378ff). Gerson said explicitly at the beginning of consideration 5 that he was talking about theological definition "per modum doctrinae". It is true, as consideration 2 (col. 9B-C) makes clear, that although the pope pronounces a "judicium auctoritativum" he is "deviabilis" and therefore can be opposed. But consideration 5, which Karlstadt used, was talking not about this possibility, but rather about a doctrinal definition ("in casu doctrinali").

[19] Tetzel's theses are reprinted in Löscher, *Reformations-Acta*, I, 517-22. Karlstadt apparently saw Tetzel's fifty theses with their vigorous assertion of papal authority only after he had written most of his theses. Thesis 344 reads: "Ad confutandas novas, quoniam indoctas, cuiusdam [i.e. Tetzel] conclusiones, ultra ea quae in principio scripsimus, ... suppositas conclusiones tractabimus." Löscher, *Reformations-Acta*, II, 99. Theses 345ff deal with the question of papal authority.

[20] "CCCXLV. Non inficiamur Rom. Pont. novas condere leges, item dispensare, et plene interpretari posse." *Ibid.*

[21] "CCCXLVI. Ubi vero aperte Dominus, vel ejus Apostoli diffinierunt; ibi

These statements, however, are not at all radical or new. They are direct quotations from canon law.[22] Avid papalists would have agreed with Karlstadt and then added that of course papal pronouncements never have contradicted scripture. The crucial step would have been to reject some papal definitions on the grounds that they actually were contrary to scripture,[23] or at least to assert that the pope had erred. But Karlstadt never asserted that before 1520. In fact, in May 1518 he still conceived of a harmony between the Bible and papal pronouncements. In thesis 358 he complained of those irresponsible theologians who interpreted the Bible according to Aristotle and then charged the Wittenbergers with heresy "because the Wittenbergers began to grasp the sense of the truth from scripture itself, and did that well according to the doctrines of the prophets, apostles *and pontiffs*." [24]

---

Rom. Pont. non novam dare legem, sed potius usque ad animam et sanguinem confirmare debet. Textus est rotundus i.e. sunt quidam XXV. q. i. quo non dabitur glosella fortior. Non obstant quae in glo. et deinde alias tanguntur. . . . CCCXLVIII. Si Rom. Pont. quod docuerunt Apostoli et prophetae, destruere niteretur, non sententiam dare, sed magis errare convinceretur. Ita Urbanus Papa in d.c. sunt quidam, in quo videat garrulus frater [Tetzel], si bene adulatus sit Rom. Pont. cujus antecessor contrarium dixit." *Ibid.*

[22] Canon 6, Causa XXV, quest. 1: "Sunt quidam dicentes, Romano Pontifici semper licuisse novas condere leges. Quod et nos non solum non negamus, sed etiam valde affirmamus. Sciendum vero summopere est, quia inde novas leges condere potest, unde Evangelistae aliquid nequaquam dixerunt. Ubi vero aperte Dominus, vel eius Apostoli, et eos sequentes sancti Patres sententialiter aliquid diffinierunt, ibi non novam legem Romanus Pontifex dare, sed pocius quod predicatum est usque ad animam et sanguinem confirmare debet. Si enim quod docuerunt Apostoli et Prophetae destruere (quod absit) niteretur, non sentenciam dare, sed magis errare convinceretur. Sed hoc procul sit ab eis, qui semper Domini ecclesiam contra luporum insidias optime custodierunt." Emil Friedberg, *Corpus juris canonici* (2 vols.; Leipzig, 1879-81), I, 1008. Karlstadt's omissions are not totally insignificant. As will be seen below, Karlstadt wanted to set the authority of scripture apart from all subsequent statements. Hence he omitted the words "et eos sequentes sancti Patres." Further although he was certainly not yet ready to assert that popes could err, he was perhaps not as convinced as Gratian that the popes always defended the Lord's church from the wolves!

[23] Cf. Luther's rejection at Augsburg in Oct., 1518, of Clement VI's bull *Unigenitus* "because it distorts the holy scriptures" (quod scripturis sanctis abutitur). *WA* II, 8.5. Cf. also Luther's statement in August, 1518, in his reply to Prierias: "Quia tam Papa quam concilium potest errare." *WA*, I, 656.32. Cardinal Cajetan could say that the Pope was *under* scripture, and that he derived its meaning from the text, and then go on to say that one arrives at the truth of scripture only by interpreting it according to the views of the fathers, councils and popes; George H. Tavard, *Holy Writ or Holy Church* (London, 1959), pp. 115-16.

[24] My underlining. "CCCLVIII. Quod Vuittenbergenses ex ipsis scripturis capere veritatis sensum instituerunt, et bene secundum prophetica, Apostolica et Pontificia decreta, non extraneum quaerentes intellectum, ob id illi, qui suo

Nor was there any rejection of the Pope as the final authoritative interpreter of scripture. One must conclude, therefore, that although Karlstadt realized the issue of the relationship between papal and scriptural authority was important and problematic, he was not yet ready to abandon papal authority. Hence, his discussion of the issue was not an announcement that he had adopted a substantially new position on the question of authority.

In what sense then was Karlstadt prepared to argue, in May 1518, that the text of the Bible is to be preferred to the authority of the whole church (thesis 12)? The appended references to canon law provide some clues. The first reference was to canon 8, dist. IX which was a quotation from Augustine. The sacred canon of the Bible "is superior to all later letters of bishops," which can be refuted if they stray from biblical truth.[25] Karlstadt also referred to canon 9 of the same distinction where Gratian quoted Augustine's assertion that the authority of bishops' writings must be distinguished from the authority of the canon.[26] Another reference was to canon 6, causa XXV, questio I, which said, as was seen above, that although the pope can establish new laws, he must not contradict scripture.[27] Karlstadt obviously wanted to underline the supreme authority of scripture, and place it above the statements of bishops and popes.

At the same time, Karlstadt still believed that the authority of scripture depended in an important sense on the authority of the church. He still subscribed to a traditional interpretation of the famous dictum of his great African mentor. "To return to thesis

---

spiritu et Aristotelico adminiculo ipsas interpretantur, eos haereticos esse invulgant." Löscher, *Reformations-Acta*, II, 100.

[25] "Quis nesciat sanctam scripturam canonicam, tam veteris quam novi testamenti, certis terminis suis contineri, eamque posterioribus omnibus episcoporum litteris ita preponi, ut de illa omnino dubitari et disceptari non possit, utrum verum vel utrum rectum sit, quicquid in ea scriptum constiterit esse? Episcoporum autem literas, que post confirmatum canonem vel scriptae sunt vel scribuntur ... licere reprehendi, si quid in eis forte a veritate deviatum est." Canon 8, dist. IX; Friedberg, *Corpus juris canonici*, I, 17. The quotation is from Augustine's *De baptismo contra Donatistas*, II, 3.

[26] "Noli frater contra divina tam multa, tam preclara, tam indubitata testimonia colligere velle calumpnias ex episcoporum scriptis ...; primo quia hoc genus litterarum ab auctoritate canonis distinguendum est." Friedberg, *Corpus juris canonici*, I, 18.

[27] See above, notes 21 and 22. The two other references to canon law in thesis 12 are to canon 5, Causa XXV, quest. 1 (Friedberg, *Corpus juris canonici*, I, 1008) and to canon 5, dist. IX: "Ego solis eis scriptorum, qui iam canonici appellantur, didici hunc timorem honoremque referre, ut nullum eorum scribendo errasse audeam credere" (*ibid.*, I, 17).

twelve,—one might adduce to the contrary the now frequently repeated statement of Augustine, 'I would not have believed the Gospel unless the authority of the church had moved me.' " [28] Karlstadt rejected Gerson's attempt to weaken the authority of the present church by interpreting "the church" as the primitive congregation of believers.[29] He preferred Scotus' view that Augustine spoke of the authority of the contemporary church which now proclaims the Gospel, not of the early church.[30] Karlstadt found most compatible with Augustine's meaning, the statement of Cardinal Alexandrinus who denied that Augustine's statement meant that the church had more authority than Christ, but nevertheless agreed that if the church were not certifying it, one would not be certain that the statements of the New Testament were made by Christ.[31] It would appear that

---

[28] "LXVIII. Ad conclusionem XII. revertendo, opponitur hoc, quod iam est frequentatum Aug. dicterium, non crederem evangelio, nisi ecclesiae me commoneret [i.e. commoveret] auctoritas. Aug. contra epist. funda. c. V[i.e. *Contra epistolam Manichaei quam vocant Fundamenti*, 5 (6)]." Löscher, *Reformations-Acta*, II, 84. Karlstadt was quite correct in pointing to the central role of Augustine's statement. Hermann Schüssler has said: "In fact, the late medieval discussions of our problem are largely identical with the history of the interpretation of Augustine's statement." "Scripture and Tradition in the Later Middle Ages: The Canonist 'Panormitanus' and the Problem of Scriptural Authority," *Concordia Theological Monthly* XXXVIII (1967), 238.

[29] "LXIX. Ad quod per Gersonem, et male respondetur, quod Aug. ecclesiam pro primitiva congregatione fidelium eorum, qui Christum viderunt et audierunt, accepit. . . . LXX. Quoniam Aug. dicit, ipsi evangelio, catholicis praedicantibus vel praecipientibus, credidi." *Ibid*. In *De vita spirituali animae*, lect. II, coroll. 7, Gerson argued that the church which possessed such authority for Augustine was the original group of eyewitnesses. "Et hic aperitur modus intelligendi illud Augustini: Evangelio non crederem nisi me auctoritas ecclesiae compulisset. Ibidem enim ecclesiam sumit pro primitiva congregatione fidelium eorum qui Christum viderunt, audierunt, et sui testes extiterunt." *Opera omnia*, III, col. 24 A-C.

[30] "LXXI. Melius illo Gersone Scotus dixisse videtur (in q.q. XIIII. ar. I. col. III.) de fide per auditum quaesita. LXXII. Licet fundamento eius credendum esse, dubitemus inficiemurque." Löscher, *Reformations-Acta*, II, 84. In *Quaestiones quodlibetales*, quaestio XIV to which Karlstadt referred, Scotus argued that the viator "ex natura sua" could acquire "credulitas acquisita" when he heard the doctrine which the church taught. This is what "fides ex auditu" means and that is also what Augustine meant by his famous assertion. *Opera omnia*, Vivès ed. (26 vols; Paris, 1891-95), XXVI, 9. It is interesting that Karlstadt added in thesis 72 that he rejected Scotus' "fundamentum" which was clearly a reference to Scotus' distinction between "fides acquisita" and "fides infusa." As Scotus' text makes clear, the former is possible "ex natura sua," but not the latter. Karlstadt, however, completely rejected the entire distinction, just as he rejected the distinction between general and justifying grace. See *Defensio*, Löscher, *Reformations-Acta*, II, 134: "Rationes Scholasticorum de fide formata et informi, et acquisita non curo."

[31] "LXXIII. Verius ad mentem Aug. accessit, qui ait, Non debes per hoc

Karlstadt wanted to affirm the traditional view that the church's certification of scripture is necessary without thereby basing the authority of scripture exclusively on the authority of the church. The latter concern apparently prompted thesis 97: "If the authority of God were not supporting the sacred letters, it would be sufficient . . . that they were once received and authorized by the church." [32] This statement clearly implies that scripture does possess direct divine authority; hence the authority of scripture is partially independent of the church.

The text of the Bible is certainly to be preferred to the statements of general councils.

> The same Gerson rightly affirms . . . that one ought to believe a man excellently learned in the sacred letters and depending on a [Biblical] text, more than a general council. He restricts this: if a council departs from a text of the Gospel through maliciousness (note that) or ignorance. However, according to Gerson, a general council can mislead and make a mistake both out of maliciousness and ignorance.[33]

Karlstadt, of course, seriously misunderstood Gerson,[34] but that does not change the fact that in the case of a general council he moved

---

concludere, quod ecclesia habeat maiorem auctoritatem quam Christus, sed nisi ecclesia approbaret, non haberemus certitudinem, quod dicta novi et vet. test. fuissent a Christo prolata aut in vet. testam. contenta. Cardina. Alexandri. contra I. T." *Ibid.*, p. 84. Cardinal Alexandrinus (Giovanni Antonio de San Giorgio) a canonist who died in 1509, had a papal ecclesiology. See Bubenheimer's discussion, "Consonantia," pp. 154-159 (also, pp. 88-90). One cannot agree with Barge: "Schon [in the *370 Conclusiones*] ist Karlstadt über die kirchliche Gebundenheit Augustins hinausgewachsen." *Karlstadt*, I, 120.

[32] "XCVII. Si Dei auctoritas sacris literis non suffragaretur, sufficeret ad convincendum et defendendum ecclesiam, illas ab hac semel receptas atque fuisse adprobatas." *Ibid.*, p. 86. Karlstadt, it would appear was beginning to grope for the view (which he stated in 1520) that Augustine's statement should be interpreted to mean that the church established the canon and thus designated what books are apostolic without thereby becoming the source of scripture's authority. See below, chapter III, nn. 39-46.

[33] "XVII. Bene tamen idem Gerson, sed rursus male tacito imitationis vestigio, affirmavit, quod in sacris literis excellenter erudito et auctoritate nitenti plus est credendum quam generali concilio. XVIII. Quod restringit, si malicia (quod nota) vel ignorantia, ab evangelica auctoritate declinaret concilium. . . . XX. Concilium autem generale, iuxta Gersonem, et ex malicia et ignorantia, fallere ac falli potest." Löscher, *Reformations-Acta*, II, 80.

[34] In *De examinatione doctrinarum*, Pt. I, cons. 1, Gerson had made it very clear that a general council's dogmatic authoritative definitions were infallible (*Opera omnia*, I, 8). In consideration 5, from which Karlstadt drew his theses, Gerson was speaking not about definition "per modum auctoritatis," but rather "per modum doctrinae" (see above, n. 18). Gerson did say that the majority at a council might

beyond the general affirmation of the superiority of scripture to the statement that a general council could err. Whereas he denied that one man armed with scripture is to be preferred to the Pope, he explicitly affirmed such a view in the case of general councils.

By defining the literal sense of scripture very narrowly, however, Karlstadt hoped to limit the possibility of a clash between ecclesiastical and scriptural authority. Only when the literal sense of scripture supports an individual doctor may he legitimately oppose a general council or a pope who has fallen into open heresy.[35] That which one infers from the circumstances of the writer,[36] or by logical deduction[37] is not the literal meaning of the text. Only that which is so clearly in the text that one can "see it with one's eyes" dare be called the literal sense of scripture.[38] Only if one possessed the clearest scriptural texts whose literal meaning was unambiguous would one dare challenge ecclesiastical authorities.

In the *370 Conclusiones* then, Karlstadt asserted the supremacy of scripture without thereby denying the church's authority. The Bible does possess a direct divine authority, but the church also certifies and approves it. Scripture's authority surpasses that of popes who dare not contradict it, but then, apparently none ever have. As a canonist whose sympathies were more papal than conciliar, he could of

---

be inclining toward a view contrary to the Gospel through ignorance or maliciousness. In this case the individual learned in scripture must speak (*Opera omnia*, I, 11 B-C). Presumably, however, the general council would adopt the scriptural view before it issued its authoritative pronouncement.

[35] "XXIII. Praemissae conclusiones verae sunt, si dicto doctoris, testimonium sanctum, secundum literalem sententiam suffragaretur." Löscher, *Reformations-Acta*, II, 80. See Bubenheimer's careful discussion, "Consonantia," pp. 130-39.

[36] "XXV. Contra Gers. negamus esse sensum literalem, qui ex intentione et circumstanciis scribentis colligit. Gers. eodem tract. Cons. VI." "XXX. Ea autem, quae colliguntur ex circumstanciis, vel scribentis intentione, extrinsecus, hoc est extra literam, intelliguntur, iuxta Ulpian. et veritatem." Löscher, *Reformations-Acta*, II, 81.

[37] "XXVI. Nec eum, qui stricte est logicalis, literalem fatemur, nec dialectica literas docuit." *Ibid.* Karlstadt called any meaning derived by logical inference or argument from the circumstances of the writer an inferred intention ("intentio colligibilis"—thesis 34) of the text. "XXXIX. Ex praemissis omnibus infertur, quod plus seu potius adherendum est habenti auctoritatem ad literam, quam habenti colligibilem, vel ad mentem. XL. Secundo infertur, quod habens auctoritatem ad literam, praeferendus est habenti auctoritatem a contrario sensu. XLI. Tercio quod argumentum a contrario sensu non est expressum, sed venit in quandam consequentiam, colligibile ex circumstanciis." *Ibid.*, p. 82.

[38] "XXVIII. Legi, sic accipiendum, non intelligi tantum sed et oculis perspici, quod scriptum est. Ita Ulpia. . . ." *Ibid.*, p. 81. "XLV. Fortius est argumentum, quod legibile [cf. thesis 28] seu literale, vel ad literam est." *Ibid.*, p. 82.

course deny the infallibility of general councils. But that was hardly radical. In short the May 1518 theses were cautious rather than revolutionary on the question of authority.[39]

Are Karlstadt's subsequent statements in 1518 and 1519 compatible with this interpretation? When Karlstadt turned to Augustine in 1517, he rejected more than a decade of preoccupation with scholasticism because he had finally become convinced that the scholastics' combination of Aristotle and scripture had produced a grossly distorted interpretation of the Bible. It was natural for Karlstadt to return repeatedly to the attack on this unholy mixture. At the end of *Ausslegung* (April, 1519), he concluded that the scriptures adduced would completely demolish the view that the unaided will could accomplish anything—unless Aristotle came to the rescue with a distinction. He denounced those "mixed-up" theologians "who mix the scriptures so excessively that one reads much more pagan than holy biblical doctrines in their books, even though divine scripture should be purely unmixed." [40]

The desire to avoid the unfortunate scholastic combination of philosophy and revelation led quite naturally to a strong emphasis on the primacy of scripture. "All things are to be referred to the measure and rule of sacred scriptures." [41] The word of God is the standard by which theologians distinguish truth from falsehood.[42] There is a vast

---

[39] The ending was not a mere formality: "Protestatur, prout est iuris, moris et stili Theologici, Insuper se aliter non sensurum, quem [sic] sacrosancta scriptura et catholica ecclesia docuerit, item, et eius decreto obediturum sese." Löscher, *Reformations-Acta*, II, 102. Earlier, Karlstadt ended a brief, vacillating discussion of indulgences with the words: "Per ista tamen nihil volo de indulgentiis contra praelatos catholicos dixisse" (thesis 342). *Ibid.*, p. 98.

[40] "Dye seind die vermengte Theoolgen [sic] sie vermuschen die schrifft mit soliger unmessigkeit, das man vil meer heydnisch dan heylig biblischen lerenn in ihren bochern vor augen liest. Wiewol gotlich schrifft rein unvermuscht sein sal." *Ausslegung*, Ev. See also theses 143-144, Kähler, p. 34*; *De sp.*, Kähler, p. 3.12-14. In "Karlstadts Protest," p. 306 (and n. 37), Kähler says that when Karlstadt speaks of "vermuschten theologen" (e.g. *Ausslegung* [1519], EivV), "vermuscht" means "geziert." The passage just quoted, however, where Karlstadt complains of those theologians because they mix scripture with pagan doctrine suggests that the word means "vermischt" and refers to the blending of Aristotle and scripture.

[41] "Ad gnomonem et regulam sanctarum scripturarum cuncta scito referenda." *De sp.*, Kähler, p. 114.3-4. As Kähler shows in his introduction (pp. 50*-51*), pp. 88ff of Karlstadt's commentary were written about the time of or a little after the date of the *370 Conclusiones*.

[42] "At ego impudentissimum putaverim ab Ecclesiae et Dei verborum loquendi regula dissentire, existimavi quippe verbum Dei velut gnomonem et regulam Theologis datam, ut secundum eam, quicquid legant et audiant, verum vel falsum,

distinction between the statements of the holy fathers and the scriptures.[43] One should obey neither ancient tradition nor ecclesiastical prelates if they urge things contrary to scripture.[44] Nowhere, however, did he charge the church, the fathers, the bishops or the Pope with actual error.

In fact, he seems to have continued in the belief, apparent in the *370 Conclusiones*, that there is a harmony between scripture on the one hand and the ecclesiastical tradition (except for the scholastics!) on the other. Incidental comments about the fathers and the liturgy assume such a congruence. When Eck quoted Scotus against him, Karlstadt sarcastically reminded him that he had tried the scholastics, but found them far inferior to the fathers (*ecclesiastici*) who had imbibed the juice of the sacred letters.[45] Karlstadt began his defense against Eck by declaring that in the previous theses he had not stated personal opininons; rather, he had merely "repeated what the Holy Spirit published through the law, prophets . . ., apostles [and] fathers." [46]

Karlstadt asserted the same congruence between scripture and the liturgy of the church. He quoted liturgical prayers repeatedly in the Augustinian commentary, in *370 Conclusiones* and in his *Defensio*. He cited and expounded selections from the mass to support his doctrine of *sola gratia*.[47] When Eck rejected his citation of the liturgical prayers as useless, he retorted that the prayers, which the fathers had assembled at the command of the church, contained an accurate compendium of scripture.[48] He warned one person who rejected his argument

proprium vel improprium in sacrarum literarum explicatione iudicarent." *Defensio*, Löscher, *Reformations-Acta*, II, 145.

[43] "Inter dicta patrum sanctorum atque scripturam (quam Ecclesiastici appellitant canonicam) δίς διὰ πασῶν fateor distare." *Ibid.*, p. 117.

[44] *Ibid.*, p. 147 (but the basic statements here are quotations from canon law).

[45] "Haec [a long list of references to Scotus] conflavi ut intelligas et me illa tentasse, meliora autem his (hoc est Scholasticis) et invenisse et tenere, hoc est Ecclesiasticos, qui verum et sanctarum literarum succum imbiberint." *Ibid.*, p. 121. In a May 14, 1518 letter to Spalatin, he expressed confidence that Eck and Tetzel represented no problem because the Bible and the fathers supported him: "Suffragatur Wittemburgen. Biblia, Occurrunt Ecclesiastici." Gerdes, p. 308. See also *De sp.*, Kähler, pp. 9.29-10.5.

[46] "Porro in meis conclusionibus, quas non paucis, D. Eckius orbitatibus confecit, nihil de meo dixi: neque meam attuli sententiam, sed eam repeto, quam Spiritus sanctus per legem, Prophetas, Agiographos, Evangelistas, Apostolos, Ecclesiasticos patres edidit." *Defensio*, Löscher, *Reformations-Acta*, II, 109.

[47] *De sp.*, Kähler, pp. 104.27-105.23.

[48] "An inutilis labor est, quem in opponendis collectis expressi? quas non sine oleo et opera sancti patres mandato Ecclesiae elaborarunt, adeoque optima consonantia, Evangelio epistolas vel prophetias copularint et illud compendio verborum

from the church's prayers that the saints merely intercede for us and do not actually bestow assistance, "to take care lest he make the church his adversary, [and] to take care lest he contradict sacred scripture." [49] Most interesting is his reply to Spalatin who had communicated the view of someone who argued on the basis of a collect that one could ask the saints themselves for assistance. The unnamed person had added that the church cannot err. Nowhere in his reply did Karlstadt question the assertion that the church—in its prayers—cannot err. "The church has not talked idly, but that man erred; he did not ponder the words of the prayer." [50] And then he gave his own interpretation and supported it with other collects. He did not, of course, grant the same authority to the liturgy as to scripture. Nevertheless, he was not yet prepared to assert any contradiction between the liturgy and scripture.

Apparently Karlstadt sensed very early that the new Wittenberg theology would require a thorough reconsideration of the entire problem of authority. In *370 Conclusiones* and later works and letters of 1518 and 1519 he examined the relationship of the authority of scripture to the authority of the church and ecclesiastical tradition. In spite, however, of increasing preoccupation with scripture and a desire to assert its primacy, he was not willing to charge the fathers, the Pope or even the church's universally used prayers with any actual departure from scripture. By asserting a harmonious agreement between them and scripture, he hoped to avoid a violent confrontation between ecclesiastical and scriptural authority.

## (b) *Indulgences*

Nor was he any more daring in his discussion of indulgences and the related issue of the penalties(*poenae*) imposed by the church after guilt is remitted. In early 1518 Spalatin quizzed both Karlstadt and

---

perstrinxerit, quod vis atque potestas et campus sacrarum literarum continet. Apage sis D. Ecki sile, mutesce, revererte, honora Ecclesiae preces." *Defensio*, Löscher, *Reformations-Acta*, II, 122. In the last part of the Augustine commentary he said that certain prayers prepared at the command of individual bishops were contrary to God's word. The prayers of the universal church, however, are "optimae ac divinae legi dei verbo consonantissimae." *De sp.*, Kähler, p. 104. 15-16. See all pp. 103.30-104.26.

[49] "Idcirco dicebam bona temporalia a nullo nisi deo postulanda esse, non a sanctis nisi ut intercessoribus. . . . Si cui hec insipiunt, videat, ne ecclesiam sibi faciat adversariam, videat, ne sanctae scripturae contradicat." *Ibid.*, p. 113.29-33.

[50] "Cui tu [Spalatin] meis verbis responde, Ecclesiam non hallucinatam, sed hominem illum errasse, qui verba Orationis non pensiculavit." Karlstadt to Spalatin, Dec. 6, 1518, Gerdes, VII, 316.

Luther about indulgences. Karlstadt declined comment since he planned to discuss the issue in a forthcoming book.[51] But Luther informed Spalatin that Karlstadt did not share his view that indulgences were worthless.[52] He began a brief discussion of indulgences in the *370 Conclusiones* by suggesting that true penance has little to do with indulgences. He condemned the pecuniary motives of indulgence hawkers, but he hastily noted that he did not want to express any conclusive position.[53] He expressed doubt about the penalties normally imposed and insisted that priests should remit both guilt (*culpa*) and penalty (*poena*) whenever parishioners requested it. If the priest refused, however, the parishioner ought to be obedient. He concluded the discussion with the cautious proviso: "In the above, however, I do not want to have spoken anything about indulgences contrary to the catholic prelates." [54] Similarly, in a letter to Spalatin in

---

[51] "Iam alterum institui edere libellum, quem te brevi spero visurum. In eo de poenitentia tractare proposui, quoniam ipsa est ea virtus, quae verbo hoc: 'Tolle crucem tuam et sequere me,' nobis praecipitur. Quae sane intellecta omnem de indulgentiis stationibusque ambiguitatem imis e pectoribus expungit ac prorsus proculcat; quae etiam non intellecta diligentiorem in sacris literis operam moratur, intellecta autem et velum et ventum navigio praestat. Propterea tibi impraesentiarum in ea parte, qua flagitabas, quemadmodum essent indulgentiae promerendae, quidve sint, modo si quid valent depromerem, respondere superfluum arbitratus sum." Karlstadt to Spalatin. Feb. 5, 1518. *WABr*, I, 141.3-142.12.

[52] "Mihi in Indulgentiis hodie videri non esse nisi animarum illusionem et nihil prorsus utiles esse nisi stertentibus et pigris in via Christi. Et si hanc sententiam non tenet Noster Carlsta[dius], certum est tamen mihi, quod eas nihil ducit." Feb. 15, 1518. *WABr*, I, 146.55-58. The meaning of the latter part of this sentence is unclear. Preserved Smith has translated it: "Yet I am certain that there is nothing in them." (*Luther's Correspondence*, I, 71). On the other hand, Luther may mean that Karlstadt sees little value in indulgences even though he considers Luther's view somewhat extreme. The statements quoted in nn. 53-54 suggest that it was primarily concern for ecclesiastical authority that gave Karlstadt pause on the question of indulgences. Hence the second interpretation of Luther's statement may be more likely.

[53] "CCCXXXVIII. Quanquam secundum sacras scripturarum auctoritates in veraciter poenitente, quod denariorum sono redimi debeat, comperias nihil, tamen de indulgentiis nihil concludo, nec eas ut divulgantur approbo. Sed improbare teneor ob id quod opimas hominum exuuias, non animas hominum diligunt atque pelliciunt. . . ." Löscher, *Reformations-Acta*, II, 98.

[54] "CCCXL. Dubito etiam, an ecclesia remissis iniuriarum obligationibus poenas exigere possit; arg. I. Si unus. Si pactum ff. de pac. iunc. c. I. de no. ope. nunc Canones iudicium legum imitantur. CCCXLI. Hoc arbitror veritati consonare quod quilibet sacerdos (nullo praelato dempto) suo subdito petenti sibi remitti, et culpas et poenas remittere tenetur. CCCXLII. Quod si non fecerit, existimo subditum praecepto etiam discipuli Domini ligari. Per ista tamen nihil volo de indulgentiis contra praelatos catholicos dixisse. CCCXLIII. Peccat tamen praelatus non dimittens." *Ibid.*, pp. 98-99.

1519, he found only the "penalty of the cross"—i.e. perpetual self-condemnation, repentance and obedience to God's commands—in the scriptures. But he was even more willing than in 1518 to accept penalties imposed by the church. "No one but a disobedient person rejects the penalty of the church, which, as Augustine witnesses, the church can impose." [55] Karlstadt fulfilled Luther's unhappy expectation by saying nothing about indulgences at the Leipzig debate. Since the papal decretal published by Cajetan in December, 1518 defended indulgences and threatened anyone who spoke otherwise with excommunication,[56] consistency as well as caution urged silence upon someone who was not yet prepared to abandon papal authority.

## 2. LUTHER'S GROWING INFLUENCE ON KARLSTADT'S THEOLOGY

### (a) *Sin*

It was noted in the previous chapter that Karlstadt, unlike Augustine, used Ecclesiastes 7:21 to argue that every good deed contains sin. Another slight but significant departure from Augustine appeared in Karlstadt's discussion of post-baptismal concupiscence. Augustine had taught that in baptism the guilt of concupiscence was forgiven and no longer imputed. Concupiscence, of course, in the sense of a continuing inclination to sin remains, but "in the case of the regenerate, concupiscence is not itself sin any longer, whenever they do not consent to it for illicit works." [57] After baptism concupiscence remains only as a tendency toward sin, not as sin itself and guilt. "There is not, to be sure, anything remaining which may be remitted whenever, as scripture says, 'The Lord forgiveth all our iniquities.' " [58]

In his Romans lectures, however, Luther designated post-baptismal concupiscence sin.[59] In his important work on Luther and Augustine,

---

[55] "In scripturis video poenam, quam Deus pro peccatis solvendam ingerit. At, haec, ut uno verbo compendiosissime edisseram, est poena crucis, velut Hiere. et Ezechiel ajunt, resipiscere, et praecepta Domini custodire. Haec poenitudo tam est intrinseca poenitenti, ut nullo remedio, nisi morte, et postremo resurrectione dividatur. . . . Poenam autem Ecclesiae quam Augustino teste Ecclesia injungere potest, nemo recusabit, nisi inobediens. At petenti ex infirmitate condonandus est cruciatus inferendus. . . ." The letter is undated, but Spalatin added a note dating it in 1519; Gerdes, VII, 327-28. Here Karlstadt suggests exemption from penalty only in the case of sickness (cf. n. 54, thesis 341).

[56] Walter Köhler has reprinted the bull in his *Dokumente zum Ablassstreit von 1517* (Tübingen and Leipzip, 1902), pp. 158-60. See chapter III, n. 62, for Karlstadt's admission in 1520 that he had not discussed indulgences.

[57] *De nuptiis et concupiscentia*, I, xxiii (25); also I, xxv (28).

[58] *Ibid.*, I, xxv (28).

[59] E.g. *WA*, LVI, 271.15-31. With regard to *concupiscentia*, Luther commented:

Adolf Hamel contrasted the position of Augustine and Luther (in the Romans lectures): "Whereas according to Luther sin is forgiven and not imputed although it still exists in the baptized (as sin!), according to Augustine the punishable aspect or guilt of concupiscence is forgiven and it remains as an inclination enticing one to sin (not as sin itself!)." [60]

Karlstadt also abandoned the African bishop, albeit with less alacrity than Luther. In his *Defensio* Eck argued that post-baptismal concupiscence should be called not sin, but merely the daughter of sin. Karlstadt's response exhibits studied carefulness. "I say with Augustine that concupiscence is sin." But he hastened to add that it is sin because it was caused by (Adam's) sin, is moved by the delight of sin and gives birth to sin. "To consent to it is to sin." [61] Eck and Augustine both agreed. By the time of the Leipzig debate, however, Karlstadt's position was clear and explicit. During the debate Eck again stated the Augustinian position: concupiscence remains after baptism as the penalty of sin (*poena peccati*) and the tinder of sin (*fomes peccati*), but not as guilt. Eck quite correctly referred to book one of *De nuptiis et concupiscentia*. But not even Augustine's authority intimidated Karlstadt this time! Was St. Paul, he queried sarcastically, baptized when he wrote Romans? If he was, then he erred in calling his concupiscence sin in Romans 7:17 ("It is no longer I who sin, but sin which dwells within me"). "After baptism, the apostle calls the con-

---

"Et de tali peccato intelligenda sunt omnia predicta, Scil.: 'Beati, quorum remissae sunt iniquitates.' . . . Hoc enim malum, cum sit re vera peccatum, Quod Deus remittit per suam non-Imputationem ex misericordia. . . Et error est, Quod hoc malum possit per opera sanari, Cum Experientia testetur, quod in quantumlibet bene operemur, relinquitur concupiscentia ista ad malum et nemo mundus ab illa. . . . Sic ergo in nobis sumus peccatores Et tamen reputante Deo Iusti per fidem." Cf. also p. 350.5: "peccatum est in spirituali homine relictum" (see all of lines 5-10).

[60] *Der junge Luther und Augustin* (2 vols.; Gütersloh, 1934-35), II, 15. Hamel discussed the point at some length on pp. 15-23. "Luther im Gegensatz zu Augustin keine Konkupiszenz kennt, die nicht irgendwie, und sei es noch so verborgen, Willensakt und darum Schuld wäre" (p. 23).

[61] "De concupiscentia, dico ipsam secundum Augustinum esse peccatum. Primo, quia peccato facta est, sicuti haec scriptura dicitur manus, quia facta est manu, et locutio lingua. Secundo dicitur peccatum, quod delectatione peccandi moveatur: Tertio, quod peccatum facit ac parit et malum nobis nolentibus ingerit, ac ad reatum rebellando nostrahit, nisi adiuuante gratia liberemur, et quod ei consentire peccare est." *Defensio*, Löscher, *Reformations-Acta*, II, 136. For Eck's statement see Greving, p. 49, thesis 19. Cf. Augustine, *De nupt. et concup.*, I, xxiii (25): "By a certain manner of speech it [concupiscence] is called sin, since it arose from sin, and . . . produces sin . . . although in the regenerate it is not actually sin."

cupiscence in his flesh sin." [62] Thus on the point of post-baptismal concupiscence, Karlstadt accepted Luther's position.

Karlstadt also adopted Luther's dissatisfaction over the traditional distinction between venial and deadly sins. Augustine had taught that whereas public penance was necessary for mortal sin, fasting, giving of alms and recitation of the Lord's Prayer atoned for venial sins. [63] According to the scholastics, unforgiven mortal sins led to eternal punishment but unforgiven venial sins merely received temporal punishment. [64] Luther, however, insisted that contrary to the scholastics, so-called venial sins were very serious and would certainly lead to damnation if God did not grant forgiveness. [65] Karlstadt stated the same position in 1519: "It is hard to fathom whether one sins mortally or non-mortally, for all sins which we do not lament and cast aside are mortal." [66] From his younger colleague Karlstadt was learning a great deal about the seriousness of sin.

### (b) *Justitia and justificatio*

In the previous chapter it was shown that in 1517 and 1518 Karlstadt had adopted Augustine's definition of justification. God justifies the sinner by inwardly transforming the will and thereby making man righteous. It was also discovered, however, that the hint of a more forensic concept of justification appeared in 1518 in connection with Karlstadt's discussion of the presence of sin in good deeds. [67] If, as

---

[62] "Postremo rogo D. D., dicat mihi, si Paulus fuerit baptizatus, vel ne, quando 'ad' Rom. epistolam scripsit. Si fuit baptizatus, tunc male appellavit concupiscentiam peccatum post baptismum, cum dicit: Nunc autem iam non ego operor illud, sed quod habitat in me peccatum. Testimonium est apostolicum, quod apostolus post baptismum concupiscentiam in carne sua vocavit peccatum: Ergo nemo reprehendendus, si modum loquendi apostolicum vel fuerit assecutus vel imitatus." Otto Seitz, *Der authentische Text der Leipziger Disputation* (Berlin, 1903), p. 244. Cf. pp. 242-245 for the entire argument.

[63] E.g. *Enchiridion*, 65, 72, 76.

[64] E.g., Aquinas, *ST*, II-1, q. 87, art. 4. Cf. also Staupitz who retained the scholastics' distinction; *Tübinger Predigten*, p. 186.27-32.

[65] E.g., *Resolutiones* (1518), *WA*, I, 608. 4-16 and 623.1-15; also the *Probationes* of the Heidelberg theses, *WA*, I, 369.11-16.

[66] " . . . unnd schwer tzuergrunden ist, ap einer todtlich oder untodtlich sundige dan alle sunde seint todtlich die wir nit beclagen und verwerffen, auch werden klein schulden gros und unvergeblich, wan wir nit vorgebenn. Es ist noch keyn dapfferer gekummen, der uns untodtlich sunden, verstendiget und erkennen leert." *Ausslegung* (1519), Ciii. Also: "Omne peccatum minutum, quod homo non iudicat, est damnabile. . . ." Thesis 7 (see also theses, 6, 8) of the 17 theses for Leipzig published on April 26, 1519. Löscher, *Reformations-Acta*, III, 289-90.

[67] See above, chapter one, nn. 71-74.

Karlstadt had come to believe by 1519, post-baptismal concupiscence is actually sin and if all good deeds are vitiated by sin, then it would be logical to expect him to begin to talk more about the non-imputation of sin than did Augustine. Further, as non-imputation of sin becomes more important, the meaning of justification is likely to shift from a divinely effected inner transformation of the will to a more forensic non-reckoning of sins. A change of this kind, via a new definition of *justitia*, appears in his writings in 1519.

His first work in 1519, *De impii justificatione*, offered a new definition of *justitia*. At the beginning he announced his intention to discuss justification in terms of two movements—mortification and descent to hell on the one hand and restoration and ascent from hell on the other.[68] In great detail Karlstadt described "mortifying justification," which is God's activity whereby he frightens, whips, wounds and mortifies the sinner.[69] This divine action, which is designed to produce shame at and confession of sin, was also called God's alien and strange deed.[70] In this stage the conscience of the sinner is so overwhelmed by the awareness of his sin that he feels completely rejected by God.[71] The means for this *descensus ad inferos* are *judicium* and *veritas*. I Corinthians 11:31 provided the definition of "judgment": "If we would judge ourselves, we would not be judged by God." One must become his own accuser (*accusator sui*).[72] If one considers oneself a sinner, con-

---

[68] "Justificationi, mortificationem, perditionem, destructionem, deductum ad inferos et ediverso, vivificationem, salvationem, instaurationem, ab inferis reductum, adscribi contendimus." *De impii justificatione, Aiii.*

[69] "Proinde, justificationem dico, a vocatione Dei oboriri sed et vocandi ordine servato, q[uando] justificaturus deus, primum terret, flagellat, conterit, sautiat, mortificat, deducit ad inferos. Deinde, consolatur, recipit, contritionem sanat, vivificat, et ab inferis reducit." *Ibid.*, B. For "mortificans justificatio," see *ibid.*, DiiV.

[70] "Deus hoc gradu: cui alias proprium est misereri et parcere: peccatorem urget, stimulat, punit, alienum opus eius, ut operetur opus suum, peregrinum opus eius, ut proprium operetur" [cf. Isaiah 28.21]. *Ibid.*, Biii.

[71] *Ibid.*, BV-Bii.

[72] The title of chapter nine was: "In hanc contritionem et conversionem hominis primam, judicio et veritate descenditur." Karlstadt continued: ". . . De iudicio ad propositum, iudicium illud est, ad quod Apostolus hortatur nos, dicens, Si nos iudicaremus, non iudicaremur a domino. . . . Justus enim in primordio sermonis, est accusator sui [cf. Prov. 18: 17]." *Ibid.*, Biii. Karlstadt had probably borrowed ideas from Luther. Gordon Rupp points out, in *The Righteousness of God* (London, 1953), p. 148, that Luther found special significance in Prov. 18:17 ("Justus in principio accusator sui est"). Luther often used the word *judicium* to designate the repenting sinner's self-condemnation before God. E.g., *WA*, III, 179.3-4, 203.1-12, 208.5-6, 16-17 (Rupp, *Righteousness of God*, p. 148, n. 4). In the *Probationes* of the Heidelberg Theses (1518), Luther used I Kings 2:6

demns and accuses oneself, then one does the truth. The sinner must reveal his wicked way to God.[73]

It was at this point that Karlstadt offered a new definition of *justitia*: "To reveal one's [sinful] way is to do righteousness (revelare viam, est facere justiciam)." Precisely this revelation (i.e. confession of sin) is righteousness.[74] A little later Karlstadt said righteousness is that by which one attributes righteousness to God and unrighteousness and confession to oneself.[75] It is clear from this section that Karlstadt was equating *justitia* with self-accusation and confession of sin.

To a certain extent the word justification still designates God's transforming activity in the Christian, for it is God's "mortifying justification" which brings the sinner to the place where he openly reveals his sin and thereby obtains that righteousness which is self-denigration *coram Deo*. In this context however, justification begins to acquire a much more intimate relationship with forgiveness and non-imputation of sins than it did in Augustine. Toward the end of the treatise, Karlstadt referred to the righteous (*justi*) who had experienced the *reductum ab inferis* as "those who had been justified

---

("Deus deducit ad inferos et reducit") to prove that God's alien work consists of his humbling and frightening the sinner (*WA*, I, 356.35-357.11). Luther had used both concepts as early as the Psalms lectures (Rupp, *Righteousness of God*, p. 146). Staupitz, too, may have influenced Karlstadt, for I Cor. 11:31 and Prov. 18:17 were important for his emphasis on *accusatio sui* (Wolf, *Staupitz und Luther*, pp. 101-3). Eg.: "Deus enim, quia iustus est, non punit iniuste nec quod iuste corrigit, repente affligit, sed expectat, Si forte seipsum homo iudicare et punire velit, quo facto ipse minime iudicabit. Scriptum namque habes j. ad cor. xj [v. 31]. 'Si nosmetipsos diiudicaremus, non utique iudicaremur.'" Staupitz, *Tübinger Predigten*, p. 177. 25-29. Also: "Sis tibi ipse iudex, ne forte dominus te iudicet et condempnet." *Ibid.*, p. 178.4-5. See also *Libellus de executione aeternae praedestinationis*, chap. 23, para. 242 where he used Prov. 18:17.

[73] "Nempe qui iudicat se peccatorem, veritatem facit. Si enim dixerimus nos non habere peccatum, veritas non est in nobis. fac veritatem, peccata tua cognita deo facientem, et venies ad lucem. sed cur ad lucem, quae illuminat omnem hominem in mundum venientem? ut manifestentur opera tua. Revela domino viam tuam, et spera in eum, et ipse faciet, et deducet velut lumen iustitiam tuam et iudicium tuum sicut meridiem [cf. Psalms 36 (37): 5-6]. In consequentibus apparet initium versiculi: revela domino viam tuam: sub aliis verbis repetitum, revelare viam, est facere justiciam, item et iudicium, de quo praeiecimus alioqui, qua ratione subiecisset. Et deducet justiciam tuam, nisi cum iuberet revelari viam, monstrasset revelationem hanc esse justiciam et judicium. Eo quidem justorum pendet justicia, quod se imperfectos, iniustos et peccatores confitentur." *Ibid.*, Biii-BiiiV.

[74] See n. 73.

[75] "Tu infirmitatem fateris, desyderas medicum, ad Christum confugis, et ipse deducit iusticiam tuam quasi lumen. haec est lucida iusticia, qua deo iusticiam, tibi iniusticiam et confusionem tribuis." *Ibid.*, BivV.

by the grace of propitiation and security." [76] Here Karlstadt connects justification with the freedom from guilt and punishment arising from Christ's propitiatory death. In another passage Karlstadt said: "Reveal your way . . . in order that you are justified." [77] Since "reveal your way" means, for Karlstadt, "confess your sins," justification is associated directly with the confession of sins. It would appear that when *justitia* begins to be conceived of in terms of humility or self-accusation, then justification refers not only to God's activity in producing this righteousness which is self-condemnation, but also to God's forgiving response to it.

The two ideas of Christ's bearing our sins and *justitia* as confession appear together in an intriguing passage. Karlstadt urges the one who confesses his sinful ways to God to believe and trust in God who will bring it to pass. But why trust in the Lord, he asks:

> Because it was he who carried our iniquities. . . . He himself who knew no sin was made sin for us so that we might become the righteousness of God in God. But what will he do? He will bring it to pass that for the one who trusts in him and reveals his evil way, that revelation will be righteousness and judgment.[78]

This passage shows clearly that the notion of *justitia* as self-condemnation (*revelare viam* here) led to a significant emphasis on divine forgiveness and Christ's sin-bearing activity. The purely Augustinian concept of *justitia*, on the other hand, did not require so great an emphasis here, because it stressed the inner transformation of the will and the emergence of a regenerate will which can love and obey God.[79] Accordingly, it would seem that the stress on *justitia* as self-

----

[76] " . . . ille te ab inferis reduxit qui deduxerat, et qui te mortificarat et abiecerat, ille te . . . vivificat et erigit. . . . letamini in domino et exultate iusti, iustificati gratia propiciationis securitatisque, et gloriamini omnes recti corde, omnes qui peccata vestra et infirmitates confitemini, iusticiam deo tribuentes." *Ibid.*, Diii-DiiiV.

[77] "Revela viam tuam, narra si quid habes, ut justificeris." *Ibid.*, BiiiV.

[78] " . . . revela ad dominum, volve super dominum viam tuam, et spera in eum, crede, confide in eum, et ipse faciet. Sed cur ad dominum? q[uod] ipse portavit iniquitates nostras. ipse est petra, quae spinosis herinaciis est refugium, ipse factus est pro nobis peccatum, qui peccatum non cognovit, ut nos essemus iusticia dei in deo [cf. 2 Cor. 5.21]. Sed quid ipse faciet? Faciet quod confidenti in eum, revelantique malam viam, revelatio illa erit iusticia, erit iudicium." *Ibid.*, Biv.

[79] Cf. Harnack's judgment: "Augustine's doctrine of infused love is indifferent to the work of the historical Christ. . . . All that leads us back ultimately to the fact that he under-estimated the significance of the forgiveness of sins." A. Harnack, *History of Dogma*, trans. N. Buchanan (7 vols.; New York, 1961), V, 91. Cf. also pp. 88ff.

accusation was helping to prepare the way for a concept of justification which focused on divine forgiveness rather than divine reclothing.

The conception of righteousness as self-accusation of sin reappeared repeatedly in Karlstadt's next work, *Ausslegung*, published in April. To the question, who can boast of a pure heart before God, the "righteous sinner" replies:

> I bring my evil before you; that is my righteousness. When man uncovers and reports his evil and villainy to God, then he does righteousness and is righteous. As it is written, the righteous one . . . is his own accuser. . . .[80]

In the very next paragraph he argued on the basis of Ecclesiastes 7:21 that every good deed, even a prayer, contains sin.[81] "Therefore, we must pray over every good work and say, 'forgive our debt.' "[82]

---

[80] "Antwurt des gerechten sunders. Ich breng fuer dich mein boszheyt. Das ist mein gerechtikeit. Wan der mensch sein boszheit und schalckheit Got endeckt und fuertregt, so thut er gerechtikeit unnd ist gerecht, als geschriben steht [cf. Prov. 18:17], der gerecht ist im anfanck seiner reed, sein selbst anclager und beschuldiger, clager und beclagter." *Ausslegung* (1519), Eii. Cf. also Ciii V.

It is obvious that Karlstadt's concept of righteousness here is very similar to what Ernst Bizer calls Luther's notion of *Demutsgerechtigkeit* which according to Bizer continued to be Luther's view until late 1518. See Ernst Bizer, *Fides ex Auditu* (3rd ed.; Vluyn, 1966), and more recently Oswald Bayer, *Promissio: Geschichte der reformatorischen Wende in Luthers Theologie* (Göttingen, 1971). However, there is a great deal of controversy over Bizer's thesis. Heinrich Bornkamm thinks that as early as the lecture on Psalm 71 (72), *justitia Dei* meant "die im Glauben an Christus bestehende Gerechtigkeit." "Zur Frage der Justitia Dei beim jungen Luther," *ARG*, LII (1961), 24. Gordon Rupp, on the other hand, thinks the conception was still essentially Augustinian through the Romans commentary (*ZKG*, LXXI, 353-54). Obviously this book should not attempt to settle (or venture a guess) on this much debated issue of Luther research. Unfortunately, this means that it is not possible to settle the precise influence of Luther on the development of Karlstadt's new conception of *justitia* as self-condemnation of sin. If Luther continued to conceive of *justitia* as *Demutsgerechtigkeit* until late 1518, then the influence on Karlstadt was probably simple and direct. But if Bornkamm is correct, the relationship is less clear. Probably one cannot safely say more than first that Karlstadt's conception of *justitia* was developing in the same direction as was Luther's and second that Luther's ideas of *judicium* and God's alien act of making the sinner *accusator sui* contributed to this development. (Cf. n. 72 above.)

[81] "Aller und yder heyligen werck auff erdreich. Seind loblich und streflich. . . . Du weist das gebeth ein gelobt werck ist. Nu lesen wir dz Asaph tzu Got clagt. O herr, wie langk tzurnestu, wyder das gebet deines knechts, alle tzornwirdige wercke, seindt strafflich nach Augustini ausszag, Hye repetir abgebraucht schrifft, auff erdrich ist kein gerechter der wol tuth und sundiget nit." *Ausslegung* (1519), EiiV.

[82] "Aber so der geheiligt geist sich Got underlegen wil, alsbald spandt die natur ir armbrust und scheust mit eygenschafft tzum tzyl. Darumb wir uber ycklliche gute werck beten mussen, und sagen, vergib uns unser schuldt." *Ibid.*, EV.

5

Earlier, Karlstadt had explicitly connected the need for self-condemnation with the presence of sin in good deeds: "As long as that severe condemnation lies upon and adheres to our misdeed which arises in good deeds—as it is written, there is no righteous man on earth who does well and does not sin—, . . . man obtains and is assured of divine graciousness and forgiveness of his sins." [83]

In the middle of the treatise there was a lengthy discussion of sin and self-condemnation. Since he thought the ordinary preachers expatiated sufficiently on the devil and worldly temptations, he said he would restrict his discussion of sin to that inner sinful desire which remains in the believer until death.[84] After discussing this enemy "named concupiscence and sin" [85] at length, Karlstadt urged constant self-condemnation. Supposed venial sins are mortal unless confessed.[86] Then he turned to the words "he imputes" and "he does not impute." He defined "non imputat" as "He forgives graciously." Using Romans 4:8, he added: " 'Blessed is the man to whom God does not attribute his sins,' to whom God reckons his guilt as if he had paid it." [87] And then he used the word righteousness (*gerechtigkeit*) with reference both to man's confession of sin and God's resulting forgiveness:

> St. John [says,] "If we will confess our sins, he is righteous to forgive our sins." His righteousness looks down from heaven as soon as truth arises in the earth. For as soon as man confesses his sin, he gives birth to truth, and God, therefore, looks at the man with righteousness, for he makes him righteous. On this point, Isaiah says, you shall confess your sin beforehand so that you become righteous. For God forgets when we remember.[88]

---

[83] "Endtlich und beschlieszlich ist uns von noten, das wir in obgemelt urteyl treten. Dann dieweil das gestreng urteil unsern miszhendelung, die sich in woltuen begeben, als geschriben. Es ist kein gerechter auff erdtreich, der woltuet und sundiget nicht. Dardurch dann nit klein vorhinderung und tzerruttung im geist, den heiligen alhie entstanden sein, obleyt und anhangt, ist der mensch gotlicher gutigkeyt und vorgebung seiner sunden habhafft und vorsichert." *Ibid.*, BiiV.

[84] *Ibid.*, C-CiiV.

[85] " . . . der veint ist, begirlikeit und sund, yn gelydern gelassen, genant." *Ibid.*, CiiV.

[86] See above, n. 66.

[87] "Was ist imputat furwurfft tzornig. non imputat vergibt gnedig. Aus itzt vertzelten wortenn, machen etzlich lacherey, unangesehen, dz sant Pauel die schrifft fur sich getzogen [:] Selig ist der, dem Got sein sund nicht furwurfft [cf. Romans 4:8], dem Got sein schuldt acht, als het er sie betzalt." *Ibid.*, Ciii.

[88] " . . . S. Johannes: Werden wir unnszere sunde bekennen, so ist er gerecht, unsere sunden tzuvergeben [cf. 1 John 1:9] sein gerechtigkeit sihet vom himel, szo baldt warheyt ym erdrich auffgeet [cf. Ps. 85:11 (Vulgate: 84:12)]. Dan es bald der mensch sein sunde bekend, so gebirth er die warheit, und darumb syhet

Since man's righteousness is his confession of sin, God's righteousness is no longer that with which he clothes man, but rather that by which he forgives man.

An interesting exchange at Leipzig contained an explicit statement of the emerging doctrine of forensic justification.[89] It also illustrated the connection of the non-Augustinian emphasis on sin in good deeds with the new concept. Eck attacked Karlstadt's assertion that even good deeds contain sin, and cited Jerome's view that David demanded that God judge him since he was innocent.[90] Hence Karlstadt was wrong in discovering sin in all good deeds. Karlstadt responded with his own interpretation of the nature of David's innocence. He interpreted David's statement that truth arises from the earth and righteousness descends from heaven (Psalm 85:11) in the way he had previously:

> When truth, i.e. confession of sins, arises in man, then the righteousness which justifies man looks down from heaven.... Therefore, when a man judges his own sins, then the God who righteously justifies and pities passes over his debt.[91]

In this passage justification does not connote God's gracious creation of righteousness in man, but rather his merciful act of forgiveness. Thus, by the time of the Leipzig debate, Karlstadt had arrived at a

---

Goth mit gerechtigkeit yn dem menschenn, dan er macht yn gerecht. Hirumb sagt Esaias [cf. 43:26], Du salt deyn sund tzufuer bekennen, das du gerecht werdest, dan Got vorgist, so wir gedencken." *Ibid.*, CiiiV.

[89] The exchange began on July 15; Seitz, pp. 229ff.

[90] "Videat novus [i.e. Karlstadt] interpres sacrae scripturae eundum 'Hieronymum adducentem' sanctum David lib. 2. contra Jovinianum, ubi inquit: David electum secundum cor Domini, qui fecit omnes voluntates eius, et qui ausus erat dicere: Judica me, Domine, quoniam ego in innocentia mea ingressus sum. Ecce hic David petiit iudicium secundum innocentiam suam." Seitz, p. 233.

[91] "Sed vellem D. D. intelligeret innocentiam Davidis et iustitiam Job, et tunc recte pro me inferret auctoritatem: Judica me, domine secundum innocentiam Job. Nam iustitia Job est iudicium, de quo paulo ante dixit: Veruntamen vias meas in conspectu eius arguam et ipse erit salvator meus. Non enim veniet in conspectu eius omnis hypocrita. Secundum hanc iusticiam, qua Job iudicat peccata sua, agnoscit et damnat, vult iudicari et iudicandus invenietur iustus. Quod David dicit: Veritas de terra orta est et iustitia de caelo prospexit: dum oritur veritas, i.e. confessio peccatorum in homine, tunc iustitia iustificans hominem prospicit de caelo. Quod apostolus dicit: Si nos iudicamus, non iudicamur a Domino; et Johannes in canonica: Si confessi fuerimus peccata nostra, iustus est deus, qui relinquit nobis peccata: Ergo quando homo iudicat peccata sua, tunc iuste iustificans deus et misericors relinquit delictum. Ita etiam David habuit innocentiam, quod peccatum suum contra se semper fuit, et quod peccata sua nota fecit deo. Et secundum istam innocentiam vult iudicari in sua iustitia." Seitz, p. 236.

doctrine of forensic justification. Luther's influence is unmistakable.[92]

The foregoing analysis suggests that the non-Augustinian ideas of sin in good deeds and post-baptismal concupiscence as sin were important in the emergence of the new definition of justification. If every act contains sin, the righteousness possessed by the "righteous sinner" must consist of self-condemnation and confession of sin. Consequently God's act of forgiveness rather than his creation of inner righteousness becomes the focus of attention. Hence justification connotes God's merciful non-imputation of sins.

### (c) *Poenitentia*

It was Luther's "Ninety-Five Theses" and the subsequent debate which aroused Karlstadt's interest in *poenitentia*. Before the outbreak of the indulgence controversy, Karlstadt had mentioned the subject only briefly and then merely to safeguard his Augustinian concern for *sola gratia*. It was the seemingly Pelagian character of Scotus' doctrine of attrition which prompted Karlstadt's six theses on penance in the "151 Theses." Scotus had taught that the sinner could produce displeasure at sin and the will to conform oneself to divine law without the aid of special grace. If this displeasure, this *dispositio*, is properly conditioned, i.e. if it lasts for a period of time designated by God, it merits infused grace and is transformed into contrition. Having learned from Augustine that the will is too depraved to be able to prepare for grace, Karlstadt simply denied that even the most perfectly conditioned attrition produced by man was a sufficient disposition for justification.[93] Further, if attrition or contrition is required, it is as an act informed by grace (*actus formatus*), not as an act

---

[92] One should hasten to point out that justification is still not defined explicitly as *per fidem ex auditu*, but that definition will soon appear. It should also be noted that the new conception of *justitia* and justification did not mean that Karlstadt could not sometimes still define *justitia* in a perfectly Augustinian fashion. E.g. ". . . liberum arbitrium nullam iustitiam facere potest, nisi Christus assumat prius peccata liberi arbitrii et ipsum transferat in regnum lucis, ut sit solus Christus bonus in bonis, in iustificatis iustus sanctificatio in sanctificatis. . . ." Seitz, p. 21. For Luther, see below, chapter IV, nn. 106-112.

[93] "Ita cognicio legis et voluntas ei se conformans non est disposicio previa ad gratiam (Contra Scotum), Ita nec attritio perfectissime circumstancionata in genere morum est disposicio sufficiens ad iustificacionem (Contra eundem)." Theses 77 and 78 of "151 Theses," Kähler, p. 24*. Cf. Scotus: "Nulla potest esse sufficientior dispositio ad istam justificationem, quam ista attritio perfecte circumstantionata in genere moris"; quoted in Reinhold Seeberg, *Die Theologie des Johannes Duns Scotus* (Leipzig, 1900), p. 404. Cf. pp. 397ff for Scotus' doctrine of penance.

of the unaided will.[94] These theses show that Karlstadt's primary reason for discussing *poenitentia* prior to Luther's "Ninety-Five Theses" was to avoid any Pelagian weakening of the doctrine of grace alone.

Luther's influence was visible in Karlstadt's *370 Conclusiones*. Since theses 102-140 were in defense of Luther's first thesis (the whole life of the believer should be one of repentance) which Eck had attacked in his first obelisk, it is not surprising that Karlstadt talked a great deal about daily repentance.[95] Eck had argued that "since the kingdom of heaven in Christ's words seems to signify the present church, . . . it is not apparent how repentance represents the whole life of believers." [96] Karlstadt thought Eck supposed the church contained many people so genuinely righteous that they did not need to repent. Karlstadt disagreed vehemently. He cited numerous liturgical prayers which spoke of constant repentance by the righteous person (*justus*) to support his argument that daily repentance is imperative.[97] Quite logically, he also supported the demand for daily repentance with his notion that good deeds always contain sin.[98] In his *Defensio*, he adduced Ecclesiastes 7:21 to defend his thesis that good deeds are sinful, and argued again that constant repentance was necessary.[99]

It was probably also Luther's influence which prompted Karlstadt to become concerned with inner repentance in 1518. Partly through the influence of Staupitz, Luther had come to believe that the most significant aspect of *poenitentia* was not some external act but rather an internal change of disposition.[100] In his *Defensio* Karlstadt reminded

---

[94] "Si contritio vel attricio requiritur ad iustificacionem tunc ut actus concomitans non previus ([Contra] multos), Ut actus formatus, non formabilis." Theses 79-80 of "151 Theses," Kähler, p. 24*.

[95] Greving, pp. 38ff.

[96] "Cum regnum coelorum in verbis Christi praesentem videatur significare ecclesiam ac tempus plenitudinis evangelicae tunc adventantis, non videtur, quomodo poentitentia omnem fidelium vitam exprimat." Greving, p. 38.2-4.

[97] See theses 102-128, *ibid.*, pp. 38-42. E.g., theses 127-28: "Tametsi evangelicae plenitudinis tempus ecclesiae advenerit, attamen universa ecclesia, quamdiu militaverit, quottidianae poenitentiae est indiga." *Ibid.*, p. 42.10-12.

[98] "Hoc vicium peccatum est, quod ecclesia sancta quottidiana confessione nec sterili dolore expiat. . . . Quod boni et mali, filii Dei, habent; semper enim, dum bene facit iustus, peccat, et bonus et malus est." Theses 132, 134; *ibid.*, p. 44.3-8.

[99] "Peccatum in bono opere vel actu, est proprie peccatum, quia scriptura vocat peccatum. Porro sic scribitur: Non est iustus in terra, qui facit bonum et non peccat, idcirco iustus benefaciendo peccat proprie et nisi fateretur se peccare, dolum in spiritu haberet et non esset beatus. Peccatum in bono opere utique est peccatum proprie. Item poenitendum, . . ." Löscher, *Reformations-Acta*, II, 146.

[100] See Luther to Staupitz, May 30, 1518; *LW*, XLVIII, 64-70; *WA*, I, 525-27. "Und darumb zu ainem beschlus fruchtbars erlangens so sol unser rew also

Eck that their debate was not about the sacrament of penance, for of course he believed in the second plank after shipwreck; rather, their controversy dealt with that inner, life-long repentance in which a man humbly belittles himself in prayer, shuts his closet door and in complete affliction of mind pours out his heart before God.[101] The non-polemical, devotional *De impii justificatione* (early 1519) was devoted almost exclusively to the inner psychological experience of self-condemnation and sorrowing over sins.[102] Karlstadt did not reject the sacrament of penance at this time. Since he had learned from Luther and Staupitz that that inner repentance which is a change of disposition is the most significant aspect of *poenitentia*, he merely said very little about it. Thus, as Karlstadt took up arms in defense of the "Wittenbergers", his statements on sin, justification and *poenitentia* began to betray more and more traces of his younger colleague's ideas.

### 3. THE LEIPZIG DEBATE AND ITS AFTERMATH

Karlstadt's most significant contribution to the Leipzig debate was simply that of provoking continued conflict between Wittenberg and Ingolstadt at a time when Luther and Eck apparently would have preferred peace. After a written, but private exchange of views on Luther's "Ninety-Five Theses," Luther, and to a lesser extent Eck, attempted to avoid further conflict.[103] While Luther was at Heidelberg

---

geschickt sein, das wir uber Unser sunden den hochsten Schmerzen mer mit den Inwendigen zehern des herzens dann auswendiger bewaynung haben." Staupitz, *Von ainer waren rechtn rew;* Knaake, *Staupitzens sämmtliche Werke,* I, 16. Steinmetz comments apropos Staupitz: "True penance is more internal than external, more a matter of inner sorrow than of outer expressions of grief." *Misericordia Dei,* p. 101. That Staupitz also influenced Karlstadt directly in his thinking on *poenitentia* is quite probable.

[101] See Karlstadt's entire discussion in Löscher, *Reformations-Acta,* II, 112-115. "Assero et confiteor ipse, sacramentalem poenitentiam cum Ecclesia, sed eam non tantum, imo et alias. ... Videsne aperte Aug. adservisse, totam seu omnem fidelium vitam esse poenitentiam. ... Sed qualem? adverte, talem, quae perpetua supplicationis humilitate subitur. ... Quid autem est homini, vel molestius vel difficilius perpetuo poenitere cum humilitate? ut sibi vilescat homo, cum oratione seu supplicatione, ut clauso ostio cubiculum ingrediatur et toto mentis affectu cor suum coram Deo effendat" (pp. 112-113).

[102] It is probable that this is the book Karlstadt had promised Spalatin a year earlier (see above, n. 51). Karlstadt also referred to the book in his *Defensio;* Löscher, *Reformations-Acta,* II, 115. I would guess that Karlstadt originally intended to discuss indulgences as he promised Spalatin, but then decided to avoid taking a public stand at this time. See Oberman's discussion of the pre-Leipzig exchange of Eck and Karlstadt on *poenitentia*: "Wittenbergs Zweifronten-krieg," pp. 346ff.

[103] In his letter to Eck on May 19, 1518, Luther urged Eck not to publish

in May, 1518, however, Karlstadt rushed into print his *370 Conclusiones*, theses 102-213 of which were specifically directed against Eck. Karlstadt's answer to Eck's plea—which arrived too late in any case—to avoid publication revealed a man eager for battle: "I have decided to endure war and tyrannical siege rather than a perverse peace at the price of disparaging the divine writings." [104] Karlstadt's published attack virtually forced Eck to defend himself. It was Eck's challenge to settle their argument in a public debate which led eventually to the important confrontation at Leipzig.[105]

Initially the debate was to be only between Karlstadt and Eck. In the fall of 1518 Luther was involved only as an intermediary arranging the details. Eventually, of course, Eck cleverly involved Luther and the Eck-Luther exchange became the significant aspect of the debate.[106] But the Luther-Eck debate, with its important consequences probably would never have occurred had not Karlstadt kept the controversy alive in 1518.

## (a) *The debate*

The accident which unceremoniously hurled Karlstadt out of his wagon into the mud as he approached the gates of Leipzig is often viewed as symbolic of his later fortunes in the verbal encounter with Eck. An analysis of the discussion, however, will show that such a view is only partly correct.

A brief sketch of Eck's pre-Leipzig understanding of the relationship between grace and free will will help clarify his statements at Leipzig. After God acts first and provides prevenient grace, the will is free to respond to God. If the will freely does what is in it (*quod in se*

---

anything against him (*WABr*, I, 178.17-34). Eck apparently was agreeable for when he heard that Karlstadt intended to publish against him, he wrote a hasty letter asking him as a friend to abandon his intention (Eck to Karlstadt, May 28, 1518; Smith, *Luther's Correspondence*, I, 90-91; Gerdes, VII, 310-311). After Karlstadt had published his *370 Conclusiones*, Luther wrote to Christopher Scheurl, a mutual friend of Luther and Eck who was trying to arrange a reconciliation, that he had not known or consented to Karlstadt's publication. Furthermore, Luther said he felt entirely reconciled to Eck and hoped for peace (June, 15, 1518, *WABr*, I, 183.5-26).

[104] "Institui mecum magis bellum et tyrannicam obsidionem sustinendam, quam perversam pacem in detrimentum divinorum documinum [!] et perniciem habendam: Susque deque habiturus, quod mihi eveniet." Gerdes, VII, 312. See the translation in Smith, *Luther's Correspondence*, I, 93-94.

[105] Eck offered the challenge in his reply to Karlstadt's theses. Greving, pp. 81-2.

[106] See Fife, *Revolt*, pp. 339ff, for the details.

*est*) then God views this disposition for grace as meritorious *de congruo* and grants justifying grace which in turn enables the believer to perform good works which merit (*de digno*) eternal life.[107] Eck's precise understanding of prevenient grace is particularly important for one's understanding of the Leipzig debate. That "divine motion" or "special assistance" which is the necessary first step toward justification is something supernatural.[108] Although distinct from man's natural powers, however, this special motion is universally and constantly available to all men.[109] God grants justifying grace if the human will, aided by this special prevenient grace which is always available to every person, chooses to turn to God. That such a view of the role of free will differed radically from Karlstadt's Augustinian stance is obvious.

When the debate opened on June 27, Eck immediately raised the issue of the role of the will in good deeds.[110] He declared that he was ready to defend the view that when aided by special grace, the will exercises an active causality in good deeds.[111] When Karlstadt replied

---

[107] See the summary of Eck's *ordo salutis* in Walter L. Moore, "Between Mani and Pelagius: Predestination and Justification in the Early Writings of John Eck" (Unpublished Th. D. dissertation, Harvard University, 1967), pp. 106-7. God's act of predestination, then, is based on his foreknowledge that particular men will freely respond to prevenient grace and then after receiving justifying grace, also will to do good works which will merit eternal life. (*ibid.*, pp. 73-74).

[108] "Unde sicut dona naturalia proprie non sunt effectus nec ratio praedestinationis, ita nec illa motio, quamvis sit supernaturalis." *Chrysopassus a Ioanne Maioris Eckio* (Augsburg, 1514), III. lix; quoted in Moore, *op. cit.*, p. 93, n. 14.

[109] "Ipsa etiam motio divina, quae praevenit et praeoccupat voluntatem, nec est effectus nec ratio praedestinationis. Quod non sit effectus probatur: est enim communis omni homini praedestinato et reprobato. Omnes enim Deus movet sufficienter. . . ." *Chrysopassus*, III, lix; quoted in Moore, *op. cit.*, p. 96, n. 21. For the constant availability, see *ibid.*, p. 98.

[110] Karlstadt and Eck debated three basic topics, but their argument over free will was the longest: 1) free will (Seitz, pp. 15-54); 2) Can man by doing *quod in se est* remove the obstacle to grace? (Seitz, 220-229); 3) Does the righteous person sin in good deeds? (Seitz, pp. 229-247). The first two issues are discussed below. For the third, see above, n. 62.

[111] "Intendo ergo probare illud esse conveniens sacrae scripturae, sanctis patribus, fidei christianae, liberum arbitrium voluntatem humanam habere causalitatem activam, vim productivam, elicitivam operis meritorii, non excludendo gratiam et speciale adiutorium dei." Seitz, p. 15. Eck's opening words had contained a reference to one of Karlstadt's theses prepared for Leipzig: "Clarissime doctor, quia una summa contentionis est nostrae propositio 11 [the Freyberger Manuskript and the first printed edition read: 14], ubi vertitur materia, quomodo liberum arbitrium se habeat ad opus bonum et meritorium." Karlstadt's 14th thesis reads: "D. Joannes non videns, quomodo bonum opus sit totum a Deo, et Dei opus. . . ." And the 11th: "Liberum arbitrium, ante gratiam per Spiritum S.

in good Augustinian fashion that the will apart from grace can do nothing pleasing to God,[112] Eck stated his conception of the will's role more clearly. He insisted first of all that since he was a Christian not a Pelagian, he knew very well that the will apart from grace could not do any good deed. The real dispute rather was about his contention that

> free will, our rational power, when helped by grace, is not deceived about its *natural*, productive and causative power. That is, the will is not merely passive in a good deed, . . . but rather cooperates with God when he helps with his grace.[113]

Karlstadt of course, promptly denied that after grace has been received the will has any "natural activity" apart from grace.[114] After a few remarks by Eck, time intervened and the session was adjourned until the next morning.

Karlstadt apparently did not spend the entire night in slumber, for when the debate resumed at seven the next morning, his exceedingly lengthy remarks were so obviously prepared beforehand that Eck complained that they were engaged in debate, not the recitation of previously composed orations.[115] Karlstadt argued at great length that everything which the believer does is actually performed by grace.[116] Therefore, he again insisted, Eck was wrong in attributing a natural activity to the will.[117] When Karlstadt finally relinquished the floor, Eck expressed amazement that Karlstadt had said his opponent believed that free will had a special operation not caused by grace.

---

infusam, nihil valet nisi ad peccandum. . . ." Löscher, *Reformations-Acta*, III, 290. Later, Karlstadt commented: "Interim salva sit conclusio mea XI." Seitz, p. 23.

[112] " . . . voluntas absque gratia spiritus sancti nihil potest facere, quod deo gratum est et acceptum, sed quidquid facit, illud est nocivum." Seitz, p. 17.

[113] " . . . verum hoc erat propositi nostri et hoc saxum volvebamus, ut liberum arbitrium vis nostra rationalis adiuta gratia naturali virtute productiva elicitiva non probaretur [first printed edition: fraudaretur], hoc est quod voluntas non haberet se mere passive ad bonum nec liberum arbitrium esset res de solo titulo post peccatum, sed potius cooperaretur deo sua gratia adiuvante." Seitz, p. 18.

[114] "Ad tertium dico, quod auctoritas ista non probat hominem concessa gratia habere specialem quandam activitatem et naturalem a gratia distinctam." Seitz, p. 19.

[115] Seitz, p. 24. Karlstadt's speech extends from pp. 20-23.

[116] "Quod autem voculam istam mecum expendit et libero arbitrio operationem adhuc aliquam propriam, quam gratia non faciat, tribuit, satis notum est intellectoribus divi Pauli, quam misere torqueat auctoritatem ejus contra manifestam divi apostoli intentionem, qui omnem actionem, quam gratia non efficit, ablegavit, cum dixit: Non ego, sed gratia dei mecum, hoc est, non sum ego, qui specialem activitatem, ut aiunt scholastici, sed gratia est, quae omnem largitur operatioem." Seitz, p. 22.

[117] "At dominus meus Eccius facit voluntatem reginam, cum dicit voluntatem habere specialem activitatem et naturalem concurrentem in bonis meritis." Seitz, p. 23.

Eck said he had never thought of such a position.[118] At this point
Karlstadt claimed that Eck had conceded and wanted to move on to
another matter, but Eck hotly denied that he had lost and urged a
postponement because of the late hour. The judges agreed.[119]

Brief asides in Karlstadt's and Eck's major speeches of the morning
point to deeper disagreements between the two assailants. After
noting that Eck now agreed that the will which had not been restored
by grace could not do anything pleasing to God, he added: "So
farewell to scholastic dispositions *de congruo*." [120] Karlstadt certainly
did not believe, as did Eck, that the will could freely choose to dispose
itself for and thus merit justifying grace. For his part, Eck noted that
he was concerned to preserve that law of freedom by which men can
choose life or death.[121] Again, Karlstadt vigorously disagreed with
Eck's doctrine of predestination *secundum praevisa merita*. The debate
might have been more illuminating if these issues had become central
at this point. Instead, they continued to argue over whether the will
has any causal activity in a good deed.

When Eck began the debate again after lunch, he did not refer to the
issue of a natural activity of the will. Instead, he used Saint Bernard to
argue that the will is not just a servant, but also an active ally of grace.
He quoted Bernard's statement that what is begun by grace alone is
accomplished by grace and the will. "Here, the holy father explained

---

[118] " . . . et magis miror, cum copiam hesternae disputationis per notarium
habuerit, quod mihi imponit contra conventa, quod asseruerim liberum arbitrium
specialem habere operationem, quam non faciat gratia, quod non cogitavi quidem.'
Seitz, p. 25. Eck meant, of course, that since prevenient grace is always available,
no good act of the will can be without special supernatural grace.

[119] Seitz, p. 25.

[120] "Et admodum mihi gratum est, quod egregius d. meus . . . asserit, liberum
arbitrium seu voluntatem lapsam gratia dei nondum erectam atque instauratam
nihil facere posse, quod deo gratum, acceptum atque complacitum sit. Valeant
igitur dispositionis scholasticae de congruo, nec prosint contritiones, quas voluntati necdum sanatae attribuunt." Seitz, p. 23.

[121] "De secundo dico me nihil inculcare toties, nisi quod velim libertatis legem
per sapientem explicatam, cuius et Cyprianus meminit ad Cornelium papam
dicens: Christus non increpavit recedentes, sed magis conversus ad apostolos
suos dixit: nunquid et vos vultis abire? Servant scil. legem, qua homo libertati
suae relictus et in arbitrio proprio constitutus mortem sibi appetit vel vitam."
Seitz, p. 24. See above, n. 107 for Eck's position on predestination. It is even
more surprising that Karlstadt did not pick up this remark and challenge Eck's
doctrine of predestination since in their pre-Leipzig polemics, Karlstadt had
rejected Eck's assertion that predestination was irrelevant to their discussion of
*poenitentia*. Karlstadt insisted that justification and predestination were intimately
related. See *Defensio*, Löscher, II, 128. Cf. also Oberman's discussion in "Wittenbergs Zweifrontenkrieg," pp. 349-356.

not only the causality but also the mode of the free will." [122] Karlstadt fortunately had Bernard's text and was able to point out that Bernard had gone on to say that grace and free will both act, but only in the sense that although the act is totally *in* the will, it is also totally *of* (*ex*) grace. Thus Bernard meant that the will's activity in good deeds is entirely of grace.[123] Karlstadt was holding his own quite well.

Eck decided to try to capitalize on Karlstadt's tendency to emphasize the passivity of the will. He declared that the activity of the first cause does not exclude the concomitant operation of a secondary cause. Hence even though grace enables the will to act, one should not conclude that the will is passive.[124] And, of course, he could cite Augustine to show that the will actually wills when grace activates it. He agreed that the will has no action (*actio*) not given by grace, but demanded that Karlstadt tell him whether the will is therefore passive.[125] Karlstadt immediately retorted that he had never denied that grace gives action (*actio*) to the will. He had merely opposed any "natural activity" of the will in good deeds.[126] Eck now ridiculously claimed that by agreeing to an activity given by grace, Karlstadt had adopted his opponent's position.[127]

Eck then went on to argue that in his *Defensio*, Karlstadt had said that in good deeds the will is completely passive and does not act, thereby denying, Eck implied, even that activity communicated by grace.[128] In reply Karlstadt restated his position most clearly:

---

[122] "Verba Bernhardi sunt ista: Sic autem ista gratia cum libero arbitrio operatur ut tamen illud in primo praeveniat, in ceteris comitetur; ad hoc utique praeveniens, ut iam sibi cooperetur, ita tamen, quod a sola gratia coeptum est, pariter ab utroque perficiatur. . . . Hic sanctus pater non modo causalitatem liberi arbitrii, sed et modum eius exposuit." Seitz, p. 26.

[123] "Sequitur declaratio Bernhardi: Totum quidem hoc, id est liberum arbitrium totum, scil. opus bonum, illa, videlicet gratia facit. Sed ut totum in illo i.e. in libero arbitrio, sic totum ex illa, scil. gratia fit. Est ergo sensus, quod gratia operatur bona opera in libero arbitrio et ita gratia habet activitatem bonorum operum, liberum autem arbitrium habet susceptionem." Seitz, p. 27. The passage is in Bernard, *De gratia et libero arbitrio*, XIV (48): "Non partim gratia, partim liberum arbitrium, sed totum singula opere individuo peragunt, totum quidem hoc, et totum illa, sed ut totum in illo [lib. arb.], sic totum ex illa [gratia]." *Sancti Bernardi Opera*, ed. J. Leclercq and H. M. Rochais (Rome, 1957-    ), III, 200.

[124] Seitz, p. 28.

[125] Seitz, pp. 29-30.

[126] "Ad primum, secundum et tertium et sextum argumentum dico, quod gratia utique dat actionem libero arbitrio neque hoc est negatum per me, sed solum hoc, quod liberum arbitrium habeat specialem et naturalem activitatem in bonis operibus." Seitz, p. 30.

[127] Seitz, p. 31.

[128] "Quarto quod clarissimus dominus doctor saepe scriptum reliquit in defen-

Since the doctor infers from [my] fourteenth thesis that [I say] that free will has no activity, I agree to his statement as far as any *natural* activity is concerned. But in the case of that activity which grace confers, I say that free will has activity.[129]

Verbally Eck was correct in his reference to *Defensio*, for Karlstadt sometimes stated his theme of *sola gratia* in terms of the complete passivity of the will.[130] In virtually all his publications, however, he had also explicitly accepted Augustine's view that when grace transforms the will, then the will genuinely wills.[131] Thus Eck was wrong in charging Karlstadt with denying to the will an activity imparted by grace.

When after intervening festivities Karlstadt arose and charged Eck with a contradiction, Eck interrupted his speech. The pro-Wittenberg editor who edited the 1519 edition of the debate hinted that it was because Eck was losing that he chose this moment to object strenuously to Karlstadt's use of notes.[132] When the judge agreed with Eck, an uproar ensued and it appeared that the debate might not continue. Eventually, however, it was agreed to go on.

When Karlstadt took the floor on July 1, he charged Eck with a contradiction. At the beginning of the debate he had attributed a natural activity to the will in good deeds, but later he denied that the will had any activity not imparted by grace. "I ask, therefore, since to have activity from another is not to have it from oneself . . . how he can reconcile this contradiction." [133] Somewhat incredibly, Eck

---

sione sua, liberum arbitrium et voluntatem pati et non agere ad opus bonum, sicut patet b. 4. facie 2 et c. 2 fac. 1 . . . et in multis aliis locis, quibus clarissimus doctor dicit voluntatem solum recipere et non agere, tamen si libero arbitrio dat activitatem sibi a gratia communicatam, sum contentus." Seitz, p. 31.

[129] "Ad primum, quoniam dominus doctor per conclusionem 14. infert, quod liberum arbitrium nullam activitatem habeat, subscribo sententiae suae quantum ad activitatem naturalem, sed quantum ad activitatem, quam gratia confert, dico, quod liberum arbitrium habet activitatem." Seitz, p. 32. See above, n. 111 for Karlstadt's 14th thesis.

[130] E.g., *Defensio*, Löscher, *Reformations-Acta*, II, 123 and *De sp.*, Kähler, pp. 42.1-43.12.

[131] "CCCCII. . . . Sine me nihil potestis facere. Ex haec auctoritas: Dominus dabit benignitatem, et terra nostra dabit fructum suum. CCCCIII. Non fit sine voluntate, hoc est non extra. CCCCIIII. Not fit sine voluntate, quia Deus facit velle et operatur velle." *370 Conclusiones*, Löscher, *Reformations-Acta*, II, 104. See also thesis 288, *ibid.*, p. 94; *De sp.*, Kähler, pp. 38.31-40.10, 94.3-37; *Defensio*, Löscher, II, 154-5.

[132] "Eccius forte sibi ipsi diffisus hic Carolostadium interpellavit, ne scheda aut libri beneficio uteretur." Seitz, p. 33.

[133] "Est autem contrarietas ista: in exordio suae disputationis dixit liberum

simply denied that he had ever attributed a natural activity to the will in good deeds. The will has a supernatural, not a natural activity.[134] And then Eck turned quickly to the philosophical distinction again. Karlstadt was wrong in arguing that activity from another (*a alieno*) is not one's own (*propria*) activity. Rather, the activity which grace communicates to the will is the will's own activity, although one does not thereby exclude the concurrence of another cause.[135]

Foolishly, Karlstadt failed to press the fact that Eck had contradicted himself. To Eck's denial that he had ever spoken of a natural activity of the will, he merely muttered, "Let the world judge," [136] and then turned to the philosophical problem. Karlstadt expressed his inability to see how two causes could both produce a good work totally, unless the one cause were passive and the other active.[137] Eck mockingly replied that anyone moderately learned in philosophy could understand how two causes—a primary and a secondary—could each produce the total effect. One should not suppose, of course, as Karlstadt did in his *Defensio*, that this position implies that the will produces one part and grace another part of a good deed. Each cause is a total cause.[138]

---

arbitrium adiutum gratia habere specialem et naturalem activitatem in bono opere, in processu autem disputationis dixit, se nunquam cogitasse liberum arbitrium habere specialem activitatem, quam gratia non praestiterit. Quaero igitur, cum habere activitatem ex alio non sit eam habere ex se, neque habere propiam [!], sed alienam, quomodo huiusmodi dictum sibi ipsi dissidens concordari debeat, ne nostra disputatio per inane emicet." Seitz, p. 34.

[134] "Respondeo et dico, neque ab exordio disputationis neque in processu unquam me dixisse liberum arbitrium habere activitatem naturalem respectu boni operis, sed opponendo contra dominum doctorem assumpsi probaturus liberum arbitrium habere activitatem, vim productivam et elicitivam boni operis adiutum a gratia, de quo me remitto ad acta notariorum. Quare addendo adiutorium gratiae non naturalem, sed supernaturalem dedi voluntati activitatem a gratia sibi communicatam, in qua sententia adhuc persevero." Seitz, p. 34. In this same speech, however, Eck included a quotation from the pseudonymous letter *ad Demetriadem* which said that man was made "ut boni et mali capax naturaliter utrumque posset et ad alterutrum deflectere voluntatem." *Ibid.*, p. 35.

[135] Seitz, pp. 34-5.

[136] "Judicet mundus" is in the first printed edition of 1519, but not in the manuscripts used by Seitz. It is probable however that Karlstadt did make some preliminary comment since the MSS begin with the word "secundo" (see next note).

[137] "Secundo quaero ex domino doctore, quomodo eiusdem operis boni possunt esse duae causae, quarum utraque totum producit, quemadmodum Bernhardus per doctorem adductus dicit, singula peragunt totum individuo opere? nisi enim altera causarum tantum passive concurrat et altera tantum active, vix intelligi potest, quomodo totum opus ab utroque sit totaliter." Seitz, p. 35.

[138] Seitz, pp. 35-6.

Karlstadt should have been able to handle this common philosophical distinction between primary and secondary causes, but for some reason he was puzzled.[139] From this point on, Eck won easily. Eck argued that grace produces the total (*totum*) good deed, but not totally (*totaliter*), for that would deny any activity to the will.[140] Karlstadt complained of Eck's using heathen weapons in theology,[141] and then lamely repeated his view that the entire (*totum*) good deed is of God.[142] To that Eck cleverly responded with a reminder that Karlstadt should be disproving, rather than supporting, his opponent's position! The debate dragged on through July 1 and 2, but it was largely dreary repetition.[143] Karlstadt did not do as well in the latter part of their first debate as he might have.

After the vigorous debate between Luther and Eck, Karlstadt and Eck returned to battle on July 14. This time Karlstadt promptly focused the central issue of the *dispositiones de congruo* by declaring: "I will defend and prove that to do what is in one is to sin, do evil, displease God, lie." [144] Eck agreed that in its own strength the will could only sin, but added that when grace assists the will, it can do good and obtain merit.[145] Although quite prepared to grant that grace (*divina motio*) precedes the will's act by which it disposes itself in a

---

[139] As an ex-Thomist he should at least have been familiar with Aquinas. See, for example, *Summa Theologica*, I, Q. 23, art. 5 and the excellent discussion in E. Gilson, *The Christian Philosophy of St. Thomas Aquinas* (New York, 1956), pp. 180-86.

[140] Seitz, p. 36 (also pp. 53-54).

[141] "Quod dominus doctor in certamine theologico se munit armis gentilibus, hoc suo more facit, sed quaestioni meae adhuc non satisfecit." Seitz, p. 36.

[142] Seitz, p. 37. Eck replied: "Rogo dominus doctor meminerit, quam agat personam, eius enim est non mea firmare, sed improbare." *Ibid.*

[143] Karlstadt expressed dissatisfaction with Eck's *totum-totaliter* distinction, but then continued to use metaphors which enabled Eck to continue repeating his distinction and insisting on a real activity of the will. E.g., see Karlstadt's comparison of the will to a stick and an axe in God's hand (Seitz, p. 52).

[144] "Restat iam disputanda tertia decima conclusio, quae est, quod 'dominus doctor cum sua maxima suorum disputatorum potest facere, quod in se est, id est obicem et impedimentum gratiae tollere' etc. Ego defendam et probabo, quod facere quod in se est, est peccare, malefacere, deo displicere, mentiri, se ictare etc." Seitz, p. 219. The material in quotation marks is from Karlstadt's 13th thesis prepared for Leipzig. Löscher, III, 290. Well before Leipzig, Karlstadt had denounced the doctrine of *dispositiones de congruo* and the use made of the distinction between general and justifying grace. See chapter one, "*Sola Gratia* and the New Pelagians."

[145] "Liberum arbitrium sicut faciendo, quod in se est, potest peccare, mentiri etc, ita faciendo, quod in se est, adiutum a gratia potest bene agere, mereri, peccatum vitare." Seitz, p. 220. Eck, of course, referred to that prevenient grace which is universally and constantly available.

meritorious fashion, he nevertheless insisted that the free will did have the power to consent to grace.[146]

Karlstadt retorted that God attributes damnation to the man who does what is in him.[147] Aware that many scholastics taught that the *facere quod in se est* preceded the infusion of justifying grace,[148] he then demanded that Eck define more precisely that grace which precedes the disposition for grace:

> The doctor has said that a divine motion precedes the disposition for grace. I fear that if that divine motion is distinguished from the grace which justifies the wicked, the excellent doctor defends with scholastic inventions clothing in which Pelagians are hid.[149]

Instead of candidly admitting that he taught that prevenient grace (which enables man to dispose himself for justifying grace) is universally and constantly available to all men, Eck attempted to sound as anti-Pelagian as possible. He insisted that a meritorious act is never possible without special grace.[150] He noted that Karlstadt had not cited any proof for his theses that it would be Pelagian to distinguish prevenient grace from justifying grace but then proceeded to state his own position so ambiguously that Karlstadt assumed that Eck had indeed accepted his own point of view.[151] And he concluded his

---

[146] " . . . quod tamen facere in se bonum semper praecedit divina motio, ut ibidem expresse declarat de Ezechiele, quem facit nobis adversari. Manifestarium est eum nobis esse concordantem: 'aufer cor lapideum et da cor carneum,' quia, ut semper diximus, bona voluntas praeparatur a domino et praevenitur et gratia facit voluntatem bene agere, tamen requiritur voluntatis acquiescentia seu consensus. Et hoc est facere, quod in se est." Seitz, p. 222.

[147] "Ex quo textu sequitur, quod deus homini facienti, quod in se est, tribuit damnationem, facienti autem, quod ex deo est, largitur coronam. "Seitz, p. 224.

[148] " . . . scholastici autem dicunt, quod facere, quod in se est, praecedit infusionem gratiae." Seitz, p. 224.

[149] "Duodecimo cum dominus doctor dixit, divinam motionem praecedere dispositionem ad gratiam, vereor, si ista divina motio distinguitur contra gratiam iustificantem impium, egregium dominum doctorem cum inventis scholasticis defendere vestitum, quo teguntur Pelagiani, qui veniunt in vestimentis ovium et intrinsecus sunt lupi rapaces." Seitz, p. 225. See above, n. 144.

[150] "Quoniam libere confiteor, nunquam fieri aliquod bonum opus meritorium sine speciali assistentia divinae gratiae et misericordiae." Seitz, pp. 227-228. See above nn. 108-109 for Eck's conception of prevenient grace.

[151] "Quod dicit vel veretur me incedere sub habitu Pelagianorum, si dispositio praecedens non sit gratia iustificans, nihil adduxit, ideo solum me excuso, esse me parvam oviculam et lupos ignorare. Hoc tamen arbitror esse de mente Augustini, quod initium salutis sit gratia et gratuita motio iustificans: primo in tertio gradu ab Augustino posito, ubi datur gratia, quae est vera charitas, ut prima sit gratia praeveniens, secunda cooperans." Seitz, p. 228. See Moore's interpretation of this statement: "Between Mani and Pelagius," pp. 135-137. Eck apparently meant that there are three steps: 1) God gives *gratia praeveniens;* 2) the will and grace then

remarks with the assurance that he had always believed that the free will of itself can only sin. Only when helped, lifted and moved by grace can it do good.[152] It is hardly surprising that Karlstadt expressed satisfaction with Eck's comments and concluded that Eck had agreed that any disposition for grace is produced by justifying grace.[153] A few days later, Luther told Spalatin that Eck had conceded to Karlstadt on this issue.[154] Thus by declining Karlstadt's demand that he define prevenient grace and by sounding as anti-Pelagian as possible, Eck confused the issue.[155]

It is difficult and perhaps irrelevant to ask whether Karlstadt or Eck won the debate at Leipzig. It is not insignificant, however, that Karlstadt was able to show that Eck had contradicted himself—verbally at least—by first asserting and then denying that the will has a "natural" activity in good deeds.[156] It is true of course that Eck could reply that from the beginning he had always asserted that grace must aid the will which performs good deeds. Presumably he used the adjective "naturalis" at the beginning because he wanted to emphasize the genuine role of the free will which was central to his view of *dispositiones de congruo* and his conception of predestination *secundum praevisa merita.* Had Karlstadt attacked Eck's view of the will's role in disposing itself for grace earlier, the first part of the Leipzig debate would have been less tedious! When he did focus this issue, Eck's

---

cooperate in producing the *dispositio ad gratiam*, 3) *gratia justificans* (= *vera charitas*) is infused.

[152] "Quare, clarissime D. D., videtis mentem meam nunquam fuisse aliam, quam quod voluerim liberum arbitrium ex se posse in malum, sed non posse ex se in bonum, nisi a gratia adiutum, erectum, tractum et impulsum." Seitz, p. 228.

[153] "Ad secundum et 14. placet mihi, quod et ultimum dictum doctoris fuit, quod liberum arbitrium ex se non potest in bonum nisi gratia erectum, tractum et impulsum. Pulchra est et vera sententia et laus deo. Quod dispositio praecedens sit gratia iustificans, mihi placet; vellem tamen, ut eo nomine abrogato uteremur vocabulo, per quod spiritus sanctus in scripturis nobis loquitur." Seitz, p. 228.

[154] *LW*, XXXI, 323; *WABr*, I, 423.97-101: "Finita itaque mea disputatione rursum cum Carlstadio tribus diebus novissimis disputavit, iterum omnia concedens et consentiens: quod facere, quod in se est, sit peccatum, et quod liberum arbitrium sine gratia nihil nisi peccare possit, et quod in omni opere bono sit peccatum, et quod facere, quod in se est, disponenti ad gratiam sit ipsa gratia."

[155] While insisting that Eck did not contradict himself, Moore admits that Eck's failure to spell out his conception of prevenient grace led to confusion at Leipzig. "Between Mani and Pelagius," pp. 163-4.

[156] Cf. Luther's report to Spalatin on July 20, 1519 that in their debate on the freedom of the will, Eck conceded everything that Karlstadt asserted. *LW*, XXXI, 320-21; *WABr*, I, 422.51-52: "In fine subdolus Homo omnia concessit, quae Carlstadius arguebat." (See also all of *ibid.*, p. 421.40ff.)

remarks were cautious and sometimes ambiguous. Karlstadt's part in the Leipzig debate was certainly not an unmitigated disaster for the Wittenbergers.

### (b) *The aftermath*

The debate arranged to end further controversy provoked a flood of violent polemics. Two of Karlstadt's three contributions to this sordid torrent were merely bitter invectives, but a third, *Verba Dei* showed that the Leipzig affair had led to marked development in Karlstadt's thought. A minor incident during the debate focused the two new emphases which emerged in Karlstadt's theology as he reflected upon the encounter with Eck.

One day as one of the Luther-Eck exchanges was about to begin, Eck came by and began a conversation with Karlstadt.[157] When Eck suggested that he and Karlstadt agreed, Karlstadt hotly denied it. He charged Eck with gross inconsistency. He said that in their debate Eck had abandoned his uncircumcised doctrine of free will and accepted his own position. In his public sermon on July 2, however, Eck had again exaggerated the natural power of free will and quoted a pseudonymous letter of Jerome to the effect that the will is "naturally capable" of doing good or evil. With some surprise Eck asked whether Karlstadt supposed that one ought to say the same thing in sermons that one asserts in theological debates. One does not say to ordinary illiterate folk what one says to learned theologians. As Karlstadt reflected on this event, the substance of *Verba Dei* took shape.[158] In reaction to Eck's belittling of the common man, Karl-

---

[157] Karlstadt described the incident at Leipzig at length at the beginning of *Verba Dei*, AiiV-Aiv. Also (more briefly!) in BV: "Dicit audacter, Certe docendum aliud in contione, ubi personam veritatis gerit, aliud in schola, ubi veritatem tutatur, Praeterea, Epistola ad Demetriadem, Hieronymo falso praetitulata, posteaque secundum Augustinum et Bedam, Pelagii haeretici fuisse, convictus erat, In aede sancta sciens, usus est, non casu vel nescientia, sed consilio principali adductus, et in ea parte maxime et pessime, quae passim ab Ecclesiasticis tractatoribus divellitur et dissipatur, docebat hominem ex naturalibus viribus facultatem habere, ad faciendum bonum, in schola idip̄m negare coactus." In his letter to Spalatin on July 20, 1519, Luther also mentioned the incident and Eck's remark. *LW*, XXXI, 323; *WABr*, I, 423.93-96: "Atque, quo maius sit monstrum: Aliud concessit in Schola, aliud Vulgo docuit in Ecclesia. Conventus autem a Carlstadio, cur sic variaret, respondit homo sine fronte, non oportere populum haec doceri, quae disputarentur." For Eck's citation of the pseudonymous letter at Leipzig, see Seitz, p. 35; for Karlstadt's reply, Seitz, p. 41; for Eck's retort, Seitz, p. 44.

[158] *Verba Dei* was written in 1519 and published in early 1520.

stadt's treatise reflected a strong faith in and a turning to the humble, unlearned person. And in reaction to what Karlstadt viewed as Aristotle's influence in Eck's disregard for the scriptural teaching on the will's impotence, he reasserted the qualitative difference between the word of God and the word of man. Using the incident with Eck as the point of departure, Karlstadt effectively developed these two themes at length in *Verba Dei*.[159]

Professor Oberman has reminded us that some of the common generalizations about the pre-Reformation situation have been seriously misleading.[160] Without ignoring this warning, however, it may still be legitimate to say, on the basis of Kurt Uhrig's work on the status of the peasantry in pre-Reformation and Reformation thought, that there was a very strong tendency in the later middle ages to despise and mock the peasantry.[161] The superior status of the cleric vis à vis the layman was of course a cause of this situation. Uhrig has also shown that the early years of the Reformation, especially Luther's writings and his doctrine of the priesthood of all believers, effected a significant change in the common conception of the layman in general and the peasant in particular.[162] Thus when Karlstadt placed great emphasis on the humble layman in *Verba Dei*, he was contributing to the Reformation's reversal of a widespread medieval attitude.

Karlstadt interpreted Eck's remark that one ought not say the same things to the learned and the ignorant to mean that one should not give the scriptures to the common people. In reply, Karlstadt declared that one of his two aims in *Verba Dei* was to show "that scripture is to be taught not only to the learned, but also to women and illiterates." [163] In Deuteronomy (e.g. chapters 4 and 32), Moses taught God's word to all the people in order that they in turn could teach their children.[164]

---

[159] Since the development of Karlstadt's thought on the Word of God continues in 1520 and is the presupposition of the break with Rome, that issue will be discussed in the next chapter.

[160] H. A. Oberman, *Forerunners of the Reformation* (New York, 1966), pp. 4-9.

[161] Kurt Uhrig, "Der Bauer in der Publizistik der Reformation bis zum Ausgang des Bauernkrieges," *ARG*, XXXIII (1936), 70.

[162] *Ibid.*, pp. 98ff.

[163] "Hoc ordine commodius mihi videor facturus, ut primum ostendam, non ferendos, qui concionibus ecclesiasticis, praestigias hominum, non syncera dei verba divulgant. secundo scripturam, sanctam non doctos tantum, sed et mulieres et illitteratos docendam." *Verba Dei*, Aiv.

[164] *Ibid.*, CiiiV-Civ. One marginal note epitomizes this section: "Universa scriptura universis Christi fidelibus noscenda." *Ibid.*, Civ.

No one fails to observe how Moses urged every believer to understand the words of God.... Today Eck deceives the faithful disciples of Christ by saying that it is wrong for the rustic person to examine God's words.[165]

Karlstadt quoted with approval Chrysostom's request that every man study the scriptures at home.[166] Unlike Eck, he wanted rustics to learn Biblical precepts and then teach other rustics.[167] The last two-thirds of the treatise is devoted to expounding his thesis that everything in scripture should be available to all, not just to the learned.[168]

Several of the factors which prompted Karlstadt's new emphasis are apparent. After Eck succeeded in having books banned from the debate, Karlstadt was definitely at a disadvantage because of his poorer memory, which Eck mocked in a subsequent writing.[169] Karlstadt's consequent embarrassment led him to identify with the unlearned. Karlstadt surmised that Eck would support his practice of not telling the masses what he said to theologians with Matthew 7:6: "Do not throw your pearls before swine." Karlstadt then proceeded to refute this argument which Eck "has thrown against us simple ones who although most eager for the divine word, are covered with shame because of our small memory and despicable ability."[170]

---

[165] "Nemo non speculatur, quam Moses singulos fidelium adhortatus est, ad intelligendum verba dei, quando illos ad erudientium diligentiam adstringit, et iubet, ut filiis suis non modo proponant, vel legenda, vel audienda, verum denarrent et exponant.... Hodie Eckius, fidos Christi discipulos fallit, dicens, nefas esse rustico verba dei perscrutari." *Ibid.*, CivV.

[166] *Ibid.*, Dii-DiiV.

[167] "Paulus electionis vas scripsit, Educate filios vestros in institutione et admonitione Christi domini, hoc est in corda et animos filiorum ingeratis domini praecepta, Eckius naeniarum pertusum vas, nedum filiis talem educationem invidet, sed etiam viris negat licere vulgariis, ut rusticum erudiat rusticus." *Ibid.*, Div.

[168] One should not exaggerate the importance of this new emphasis as Barge did when, with reference to *Verba Dei*, he spoke of "der religiöse Appell an die Masse" and compared it with Luther's *An den christlichen Adel* (*Karlstadt*, I, 173). One hardly appeals to the German masses in a latin treatise! Nor is the new emphasis on the common man given the important theological grounding which Luther supplied in his work with the doctrine of the priesthood of all believers. On the other hand, it is not insignificant that Karlstadt emphatically stated the idea of the necessity of scripture being accessible to everyone several months before Luther made his effective popular appeal.

[169] "Carlstadium minus aptum disputationi, quod pronunciacio esset ei gravis aspera et hiulca: memoria esset illi vel nulla vel parva, discursus modicus." *Contra Martini Ludder obtusum propugnatorem Andream Rodolphi Bodenstein Carlstadium*, Eiii; quoted in *Karlstadt*, I, 153, n. 67.

[170] "Scriptum est inquit Eckius Mathei ca. vii Ne detis sanctum canibus, et ne proieceritis margaritas ante porcos, nequãdo hii conculcent pedibus suis, Ergo

More important was the entire content and outcome of the debate. Karlstadt believed that Eck had evaded the biblical teaching on free will by means of philosophical subterfuge. It seemed that the learned theologians of his day stood opposed to the straightforward biblical truths. In light of this intransigence of the learned, Karlstadt, not surprisingly, turned to the common man.[171]

> The simple come to the word of God piously and reverently respect it and kiss it with the greatest awe. But the chatterers never treat the divine scriptures sincerely and never fail to fence it in with their thornbushes. . . . They cover the law of God with thorny syllogisms.[172]

Karlstadt concluded that the simple and unlearned are especially prepared for God's word precisely because they are not learned.[173] Karlstadt, however, did not intend an obscurantist attack on learning in general. It is quite legitimate to read and study pagan authors, as long as one views their ideas as mere human philosophy and does not insinuate them into Christian faith.[174] It was because Karlstadt thought Eck introduced heretical Aristotelian notions about free will into theology that he attacked learning. As such, he saw Eck as a "verbose theologian inferior to many peasants." [175] Thus the initial preoccupation of the man who was later to style himself a "new layman" with the religious virtues of the simple layman seems to have resulted partially from the fact that in his early years as a proponent of the new

---

ad homines simplicianos ac barbaros et insipientes non iactamus illud nobile margaritum, quod est dei verbum. . . . Syllogismus est, ex Eckiana modestia profectus, quam ipse a se exorsus? adversus nos simplices, parva memoria, ingenioque despicabili propudiosos, at verbi divini cupidissimos iactavit." *Verba Dei*, DivV-E.

[171] Cf. Luther's similar move in 1520 in the opening paragraph of *An den christlichen Adel*. Luther expressed the hope that God might help his church through the efforts of the laity, since the clergy had grown quite indifferent. He turned to the laity to see "ob Got wolt doch durch den leyen standt seiner kirchen helffen, seintemal der geistlich stand, dem es billicher geburt, ist gantz unachtsam worden." *WA*, VI, 404.14-16.

[172] "Nam simplices religiose adeunt dei verbum, reverenterque suspiciunt, et summa reformidatione exosculantur, Argutatores autem nusquam non insyncere divinas scripturas tractant, et nusquam non suis spinetis obsepiunt, commiscentes caelum terra, divinum verbum humano figmento. . . . Rectius igitur formidandos docuisse Christus aestimatur, qui ventrem sapientia plenum habent, Et sapientes et fortes porcis contulisse. quandoquidem spinosis syllogismis legem dei involvunt, atque eam ad hominum sapientiam flectunt." *Verba Dei*, EV.

[173] "Vae, quod parvulos et simplices, nudos et vacuos, et ob id dei verbo praeparatos, sacrarum literarum noticia spoliatis atque impeditis." *Ibid.*, Eii.

[174] *Ibid.*, FV. See also *ibid.*, Fiii (below chapter III, n. 5).

[175] "Verbosum Theologum, multis subrusticis inferiorem." *Ibid.*, FiiiV.

theology, it appeared that the scholars of his day opposed the recovery of biblical truth with clever syllogisms and pagan wisdom.

A "celebrated and pure defender of the scriptures" named Erasmus was a third factor in Karlstadt's demand that all laymen read and study the Bible. He quoted with obvious approval Erasmus' demand that the scriptures be available in the vernacular for the uncultivated.[176] He was so enamored with Erasmus' idea of the farmer reflecting on God's word while ploughing and the traveller while walking that he placed this and similar statements in parallel columns alongside the Deuteronomic injunction (6:6-9) to meditate on God's law at every moment of the day.[177] Thus at a time when the Leipzig debate had produced exasperation with the wise of this world, the authority of the famous humanist encouraged him to turn to the simple layman.[178]

---

[176] "Erasmus inclytus et syncerus scripturarum assertor, divina quoque vir sapientia emisit, quae illis apponere volui, Erasmica, de quibus nunc memini, haec sunt [:] Vaehementer enim ab istis dissentio, qui nolunt idIotis, legi divinas literas, in vulgi linguam transfusas. . . ." *Ibid.*, D.

[177] *Ibid.*, Diii-DiiiV.

[178] Rupp wrongly dates the beginning of Karlstadt's emphasis on the importance of the simple, believing laymen at the time of the break with Rome one year later ("Karlstadt," p. 310). It should be noted that even before Leipzig, Karlstadt could demand that laymen study the Bible in the vernacular and point out that the unlearned accept the doctrine of *sola gratia* more easily than "vermuschten" theologians—i.e. those who mix Aristotle with scripture. *Ausslegung* (1519), EvV-Evi and EivV. The importance of Leipzig, however, is shown by the fact that whereas in *Ausslegung* (April, 1519) this is merely a passing remark, in *Verba Dei*, it is one of two basic topics of a lengthy treatise.

CHAPTER THREE

# THE BREAK WITH ROME
## (1520)

### 1. SOLA SCRIPTURA

In the previous chapter it was seen that Karlstadt's position on the problem of authority in 1517-1519 was a good deal more conservative than has usually been suggested. It is not at all certain that Karlstadt would have broken with the papacy even as late as 1519. In October, 1520, however, when his name unexpectedly appeared along with Luther's in the famous bull of excommunication, Karlstadt attacked the papacy with zest. It was the development of Karlstadt's thought on the problem of authority—a development which occurred as he reflected upon the Leipzig affair—which prompted Karlstadt to react differently in 1520 than he would have in 1519.

One of the two major themes of *Verba Dei*, Karlstadt's second post-Leipzig polemic, was the radical difference between the "illusions of men" and the "pure word of God." [1] Karlstadt was convinced that Eck's unbiblical position on free will and its active role in good deeds had resulted from his glossing the scripture with Aristotle. [2] Especially in his public sermon, where he allegedly contradicted what he affirmed in the debate, Eck declared not the word of God but the word of Aristotle. [3] In response Karlstadt insisted that the word of God must be separated from all other words. [4] There is a qualitative difference between human and divine sayings.

---

[1] *Verba Dei*, Aiv (see chapter II, n. 163). The other major argument of *Verba Dei* has been discussed in the preceding chapter.

[2] "Non autem de iis cogitavit, qui glossant scripturas per Aristotelem, et hominem sibi constituunt bonorum operum authorem minus principalem. huic novissimo in *Epistola* reclamavi, et aliis iamiam prorsus reluctandum duco." *Verba Dei*, BiiV-Biii. Karlstadt referred to his first post-Leipzig polemic against Eck. See Verzeichnis, No. 24.

[3] For this incident, see chapter two, n. 157. At the end of his lengthy discussion of Eck's objectionable sermon, he said: "Simplicibus autem, vel concionibus illis ad audiendum dei verbum, convenientibus, non dei, sed Aristotelici cordis verbum proponit, et suadet." *Verba Dei*, Aiv.

[4] "Praeterea et hoc elicio, verbum dei ab omni alio verbo et sermone discretum, atque ab universa natura aliena vindicatum et assertum, Eckius contra David, non erubescit dicere, dei verbum et feculentis et verbosis gentilium voculis et sententiis miscendum." *Verba Dei*, FiiV.

Let him who has a dream express the dream, and him who has the word of God declare that. Let him who has invented a reason, a distinction of Thomas or formal distinctions of Scotus confess that these are illusions of men. . . . But let him who was sent and delegated by God, speak the . . . words of God.[5]

Not only did Karlstadt declare his determination not to depart one straw from the word of God;[6] he also urged people to refuse to listen to preachers who speak their own rather than God's words.[7] In fact, he even suggested that Christian people ought to try to remove such dreamers.[8] "To stand in that place where the people . . . expect and desire to learn the word of God . . . and blab out chaff as if it were wheat and the little sayings of the philosophers as if they were the divine word is, I think, no more to be allowed and permitted than that which is most infamous." [9]

One should be careful, however, not to exaggerate the importance of *Verba Dei*. In this treatise Karlstadt did not attack papal authority or accuse the church or its general councils of error. This work is important not because it represents a radical departure from Karlstadt's previous position, but rather because it shows that the Leipzig debate had strongly reinforced his pre-Leipzig inclination to emphasize the primacy of the scriptures.

It appears that the 1519 debate prompted him to undertake a deeper more thoroughgoing examination of the problem of authority, an issue with which he had already wrestled at considerable length. As early as the last page of his first polemic against Eck published in

---

[5] "Advertat Eckius animum huc, qui habet somnium exponat somnium, qui habet dei verbum, efferat ipsum, qui, rationem, distinctionem Thomae, formalitatesque Scoti excogitavit, testetur esse praestigias hominum, qui gentium decreta spargit, esse eiusmodi nedum fateatur, sed etiam palam profiteatur, non doceat ea tanquam Christi discipulus, sed velut philosophi lector. Qui missus et delegatus est a deo, verba dei, divinam commentationem eloquatur." *Verba Dei*, Fiii.

[6] *Verba Dei*, BiiV.

[7] "Audiendum haud esse Concionatorem in aede sacra, sua, non dei verba crepantem." *Verba Dei*, Aiv. Also: "Arcentur itaque Praedicatores per sui contemptionem derisumque, qui audent, non dei, sed sua verba crepitare." *Ibid.*, AivV.

[8] " . . . nolim Iudaice et perfide infoelicibus praedicatoribus usu venire, verum spiritaliter, quemadmodum Niniven testatur subversam Augustinus. Non possum tamen non dehortari Christi populum (quorum interest publice Christianos habere declamatores) ut exigant, illiusmodi somniatores utcumque a veritatis itinere abalienantes." *Verba Dei*, BivV.

[9] "Verum eo loci stare, in quo populus extra pericula nondum constitutus, dei verbum expectat, atque perdiscere cupit, eo inquam loci consistere, et inde pro tritico paleas, pro divino verbo verbula philosophorum effutire, non minus licere phasque fore arbitror quam quod est scelestissimum." *Verba Dei*, FV-Fii.

October, 1519, Karlstadt had announced that he was occupied with the proceedings of the debate and would write a book on the problem of the "canonical writings." [10] When he finally published the results of his extensive thought and research in August, 1520, it was obvious that he had changed his mind on the fundamental question of authority.[11] The harmony between scriptural and ecclesiastical authority which he had hoped to preserve no longer seemed plausible. Not even the news of Luther's condemnation deterred him from publicly opting for *sola scriptura*.[12]

Karlstadt prefaced his volume on the canon with a substantial, sytematic treatment of several basic aspects of the problem of authority. He began with a discussion of the dignity or authority (*majestas*) of scripture. Numerous biblical texts prove that scripture derives its authority from the fact that it is the word of God.[13] "Sacred scripture is a divine oracle which has travelled from God to men." [14] As such it possesses divine authority to which layman and priest, king and bishop, emperor and pope must submit.[15] Scripture judges all things, but is judged by no one.[16] Scripture is superior to universal councils, blessed pontiffs, universal custom and the prayers of the church.[17] Citing the thesis derived from Gerson that he had considered and then rejected in 1518, he now agreed wholeheartedly that one man armed

---

[10] "Ad disputationis acta manus verto, aptoque, utpote ad operas et lucubrationes libellorum, de peccatorum meritis, vel de peccatis bonorum operum, de gratia et li. arbitrio, de scripturis Canonicis scripturus." *Epistola Andree Carolostadii adversus ineptam et ridiculam inventionem Joannis Eckii* . . . (Verzeichnis, No. 25), CvV.

[11] *De canonicis scripturis libellus;* Verzeichnis, Nos. 34, 35. I have used the reprint in K. A. Credner, *Zur Geschichte des Kanons* (Halle, 1847), pp. 316-412 (hereafter cited as Credner).

[12] Karlstadt finished *De canonicis* on August 18, 1520. Credner, p. 317. Luther apparently learned about the bull sometime between August 3 and August 14. See H. G. Leder, *Ausgleich mit dem Papst? Luthers Haltung in den Verhandlungen mit Miltitz 1520* (Stuttgart, 1969) p. 17.

[13] "Maiestatem sacrae scripturae divinam esse, Augustino de civitate dei placuit asseveranti: Deum per ora prophetarum locutum atque sanctam scripturam ab Angelis ministratam de coelo descendisse, quae omnia divinis testimoniis possunt confirmari." Credner, p. 317.

[14] "Constat itaque scripturam sanctam divinum esse oraculum, a deo ad homines profectum." Credner, p. 318.

[15] Credner, p. 319.

[16] "Accedit his, quod ex sacris literis de omnium et singulorum sententiis iudicamus, ideo pronunctiamus ipsam omnium reginam et dominam et iudicem omnia iudicantem, a nullo autem iudicari." Credner, pp. 320-21.

[17] For councils, see Credner, p. 331; pontiffs, p. 330; universal custom, pp. 337-41; prayers, p. 342 (and n. 38 below).

with canonical scripture must be believed rather than the Pope. Nor was he afraid to denounce a certain "swinish, sordid and infamous animal of Rome" for calling Gerson a heretic.[18] "Therefore, O crocodile, do not condemn Gerson as a heretic, for we judge according to the word and power not of man but of God." [19] Nor was the notion that scripture is insufficient and lacks some precepts necessary for salvation compatible with his view of scripture's authority. Those who place any additional commands not contained in scripture upon Christians ignore Isaiah's denunciation (29:13) of those who attempt to worship God with the commands of men.[20] Scripture is superior to all human words because its authority comes directly from God Himself.

Nor was Karlstadt content to assert the theoretical supremacy of scripture. He no longer conceived of a harmony between scripture and ecclesiastical tradition. Instead he declared that Popes, councils and fathers could err and in fact had done so.

> Indeed the foolishness of those declaring that the Pope is above a council and cannot err as Pope astounds me, since they themselves are accustomed to remove popes as popes from their place and dignity because of heresy. If the Roman pontiffs do not sometimes err as popes, why do we know from reliable reported history that many were expelled from the papacy. Grant, therefore, that a Pope can err, deceive and be deceived.[21]

---

[18] "Fuit quoddam spurcum, sordidum et propudiosum animal Rome. Nimirum homo erraticus, sanc talis, in quo sorduit sanctae theologicae nomen, cuius non paucos novi consectatores, ille dicebat, condemnandus est Gerson, qui scripsit: Dicto doctoris autoritate canonica munito, plus quam declarationi Papae credendum est." The same of course is true for councils for he immediately added: "Et alibi sic: In sacris literis excellenter erudito, atque authoritatem catholicam proferenti, plus est credendum, quam generali Concilio." Credner, p. 331. See above, chapter two, "The Problem of Authority" for Karlstadt's examination of these same theses in 1518 (the theses are in nn. 16, 33).

[19] "Itaque noli bestia Crocodilina Gersonem quasi haereticum condemnare, quia non ex hominum sed ex dei verbo et potestate pendemus." Credner, p. 333. Bubenheimer has shown not only that Karlstadt was referring to Prierias, Master of the Sacred Palace, but also that Karlstadt apparently debated with Prierias in Rome in 1516. "Consonantia Theologiae et Jurisprudentiae," pp. 64-80.

[20] " ... qua via igitur Pontifices sacris literis suam prudentiam attulerunt? qua lege et Theologiste sapientiam suam illis implicuerunt. ... Bone deus, bona datis verba, atque tandem persuadebitis, non omnes praeceptiones (ad vitam perpetuam indipiscendam) necessarias, in divina lege conscriptas, atque consequenter non esse sufficientem legem divinam. ... Saltem a vobis Esaias nos ammovebit, quod dominus per eum loquitur: "Timuerunt me mandato et doctrinis hominum" [Is. 29:13]. Illud ipsum propositum statuendarum legum, quibus deus hominum mandatis et doctrinis excolitur, dominus reiecit." Credner, 323-24.

[21] "Equidem quorundam fatuitatem demiror, decernentium: Papam esse

Twice he accused the Popes of mixing their own ideas with the pure teachings of scripture.[22] To be sure, Karlstadt still believed the Pope should have an important place in the church.[23] Even *qua* pope, however, he is fallible. Indeed many have erred.

Karlstadt now adopted the conciliarist position that a general council is superior to the Pope.[24] Unlike most conciliarists, however, he insisted that even a universal council could err. Karlstadt used Augustine's argument that subsequent general councils emend earlier ones to support his view that "God purposely allows a plenary council to go astray sometimes." [25] Nor are the fathers free from error. Even Augustine, Jerome and Ambrose contain many things which one doubts and more which one must reject.[26] Karlstadt, of course, used both Augustine and Jerome a great deal in this work but this was partly a tactical move: "Since many are more quickly moved by

---

supra Concilium et errare non posse tanquam papam. Quando illi ipsi soleant pontifices, tanquam papas, propter haeresim et loco et dignitate movere. Si quasi papae Romani pontifices interdum non aberrant, cur papatu permultos historica fide scimus depulsos? igitur date, papam errare posse, fallere fallique." Credner, pp. 334-5.

[22] "Quid hic pontificibus, quid nonnullis doctoribus dicam, qui farinas suas sacris libris immiscuerunt, qui repurgatum triticum, qui casta et emuncta domini eloquia suis doctrinis, suis traditionibus foedaverunt." Credner, p. 322. See also, n. 20.

[23] He argued that one learned person with scripture can oppose a council, even though he is vastly inferior to a council or the Pope ("quamquam sit incomparabiliter inferior Concilio vel Romano pontifice"). Credner, p. 333.

[24] "Consequitur ergo quod Pontificiae decretales dispositioni totius consilii subiiciuntur, et quod magis pro concilio, quam Papa praesumendum est." Credner, p. 335.

[25] "Nunc autem si verum Augustinus scripsit, quod certe communis Ecclesia confitetur, oportet concedamus, Concilium plenarium aberrare posse, et quod non omnia spiritus sanctus fuerit elocutus, et quod consulto patiatur deus interdum deviare plenarium concilium; alias priora posterioribus conciliis non sanarentur." Credner, p. 334. This is part of a long discussion (pp. 330ff) which Karlstadt introduced with the important quotation (pp. 330-31) from Augustine's *De baptismo contra Donatistas*, II, 3-4. Karlstadt had been pondering the implications of this passage for a long time (see above, chapter II, nn. 16 and 25). Nowhere in this text, however, does Augustine say that a plenary council can err. Augustine probably thought that the "emended" view of a later council was a supplement to, but not necessarily a contradiction of the earlier council's statement. Karlstadt, however, found it expedient to have the support of Augustine, whom as he explicitly noted, everyone considers free of heresy (Credner, p. 332).

[26] "Absque mora credimus, omnia, quae legimus, esse vera in catholicis scripturis. In Augustino, in Hieronimo, in Ambrosio, in Gregorio, in Cyrillo, in Chrysostomo et in caeteris scriptoribus, multa comperimus, quae dubitamus, plura videmus obeliscis expungenda, non pauca itidem boni consulenda." Credner, pp. 327-28.

Augustine's doctrine than by sacred letters, I shall adduce his main argument." [27] Popes, general councils and the fathers have erred.

Even more significant, perhaps, was his new position on the question of the legitimate interpreters of scripture. Some, Karlstadt suggested, may say that episcopal authority is superior to scriptural authority since "the pontiffs have the authority to interpret scripture." [28] Karlstadt replied that the interpretation of scripture is according to scripture's own content. "The bishops and doctors are obliged to do their exposition through sacred letters and to remain within the enclosures and walls of scripture." [29] The only one who discloses the meaning of scripture is the lamb of God who is born, lives, dies and rises from the dead under the shell of the scriptural letter.[30] In spite of the obscure phraseology, the meaning seems to be that scriptural interpretation becomes possible as one takes the story of Christ as one's guide through scripture and then interprets one part by means of another. In *Welche bücher*, a German popularization of *De canonicis*, published in November, it is clear that the interpretation of obscure passages by means of Christ means that one should concentrate first on the scriptures which depict Christ and then use

[27] "Porro quamquam hoc satis perspectum sit ex assumptis nunc, postremo tamen quia permulti citius ad Augustini doctrinam, quam sacras literas stupescunt, illius firmamentum depromam." Credner, p. 330.

[28] "Coniectura iam colligo, dicturos aliquot fratres, autoritatem Episcoporum esse maiorem et superiorem scriptura sancta, et id tali argumento. Fatemur, dicent, neque sanctimonia neque doctrina sanctos patres ab erroris suspitione liberari, sed de auctoritate non idem rati. Pontifices enim interpretandae scripturae autoritatem habent. . . . Obligantur ergo Episcopi et doctores expositionem per sacras literas facere, intraque septa et parietes scripturae manere. Cur enim scriptum est: 'Qui aperit et nemo claudit, qui claudit et nemo aperit,' nisi sit, qui solus aperiat, qui solus claudat. Agnus scilicet ille immaculatus, qui sub literarum cortice nobis nascitur, vagit, flet, spirat, patitur, cruci affigitur, moritur, resurgit, ad coelos ascendit, sedet ad patris dexteram." Credner, pp. 328-29.

[29] See n. 28. See also Credner, p. 322 and p. 318: "Ideo iure sacrilegium incurrunt, qui sacram scripturam prophanant . . . quod vitium evitabunt ii, qui omne studium eo conferunt, ut sacris literis inserviant, et suos sensus illis componant, et intra scripturarum septa se continent, neque vel interpretando vel assumendo, scripturarum normas egrediuntur." Credner, p. 318.

[30] See n. 28. The notion of Christ living under the shell of the scriptural letter is merely a reflection of his general view that all written texts constitute the shell of which the ideas or concepts are the kernel or soul. "Etenim ut a corporibus fluunt simulachra atque se in oculos conferunt, eisque tum videndi sensus fit, ita contra ab animo cum oratione defluit simulachrum mentis, quod sub elementis vivit et scriptoris exprimit spiritum, ut ne minore quidem opera hominem alioqui notum internoscas facie, quam sermonis stylo." Credner, p. 366. Thus the statement about Christ living under the shell means that the substance signified by the written letter is Christ.

precisely these passages to explicate obscure texts.[31] Karlstadt went on to say that when faced with an obscure passage, neither a band of angels nor a group of the most eminent authoritative men would be of any help unless Christ were present. The next lines explain how Christ is present:

> When, therefore, I have an obscure text, I will never disclose its meaning properly unless I select that divine word from another place [in scripture]. Rightly, therefore, I asserted that the exposition of scripture ought to be within the sacred letters, and not brought from outside and sewn together with a foreign patch.[32]

Not papal authority but the assistance of other biblical texts provides the proper interpretation of difficult passages.

The conclusion which Karlstadt drew from this hermeneutical principle is most important.

> Under the letters Christ lives, breathes, speaks and explains to all in common. Therefore, the interpretation of scripture will belong to all Christians, and all will act vigorously because the Lord is with us in the scriptures.[33]

Since the proper interpretation of scripture requires not some special authority, but rather merely the comparison of the various texts which

---

[31] "Ich ratt auch nyemandts, das er sich erstlich uff die schwerste, dunckele und verdeckte bücher heiliger schrifft lege, uff das er sein arbeit und zeit nicht unnützlich verlire, oder finsternuss durch finsternuss verkere, aber etwar einen verstant thün fassen der heiligen schrifft und heiligen geist (dero in der schrifft, wie er vorzeiten durch menschen redt, noch redet und leret) züwider und engegen sein. Dann es ist kein neyn, das etliche bücher Allegorien, figuren und verdeckte sententz haben, welche durch warheit und licht (das man hin und her in der schrifft findt) solten erklert und erleucht werden. Darumb sol der christlich leser vor allen dingen Christum in der schrifft süchen, das ist, solche schrifften lesen, die Christum mit seinem leiden, mit seiner krafft, mit seiner gütigkeit, mit seiner heiligkeit abmalen, und für die augen dess lesers setzen, so kan er nicht irren, . . . Derhalben, sollen sich die menschen erstlich, uff klar wort Christi legen, die selb innemen, und wie ein liecht zü allen verborgen schrifften tragen, und erleuchten." *Welche bücher* (Verzeichnis, No. 48), Biv.

[32] "Nam dum non adest sacras literas interpretaturo radix de tribu Iuda, clausam scripturam, obsignatum fontem, sitibundus inspicit, etiamsi de Angelorum vel hominum (maxima autoritate praestabilium) agmine fuerit, nihilque efficiet. Quippe, si literas calluerit, dicet: Legere non possum, quia signatus est; si illiteratus dicet: Literas nescio. Ubi ergo scripturam clausam teneo, nunquam foeliciter eam reserabo, nisi verbum illud divinum ex alio loco desumpsero. Recte propterea asseveravi: Expositionem scripturae sanctis literis intrinsecam esse debere, non extrinsecus allatam, et velut alienam commissuram consarcinatam." Credner, p. 329.

[33] "Nunc Christus omnibus in commune sub literis vivit, spirat, loquitur, et exponit: proinde ad omnes Christianos pertinebit scripturarum interpretatio, et viriliter agemus omnes, quia dominus nobiscum in scripturis." Credner, p. 329.

speak of Christ, any Christian can engage in biblical interpretation. He did add one qualification, but this qualification did not modify his belief that the layman has as much right to interpret scripture as does a member of the ecclesiastical hierarchy.

> I have also said that the interpretation of scripture belongs to all. I want that understood thus—all to whom the Lord bestows that gift of interpreting scripture are able to interpret it, whether they be laymen or clerics, secular or religious.[34]

In *Verba Dei* he had urged all laymen to read the Bible; in *De canonicis*, he affirmed their right to interpret it.

Karlstadt emphasized the layman's right of interpretation several times in the first thirty pages. When Augustine said, in the passage from *De baptismo*, that someone more learned in scripture could refute any bishop's letters, he meant that anyone at all armed with scripture could refute the errors of bishops—indeed even a general council composed of all bishops.[35] Similarly there is no Christian who may not judge papal decretals by the standard of canonical scripture.[36] "Whoever is skilled in theology, even if he is inferior to many dignitaries, is able to judge the letters of the Pope according to the law of God, and, if he despises modesty, is able to resist him to his face as Paul did Peter." [37] Those who discover errors in the church's prayers may pronounce them heretical.[38] Karlstadt's new belief that any Christian possessed the right to interpret scripture would become important when threatened with papal anathema.

The body of *De canonicis* offered a careful and perceptive analysis of

---

[34] "Addidi quoque ad omnes interpretationes scripturae pertinere. Id sic intellectum volo, quod omnes, quibus dominus deus illud muneris interpretandae scripturae largitur, possunt scripturam interpretari, sive sit laicus, sive clerus, sive prophanus, sive sacer." Credner, p. 329.

[35] "Hoc prior Augustinus et posterior Gerson, scripsit, neque orationem Augustinus ad paucos, vel Episcopos, vel doctores, vel fraterculos complicuit, sed de uno quolibet loquitur, licere ei per sermonem sapientiorem, id est per Canonicam scripturam errata Episcoporum omnium, id est generalis Concilii refellere." Credner, p. 333.

[36] Credner, p. 321.

[37] "Item quod quilibet in Theologia peritus, etiamsi multis nominibus est inferior, potest, secundum dei legem de literis papae iudicare, atque illi, si modestiam contemnat, in faciem sicut Paulus Petro resistere." Credner, p. 335. In the German version, he said that even the peasant who has just left his plough can correct a council. *Welche bücher*, Ciii (see below, chapter IV, n. 156).

[38] "Repugnantur quoque vitiosae Orationes Ecclesiae sacrarum literarum iuditio atque certitudine eatenus, qua licebit errores invenientibus preces aliquot Ecclesiae haereticas pronuntiare, atque velut pestes eliminare." Credner, p. 342.

the number, authorship, date, etc. of canonical books. Two issues, the role of the church in the establishment of the canon and the dispute apropos James, are of particular interest.

Karlstadt saw very clearly that, at least in the case of some books, it was the church which had decided what would be deemed canonical and what rejected as non-canonical. In his discussion of the books of the Apocrypha[39] he argued that biblical books acquire authority either from their authors or from usage.[40] Thus, in the case of the New Testament, the four gospels, which contain the words of Christ, and the epistles of Paul, Peter and John, which were clearly written by apostles, rank higher than books whose authorship is doubtful.[41] Consequently the Gospels and epistles derive their authority from their authors (and of course, the Holy Spirit who spoke through them). In the case of books whose authorship is disputed, however, the church both decides which are canonical and which not and also bestows authority on the former through universal agreement and ancient usage.[42] If the church includes a book in the canon, it has authority.[43]

---

[39] Karlstadt respected these books, but denied their canonicity and authority in theological debate. "Idem opinor, de Tobia atque de caeteris [the other books of the Apocrypha] pronuntiare possumus, videlicet quod ad contentionem non valeant." Credner, p. 376. See also p. 377.

[40] "Nam libri capiunt autoritatem vel ab ipsis autoribus, vel ab usu." Credner, p. 348.

[41] Matthew, Mark, Luke, John and Acts belong in the first rank. "Dise bücher seint die aller höchste, sonderlich die iiii Evangelien, dann in den selben redt Christus sein wort selber, und fürt uff in seinen vatter." After listing the letters of Paul, I Peter and I John, he added: "Dise Episteln seind on einigs widerred, von den aposteln (wie angezeigt) geschriben." Then he turned to the books in the *Dritt Ordenung*: "Die folgende bücher, hab ich in das dritt glid, Biblischer schrifften derhalben gestelt, das von iren werckmeistern gezweiffelt wirt, und noch nit allenthalben beschlossen, wer oder welche, sy geschriben oder gemacht." *Welche bücher*, CV-Cii. For Karlstadt's elaborate classification, see also Credner, 349ff (especially pp. 380-82, 407-412).

[42] "Ambigentes quoque de multis aliis epistolis permulti plane loquuntur, quas tamen non nescit Ecclesia, sed certe cum gratia custodit et veneratur, qua propter fatendum duco, quod totus consensus et antiquus usus apocryphiam sustollit, et libris ἀνώνυμοις καὶ ἀδεσπότοις autoritatem impertit, et, ut ita dicam, luce quadam illustratos ab omnibus suspitionum tenebris asserit." Credner, p. 349. See also, p. 375.

[43] "... non enim consequitur: eius libri fertur autor ille vel iste; igitur liber istius modi est Canonicus, quoniam, ut video sentire Augustinum, multa sub manibus prophetarum et Apostolorum feruntur, quae omnia a Canonica veritate abhorrent. Quamobrem neque nomen autoris firmum librum, neque incertus autor Apocryphum libellum facit, sed oportet, quod illum Canon habeat, hunc vero respuat." Credner, p. 348.

Karlstadt, however, was not abandoning his belief that scripture is authoritative because it is an oracle of God. In the German version, he underlined this fact:

> I say earnestly and truly that everyone should believe the church because of holy scripture, and not believe scripture because it is used in the church. For we believe biblical books because the Holy Spirit spoke them to the church. Notice here that the pope uses . . . this saying of Augustine ("I would not believe the gospel unless I believed the church") wrongly and contrary to Augustine's intention. For with that he argues that no one should believe that scripture is righteous and true and good unless he believes the church.[44]

Karlstadt was aware that there were many books that falsely claimed to be of apostolic authority.[45] Therefore we need the church to tell us which books are genuinely apostolic and which are not. That is the proper interpretation of Augustine's famous statement:

> The meaning of that [Augustine's dictum] is that from the reception of books we know that some are evangelical and others are inconsistent with evangelical authority. Similarly, as the church witnesses, we learn how many and which letters are apostolic.[46]

---

[44] "Für das vierd sag ich mit ernst und warheit, das ein yeglicher, der kirchen, von wegen heiliger schrifft glauben sol, und nit der schrifft derhalben glauben, das sy in der kirchen geübt, dann wir glauben Biblischen büchern das sy der heilig geist zü der kirchen geredt. Alhie höre, das der Bapst dise red Augustini (Non crederem evangelio nisi crederem ecclesie) unrecht und wider meinung Augustini, mit dem hören zü seinem vortel gebraucht, Dann er zeucht sy dahin, es solt keiner der schrifft glauben, das sy gerecht und warhafftig und güt ist, er glaub dann der kirchen." *Welche bücher*, CiiiV. For Karlstadt's previous discussion of this dictum of Augustine, see above, chapter II, nn. 28-31.

[45] See above, n. 43.

[46] "Hac in re nihil possumus ex Bibliis vel refellere, quoniam super ea ex usu antiquissimorum patrum pronuntiamus neque valemus diversum quiddam dicere, quam quod asseveravit Augustinus: Non crederem, dicens, Evangelio, nisi crederem ecclesiae. Cuius sensus est, quod receptione librorum scimus aliquot esse Evangelicos et aliquot ab Evangelica maiestate abhorrere, ita similiter Ecclesia testante didicimus, quot et quae sint Apostolicae epistolae." Credner, p. 408. See the similar statement in n. 44 above. The role of the church seems to include both the ranking of biblical books and, more important, the specification of which books actually were written by apostles or Evangelists and which are pseudonymous. In the passage quoted in n. 43 above, where Karlstadt said that some books allegedly written by apostles and prophets are inconsistent with canonical truth, he used the same verb (*abhorrere*) as in the passage here. Presumably then when he says that "aliquot ab Evangelica maiestate abhorrere," he refers to pseudonymous gospels and epistles that have been excluded from the canon. The church tells us which books are genuinely apostolic. In this connection, it is significant that he mentioned that no one challenges the authorship of the epistles of Paul, I Peter and I John (see n. 41 above).

By indicating which books are from the evangelists and apostles, the church shows which books already possess divine authority. With this solution Karlstadt was able to give Augustine's dictum a satisfactory interpretation and avoid the assertion that the scripture derives its authority from the church.

*De canonicis* also contained Karlstadt's first public disagreement with Luther since his adoption of Augustinianism in 1517. In August, 1519, Luther published the statement that the style of James was incompatible with apostolic authorship.[47] Karlstadt reported that when he undertook lectures on James in 1520, a certain presbyter (Luther's name was never mentioned) rejected the epistle on the grounds that its authorship was uncertain. This good priest's satirical opposition to the book apparently decreased Karlstadt's audience, and seriously threatened their old friendship.[48] Karlstadt adduced several reasons for maintaining the canonicity of James. In spite of the uncertainty about James' authorship and a consequent delay in its universal acceptance, the vast majority of the ancients accepted the book and the universal church eventually considered it canonical.[49] Both the Latin and Greek fathers, anyone of whom has more authority than six-hundred contemporaries, accepted the book as a divine oracle.[50] If mere uncertainty about whether James the apostle wrote the book were a sufficient reason for rejecting it, then many other biblical books would also be non-canonical.[51] Without engaging in any detailed discussion of the theological problem, Karlstadt declared in

---

[47] "Quod autem Iacobi Apostoli epistola inducitur 'Fides sine operibus mortua est' [James 2:17], primum stilus epistolae illius longe est infra Apostolicam maiestatem nec cum Paulino ullo modo comparandus, deinde de fide viva loquitur Paulus." *WA*, II, 425.10-13.

[48] "Hodie huius rei specie [uncertain authorship], ni fallor, propter Carolstadium, male Iacobus audit. . . . Magnus videri vult, qui dixit eam epistolam Hieronymi non Iacobi fuisse, qua tamen facetia homo ridiculus (quanquam gravitatem simulet) imprudens ostendit, quam accurate Hieronymi gustaverit stylum, quot denique lineas in eo traxerit. Nenias illius boni sacerdotis, veteris amicitiae nostrae discidia aliquamdiu sum passus, neque iam amicitiam bene conservatam ledere conabar. . . . Verum non possum non diluere frivola illius presbiteri argumenta, quibus eruditam Iacobi epistolam obruit, odio fortasse mei incensus; . . . demus autem esse Iacobi, sed non Apostoli. Licuit ideo illi auditores fastidiis Iacobinae Epistolae inflammare? atque ab auditorio subtrahere?" Credner, pp. 371-2.

[49] Credner, pp. 402, 404-405, 375.

[50] " . . . superabo, tam copia veterum scriptorum, quam illorum dignitate et eruditione, quoniam certius est Hieronymi super eiusmodi lite atque aliorum eius similium iudicium, quam sexcentorum nostratium." Credner, p. 405.

[51] Credner, pp. 375, 403.

regard to the content that the epistle contained nothing which contradicted other books such as Paul's epistles.[52] Karlstadt sharply attacked the subjectivism of Luther's position:

> If it is permissible to make something great or little as one pleases, it will happen at last that the dignity and authority of [biblical] books depends on our power. And then, by whatever right any Christian is allowed to reject my ideas, I have the same right . . . to esteem my own highly and trample down those of others.[53]

"Brother, I beg you, am I not able to say the same about all scripture if I follow you? Would this be reverence for sacred letters?" [54] Luther ought to accept the canon adopted by the universal church.

In spite of the disagreement over James, however, Karlstadt continued to adopt Luther's ideas. His new position on the problem of authority finally enabled him to accept Luther's attitude toward indulgences in *Von vermügen des Ablas* published just a few days before *De canonicis* in August, 1520. At the beginning of the treatise he demanded that someone prove from scripture that indulgences are legitimate.[55] He used the principle of the sufficiency of scripture to reject the demand that he show where the Bible forbids indulgences.[56] One dare not preach anything not taught in scripture. It is disgraceful

---

[52] "Scripsit quaedam Iacobus de operibus et fide, quae in Paulo, in Evangeliis, in prophetis, nisi conniveamus, cernere cogimur." Credner, p. 402. See also nn. 53 and 54. At one point Karlstadt seemed to accept the thesis that the book contains some unacceptable statements: "Dicant verum qui dicunt esse quaedam in epistola Iacobi abscindenda." In that case one should imitate the carpenter's hatchet which polishes rather than destroys. Credner, p. 398. Probably, however, Karlstadt did not really accept the idea that some statements of the book must be discarded. He meant, rather, that if some felt compelled to take this position, then they should at least keep the rest of the book.

[53] "Postremo demiror, eiusmodi orationem gladiis iugulatam placuisse, Iacobi vero epistolam displicuisse, quae nihil sententiarum usque habet, quod non possit canonicis literis communiri. Si phas (fas) est vel parvum vel magnum facere, quod placet; futurum tandem erit, dignitates et autoritates librorum e nostra pendere facultate, atque tum, quo iure cuivis Christianorum mea licuerit reiicere, eodem est mihi, quod autumo, concessum mea magni facere et aliorum proculcare." Credner, p. 390.

[54] "At, quaeso, si fas tibi fuerit dicere, mallem ego propter malum intellectum epistolae Iacobi totam epistolam repudiare, quam eius sensum contra Paulum sinere torqueri? vel magis vellem negare epistolam, quam glossis curiosis defendere? Precor, frater, nunquid idem de scripturis universis, te sequens, possum dicere? Sed haeccine ad sacras literas reverentia?" Credner, p. 402.

[55] "Derhalben hab ichs von nöten geacht, eiling, . . . zü fragen, ob der ablas, de iure divino sey, das ist ob die heilig schrift clar ausssag, das der Ablas, nach inhalt götlichs worts, etwas vermüg." *Ablas* (Verzeichnis, No. 29), AiiV.

[56] *Ibid.*, BV. See also n. 57.

to suppose that God would have given us a law so insufficient that it would not reveal all that we must do.[57] Consequently, he felt compelled to reject the Church's doctrine of indulgences even though he was quite aware that many popes had written about it.[58] The last comment could have been an allusion to the papal bull of 1518 published by Cajetan which clearly taught that an indulgence removed divinely imposed temporal punishment.[59] But Karlstadt was not bound by this decretal because he now believed the Pope to be fallible. He simply asserted that when God forgives sin, He adds no further requirements except that one must go and sin no more.[60] God does not impose temporal punishments. Indulgences are mere human inventions.[61] Thus his long silence apropos indulgences, which he candidly admitted at the beginning of the little work,[62] was finally broken because of his new belief in *sola scriptura*.

## 2. THE ACTUAL BREAK

During the first six months of 1520 the papal curia was busy formulating its condemnation of the German heresiarch. After formal

---

[57] "Nün lass ichs wol geschehen, das man heimliche sünd einsaltze mit zeytlichen straffen, die ablass abnimet. Ich weiss aber nit, was ich sagen sol zü dem wort Gottes. Esaias. am xxix. capitel [v. 13]: Sie haben mich geförcht mit menschen gebotten und leren. . . . Es ist Gott auch schimpflich, das er ein ungenügsam gesetz und leer geben hett, wann uns nit alles, das wir thün sollen, in seynem gesetz angezeigt wer." *Ibid.*, BiiiV. So too in *Von geweychtem wasser und saltz* (Verzeichnis, No. 33), of August 15, 1520: "Die weil nuhn, die styhm Christi sonderlich und eyniglich in der heiligen schrifft beschlossen . . . unnd gnugsam begriffen, Sollen Christglaubige schefflein kein pfeuffen oder gedon einnemen, oder einer zusag gefolgig sein, die nit ist in der schrifft woll zuweysen" (CV-Cii).

[58] "Ich hab kein zweifel, dz vil Päpst und vil münich vom ablass geschriben, dann wo es dienlich were, ich wolt dich wol in die schül füren. . . . Was darffstu mich zü menschen weisen, füre uns in die schrifft, lere uns durch göttliche schrifft." *Ablas*, AivV.

[59] See Fife, *Revolt*, pp. 306-7.

[60] "Du solt auch wissen, Wann Gott der herr, dem sünder, der sich bekert, sünd, schuld, unnd pein verzeihet und vergibt, dann so bleibet nit mer, das der mensch schuldig ist zü thün, dann das jhenige, daran vergebung der missethat und der sünde hanget und steet. . . . Möcht yemants fragen, was ist das selbe, dem vergebung der sünde, also innerlich und wesenlich eingebildet ist. Darzü antwurt ich, das ist, das uns Christus zü einer person gesagt, ging hien, und sünde nit mer." *Ablas*, Bii-BiiV.

[61] "Ich kan auch sagen, Ablass ist auss menschen gedencken entsprossen, hüt dich vor den esten." *Ibid.*, Biiii.

[62] "Wiewol ich ye und ye mich beflissen hab, gar wenig oder nichts gegen dem Ablass züsagen, Doch dringen mich die heiligen growen münich, und verkünden mir, das ich still schweig." *Ibid.*, Aii. See chapter II, nn. 51-56 for his earlier position and hesitation.

publication of the bull *Exsurge domine* at Rome on June 15, John Eck, who had been influential in its formulation, travelled north to publish it in Germany. A notary's records show that on September 21, 1520 Eck had exercised his authority to add the names of Luther's support-ers.[63] Karlstadt was among them. Although an official copy of the bull did not arrive in Wittenberg until about October 10, Karlstadt received secondhand information about the bull which he considered sufficiently reliable to warrant publication of a list of conditions under which he would submit to a trial.[64] Karlstadt announced his intention to avoid placing himself at the mercy of the pope who occupies the chair of the "faith-breaking rascals" who treacherously ignored the safe-conduct of John Hus.[65] Since hardly any contemporary bishops are familiar with scripture, his judges must consist of unbiased prelates and biblically literate laymen. He will not tolerate any Dominicans or Franciscans, both because they have quarrelled with him, and also because they have no desire for pure, clear and unadul-terated scripture.[66] Most important, of course, he will accept no refutation of his teachings unless it is based on scripture. Papal scriptural interpretations, which have often erred, have no more authority with him than those of a layman because valid exegesis results only when one interprets scripture by scripture.[67] As Luther said in a letter of October 3, Karlstadt had indeed cast his die and was

---

[63] See Barge, *Karlstadt*, I, 219, n. 101 for the documentation.

[64] The brief work is called *Bedingung*; Verzeichnis, No. 37. The date is about the end of September. See Barge, *Karlstadt*, I, 223, n. 112 and Bubenheimer, "Con-sonantia," p. 185, n. 3.

[65] "Ich wil auch yren brieffen und siegeln, so mir villeicht bischoffen oder bebstlich heilickeit zuschicken möchten, nit vortrawen dan yre vorfaren haben obgenanten doctor Joan. huss keinen glauben gehalten, so besitzen sie nun die stulen solcher glaubbruchiger freveler, darumb zuforchten, der weyn stinck nach dem fass." *Bedingung*, AiiV. See also Aii.

[66] *Ibid.*, AiiV-AiiiV.

[67] "Zu dem sechsten, sprech ich, So die heylige schrifft verborgen und dunckel, odder eine widder die andern ym scheyn stossen ist, wert ich Bebstlicher hey-lickeit und Bischofliger wirden, nit mehr nachlassen, heylige schrifft aussztulegen, oder zu vereynen, dan ich einem fleyssigen leyhischen zuhörer des wort Gottis, gestaten werde, es sey dan dz Babst und bischoffe, ernstlichen beweysen, das sie die heyligen geschrifft, in yrem eygen safft wol vorsucht und gelernet haben. Sunst sag ich, das sie durch yre hohen, nit gelerter sein, und geschicht vielmals, das ein handtwercks man, mehr von der schrifft, den ein Bischoff weyss. Dartzu weyss ich, das der Babst auch yrren kan, und sol affterglaubens und ketzerey halben, seiner wirden entsetzt werden. Weyl dan dan diesem also, folgt, das der babst die schrifft zeytten bösslich glossert, und zu seinem vorteyl ausslegt, und das yhnen nit zuglauben, er hab den die stymme und wort Christi in seiner leer." *Bedingung*, AiiiV-Aiv.

taking courage against the Pope.[68] His doctrine of scripture had developed to a point where it was theologically impossible for him to do otherwise.

The bull finally arrived in Wittenberg on October 10.[69] In an accompanying letter Eck noted the inclusion of Karlstadt and then added that by virtue of especially granted power, he would absolve Karlstadt from all penalties, if he would foreswear all heresy. But if he proved obdurate, then the deserved punishment would surely come.[70] Karlstadt replied with a quiet, inspiring confession of faith, a sharp attack on the papacy, and a legal appeal to a general council.

His *Missive von der aller hochste tugent gelassenheyt*, written the day after the bull and letter of Eck arrived, was an almost devotional epistle to his mother, brothers and sisters, and friends explaining why he could not accept their advice that he submit to the Pope.[71] To submit to the Pope would mean denying that word through which he had been born anew.[72] Through faith in its promises he hoped to obtain eternal peace.[73] Since his statements were rooted in the Bible, he could not renounce them.[74] Karlstadt begged his mother and other relatives to understand the fact that he had to choose either physical death by obeying God or spiritual death by disobeying God's word.[75] But if

---

[68] "Carlostadius et ipse iacta alea in pontificem Ro. cornua sumit." *WABr*, II, 191.29-30. Contrary to Barge (*Karlstadt*, I, 230), this brief comment by Luther does not prove that Karlstadt was already writing *Von Bepstlicher heylickeit*, his violent attack on the papacy, published on Oct. 17. Luther may have been referring to *Bedingung* or to private conversations with Karlstadt.

[69] See *Karlstadt*, I, 220-21 and Otto Clemens' discussion in *WABr*, II, 193-4.

[70] Eck to the rector of the University of Wittenberg, October 3, 1520; *Dr. Martin Luthers Sämmtliche Schriften*, ed. J. G. Walch (St. Louis, Mo., 1880-1910), XV, 1572.

[71] I have used the fifth (1521) edition (Verzeichnis, No. 42). There is no evidence that his mother, etc. visited him at Wittenberg at this time as Barge (*Karlstadt*, I, 225) says.

[72] "Du hast mich, ubermiltiglich, an alle vordienst mit dem wort deyner warheyt wider geborn. . . . Sie sagen, ich sol dein wort widerruffen, und vorleugnen, und bedrawen mich, mit absunderung, mit bann, mit vormaledeyhung, mit vorlust eer und guts, mit beraubung leyb und lebens." *Missive*, Aii.

[73] " . . . ia ich hoff yn Gottis zusagung. Gib nit zu, das sie mir deyn wort, der warheit, auss meynem hertzen reussen. Dan die, sso dein gesetz lieben, die sich an dein wort und rede hefften, und darauff lassen, und bawhen, die haben vill frides, pax multa diligentibus legem u. und werden ynn ewickeit nit vorlassen." *Ibid.*, Aiii.

[74] *Ibid.*, Aiv.

[75] "Darumb meynn mutter, bruder, schwester, öhmen, bassen, schweger, geschweyhen und alle liebe freundt ynn Christo, Ich bitt yhr wollet euch nit vorseren, und nit betrüben, von der tzeytliche schandt, und meyner anfechtung. Das mich auff alle seyten engst umbgeben. Zween tödt sehe ich vor augen, eynen

they persisted in insisting "dear son, follow the Pope," he would
follow Christ's injunction to forsake father and mother.[76] In spite of
his firm resolve, however, he was obviously fearful at the very
real prospect of death: "O God, my Lord, . . . leave me not. Depart not from me, for sadness, affliction and temptation are very
close to me. Nothing is nearer than anxiety." [77] The "hellish temptations" were so severe that he felt forsaken by God; but he was able
to take comfort in the memory that Christ had also felt forsaken on
the cross.[78]

The mystics' concept of *Gelassenheit* offered a useful medium for
emphasizing his intention to forsake all things if necessary.

> I will willingly deprive myself of my archdeaconate, [and] all goods that
> I have. I will forsake father and mother, brother and sister. I will
> renounce everything in body and soul which draws or removes me
> from divine promises. I know that I must be renounced.[79]

If taking one's cross and following Christ results in death at the stake,
so be it.[80] But he concluded on a confident note: "I will . . . flee no
violence, and will have greater confidence in God that He will

---

muss ich leyden, auff der rechten seytten trawet mir der todt, meynen geyst tzu
todten und erwurgen, und mich ewiglich zu peynigen. Auff der lincken, steht der
todt meynes fleysch, eynen muss ich annehmen." *Ibid.*, AiiiV.

[76] "Warumb solt ich mich und yhr mit mir auch nit erfreyen umb wegen uns-
sers erlössers zu leyden? . . . Darumb freyhet euch mit mir, das mich Gott berufft
umb seynes worts wegen zu leyden. Werdet yhr aber euch weych machen, und
understehen, mich abtzuhalten, sso werd ich euch sagen . . . ich kenn euch nit. . . .
Und wo yhr sprechen durfft, lieber Son oder ohm folge dem Bapst, sso darff ich
widersagen, wer bistu? behut mich Gott vor dir, und deynem rath. . . . Ich kenn yn
diser sach weder vatter, noch mutter. Ich folge eyniglich gottlicher schrifft."
*Ibid.*, AivV-B.

[77] "Nu o Gott meyn herr, mein schöpffer, mein erlösser, mein zuflucht, mein
leyb, und mein leben, varlas mich nit. Nit weych von mir. Dann betrubnus,
anfechtung und vorsuchung ist mir das aller nehest, nichts ist mir neher, dan
angst." *Ibid.*, AV.

[78] *Ibid.*, AiiV-Aiii.

[79] "Das will ich gern thun, ich will mich meynes Archidiaconat, aller gütter,
sso ich hab, guttwilliglich erwegen, vatter und mutter, brüder unnd schwester
vortzeyhen, alles gelassen an leyb und seel, das mich von gottlichen tzusagungen
zeuget oder fernet. Ich weyss das ich gelassen seyn muss und das ich alle creaturen
gelassen muss, und darff keynem Engell vortrawhen, sso er mich andernn lernen
odder gebenedeyhen wil, dan yn der Biblien beschrieben ist." *Ibid.*, B.

[80] "Nu sagt Christus, das wir das creutz annehmen, und yhm nachfollgen
sollen. . . . Derhalben solt yhr euch nit bekümmern, ob ich gleych auff eynen rost
gebunden und vorbrant würd. Ist doch Christus ein reyner mensch und Gott
gewest, und hatt sich nit geschemet an eynem galgen zu hangen und sterben."
*Ibid.*, BiiV.

graciously preserve me in His word, and grant eternal life after I have suffered death." [81]

On October 17, five days after the letter to his relatives and friends, he completed a voluminous attack on the papacy called *Von Bepstlicher heylickeit*.[82] Coming after Luther's *Address to the German Nobility* and *Babylonian Captivity*, it was mere anti-climax. Karlstadt borrowed the doctrine of the priesthood of all believers,[83] urged the secular nobility to reform the church,[84] appealed to German nationalistic sentiment,[85] and argued that the Pope had led Christendom into *Egypt!* [86] A good deal of the criticism of the Pope was either petty or conventional. At each annual celebration of the elevation of the reigning Pope, they burn more candles than on ten Easters.[87] Contrary to the example of Peter with Cornelius, the Pope insists that Emperors and kings lie at his feet.[88] Indeed his entire style of life is the very opposite of that humble manner exhibited by Christ. The attack on the luxury enjoyed by the Pope and his love for the German money-bag was conventional,[89] although the justification of this attack in terms of the consequent neglect of the poor was perhaps less common.[90]

In spite of a good deal that was innocuous or commonplace, however, the work did contain some vigorous statements about the Pope. Popes have erred, do err, and will err as long as the world stands.[91] The Pope can err in his interpretation of the scriptures and

---

[81] "Auff disse und andere trostlichen zusagungen, will ich stehen, wie auff eynem felss. Inn Christo, mit glauben und hoffnung und lieb sso vill mir vorlihen wirt, vest bleyben, und keyne ungestümheit fliehen, und ynn Gott grösser zuvorsich seyn, er werde mich gnedig yn seynem wort halten, und nach erliden todt, mit ewigem leben vorsehen. Das helff, mir und uns allen der guttig Gott. Amen." *Ibid.*, Biv.

[82] Verzeichnis, No. 44. Since he says on p. Fiv that he saw the papal bull yesterday, he must have been working on this treatise some time before October 10.

[83] *Von Bepstlicher heylickeit*, DiiiV-Div.     [84] *Ibid.*, Eii, Giii.

[85] *Ibid.*, GiiiV.

[86] *Ibid.*, Biv. See also, n. 90.

[87] *Ibid.*, CV. See below, n. 90.

[88] *Ibid.*, DV.

[89] *Ibid.*, BiiiV, GiiV.

[90] "Nun horent noch eynsz, am Jartag der erwelung unnd kronung, als ein Bapst erwelt unnd gekront ist, mussen die Cardinalen, Bischoffen, und grosse burger zu Rom, bey vorlust aller Bepstlicher genadenn, kertzen und vasz vorbrennen, und mehr wachs, dan sie an tzehen Ostertagen zurschmeltzenn. . . . Auch leyden viel arme hunger, welche der Bapst, mit solchem unnutzlichen gelt, wol speyszen kundt. Aber er furet uns mit drew wortten und ernst in Egypten." *Ibid.*, CV.

[91] " . . . alle Bebst sunder sein, und haben geyrret, und irren noch, und werden yrren sso lang die welt steht." *Ibid.*, Aii-AiiV.

cause God's people to go astray in matters of faith.[92] Since he perverts scripture, the Pope is the enemy of God rather than the vicar of Christ.[93] Indeed, the present Pope is a heretic who should be deposed.[94] Karlstadt, however, was not prepared to reject the entire institution of the papacy. He could still speak of "St. Peter and his successor." [95] He stated most emphatically that the pope possessed no authority once he stepped beyond his biblical commission and failed to govern Christians according to scripture. But he also said that "the pope should have the divine book in his hand and govern all Christians from it." [96] Indeed, if the Pope would only return to Christ and His word, he would be glad to kiss his foot.[97] Karlstadt never defined the extent of legitimate papal authority, but he certainly assumed that a reformed Pope submissive to scripture ought to govern Christendom.

Two days later Karlstadt made his rejection of papal authority official. He summoned an imperial notary to his dwelling and lodged an official appeal from the pope to a future general council.[98] The break with Rome was complete.

---

[92] "Ja ich darff yhm wol ansagen, das der Bapst mit allen seinen anhenger (das ist seinen Concilio) in der geschrifft durch unwissenheit kan yrren und sundigen, dartzu Gottis volck ym glauben yrren machen, als Levitici ym. iiii. capittel geschrieben." *Ibid.*, Fiv.

[93] "Nu die weil er die schrifft gar umbkeret, so sollen wir yhn hynfur auch keinen Commissarien Christi, sonder einen feynd Gottis nennen." *Ibid.*, Fii.

[94] "Ich weyss aber wol, das er widder das gotlich gesetz und greufflich geyrret, und will das reden und schreyben. Ich will mich auch unterstehen so bald mir die artikel, die er zuverdamen furnemen sol, behendet werden, sein bepstlich heylickeit, als einen ketzer, der von seinen stuel und eren abtzusetzen ist, anklagen." *Ibid.*, BV-Bii.

[95] "Wir halden alle, das der Befehlhaber oder ein Anwald, den befehl sunderlich, und vor allen behertzen, und aussrichten sol, den yhm sein her, in grosser not und in seinem abgehen oder abstehen befihlet. Christus . . . sanct. Peter, und seinem nachfolger, ym ende seines abstehens und vor seinem tod (yhm und allen iungern) befohlen, das der mit diensparckeit allen menschen sol dienenn, dero der hochste will sein odder ist." *Ibid.*, Fii.

[96] " . . . so bald er auss inhalt das [= des] beuelhs geet, ist sein macht vorloschen und unpundig. Ehr solt auch fur keinen stathalder gehalten werdenn. Das gotlich buch sol der Bapst in seiner hand haben, und alle Christen darauss regieren." *Ibid.*, Bii-BiiV. See also, n. 95.

[97] *Ibid.*, FivV.

[98] *Appellation* (Verzeichnis, No 45). See Bubenheimer's careful discussion of this legal document. "Consonantia," pp. 253-272.

# CHAPTER FOUR

# KARLSTADT'S MATURE WITTENBERG THEOLOGY
## (1520-1521)

In chapter two, it was seen that the Augustinianism of Karlstadt's earliest "Reformation" writings underwent modification in late 1518 and 1519. We have also traced the way Karlstadt's position on the problem of authority developed in such a fashion after the Leipzig debate that in 1520 he was able to break with the papacy. The task of the present chapter will be to discuss the basic aspects of Karlstadt's theology in the period after Leipzig and before the abrupt nullification of Karlstadt's reforms by Luther upon his return from the Wartburg in early 1522.

Both because of the eventual conflict between Luther and Karlstadt and also because of specific disagreements about the canonicity of James and the propitious moment for introducing practical reforms, there has been an attempt to discover fundamental differences in the theology of the two men during the period of their relatively harmonious cooperation through 1521. Barge argued that from 1520 on, there was a fundamental divergence based on a different religious experience.[1] Barge's primary example was the differing importance of forgiveness and sanctification in the two theologies. Barge believed that whereas the experience of forgiveness was fundamental for Luther, the crux of Karlstadt's religious experience and theology was inner renewal and sanctification.[2] More recently, Hillerbrand has restated the same point in terms of a continuing Augustinianism in Karlstadt which prevented him from adopting Luther's forensic conception of the Gospel as "favor dei." [3] By outlining Karlstadt's

---

[1] "Und doch ist das religiöse Empfinden beider Männer Anfang 1520 schon nicht mehr auf den gleichen Ton gestimmt! Für Luther, . . . stand im beherrschenden Mittelpunkte des Heilsvorganges die den Gläubigen erlösende Sündenvergebung. . . . Das Bewusstsein, mit Gott versöhnt zu sein, ist ihm [Karlstadt] nur die erste Staffel zu einem neuen, höheren seelischen Habitus, in dem der Gläubige der göttlichen Vollkommenheit teilhaftig werden und sie bewähren soll. . . . Die Versöhnung mit Gott bildet ihm nur die Voraussetzung der inneren Heiligung." *Karlstadt*, I, 182-3.

[2] In addition to the previous note, see also *ibid.*, pp. 199, 208.

[3] "Carlstadt's inability to utilize the term 'evangelium,' as *favor dei*, meant that he was unable to apprehend what was indeed the most crucial aspect of Luther's

mature theology of 1520 and 1521, it will be possible to determine the validity of the attempt to explain the later break in terms of earlier theological differences.

## 1. THE WORD OF GOD

After the development traced in the previous chapter, Karlstadt's thinking on the problem of authority changed very little in the years under consideration. From 1520 on he constantly repeated the demand for *sola scriptura*.[4] Christians believe the words of holy scripture because the Holy Spirit spoke them to men who wrote them down.[5] Whereas formerly the Holy Spirit spoke directly to men, he now speaks through scripture.[6] The only aim of his writing, he informed his readers, was to bring them to scripture.[7] He compared both the ancient prophets and contemporary preachers to mere tubes through which the divine word flows in order to emphasize the point that man must not add anything to the authoritative word of God.[8] The sole authority of scripture continued as a fundamental dogma for Karlstadt.

### (a) *Exegesis of the word*

Karlstadt's concern for proper exegetical method began very early. In the *370 Conclusiones* of May, 1518, the work in which he first raised the problem of authority at length, he quite naturally discussed the problem of exegesis. Already in this set of theses he outlined the two basic exegetical principles which he was to continue to stress thereafter—viz. literal interpretation and the explication of one scripture by another.[9]

---

new theology." "Karlstadt," p. 383. Hillerbrand, however, warns against an exaggeration of the differences.

[4] *Ochssenfart*, AiiV-AiiiV is a good example.

[5] *Welche bücher*, CiiiV (see above, chapter III, n. 44).

[6] *Welche bücher*, Biv (see above, chapter III, n. 31).

[7] "Ich wil auch nit weyter geschrieben haben, oder hinfurd schreyben, dan das ich die leser meyner buchlein von mir yn die schrifft breng, auff das sie mich frey urteyln durch die schrifft, sollen mir auch nicht weyters glewben, dan sie in der schrifft grundes vernemen." *Beyden gestaldten*, D.

[8] "Niemand soll sich lassen kumern, das die schrifft tzeiten spricht. Gott oder der h. geyst hat durch den mund seyner Propheten geredt. Dann die schrifft verbirget ye nit, das Got sein wort allein aussredet wircklich. Und das seine Propheten allein roher oder pfeuffen gewest sein, welchen Got sein wort eingeplassen, und seinen gesanck aussgesprochen oder geseungen hat." *Malachiam*, BiiiV. See also BiiV.

[9] For his discussion of the literal meaning of scripture, see above, chapter II,

In subsequent writings Karlstadt assumed that literal exegesis was necessary and talked more about the other principle. As has already been seen, the principle of the interpretation of scripture by other scripture enabled him to reject the role of the Pope as authoritative interpreter in his book on the canon in 1520.[10] Thereafter, he often restated it.[11] In his work on the very difficult passage in Matthew 11:12, he consciously enunciated and then successfully followed this principle. He explicated the text by examining first the verse itself in its immediate context, then other texts in the Gospels, and finally other scriptural passages.[12] In a book in early 1522 he added the suggestion that if the examination of surrounding texts and other scriptures does not help, then one should ask God for help, or be silent.[13]

Emphasis on the literal sense of scripture did not preclude the use of allegory.[14] Although Karlstadt did not use the full medieval mechanism of the fourfold sense of scripture in any of his publications, he always defended limited allegorical exegesis. In *370 Conclusiones* he simply accepted Augustine's view that one should interpret allegorically not only obviously figurative passages but also those whose literal sense is absurd.[15] And his writings frequently contained alle-

---

nn. 35-38. Karlstadt also alluded to the fact that one should interpret the scripture by means of other scripture: XLVII. Scriptura etenim idem quod uno loco abscondit, in alio aperit, seu ostendit." Löscher, *Reformations-Acta*, II, 82. See also thesis 92 (*ibid.*, p. 86) where he applied this principle.

[10] See above, chapter III, nn. 28-34.

[11] *Welche bücher*, Biv-BivV (see above, chapter III, n. 31). "Darauss ist leichtlich abtzunehmen, das kein texte, one beysetzung und vergleichung anderer texten, sso von eyner materien reden, gnuglich verstanden wirt." *Gelubden*, FivV. Cf. also *Ochssenfart*, B.

[12] The following is the most important methodological reference: "Warhafftig ausslegung disser red. Das reich Gotis leydet gewald. Nach obgesagten Opinionen, wil ich mein gutduncken auch furtragen, und Orstlich auss aller nehysten umbsteend der schrifft. Darnach, mit tzusetzung Ewangelischer reden. Und endtlich, mit einen kleinen durchlauff etzlicher schrifften beweisen." *Berichtung*, BV. See also, BiiiV-Biv.

[13] "Wan die schrifft dunckell ist. und mogen sie nit ausslegen, durch hylff der umbsteende schrifft, ader andere heilige schrifft, sollen sie vil liber nicht wissen, dan frevelich etwass aussprechen. Got sollen sie umb rath fragen. Wie Moses gethan hat. aber [= oder] sollen still schweigen." *Malachiam*, Biii.

[14] So too Luther; cf. M. Reu, *Luther's German Bible* (Columbus, 1934), p. 132 and Holl, *Gesammelte Aufsätze*, I, 553ff.

[15] "LXXVII. Proprietati seu verborum sono, in sacris literis est semper adherendum. Aug. de spiritu et litera c. II. LXXVIII. Restringitur, seu limitatur haec, nisi quispiam docere potuerit, verba aliter quam sonant, accipi posse. LXXIX. Hoc autem per simplicem negationem, vel ignorantiam, vel quod fedius est, per futilem pertinaciam, non docebit quisquam, sed per assignationem absurditatis vel

gorical exegesis.[16] Karlstadt applied his principle of the interpretation of scripture by scripture to the question of allegorical interpretation. Since there are figurative passages in scripture, one should interpret these obscure texts by means of the clear words of Christ.[17] The task of the preacher is to explain the mysteries of the Old Testament by means of the New and then adorn the New with allegories from the Old Testament.[18] One reason Karlstadt continued to accept allegorical exegesis was precisely his acceptance of the absolute authority of scripture. He defended tropology by pointing out that if the method were illegitimate, many of St. Paul's arguments would be useless.[19]

In keeping with his emphasis on the literal meaning of scripture, however, Karlstadt carefully limited the role of figurative interpretation. No figurative exegesis gives authority to a theological argument unless the figure is explained elsewhere in scripture. In that case it is the literal explanation and not the allegorical passage which is authoritative.[20]

> Nor dare you bring forward figurative passages and obscure scriptures. I want to have clear and lucid scriptures. . . . I do not thereby want to deny that prophets and apostles have interpreted figurative passages, but I will not grant that you may interpret ancient figures of speech according to your own whim. You yourself must confess and say according to Saint Thomas: scriptura symbolica non est argumentativa. . . . Therefore, you dare not think that you will wound me with exegesis of figures of speech, unless scripture has interpreted your figures of speech.[21]

---

figurati sermonis. De Ser. Do. in mon. lib. I. h. et de spiritu et litera c. IV."
Löscher, *Reformations-Acta*, II, 85. Cf. also *De sp.*, Kähler, pp. 32.8-33.16. Luther also allowed allegorical exegesis in the case of passages whose literal meaning was absurd (Holl, *Gesammelte Aufsätze*, I, 553, n. 6). So too Augustine; see *De spiritu et litera*, iv (6) and *De doctrina Christiana*, III, x(14) and xii (18).

[16] E.g. *Auslegung* (1519), DiiV; *De impii justificatione*, B-Bii; *Verba Dei*, CV; *Empfahern*, b.

[17] *Welche bücher*, Biv (see above, chapter III, n. 31).

[18] "Quinimo, secretissima veteris legis mysteria, novae legis lumine quasi nitidissimo Phoebo perfundere et illustrare et mutuo vetustis antiqui testamenti translationibus et allegoriis tanquam stellis quibusdam novuum testamentum exornare, officii praedicatorii, vel explicatoris literarum proprium existit." *Verba Dei*, F.

[19] "Etenim nisi ad eas res, et personas coaptari lex posset, quae quandoque erunt similes, multa tropologiae dulcissima argumenta periissent . . . frustra Paulus argumentaretur pleraque. . . ." *Super coelibatu*, Aiv.

[20] "Szo schleusset auch keyn figurliche ausslegung, sie wer dan yn der Biblien begriffen, und alsdan beschleusset sie nit, als figurlich erklerung, ssondernn als geschriebener text." *Beyden gestaldten*, CivV.

[21] "Jr dörfft mir auch nit figuren und dunckel schrifften hertragen. Ich will klare und liechte schrifften haben so will ich auch mit klaren schrifften antworten,

Thus Karlstadt's discussion of figurative exegesis also illustrates the fact that his two central exegetical principles were the importance of the literal meaning of scripture and the interpretation of one scripture in light of another.

### (b) *The Old Testament*

Before discussing one final aspect of Karlstadt's exegetical method, the notion of the inner sense or spirit of the letter, it is necessary to understand his attitude toward the old law. To what extent is the Old Testament normative and authoritative for Christians? Karlstadt's earliest writings published after he had purchased his copy of Augustine's works at Leipzig reflected the Augustinian position that the law reveals man's weakness "so that grace may restore the will and the restored will may fulfil the law." [22] In the first ("151 Theses"), Karlstadt agreed with Augustine that "grace makes us lovers and doers of the law." [23] Karlstadt continued to think in these terms for the rest of his life. After grace, the believer is a friend of the law.[24] Thus Karlstadt's attitude toward the law was a function of his Augustinianism. It should be added that Karlstadt may have gone beyond Augustine apropos the normative character of the law, for it is not

---

und mit solichen, das yederman sehen und hören kan, das ich on frevell und unstreflich schreib oder red. Domit will ich nit leuncken, das Propheten und Aposteln figuren aussgelegt haben. Aber ich werde dir nit gesteen, das du alte figuren, nach deinen wolduncken, ausslegest, jr müest ye selber bekennen, und secundum sanct Thomam sagen. Scriptura symbolica non est argumentativa. Auch ist euch bewüst, das Hieronymus tropologiam selber verlacht. Dorumb dörfft jr nit gedencken das jr mich mit aussleg der figuren werdet verletzen, es wer dann, das die schrifft jre figuren aussgelegt het." *Ochssenfart*, AiiiV-Aiv. Karlstadt, who began his theological career as a Thomist, accurately reflected Aquinas' position. See *Summa Theologica*, I, Q. 1, art. 10, especially ad. 1. Karlstadt's agreement with Aquinas here is not surprising since the angelic doctor stressed the literal sense far more than did many medieval exegetes. See Beryl Smalley, *The Study of the Bible in the Middle Ages* (Oxford, 1952), pp. 300-305. Unlike Karlstadt, of course, Aquinas did use the scheme of the fourfold figurative sense of scripture.

[22] Aug., *De sp. et lit.*, ix (15).

[23] "'Gratia facit nos legis dilectores' et factores." Thesis 85 of "151 Theses," Kähler, p. 25*. Karlstadt was quoting from Augustine's *De grat. et lib. arb.*, XVIII (38). So too *Defensio*, Löscher, *Reformations-Acta*, II, 123.

[24] "Redempti per Christum non sunt sub legis tyrannide: neque pondere eius premuntur. Amicus legis est: qui mente servit legi dei. ... Sic ego Paulum legis amicum verius dixero quam servum: Quamquam faciat et serviat legi. Quoniam Christus discipulos suos voluit amicos appellare: si facerent praecepta." *De legis litera*, Bii. Also: "Sic non servus legis, sed amicus es faciens, quae praecepit tibi." Thesis 12 of 46 theses written in the middle of 1521; reprinted in Jäger, *Carlstadt*, p. 207. Cf. Aug., *De gratia Christi*, I, xiii (14); After grace the believer can "live with law as his companion."

entirely clear precisely what parts of the old law are binding upon Christians in Augustine.[25] It is not difficult, however, to see how the Augustinian thesis that grace enables one to perform what the law demands could lead to considerable emphasis on the normative character of the old law.

Karlstadt took this path. In his "151 Theses" in 1517, he agreed with Augustine that the Decalogue, except for the Sabbath command, is normative for Christians.[26] Beginning in early 1520, the application of other Old Testament texts to the Church became rather frequent. What Ezekiel said to the Israelites, he asserted, should be referred to the Church.[27] After quoting Deuteronomy and Joshua, he rejected the counterargument that these texts are not applicable because they are part of the old law. Christ led the Jews to the law when he was asked what one ought to do to gain eternal life.[28] Passages from Deuteronomy were applied directly to the Pope.[29] Most well-known, perhaps, is

---

[25] J. Plagnieux's thesis is that "la loi, comme institution de salut, est supprimée. ... Mais comme obligation morale, La Loi subsiste. (Rien, à peu de chose près, n'est supprimé de ce qu' elle ordonnait.)" "En tant que norme de vie chrétienne, la loi n'a rien perdu de sa puissance d'obligation." J. Plagnieux, "Le Chrétien en face de la Loi d'après le *De Spiritu et Littera* de Saint Augustin," *Theologie in Geschichte und Gegenwart: Michael Schmaus zum sechzigsten Geburtstag*, ed. J. Auer and H. Volk (München, 1957), pp. 730-32. This may be somewhat overstated. In *Epistolae ad Galatas Expositio*, 19, Augustine distinguished the still binding moral law (*mores*) from the no longer normative ceremonial laws (*sacramenta*) without, however, clearly defining the extent of the former. His examples of binding Old Testament moral law tended to come from the Decalogue, all of which is binding except the command apropos the sabbath (e.g. *De sp. et litera*, xiv (23), xxi (36).

[26] "Decalogus 'excepta sabbati observacione' 'a Christiano est observandus'...." Thesis 101 of "151 theses," Kähler, p. 28*. Cf. *De sp. et lit.*, xiv (23).

[27] With reference to Ezek. 13:3, Karlstadt said: "... quae tunc populo Israeli dicebantur, ea ad Ecclesiam, et viros apostolicos, referri debebunt." *Verba Dei*, BV (see B-BV for the context).

[28] "Sed repugnabunt, dicentes, deum hoc hodie non iubere, sed in veteri lege, neque nobis hanc commentationem hodie delegari, At illis obgero, quod Iudeos magnopere ad legem Christus diduxit, Scrutamini scripturas ait, .... Interrogantibus quod facerent ut salvarentur, Respondit, in lege quod scriptum est? Preterea percunctanti de maximo mandato dei ..., quod ... demonstrabat nisi quod in mandatis dei scribitur, Diliges dominum deum tuum et c. Io:V.Si crederetis Mosi, crederetis et mihi, ille de me scripsit [John 5:46], Novissime dixit, In exempo, habent Mosen et prophetas. Habemus igitur dei mandata et praecepta, quae in libris nobis leguntur divinis, illa prodicemus oportet, si necationem aufugere malumus." *Verba Dei*, Bii. In addition to this passage, Karlstadt also referred to Matt. 19:16ff in *Abtuhung* to support his view that the old law was still authoritative: "Christus tzeiget dem das gesetz, dero froget. Wass sol ich thun. auff das ich, yn das ewig leben gehn? Warumb solt ich dich disses fals auch nit, in das gesetz Moisi fhuren?" Lietzmann's edition, p. 22.4-6.

[29] He applied Deut. 17:15-21 directly to the Pope in *Von Bepstlicher heylickeit*,

his use of Leviticus 27 and Numbers 30 to authorize the abandonment of monastic vows.[30] After noting that Leviticus commanded priests to marry and that I Timothy 3 did the same for deacons and bishops, he added that "we can see from the previous statements how all things in both old and new [Testaments] agree, and how the law, the Gospel and Paul speak with one mind and one voice." [31]

Karlstadt dealt with the normative character of the old law most clearly in his work on images. Some "image-kissers" may say that the old law's prohibition of images is irrelevant because we follow the new law. But this is heresy. Such a view belittles the doctrine of Christ both because He fulfilled the Old Testament prophecies and, more important, because He proved His doctrine by citing Moses.

> Nor did Christ break the smallest letter in Moses. Further, he did not make one addition to or subtraction from the law of Moses. Briefly, Christ did not pull down anything which pleased God in the old law. Christ remained in the will and content of the old law.[32]

BiiV ("konig der Juden, das ist, der gleubigen") and BiiiV: "Der bapst lebet wissentlich, wider das alt und new gesetz, der wegen er sundigt, und von notten yrret. Dan Got hat durch Moysen in obberurten xvii. capittel der andern ehe gesagt, der konig der glaubigen sol nit vil pferd zu sich sameln [cf. Deut. 17:16]." And then Karlstadt denounced the Pope's many horses.

[30] See both *Gelubden* and *Super coelibatu*; especially *Gelubden*, DiiiV and G. The text of Numbers 30, which allowed a father to reject a daughter's rash vow, he applied directly to the current monastic practice of "luring" children to the monasteries and ignoring parents' wishes (G). Leviticus 27:1-8 authorizes monks and nuns to redeem their vows and marry: "Ich weiss nit was die Monichen Nonnen und pfaffen Gott mehr geloben mogen, dan yhre seelen. Das selbe gelubd sollen sie halten, nach ordenung der schrifft, die yhn macht gibet yre seelen zu loesen. Nemlich, sso ein Monich oder Nonn in dem xx iar biss auff lx iar, Gott yhre seel gelobt hatt, sso magk er oder sie, sich loesen mit l. odder xx. siclos wie gesagt [cf. Lev. 27:3-4]." *Gelubden*, DiiiV. It is true that Karlstadt offered a number of other reasons for rejecting vows, but one simply cannot accept Barge's statement that "geben alttestamentliche Vorschriften bei Karlstadt nie das Fundament ab für seine religiösen Gedankengänge: er bedient sich ihrer nur als willkommener Belege für die Richtigkeit der eigen Aufstellungen" (*Karlstadt*, I, 266). This is most clear, perhaps, in his work on images. He did offer many substantial arguments against images in addition to the exegetical one, but then he insisted that even if one could show that images are useful to laymen, he would still not allow them because God prohibited them in scripture: "Sih, ap ich tzugobe, das Leyhen ehtwass nutzes und seligbarlichs aus bildern kondten lernen. Dorfft ich doch das mit nicht gestaten, wider verbot der schrifft und wider gotlichen willen. Die schrifft spricht klar auss das Got bilder hasset und neydet." *Abtuhung*, ed. Lietzmann, p. 11.15-18.

[31] "Superioribus ex dictis videre quimus, quam omnia consonant et vetera et nova, quam una mente, unaque voce, conclamant, et lex, Evangelium et Paulus." *Super coelibatu*, D.

[32] "Etliche bildekusser sprechen. Das alhte gesetz verbeut bilder, und das neuwe nit. Aber wir volgen dem neuwen, nit dem alten gesetz. Liebe brüder behut

Karlstadt was not unaware of the problem posed by the Pauline teaching that faith antiquates the law. He noted that he who can harmonize this statement with the other Pauline dictum that "by faith or grace we establish the law" (Romans 3:31), understands Moses, the prophets, Christ and Paul. But he declined to explain to what extent the old law is no longer binding both because of lack of time and because the enemies of the law would not understand any-way.[33] In light of his vigorous defense of the authority of the old law in the Church, this omission was unfortunate.

Karlstadt, of course, believed that there was a significant difference between the two testaments which together make up "the law of God." [34] The ceremonial law, certainly, is no longer binding. It was noted above that he assigned to the preacher the task of explaining the mysteries of the Old Testament by means of the New Testament.[35] In comparison with the New Testament sun, the Old Testament is a mere star.[36] The relative superiority of the New Testament, however,

---

euch Got, vor diesem ketzerischen sermon und wort. und das ihr ye nit sprecht. Wir volgen dem alten gesetze nit. ader nhemen ess nit ahn, dan das gehort den unchristen tzu. und bricht und verkleindt die laher Christi. Dan Christus beweys-set seyne laher aus Moise, und Propheten. Und spricht das ehr nicht komen sey, das gesetz tzu brechen, sonder tzu erfullen. Ehr hat auch seyne Junger gelert, wie das er hab mussen leben und leyden, auff das die schrifften erfulth wurden, Chris-tus hat ouch nicht den aller kleynsten buchstaben, ym Moyse verbrochen. Ehr hat auch keynen tzusatz, und keynen abbruch dem gesetz Moysi gethan. Kürtzlich Christus hat nichts nyder gelegt, das Gott ym alten gesetz behagt hat. Christus ist im willen und inhalt altes gesetzes bestanden. Wer disse tzwen sprüch tzesamen fügen kann. Nemlich. Fide legem antiquamus. Fide vel gratia legem stabilimus. Der versteht Moysen Propheten, Christum, und Paulum. In dem artickell. das. alth gesetze unpundig ist. Jtzo ists tzuvil, das tzu erkleren so weyss ich auch dz mich die gesetz feinde nit versten wurden." *Abtuhung*, ed. Lietzmann, p. 21.15-32.

[33] See previous note.

[34] Karlstadt frequently referred to the Bible as the *lex dei*. E.g. *Verba Dei*, bii: "Igitur et tale evangelium quod in lege domini non offenditur, est anathema." Cf. also *ibid.*, CiiV. In *Welche bücher*, CV, he spoke of the "drey stelh oder ord-nungen neüwes gesatz." See also, n. 18 above. See further Bubenheimer's sug-gestion that Karlstadt's juridical training and interest contributed significantly to the importance of his conception of the Bible as the *ius divinum*. "Consonantia theologiae et iurisprudentiae," pp. 234-43, 245. That such a conception could sometimes lead to a legalistic attitude is hardly surprising. He could insist, for instance, that since the verb in I Timothy 3:2 ("the bishop must be the husband of one wife") is present tense, it is not adequate that a nominee was married at one time. He must have a wife at the time of his elevation to the episcopacy! *Super coelibatu*, Diiii. See also above, n. 30.

[35] *Verba Dei*, F (see above, n. 18).

[36] "Wellcher wissen und lernen will, Was in disses hochwirdigen Sacraments unwirdig macht, der müss achtung haben auff die historien, Geschycht, und gschrifft alttes gesetzes und fleissyg auffsehen, was die Juden unwirdig gemacht

by no means precluded a significant normative role in the Church for all but a presumably insignificant and never clearly defined part of the Old Testament.

### (c) *The spirit and the letter*

Gordon Rupp has noted that in the early years of the Reformation when the doctrine of the word was the significant issue, the contrast between the inner and the outer word, between the spirit and the letter, was very important.[37] Karlstadt illustrates Rupp's point. Any discussion of Karlstadt's exegesis must consider this problem both because Karlstadt wrote a treatise called *De legis litera sive carne et spiritu* and also because scholars have asserted that his conception of the spirit of the law involved a spiritualist dissipation of scriptural authority. Hayo Gerdes has argued that according to Karlstadt one cannot understand the spirit of the law by means of the reason. Rather, since God is Spirit, man grasps the inner sense of the law only in the ground of the soul by means of the Spirit.[38]

It is very important to notice that Augustine used the spirit-letter dichotomy of II Corinthians 3:6 ("The letter kills but the Spirit gives life") in two very different ways. He taught that this text does pertain to the fact that one must not take figurative passages literally.[39] In the case of all texts whose literal meaning is shameful, one must understand them spiritually and remove the "kernels from the husk." [40] In this dichotomy the content is the variable. In his great work called *De spiritu et litera*, however, Augustine explicitly stated that although II Corinthians 3:6 does pertain to the question of figurative exegesis, its more important meaning is related to the dichotomy of law and grace.[41] The letter of the law merely reveals sin. Grace on the other hand transforms the will and enables man to keep the law. Here the only variable is the will's power to do what the content of the law requires. Karlstadt followed Augustine in using the spirit-letter dichotomy in both these senses. Even though Karlstadt sometimes

---

hat göttlycher züsagungen, Unnd darnach das New testament gegen dem altten vergleychen, Gleych als wann ayner die Sonne gegen den stern des hymels stöllet." *Predig* (Dec. 25, 1521), AV.

[37] Rupp, "Word and Spirit in the First Years of the Reformation," *ARG*, XLIX (1958), 13.

[38] H. Gerdes, *Luthers Streit mit den Schwärmern um das rechte Verständnis des Gesetzes Mose* (Göttingen, 1955), pp. 28-29.

[39] *De doctrina christiana*, III, v. (9).

[40] *Ibid.*, xii (18).

[41] *De sp. et lit.*, iv (6).

confused the two different dichotomies, it is essential to bear in mind their basic difference. Gerdes' failure to distinguish these two very different conceptions resulted in a distortion of Karlstadt's position.[42]

Gerdes is quite correct in suggesting that it was Karlstadt's view of the normative character of the old law which forced him to develop some mechanism for handling laws later abrogated by the prophets or the New Testament.[43] His treatise on the letter and the spirit of the law was an attempt, albeit an extremely confused one as will be seen, to find some solution.[44] Thus one would expect this treatise to deal with the first of the two Augustinian dichotomies connoted by the words "the spirit and the letter." The following summary of the treatise will attempt to ascertain both the new content that a spiritual understanding of the law provides, and also the method for discovering that new content called the spirit of the law.

Karlstadt introduced the problem by pointing out that whereas Leviticus clearly and explicitly demanded physical sacrifices, both Isaiah and David denied that God desired such sacrifices.[45] Karlstadt concluded that the spirit or will of the law demanded something other than what the flesh (or shell, skin, letter, etc.) required. He then declared that although the shell of the law is clearly visible to the eyes, "the spirit is acquired only by the soul."[46] At first glance this assertion might appear to be a clear confirmation of Gerdes' view that the spiritual content of the law is given to the spirit of man quite apart from the mediation of the word. But in fact Karlstadt obtained the spiritual content of the law pertaining to physical sacrifice precisely from scripture. He proceeded to argue that when the Jews failed to

---

[42] Many of the texts cited in Gerdes, *Luthers Streit*, p. 29 and n. 11 to support his interpretation of Karlstadt's exegesis actually pertain only to the law-grace dichotomy. This is true of all the texts cited from Kähler, p. 28*. It will be shown below (see chapter VII, nn. 183-6) that this is also true of the important text from *Sermon vom Stand*, bV.

[43] Gerdes, *Luthers Streit*, pp. 26-30.

[44] *De legis litera sive carne et spiritu* (Sept. 30, 1521).

[45] *Ibid.*, Aii.

[46] "Testatur iis Esaias: non quaesiisse id legis spiritum et voluntatem: quod plane litera et caro praeceptorum exquirit quippe nemo non cernit: quam accurata diligentia dominus per Mosen legem victimarum ediderit. Quanta contestatione sabbatum caeterasque festivitates instituerat. Tamen per Esaiam dicit: aliud victimarum et festivitatum nomine conquisitum neque idem corticem legis: et eius spiritum desyderavisse: Legis caro et litera: sive cortex, cutis, seu velamen, bractea et pellis est. quam oculis inspicere, manu, calamoque formare possumus. Spiritus autem solo animo colligitur: neque vere spiritus nobis est: nisi divina vi et digito: cordi insculpatur." *Ibid.*, Aii-AiiV.

perceive the spirit of the law, God sent prophets and interpreters to recall them to the law's true intention.[47] Isaiah demanded purification of the heart and David showed that God required a contrite heart. Karlstadt concluded that although the flesh or letter of the law demands something physical, the essence of the spirit of the law has always been the demand for purification of the heart through faith.[48]

Karlstadt explained this further. The spirit of the law is identical with the will of God.[49] "If anyone diligently pays attention to the divine will, he perceives that God desires nothing more eagerly and strongly than that we have hope, trust and love and above all faith in him." [50] This understanding of the divine will, however, he obtained from other scripture. He defined the will of God by quoting Christ who said that the will of His Father was that men have faith in Him and thereby obtain eternal life (John 6:40).[51] "Therefore the divine will which is hidden under the flesh of the law, just as the soul is hidden under the body, vigorously and especially promises and demands faith." [52] Since the spirit of the law is the demand that we have faith, "we fulfil it to the extent that we believe that Christ freed and redeemed us from the curse of the law." [53]

---

[47] "Caeterum non referebat legis cutis: divinae leges [=legis] spiritum: sed occultavit et abstrusit. Quo opinor (ut revocarent ad spiritum) prophetas et interpretes delegatos a deo." *Ibid.*, AiiV.

[48] "At illa legis pelle Esaias: et ante eum nonnulli alii submoverunt. Esaias ait. Lavamini: mundi estote [1:16]: nisi enim sordes cordis primum elueritis: contaminatum offeretis, quicquid offertur. . . . David itidem repositum victimarum spiritum prodidit. dicens Si voluisses sacrificium dedissem: utique holocaustis non delectaberis: sacrificium deo spiritus contribulatus cor contritum et humiliatum non despicit deus [Psalm 51:16-17 (Vulgate: 50:18-19)]. . . . Vere spiritualis est lex nos autem carnales: Spiritusque legis semper et nusquam non vult per fidem nos emundari." *Ibid.*, AiiV.

[49] "Nunc fortiter: neque tamen temere: uno verbo legis spiritum effundam. Spiritus legis voluntas est dei. Nempe quid potest esse maius: in quolibet lege (etiam privata) quam legis voluntas?" *Ibid.*, Aiii.

[50] "Nunc si quis diligenter voluntatem divinam animadvertit: nihil cernit studiosius et vehementius deum velle: quam quod in se spem fiduciam et charitatem et ante omnia fidem habeamus. Propterea ait Christus. Haec est voluntas patris mei: ut is: qui videt filium et credit in eum non pereat: sed habeat vitam aeternam [John 6:40]." *Ibid.*, Aiii.

[51] See previous note.

[52] "Voluntas ergo divina: sub legis carne: sicut anima sub corpore latens: summopore et praecipue fidem promittit et exigit." *Ibid.*, AiiiV.

[53] "Hisce constat fidem exegi: quae corda purificat: et spirituales nos facit adeo ut spiritu spiritum legis id est per fidem dei voluntatem complectamur: fides nos facit spontaneos et voluntarios et conformes voluntati legis: quam Christus adimplevit. Atque nos eatenus implemus: quatenus credimus Christum nos a legis maledicto liberavisse: et redemisse: et iustitiam nobis factum." *Ibid.*, AiiiV.

The same kind of contrast was developed in the case of circumcision. When the Jews were preoccupied with circumcision of the letter (i.e. of the flesh), Moses showed that true circumcision was that circumcision of the heart effected by the Spirit. Man, of course cannot effect this transformation of the heart. God performs it as one believes. Thus although the flesh of the law speaks of physical circumcision, the spirit or will of the law demands spiritual circumcision.[54]

Karlstadt next turned to the problem of the Christian's relationship to the law. He attempted to elucidate the Pauline notion that those serving in the Spirit are no longer under the law but yet actually fulfil the just requirement of the law. If one fulfils the just requirement of the law, then one actually is a slave of the law's just requirement.[55] One must realize, however, that for Paul, being under the law generally signifies being a slave of sin.[56] The man, however, who has been redeemed through Christ willingly serves the law. "Thus I would more truly have said that Paul was a friend rather than a slave of the law, although he performs and serves the law." [57]

At this point he digressed and actually discussed the second of the two basic dichotomies noted above. Using the terminology of this treatise, he discussed the contrast between law and grace. Whenever the Jews tried to follow the law by means of works, the results were always disastrous. "While practicing the law through works they never came into the spirit of the law"—i.e. they missed the fact that the central point of the law is faith.[58] Since they tried to obey the law by

---

[54] "Nempe: ut Iudaei: in minuciis pendentes: magnificaverunt: glandis circumcisionem: quasi tum legem custodierint: errorem illorum Moses. Deu. x. emendare cupiens: dixit. Circumcidite praepucium cordis vestri: quo plane praecepto sensum circumcisionis expromsit: et ad principium eius revocavit: scilicet ad fidem quam Abraham habuit antequam circumcisionis carnalis praeceptum audiret. . . . Ergo ex iis inferam Circumcisionem carnis et literae esse: quam caro legis eloquitur: Circumcisionem spiritus esse quam praecipue legis exquirit voluntas." *Ibid.*, AivV-B.

[55] "Quod dixi. Servientes spiritui et voluntati legis: exemptos esse a carne et litera legis sic opinor tractandum Paulus adseverat positos sub lege non esse sub gratia. Ro. vi. Atque rursus. Iustificationem legis impleri secundum spiritum: Rom.ii et viii. Ergo spiritu iustificationem legis implens: servus est iustificationis legis. Sicut servus est iusticiae: qui iusticiam facit: Roma. vi. Nunc Paulus dilucido sermone ait. Mente servio legi dei. Rom. vii. At qui certe: servus fuerit qui servit. Consequentur dabis: Iustum legis fore servum. . . . Pugnant autem eundem: esse legis addictum ac servum: et a lege liberatum." *Ibid.*, B-BV.

[56] "Addo quod idem Paulus facit istec idem significare: Esse in carne: esse sub lege: Secundum carnem vivere: Et extra gratiam esse." *Ibid.*, BV.

[57] *Ibid.*, Bii (see above, n. 24).

[58] "Nunquam bene cessit Iudaeis: multitudini hominum: aut suis viribus

themselves, they merely wounded themselves. "They dwelt within and served the oldness of the letter, not the newness of the Spirit." Believers, on the other hand, are made new by faith and then fulfil the just requirements of the law.[59] At this point Karlstadt abruptly announced that he had departed from his theme, although he lamely tried to insist that the problem of the letter and spirit of the law is related to the fact that man must be renewed by the Spirit before he can follow the law.[60]

He returned to his theme with the assertion that "in any law at all there is spirit and newness." It is particularly easy to separate the letter from the spirit in ceremonial law.[61] At this point Karlstadt stated most clearly the method for separating the spiritual content from the letter. "It is not granted to anyone at all to perceive the difference between age and newness, letter and spirit in any law at the first meeting as one says or at the first glance; for that pertains to a man of *extensive reading*." [62] He quickly added that even a great deal of

---

fidentibus id quod historiae passim attestantur. Neque potuit: neque debuit illis succedere quando legem operibus consectabantur. Quippe per opera legem colentes: illi nunquam in legis spiritum veniunt: quia non noverunt quae Christus a patre audivit. . . . Neque fieri potest ut in legem iusticiae venias si operibus accedis: quia summa legis est credere deo. Ut credas: haec est radix, petra, corpus et fastidium [=fastigium] legis." *Ibid.*, BiiV.

[59] "Quanto acrius intendimus actionem tanto vehementius lex vulnerat. Ad legem iusticiae Israel ideo non pervenit, quia legem iusticiae non ex fide: sed ex operibus sectabatur Ro. x. Iccirco per vetustatem literae: non per novitatem spiritus ambulaverunt et servierunt. Credulus autem: mortuus est legi: in qua tenebatur incredulus: et secundum novitatem spiritus ambulat atque servit. Ro. vii. hoc est factus per fidem novus homo. illi servit in lege dei. quod ad novos homines pertinet: ut iustificatio legis in iis tantummodo impleatur: qui non secundum carnem sed spiritum versantur. Ro. viii." *Ibid.*, Biii. Karlstadt does not go beyond this kind of general statement to define the content of the just requirement of the law which the believer fulfills.

[60] "Alio raptus sum: sed tamen in campum haud remotum quia dicere volebam interesse inter legis literam et spiritum: at proxime tractata: eo plane tendent: quod nemo legis literam in sui salutem: assequi potest: nisi primum legalem illum spiritum attingat: et illi per novitatem spiritus compingatur." *Ibid.*, BiiiV.

[61] "Itaque in qualibet lege spiritus est et novitas: quam potissimum debemus degustare. Atque in ceremoniali lege facilius est videre: literae vetustatem: a novitate spiritus distare. Verum enim vero non cuiuis licet primo congressu ut dicitur vel intuitu qualibet in lege vetustatem et novitatem: literam et spiritum discriminatim nosse. Quoniam id est hominis multae lectiones [read lectionis?]. Sed non sufficit lectio multa: nisi spiritum dei habeas. Possumus quidem multi de scripturis loqui: alios docere: alios inflammare: et ipsi nos ipsos non docere et frigescere. Ro. ii. Animalis homo non praecipit quae dei sunt. Etiamsi veritatem audit: tractatue: non sibi sapit intus veritas: non in veritate iocundatur: non in dei gloriam venit: ingratus permanet: atque sic cor insciens obtenebrescit: Ro. 1." *Ibid.*, BiiiV.          [62] My italics (see previous note).

reading is insufficient without the Spirit of God but it is clear that the insufficiency pertains to one's personal appropriation of the word of God, not to one's discernment of the difference of content between the spirit and the letter of the law. Many who teach others about scripture are cold and ungrateful themselves. They fail to understand it inwardly, i.e. they do not rejoice in it.[63]

> Certainly we are able, God willing, by constant reading and careful precision to distinguish the newness and spirit of the law from the letter and oldness. But the mysteries of God do not become sweet to us, good God, unless the Spirit of Christ is bestowed upon us. The heart remains ignorant while the mouth utters the secrets of the law. . . . We have what God revealed, but the heart is far away, because we do not have the truth in truth, i.e. in the Spirit.[64]

In light of this important passage we must conclude that Gerdes was incorrect in asserting that the content of the spirit of the law was available only to the soul and not to the reason.[65] One obtains the spirit of the law by rational study of scripture. Further this explicit statement corresponds with the discovery that in the place where it seemed that Karlstadt might mean that the spirit of the law is accessible only to the soul, he immediately defined the content of the spirit of the law by adducing other scripture. In short, in 1521 at least, Karlstadt's notion of the spirit of the law may have been somewhat novel, but it had not led to a spiritualist abandonment of *sola scriptura*.

The concluding paragraph reveals the extent of Karlstadt's confusion in this treatise. In spite of considerable obscurity the reader must conclude that when Karlstadt spoke of the difference between the letter and the spirit of the law, he intended to refer to some dichotomy other than the second Augustinian contrast between the demanding law and that regenerating grace which fulfils the law. But

---

[63] *Ibid.* (see n. 61).

[64] "Possumus certe: deo volente: assiduitate lectionis et acri adhibito delectu: novitatem et spiritum legis a litera et vetustate discernere. Sed deus bone: non dulcescunt nobis legis mysteria: nisi Christi spiritus nobis imperciatur: cor insciens manet: dum os arcana legis eloquitur. Veritas in ore: veritas in impietate et iusticia [read iniusticia with the other edition]. Quod deus revelavit habemus cor autem longe abest: quia veritatem non habemus in veritate: hoc est in spiritu." *Ibid.*, BiiiV-Biv. A passage from AiiiV (quoted in n. 53 above) should be interpreted in light of this passage. To embrace or appropriate the spirit of the law by the spirit is identical with coming into a right relationship with the will of God by faith. The passage does not mean that the content of the spirit of the law is accessible only to the spirit and not the reason of man.

[65] Gerdes, *Luthers Streit*, pp. 28-29. It remains to be seen whether Gerdes interpretation is correct for the post 1521 writings.

the last paragraph does not support this conclusion. He again declared that "any law whatsoever and every precept has flesh and soul or letter and spirit." [66]

> I think that the oldness and flesh of the law consists in the fact that the carnal man is accustomed to proceed with that which is written when he hears the precepts of God, i.e. to rashly stand in what he hears and think that to have heard the law is enough for him. It is clear that the pompous Jews did that.... They knew that which was written, but did not know the power of the Lord.... No wonder he showed by that word that the letter of the law is insufficient; rather there is need for power by which they receive such a mind [to keep God's commands]. That is what Moses stated openly about circumcision. ... Therefore the spirit of the law is hidden and inwardly gives joy to the mind for we obtain the spirit not by works but by faith, not by oldness but by newness— i.e. we are joined to the will of God by faith and trust.[67]

Here the variable is not the content but the ability of man's will. If one interpreted the entire work on the basis of this last paragraph, one would have to conclude that the entire treatise was intended only as a discussion of the law-grace dichotomy. One can only conclude that this important work is somewhat unclear.

## (d) *The word as means of grace*

The writings of 1520 and early 1521 stressed the role of the external word in the communication of grace far more than had the preceding publications. Whereas formerly Karlstadt had both assumed the necessity and pointed out the insufficiency of the external word,[68]

---

[66] See n. 67.

[67] "Nunc breviter quelibet lex: et omne praeceptum carnem habet et animam sive literam et spiritum.... In eo vetustatem et carnem legis opinor consistere: quod carnalis homo solet: in literaturam ire: audiens dei praecepta: hoc est. Temere stans in eo quod audit: arbitrans satis sibi esse: legem audisse. Id quod constat tumidos Iudaeos fecisse. ... Illi audacter fortiter literam sermonis acceperunt. Literaturam noverunt. Potentiam domini non noverunt.... Nimirum eo sermone [Deu. 5:27, 29 just quoted] demonstravit: non sufficere legis literam. Sed potentia opus esse: qua talem mentem capiant. Id quod et Moses de circumcisione palam disseruit: et omnes post eum prophetae docuerunt. Itaque spiritus legis est occultatus et intrinsecus oblectat mentem: quia spiritum non operibus: sed fide: non vetustate: sed novitate contingimus: hoc est voluntati dei fiducia atque fide iungamur: caetera alias." *Ibid.*, Biv. Cf. also *Super coelibatu*, Bii, where the spirit of the precept is precisely the divinely bestowed power to obey it.

[68] See above chapter I, nn. 43-59. *Ausslegung*, written in 1519, contained the last of Karlstadt's early Augustinian statements on the insufficiency and powerlessness of the external letter apart from grace. Scripture is a road sign (DV) which points out man's disobedience and sinful inability to change (Diii). "Aber alle und yegklich vorgemelt heiligenn schryfften toden den menschen, dan sie

he now spoke only of the former. "Fides ex auditu" became a constant theme.

It was in *Verba Dei* that this new emphasis on the external word first appeared. It is precisely because faith is impossible apart from hearing the word of God that the preacher must be exceedingly careful to proclaim God's word rather than that of Aristotle.[69] When faced with excommunication in 1520 he explained to his relatives that the Pope wanted to take away that word through which he had obtained faith.[70] Karlstadt underlined the importance of the external word by contrasting its significance with that of lesser things. The people foolishly grant excessive honor to stone churches and consecrated eucharistic utensils even though they cannot help us taste Christ. They should be more concerned with scripture because one may "scoop up, sample and taste the true Spirit of Christ through industrious reading or hearing."[71] Indeed, Christ dwells a thousand times more powerfully and efficaciously in his word than in a stone cathedral.[72] Legitimate tasks such as the burial of relatives, hospitality,

---

verbieten sunden und tzeygen Christum aber helffen dem menschen nit weyter. Darumb muss der sunder in der schrifft sterben, wan er in ire, andere hulff suchet dan scheynliche antzeygung gotliches willen und unsere kranckheyten. Dan der bustaben, an gotlich genad held den ungutigen gefangen" (Div).

[69] "Deinde populi plurimum interest, audire verbum dei. ... Sed constat, sine auditu neminem credere, Item absque praedicante, nullum audire. ... Apostolus dixit, fides est ex auditu, Iccirco quomodo audient sine praedicante? quomodo praedicabunt nisi mittentur? fides enim per verbum Christi, Non dicit per verbum Aristotelis, per verbum nostri cordis, sed per verbum hominum, sed per verbum Christi, fides est ex auditu, Proinde nemo recte et syncere credit, nisi qui recte et syncere audit. Hoc autem factu impossibile est, nisi sit contionator, qui ita praedicat, sicut auditores oportet audire." *Verba Dei*, BiiiV. Explicit references or obvious allusions to Romans 10:14-17 became frequent. In addition to the long discussion here, cf. also *Verba Dei*, C, CiiiV; *Missive*, Aii; *Super coelibatu*, Biii: "Haec fides unico verbo inspiratur et adservatur, teste Apostolo. Fides ex auditu, auditus per verbum Christi."

[70] "Du hast mich, ubermiltiglich, an alle vordienst mit dem wort deyner warheyt wider geborn. ... In deynem wort, idest, In deynen zusagungen und vorheyschung hastu uns geystlich, das ist ym glauben, yn lieb, in trost und yn hoffnung zu dir geborn, und lebendig gemacht. ... Der glaub hanget an deynem wort, als Paulus geschrieben. Der glaub ist auss dem gehör deynes worts.' *Missive*, Aii. See also chapter III, n. 72.

[71] "Die heylige geschrifft ist Got nichts mynder voreynet und eygen gemacht, dan ein kelch odder altar, und konden in der schrifft lessen, odder horen lessenn alles das, das uns von noten, und mugen auch den rechten geyst Christi durch fleyssig lesung oder anhorung schopffen, versuchen und schmecken." *Bepstlicher heylickeit*, Eiv.

[72] "In der summa, Christus wanet in seinen wort, und heyliger geschrifft, mit leyden, tod, und leben, und hersung, und einwanet tausent mal krefftiger und wircklicher, und allenthalben lebendiger, dan in einen steynern hauss. Szo hat

assistance to the unfortunate, and even baptism should be neglected in order to preach the word, because faith is poured in and preserved through the word of Christ. Paul said he was sent to preach not to baptize.[73] The Spirit works through the external word:

> Christ says that no one becomes incorporated into God's kingdom unless he is born again of water and the Spirit. It follows that God's word is a fountain out of which [the] Divine Spirit flows into the believers and renews them and makes them a kingdom of God.[74]

Karlstadt obviously had adopted Luther's conception of the external word as the means of grace.

Not until *De legis litera sive carne et spiritu* written in September, 1521 did Karlstadt mention the insufficiency of the external word which he had discussed in his Augustinian writings of 1517 and 1518. In this work, however, he again insisted that even "extensive reading

---

er uns auch an sein wort gepunden." *Ibid.*, F. It should be noted that Jäger (*Carlstadt*, p. 156, n. 1) is incorrect in arguing that in *Bepstlicher heylickeit*, Dii Karlstadt conceived of an inner drawing of man toward Christ which precedes the external offer of grace. Jäger adds that this would necessarily lead to an abandonment of the external means of grace. In this passage Karlstadt was arguing both that Christ's atonement was efficacious only for those predestined by the Father and also that no one comes to Christ unless the Father draws him. He concluded: "Christus keinen mit seinem blut besprenget odder erlosset, er sey dan *vor* von dem vatter getzogen" (my italics). This passage may mean merely that Christ forgives only the predestined. Or, it may also mean that forgiveness never occurs unless the Father first draws one toward Christ. But that by no means implies that the Father's activity precedes the external word.

[73] "Baptizationem similiter caedere [=cedere] predicationi, videtur Paulus astruere, dicens, Non misit me Christus ut baptizarem sed ut Evangelizarem. . . . Neque alia re poterat gloriam Christi, plus illustrare, quam verbo. Eo piscabatur homines. Eo genuit sanctos in Christo. . . . fides per verbum Christi infunditur, atque per verbum conservatur. . . . omnia externa locum dant verbo. Ideoque si cursum et operam verbi praepediunt, arcenda sunt ipsa, quae possunt utcunque impedire verbum. Consistent nupciae, stabit hospitalis pietas. Tenebit gradum sepultura. Retrahet pedem succursio miserorum." *Super coelibatu*, C; see all of BiiiV-Cii. When Karlstadt said that "omnia externa locum dant verbo," the "word' under consideration was precisely external preaching. It should be noted that when Kriechbaum (*Grundzüge*, p. 29) uses Karlstadt's assertion in the German edition that "Warheit ist an kein leiplich oder sichtbarlich ding gepunden" (*Gelubden*, Fii) to argue that Karlstadt believed in an "unvermittelte Wort Gottes" at this time, she is mistaken. Karlstadt was arguing here that true worshipers who worship in the Spirit are not bound to a particular place of worship such as a given cloister.

[74] "Das saget auch Augustinus, und steet Apocalypsis am. tzwentzigystem geschriben, Wie die vernewten, yn dem gelauben, Gotis reich sein. Der wegen saget Christus. Das keiner, Gotis reich eingeleibt wirdt, ehr sei dan, wider geborn, Auss dem wasser und geist. Darauss volget, das Gotis wort, ein born ist, daraus gotlicher geist, yn die glawbige fleusset, und vernawhet sie, und macht sie, ein reich Gottis ader der hiemeln." *Berichtung*, BiiiV. See also C (n. 147 below).

is not sufficient unless you have the Spirit of God." Many who can discuss the scriptures and excite others are cold and do not rejoice personally in the truth.[75] "The mysteries of God do not become sweet to us. . . unless the Spirit of Christ is bestowed upon us. . . . We have what God revealed, but the heart is far away." [76] Karlstadt insisted on the same point in some theses on October 17. Merely hearing the promises announced does not make one a son of God because the Gospel of the cross was an offense to the Jews and foolishness to the Greeks. Faith is also necessary.[77] "The word of the promise does not bring it about that sin does not condemn us, for nothing is useful to those who do not have faith joined to the word." The promise makes a comforting declaration, but God alone justifies.[78]

One should not assume, of course, that Karlstadt had abandoned his belief in the mediation of grace via the external word. A month after *De legis litera* he declared that faith comes from the word.[79] Although not mentioned as frequently and explicitly as before, subsequent works still contained statements indicating that the righteous person becomes alive in the word of God.[80] He had not

---

[75] *De legis litera*, BiiiV (see above, n. 61).

[76] *Ibid.*, BiiiV-Biv (see above, n. 64). In the famous Dec. 25 service, too, he reminded his listeners briefly that merely hearing the Gospel is useless unless one also believes; *Predig* (Dec. 25, 1521), Aiv.

[77] "Deinceps ipsummet crucis Evangelium Iudaeis offendiculum et Graecis stulticiam fuisse (3). . . . Sicuti non sunt facti Christi fratres, vel filii dei, qui Christum viderunt et audierunt (5). At ii qui eum receperunt (6). Ita non est promissionis filius qui audit promissionem (7). Atqui soli promissionis sunt filii, qui credunt annuncianti (8)." Reprinted in Barge, *Karlstadt*, I, 484.

[78] "Evangelium illud. Filium suum pro nobis omnibus tradidit, et omnia nobis in eo donavit (Ro. VIII) laetos nos facit, quod licet malum adiaceat, tamen per Christum non damnat (21). Porro sermo promissionis non facit, ne peccatum nos damnet, quia nihil profuit iis, qui non habuerunt fidem coniunctam sermoni. he. IIII (22). In summa, Promissio declarat promittentem id posse et velle dare, quod promittens spondet. Deus unus iustificat (23)." *Ibid.*, p. 485. It is neither helpful nor correct, however, to say as E. Wolf does on the basis of these theses that "Karlstadt traut dem Wort Gottes nichts zu." "Gesetz und Evangelium in Luthers Auseinandersetzung mit den Schwärmern," *ET*, V (1938), 105. Karlstadt has only said that the external word is insufficient.

[79] "Der glawb ist auss den wortten, Ro. 10." *Beyden gestaldten*, CiiiV.

[80] "Wan ich gleich bekennet, das bildnis erleubt weren, das doch keyn Crist kan bekennen. Doch ist kein trost, dan in dem wort Gotis. darin der gerecht lebendig gesund und selig wirt. Drumb ists unvergleichlicher weiss mer, dz du einen beide evangelien fursagest, welche der her tzur letzt, und vor seinen tod geben hat. Nemlich dastu eynen krancken vorsagest inhalt und meynung disses trosts. Mein leip wirt fur euch gegeben. . . . Disse evangelia haben eynen lebentigen geyst." *Abtuhung*, ed. Lietzmann, pp. 10.35-11.2. Images are not the layman's books because they cannot, unlike the word of God, make people Christ's disciples (*ibid.*, p. 9.24-31). Cf. also *Malachiam*, B.

denied that the Spirit flows from the fountain of the divine word. He had, however, issued a warning that the Spirit's activity does not automatically accompany the external word.

## 2. JUSTIFICATIO AND JUSTITIA

By 1517, Karlstadt had adopted a thoroughly Augustinian notion of justification as God's creative act whereby he clothes man with actual righteousness.[81] By 1519, however, a non-Augustinian emphasis on the omnipresence of sin in the believer led to a new conception of the believer's righteousness as self-condemnation.[82] As the emphasis focused on forgiveness of sins, Karlstadt came to view justification as God's merciful pardoning of sins. It is this imputed righteousness which appears most frequently in the writings of 1520-1521.

### (a) *Imputed righteousness*

Karlstadt continued to discuss righteousness in terms of self-condemnation because of sins in 1520. "The righteous and true saints are not only sinners; they also . . . condemn and accuse their sins." [83] Even the nearly perfect believer has daily sin which is so serious that it would lead to eternal damnation.[84] Sinful concupiscence is in all holy men during this life. Hence the self-hatred and self-condemnation which God inspires is necessary, "for God will be gracious when you are harsh to yourself." [85] Man should bewail and grieve over his sins. "At that moment when the sinner says, 'I want to confess my sin

---

[81] See chapter I, "Justitia and justificatio."

[82] See chapter II, "Sin," and "Justitia and justificatio."

[83] "Die gerechten und warhafftigen heyligen, seint nicht allein sunder, ssonder sie fulen und empfinden, und urteylen und beschuldigen yhre sunde." *Bepstlicher heylickeit* (Oct., 1520), FiiV-Fiii. So too *Ablas* (Aug., 1520), BiiiiV.

[84] "Erschrecklich also, das die tegliche sunde, so sie nit vorgeben werden, uns arme sunder, von dem teyl, ewigs leben, endtrben. . . . Wiewol auch die gerechte menschen die auch sonste reyne seint mit solchen fuessen, Gott dienen und wol thuen. Dennoch beflecken sie sich. und sundigen, Mit sunden, die sie, neyden und hassen, die sich auch nit fliehen, nach umbgeen mugen, von den sunden weschet sie Christus. . . ." *Wasser und salcz* (Aug., 1520), Biii (see all of Biii-Biv).

[85] "Disse kranckheyt ist, in allenn heyligen menschen, so alhie leben und ist genant von Paulo, die sunde der glider. Item concupiscentia. i. [id est] begirlickeit. . . . sso steet in dir, ein bitterkeit auff, und [du] hast ein hass unnd neidt uber dich selber, und wollest gern auss dir auss geen und wegfliehen. . . . es macht dich recht demutig bey dir und forchtsam bey Got. Item lasset keinen todt hynfur, das ist, die unreinickeit, deynes hertzenn, wirt dir nit zu schadenn, unnd dem todt gereichenn, dan Got wil gutig sein, wan du, dyr selber scharff bist. . . . Disse flucht. von sich selber, ist ein saltz, das Got eingibt. . . ." *Ibid.*, BiiiV-Biv.

against myself,' immediately God forgives the sin." [86] Through 1521, Karlstadt continued to assert this view that the righteous person is he who has divinely bestowed self-accusation. [87]

In 1521, Karlstadt talked less about self-condemnation and a great deal more about the fact that faith in Christ is reckoned as righteousness. The sacramental wine signifies forgiveness of sins. It assures one

> that Christ has not forgotten his promise . . . and that at that moment his blood has drowned and obliterated my sins. If I believe that, then God is present and reckons (schatzet) this faith to me for righteousness. [88]

All through his work on the proper reception of the sacraments, he insisted that one must not abstain from the sacrament because of sin. One should not try to prepare oneself, for this is to attempt to go to God with good deeds. All one needs is faith in Christ's promise of forgiveness.

> Paul wrote: "To him who does not work, but believes in him who makes the evil one righteous, faith is reckoned as righteousness [Romans 4:5]." If you want to become distant from God, then come with your works and piety. If you want to approach God and become righteous, then come with confession of your sins. [89]

---

[86] "Dann wiewol es unmügelich ist, das der mensch alle seine sünde ersinne. doch sol er die misstheten, die er, auss fürsatze, gethon, mit grossem ernst und fleiss, für sein gestreng gericht und urteil tragen, die mit seüfftzen, leid, widerwillen, verdriess und leiden beweinen. . . . Ja in dem nün, wann der sünder spricht, ich will mein sünde, wider mich bekennen, als balde. vergibt im Got die sünde." *Ablas*, Biii.

[87] E.g. *Berichtung* (July, 1521), Civ.

[88] "Demnach sag ich, das der weyn eygentlich und sonderlich vergebung der sunden bedeut. . . . Das wort muss ich erstlich drincken odder essen, ehr ich den kelch trinck, das ist, dem wortt muss ich, on alle widderreed, glauben, Darnach magk ich das tzeychen disses worts nemen, dadurch ich eygentlich weyss, das Christus seyner tzusag nit vergessen hatt, und das er, seyne wort wil erfullen, und das seyn blut gleych meyne sunde erseufft und aussgetilget hat. Wan ich das glaub, sso ist Got alhie und schatzet myr dissen glauben fur gerechtickeyt, und wyl meyner sunden yn ewigkeit nit mer gedencken oder straffen. . . . In solchen glauben solt ich frid haben tzu Gott durch Christum." *Beyden gestaldten* (Nov., 1521), Div.

[89] "Dan wie einer nit wol gehen kan, mit krancken fuessen, also kan ein sunder, nit wol, oder nit an schaden zu Got kummen, mit werckenn, eher er gesunthet erlanget hat. Dat ist die ursach des spruechs Esaie. Ich wil eur gebet nit horen u. das die selben gleyssner, wie unsser Monichen und pfaffen, und andere heyligen fresser mit den wercken anfahen zu Got gehen. Derwegen Paulus geschrieben. Dem yhenen, dero nit arbeit, gelaubet aber, in den dero den ungutigen gerecht schafft, wurd der glaub zu der gerechtickeit geschatzt. Wiltu Got fern werden, sso kum mit deinen wercken und frumkeit, wiltu Got nhaen und gerecht werden, so kum mit bekentniss deyner sunden. . . . und merck dastu auff erdtrich nichts anders bedarffest, wan du das sacrament wirdiglich wilt empfahen, dan dastu dich

His emphasis on faith reckoned as righteousness led to the assertion that the believer fulfils the law through faith. Precisely in his work on the letter and spirit of the law, he declared:

> Faith makes us spontaneous and docile and in agreement with the will of the law which Christ fulfilled. And we fulfil it to the extent that we believe that Christ freed and redeemed us from the curse of the law and was made righteousness for us.[90]

"The will of God is that we believe that Christ is our redeemer, our righteousness and the fulfillment of the law." [91] It should be clear from the earlier discussion of the normative character of the old law that Karlstadt did not mean that the believer does not obey the law. Rather he meant that no man perfectly fulfils the law because all good deeds contain sin. In some theses of 1521 he urged believers to do those good deeds urged by the divine commands.[92] He added however, that faith must be present to counteract the sin present in good deeds: "Even works done in faith would be evil, but God does not impute this evil in consideration of faith." [93] Christ's imputed righteousness covers this sin. "To the extent that we believe that Christ freed us from the curse of the law and was made righteousness for us, we keep the commands of God." [94] The Christian should certainly live according to the divine commands. But since sin always taints good deeds, perfect fulfillment of the law must be reckoned to him who believes in Christ.

---

deiner schuld und sunden schuldig bekondest." *Empfahern* (June, 1521), biiV-biii. Also: "Wer das wirdiglich wil essen, der muss nicht mer thun, dan wunden seyner sunden, und bosshafftig leben fuelen, und vestiglich glauben den worten, das der leyp Christi (den er essen wil) fur seine sunde und krancheiten gestorben ist." *Ibid.*, cV.

[90] *De legis litera* (Sept., 1521), AiiiV (see above, n. 53).

[91] "Quoniam eadem est voluntas legis dei [margin: Eadem voluntas dei et legis]. Nunc dei voluntas est: ut credamus Christum redemptorem nostrum: iusticiam nostram: legisque impletionem." *Ibid.*, AivV.

[92] "Christianus est ad omne opus liber (1). Faciat ergo cum Saule, quaecunque invenerit manus sua (3). Sola haec plane opera bona sunt, quae fiunt secundum mandata Dei (5). Sic non servus legis, sed amicus es faciens, quae praecepit tibi (12)." Reprinted in Jäger, *Carlstadt*, p. 207. For the date and authorship of these theses, see below n. 133.

[93] "Opera, etiam in fide facta, mala fuerunt, sed hanc malitiam intuitu fide non imputat Deus (40)." *Ibid.*, p. 208.

[94] Thesis 14 (see below, n. 136). Karlstadt made the same point in another set of theses perhaps from late 1520: "Omne ergo hominis opus, omnis humana justitia, viribus naturae parta, peccatum est (2). Maledictionem sustulit Christus, factus pro nobis maledictum (3). Justitia itaque credentibus Christus est" (4). Barge, *Karlstadt*, I, 473.

Although the word "justification" was not usually used in his frequent discussions of imputed righteousness, it is clear that in 1521 Karlstadt accepted a doctrine of forensic justification similar to that of Luther's.[95] Occasionally, however, he did use the word. "Faith alone justifies." [96]

> He who believes in the Son whom God made Redeemer and Reconciler will be justified (justificabitur) and will have eternal life. "He who believes will not be condemned." ... All profit and all salvation depend on faith.[97]

Justification is no longer viewed as God's inward transformation of man; rather it is his merciful non-reckoning of sins to the believer. So important in fact had imputed righteousness become that Karlstadt gave the words "holy," "purify" and "sanctify" a forensic connotation in his famous December 25 sermon.[98]

The focus of Karlstadt's theology had obviously shifted. Whereas infused grace was central in the earlier period, forgiveness of sins through faith was now his constant theme. Further, whereas the earlier Augustinian writings had paid scant attention to the role of Christ, the above passages show that Christ's death on the cross was a very frequent topic.[99] The change must be credited to Luther and his forensic doctrine of justification.

---

[95] For Luther, see below nn. 106-112.

[96] "Sola fides justificat, nullorum operum neque bonorum neque malorum respectu" (thesis 33). Jäger, *Carlstadt*, p. 208. The intention is clearly forensic for in thesis 40 he referred to the non-imputation of sin because of faith (see above, n. 93).

[97] *De legis litera*, Aiii (see below, n. 124). So too thesis 23 from Oct. 17, 1521; Barge, *Karlstadt*, I, 485 (see above, n. 78). Cf. also theses 81-82, *ibid.*, p. 488.

[98] "Wann du Gottes trostlich züsagung mit glauben ein nimbst, wirstu rain und sauber, als Christus bezeügt sprechent. Ir seyt yetz rain von wegen des sermon, so ich eüch gesagt hab. Joan.xv. Gottes wortt rainiget und hailiget alle, die es jm glauben empfahen.... Ain yeder, der jn mich gelaubt der wirt selig, ob er wolt sagen. Du bedarffest kainer arbait und mü, dir ist auff erdtrich nicht von nöten, dann dz du mich ansychest, und glaubest, das ich, von meynem vatter geschickt bin, disse welt selyg zü machen. Sich wie dich Christus seyner selygkayt tayl-hafftyg macht. so du glaubest. Sych wie er dich Durch sein verhayssung hayliget und rainiget. Sich noch meer, das Christus vor dir steet, Unnd endthebt dich aller deyner arbayt, Unnd nymbt allen zweyfell von dir, daz du ye gewisslych soltest wyssen, Das er dich durch seyne wort selig macht. Nun müss Got ye sünd verge-ben. So er hailig macht, als geschriben. Selyg seynd die, Dien jr sünde vergeben seynd. Wellycher nun göttlycher warhaytt und gnad verkündigung glaubt, der ist hailig, Unnd ist unmüglych, das jm Christus nit sage. Stee auff, dein glaub hat dich selig gemacht. Ste auf deine sünde seind dir vergeben." *Predig* (Dec. 25, 1521), Bii-BiiV.

[99] See above, chapter I, n. 135. In 1520, on the other hand, he insisted: "Das ist offentlich, das Got allein durch Christum, alle sein gaben in seinen erwelten wircket." *Antwort . . . geweicht wasser*, aiv.

(b) *Inner righteousness*

One must not conclude, however, that Karlstadt had forgotten St. Augustine. He did not always use the word righteousness in the sense of Romans 4:5. Sometimes, albeit less frequently, the word connoted an inner transformation of man. Christ's blood is a medicine which destroys sin and brings righteousness and newness of spirit.[100] In *De legis litera* he referred to the righteousness which pertains to new men and in fact makes them new. [101] Karlstadt had certainly not lost interest in that inner transformation wrought by grace.

He used various metaphors such as rebirth, renewal, and spiritual circumcision to discuss the inner regeneration and sanctification of man by grace. Under the heading "How Holiness Happens in This Life," he explained that holiness is incomplete on earth. Although man's spirit experiences a rebirth, he still possesses only a very imperfect holiness in this life.[102] In his work on vows Karlstadt discussed the inner transformation in terms of a spiritual circumcision of the heart. God circumcises the heart by cutting away all love for creatures in matters which pertain to God.

> God circumcises your heart first with prohibitions, commands and demands. . . . Afterward, he sends His Spirit and breaks stony hearts and gives a new spirit and a new heart and circumcises your heart so that you may love God with your whole heart and soul.[103]

---

[100] " . . . das fleisch unnd bluet Christi, sso du einniembst, deine sunde todtet, und dir zu einer ertzney sey, und zw gerechtickeit unnd newheit deynes geystes." *Empfahern*, Ciii.

[101] "Quia lex quevis [quaevis]: modo sit divina: lex est iusticiae: Ro.x. non inquam iusticiae quae ex operibus est: quia ex operibus legis non iustificatur omnis caro. Ro. iii. sed iusticiae: quae est per fidem. Ro.x. Haec iusticia ad homines novos pertinet. Imo novos facit." *De legis litera*, BiiiV.

[102] "Durch glauben, hoffnung und liebe, wurt der geyst widder geboren, aber der leyp wurt nit ehr geborn, dan nach seinem sterbenn unnd aufferstehung, alsso wurt keyner volkumlich unnd gantz heylig, ssonder allein in anfengenn. . . . welcher aber in die warheit gotlicher zusagung kumbt, der hat allein anfeng geistlicher heylickeit." *Bepstlicher heylickeit*, Aiii. See, too, *Verba Dei*, Cii, and *Missive*, Aii (see above, n. 70) for other references to spiritual birth and rebirth.

[103] "Alle creaturen müssen von hertzen abgeschniden sein. Das ist, wir sollen Gott auss gantzem hertzen lieben. . . . Das heysset sich geystlich beschneyden. wan eyner mit gantzem hertzen allein Got liebet. . . . Alsso beschneyt Gott dein hertz erstlich mit verbot, gesetz, und foderung, sagende. Du solt sie wider anbeten, noch ehren. Darnach sendet er seynen geyst und bricht steynern hertzen, und gibt eynen newen geyst, und ein new hertz, und beschneydt dein hertz, auff dastu Gott, mit gantzem hertzen, aller seel lieben mogest." *Gelubden*, CV-Cii. So, too, *De legis litera*. Aiv-B.

When the word of God gives him a new character or spirit, it enables him to walk according to the divine commands.[104] Faith effects this inner renewal: "Faith makes one spiritual, for it unites the believer with Christ, in whom all creatures become new and spiritual." [105] Through the hearing of the word which produces faith as the Holy Spirit acts, man becomes genuinely although not perfectly righteous.

How similar was Karlstadt's conception of *justificatio* and *justitia* to that of Luther? In the Romans commentary, Luther said that "the righteousness of scripture consists rather in the imputation of God than in the essence of the thing." Since man remains a sinner throughout his life, he is righteous only through faith in the word of him who mercifully reputes him righteous in spite of his sin.[106] In *The Freedom of a Christian* (1520), Luther outlined the relationship between faith and works:

> In doing these works, however, we must not think that a man is justified before God by them, for faith, which alone is righteousness before God, cannot endure that erroneous opinion. . . . Since by faith the soul is cleansed and made to love God, it desires that all things, and especially its own body, shall be purified. . . . Nevertheless the works themselves do not justify him before God, but he does the works out of spontaneous love in obedience to God. [107]

---

[104] "Das wort Gotis wendet den anhorer, oder den yenen, dero ehs begeret, ansich, nimbt yme eigen art, und giebt seine." *Berichtung*, Aiii. Also: "Der geyst strebet wider fleisch, und Got thet der natur gewalt, welcher guten willen, und gutte werck, yhn uns schaffet. Der das steinern hertz, weich macht, und giebt uns ein nawen geyst, und macht, das wir yhn gotlichen geboten wandern und gehen, und macht, das wir machen" (AivV).

[105] "Der glaub macht geistlich, dan er vereyndt die glaubige mit Christo, in wilchen alle creaturen new und geistlich werden." *Anbettung*, Aii.

[106] "Iustitia et 'Iniustitia' multum aliter, quam philosophi et Iuristae accipiunt, in Scriptura accipitur. Patet, Quia illi qualitatem asserunt animae etc. Sed. 'Iustitia' Scripture magis pendet ab imputatione Dei quam ab esse rei. Ille enim habet Iustitiam, non qui qualitatem solam habet, immo ille peccator est omnino et Iniustus, Sed quem Deus propter confessionem iniustitiae suae et implorationem Iustitiae Dei misericorditer reputat et voluit Iustum apud se haberi. Ideo omnes In iniquitate i.e. Iniustitia nascimur, morimur, Sola autem reputatione miserentis Dei per fidem Verbi eius Iusti sumus." *WA*, LVI, 287.16-24. So too *WA*, VIII, 92.38-93.9, Cf. Karlstadt's statement in n. 93 above.

[107] "Verum ea opera oportet non ea fieri opinione, quo per ipsa coram deo iustificetur quisquam: hanc enim falsam opinionem fides non feret quae sola est iustitia coram deo. . . . Cum enim anima per fidem purgata sit et amans dei facta, vellet omnia pariter purgari, praecipue corpus proprium, ut omnia secum amarent et laudarent deum. Ita fit, ut homo exigente corporis sui causa ociari non possit cogaturque ob id multa bona operari, ut in servitutem redigat. Nec tamen opera ipsa id sunt, quo iustificetur coram deo, sed gratuito amore ea faciat in obsequium dei." *LW*, XXXI, 359; *WA*, VII, 60.19-28.

Through faith man is justified by the merits of Christ.[108] Justification by faith alone then consists of God's merciful imputation of Christ's merits to the believing sinner.

It is abundantly clear that this forensic conception of justification by no means entailed a rejection of the inner transformation of the believer. Faith inevitably cleanses the soul and produces works of love toward neighbour.[109] In his polemic against Latomus (1521), Luther carefully spelled out the "two goods of the Gospel," namely grace and the gift of inward renewal. [110] Grace is that *favor Dei* which forgives man's sins and makes him accepted before God.[111] The gift, on the other hand is infused in man who then experiences partial inward healing. Although the believer possesses both these goods, they must be sharply distinguished.[112]

Clearly both Luther and Karlstadt believed both that man is justified by faith alone when the righteousness of Christ is reckoned to him and also that such faith results inevitably in inward renewal. Karlstadt's continuing concern for inner righteousness in no way validates Barge's assertion that in 1520 and 1521 Karlstadt and Luther differed markedly in that the former emphasized regeneration whereas the latter stressed forgiveness.[113] As has been discovered above, Karlstadt said more about that forensic righteousness which is

---

[108] "Hoc enim cognito scies, Christum necessarium tibi, qui pro te passus et resuscitatus est, ut in eum credens alius homo hac fide fieres, donatis omnibus peccatis tuis et iustificato te alienis meritis, nempe Christi solius." *LW*, XXXI, 347; *WA*, VII, 51.31-34. The commandments are fulfilled through faith alone: "Hoc nomine fides sola est iustitia Christiani hominis et omnium praeceptorum plenitudo." *LW*, XXXI, 353; *WA*, VII, 56.5-6. Cf. Karlstadt's similar statements in nn. 90, 91, 94 above.

[109] Cf. Gerhard Ebeling's comment: "The formula 'by faith alone,' although it excludes love as the basis of justification, is far from excluding love as the consequence of justification." *Luther: An Introduction to His Thought*, trans. R. A. Wilson (London, 1970), pp. 172-73.

[110] "Habemus ergo duo bona evangelii adversus duo mala legis, donum pro peccato, gratiam pro ira." *LW*, XXXII, 228; *WA*, VIII, 106.35-37.

[111] "Gratiam accipio hic proprie pro favore dei, sicut debet, non pro qualitate animi." *LW*, XXXII, 227; *WA*, VIII, 106.10-11.

[112] " . . . sicut dixi, gratia a donis secernenda sit, cum sola gratia sit vita aeterna Ro. vi. et sola ira sit mors aeterna. Veniamus tandem ad institutum. Iustus et fidelis absque dubio habet gratiam et donum: gratiam, quae eum totum gratificet, ut persona prorsus accepta sit, et nullus irae locus in eo sit amplius, donum vero, quod eum sanet a peccato et tota corruptione sua animi et corporis. . . . Remissa sunt omnia per gratiam, sed nondum omnia sanata per donum. Donum etiam infusum est, fermentum mixtum est, laborat, ut peccatum expurget." *LW*, XXXII, 229; *WA*, VIII, 107.11-23.

[113] See above, nn. 1-2.

imputed to man for the forgiveness of sins in these years than he did about inner righteousness. Nor can one agree with Hillerbrand that "Carlstadt's inability to utilize the term 'evangelium,' as *favor dei*, meant that he was unable to apprehend what was indeed the most crucial aspect of Luther's new theology." [114] It is true that Karlstadt used the word "Gospel" only very infrequently.[115] But he spoke of precisely the same thing in terms which Luther also used. Christ's righteousness which is imputed to the one who believes is precisely what Luther meant by *favor dei*. Both in the definition and the importance of forensic righteousness, Karlstadt differed hardly at all from Luther in 1520 and 1521.

### 3. The Ground of Eternal Life

The fundamental agreement of Luther and Karlstadt can be demonstrated further by asking on what basis Karlstadt now believed man ultimately obtained eternal life. In chapter one it was shown that he had adopted the Augustinian conception which viewed eternal life as the reward of good deeds. These good deeds, of course, are solely the product of divine grace. Nevertheless they are also man's deeds because his transformed will performs them.[116] For Luther, on the other hand, even the Christian's best deeds are marred by sin; hence, eternal life can only be an unmerited gift graciously granted to the believer.[117]

---

[114] "Karlstadt," p. 383.

[115] Hence it is hardly helpful when Kriechbaum devotes almost one third of her study to the category "Law and Gospel" (*Grundzüge*, pp. 39-76). It is interesting, however, that in the writings under consideration, Karlstadt used the word several times as a synonym for "promise." E.g. *Beyden gestaldten*, Biv, CiiiV, Eiv. Cf. also *Abtuhung*, ed. Lietzmann, pp. 10.37-11.2 (see above, n. 80). In theses 21-23 of Oct. 17, 1521 Karlstadt used the term Gospel and summarized its content in terms of God's justifying the one who has faith in the word of promise and believes that God handed over his Son for our sins (see above, n. 78). But Karlstadt seldom used the term.

[116] See above, chapter I, "Salvation as the reward of good deeds."

[117] After defining "gratia" as "favor Dei" and "donum" as the infused gift which heals the soul, he noted: "gratia a donis secernenda sit, cum sola gratia sit vita aeterna" (see above, n. 112). A bit later, Luther discussed the problem of sin in the believer and in good works and argued that the believer can go before God's face only because God does not impute his sin: "Nihil differt peccatum a seipso, secundum naturam suam, ante gratiam et post gratiam, differt vero a sui tractatu. . . . Ita dico et doceo, ut omnis homo in omni opere suo sciat se tantum habere de peccato, quantum in ipso nondum est eiectum peccatum, qualis arbor, talis fructus, ne glorietur coram deo de mundicia sua in seipso, glorietur autem in gratia et dono dei, quod faventem deum habet, qui hoc peccatum non imputat, insuper donum dedit, quo expurget. Veritatem ergo confiteatur, quod si secundum

Although Karlstadt no longer described heaven as the reward of divinely bestowed good deeds in 1520, his thought still seemed somewhat Augustinian at this point. In *Verba Dei* he spoke of the spiritual relatives of Christ and stressed the latter part of Luke 8:21: "My mother and brothers are they who hear the word of God *and do* it." Christ insisted on the latter part "lest any slothful listener think that it is enough to hear [God's Word]." [118]

> Nor is this [hearing the word] sufficient for the attainment of beatitude; rather, it is also necessary to keep it. Thus they who hear and keep it are clearly the brothers of Christ, coheirs and heirs through the word of God.[119]

Karlstadt hastened to place this teaching within the larger framework of the doctrine of predestination. Only the elect are made hearers and doers of the word.[120] "Doing" the word, however, is necessary for beatitude. Several times he alluded to Jesus' encounter with the young man who asked Jesus what he should do to gain eternal life, and was told: "If you would enter life, keep the commandments." [121] After being forgiven by God one must, as Jesus told the young man,

---

naturam operis, citra gratiam, iudicandus esset, non posset subsistere ante faciem eius. Nunc, quia in gratia nititur, nihil est, quod eum accusare potest." *LW*, XXXII, 229-30; *WA*, VIII, 107.26-28, 108.2-9.

[118] "Attollat oculos in superna, et conspectis circumstantiis, reperiet, Christum, priusquam concluderet, de discipulis dixisse, Ecce mater mea etc [cf. Matt. 12:46-50 and Luke 8:19-21]. auditores materna et fraterna gloria tu[m] condecorans. Conclusit autem, postea continuo, Qui facit voluntatem patris mei, ille est frater et mater, ne quis socors auditor arbitraretur, sat esse, si audiat. Necessarius est auditus, quod sine auditione non contingit fides, quae patris Christi voluntatem facit et exequitur." *Verba Dei* (late 1519), C.

[119] "Concludo igitur, auditorem ardentem, et divini amantem verbi Christi, Sorori fratrique matrique aequiparari, si dei verbum audit atque custodit. . . . Non legimus qui audiunt verbum Aristotelis, definitiones Petri Hispani . . . sed qui audiunt dei verbum. neque hoc sufficit consequendae beatitudini, verum necessum est et custodire illud. Nempe, qui audiunt et custodiunt, plane sunt Christi fratres, cohaeredesque, haeredes verbo dei." *Ibid.*

[120] "Ad illum partum, non nostra gradimur facultate. ipse enim nos, elegit et posuit, ut eamus auditum verba dei, fructumque facturi. Nulli certe divinos sermones capiunt, nisi quibus datum est ut intelligant. . . . Quod rursus testatur Moses XXVII. dicens Hodie factus es populus domini dei tui, audies vocem eius et facies mandata [cf. Deut. 27:9-10], Ideo audient et facient, quia sunt electi et facti auditores et factores." *Ibid.*, Cii. That Karlstadt continued to believe most firmly in predestination can be seen from *Von Bepstlicher heylickeit*, Dii where he taught a doctrine of limited atonement: "Das aber Christus sein gebet und leydenn, allen den yhenen gondet, welchenn es der vatter gondet, und die ewiglich vorsehen seint, kan ich beweren alsso, Christus saget, Ich bit nit fur die welt, sonder fur die, welche du mir gegeben hast."

[121] Matt. 19:16-22; cf. Luke 10:25-28.

enter into all God's commands "which serve for life." [122] The righteousness which makes this possible is of course from God, not men.
"God alone inspires in them the goods which bring them to blessedness." [123] It is still infused goodness or righteousness, however, which
obtains salvation.

That Karlstadt had adopted a more Lutheran conception by the
fall of 1521 is obvious. Precisely in *De legis litera* where he insisted
most clearly that the Christian must obey the law, he also underlined
the fact that eternal salvation depends solely on faith. God's most basic
demand is faith.

> Therefore Christ says, "This is the will of my father, that anyone who
> sees the Son and believes in him does not perish but has eternal life"
> [cf. John 6:40]. And at another place [Christ said]: "He who does the
> will of my father will enter the kingdom of heaven"—i.e. he who
> believes in the Son whom God made Redeemer and Reconciler will be
> justified and will have eternal life. "He who believes will not be con-
> demned. He who does not believe is already judged." All profit and all
> salvation depend on faith.[124]

---

[122] "In dem XVIII. cap. Ezechielis. hab ich ein schrifft oben erzelt, also lau-
tende. So der ungütig, alle sein sünden berewet, unnd bewart alle mein gebott,
und übet sich in dem urteil unnd gerechtigkeit, so will ich keiner missthat, noch
keines übels gedencken [vv. 21-22]. Diss ist ein tröstliche Gottes zůsagung,
dodurch die warhafftige zůker angezeiget ist, und lauter gesagt, was, *nach* vergebung der sünde, der sünder thůn und wircken sol. . . . Soll nůn der mensch alle
gebott bewaren, so müss er sie wol lernen, wann er dann begert, die *gebott, des
lebens* zů wissen, spricht Christus, du sagst, welche gebott zů dem rechten leben
weisen, ich frage dich, was ist im gesetz geschriben [cf. Luke 10:26], also füret
Gott den menschen in götlich gebott, darumb ist von nöten, dz sich der sünder,
mit höchsten vleiss, auff die schrifft leg, und hencke sich festigklich an götliche
zůsagung und geen in allen gebotten Gottes, er müss das kreütz Christi, darinn alle
gebott und weissheit, *so zům leben dienen,* behalten sein, auff sich nemen, und
seinen willen auss dem creütz schöpffen." *Ablas* (Aug., 1520), Biiii-BiiiiV (my
italics). The last sentence may contain an allusion to the fact that all good deeds
contain sin; hence all commands must be kept in the cross of Christ. For another
allusion to Matt. 19:17, see n. 129 below.

[123] "Das lernen die yene, sso Got quelet und kranck macht, das sie auss freyhem
willen unnd eygen krefftenn nicht mugen wircken, unnd das sie durch eygen
krefften zu keyner gerechtickeit kummen, sonder das yhn Got allein eingiebet
gutter, die sie zu der selickeit brengenn." *Antwort . . . geweicht wasser* (Oct., 1520), aiii.

[124] For the first part of this statement, see above, n. 50. "Propterea ait Christus.
Haec est voluntas patris mei: ut is: qui videt filium et credit in eum non pereat:
sed habeat vitam aeternam [John 6:40]: Et alibi qui facit voluntatem patris:
hic intrabit regnum coelorum [cf. Matt. 7:21]: hoc est qui credit in filium quem
deus posuit redemptorem et reconciliatorem is iustificabitur: et vitam vivet
aeternam. Qui credit non damnabitur. qui non credit iam iudicatus est [John
3:18]. totum lucrum et omnis salus in fide consistit: tota damnatio et omnis
infoelicitas incredulitati reputatur." *De legis litera* (Sept., 1521), Aiii.

It was seen that in 1520 in *Verba Dei*, Karlstadt had argued that the Christian must keep the commandments in order to obtain salvation. [125] Now, however, he has learned from John 6 to define doing the will of God as believing in the Son. Eternal life depends solely on faith.[126]

The chronology of Karlstadt's acceptance of this different viewpoint is not entirely clear. As early as the summer of 1520 he gave instructions for comforting the dying whom Satan terrorizes with previous sin, and the advice would seem to presuppose the later viewpoint.

> You should hold fast that comforting word in your heart: Christ seeks sinners. Christ came to help those who are evil. As Peter says, Christ came so that he would take our sin upon himself and pay for it. . . . While you depend on these words, the devil cannot injure you; rather you come out of the battle into eternal peace.[127]

The earlier viewpoint, however, seems to lie behind statements in another tract of the same date.[128] As late as the German work on vows (June 24, 1521), there is at least a hint of the older conception.[129] In the latin work of almost the same date, however, Karlstadt condemned the monks for supposing that salvation depends on works. "That which pleases and obeys God is faith alone." Faith is the food of life;

---

[125] See above, nn. 118-119.

[126] "Nunc palam est: Christum inter omnia: primum hoc velle ut per eum in eius patrem credamus: tumque nullam condemnationem credentes metuamus. Ideo dixit. Qui sermonem meum audit: et credit ei: qui me misit: habet vitam aeternam: et in condemnationem non veniet. Joannis.v. [v.24]." *De legis litera*, Bii.

[127] "Wann sie der Teuffel yn todtez notenn, anfeelt sprechende, wiltu Gott anruffen oder vortrawhen, weystu nit wie du wider yhn gehandelt. Dan soltu dem Teuffel ein schniplin, und weniger dan ein meiglin bietten. Aber du solt das ubertrostlich wort, in deynem hertzen vest halden. Christus suchet sunder. Christus ist kumen, den bossen zu helffen, wye Petrus sagt. Christus ist kumenn, auff das er, unsser ssund auff sich, leget, und betzalet. als Esaias. Christus macht yhm, unsser sunde aygen, wie Paulus gesagth. Die weyl du in dissenn worthenn hangest, mag dyr der Teuffel nicht schadenn, sonder du kumest, auss dem streyt tzu ewygem fridt." *Wasser und salcz* (Aug., 1520), Ciii. Cf. also, *Beyden gestaldten* (Nov., 1521), EiiiV.

[128] See above, n. 122.

[129] "Aber wir sehen, wie monichen, nonnen und pfaffen, allen yhren vleiss, alle seligkeit, allen verlust, auff yhr katzen gebet und himpellischen cerimonien stellen. . . . sie dienen Gott nit, und glauben Gott nicht. Derhalben sie nit selig werden, dan die schrifft sagt. Wilcher nit glaubt, der ist verloren. Item wiltu zum leben eingehn, bewar Gottis gebott." *Gelubden*, FiiV. It is possible of course that Karlstadt meant that one keeps the commands by believing (see below, n. 136).

unbelief is the food of death.[130] Similarly, in his work on the sacraments dated June 24, 1521 he declared: "It is impossible that one who firmly and constantly believes in the divine promise should perish." [131] A month later he insisted unequivocally that "no one comes into divine rest unless he believes in the promise apart from works." [132] From July, 1521 on, Karlstadt's works reflected only the new viewpoint.

In the late summer of 1521, in some theses on faith and works, Karlstadt made a significant attempt to harmonize his belief in the necessity of keeping the commands with his more recent view that eternal life depends on faith alone.[133] After urging obedience to the commands,[134] he insisted that such deeds would contain sin unless one exercised faith at the same time.[135] He then interpreted "keep the commands" in the fashion already noticed in *De legis litera*.

> Christ taught us this: "If you want to enter into life, keep the commands" [Matthew 19:17]. To the extent that we believe that Christ freed us from the curse of the law and was made righteousness for us, we keep the commands of God. He who thinks that he keeps the commands of God without this faith acts as a good Jew but not as a Christian.[136]

---

[130] "Vos omnem salutem in operibus sitam opinamini. Ego nihil salutis, plurimum damnationis operam vestram habere non dubito. . . . Id quod deo placet et obsequitur una fides est, a qua ne quidem caritatem, aut fiduciam, vel spem, vel timorem dei divellam. Nihil est quod divinam maiestatem laedit, quam fallax incredulitas. Nulla re magis oblectatur deus quam fide. . . . In summa. Sicut sola fides inservit deo. Ita una infidelitas adversus deum tumet. Fides, cibus est vitae, haud deperiens. Incredulitas cibatus est mortis, assidue disperdens." *Super coelibatu* (June 29, 1521), BiiV-Biii.

[131] "Es ist unmuglich das einer verderb, der gotlicher zusag festiglich und bestendiglich glawbet." *Empfahern*, civV.

[132] "Quemadmodum nullus in divinam requiem venit nisi credat absque operibus promissioni." Thesis 6 of the July 12, 1521 theses, reprinted in Otto Clemen, *Beiträge zu Reformationsgeschichte* (3 vols.; Berlin, 1900-1903), I, 34.

[133] The theses are not explicitly attributed to Karlstadt in the original, but there is unanimous agreement that they are Karlstadt's (Barge, *Karlstadt*, I, 481; Jäger, *Carlstadt*, pp. 207-9; Kriechbaum, *Grundzüge*, p. 76; E. Fischer, *Geschichte der evangelischen Beichte*, II, 129ff). Barge dates them in August or September, 1521 (*Karlstadt*, I, 481). Jäger (*Carlstadt*, pp. 207-9) has reprinted them.

[134] See above, n. 92.

[135] "Sic ea [praecepta] faciens confide et certus sis Deo placere (10), quia ubi dubitaveris, jam mala forent et sine fide (11)." Jäger, *Carlstadt*, p. 207. These two theses should probably be interpreted in light of thesis 40 (see below, n. 139) where Karlstadt argued that all good deeds contain sin, but God does not impute the guilt to the believer because of his faith.

[136] "Id Christus nos docuit: 'si vis ad vitam,' inquiens, 'ingredi, serva mandata' [Matt. 19:17] (13). Eatenus mandata Dei implemus, quatenus credimus Christum

The primary way one "keeps the commands" is by believing that Christ's death covers the sin in one's inadequate attempts to keep the law.

After a discussion of the authority of custom, Karlstadt turned to the question of heavenly rewards. He insisted, probably on the basis of Philippians 2:16, that "good works do not lack their reward." [137] He who despairs of reward is ignorant of God's mercy[138]—i.e. ignorant of the fact that God does not impute the sin in good deeds if one has faith.[139] Belief in rewards, however, by no means involved adherence to the thesis that ultimate acceptance with God depends on works. "For works are rewarded although they do not justify. Faith alone justifies without respect to any works whether good or bad." [140] At this point, however, Karlstadt wanted to guard against the view that true faith might exist without works. "Just as it is impossible in this life that faith is without works, so it is impossible there that faith is rewarded apart from its works." [141] This means only that true faith is always accompanied by good deeds which will also receive their reward. That Karlstadt did not intend to assert that faith and works together are the ground of eternal life is clear from the next theses. Just as good fruit reveals a good tree, so too good works reveal that righteousness which is of faith. This is clear from Jesus' parable of the last judgment: "Christ in Matthew 25 judges the works of men as if they were signs of faith and unbelief—although of course faith or unbelief would be judged first." [142] Presumably by declaring that

---

nos a maledicto legis liberasse et pro nobis factum justitiam (14). Qui sine hac fide mandata Dei servare se putat, is bonum Judaeum agit, sed non Christianum" (15). *Ibid.*, pp. 207-8. For the similar passage in *De legis litera*, see above, n. 53. Thesis 14 is almost a direct quotation!

[137] "Certus tamen esto, opera bona non carere praemio (29). Sic Paulus non in incertum se currere gloriatur [cf. Phil. 2:16] (30)." *Ibid.*, p. 208.

[138] "Non sperare praemium, est desperare et ignorare misericordiam Dei (31)." *Ibid.*, p. 208.

[139] "Opera praemiantur non quia opera, sed quia in fide facta (39). Opera, etiam in fide facta, mala fuerunt, sed hanc malitiam intuitu fidei non imputat Deus (40)." *Ibid.*

[140] "Opera enim praemiantur, quantumvis non justificent (32). Sola fides justificat, nullorum operum neque bonorum neque malorum respectu (33)." *Ibid.*

[141] "Ut impossibile est in hac vita, fidem sine bonis operibus esse (34), ita impossibile est et alibi fidem praemiari absque suis operibus (35)." *Ibid.*

[142] "Ut bonitas fructus arborem bonam, sic opera bona declarant hominis justitiam, quae est ex fide (36). Hinc Christus Matth. XXV. hominum opera, tanquam fidei et incredulitatis indicia, judicat (37):—licet primum judicetur fides aut incredulitas (38)." *Ibid.* The notion of a righteous life as the sign of faith appears again in his work on images and begging. He began the second section

faith is judged first, Karlstadt meant what he had emphasized earlier, namely that eternal salvation is by faith alone apart from all works.[143]

One might summarize Karlstadt's position in this way. Eternal life depends solely on faith because all good deeds contain sin and, therefore, cannot merit salvation. Eternal life, however, will be granted only to that faith which produces good deeds. And because God graciously forgives the sin in good deeds, one can even say that they receive rewards—albeit not, as Augustine taught, that reward which is eternal life. Without abandoning his emphasis on the importance of a genuinely righteous life, Karlstadt had abandoned the Augustinian notion that eternal life is the reward of divinely bestowed good deeds. Again the influence of Karlstadt's younger colleague is obvious.

## 4. The Church

Karlstadt devoted some thought to both the nature and the organization of the Church during these years. Since he equated the "kingdom of God" with the Church, his exegetical tract on the text "the kingdom of heaven suffers violence" (Matthew 11:12) provides his most explicit statements. "The kingdom of heaven is Christ and all those who are incorporated into Christ by faith." [144] Karlstadt then proceeded to compare the believer to a temple in which God dwells. Faith is the means by which Christ (or God) dwells and rules in the inner man.[145] His conception of "incorporation" into Christ became clearer a little later when he argued that those who have been renewed (*vernewten*) by faith compose God's kingdom.

> Therefore, Christ says that no one becomes incorporated into God's kingdom unless he is born again (widergeborn) of water and Spirit. If follows that God's word is a fountain out of which [the] Divine Spirit flows into the believers and renews them and makes them a kingdom of God.[146]

which rejected public begging and urged a different kind of Christian charity with the observation that the presence of many poor beggars in a city is a sure sign (*ein gewiss tzeichen*) that there are few Christians there, for Matt. 25 teaches that those who do not help the needy go to eternal damnation (*Abtuhung*, ed. Lietzmann, pp. 23.4-24.5).

[143] See above, n. 140.

[144] "Das reich Gotis, ist Christus, und alle, so Christo eingeleibt sein mit glawben." *Berichtung*, BiiV.

[145] "Sihe wie vergleicht Got, die menschen eynem konigreich, ehr nennet menschen, seinen tempel, und koniglichen Sahl, der alle tzyr inwendig hat. Der halben spricht Got. Ich werde yhn ynen wonen und wandern. Wie wonet Got? Durch den glawben. . . . Also regiret Got, vermittelst des glawben, yhn seinen ausserwelten, welcher hauptman yst Christus." *Ibid.*

[146] *Ibid.*, BiiiV (see above, n. 74).

It is the inner experience of regeneration or renewal which makes one a genuine member of the Church.

Since the Spirit effects this renewal only when one has that faith which comes by hearing, the proclamation of the word is the one external thing Karlstadt indicated as essential to the Church. "The Church can by no means live, exist, and bear fruit without the proclamation of God's word." [147] In addition to being the source of the Church's very existence, the word is also the basis of its unity. Division arises in the body of Christ when the "one word of God" is ignored.[148] The pernicious notion of the friars who suppose that all heresies have arisen from the Bible is mistaken, for scripture leads to unity.[149] In essence, then, the Church consists of all who have been renewed through faith in that word which unites all members into one body in Christ.

Karlstadt's remarks on the organization of the Church were more numerous. The most basic and significant aspect of this part of his ecclesiology was undoubtedly his constant emphasis on the dignity and role of the simple layman. It was seen previously that in early 1520 Karlstadt had stressed the importance of the ordinary layman (*Verba Dei*) and then a few months later in his work on the canon, granted him the right to interpret scripture.[150] Consequently it is not at all surprising that Karlstadt quickly adopted Luther's doctrine of the priesthood of all believers which provided a theological grounding for his previous emphasis. "Faith in Christ makes all believers priests or pastors." [151]

---

[147] Karlstadt used the parable of the vineyard in Luke 20:11-27 in his discussion of the church. "Der weinberg ist die Christlich kirch, von dem fleisch und blueth Christi gepflantzt, Die knecht seind, prediger aber verkundiger Gotis wort, Der Soen ist Christus, die alle mügen frücht aus dem weinberg brengen sso sie Gotis wort leren. Dan die kirch, aber weinberg, kan one gottliche wort, weder leben nach frücht tragen, Alles leben, und alle frücht steen und wachsen yn dem wort des glawben, lieb, und hoffenug. . . . dan die kirch magk mit nicht, one verkundung Gotis wort leben, besteen, und frucht tragen." *Ibid.*, C. See also Biii.

[148] "Dan wan ein versamelung gottlich wort verlosset, ists umb sie gescheen. Sie muss von noten tzweispeltig und in seckten geteilt werden. Ursach, Wan sie nit in Christo versamelt sein, sso ist Christus nit in irem mittell." *Sendbryff* (Dec. 10, 1521), Aii. Also: "Sich das der einige und gantzer leib anfengklich und endlich in einem wort Gotis steht. Dann ein hertz, ein gemüth, ein meinung, und will kumpt auss dem eine wort des glawbens." *Ibid.*, AiiV.

[149] "Das weiss ich, das unbegreufflich ist, das einer ein ketzer durch die schrifft werd, die von wegen des glawbens und eynnigkeit geben ist." *Ibid.*, Aiii.

[150] See above, chapter II, "The Aftermath," and chapter III, nn. 33-38.

[151] "Nun hore lieber text, wie santt Peter saget, das alle Christen, ein geystlich hauss, und heylig priesterschafft seint, ya ein heylige unnd konigliche priester-

The continued obstinacy of the learned, the religious, and the ecclesiastically powerful encouraged Karlstadt's inclination to idealize the humble worker. Poor laborers pray more earnestly than do lazy monks and nuns.[152] A craftsman often knows more about the Bible than a bishop.[153] He urged daily study of scripture upon laymen in order that they need not depend on the hypocrites.[154] Karlstadt declared his readiness to have even a little child teach him from scripture.[155] The Pope should not be ashamed to listen to an informed Christian farmer, and a general council should give heed to the peasant who has just left his plow.[156] Karlstadt's reference to "us laymen" in his Christmas Day sermon in 1521, was symbolic of his close identification with the common man.[157]

Karlstadt denounced the privileged position of the clerics and granted laymen the right to perform all tasks previously reserved for the ordained. The reason the Pope allows only the clergy to take the sacrament in both kinds is that he wants "himself and his clerics to be esteemed more highly than laymen." [158] Karlstadt retaliated by asserting the layman's right to judge theological disputes and attend

schafft [cf. I Peter 2:5]. Darauss folget, das der glaub in Christum alle glaubigenn zu priestern odder pfaffen macht, unnd das die pfaffenn, nicht newes enphagen, wan sie geweicht werden, ssonder sie werden allein zu dem ampt und diensperckeit erwelt." *Bepstlicher heylickeit* (Oct., 1520), Div. So too *Super coelibatu* (1521), D. Luther stated the doctrine earlier in his *To the Christian Nobility of the German Nation* (*WA*, VI, 404ff) published in August, 1520 (see below, n. 163).

[152] "Zu dem andern, weil Gott ein geist ist, sollen wir ome [sic] ym geiste dienen, wie Paulus sagt. Dem ich im geist diene Ro.i. Das thun arme arbeiter vil besser. dan mussige Monichen und Nonnen." *Gelubden*, FV.

[153] *Bedingung*, Aiv (see above, chapter III, n. 67). See also Aiii.

[154] " . . . alle leyhen sollen, alle tag, das wort Gottis lernen, die Biblien selber leessen oder horen lessen . . . dz sie nit, an den gleissnern, an den holtzschugern hangen." *Wasser u. salcz*, BivV.

[155] "Ich wold mich, nit allein grossen hanssen (welche namen titel und ampt Biblischer kunst inhalden, als Bischoffen und Theologen seint) sunder auch ein klein kind lassen lernen und weyssen durch heylige schrifft, wo ich ungerecht . . ." *Appellation*, Aiii; *Ablas*, Aiv.

[156] " . . . [Der Papst] solt sich nicht schemen, von einen Christlichen unnd vorstendigen Ackerman zuhoren und lernen." *Bepstlicher heylickeit*, FivV. "Das ander, sag ich, und ist war, das Biblische schrifft ein gemein Concilium überwindt, und so ein bawer vom plug, dem Concilio ein schrifft könt zeigen, das sein sinn güt, und dess Concilii böss were, so solt das Concilium dem bawren weichen und ere geben, von wegen Biblischer schrifft." *Welche bücher*, Ciii.

[157] "Uns leyeen" *Predig* (Dec. 25, 1521), BiiiV.

[158] "Der Bapst hatt alleyn seyne Pfaffen beyder gestaldten wyrdig gemacht, die leyhen macht er des kelchs unwirdig, und thut das auss lawterem frevel, und muttwill, das er unnd seyne pfaffen, höher geacht werden, dan leyhen, wye wol er das nit gesteen wyl." *Beyden gestaldten*, DiiV.

general councils, [159] to hear confession and grant absolution regularly rather than merely in the case of necessity,[160] and to celebrate the Eucharist privately.[161] The authority to bind and loose applies to all Christians.[162] Karlstadt's theological basis for these views was, of course, the doctrine of the priesthood of all believers and the inference concerning ordination which Luther had drawn.

> It follows that faith in Christ makes all believers priests or pastors and that the pastors receive nothing new when they are consecrated. Rather they are merely elected to the office and to service.[163]

Karlstadt thus accepted Luther's removal of the qualitative difference between clergy and laity.

He still believed, nonetheless, that ecclesiastical officers were intended by God. Since Paul interchanged the words "bishop" and "presbyter" in Titus 1:5-10, both words must connote the same office.[164] Further, since Paul mentioned only bishops and deacons in I Timothy 3, there must only have been these two offices. Hence all parish priests (*parrochi*) are bishops.[165] Ecclesiastical officers, of course,

---

[159] *Bepstlicher heylickeit*, FivV (see above, n. 156), Gv; *Welche bücher*, Ciii (see above, n 156); *Bedingung*, Aiii; *Appellation*, Av: "Appellir ich zu dem allerheylgsten Christlichen und gemeynem Concilio (das nicht allein Bischoffen und prelaten, sunder auch weltlich hern und alle leyhen, so einen reynen, guten vorstand heyliger schrifft haben)."

[160] "Extra casum necessitatis (permittente Evangelio) possumus laicis confiteri et ab eis iure divino absolvi (29)." Thesis 29 of the July 12, 1521 theses. The Pope wrongly limited the right of hearing confession to a few hooded ones (thesis 30). Clemen, *Beiträge zur Reformationsgeschichte*, I, 36.

[161] This seems to be the implication of thesis 113 (of the Oct. 11, 1521 theses) where Karlstadt argued that one should not suppose that every aspect of the original celebration by Christ and the Apostles is normative, for if it were, laymen could not celebrate privately. "Si ex Christi caena legem et formam veritatis sumere liceret, sequeretur, quod laici non possent privatim celebrare, neque sacramentum accipere, quia cum Christo soli episcopi accubuerunt (113)." Barge, *Karlstadt*, I, 489. See also Köhler, *GGA*, p. 513.

[162] "Dartzu wollen wir dem selben gar nicht gestehen, das allein gesagt sey dem bapst, Allis das du aufflosest auff erdtrich u. dan Christus hat das zu allenn Christen gesagt." *Bepstlicher heylickeit*, CiiiV.

[163] *Ibid.*, Div (see above, n. 151). So too Luther earlier in *An den christl. Adel deutscher Nation*, *WA*, VI, 407.10ff. E.g. "Szo folget ausz dissem, das leye, priester, fursten, bischoff, und wie sie sagen, geistlich und weltlich, keynen andern unterscheyd ym grund warlich haben, den des ampts odder wercks halben. . . ." *Ibid.*, p. 408.26-28.

[164] After quoting Titus 1:5-7, he added: "Hic Paulus Episcopos et presbyteros pares facit officio, titulo, dignitate, et authoritate. Immo eosdem quos paulum ante nuncupavit Presbyteros paululum post nuncupat Episcopos." *Super coelibatu*, DiiiV. So also, Diii.

[165] After quoting from I Timothy 3:8-15, he added: "Nunc autem dum non

possess authority only to the extent that they speak according to their divine commission.[166] The mistake of the Pope was to suppose that he was a vicar of Christ rather than merely a messenger proclaiming the truth contained in his commission.[167] As they depend on scripture, however, bishops have considerable authority.[168]

Developments at Wittenberg in early 1522 may have influenced Karlstadt's statements on the calling of the minister. Since the electoral court had opposed the innovations in Wittenberg in late 1521 and early 1522, it was no surprise when Karlstadt, one of the most active leaders, received a warning letter from the elector's adviser, Hugold von Einsiedel.[169] Karlstadt's first statement apropos the minister's calling was in his response to Einsiedel's demand that Karlstadt not insinuate himself where he had not been called to preach. Our archdeacon first insisted that he had been sufficiently called, and then added that he would consider himself bound to preach even without such an official call. "The word has fallen upon me with great suddenness; woe is me if I do not preach." [170] In his work on the prophet Malachi published two weeks later, he offered the hypothesis that Malachi may have been an uncalled (*unberuffen*) man like the peasant Amos. Noting that the word "Malachi" means "my messenger," he asserted that "anyone who proclaims God's word and is driven by the Spirit of God to proclaim the divine word

---

alios ministros norit Paulus in Ecclesia dei, quam Episcopos et Diaconos, atque sic clanculum asseveranter doceat. Omnes in domo dei clericos, aut Episcoporum, aut Diaconorum functiones peragere. Consequitur quod omnes Presbyteri sunt Episcopi, caeteri autem Diaconi. Sic Parrochi sunt Episcopi." *Ibid.*, D.

[166] "Damit wir abei clueg werden, und glauben keynem pfaffen odder Monichen, er kon uns dan gottlichen bevelh zeygen, spricht die schrifft. Moises hatt das ertzelet, das yhm Gott bevolhen oder geboten." *Gelubden*, Dii.

[167] "Darab soll yderman betrachten, das erdicht und erlogen worthlin Vicarius. Welches, Bepst erdicht haben, und konden nymer mher, in gotlichem bevel antzeigen, das sie stathalter oder vicarien Gottis seind, Wan sie Gotis wort predigten, und lerten das selb reyniglich one tzusatz und eynmüschung yrer dreber, sso weren sie Gotis boten, und mit nicht Gottis Vicarien oder stathalter." *Malachiam*, AiiiV.

[168] For instance on the basis of I Timothy 5:11 and Numbers 30, he concluded that the bishop possessed divine authority to accept or reject all vows (*Super coelibatu*, Aiv-AivV).

[169] For Einsiedel, see N. Müller, *Die Wittenberger Bewegung* (2nd. ed.; Leipzig, 1911), 372-76. His letter to Karlstadt, Feb. 3, 1522, is in *ibid.*, pp. 177-78.

[170] " . . . versehe mich, ich sey alsso gnugsam daczu beruffen, wie wolh ich mich an dass auch sonste schuldig erkandt, Gotis wort czu predigen. Bin ich doch unwirdigc doctor, war umb solt ich nit predigen? Gestrenger her, mir ist dass wort vast in grosser swindikeit eingefallen: We mir, wen ich nit predigen!" Karlstadt to Einsiedel, Feb. 4, 1522, *ibid.*, p. 181.

may be called 'Malachi'." [171] The course of events, apparently, had led Karlstadt to believe that the essence of the minister's call consists not in some official authorization, but rather in an inner compulsion to preach given by the Holy Spirit.

## 5. The Sacraments

Karlstadt's position on the sacraments in 1520 and 1521 illustrates further his great indebtedness to Luther. Although he did not explicitly reduce the number of valid sacraments as did Luther in *The Babylonian Captivity of the Church*, he completely ignored all but the Eucharist, baptism and confession. Nor did these three receive equal attention. Apart from the occasional comment that baptism is useless apart from faith,[172] he did not discuss the sacrament of baptism. Although the discussion of confession was somewhat original, it was not extensive. Only the sacrament of the Eucharist received considerable treatment.

### (a) *The Eucharist*

From Luther Karlstadt had learned to stress the centrality of faith, to conceive of the Eucharist in terms of sign and promise, and to reject the Catholic notions of transsubstantiation and the Eucharistic sacrifice. Only in a few areas such as the elevation of the elements, the problem of taking only one kind, and the specific signification of the bread and wine did Karlstadt's statements depart from previously published ideas of Luther.

Karlstadt asserted the centrality of faith by reiterating the view that faith is the only thing which makes the recipient worthy of receiving the sacrament.

> If you had committed the sins of all the world you would be just as well, indeed better, suited than the most holy, if you believed the word. . . . Man should repulse all other preparation and consider well how his heart is prepared in faith.[173]

---

[171] "Ich acht dz der mensch (den Got Malachias nent) etwar eyn schlecht unberuffen man gewest ist. wie Amos, oder ein bawr, scheffer oder hirt (wie Amos) welchem Got den nhomen Malachias tzugeeignet hatt. . . . Malachi hebraisch, heyset auff teutzsch. Meyn bott, Mein geschickter, Mein beveltrager, Meyn werber und verkundiger. In der summ. Ein yeder dero Gots wort verkundiget, und von dem geist Gotis, getriben wirt tzu verkundigung gotliche wort. der mocht Malach genent werden." *Malachiam*, Aii-AiiV.

[172] "Nunc si nihil valet baptismus sine fide. Inferam baptizationem nihil valere sine verbo, quia fides per verbum Christi infunditur." *Super coelibatu*, C (see also, n. 73 above). Cf. also the similar statement about holy water, *Wasser u. salcz*, Aiii.

[173] "Wan du aller wellt sunde begangen hettest, bistu gleych sso wol, ya besser

Nor can one prepare for the sacrament by fasting, confession or prayer.[174] Unbelief is the only valid impediment, faith the only legitimate preparation.

Luther's schema of sign and promise was adopted by Karlstadt in his major works on the Eucharist.[175] He used Luther's illustration of the rainbow to explain the fact that the external sign points to the divine promise.[176] The signs of the bread and wine, of course, do not in themselves make one righteous. John 6:63 proves that even the very flesh of Christ is useless when used externally. The role of the external Eucharistic signs is to remind the communicant of God's promise and thus to strengthen his faith in that divine pledge.

geschickt, alss der heyligist, wann du dem wort glawbest, unnd durch tzeychen sicher und gewiss wirdest. Widerumb, wan du nit glawbest, und sicher wirdest, sso lesterstu Gott. . . . Es sollt auch der mensch alle andere bereitung tzuruck-schlahen, und sich woll endsynnen, wye seyn hertz ym glawben bereytt ist." *Beyden gestaldten* (1521), EivV. Also: "Minus offendit meretrix afflicta manducando carnem Christi, quam justus aliquis pharisaeus suae justitiae conscius." Thesis 16 of the July 19, 1521 theses. Gerdes, I, 41.

[174] "Der halben sol niemant dencken wie er sich dises Sacraments wirdig und empfencklich künd machen, durch beten, Fasten, Beychten, Casteyen. und der gleychen, dann ob du disse stuck alle sampte, und aller welt rew und güt übung hettest, und mangelt dir der glaub, so bistu dises Sacraments unwirdig, und mit nicht darzü geschickt." *Predig* (Dec. 25, 1521), Aiv. So Luther earlier in *Baby-*. *lonian Captivity* (1520), e.g. *LW*, XXXVI, 40, 42, 46; *WA*, VI, 515.27-28, 527.8-23, 520.2-6: ". . . cavendo, ne fidutia confessionis, orationis, praeparationis quisquam accedat, sed his omnibus desperatis in superba fidutia promittentis Christi. Quia, ut dictum est satis, verbum promissionis hic solum regnare debet in fide pura, quae est unica et sola sufficiens praeparatio."

[175] Luther used this schema in *Babylonian Captivity* (1520); e.g. *LW*, XXXVI, 44; *WA*, VI, 518.10-23. Barge (*Karlstadt*, I, 283) noticed this fact and admitted Luther's probable influence but attempted to minimize it by adding that even before Luther's *Babylonian Captivity* Karlstadt had used the notion of external signs of spiritual reality in *Wasser u. salcz*. Actually, however, Karlstadt spoke of the sign and the thing signified in *Wasser u. salcz* (Aug., 1520), AiiV-Aiii in a fashion very similar to Luther's usage of "sign" and "significance" in his Dec., 1519 sermon on *The Blessed Sacrament*(*LW*, XXXV, 49-50; *WA*, II, 742.5-23, 743.7-8). Neither Luther's *The Blessed Sacrament* nor Karlstadt's *Wasser u. salcz* focused the concept of the promise (or covenant) in the way their subsequent writings did. Later, Karlstadt adopted the sign-promise (or covenant) schema of Luther's 1520 publications. One cannot speak of any originality on Karlstadt's part. Karlstadt used the later schema in *Empfahern* (1521), biiiVff; *Anbettung* (1521), Bii-BiiV; *Beyden gestaldten* (1521), AiiiVff.

[176] "Sihe alda haben wyr erstlich, das Evangelium ist das die froliche tzusag, nemlich disser meynung. Ich vorheysch euch, das ich die gantz erden nicht will mit wasser vortilgen. . . . Das ist die satzung und tzusag, nach der selben gab Gott auss gnaden, eyn tzeychen, das tzwischen Gott unnd den menschen sollt mitteln, also das der regen bog das selbe tzeychen seyn sollt, wilches er ynn die gewolcken setzen wollt, unnd sollt eyn tzeychen gottlicher tzusag odder vorbundniss seyn." *Beyden gestaldten*, Biv; cf. Luther in *LW*, XXXVI, 43; *WA*, VI, 517.38-518.4.

> Signs do not make us righteous or pious, but rather merely give birth to and inspire certain assurance. . . . Signs suppress the old Adam, trouble and quench his unbelief and break doubt, and produce assurance in the promise which you have previously believed. . . . They give birth to certain assurance.[177]

Since the promise of the sacrament is that God forgives sins and since the sign strengthens one's faith in that promise, Karlstadt could say that one obtains forgiveness of sins through the sacrament of the cup.[178]

In addition to adopting Luther's discussion of the Eucharist in terms of sign and promise, Karlstadt also followed his rejection of the Catholic idea of transsubstantiation. In October, 1520 Karlstadt could still speak of Christ's presence in the form of bread,[179] but a year later he denounced the "dream of transsubstantiation." [180] Since Christ took bread and said "*This* is my body," one must admit that the baker's bread remains after consecration.[181] Karlstadt, of course,

---

[177] "Zum funfften ist tzu mercken, das uns tzeychen nit gerecht oder frum machen, ssondern alleyn gewissliche sicherheyt gebern und eyngeben. . . . Dastu kurtz yn dissen grund trettest, sso merck, das das sichbarlich fleysch Christi keynen heylig, gerecht und frum macht. Das Christus selber leret, sprechend. Caro nihil prodest Joh.6. Das fleysch ist nicht nutz, ssonder der geyst. Nu kan niemandt leucken, das Christus uber alle creaturen erhocht ist, und ist doch nicht nutz sso er alleyn eusserlich gebraucht wirt. Wie mocht dan eyn creatur odder tzeychen dich gerecht und heylig machen? Drumb wisse und vorstehe, das tzeychen, den alten Adam niderdrucken, engsten und dempffen seynen unglawben, und brechen den tzweyffel, und machen sicherheyt yn der promission wilcher du vor geglawbt hast, als gesagt yn disser erklerung, und oben das sie gewisse sicherheyt geberen." *Beyden gestaldten*, CV-Cii. So too *Empfahern*, ciiV; *Anbettung*, Bii. Earlier Luther had stated the same view that the purpose of the sign is to strengthen faith: *LW*, XXXVI, 51; *LW*, XXXV, 86, 91; *WA*, VI, 523.6-7, 358.35-37, 363.20-23.

[178] "Kürtzlich ich wolt ainem raten das er vest vor dissem sacrament fliehen sol, so er nitt glauben kan, das er durchs sacrament des kelches, nitt kan oder wil, vergebung der sünden bekommen. . . . Got will gleich sagen. weil du nit glaubest das ich zü dir red, und sag, der halben solttestu meines trost verlustyg seyn." *Predig* (Dec. 25, 1521), BiiiV. The opposite is true, of course, when one believes: "Item ich weiss das mir Got meine sunde gewisslich durch das hochwirdig sacrament wurt vergeben." *Empfahern*, biii.

[179] In describing a procession at Rome, Karlstadt noted: "Das hymeln unnd erdtrich erhelt, das mag unsser Bapst nit halten, es muss vor yhm furtrabenn, Christus, der muss alleinn auff einem pferd sitzenn, auff das ehr yhe ein reutter in gestalt des brottes werd." *Bepstlicher heylickeit*, Cii.

[180] "Mendacium ex carybdi collapsum est in Scyllam, quoniam negans illam propositionem Panis est corpus Christi finxit somnium transsubstantionis [sic]. . . ." Thesis 35 of the Oct. 17, 1521 theses; reprinted in Barge, *Karlstadt*, I, 485-6.

[181] " . . . dan gleych das brot, das der becker gemacht und gebacken hat, bleybet auch nach der gebenedeyung brot, Dan wan gesegnet brot nit das brot blieb, das der priester vor der consecration yn seyn hende nimpt, sso mocht

had not rejected the real presence any more than had Luther. The Incarnate One who was both true man and true God provides an analogy to the consecrated wafer which is both bread and flesh.[182] Karlstadt confessed that belief in the physical presence of Christ in the sacrament was "very bitter and difficult for me and my old Adam." But since the word declared this truth, he believed it.[183] And since he accepted the real presence of Christ, he continued to defend adoration of the sacrament after others in Wittenberg wanted to reject this practice in 1521. "I do not see why the bread should not be adored since we ought to and can adore the body of Christ. We can say to Christ, 'My Lord, my God,' as Thomas said. . . . The bread is Christ; therefore we ought to adore the bread." [184] Such adoration, of course, is idolatry if one cannot believe that Christ is truly present. One adores the Incarnate One, not the bread.[185]

The adoption of much of Luther's new Eucharistic doctrine did not prevent Karlstadt from enunciating a few ideas on his own. To Luther's life-long annoyance Karlstadt rejected the elevation of the sacrament. He accepted Luther's rejection of the Eucharistic sacrifice,[186] and then concluded, unlike Luther, that since elevation was part of Old Testament sacrificial ritual, it should be rejected.[187]

Christus yn keynen weeg warhafftig gesagt haben, nembt hyn, das ist meyn leyp." *Beyden gestaldten* (1521), AiiiV. So too *Anbettung*, Biii. So too Luther earlier in *Babylonian Captivity, LW*, XXXVI, 34; *WA*, VI, 511.21-33.

[182] "Das brott ist gleich woll das brott, das der becker gebacken hatt, ob es der leyb Christi geworden ist. Wie auch Christus gleich der mensche bleibt. den er in mutter leyb empfangen hat, ob gleich der selbe menschlich leyb Gott ist." *Anbettung*, Biii; Luther had developed this earlier; *LW*, XXXVI, 35; *WA*, VI, 511.34-512.6.

[183] " . . . alsso ists der natur auch unglaublich, das ein mensch Gott sein soll, und das naturlich brot der leyb Christi soll sein. Aber dem glauben seind sie beyde leicht und glaublich. . . . Ich hab auch keynen tzweyfel. an dem wort Christi, und glaub yhm, ob mirs. und meinem adam tzusawer und wichtig ist." *Anbettung*, AivV.

[184] "Caeterum non video cur non debeat adorari panis, quando Christi corpus adorare debemus et possumus (43). Possumus Christo dicere dominus meus, deus meus, sicut Thomas dixit . . . (44). Atqui probatum fuit, panem esse Christum ergo panem adorare debemus (45)." Theses 43-45 of the Oct. 17, 1521 theses; reprinted in Barge, *Karlstadt*, I, 486. So too *Anbettung*, AiiiV-Aiv.

[185] "Wir faren aber furt durchs brot in Christum. des leyb, brot ist, alsso eren wir das brot, und eren es nit. Wir eren es das wir wissen, das brot der leyb Christi ist, und eren es nit, das wir nit im brot, sonder in Christo hafften." *Ibid.*, B.

[186] Thesis 51 (see n. 187) of the Oct. 17, 1521 theses. So too Luther earlier in *Babylonian Captivity; LW*, XXXVI, 51ff; *WA*, VI, 523.8ff.

[187] "Hoc plane fatebor, sacerdotes cum Christo ludere et salvatorem deridendum exponere, quando sustollunt panem qui est Christus et subtrahunt esurientibus qui circumstant (50), Quandoquidem panis ille non oblatio neque hostia sed

Karlstadt also went one better than Luther apropos the Catholic practice of withholding the cup from the laity. Whereas Luther was content to condemn the hierarchy for withholding the cup, Karlstadt condemned as sinful any communicant who took only one kind.[188] It may have been to justify his statement in July that communicating in one kind is sin that Karlstadt subsequently enunciated the idea that the bread and wine signify two distinct promises. Whereas the cup is the sign of the promise that God forgives one's sins, the bread signifies the promise that the believer will be victorious over death and experience the glory of the resurrection.[189] The notion of two distinct promises was not, however, Karlstadt's only reason for recommending abstention rather than communication in one kind. He also cited Jesus' command (Matthew 26:28): "Drink of it, all of you."[190] In spite, however, of these few points at which Karlstadt diverged from Luther, his statements on the Eucharist in 1521 were essentially a repetition of the ideas of his younger colleague.

## (b) Confession

Until the famous Christmas sermon of 1521, Karlstadt's sparse references to confession were also a reflection of Luther's views. In a set of theses in July he repeated Luther's assertions that confession

---

cibus non proprius (51). In sacrificiis olim duas fuisse elevationes non inficior, sed communis. unam thruram appellatam, quae erat sursum deorsumque, sicut nunc panem et calicem infoelices sacrificuli elevant (52). Alteram Thnupham nuncupatam, quae erat dextrorsum et sinistrorsum, antrorsum et retrorsum, quemadmodum benedicunt pplō (populo?) Chaldaei (53). Neutra sublevatio pani et vino congruit, quia non sunt sacrificia neque symbola in illud proposita (54)." Theses 50-54 of the Oct. 17, 1521 theses (Barge, *Karlstadt*, I, 486-7). Luther on the other hand, justified elevation; e.g., *LW*, XXXVI, 53-54; *WA*, VI, 524.21-35.

[188] "Non sunt Bohemi, sed veri Christiani panem et poculum Christi sumentes (9). Qui solo pane vescitur, mea sententia peccat (10)." Theses 9, 10 of the July 19, 1521 theses (Gerdes, I, 41). So too thesis 71 of the Oct. 17, 1521 theses (Barge, *Karlstadt*, I, 487). Luther said precisely the opposite in *Babylonian Captivity*: *LW*, XXXVI, 27; *WA*, VI, 507.6-10.

[189] "Beneficium remissionis peccatorum annunciatur per promissionem cui poculum est signum (75)." "Debemus ergo mortis victoriam et ressurectionis gloriam credere nobis futuram, dum promissionem, Hoc est corpus meum, quod pro vobis traditur, et panem illius signum sumimus (80)." Theses 75, 80 of the Oct. 17, 1521 theses (Barge, *Karlstadt*, I, 488); *Beyden gestaldten*, Dff.

[190] "Ich wil dir Bapst, und du neid, ein ander item furhalten, Christus spricht zu allen den yene so sein brot gessen haben, und saget noch heuth in der schrifft zu denen die seyn brot essen. Ir solt allesampt auss dem kelch trincken. Matt. 26 [v.28]. Also haben auch alle empfaher des brots auss dem kelch gedruncken. Marci 14." *Beyden gestaldten*, Dii. Luther had developed this exegetical argument earlier: *LW*, XXXVI, 20; *WA*, VI, 502.29-36.

was not a matter of biblical (and therefore divine) command, that one can confess to a layman regularly, and that the person confessing is free to omit sins which he does not want to mention.[191] In his Christmas sermon six months later, however, Karlstadt went well beyond Luther. Whereas Luther had continued to insist that confession is useful although not necessary,[192] Karlstadt condemned the practice not only because of the abuses and the absence of divine institution, but also because he felt it detracted from the Eucharist.[193] Christ's promise apropos the cup was that His blood was shed for the forgiveness of the sins of those who believe His promise. "If you want to have forgiveness of sins before you receive the sacrament, . . . you must not believe the words of Christ at all." [194] Such people believe the invented words of miserable clerics more than the promise of Christ.[195] To counteract this problem Karlstadt rejected confession and announced his belief that one does not obtain forgiveness of sins in oral confession.[196] He knew of no word of absolution except that contained in the promise of the cup.[197] Thus in order to reinforce the

---

[191] "Confessio peccatorum (quam extorserunt Pontifices) non est de iure biblico, quod solum est divinum (25). Potest quis confiteri ea et quot voluerit peccata, etiam singula nulla, et nihilominus absolutionem petere, si se sacerdoti ostendat (26)." Theses 25-26 of the July 12, 1521 theses. Clemen, *Beiträge zur Reformationsgeschichte*, I, 36. See above, n. 160 for thesis 29. Theses 25-31 all pertain to this issue. For Luther, see E. Fischer, *Zur Geschichte der evangelische Beichte*, I, 118ff and II, 3ff.

[192] *Ibid.*, II, 82.

[193] " . . . acht ich dz die yene so jre augen auff die beicht keren. dz sy dissen worten des kölchs so wienig vertrauen, so vil sy der beicht getrauen, und als vil sy an der beicht kleben, so vil seind sy von disem sacrament fremd. Dann jr beycht thünd sy darumb daz sy vergebung der sunden nit jn empfahung des sacraments süchen dz ist verlich und schedlich." *Predig* (Dec. 25, 1521), Biv.

[194] "Ich frag dich ob Chrystus warhafftig spricht. Nembt hyn und trincket. dz drinck vass, ist das new testament, jn meinem blütt, das vergossen wirt, für eüch und vill, jn vergebung der sünden. . . . Glaubestu das Christus disse red recht und warhafftiklych gesagt hat. So müstu ye glauben, das er die sünde vergybt So du seyne wort vassest, Dien er dien kölch zü hat gegeben. . . . Wann du vergebung der sünden, vor wilt haben ee du dz Sacrament empfast und darnach des Sacrament brauchen. So müst du ye den wortten Christi kaynenn glauben geben." *Ibid.*, Biii.

[195] "Es ist nichts dann des Teüfels spil und Entchristis lochen das mir dz wort des kölches nit so vil gelten sol, als ain erdicht form aines ellenden pfaffen." *Ibid.*, BiiiV. The priest's words of absolution in private confession are "erdicht" because private confession is not "de iure biblico" (see above, n. 191).

[196] "Ob gleich vergebung haimlicher sünden jn den oren beichten erlangt wurt (das ich nit glaub) müstu ye sünde mit dir tragen welche dir das Sacrament abnemmen möcht." *Ibid.*, Biii.

[197] "Disse wort, Alles das jr pyndett, Soll gepundenn seynn. Alles dz jr lösset, sol gelösst werden, gehören auff offenliche sunde. und ob sy gleich andere sünd begriffen, kanstu mir kayn gewisser wort, der absolucion fürlegen, dann

assertion that worthy reception of the Eucharist depends solely on faith, not on previous fasting or confession, Karlstadt publicly attacked confession itself before his huge audience on Christmas day, 1521. As a result of this sermon oral confession decreased significantly at Wittenberg for some time.[198]

## 6. CONCLUSION

What evidence has been discovered to support the view that the later quarrels of Luther and Karlstadt can be traced back to fundamental theological differences in 1520 and 1521? Some theological disagreement was certainly present in these years. Most important, perhaps, was Karlstadt's repeated emphasis on the normative character of the Old Testament for the Christian. Luther was to become increasingly unhappy with this emphasis on the Old Testament. Also potentially productive of disagreement was Karlstadt's notion, which developed in the course of the Wittenberg Movement, that the minister's call is essentially an inward activity of the Spirit, not an external act of man. Less important although more explicit were the disagreements over the elevation of the elements and the legitimacy of partaking of only one kind. Finally, Karlstadt rejected oral confession whereas Luther continued to teach that non-compulsory confession was useful.

The areas in which Karlstadt and Luther agreed, however, were far more numerous and important. They both affirmed the doctrine of *sola scriptura*, the necessity of literal exegesis, and the external mediation of grace via the word. Karlstadt, it is true, sounded the Augustinian note that the word alone is insufficient without the Spirit, but he constantly affirmed the necessity of external proclamation. Nor did his work on the Spirit and the letter involve a spiritualist dissipation of *sola scriptura*. In these years Karlstadt's primary conception of *justitia* was of that imputed righteousness which is reckoned to the believer

---

dise seind, so ob vom kölch gemelt seind." *Ibid.*, Biii-BiiiV. The biblical authority to bind and loose, then, pertains to public sins. Furthermore, this authority is exercised only *in the congregation*: "Darauss volget das kain pfaff *an* [=ohne] *einen Christlichen hauffen*, kan binden. Dann Pa. spricht congregatis vobis et spiritu meo I. Co. V [v.4]. und Christus saget. Dic ecclesie. Si non audierit ecclesiam. u. volget. Alles daz jr bindet oder lössen werdet, dz ist gepunden oder erlösst. Ma. xviii [vv. 18-19]. So hat Christus Petro die schlüssel geben, alls er *für dyen gantzen hauffen* antwurt. Math. xv." *Ibid.*, Biv (my italics).

[198] Fischer assembled the evidence in *Geschichte der ev. Beichte*, II, 155-169. Not even Luther's encouragement of confession after his return in 1522 was sufficient to reinstate widespread adherence to the old practice immediately. *Ibid.*

who trusts in Christ's promise. Although Karlstadt used the words "justification" and "Gospel" less than Luther, he clearly taught a doctrine of forensic justification. As was shown above, it is simply incorrect to argue that the doctrine of forensic justification was significantly less important for Karlstadt than for Luther at this time. It is true, of course, that Karlstadt continued to place considerable albeit less emphasis on inner righteousness which he discussed in terms of spiritual circumcision and regeneration, but this aspect of *justitia* was certainly not foreign to Luther's thought either. Further, by 1521 Karlstadt abandoned the Augustinian conception of eternal life as the reward of divinely bestowed good deeds and adopted Luther's view that since all good deeds are tainted with sin, faith alone can be the ground of eternal salvation. This change proves that Luther's forensic conception of justification was continuing to influence Karlstadt's theology in a fundamental way through 1521 and the Wittenberg Movement. Luther's influence was also plainly apparent in Karlstadt's statements on the priesthood of all believers and the Eucharist. Karlstadt was quick to adopt Luther's doctrine of the priesthood of all believers to undergird his earlier emphasis on the important role of the layman in the church. And, apart from the exceptions noted above, his Eucharistic statements were largely a repetition of Luther's ideas. One can only conclude that apart from a few significant exceptions (e.g. the normative character of the Old Testament and the call of the minister), Luther and Karlstadt were in fundamental theological agreement through the period of Luther's sojourn at the Wartburg.

# CHAPTER FIVE

# FROM THEORY TO PRACTICE
## (June, 1521 to February, 1522)

That Karlstadt moved to implement the new ideas in the second half of 1521 reflected an increase of courage, not a decrease in danger. Much was different in the summer of 1521. Luther had made his daring stand at Worms and was now secluded in the land of the birds, safe from the imperial edict. A rump diet had banned Luther and his followers and ordered them seized. Anyone who wrote against the Roman faith, the papacy, the clergy or scholastic theology was to be executed.[1] It is not surprising, therefore, that the Elector was extremely worried when Karlstadt unexpectedly reappeared in Wittenberg in June, only weeks after a trip to Denmark had seemed to relieve the Elector of the second of his all-too-well-known theologians.[2] Spalatin's attempt to persuade Karlstadt to return to Denmark failed and Karlstadt remained in Wittenberg.[3]

Karlstadt's mood was apparent in his work on monasticism. After condemning numerous abuses, he noted Paul's command not to offend other Christians. "Up to the present we have born the weakness of the monks." While keeping the numerous practices apropos food, fasting, candles, vows, etc., they had proclaimed the insignificance of externals. But no change had resulted from this tolerance. "On that account I think that at last those persons must be abandoned lest their voluntary prison destroy our liberty."[4] The political situation was hardly favorable in the summer of 1521, but Karlstadt was ready to act.

---

[1] Schwiebert, *Luther and His Times*, p. 511.

[2] Barge has discussed this trip at some length (*Karlstadt*, I, 249-263). Karlstadt left for Denmark after Luther went to the Wartburg, and returned on June 20 (*ibid.*, I, 470).

[3] See the documents in Otto Waltz, "Epistolae Reformatorum," *ZKG*, II (1878),128-30.

[4] "Tuliamus nos hactenus Monachorum imbecillitatem, temperavimus nobis cibis, multiplicavimus poculas, ieiunavimus, cecinimus, luximus, atque assidue praedicamus iuxta externa neminem iudicari debere, sensimus acerbitatem votorum. . . . nemo desciscit a iugo captivitatis, nemo pondus excutit. Ideo tandem relinquendos puto, ne nostram libertatem exedat illorum spontaneus carcer." *Super coelibatu* (June, 1521), CiiV.

### 1. KARLSTADT'S REJECTION OF THE EXTERNALIZATION OF RELIGION

Karlstadt's critique of the religious externalism of his day helped determine the precise form of his attack on religious praxis. In the chapter called "Religious Thought Crystallizing into Images," Huizinga has argued that the tendency for religious devotion to find a visible, external expression was particularly strong in the latter middle ages. Pierre d'Ailly complained of the rapidly increasing number of churches, festivals, saints, holy days, images and paintings. "By this tendency to embodiment in visible forms all holy concepts are constantly exposed to the danger of hardening into mere externalism." [5] Convinced that much of the religiosity of his day was sheer externalism, Karlstadt reacted against it very sharply.

Karlstadt's earliest attack on externalism was an Erasmian objection to the practice of esteeming the saints' relics more than their books. In 1518 he announced his agreement with "our most learned Erasmus," and then quoted his charge that people kiss the saints' handkerchiefs and neglect their books.[6] Although the attack on externalized religion began rather early, the critique became constant and extensive only in 1520. From *Verba Dei* on, he repeatedly showed how externals were both useless without faith and understanding, and also insignificant in comparison with the word of God. He constantly supported his thesis with John 6:63: "It is the spirit that gives life; the flesh is of no avail."

In his book on consecrated water and salt, he denounced the view that holy water blots out venial sins.

> If you poured the whole Tiber, Elbe, Rhine and Danube over one sinner, you would not wash away one venial sin from him. . . . For water without faith cannot touch the soul.[7]

---

[5] J. Huizinga, *The Waning of the Middle Ages* (Garden City, New York, 1954), pp. 152-3. For the amazing amount of church construction, cf. Johannes Janssen, *History of the German People at the Close of the Middle Ages*, trans. M. A. Mitchell and A. M. Christie, I (St. Louis, 1896), 170-83. For the religious intensity which drove people to undertake pilgrimages, cf. W. Waetzoldt, *Dürer and His Times*, trans. R. H. Boothroyd (London, 1950), p. 29.

[6] *De sp.*, Kähler, pp. 100.31-101.1 Cf. also *Bepstlicher heylickeit*, EivV.

[7] "Schuttestu die gantz Tyber und Elb, Rein und Thonau uber eynen sunder, du wurdest ym kein teglich sund abwaschen, seynt doch alle ding durch Gott gebenedeyet, was solt dir gebrechen, das du dem Bader ii pfenning in dz bade gebest, und wuschest leyb unnd seel, gar wol und reyn, dan szo du nith glaubst, was durch wasser bedeut und angetzeigt ist so wurstu nit selig Marci ultimo. Und ist wasser, nit anders oder meher, dan wasser. Und ist gar nicht besser dann des baders wasser, dan wasser sonder glaubem, magk die seel nit anruren. *Wasser und salcz*, Aiii.

Karlstadt was disturbed that the people blindly attached themselves to water and salt when they should have hoped only in God. It is faith, not physical water which effects forgiveness of sins.[8] In his reply to his opponent's rebuttal that consecrated water has power from the blood of Christ, Karlstadt referred to Christ's dictum that the flesh is useless and again insisted that the one thing needed is faith.[9] John 6:63 shows that even the flesh of Christ in the sacrament is useless apart from faith.[10]

Karlstadt was most impatient with the interminable, unintelligible prayers of the monks and nuns. The religious suppose that the best acts are long prayers, eternal church attendance, and the hearing of mass. "Clerics, monks, and nuns babble all day and night, chatter like magpies, and do not know what they pray." They cannot possibly say such long prayers with faith![11] They should explain the content of

[8] "Ich sag nit das geweycht wasser und saltz dem menschenn schaden bring . . . sondern ich vorlach allein den nerrischen und plintten gebrauch, das sich dye menschenn an wasser und saltz, anhefften, und hangen mit hoffnung, in worten und tzusagungen, die yn menschen zugesagt, do sie mit hoffnung allein in Gottis worten bleyben solthen. Sie steent ym wasser stil, und solten doch das hertz auff in Gott tragen." *Ibid.*, AiiiV. "Es ist auch nit tzubergen, dz der glaub der erweckt wurt, in ubung des wassers, sunden vorgibt, und wirckt alles das alle benedeyhung des wassers antzeigen, dan es muss ye sein, das sonder glauben, kein selickeit kompt." *Ibid.*, AivV.
[9] "Weistu nit du grober dolper, das Christus gesaget, welcher nit glaubet der ist vordampt, ap er Christo ym fleisch unnd plut stund? Weistu abermals nit, das Christus niemant wil helffen er glaub dan? Derhalben er offt gesagt, Euch geschehe wie yhr gleubt Matth. ix. Christus spricht caro das fleisch taug nicht, der geist ist dero lebendig macht Johan. vi." *Antwort . . . geweicht wasser*, BV-Bii. cf. also Bii-BiiV.
[10] "Dastu kurtz yn dissen grund trettest, sso merck, das das sichbarlich fleysch Christi keynen heylig, gerecht und frum macht. Das Christus selber leret, sprechend: Caro nihil prodest Joh. 6. Das fleysch ist nicht nutz, ssonder der geyst. Nu kan niemandt leucken, das Christus uber alle creaturen erhocht ist, und ist doch nicht nutz sso er alleyn eusserlich gebraucht wirt." *Beyden gestaldten*, Cii. Cf. also CV, Ciii, CiiiV.
[11] "Nun, sso ich ampt, werck, und leben, der vermeynten geistliche anseh und ermess (der yenen, mein ich, die ynn unstrefflichem und wolscheinlichem leben, bey den menschen gehn und frum gehalten sein) sso find ich kein furtrefflicher werck, dan lang gebeth, ewig kirch liegen, messe horen und lessen, der doch keynes vor Gott gutt ist. Christus verbeut lang gebet, und spricht. Ihr solt nit vil redende sein (sso yhr betend) wie die Heyden. Matth. vi. So schwatzen Pfaffen, Monichen und Nonnen den gantzen tag und nacht, kotern wie Elssdern, wissen auch nit was sie beten, beten mehr und anders, den Got haben wil. . . . Wie ists muglich, das sie solch lang gebeth ym glauben sprechen. Szo brengen sie wenig glauben und vill wort, der doch keynes Gott gefelt odder yhe beheglich gewest. Christus spricht. Ihr solt nit offenbar beten, wie die gleyssner, sonder heymlich, dan Gott sicht im verborgen und heimlichen. Matth. vi. Gott urteylt das hertz, nit das angesicht. Joh. viii. Got ist ein geist, und soll geistlich geehrt werden. Johan. iiii. Wir tolhe narren haben uns gar darauff lassen bereden, das wir fur gnug

their prayers to the people, for Paul preferred to say five words intelligibly rather than five thousand in an unintelligible tongue.[12] The foolish masses suppose that all that is required of the clergy is lengthy, public prayer. In reality, however, God is a Spirit and should be worshipped spiritually. "All visible and external acts of worship are useless." God esteems only the spirit.[13] The kind of prayer Karlstadt desired is clear from another passage where he insisted that Christians pray not only with the spirit, but also with the mind and the understanding.[14] Genuine prayer involves the reason, but is independent of all external things. Karlstadt, of course, did not intend to abandon all external worship: "We by no means reject vocal prayers which proceed from the heart, but rather the sonorous kind which only the vocal cords blow through the cheeks." [15] But he did want to avoid the mechanical recitation of liturgical phrases devoid of both inner religious devotion and intellectual comprehension.

Karlstadt frequently contrasted the uselessness of externals with the importance of the word. He condemned those who esteem stone churches and silver monstrances more than the word of God even though it is only through the latter that one comes to Christ.[16] The

---

achten, sso wir offenlich am tag, vor allen leuthen, singen, schreyhen, aber beten. . . . Ich geschweig, das alle sichtparliche und eusserliche Gottis dienste, nit nütz sein. Und das Gott den geist allein tewr schatzet, als Christus sagt. Johannis vi. Das fleysch ist nit nütz." *Gelubden*, EivV-FV. The discussion continues to Fii.

[12] "Das lass ich geschehen, das Monichen und Nonnen offenlich vor den leuthen, yhr gebet erstlich in der Biblien tzeigen, dar nach die leuth, sso umbstehen, inhalt yhrs gebets leren, und thun das kurtzlich. Wie Paulus sagt. Ich wil lieber funff wort, verstendlich und vernemlich in der kirchen, also beten, das ich andere menschen leer, dann funff tausent wort, in eyner tzunge reden, wilche die umbsteher nit vernhemen. i. Cor. xiiii. Unssere Pfaffen, Monichen und Nonnen verstehent yhr gebeth selbst nit, wie konden sie vernemlich beten?" *Ibid.*, FV. Cf. also theses 24 and 26 from the March, 1521 theses; T. Brieger, "Thesen Karlstadts," *ZKG*, XI (1890), 482.

[13] *Gelubden*, F (see n. 11 above).

[14] "Ethnicorum est absque intellectu multa offundere. Christianorum vero non modo spiritu, sed mente, nedum ligua [sic] et sibilo, sed corde et intellectu precari." *Super coelibatu*, CV.

[15] "Orationes vocales ex corde procedentes haud abjicimus (28). Sed sonoras, quas sola arteria per buccas parturit" (29). Theses 28-29 of "De cantu Gregoriano disputatio" (reprinted in *Karlstadt*, I, 493).

[16] "Steynerin kirchen und silberin kelch ehren die leut darumb, das sie Got eygen gemacht seint, und alsso geheyliget, und konden doch keinen geist Christi auss ynen durchlessen odder ansehen, erlernen, odder richen odder schmecken. Die heylige geschrifft ist Got nichts mynder voreynet und eygen gemacht, dan ein kelch odder altar, . . . und mugen auch den rechten geyst Christi durch fleyssig lesung oder anhorung schopffen, versuchen und schmecken." *Von Bepstlicher heylickeit*, Eiv. See too *Verba Dei*, CV-Cii.

monks are so preoccupied with the external paraphernalia of the altar that they lose sight of the word of God.[17] With reference to the Eucharist, Karlstadt asserted that it is the word of promise, not the physical, external sign which is useful. Just as the flesh of Christ is useless (John 6:63), so too the visible bread is in vain unless one feeds on the promise in one's heart. "He who feeds thus on the promise truly eats; nor does he need anything external at all." [18] The word itself, of course, is external. And it is far from useless.[19] In the work on images he decried those who are preoccupied with the wooden crucifixes which teach how Christ died, but not why he died. Images which only depict how Christ hung his head are mere useless flesh. That which vivifies is precisely the word. "Christ had words of eternal life. . . . God's word is spiritual and it alone is of benefit to believers."[20] By denouncing the various forms of religious externalism, Karlstadt hoped to reassert the primacy of the word.

He also hoped that a genuine inner devotion would develop. Prayer is the elevation of the mind to God, and it happens most successfully "in the heart, for God is Spirit." [21] It is faith rather than external acts, and the word rather than physical objects which are important for the Christian. Convinced that externals were not significant, Karlstadt dared to urge the Wittenbergers to change them.

---

[17] "Piaculum grande censetis admitti, siquis lampadum concinnator, restinctos lychnos sinat fumigare donec audit dei sermonem. Altaria vestra amicitis variis, in cultu externorum anxie laboratis, atque ad illam superstitionem vehimini in curribus Pharaonis, . . . hoc est seniorum vestrorum traditionibus, . . . qui a mandato et verbis vitae aeternae vos diripiunt." *Super coelibatu*, Cii.

[18] "Quoniam sicuti Christi caro nihil prodest, ita nec panis visibilis (95). Spiritus est qui vivificat, spiritus fidei, cuius verbum est sermo promissionum (96). Porro qui sic commedit promissionem iste vere manducat, neque illi opus est qualibet re externa. Ergo citra panis et poculi sumptionem iustificatur" (97). Theses 95-97 of the Oct. 17, 1521 theses (*Karlstadt*, I, 489).

[19] This is even clearer in *Super coelibatu*, C where Karlstadt declared that "all external things give place to the word." He was talking about public preaching. See above, chapter IV, n. 73.

[20] "Auss dem bild des gecreusigten Christi lernestu nicht, dan das fleischlich leyden Christi, wie Christus seine heubt geneigt, und der gleichen. Nhu sagt Christus, das sein eygen fleisch nit nutz sey, sonder dz der geist, nutz sey und lebendig thun machen. Szo spricht auch Petrus. Das Christus, worte hat gehabt, des ewigen lebens und gaistes. Dieweil nun dye bilder stum, und taub seind, konden weder sehen noch horen, weder lernen oder leren, und deuten, auff nichs anders dan uff lauter und blos fleisch, das nicht nutz ist. Volget vestiglich, das sie nicht nutz seind. Aber das wortt Gottis ist geystlich, und allein den glaubigen nutze." *Abtuhung*, ed. Lietzmann, p. 9.7-15.

[21] "Oratio est elevatio mentis in deum (1). Haec est optima, quae corde fit, deus enim spiritus est (2). Theses 1-2 of "De cantu Gregoriano" (*Karlstadt*, I, 492).

## 2. Karlstadt's Role in the Wittenberg Movement

The busy pens of Luther and Karlstadt had created a large number of people, both clerical and lay, who were eager for change. If the electoral establishment feared change, the Wittenberg city council was less cautious. Students, of course, are ever impatient. The result was the Wittenberg Movement of late 1521 and early 1522.[22]

In spite of Luther's frequent condemnation of the theology and praxis of the Mass, no one had actually modified current practice. First some Augustinian monks and then a junior faculty member and his eager students changed that. On September 29, Melanchthon and his students took the sacraments in both kinds at the parish church. Repeatedly apparently in the following weeks people both inside and outside the academic community partook of both kinds at various services.[23] Still more significant in its effect was the spirited sermon of

---

[22] The account of the Wittenberg Movement advanced by Hermann Barge in his two-volume work on Karlstadt sparked a bitter academic quarrel at the turn of this century. In reply Karl Müller, professor of theology at Tübingen, argued in *Luther und Karlstadt* (Tübingen, 1907 [hereafter cited as *LuK*]) that Karlstadt was far less original and a great deal more culpable than Barge had supposed. Barge offered an angry 366 page retort: *Frühprotestantische Gemeindechristentum in Wittenberg und Orlamünde* (Leipzig, 1909 [hereafter *FG*]). The same year M. von Tiling wrote a relatively unimportant article on the dispute—"Der Kampf gegen die missa privata in Wittenberg im Herbst 1521," *Neue kirchliche Zeitschrift*, XX (1909), 85-130. Three years later Walther Köhler reviewed the debate in a lengthy article the irenic tone of which provided a welcome contrast to the sharp polemic and petty haggling of the Müller and Barge volumes. The work has no title. It appeared in *Göttingische gelehrte Anzeigen*, CLXXIV (1912), 505-550 (hereafter *GGA*). Köhler's careful reassessment was made possible by the extensive documents published by Nikolaus Müller first in *ARG*, VI-VIII and then in *Die Wittenberger Bewegung 1521 und 1522* (2nd ed.; Leipzig, 1911 [hereafter *WB*]). Although Köhler's article was generally accurate, it did not provide a descriptive account of the Wittenberg movement, but rather only a sound adjudication of the numerous disagreements between Barge and Müller. Recently Wilhelm Neuser has provided a good general description in *Die Abendmahlslehre Melanchthons in ihrer geschichtlichen Entwicklung (1519-1530)* (Neukirchen-Vluyn, 1968), pp. 114-213. The following account will focus on Karlstadt's role.

[23] *WB*, No. 4, p. 17, No. 6, p. 23 and No. 25, pp. 61-2; cf. also *LuK*, p. 6 n. 3 and *GGA*, p. 508. Even Müller believed that the partaking of both kinds before Dec. 25 occurred only at small private gatherings (*LuK*, p. 30). Neuser, *Abendmahlslehre Melanchthons*, pp. 128-9, however has shown on the basis of *WB*, No. 25, p. 62 that this occurred also at public services. On November 4, conservatives reported the following: "Aber jungst am tag omnium Sanctorum [1 November] der Capellan in der pfarrkirchen dem gemeynem volck, jungk und alt, das heilig, hochwirdig sacrament under beider gestalt sollen gereicht haben" (*WB*, No. 25, p. 62). Presumably this was not a private gathering. One must not assume, however, that the cup was easily available at all times. In his theses of October 17, Karlstadt argued that the private mass be retained in order that those who could

Gabriel Zwilling, Luther's fellow Augustinian, on October 6. He rejected the idea of sacrifice, condemned the elevation of the host, and demanded that the numerous daily private Masses be replaced by a very few communion services. It is a sin to celebrate a private Mass. When the conservative prior balked at change, the eager monks simply stopped saying Masses.[24] Concerned lest tumult arise, Frederick the Wise ordered a committee, which included Karlstadt, to advise him.[25]

Before the commission sent its report to the Elector, an important public disputation on the disputed issues took place under Karlstadt's leadership. In the theses which he prepared for the debate, Karlstadt adopted a middle position between the impetuous Augustinians and the conservatives. He repeated many ideas which he had learned from Luther. Faith in the promise is the most fundamental aspect of the sacrament.[26] Although the body of Christ is genuinely present, transsubstantiation is a worthless dream.[27] The Mass is not a sacrifice, but rather a food for all.[28] Karlstadt agreed with the Augustinians that the elevation of the host was an evil practice,[29] but disagreed with their condemnation of the adoration of the elements. "We can say to Christ, 'My Lord and my God!' . . . The bread is Christ; therefore, we ought to adore the bread." [30] He agreed with Melanchthon and the monks that all should partake of both kinds, but added his peculiar notion that taking only the bread is sin.[31] Since he who meditates on the promise "does not need anything external" except the word,[32] there is

---

not obtain the cup in a public service might receive the wine by celebrating a private mass (theses 105-107; see below, n. 35).

[24] *WB*, No. 10, p. 28 and No. 3, pp. 14-15.

[25] *Ibid.*, No. 14, p. 32.

[26] Theses 90-94, *Karlstadt*, I, 488 (see below, n. 33). Cf. also: "Quid brevius, quid tantopere totque modis optandum et osculandum quam hoc. Qui credit non damnabitur. Joan. III. Qui sermonem meum audit et credit ei qui me misit, habet vitam aeternam et in condemnationem non veniet. Joan. VI. Quem eiusmodi annunciationes bonorum non exhilerarent? . . . (16). *Ibid.*, p. 485. See all of the first 24 theses, *ibid.*, pp. 484f.

[27] "Mendacium ex carybdi collapsum est in Scyllam, quoniam negans illam propositionem Panis est corpus Christi finxit somnium transsubstantionis [sic!]. . . ." Thesis 35, *ibid.*, p. 485f. See all of theses 25-42.

[28] " . . . panis ille non oblatio neque hostia sed cibus non proprius." Thesis 51, *ibid.*, p. 486.

[29] Theses 50-54, *ibid.*, pp. 486f (see above, chapter IV, n. 187).

[30] Theses 43-45, *ibid.*, p. 486 (see above, chapter IV, n. 184).

[31] "Ideo a peccato neminem possum asserere unam speciem capientem." Thesis 71, *ibid.*, p. 487. Cf. also theses 72-81. See too chapter IV, n. 188.

[32] See above, n. 18.

no danger in abstaining completely if the priest withholds the cup.[33] Partially because the cup was still not completely accessible, Karlstadt disagreed with the Augustinians' rejection of private Masses. He no longer, of course, accepted the medieval theory that a private Mass was a sacrifice and good work which benefited the founder and those who stood around and watched.[34] But he did believe that until there was total freedom and opportunity to communicate in both kinds in the public worship services, it was permissible for not only one individual priest, but also a layman to have a private communion service alone in order to circumvent the existing tyranny.[35]

Perhaps because the nature of the report to the Elector depended upon its outcome, the public disputation was unusually lively. Melanchthon, Jonas, Karlstadt and the monks all stated their views forcefully. Concerned for public order and the more conservative brother, Karlstadt clashed with Melanchthon who was in a hurry.

---

[33] "Nihil periculi fuerit non sumere, modo forti sis fide (90), quia promissiones potest quis iure, absque signo, commedere (91). . . . Nemo profecto salubriter signis pane et vino utitur, nisi prius corde molli promissionibus vescatur (93). Prius edendus est promissionum sermo, tum panis et poculum sumendum (94)." *Ibid.*, p. 488.

[34] "Errare plebem fateor astantem si privatim celebrantis putat sibi manducationem conferre (115). Sicut errat qui se putat saturari, dum videt alium manducare" (116). *Ibid.*, p. 490.

[35] That Karlstadt preferred that people partake at public services is clear from theses 64-65 and thesis 111. But he also thought private Eucharistic services were permissible. "Itaque non est certum (quamquam plures legimus concoenatos Christo sacramentum instituenti et in Corinthijs a multitudine celebrari) an vetuerit Christus, ne solus sumat (105). Alioqui dubium erit, num sit necessum semper XIII comprandere, quando Christus cum duodecim discipulis accubuit. Lucae XXj (106). Hoc ansam praestat excusationis, ut illi qui per tyrannidem non possunt utrumque signum accipere, privatim celebrent missas, ut capiant utrumque (107). . . . Volo quam proxime communioni publicae tanquam minus suspectae et facto Christi accedas (111). Verum non illum condemno qui privatim celebrat, propter hoc quod Christus dicit. Accipite et non dicit accipe (112). Si ex Christi caena legem et formam veritatis sumere liceret, sequeretur, quod laici non possent privatim celebrare, neque sacramentum accipere, quia cum Christo soli episcopi accubuerunt (113). Videntur facilitatis crimine leborare [sic!], quotqnot [sic!] affirmant non esse Christum cum signis eius, qui solus et fide celebrat (114)." *Ibid.*, p. 489. There has been considerable debate over the interpretation of theses 100ff. Köhler (*GGA*, pp. 509-13) and Barge (*FG*, pp. 18ff) rightly reject Müller (*LuK*, pp. 11-14). See also Neuser, *Abendmahlslehre Melanchthons*, pp. 138-9, n. 110. Neuser, however, in rightly stressing Karlstadt's concern to avoid tumult as one reason for defending the private Mass, tends to overlook Karlstadt's explicit statement in thesis 107 that he wants to preserve the private Mass in order that they who cannot receive both kinds because of tyranny can celebrate privately in order to receive both.

Karlstadt insisted that all the Wittenbergers must first be persuaded by preaching. Melanchthon, on the other hand, objected that there had been enough preaching. It was time to act! Turning to Karlstadt who was presiding, Melanchthon exclaimed with frustrated annoyance: "I know that your lordship also wants the thing changed." Karlstadt's retort breathes the spirit of caution: "By all means but without tumult and without giving opponents an opportunity for slander." [36] In order to prevent disorder, Karlstadt urged that no action be taken without the consent of the Wittenberg magistracy.[37] Orderly change would be possible if they proceeded cautiously.

The commission's official report, sent to Frederick on the 20th, shows that Karlstadt had succeeded in defending private Masses, but had not convinced the others that partaking of one kind was sin. The report sympathized with the monk's demands, but urged that the Mass be changed rather than simply ended. Whereas Karlstadt had spoken of the consent of the Wittenberg city council, the report urged the Elector to change the present abuses in the Mass.[38] Frederick, however, had no intention of meddling with the liturgy at the suggestion of a few small-town professors in Wittenberg! That was a matter for the whole of Christendom. He requested that other members of the university and All Saints investigate the matter further.[39]

Confronted with an electoral *Nein!*, Karlstadt turned to writing tracts, the Augustinians jumped over their monastery walls and the people rioted. During November Karlstadt published two Eucharistic tracts in which he restated the views propounded in the October 17

---

[36] "Scio et dominacionem vestram rem immutatam velle. Respondit Karolstadius: maxime, tamen sine tumultu et Adversariorum calumniandi ansa." *WB*, No. 18, p. 48. No. 15, pp. 32-34 has another contemporary report of the debate. The latter observer was impressed with Karlstadt whom he said "altum sapit in Theologia" (p. 33). Neuser's comment captures Karlstadt's cautiously progressive mood: "Noch wünscht er [Karlstadt] keinen Abbau der Institutionen, wie ihn die Abschaffung der Privatmesse mit sich bringen musste. Er will grundlegende Änderungen, aber vorläufig keinen Umbruch" (*Abendmahlslehre Melanchthons*, p. 138).

[37] "Adhortabatur item, ut, si omnino missam sublatam vellent, facerent id cum consensu magistratus Wittembergensis, ne quid offendiculi inde nasceretur in vulgo." *WB*, No. 15, p. 34.

[38] The report is in *WB*, No. 16, pp. 35-40. Barge (*Karlstadt*, I, 324 and *FG*, p. 33) lacked sufficient evidence for his assertion that Karlstadt was the report's author (so *LuK*, p. 17 and *GGA*, p. 515). Neuser, *Abendmahlslehre Melanchthons*, p. 116, n. 8 thinks that Melanchthon wrote it.

[39] *WB*, No. 20, pp. 50-52.

theses.[40] He continued to oppose both the conservative Catholics and the eager Augustinians.[41] Many monks for their part refused to say the endowed Masses and left the monastery.[42] Laymen, too, were caught up in the excitement of the revolutionary times. Young student radicals and eager citizens who found it hard to wait for change through the normal channels took direct action against the conservatives on December 3. Groups of students and townspeople forcibly entered the parish church, threw away the missals and drove the priests from the altar. The next day they threw stones into the Franciscan cloister during Mass and pulled down the altar.[43] Reacting characteristically, Frederick showed leniency toward the rioters and demanded still another report from his theologians and clerics.

He received three. The original committee which included Karlstadt and Melanchthon, demonstrated their commitment to genuine change by again urging the Elector to end the abuses in the Mass. They agreed that they were only small in number but argued that this was insignificant since they were armed with God's word. Christ sent out a few unlearned disciples to preach his Gospel.[44] The Catholics, on the other hand, rejected all the proposed innovations and stressed the authority of the universal church. And the humanist, Otto Beckman, contributed a refutation of the Reformers.[45] Faced with divergent counsel, the Elector did nothing—or rather he in effect sided with the conservatives. On December 19, he ordered his representative to forbid the university and foundation to introduce any innovation in the Mass.[46]

---

[40] Gordon Rupp suggests that the moderate tone of these treatises may be explained by the fact that Karlstadt "was, after all, Dean of the Faculty of Theology." *Patterns of Reformation* (Philadelphia, 1969), p. 96. Actually, however, Karlstadt was no longer dean. He was dean in the summer of 1521, but the new dean always took office on October 18. See my "Karlstadt and Luther's Doctorate", *Journal of Theological Studies*, XXII (1971), 169.

[41] E.g., see his insistence on worshipping the sacrament in *Anbettung*, AiiiVff.

[42] *WB*, No. 28, p. 68 and No. 31, p. 71.

[43] *WB*, No. 32, p. 73 and No. 68, pp. 152-3. Müller is right (*LuK*, P. 26, n. 5) in insisting that the rioters included more than students (cf. *Karlstadt*, I, 350). To speak of "the instigator being Luther's colleague, Karlstadt" is pure fiction. Joseph Lortz, *The Reformation in Germany*, trans. Ronald Walls (New York, 1968), p. 347.

[44] *WB*, No. 43, pp. 84ff.

[45] *WB*, No. 44, pp. 91ff and No. 51, pp. 107ff.

[46] *WB*, No. 56, p. 124. He did, however, explicitly permit continued debate via sermon, disputation and tract.

At this point Karlstadt seized the initiative. He announced that he would celebrate a public, evangelical Mass at the important New Year's Day festival. Why did Karlstadt, who had urged caution upon Melanchthon in October, now defy the Elector? The excitement of the times undoubtedly infected Karlstadt. The title page of his November 30 work on the Eucharist contained a reference to the "Christian city of Wittenberg." [47] The unruly crowd of citizens which forced its way into the city council in mid-December and demanded in its Six Articles that the old Masses be ended and that all be allowed to partake of two kinds, underlined the fact that many Wittenbergers wanted changes in public worship.[48] In his open letter published on December 10, he noted that the common man wanted a Christian Mass and "other suitable and evangelical services." [49] Thus the people of Wittenberg probably encouraged him to act.

In addition he received a nudge from the conservatives at All Saints. Sometime in the fall of 1521, Karlstadt followed the example of the Augustinians and refused to officiate at Mass. He even declined to celebrate the important festival Mass of November 21 reserved for the Archdeacon of All Saints.[50] Conservative colleagues from All Saints willingly substituted for him until he preached a particularly vigorous sermon against the old Mass. Then, in retaliation, they agreed not to take his place henceforth in order to force him either to celebrate the traditional Mass again or to neglect his canonical duties. Karlstadt's response was hardly to their liking. He decided that if he had to say Mass, then he would officiate on New Year's Day at an evangelical one performed according to Christ's institution.[51] The

---

[47] On the title page of the first edition (Verzeichnis, No 71) of *Beyden gestaldten*, are the words: "Gedruckt in der Christliche statt Wittemberg."

[48] See *WB*, No. 68, p. 161ff for the six articles and *WB*, No. 54, p. 120 for a description of the event. See *LuK*, p. 38, n. 4 and *FG*, p. 48, n. 1 for the date (they agree!). The incident at the council occurred before December 15.

[49] Karlstadt denied that the laymen were obsessed with changes because of financial considerations: "Fur den gemeinen mann sag ich, das ich keinen verhort, der heller oder pfennig von den pfaffen begertt. Allein bitten sye, das ein Christliche Mess und andere tzimliche und Ewangelische dinst gehalten werden." *Sendbryff* (Dec. 10, 1521), AiiiV.

[50] This is clear from *WB*, No. 68, p. 153 where it is reported that Karlstadt had not celebrated Mass for a long time and had not taken "ettliche festa" reserved for him. Since the "Ordnung der Stiftskirche" (*Karlstadt* II, 527) shows that he had only one festival Mass reserved for him from October to New Year's, he must have skipped the November one. He would also have normally read some regular Sunday Masses.

[51] *WB*, No. 68, pp. 153-4.

conservatives had unwittingly pushed Karlstadt a little closer to a more radical stance.

On either December 15 or December 22 in a Sunday sermon, Karlstadt announced his plans for the coming New Year's Day festival.[52] And then, perhaps because he had heard reports of the electoral prohibition, but possibly for the sake of his fellow Reformer Jonas, he moved up the date to Christmas.[53] Legally, Frederick had every right as patron of the foundation of All Saints to prohibit Karlstadt's action. But Karlstadt was now ready to defy the Elector in order to initiate change.[54]

Unfortunately for Karlstadt's later reputation, violence flared up again on Christmas eve. A riotous crowd pushed its way into the parish church, destroyed the lamps, threatened the priest and sang popular songs. When a guard arrived they assisted the choir from outside and then went to All Saints. Here they wished the conservative priest pestilence and hell fire! [55]

The violence, however, did not preclude—it may in fact have guaranteed—a huge audience at All Saints on Christmas day. Karlstadt officiated in a plain secular gown and addressed his listeners as fellow laymen.[56] In his sermon on the Eucharist he insisted that the only preparation necessary for taking communion is faith in the two promises of the Eucharist. Neither gross sin nor failure to fast or confess should keep one from the sacrament. "Although you have not

---

[52] *WB*, No. 57, p. 125.

[53] In an undated letter which probably was sent between Dec. 22 and 25, the electoral advisers refer to Karlstadt's announced plan and order the electoral representative in Wittenberg to forbid it. Müller (*LuK*, pp. 42-3) argued that Karlstadt changed the date in order to present the Elector with a *fait accompli* when the prohibition arrived. Barge, however, (*FG*, pp. 62, 65 and 73) pointed out that Karlstadt could only have made his announcement on Dec. 15 or 22. If he did so on the first Sunday, the prohibition would have had time to reach him before Dec. 25. If he did so on Dec. 22, he would already have known of the general Dec. 19 prohibition (*WB*, No. 56, p. 124). Hence in either case he was defying a clear electoral prohibition. It is possible therefore, that he celebrated the Christmas Mass for Jonas because Jonas did not yet want either to defy Frederick or celebrate the old Mass (see especially *FG*, p. 62).

[54] A few weeks earlier he had declared that with regard to the sacrament, one must consider only scripture and not the views and acts of Pope, bishop, prince or burgomaster. *Beyden gestaldten*, DV-Dii. Cf. *LuK*, p. 44 for an accurate description of the legal situation.

[55] *WB*, No. 61, p. 133-34. Since the report comes from the Catholic members of All Saints, it was certainly no worse than they said. But that was rather disorderly.

[56] See *WB*, No. 73, p. 170 for Karlstadt's gown, and *Predig* (Dec. 25, 1521), BiiiV for his "uns leyeen." In *Karlstadt*, I, 358, n. 103 Barge proves that the historic occasion occurred at All Saints.

confessed," he assured his excited audience, "you should nevertheless go joyfully in good confidence, hope and faith and receive this sacrament for it must certainly be true that faith alone makes us holy and righteous." [57] And then, as the breathless crowd watched, he read a simplified Latin Mass, omitting all references to sacrifice. For the first time in the Reformation, the words of institution were spoken in German in a large public service. He omitted the elevation of the host. The tension reached its peak when each communicant took the bread and cup in his own trembling hands. One frightened layman was so terrified by this innovation that he dropped his wafer and was too terror struck to pick it up again.[58] Karlstadt had celebrated the first evangelical Mass in an important public worship service.

Karlstadt's daring act increased the tempo of change. Public evangelical Eucharistic services occurred again on New Year's Day, the next Sunday and Epiphany (January 6). The sermons which Karlstadt gave every Friday were so well attended that one important eyewitness reported—undoubtedly with some exaggeration—that almost all the Wittenbergers attended, including those who had previously come to hear sermons not at all or very infrequently.[59] His sermons were so excellent that "everyone said it was not the same Karlstadt." [60]

The day after his historic Christmas mass, Karlstadt increased the momentum of change in another area by implementing his theoretical rejection of clerical celibacy. Jonas and Melanchthon witnessed his engagement to the daughter of an impoverished nobleman.[61] When he invited the Elector to his January 19 wedding, he explained that he had acted not only because God had called priests to the married life, but also because he hoped to encourage priests to marry their "cooks." "I also take into consideration the fact that many poor, miserable and lost clerics who now lie in the devil's prison and

---

[57] "Ob du gleych nitt hettest gebeycht, Solst du doch frölych inn gütter züversicht, hoffnung, und glauben zügeen, Unnd dysses Sacrament empffahen, dann es müss ye war seyn, Das der glaub unns allain hailig und gerecht macht." *Predig* (December 25, 1521), Aiv.

[58] Karlstadt did. *WB*, No. 61, p. 132, No. 68, p. 154 and No. 73, p. 170.

[59] *WB*, No. 68, p. 163.

[60] " . . . hatt er vorher auch lang nye gepredigt, Nun dreymal wieder an predigt, das all menschen sagt, es sey nymer der Carlstat, also Kostliche dingk predigt er nun. . . ." *Ibid.*, pp. 153-4. This remark refers to sermons preached just before the December 25 service, but it almost certainly is applicable to Karlstadt's post December 25 sermons also.

[61] *WB*, No. 68, pp. 155-9 and No. 73, p. 170.

dungeon might without doubt be counselled and helped by a good model and example." [62] Less sincere and vastly more amusing was the action of an unfriendly reader of the letter who took the opportunity to publish a satirical wedding Mass including a prayer that through Karlstadt's fruitful marriage they might be kept from all dangers of harlotry.[63] Whatever his motive may have been, Karlstadt was successfully challenging and changing the age-old institution of clerical celibacy.

Just after Christmas, three radicals from Zwickau burst on the Wittenberg scene, caused a stir for a short time and then disappeared. Since Professor Rupp believes these "Zwickau Prophets" had a significant influence on Karlstadt, it is important to examine their ideas, the documentary evidence for their contacts while at Wittenberg, and the alleged congruence of Karlstadt's and their thought.[64]

The Zwickau Prophets had been connected with Thomas Müntzer before he left Zwickau in April, 1521. Under severe pressure from the Zwickau authorities they fled to Wittenberg around Christmas, 1521 and promptly began propagating their ideas.[65] They rejected infant baptism on the ground that infants lack faith.[66] They claimed to hold direct conversations with God and to receive special revelations from

---

[62] " . . . so betracht ich auch in ansehung das vil arm ellend und verloren pfaffen yetz in des teüfels gefengknuss und kercker ligen, denen on zweyfel durch güt vorbild und exempel möcht geraten und geholfen werden." Karlstadt to the Elector, *Sendbrief* (Jan. 5, 1522), Aii; *CR*, I, 539. This letter was published, perhaps without Karlstadt's permission (cf. *Karlstadt*, I, 365 and n. 123), in six different editions (Verzeichnis, Nos. 81-86).

[63] Quoted in Barge, *Karlstadt*, I, 366.

[64] Gordon Rupp has said that "Karlstadt was won over for a time by them." "Word and Spirit in the First Years of the Reformation," *ARG*, XLIX (1958), 20. Cf also: "There is not much evidence about Karlstadt's contacts with these men, but they must surely have been influential , so congenial were their doctrines to the movement of his own thoughts and actions in recent weeks." Gordon Rupp, "Andrew Karlstadt and Reformation Puritanism," *Journal of Theological Studies*, N.S., X (1959), 316. In his most recent book, he argues that "the initiative" apropos the Zwickau prophets fell to Karlstadt. He notes that there is only one enigmatic reference to Karlstadt's association with them, but adds: "The fact that he soon began to speak in much more extreme and radical terms, and that he began to lecture on Malachi, suggests that he found them congenial" (*Patterns of Reformation*, p. 101). Also: "It looks as though Karlstadt's head was turned by the Zwickau prophets" (*ibid.*, p. 113).

[65] Paul Wappler has written the best account of their activities and ideas: *Thomas Müntzer in Zwickau und die "Zwickauer Propheten"* (2nd. ed.; Gütersloh, 1966). The following discussion of their ideas is based on this work and the documents in Müller's *WB*, Nos. 59-60, 62-4, 68.

[66] See Luther's reply (Jan. 13, 1522) to Melanchthon's troubled letter in *WABr*, II, 424-7, and also *WB*, No. 64, pp. 140-43.

him via dreams.[67] The Scripture, they announced, is not powerful
enough to teach man: "Man must be taught by the Spirit alone. For if
God had wanted man to be taught by scripture, he would have sent
down the Bible to us from heaven." [68] The inward voice of God has
no connection with Christ or the Gospel. Their commission to teach
came via a "clear voice of God." [69] They claimed prophetic insight
into the near future which was to see a great Turkish invasion, the de-
struction of all priests and the end of the world.[70] They even antici-
pated using the sword against the godless.[71]

When one examines the documents of the Wittenberg Movement,
one discovers first that these prophets produced quite a stir in Wittenberg for a few days at the end of the year and then retreated into
obscurity, and second that it was Melanchthon and not Karlstadt who
was preoccupied with them during their moment of fame. It was
Melanchthon who urged the Elector to allow Luther to return in
order to meet the new prophets.[72] One person living in Wittenberg
reported apropos Melanchthon's attitude toward one of the prophets
that "Philip continually clings to his side, listens to him, wonders at
him and even venerates him most highly." [73] Whereas virtually every
report of the prophets relates Melanchthon's great interest,[74] there is
only one report which connects Karlstadt with them. On January 1
Stübner, the only educated member of the trio, was apparently

---

[67] "Cum deo familiaria colloquia" (*WB*, No. 59, p. 129). Apropos one of the
men, one report said, "man sagt, er hab vill Offenwarung von Gott" (*WB*, No.
68, p. 160). "Praedicabat sibi per somnia ostendi a deo quae vellet" (quoted in
Wappler, *Müntzer*, p. 47, n. 199).

[68] "Etlich geben an, als were die gotlich schrifft zur lare der menschen un-
crefftig. Dan der mensch must allein durch den geist gelerneth werden. Dan hett
Gott den menschen mit geschrifft wellen gelernt haben, so hett er uns vom himmel
herab ein Biblien gesandt." *WB*, No. 64, p. 143. Also: "Oportere nos remoto
Christo, remoto evangelio vocem dei patris in cordibus nostris audire" (quoted in
Wappler, *Müntzer*, p. 68, n. 282).

[69] *WB*, No. 59, p. 129.

[70] *WB*, No. 68, pp. 160-61.

[71] "Dixit eorum nuper quidam ipsis nullos fidem facere, Ideo gladio se brevi
pugnaturum, quem aduc Philippus judicare noluit aiens prophetam fuisse olim,
qui plures eciam ferro jnterimisset." *WB*, No. 63, p. 136. See also Neuser, *Abendmahlslehre Melanchthons*, p. 160.

[72] December 27, 1521, *WB*, No. 59, p. 129.

[73] "Continuo eius lateri Philippus adhaeret, ei auscultatur, admiratur adeoque
summe veneratur et pene perturbatus, quod viro illi satisfieri a nullo possit."
Ulscenius to Capito, Jan. 1, 1522; *WB*, No. 62, p. 135. The "prophet" involved
was Markus Stübner who had been a student of Melanchthon.

[74] See also *WB*, No. 64, p. 137ff and No. 68, p. 160.

staying at Karlstadt's place.[75] Since, however, Melanchthon's friend and biographer, Camerarius, makes it very clear that Stübner stayed with Melanchthon, one must assume that Stübner lived only briefly with Karlstadt during Melanchthon's absence for negotiations with the Elector on January 2.[76] If Karlstadt actually did show the same interest as Melanchthon in the Zwickau prophets, it is extremely surprising that none of the contemporary documents contain any indication of it. Lacking such evidence it is very precarious to argue that they "must" have influenced Karlstadt unless it is possible to show convincingly that Karlstadt's words after late December, 1521 began to reflect the ideas of the newcomers.

Do the three treatises published by Karlstadt in January and February 1522 reveal any influence from the Zwickau Prophets? Of the invalidity of infant baptism there is not a word. Nor is there any apocalyptic speculation. Most important, two of the three treatises contain a reaffirmation of *sola scriptura!* Sometime in late January or early February Karlstadt wrote a treatise against a Catholic opponent. This treatise is one of his clearest declarations of the sole authority of the written text of scripture.[77] On February 18, he published some of the material he had recently preached at Wittenberg.[78] Unlike the

---

[75] *WB*, No. 63, p. 136. Neuser (*Abendmahlslehre Melanchthons*, p. 159) asserts that the other two prophets, Storch and Drechsel were staying with Karlstadt. His reference, however, is to the following statement of Felix Ulscenius to Capito, Jan. 1, 1522: "Vir [Stübner], de quo heri scripseram, apud d. Karolstadium conversatur, qui aduc alios duos habet familiares nunc absentes" (*WB*, no. 63, p. 136). The one who has two other close friends is obviously Stübner. The statement does *not* say the other men stayed with Karlstadt. Thus there is no evidence to support the suggestion that Storch and Drechsel stayed with Karlstadt. In both this letter and the one cited in the following note, Ulscenius reports Karlstadt's numerous activities: his innovative Christmas Eucharist, his coming marriage, his preaching and his Eucharist at the *Pfarrkirche*. But there is just this one reference to Karlstadt's connection with the prophets. One receives the impression that Karlstadt was much too busy with various innovations to be very concerned with the Zwickau Prophets.

[76] "Marcus . . . Wittenbergae aliquantisper mansit, quem et nos ibi vidimus et cum eo sumus saepe collocuti. Receperat autem eum ad se Philippus Melanchthon. . . . Itaque hic hospitem quidem habebat Philippum. . . ." Camerarii *Vita Melanchth.*, pp. 48f; quoted in Wappler, *Müntzer*, p. 65, n. 269. Also: "Philippus Melanchthon tunc quoque fovebat apud se Marcum." Camerarii, *Vita Melanchth.*, p. 50; Wappler, *Müntzer*, p. 66, n. 272. Melanchthon went to seek the Elector's advice on the best way to deal with the prophets (see *WB*, No. 64, pp. 137ff).

[77] *Bit . . . Ochssenfart*; see especially AivV-B. Eg.: "Wiltu sprechen, Die von Wittenberg, handeln übel und ketzerisch mit der Messe, so müstu das durch gezeügnus hey. schriffte war machen und beweysen, . . . Dann die heilig schrifft ist reich, warhafftig und gnugsam zü zeügen und bindet unss an jr eygen zeügknuss."

[78] *Malachiam*, AV.

Zwickau Prophets, he insisted that "God puts a great deal of emphasis on the proclamation of his Word." Not to esteem God's word is to blaspheme.[79] He spoke at some length of the way that God gave His word to the prophets via immediate revelation, but there was no indication that direct revelation continued after the close of the canon. In fact, he stated at the end that

> all preachers should always state that their doctrine is not their own, but God's. And they should ... say with great earnestness: "God has spoken this." ... They can discover nothing out of their own heads. If the Bible is at an end, then their knowledge is also at an end. They cannot invent anything new. ... No spiritual man can reproach them for that.[80]

Such a position was hardly compatible with the thought of the Zwickau Prophets. In fact, the last sentence was probably a direct reference to their belittling of the Bible.

In light of Karlstadt's explicit statements soon after the prophets' stay in Wittenberg, one must use with caution his statement written months later in a letter to Müntzer: "I said more here about visions and dreams than any other professor." [81] Since Karlstadt did not expand on this comment at all and say what he had said about dreams and visions, one dare not assume that he had accepted the idea of special revelation via dreams. In his work on Malachi, in fact, in roundly condemning the popes for teaching things other than the Bible, he denounced the popes for allegedly teaching "their dreams as divine doctrine." [82] It is true that he did not intend to assert that the

---

[79] "Domit tzeiget Christus an, dz Got vil an verkundigung seines wortes gelegen ist. Wie ich offt gesagt hab, dz wir Got smehen und lestern, wan wir sein wort nit wol achten." *Ibid.*, Aiii.

[80] "Alsso solten alle Predigern stetz bedingen, das ire laher, nicht ir selber ist, sonder Gotis. Und solten disse bedinghung mit hertzen thun. Und mit grossem ernst sagen: Das hat Got geredt. Und solten gern horen, das man yenen saget: Du kanst nicht dan Gotis wort, oder: Ire laher, ist nit ire laher. Sie konden nicht auss iren kopffen finden. Wan die Biblien aus ist, sso ist ir kunst auch auss. Sie konden von sich gar nicht erdencken. Sie konden nit etwass newes erdichten. Soliche reden solten sie gern horen, und der welt narren willicklich sein. Die Evangelisten Gotis sollen offenlich bekennen, dz ire laher, wort, und kunste, Gotis ist, und nichts ir eygen. Das kan ynen ouch kein geistlicher mann verargen." *Ibid.*, BiiiV. Thus it is hardly convincing when Rupp (*Patterns of Reformation*, p. 101) cites the fact that Karlstadt began lecturing on Malachi to support his assertion that Karlstadt found the Zwickau Prophets congenial!

[81] "Hic [Wittenberg] plus de visionibus et somniis dixi quam aliquis professorum" (Dec. 21, 1522). G. Franz, ed., *Thomas Müntzer: Schriften und Briefe* (Gütersloh, 1968), p. 387.

[82] "Gotis wort ist einer vesten last und gewycht vergleicht. Menschlich wort

popes claimed special revelations via dreams. On the other hand, it is unlikely that he would have used this terminology if in the previous month he had come to believe in the validity of special revelation via dreams and visions. Sometime in early 1522 at Wittenberg he presumably made some favorable comments about visions for someone—maybe only the biblical prophets—but one can be fairly certain, in light of his more explicit treatises, that he did not claim any special revelations for himself or others.[83]

In fact, the only place Karlstadt came at all close to approximating the ideas of the prophets was in his description of his call to preach. The prophets laid claim to a clear voice of God which authorized them to teach. Karlstadt, when challenged by an Electoral official, retorted: "The word has fallen upon me with great suddenness; woe is me if I do not preach." [84] And in *Malachiam* he again declared that anyone who is "driven" by the Spirit of God to proclaim the divine word is a messenger.[85] It is not impossible that the Zwickau Prophets prompted Karlstadt to stress the role of the Spirit in the minister's call. On the other hand, it is equally possible that it was the course of events rather than the new prophets which prompted the emergence of this new idea. At any rate it is essential to note that there was still a vast difference between Karlstadt's position and that of the Zwickau Prophets, for it was precisely the written biblical word which the Holy Spirit allegedly compelled and authorized Karlstadt to preach. Karlstadt's treatises and letters through February, 1522 at least, offer virtually no basis for asserting a similarity of thought between Karlstadt and the Zwickau Prophets. Thus if the radical left in the Wittenberg Movement is represented by the Zwickau Prophets with their belief in special revelations and their favorable attitude toward the sword as an instrument of change, it is clear that Karlstadt was still very much a moderate. In fact he was still busily working at change from within the system.

In extended consultation with the leading Reformers including Karlstadt and Melanchthon (who was still very eager for further

---

seind dem wind, staub, und leichtem rauch vergleicht. Drumb müssen alle Bepst, ym iunsten gericht antwort geben. Die sie ire dreume fur gotliche laher geleret, und die underthan getzwungen haben tzubewarung menschlicher gesetz." *Malachiam*, AivV-B. See also AiiiV-Aiv for his attack on the popes.

[83] For evidence that this was also true of Karlstadt in 1522-1524, see below chapter VII, nn. 249-254.

[84] Karlstadt to Einsiedel, Feb. 4, 1522 (see above, chapter IV, n. 170).

[85] *Malachiam*, Aii-Aiii (see above, chapter IV, n. 171).

innovations), the Wittenberg magistracy worked out an important decree which it enacted about January 24.[86] The measure covered many aspects of religious activity at the parish church. Since many priests celebrated the Eucharist differently after Karlstadt's modification of the Mass on December 25, the council wanted to introduce a uniform Eucharistic celebration.[87] The basic ideas behind Karlstadt's changes at Christmas had a common core from Luther, but it was Karlstadt who had implemented them. Thus it was fitting that the council's regulation of the Mass followed the pattern of Karlstadt's earlier service.[88] After the words of institution in German, the communicant was to take the bread and cup in his own hands. Private Masses were abolished. The images, whose removal Karlstadt had advocated since the previous summer, were to be taken from the churches under the direction of the city council.[89] Thus by January, 1522 significant modifications of religious life had been introduced.[90] So elated was Karlstadt with the new reforms that he reviewed them in his next publication and declared that God Almighty had stirred up the rulers' hearts and was effecting his work through them.[91] Genuine change within established structures seemed possible.

The measures adopted in January, however, represented the zenith of Karlstadt's success at Wittenberg. Governmental reaction to his

---

[86] *WB*, No. 74, p. 173 ("Philippus ardentissime rem agit") and No. 93, p. 194.

[87] *WB*, No. 93, p. 194.

[88] So *LuK*, pp. 51, 65-6. The details are in *WB*, No. 75, p. 174 and the actual decree is reprinted by H. Lietzmann, ed., *Die Wittenberger und Leisniger Kastenordnung* (Bonn, 1907), pp. 5-6 (section 14).

[89] *Ibid.*, p. 5. Neuser (*Abendmahlslehre Melanchthons*, p. 166) thinks the council's decision to remove the images probably occurred before Jan. 24. Section 13 speaks of "die bild in der kirchen" although the council had no authority over All Saints. *WB*, No. 93, p. 195 makes it very clear that the council intended to supervise the removal! For Karlstadt's earlier views, see *Gelubden*, CV and thesis 12 of July 22, 1521; T. Kolde, "Wittenberger Disputationsthesen," *ZKG*, XI, 463 (for the date of this thesis, see Barge, *Karlstadt*, I, 480).

[90] Both the theologians and the city council were also concerned to alleviate some of the town's social evils. See K. Pallas, ed., "Die Wittenberger Beutelordnung vom Jahre 1521 und ihr Verhältnis zu der Einrichtung des Gemeinen Kastens im Januar 1522. Aus dem Nachlasse des Professors D. Dr. Nic. Müller-Berlin," *Zeitschrift des Vereins für Kirchengeschichte in der Provinz Sachsen*, XII (1915), 1-45, and XIII (1916), 100-137. See also the interesting Marxist-oriented analysis in Gerhard Fuchs, "Karlstadts radikal-reformatorisches Wirken," *Wissenschaftliche Zeitschrift der Martin-Luther-Universität Halle-Wittenberg*, III (1953-54), 530-31.

[91] "Edeler wolgeborner, gnediger her, E.g. gebe ich tzuerkennen, das der almechtig lebentig, und starck Gott, unsserer regenten hertze erweigt, und sein werck in yenen gewirckt hat." *Abtuhung* (Jan. 27), ed. Lietzmann, p. 3.11-13.

allegedly revolutionary preaching and to the disorderly removal of images was to squelch his influence abruptly. Before this happened, however, he published his arguments against images on January 27.[92] His basic thesis was that the people do in fact trust in images and thus transgress the biblical command to trust in God alone who is One. "God forbids all kinds of images because men are thoughtless and inclined to worship them. Therefore, God says, 'You shall not worship them; you shall not honor them either.' "[93] Karlstadt's argument was legalistic in a sense. God's prohibition in the decalogue is the authority for removing them. Even if they were helpful, the prohibition would preclude their use.[94] And yet much of the treatise was a convincing argument that the people did in fact place in images the hope and trust which belongs to God alone.[95] The legal prohibition has a rational basis.

In spite of his elation over the council's decision to remove the images, Karlstadt was disappointed that they had not yet acted. He attempted to encourage prompt action by warning those in power that if they should fail to follow through with their decision, God would punish them.[96] On the other hand, if they do drive the wooden images from the church, they will deserve high praise. The story of Josiah proves that the secular rulers have authority to force the clergy to remove things condemned by scripture. "Therefore our magistrates should not wait until the clerics of Baal begin to remove their . . . logs [i.e. images] and obstruction. For they will never begin. The highest secular hand should command and act."[97] Karlstadt wanted immediate action by the city council.

---

[92] *Ibid.*, pp. 3-22. Although Karlstadt explicitly dated it "Montags nach Conversionis Pauli, 1522," (Lietzmann, p. 4.18), i.e., Jan. 27, the date has been confused. Rupp dates it on Nov. 30, 1521 ("Karlstadt," p. 315), and Williams (*Radical Reformation*, p. 42) on Jan. 22.

[93] "Sih wie Got allerley bilder verbeut, darumb das menschen leychtfertig seind, und gneigt, sie antzubeten. Der halben spricht Got, du solt sie nit anbetten, du salt sie auch nit eheren." *Abtuhung*, ed. Lietzmann, p. 7.24-26.

[94] *Ibid.*, p. 11.15-18 (see above chapter IV, n. 30).

[95] *Ibid.*, pp. 6.16-25, 11.35-12.4, 17.28-19.37 (19.3ff is especially important).

[96] "Ich hette auch gehofft, der lebentig Got solt seine eingegeben werck, das ist guten willen tzu abtuhung der bilder voltzogen, und yns eusserlich werck gefurt haben. Uber ess ist noch kein execution geschehen, vileicht derhalben, das Got seinen tzorn uber uns last treuffen, yn meynung seinen gantzen tzorn ausstzuschüden, wu wir alsso blind bleiben, und forchten unss vor dem, das uns nicht kan thun. Das weiss ich das die Obirsten derhalben gestrafft werden." *Ibid.*, p. 20.21-27.

[97] "Der konig Josias hat dem Obirste pontifex, und den andern pfaffen geboten, auff das sie alle vass, linden, und der gleichen Baal auss wurffen, und er verbrandt

Sometime before February 3, the council met Karlstadt's demand by announcing the date on which it would remove the images. Given the excited mood of the people, this announcement unfortunately produced further rioting on or before the appointed day. A crowd pulled down and burned many images.[98] It may have been political considerations which prompted electoral intervention at this point.[99] Convinced that Karlstadt's and Zwilling's preaching had helped foment the rioting, Einsiedel (the Elector's representative in Wittenberg) informed Karlstadt in a letter of February 3 that he should be careful to exercise discretion in his preaching lest riots (*Aufruhr*) occur. Furthermore, he should not preach in places where he had not been called.[100]

How fair were these two implicit charges? In his reply to Einsiedel on February 4, Karlstadt insisted that he hated and forbade disorderly tumult.[101] Müller, however, has argued that this denial is irrelevant because we do not know if Karlstadt considered unauthorized removal of images riotous activity.[102] Einsiedel repeatedly referred to Karlstadt's "tumultuous" preaching.[103] Even more important, he charged

---

sie ausswenig der statt Hierusalem. Darauss sal yderman mercken, wie die pfaffen, den konigen untherdenig sollen sein, auss gotlichem rechten. Derwegen solten unssere Magistraten nit erwarten, biss die pfaffen Baal, ire gevess Klotzer, und verhindernis anfahen ausstzufüren. Dan sie werden niemer mher anfahen. Die obirste weltliche hand soll gebieten und schaffen." *Ibid.*, pp. 20.38-21.5.

[98] Since the allusions to the actual disorder are very brief, it is difficult to assess its extent. The evidence is in *WB*, No. 92, p. 191 and No. 93, p. 195. There is no evidence to warrant the statement that Karlstadt and Zwilling "led a mob to the Town Church, despoiled the gravestones, and vandalized images." C. L. Manschreck, *Melanchthon* (New York, 1958), p. 79.

[99] Barge and Müller disagreed over who made the first move and why, and Köhler (*GGA*, pp. 527-8) argued that Barge failed to prove that the Jan. 20 mandate of the Nürnberg diet which was directed against the religious innovations in Germany was the initial cause of the intervention. Cf. Neuser, *Abendmahlslehre Melanchthons*, pp. 177ff, for a recent discussion of the political pressure on the Elector. Certainly allusions to the mandate of Jan. 20 are detectable after the Electoral intervention in Wittenberg had begun. Christian Beyer, the Wittenberg Burgomaster, may have helped precipitate Einsiedel's action (*WB*, Nos. 75-77, 79-80, pp. 174-7).

[100] *WB*, No. 81, pp. 177-8.

[101] "Dass wil ich mich auch berumen, dass ich auffrur hasss und flih. Got geb, dass meine angeber nit mit der czeit eynen auffrur werden erwecken, der nit gut wirt. Ich verbit auffrur." *WB*, No. 83, p. 181.

[102] *LuK*, pp. 68ff. Köhler agrees (*GGA*, pp. 526-7).

[103] "Ungestumen predigen Karlstat" (*WB*, No. 80, p. 177) and "uffrurigenn predig" (No. 97, p. 204). In *ibid.*, p. 205, Einsiedel reported that Karlstadt could not deny that the previous "auffrur" had resulted from his and Zwilling's preaching. But this must be viewed together with the fact that in the negotiations with

that Karlstadt and Zwilling had declared that if the government failed to act, then "dye gemein" had power to do so.[104]

Was Karlstadt beginning to despair of change through duly constituted channels? It is extremely unlikely that Karlstadt called on "the common man" to form a riotous crowd and pull down the images. In his work on images, as has been noted above, he had indeed called for their prompt removal, but he explicitly stated that this task was the duty of the rulers. In discussing their failure to act, he had mentioned the possibility of divine punishment but not the legitimacy of plebeian intervention.[105] Furthermore, it is possible that even though only Zwilling called for direct action by the masses (*dye gemein*), Karlstadt was tarred with the same brush.[106] In subsequent negotiations, the committee (which included Karlstadt but not Zwilling), insisted that only the established government had the authority to remove images. And they denied all responsibility for the rioters' behavior.[107]

How accurate was the charge of unauthorized preaching? It has generally been assumed that Einsiedel's reference to unauthorized

---

Einsiedel, the committee (which included Karlstadt) denied all responsibility for this riot (*WB*, No. 93, p. 195).

[104] "Sye sagenn, das dye gemein woll macht habe, in Nachlessigkeyt der oberkeyt" (*WB*, No. 89, p. 186). This document dates from Feb. 8, 1522.

[105] See above, nn. 96-97.

[106] As n. 104 shows, Einsiedel said on Feb. 8 that Karlstadt and Zwilling both taught that when the government delayed, the people had the right to act. Einsiedel's first letter (Feb.3) to Karlstadt, however, was very general (*WB*, No. 81, pp. 177-8). It did *not* accuse Karlstadt of calling for direct action by "dye gemein." The same day, however, Einsiedel did make precisely this charge against Zwilling in a letter to Melanchthon: "So jch dan bericht, das magister Gabriell sich zu weyllenn mit auffrurischen wortenn vornemen lasss, mit unterweyssung, wie diss oder das solt vnnd mocht durch dye gemein geandert werden" (*WB*, No. 82, p. 179). Neuser (*Abendmahlslehre Melanchthons*, p. 174) also notes this difference in the two letters of Feb. 3. It is possible that Zwilling's more radical statements were subsequently attributed unfairly to Karlstadt as well as himself. Zwilling apparently was also quite ready personally to lead some rather violent activity. ". . . hat er [Zwilling] folgends freitags [10. Januar] mit etzlichen monchen ein fewer jns Augustiner closter hof gemacht, jst jn die kirche mit jnen gangen, hat die holtzern altaria zu grund abgebrochen, dieselbigen mit jren und sonst allen andern tafeln, gemalten und geschnitzten bildern, Crucifixen, fannen, kerzen, leuchtern, etc. allezumal dem fewer zu getragen, dorein geworfen und vorbrandt. . . ." Johann Pfab to Hermann Mühlpfort, early 1522; Ernst Fabian, "Zwei gleichzeitige Berichte von Zwickauern über die Wittenberger Unruhen 1521 und 1522," *Mitteilungen des Altertumsvereins für Zwickau und Umgegend*, XI (1914), p. 30. (For this reference, I am indebted to Professor Johannes Wallmann.) There is no evidence that Karlstadt engaged in this kind of activity.

[107] *WB*, No. 93, p. 195.

preaching referred to sermons at the parish church where Karlstadt had no specific authorization to preach.[108] He did in fact hold one evangelical mass there on January 1, but he did so with the consent and assistance of the parish minister![109] The documents contain no explicit reference to any further sermons at the parish church.[110] Karlstadt, at any rate, apparently thought Einsiedel was objecting to the new sermons at All Saints which he had substituted for Vespers. He correctly informed Einsiedel that he had the right to preach at All Saints, and to undertake the new sermons at the time of Vespers.[111]

---

[108] Rupp speaks of Karlstadt's "illegal intrusion into the parish church" (*Patterns of Reformation*, p. 107).

[109] The following passage seems to have been largely overlooked in previous discussion. "D. Karolstadius die Circuncisionis [January 1] duas habuit conciones de sacramento Eucharistiae et in parochia [parish church] *consenciente ac administrante Parocho* [Simon Heins, the parish minister] populum pane ac vino cibavit" (*WB*, No. 63, p. 136). It is not made explicit, but the sermons need not have been in the "parocia" since they are related before the "et." Furthermore, in an official statement sent to Einsiedel on Feb. 13, 1522 by Melanchthon, Jonas, Karlstadt, Amsdorff, etc., it was stated: "Karstat eyns yn dem stifft das ander mal in der pfar dy messe vorendert (*WB*, No. 93, p. 194).

[110] Müller (*LuK*, p. 69 and n. 5) implies frequent sermons by Karlstadt at the parish church, but cites no evidence other than Einsiedel's vague statement of Feb. 3 which does not mention the *Pfarrkirche*, and an accusation of Luther made in 1524 (*WA*, XV, 338)!

The following statement of Einsiedel from Feb. 14, 1522 is unclear: "Nachdem auch doctor Karlstat zugesagt, sich hinfurder dergleichen predigens zuenthaltenn . . . [and since Zwilling has left town], So vorhoff jch, es werde woll bey der ordnung, So syeder der zeit abegeredt unnd sye unns jetz ubergebenn, bleybenn, Sonderlich weill sich Ambstorff, welcher jetz prediger in der pfarkirchen ist, Erbotten, das volck dazu zuundterweyssenn" (*WB*, No. 97, p. 205). This could mean that, according to Einsiedel, order had been disrupted both by the tumultuous character of Karlstadt's sermons and the fact that they were preached at the parish church without authorization. Since Amsdorf had now replaced him there, Einsiedel hoped for an end to disorder. The stated reason, however, for Einsiedel's high expectations for Amsdorf is that he had offered to instruct the people— probably about the evil of *Aufruhr*. "Dergleichen" probably pertains not to the location of Karlstadt's sermons, but to their character. Thus this passage does not provide any clear proof that Karlstadt had preached at the parish church other than on January 1, at the introduction of the new mass when he had the consent of the parish minister.

[111] *WB*, No. 83, pp. 180-1. These sermons were obviously at All Saints. Another document proves that "die Pfaffen" (probably the conservatives of the chapter) objected to Karlstadt's sermons at Vespers (*WB*, No. 68, p. 163). On Feb. 13 Frederick insisted on knowing "worumb nicht wesper gehaltten ader plallirt [=psalliert] werde." (*WB*, No. 92, p. 192). Since the regulations of the chapter state that "die predicature yn der stiefftkirchenn sall der Archydiaconus vorsorgenn" (*Karlstadt*, II, 528), Karlstadt did have the right to make these changes. The statement from Feb. 8 that Karlstadt "zu predigenn unerfordert eyndrynngen" (*WB*, No. 89, p. 186) is Einsiedel's mistaken interpretation of either Karlstadt's Vesper sermons or his Mass at the parish church or both.

Thus there is absolutely no clear evidence that Karlstadt preached where he had not been "called" in early 1522.

The governmental machinery, however, had already begun to move because significant innovation at Wittenberg was politically inexpedient. On February 2 Einsiedel had reported Karlstadt's allegedly tumultuous preaching to the Elector who had then instructed him to negotiate with the city council, university and chapter in order to prevent further disorder.[112] After preliminary meetings, important negotiations took place on February 13 between Einsiedel and a committee from the university and chapter. It included Karlstadt and Melanchthon. In his instructions for these negotiations, Frederick the Wise indicated that he wanted the elevation of the host restored, the handling of the sacrament by the communicant in his own hands ended, further removal of images prohibited and the private Mass permitted. Further, most of the innovations of January 24 were to be discussed. Above all, further riot was to be prevented. Finally, "if one could arrange it so that Karlstadt would not preach, that would not be amiss." [113] The negotiations did not result in a total return to the situation which existed before January 24, for some aspects of the council's decree were accepted. The committee, however, acquiesced in all Frederick's specific demands.[114] Karlstadt for his part at least agreed to abandon the kind of preaching which had proved disturbing; he was probably also forbidden to preach at all.[115]

---

[112] *WB*, No. 80, p. 177. Einsiedel's letter of Feb. 14 (*WB*, No. 97, pp. 203ff) contains the best narrative of subsequent events. See too Müller's reconstruction (*LuK*, pp. 73ff).

[113] *WB*, No. 92, 192-3. "Wu man Karolstat vermocht, das er nicht prediget, so were es nit Ungut" (p. 193).

[114] *WB*, No. 97, p. 205 and No. 95, p. 201. See too *LuK*, pp. 79-80.

[115] The three bits of evidence are not entirely clear. Barge says that Karlstadt promised "sich fürderhin des Predigens zu enthalten" (*Karlstadt*, I, 412 and *FG*, p. 121), but Müller rightly shows (*LuK*, p. 77, n. 3) that Barge omitted an important word: "Karlstat zugesagt, sich hinfurder *dergleichen* predigens zuenthaltenn" (*WB*, No. 97, p. 205). One could conclude from this statement that he was allowed to preach provided that the sermons were not "tumultuous." On March 19, 1522, however, Luther told Link via letter: "Certum est, ei interdicere suggestu [pulpit], quod ipse temeritate propria, nulla vocatione, invitis Deo [!] et hominibus conscendit" (*WABr*, II, 478.7-9). If P. Smith's translation, "he will be forbidden to enter the pulpit" (*Luther's Correspondence* [2 vols.; Philadelphia, 1918], II, 112), is correct, then there presumably was a prohibition directed against Karlstadt sometime after March 19, 1522. It is true that the statement does not specify what pulpit is denied Karlstadt. Conceivably it was only that of the *Pfarrkirche*. On the other hand, since the word "pulpit" is not qualified at all, it tends to

The final act of the Wittenberg Movement opened when Luther returned home on March 6.[116] In eight forceful sermons beginning the following Sunday, he quickly regained control of the reformation in Wittenberg and satisfied the Elector's concern for law and order. In addition to the changes already agreed to in the negotiations with the Elector's representative on February 13, several other traditional practices were restored.[117] Even though the committee had insisted strongly that the Eucharistic words of institution should be in German because "taking communion is in vain without an understanding of the word," [118] Luther restored the old custom. He again spoke the

imply a general prohibition. Enders has noted that since preaching at All Saints was part of his official duties (and rights) as Archdeacon, it is puzzling how this task could be removed without depriving him of the archdeaconry. *Dr. Martin Luthers Briefwechsel* (19 vols.; Stuttgart and Leipzig, 1884ff), III, 317. On the other hand, Karlstadt later used precisely his position as archdeacon to argue that he had wrongly been prohibited from preaching in 1522! In the angry exchange at Jena in 1524 Karlstadt charged that Luther had fettered him hand and foot in 1522. When Luther asked "when", Karlstadt added: "Was das nicht gebunden unnd geschlagenn, do ir alleine wyder mich schrybt, druckt unnd predigt unnd verschuft, das mir meine bücher auss der druckerey genomen und ich zuschreyben und predigen verbotten wart? Het ich so frey dürffen schreyben und predigen als eben ir, fürwar ir solt es erfarn habenn was mein geyst aussgericht hette." *WA*, XV, 337.30-338.2. When Luther asked why he wanted to preach where he had not been called, Karlstadt replied: "Wann wir von der menschen beruffung wöllen reden, so weyss ich wol, das mirs von wegen des Archidiaconats was gebüren." *Ibid.*, p. 338.4-5. This statement can only pertain to preaching at All Saints, because Karlstadt could not assert that his archdeaconry gave him the right to preach at the parish church. The statutes did no such thing, but they did put him in charge of preaching at All Saints (see above, n. 111). Hence, Karlstadt presumably was objecting to a prohibition against his preaching at All Saints. It is true that Luther then went on to ask who commanded Karlstadt to preach at the parish church. But Karlstadt's reply was not that his archdeaconry authorized that, but rather that the same people attended both places. Probably then, Luther turned to Karlstadt's preaching at the parish church because he thought he had a legitimate argument there whereas he knew Karlstadt was right in the case of the prohibition concerning All Saints (the entire incident is in *WA*, XV, 337.29-338.10). One cannot, however, be absolutely certain about this reconstruction. Apart from this cautionary note, however, I agree with Barge (*FG*, pp. 306-8). Hillerbrand ("Karlstadt," p. 387) also agrees with Barge.

[116] Since his return was not prompted by any new activity on Karlstadt's part, the various reasons for the return are more appropriately discussed in a volume on Luther than in a work on Karlstadt.

[117] Müller, *LuK*, pp. 106-8

[118] "Dy weil aber nwe man hath orden mussen, do hath es Christlich anderss nit gescheen mogen, Dan das dy wort der gebenedeiung czu dewtzsch vom prister gesprochen werdent, auss ursach, Das alles Communicirn vorgebens ist on vorstandt der wort der gebenedeyung. Dan alle krafft des sacraments sthehet yn dyssen worten, und ist gebotten ym evangelio: das thut yn meym gedechtnuss." *WB*, No. 93, p. 196; Feb. 13, 1522.

words of institution softly in Latin while facing the altar. The cup
was again denied to the laity in public services, although special
services were made available for those who wanted both. Luther, of
course, was not opposed to the new practices which he abolished, but
he was unwilling to tolerate changes until the word had first been
preached. Only after the word had convinced the weak (and the
princes) should old customs and practices be changed.[119]

Luther did not condemn Karlstadt publicly, but his sermons and
actions inevitably wounded his colleague deeply. In his first sermon
Luther criticized the fact that the Mass had been changed suddenly
without the approval of the authorities.[120] The practice of placing
the sacrament in the hands of the communicant received Luther's
particularly vigorous condemnation.[121] In both cases Luther was
criticizing Karlstadt's action of December 25. Privately Luther said
of Karlstadt that "since he did not come from God, so he did not
teach the things of God." In fact, he had returned to Wittenberg to
"destroy this theatre of Satan." [122] With Luther's return, then, Karlstadt's significant role in Wittenberg ended. So did Karlstadt's
initially successful attempt to introduce rapid change by working
within established structures.

---

[119] See below chapter VI, nn. 95-100, 108.

[120] *WA*, X/3, 9.7-13 (see below, chapter VI, n. 110). See also Müller, *LuK*, p.
106.

[121] *WA*, X/3, 42.4-45.8; *LuK*, pp. 106-8. Barge is surely correct in insisting that
the communicant's taking the sacrament himself was a clear way of symbolizing
the end of priestly mediation of grace (*FG*, p. 201).

[122] "Satanas fecit irruptionem in hanc caulam meam. . . . Carlstadius et Gabriel
horum autores fuerunt monstrorum. . . . Ideo sicut ex Deo non venit, ita ex Deo
non docuit. . . . Haec causa coegit me redire, ut, si Christus velit, hanc scenam
Satanae destruam." Luther to Link, March 19, 1522, *WABr*, II, 478.2-13. Since
the relationship between Luther and Karlstadt after March, 1522 provided
the background for Karlstadt's move to Orlämunde, the details will be left for the
next chapter.

# CHAPTER SIX

# THE MOVE TO ORLAMÜNDE AND EXPULSION FROM SAXONY

## (1523-1524)

### 1. KARLSTADT'S POSITION AFTER LUTHER'S RETURN

Within a few short weeks Karlstadt fell from the position of a successful leader of a reform movement to that of a man suspected of connections with Satan and sedition. In mid-March Luther asked Spalatin to pray that he would be able to tread underfoot the Satan in Wittenberg. Karlstadt, he added, was finding it hard to abandon his views.[1] At this point Karlstadt could have apologized for his excessive zeal and worked behind the scenes as one of Luther's important lieutenants to foster as much change as possible. Then as now, however, the rigidity and slowness of existing structures sometimes radicalizes those who press unsuccessfully for rapid change. Disillusionment over the pace of change at Wittenberg was eventually to lead Karlstadt to seek another location to develop his program. But the emergence of a more radical stance took time.

Karlstadt's first move was to vent his anger by writing a tract in defense of the innovations Luther had dropped. He condemned the tyrants' refusal to allow the layman to take the chalice in his own hands, demanded that the words of consecration be spoken loudly in German on pain of mortal sin, rejected preparatory confession as a papistic ulcer and denounced the papist defense of elevation. In order to soften the impact, however, he referred to Luther as his friend and directed his explicit attack against the Catholic, Ochsenfahrt, who continued to defend the Eucharistic sacrifice.[2] Karlstadt's language

---

[1] "Tu fac ores pro me et iuues Satanam istum conculcare, qui se erexit Vittembergae adversus Evangelion sub nomine Evangelii. Cum angelo in angelum lucis verso iam pugnamus. Carlstadio difficile erit sensum caedere, At Christus coget eum, si non cesserit sponte." Luther to Spalatin, March 13, 1522; *WABr*, II, 471.19-23. Cf. also chapter V, n. 122. See also Luther to Kaspar Güttel, March 30, 1522; *WABr*, II, 491.5-16.

[2] Barge has reprinted the censor's excerpts (*Karlstadt*, II, 563-5). "Non est prohibendum laicis ne in manus calicem suscipiant, exemplo cene domini. Qui hoc prohibuerint, tyranni sunt" (p. 563). "Minister sacramenti vertat se ad populum et ad populum loquatur. Non secreto verba dicenda consecrationis. . . . Qui non vertunt se ad populum his verbis, faciunt populum peccare mortaliter"

was no more violent than Luther's letters, but it was intended for the public. Luther felt compelled to warn Karlstadt privately that he would attack him in print if he published the tract.³ The university, for its part, used its established power to seize Karlstadt's half-printed work and forbid its publication.⁴ In spite of his December 19, 1521 agreement to permit continued written debate apropos the Mass, the Elector accepted the university's decision, although he urged decent treatment for Karlstadt.⁵ Karlstadt was furious.⁶

In time, however, he apparently calmed down for he continued with his academic duties for a time. He was dean of the theological faculty for the winter semester 1522-1523.⁷ Luther noted on January 2, 1523 that Karlstadt's lectures were "excellent" and numerous enough although not very regular.⁸ One cannot assume from Luther's favorable comment that all friction had disappeared for that same day Melanchthon expressed the fear that Karlstadt might injure the evangelical cause to avenge a private affront.⁹ Most of the time, however, there was probably little visible friction.¹⁰ Karlstadt apparently decided to swallow his resentment.

---

(p. 564). "Diabolus est confessionis pater, in qua nichil boni. Ex ovili detrudes oves Christi fistula papistica, dum doces confessionem. Amicum [!] habeo qui putat ante eucharistiam confitendum . . ." (564). "Utcunque excusant papiste, elevatio tamen non bona est" (565).

³ Luther to Spalatin, April 21, 1522; *WABr*, II, 509.11-12. Luther denied, however, that he urged the university to act.

⁴ University to the Elector, April 27, 1522; *Karlstadt*, II, 562-3.

⁵ See chapter V, n. 46 for the Elector's December statement. The Elector to the University, April 30, 1522; *Karlstadt*, II, 565-6. Müller (*LuK*, p. 133) explains the Elector's letter differently, but Barge's rebuttal is decisive (*FG*, pp. 217, 318).

⁶ The university informed the Elector in its letter of April 27 that he planned to attack them in print, but he apparently repented (*Karlstadt*, II, 563). The Jena confrontation in 1524, however, provides an illustration of how much he resented this censorship (see above, chapter V, n. 115). Another book on images which he had written against Emser was also suppressed, perhaps by Karlstadt himself (*Gemach*, Hertzsch, I, 90.8-12).

⁷ See my "Karlstadt and Luther's Doctorate," *JTS*, XXII (1971), 169, n. 2.

⁸ "Quamquam Philippi et Carlstadii lectiones, ut sunt optimae, ita et abundent, Tamen et Pomerani nolim abesse, quod Carlstadii sit incerti temporis." Luther to Spalatin; *WABr*, III, 2.43-45. Barge (*Karlstadt*, II, 3) understood this to mean that they were well attended, but I have followed Smith, *Luther's Correspondence*, II, 156.

⁹ "Quae de Alphabeto [Karlstadt] scribis, nonnihil commoverunt. Vereor enim ne vir ille privatam contumeliam, quam putat, ulturus, novo scandalo caussam [sic] evangelicam oneret." Melanchthon to Camerarius, Jan. 2, 1523; *CR*, I, 599.

¹⁰ So Hillerbrand, "Carlstadt," p. 387, and Müller (albeit somewhat too insistently), *LuK*, p. 135. In a letter to Paul Speratus Luther sent Karlstadt's

## 2. DID KARLSTADT EXPERIENCE A CONVERSION AFTER LUTHER'S RETURN?

Erich Hertzsch has suggested that in spite of Karlstadt's acceptance of a new theology in 1517, he had nevertheless experienced very little inner ethical renewal. Only after the radical, abrupt change in Karlstadt's position resulting from Luther's return to Wittenberg did Karlstadt undergo a "conversion." [11] Although the evidence for such a view is hardly adequate,[12] it is clear that Karlstadt experienced a substantial alteration in his basic life-style. Our professor rejected his doctoral title and adopted the role of peasant. In the introduction, it was noted that Karlstadt may have had an inferiority complex which led to a desperate search for tangible signs of success and status. Apparently, Karlstadt interpreted his fall from power as divine chastisement for this intense love of honor and status.[13] In response Karlstadt made an honest attempt to adopt a more simple life-style and forgo angry polemic.[14]

Karlstadt attempted to disentangle himself from what he had come to see as self-seeking competition in the university by a dramatic move which would have delighted some contemporary student radicals. On February 3, 1523 after promoting two students, Karlstadt made the startling announcement that henceforth he would not take part in the granting of academic degrees. Apparently so stunned that he said nothing at the time, Luther later noted in the dean's book that Karlstadt appealed to Matthew 23's injunction against calling anyone master or father.[15] Karlstadt's reasons were clearer in one of the two treatises published a few weeks later under the inscription, "Andreas Karlstadt, a new layman." He confessed that formerly he had studied in order to write well and win disputes. Now, however, he saw that it

---

greetings along with Melanchthon's (*WABr* II, 531.32). Karlstadt was invited to Link's wedding along with all the other Wittenbergers in April, 1523 (*WABr*, III, 53.2-5).

[11] Hertzsch, *Bedeutung*, p. 16 and "Luther und Karlstadt," pp. 94-6.

[12] Hillerbrand, "Carlstadt," p. 387.

[13] On December 21, 1522 he reminded Müntzer that when one feels pierced by the blow of one's enemy, one can be very certain that God is chastising one "by all means because of sin:" "Verum si interdum et sibimetipsi plaga inimici percussisse videtur, id itidem cum iudicio factum adseverat, quippe quod propter peccatum." (Karlstadt to Müntzer; Franz, ed., *Müntzer: Schriften und Briefe*, p. 386.25-27). See the Introduction for a discussion of the thesis that Karlstadt may have had an inferiority complex.

[14] After the initial outburst against Luther, Karlstadt managed to forgo violent polemic until publicly challenged by Luther.

[15] Förstemann, *Liber decanorum*, p. 28.

was very wrong to study scripture for the selfish purpose of knowing it better than another.[16] More directly, he argued that people seek nothing but the praise of men in the universities. They become masters or doctors and give presents for the sake of worldly honor. They arrogantly refuse to sit with those who possess fewer degrees. "Although I or someone else should want to deny this, God would still . . . convince us that we . . . bow the knee, pay money, and establish festivities and costly meals for the sake of university glory in order that we have authority with the people and are respected." [17]

Karlstadt preferred to adopt the role of a peasant. Sometime in 1523 he put aside his academic dress, adopted the felt hat and gray garb of the peasants and urged his neighbors to call him "brother Andrew." [18] Disillusioned with the intellectual elite, Karlstadt moved to identify with the people. In reply to Luther's satirical reference to the

---

[16] "Ich wenet ich wer ain Christ gewest wann ich tyeffe und schöne sprüch auss Hiere. geschrifft klaubet, und behielte sy zü der disputation, lection, predig, oder ander reden und schreyben. . . . Was ist dise weysshait anders, dann ain weysshait in menschen augen. Wann wir die schrifft und andere creaturen (auss wölchen wir Gott solten erkennen und lieben) zü unserm lust eintragen, und wöllen etwas vor aynem andern wissen, als layder vil layen yetz die schrifft fassen und lernen, das sy in zaichen wol leben und reden etwas vor ainen andern wissen, ist das nitt ain weysshait in unsern augen?" *Sich Gelassen*, bV-bii.

[17] "In den hohen schülen was süchet man anders dann eere von den andern. Derhalben wirt ainer Magister, der ander Doctor und dartzü Doctor der hayligen geschrifft, geben auch gütt und gab umb die eere die Christus seinen leeriungern verbotten hat und wöllen dannocht die jhenen sein, die Christlichen glauben leren, und erhalten, wöllen unsere mayster und Doctores genennt seyn, wie wol sy Doctorliche eere mitt sollichem geytz und frass süchen, das sy alle andere gleychmessiger leer neyden und vervolgen, wann sy jre eere erkaufft haben, und wöllen auch kaynen lassen auffkommen, oder bey sich lassen sitzen der nit gleychen namen hat, und ob ich oder ain ander das wölten vernaynen, wurden unns doch Gottes augen mitt jrem durch scheynenden blick treffen unnd uberzeügen, das wir von wegen universistetischer glorien nider knyehen, gelt geben, hochtzeyt oder kostliche maltzeyt auffrichten, als darumb das wir bey den leütten ain authoritet haben, und angesehen werden, und wöllen dannocht nitt hören das wir ungleubig seind." *Ibid.*, eiiiV. Contemporaries who fear that professors sometimes pursue publications and lucrative positions more ardently than truth will empathize with Karlstadt's attack on the academic world.

[18] "Wie dunckt dich nü? ists nicht eyne feyne newe geystliche demut? grawen rock und filtzhut tragen, nicht wollen Doctor heyssen sondern bruder Andres und lieber nahbar wie eyn ander baur, dem richter zu Orlamünde unterworffen seyn und gehorchen wie eyn schlechter bürger. . . ." *LW*, XL, 117; *WA*, XVIII, 100.27-101.1. Luther was describing the situation at Orlamünde but Karlstadt may very well have done this sooner, for he seems to have become involved in farming before going to Orlamünde permanently (see below n. 20). Here too one thinks of the emphasis which the contemporary radical places upon external signs of his rejection of established values and mores.

peasant's garb, he noted that his gray cloak, unlike Luther's cowl, did not announce a suspect holiness. Furthermore, costly clothes deceive simple people who consider the cheaply dressed man a fool and the man in velvet intelligent regardless of their respective ability.

> Now if I can endure the fact that the world despises me, what concern is it of Luther's? . . . Doctor Luther should also know that I (God be praised) have a horror of adornment which once almost seduced me and brought me into sin. I thank God for that although no garment damns me or makes me holy.[19]

Peasants' clothing is more in keeping with Christ's example than satin, silk and velvet.

The trustworthy evidence is sparse, but it appears that Karlstadt did at least a little farming at this time.[20] "Would to God that I were a true peasant, husbandman or craftsman," he told Luther in early 1525. Aware of his position as a member of a privileged professional class, he confessed the guilt he felt for having lived from the labor of impecunious peasants without having given anything in return. Farming is an "honest mortification of the flesh."

> I thank God that his divine grace has graciously brought me to the frame of mind where I would gladly do [peasants'] work now without dread of what the whole world says. What do you think Luther? Are not blisters on your hands more honorable than golden rings?[21]

---

[19] "D. Luther: Sy tragen grawe Röcke. Carolstat: Was schadt mir ein gemeyn kleyd, geb ich doch durch einen grawen Rocke kein anzeyg verdechtlicher heyligkeit, als D. Luther mit seyner heyligen Cappen thut. . . . Aber das weyss ich dannocht wol, das man vil einfeltige lewtte mit köstlichen Kleydern betreügt, und das vil narren nach den Kleydern, die person, die kunst, und die heyligkeit urteylen, Der geringe Kleyder tregt, der ist der wellt Narr und Aff, wie geschickt er ist, wenn aber ein Narr einen Samet antrüg, er wurd für redlich und klug gehalten. Nu wenn ichs leyden kündt das mich die wellt verachtet, Was lygt denn D. Luthern dran? . . . Nu soll D. Luther dartzu wissen, das ich, Gott lob, einen grawen hab, gegen dem schmuck, der mich zeytten fast belusten thet, und zu sünden bracht, und ich danck Got drumb, wiewol mich kein Kleyd verdampt oder heylig machet. . . . Ein stoltz Kleyd das fürdert das stoltz fleysch." *Anzeig*, Hertzsch, II, 94.12-95.8. Cf. also *Dialogus*, Hertzsch, II, 39.11-21 where Karlstadt mocked the proud clothes of the clerics.

[20] In a Dec. 21, 1522 letter to Müntzer, Karlstadt said: "Deducam te in novum meum hospitium, quod in rure comparavi." Franz, ed., *Müntzer: Schriften und Briefe*, p. 387.12. Müntzer addressed his July 29, 1523 letter to "Carolostadio in Worlitz agricolae" (*ibid.*, p. 393.1). See Barge (*Karlstadt* II, 14, n. 26) and Jäger (*Carlstadt*, pp. 301-2) for the unreliability of Fröschel's report.

[21] "Wölte Got das ich ein rechter Bawr, Ackersman oder handtwercksman were, das ich mein brot im gehorsam Gottes ess, das ist, im schweyss meines angesichts, Ich hab aber der armen lewt arbeyt gessen, den ich gar nichts darfür thon hab, hab sy dartzu nicht zu recht hand gehabt, noch vermöcht handthaben [=schützen], Jedoch nichts destmynder ire arbeytt in mein hauss genommen,

Karlstadt apparently saw the adoption of the peasant's role as a way of escaping his former dependence on academic status and expensive clothing.

Evidence from late in 1523 indicates that he was also attempting to avoid angry polemics. In explanation of his recent literary silence in 1522-3, he noted that to be silent was more advantageous to himself than to write or preach. He lamented the fact that the vicious attacks of the Catholics had prompted the evangelicals to excessively sharp, scornful rebuttals.[22] "I cannot answer their useless, scornful words without arrogance," he confessed. "I hardly write without speaking scornfully." [23] Karlstadt's silence, of course, was related not only to his inner self, but also to the absence of a press! When a press at Jena became available in late 1523, he used it. The kinds of things he then published, however, suggest that the words of *Ursachen* must be taken with some seriousness. In spite of his resentment against Luther, Karlstadt chose to develop his own theological emphasis without directly attacking Luther. Only one of the treatises published during his stay at Orlamünde was devoted directly to the issues over which he and Luther had clashed, and even this treatise was not violent at all. Luther was not mentioned.[24] Karlstadt did not publish *Gemach*, his

---

vermöcht ichs, ich wölt inen alles widergeben, das ich entpfangen. Gott hatt Adam ein gebott geben, das er arbeytten soll, und das gebott lauttet von der arbeyt des feldes.... Und solche arbeyt ist ein redliche tödtung des fleysches.... Das will ich aber Got dancken, das mich seyn götliche genad, auss gnaden, zu dem gemüet gebracht, das ich yetzt one schew, aller welt rede unnd wort, gern wolt arbeyten. Wie meynstu Luther ob uns blassen nicht eerlicher in den henden stünden, denn guldene rewffe?" *Anzeig*, Hertzsch, II, 95.21-96.5. This again is from 1525, but if Karlstadt was a farmer in 1523, this statement applies to that period also.

[22] "Vor allem wisset yhr die uberschwenckliche bossheit diser zeytten in wellichen die lieb erkalt und erloschen.... Man hört grymmig zeen klappern, unnd sihet die auffgesperte rachen der Lawhen unnd Beren, derhalbenn die Evangelische prediger vorursacht, widerumb etwas zu vil scheltenn und hönen. Vorgessen auch das sie nit ubel reden sollen, sondern nur ubel hören, und schemen sich nit das sie yhr büchleyn mehr mit scheltworten erfüllen, dan mit götlichen reden und schrifftlichen ursachen ires syns unnd vorstands." *Ursachen*, (Dec., 1523), Hertzsch, I, 3.20-30.

[23] "Auch ist es euch unverborgen, das ich mich schwerlich vor inen bergen kan, und das ich uff ir unnütze scheltwort one uppikeit nit antworten kan, dadurch ich den unverstendigen, einen strick ires erkentnis möcht legen (als etlich than haben) unnd mich ein ursach setzen, des abbruchs götlicher liebe.... Da habt ir ein ursach, worumb ich biss her, in gutem frid unnd stil gesessen bin, unnd hinfurt sitzen wolt. Nemlich das ich one hönreden schwerlich schreiben, und durch böse wort, meine brüder ergern möcht." *Ibid.*, p. 5.3-14.

[24] *Vorstandt* was an attempt to refute the allegedly widespread use of Romans 9:3 to support the thesis that brotherly love can compel one to delay implemen-

direct reply to Luther's demand to proceed slowly enunciated in the eight sermons of March 1522 until after his expulsion from Orlamünde in the fall of 1524. This delay suggests that he made a serious attempt in 1523 and early 1524 to avoid bitter polemic. That Karlstadt's attempt was ultimately unsuccessful is abundantly clear from the violence of the Eucharistic writings which Luther dared him to publish. Nevertheless, if one speaks of a conscious attempt to change rather than a conversion, Hertzsch's basic thesis is both defensible and illuminating.

### 3. KARLSTADT'S INCREASED INTEREST IN THE GERMAN MYSTICS

That Karlstadt turned to the mystics' writings with intense interest at this time is hardly surprising. As occasional passages from 1518 on indicate, he had been reading them for a long time. In 1522 and 1523, however, they were particularly appropriate to his situation and concerns. At a time when external activity via pulpit and pen were severely restricted, they encouraged him to look inward. Their great emphasis on the abandonment of the egocentric self must have proved helpful at a time when he was struggling to conquer an unpleasant, selfish personality. That Tauler esteemed the *Lebenmeister* more highly than the *Lesenmeister*, may have hastened Karlstadt's increasing disenchantment with the vanities of academe.[25] Nor would Karlstadt have been displeased by the fact that the mystics used the language of the layman.[26] At the beginning of the work on *Gelassenheit*, he noted that the word "gelassen" was used frequently by the Brandenburg peasants.[27] The mystics must have proved congenial companions when Karlstadt escaped to rural solitude.

---

tation of a divine command. Karlstadt kept the discussion at the abstract level except for one reference to "cursed images" (Aii). *Von manigfeltigkeit*, Biiif is a good illustration of the way Karlstadt developed his own views without attacking Luther. In this section, he referred briefly to (unnamed) frivolous people who did not take sin seriously, and then went on to develop his emphasis on the great importance of obeying God's law. The first edition of *Fürbit Marie* (Bl. 6V, lines 24-25) is the only place where Karlstadt names Luther directly, and the reference is positive.

[25] See for example Vetter, 196. 28ff; cf. also Bernd Moeller, "Tauler and Luther," *La Mystique Rhénane*, p. 166.

[26] Kähler points this out in "Karlstadts Protest," p. 306.

[27] "Ob das wort gelasen und gelassenhait, urspründlich hye in Sachssen, oder anderen landen erschollen ist, ist mir nit bewüst. Das wayss ich aber das die Merckische pawren brauchen, unnd halt es dafür, das bey inen gemayner und breüchlicher sey dann bey andern." *Sich Gelassen*, aii. He added however, that he obtained the word from writers rather than directly from the peasants.

That Karlstadt had been reading the mystics was clear as early as 1518.[28] Through 1521, however, mystical references were very occasional and relatively insignificant. Karlstadt's first publications after the long silence of 1522, however, were full of mystical thought and language. *Sich Gelassen* was a lengthy discussion of *Gelassenheit*, a central concept of the German mystics. The writings of 1523 and 1524 indicate that Karlstadt had become fascinated with the German mystics. The next chapter will examine the extent of their influence on his theology.[29]

## 4. THE MOVE TO ORLAMÜNDE

In addition to some continuing tension between Luther and Karlstadt, the latter's involvement in ecclesiastical abuses prompted him to leave Wittenberg when an opportunity arose in 1523.[30] Unlike

---

[28] See theses 181ff of the *370 Concl.* finished on May 9, 1518. See above chapter I, n. 29. In *Ausslegung* (1519), he spoke of *Gelassenheit* and the renunciation of "I," "you," "mine" etc. (AivV, B, Bv, EiiiV). *Missive vonn der aller hochste tugent gelassenheyt* (1520) provides a moving application of mystical language to Karlstadt's decision to dare papal excommunication and support Luther. *Gelubden* (1521), Biv, Cii-CiiV contains a little mystical terminology.

[29] It is important to attempt to determine what mystics Karlstadt read. That he read Tauler's sermons is clear because he bought a copy in 1517 (*Karlstadt*, I, 147) and underlined it extensively and made many notations (Kähler, "Karlstadts Protest," p. 311, n. 40). He never mentioned Tauler by name, however. Publication and analysis of his marginal comments would aid greatly in further discussion of Karlstadt's "mysticism." *Theologia Deutsch*, on the other hand did receive explicit mention in *Sich Gelassen*, aV, dii, diiiV (see below, chapter VII, n. 121). *Sich Gelassen*, aivV-b contains a paraphrase of *Theologia Deutsch*, chap. 24. Parts of lines 15-16 of *Sich Gelassen*, b are quoted verbatim from *Theologia Deutsch*; cf. H. Mandel, ed., *Theologia Deutsch* (Leipzig, 1908), p. 49.5-6. There are undoubtedly other similar instances. No other mystics are mentioned. It is possible, however, that Karlstadt read Suso's *Büchlein der Wahrheit*, for his description of the five-fold nature of man in *Sich Gelassen*, ciii is strikingly similar to Suso's in Karl Bihlmeyer, ed., *Heinrich Seuse : Deutsche Schriften* (Frankfurt am Main, 1961), pp. 334.30-335.3.

[30] Financial considerations may also have been present at the beginning for in his original request to Duke John he asked that he be allowed to go to Orlamünde either as pastor (i.e. probably with the full Orlamünde stipend) or at least as conventor with a fitting salary (see below n. 41). Eighty gulden of Karlstadt's annual salary of 129 gulden came from the Orlamünde parish. Barge gives the details of a 1514 document in the Weimar archives (Reg. O Nr. 159) which lists the archdeacon's income (*Karlstadt*, I, 44). From at least 1521 on, however, Karlstadt's vicar had not been forwarding the designated amount to Wittenberg. In June, 1521, Karlstadt wrote to Spalatin (probably) and noted: "Mein conventor bezalt mich übel" (Waltz, "Epistolae Reformatorum" *ZKG*, II, 129). Twice in 1522 Karlstadt had to engage in legal negotiations with his vicar because of failure to forward the stipend. Johannes Trefftz, "Karlstadt und Glitzsch," *ARG*, VII (1910), 348-50. In the spring of 1524 when Karlstadt considered returning to Wittenberg, he insisted that the university must bear the responsibility of collect-

Luther and Melanchthon, Karlstadt continued to be financially dependent on ecclesiastical structures vigorously condemned by the reformers. He had condemned the corrupt status quo without disentan-
gling himself from its economic benefits. He still earned thirty-four
gulden annually from endowed private masses and vigils. And he
continued to hold the Orlamünde parish as a sinecure. Sometime in
the spring of 1523 some brethren rebuked Karlstadt so sharply for his
continued involvement in these two evils that his ears rang. In order
not to give further offence, he asked Duke John for permission to go
to Orlamünde as pastor.[31] Nor would he have been oblivious to the
fact that such a move would give him the opportunity to develop an
alternative to Luther's Wittenberg.

The problem of the legality of Karlstadt's move to Orlämunde
has occasioned bitter controversy. In December, 1524 Luther charged
that Karlstadt forced his way into Orlamünde like a wolf, drove out
the properly established pastor and settled there without the knowledge or consent of the prince or university.[32] Barge attempted to
show that Luther was completely mistaken while Müller tried to assert
Luther's essential accuracy. Fortunately a few subsequently published
documents help to clarify at least some of the aspects of legality.

About May 26, 1523 the Orlamünde council and Karlstadt both
wrote letters to Duke John requesting permission for Karlstadt to be
pastor at Orlamünde for one or two years.[33] In transferring the request
to the Elector, Duke John noted two problems concerning which he
recommended consultation with the university. As archdeacon,
Karlstadt was obliged to lecture at the university. Second, the Orla-

---

ing the stipend from Orlamünde; otherwise the past would repeat itself and he
would become a beggar. Karlstadt to Duke John, April 19, 1524 (Hase, p. 95) and
Karlstadt to the Elector, May 22, 1524 (Hase, p. 106). Since he had just taken a
wife, Karlstadt could hardly afford the loss of part of his salary. Thus even though
leaving Wittenberg involved forfeiting at least 34 gulden from "Präsenzen," it may
very well have appeared that the increased certainty of the Orlamünde income
would at least offset this loss. Köhler points out that this financial concern was
hardly blameworthy (*GGA*, p. 534). Barge (*FG*, p. 232) tries to avoid admitting
any financial motive. That the financial motives were quite secondary is clear from
the fact that Karlstadt was apparently willing to accept a vicar's meager income
(see below, n. 44).

*Präsenzen* was the income given to priests who officiated at or were present at
private masses and vigils. If one was legitimately absent, it was called "absenzen."
Otherwise, it was forfeited. See Müller, *LuK*, p. 140, n. 1.

[31] May 26, 1523; Hase, pp. 91-2.
[32] *LW*, XL, 111; *WA*, XVIII, 94.13-28.
[33] Hase, pp. 89-92.

münde pastorate was incorporated into All Saints.[34] In reply the Elector said Karlstadt was free to leave Wittenberg since he was going here and there in the country most of the time anyway. Not realizing that Karlstadt wanted to avoid the income from the private Masses, he noted that Karlstadt would of course not receive "obsenz oder presenz." The Elector, however, indicated two explicit conditions. The second of these was that he secure the agreement of the present vicar.[35]

Apparently the Elector did not know that the previous conventor, Glitzsch, had left Orlamünde about May 1, 1523. On April 9, 1522 Glitzsch and Karlstadt's lawyer had appeared before Duke John to negotiate Glitzsch's failure to pay the stipend which was due. Because of future financial losses envisaged in the pastorate, Glitzsch also indicated his desire to leave Orlamünde. He agreed to pay his debts and leave by the end of September, 1522.[36] Glitzsch, however, reneged

---

[34] "Unns hat doctor Carolstat von witenberg alhie angesucht und gebeten, das wir ime gestaten wolten, ein jar oder zway auf der pfarn zu Orlamunde, wo er nit solt perpetuirt werden, oder aufs eusseiste als eynen Conventorn umb Zinss und ertregliche pension sizen zu lassenn. . . . Die weil wir aber wissen, das solche pfarren dem Stifft zu witenberg unnd villeicht seiner prebenden des Archidiaconats daselbst eingeleibt, unnd incorporirt, so haben wir ime darauff zu antwort geben lassen, das wir nit wusten, was dem Capitel und auch der universitet daselbst und zuvorderst Eur lieb, dieweil der Archidiaconus zu einer lection in der universitet verbunden, inen zu Orlamunde als ainen pfarner oder umb pension zu residiren lassen gelegen sein wold." Duke John to the Elector, June 2, 1523; Hase, p. 92. The last point may have been a reference to the fact that the university had the right of nomination to the Orlamünde pastorate. The Elector then confirmed and the bishop installed the pastor. That this was the legal procedure is clear from the bull of Julius II, cited by Martin Wähler, *Die Einführung der Reformation in Orlamünde* (Erfurt, 1918), p. 49. See too the University to the Elector, Feb. 26, 1518; Barge, *Karlstadt*, II, 568-9.

[35] "Wie wol uns nit entgegen, das sich doctor Karlstat von Witenberg begebe, weil er doch sonst dy mere zeit im land hin und her zeuhet, besorgen wir doch, wo er uf der pfarr sein wolt, das capitel werd ym nach vermog der statuta kain obsenz oder presenz volgen lassen, es wer dan sach, das er sein prebend zu Witenberg verlassen und dy pfarr als ein Conventor inhaben, und die pflicht daran thun wolt; in massen der vorige sein conventor getan hat. wo er es in dermassen annemen vil, auf der pfarr sein wil, und e.l. es auch gut ansehn, so ist es uns nit entgegen, doch das es mit bewilligung des iczigen conventors beschee. . . ." Elector to Duke John, no date, but certainly early June, 1523; Hase, p. 93. The first condition will be discussed presently.

[36] Trefftz, "Karlstadt und Glitzsch," *ARG*, VII, 348-9. There is no indication in the document that Karlstadt pressured Glitzsch to leave. Glitzsch agreed to tell Karlstadt of a suitable replacement. Glitzsch's letter to the university, April 4, 1526 (*Karlstadt*, II, 569-71), is unreliable. As Barge has shown (*FG*, p. 325) Glitzsch copied Luther's *Against the Heavenly Prophets* which is inaccurate. Barge's (*Karlstadt*, II, 98-9), Müller's (*LuK*, pp. 147-8), and Köhler's (*GGA*, p. 536) discussions of Glitzsch are incorrect in light of Trefftz's documents.

on both points and a second legal document was drawn up by Duke John on October 14. Glitzsch was allowed to stay until May 1, 1523 on condition that he pay the money owed. This time, however, Duke John encouraged Glitzsch's resolve by stating his readiness to have a ducal agent aid Karlstadt if Glitzsch again failed to keep the agreement.[37] Thus one cannot speak of Karlstadt's displacing a duly appointed pastor, for Glitzsch was legally bound to leave the Orlamünde pastorate before Karlstadt asked for permission to go there.

One could wish that it were as easy to decide if Karlstadt met the Elector's second condition. The Elector indicated that Karlstadt should "abandon his prebend at Wittenberg and possess the pastorate as a conventor." If Karlstadt would be willing to have the pastorate in the same way as the previous conventor, then he would not be opposed.[38] There are two issues here. First, what did becoming a conventor involve, and did Karlstadt act accordingly? Second, did Frederick intend Karlstadt to resign as archdeacon?

As archdeacon Karlstadt received eighty gulden from Orlamünde, only seventeen of which returned there as salary for his vicar. By insisting that Karlstadt possess the pastorate in the same fashion as the previous conventor, the Elector very likely meant that Karlstadt would have to be satisfied with the meager income of seventeen gulden. Did Karlstadt meet this stipulation? That he intended to in mid 1523 is very probable; that he in fact did not is clear.[39]

In order to understand what happened, the financial problems of the Orlamünde pastorate are important.[40] As early as June, 1521, Karlstadt reported that the Orlamünde vicar had failed to forward the income from Orlamünde to him. When in 1523 the Orlamünde council petitioned Duke John to allow Karlstadt to come to Orlamünde, they explained that the house and fences were in bad repair.

---

[37] Trefftz, "Karlstadt und Glitzsch," *ARG*, VII, 349-50. Luther obviously did not know of these two legal agreements with Glitzsch. If he had, he would hardly have accused Karlstadt of driving out a duly established pastor.

[38] Hase, p. 93 (see above, n. 35).

[39] In a letter which no one else who has worked on this problem has used, Hans von Taubenheim informed the Elector on Oct. 2, 1524, that Karlstadt resigned the archdeaconry on July 22, 1524 and that he "has had and has retained 80 gulden annually from the parish at Orlamünde but he has neither preached nor lectured [at Wittenberg] during the past year although that was the reason this stipend of 80 gulden was attached to the archdeaconry." Thus Karlstadt did not go as conventor and receive only 17 gulden in income. See the Appendix for this letter.

[40] See above, n. 30.

The vineyard was in very bad condition because Glitzsch had used the manure intended for it to fertilize his own property. The fields likewise were so "starved" that they should lie fallow for a year. They would yield nothing for two years. Finally, Glitzsch had cut down so much wood that the next pastor would have to buy firewood. To remedy this situation, they asked that Dr. Karlstadt come "since he would pay no stipend." They added that if he should have to forward the regular amount to Wittenberg, things would be difficult.[41]

The Elector, however, apparently did not think it necessary for Karlstadt to get more than the vicar's salary. Since Karlstadt's request to Duke John indicated that he had no intention of going to Orlamünde without the prince's agreement, it is probable that Karlstadt intended to follow the Elector's stipulation when he went to Orlamünde in 1523.

In fact, however, the Orlamünde council's predictions proved correct. On April 19, 1524 Karlstadt explained to Duke John that the Orlamünde pastorate had yielded virtually no income.[42] In the

---

[41] After listing all the ways that Glitzsch had allowed things to disintegrate, they continued: "Dar auff welten ewr f. g. beherczigen ap man den vorigenn Conventor, wie recht, dringen und czwingen, das ehr briffe, vass, bette, das abgebrochene haus, weynberge und arteckere erstaten und bessern solt, das yme zu armut villeicht gereichen mocht, oder das der Doctor Carolstat bey unss eyn czeit wonen mocht, und das ehr selber soliche schaden erfullen solt, angesehen das ehr keyne pension gebe; wu aber Doctor Carolstat kegen wittenbergk ein pension reichen muss, hetten e.f.g. zu beherczigen, das dy zu felle abfallen, als opfer, tauffpfennige, grabrecht, beichtpfennige und das opfer am opferfest, do von man muss eyn Cappellan und schulmeister halten. Die weil nun sollichs sint abgefallen, wue man die pension von voll solt reichen, sso kunden wir wider Capellan noch schulmeister erhalden." Orla. Council to Duke John, May 26, 1523; Hase, p. 90. In his letter to Duke John of about the same date, Karlstadt asked for permission to be pastor "or at least a conventor with a fitting and tolerable stipend." "Derhalben e. f. g. ich yn unterteniger not und demuth bitt, e. f. g. geruhen mich ein Jar lang oder czwey, wo ich nicht sold perpetuyret werden, als einen pfarhern czu Orlamund lassen sitzen, Oder uff ewserste und letzte als ein Conventor umb czymlich und ertregliche pension annehmen, das ich auss armut bitt. . . ." Hase, p. 91. I.e., in light of the financial problems he wanted more than the 17 gulden even if he was to be conventor. In n. 43 below, there is further evidence that this was a valid demand.

[42] "E. f. g. darff ich auch nicht bergen, das disse pfar den Sommerlang nur vir alte schock an gelde eynkomen hat. . . . Es stehet drauff, das eynen newen Conventor, der sich den Sommer herfuget, ergehen mocht, als mir vorm Jar. Ich muste mher winczerlons geben, dan mir Got weyn bescheert. Auch verdarb mir das hew, das aber ich davon brachte, kostet mich mher geldes, danns wirdig war. . . . Der wegen besorg ich, das sich eyn Conventor mit eynem solchen schweren anfangk in schuld brengen möcht, als ich gethan." Hase, p. 95. Karlstadt's elaboration of his financial problems in this letter was probably an explanation of why he had not forwarded the usual payment to Wittenberg.

summer of 1523 he had harvested very little hay and the cost of paying grape-pickers had exceeded the value of the crop. Although he had over fifty loads of manure placed in the fields, the effect was hardly noticeable. If someone were to replace him, compensation for all the improvements he had made would amount to one year's total income. Apparently because of its decayed condition, the Orlamünde pastorate provided virtually no profit to forward to Wittenberg.[43] That Karlstadt was quite willing to be a mere conventor is quite clear, however, from his letter of May 22, 1524 to the Elector. He expressed his eagerness to administer the pastorate as a conventor and enjoy a meager livelihood. He was willing to allow the Elector to direct all income elsewhere and give him "nothing more than what belongs to a miserable servant." [44]

It was only when the Elector's categorical rejection of this request made it quite clear that he had no choice but to abandon Orlamünde that Karlstadt adopted a legal attitude and asked that his salary as archdeacon be paid through the date of his resignation from the archdeaconry.[45] And that is the way the financial problem was eventually settled.[46] Thus Karlstadt did not, in fact, meet the Elector's

---

[43] *Ibid.*, pp. 95-96. There is other evidence that the Orlamünde pastorate was such that it could ill afford to send 80 gulden to Wittenberg. By March 1525 already, Karlstadt's successor, Glatz, was asking to resign unless Wittenberg would demand only what the pastorate produced: "Glacius cupit deserere turbulentam ecclesiam [Orlamünde], et tamen adduci potest, ut maneat, si nihil exegerint nostri canonici praeterquam res fert." Melanchthon to Spalatin, March 24, 1525; *CR*, I, 730. In Oct., 1526 the rector of the university informed the Elector that Orlamünde had been trying to have its excessively high payment (80 gulden) to Wittenberg lowered. Sometime in 1526 an investigation of the actual income of the pastorate was made. Barge has reprinted the letter (*Karlstadt*, II, 572-4).

[44] "Bin ich sso gut und geschickt von E. Curf. g. geacht, das ich armer gedachte pfarr, als ein Conventor verwesen kan, sso beger ich nit reich davon czu werden noch grosse, sondern ein schlechte und geringe narung czu haben.... Und bewillig bedechtigleich drein, wils auch williglich und gern gescheen lassen, das E. curf. g. alles einkommen anders wohin ordenen und schaffen thun, und gebe mir nichts mehr, denn das einem schlimmen knechte gehort." Hase, pp. 105-6.

[45] Karlstadt to the Elector, June 8, 1524; Friedensburg, "Der Verzicht Karlstadts", *ARG*, XI, 71.

[46] "Das corpus gelt ist yme dis jar allenthalben umb frydens und aynikeit willen zufolgen nachgelassen." He also had retained the 80 gulden from Orlamünde. Hans Taubenheim to the Elector, Oct. 2, 1524 (see the Appendix). The university indicated the same in its letter of c. Aug. 22 to the Elector (Hase, p. 112). Karlstadt owed the university 32 florins. By allowing Karlstadt to keep "was des archidiaconats Corpus ime gehorig," he was able to repay two-thirds of the debt. The rest was forgiven. Karlstadt obviously did not receive the "presenz" for the time he was in Orlamünde for this amounted to 34 gulden annually (*Karlstadt*, I, 44).

stipulation that he accept the Orlamünde pastorate as conventor. The financial reasons for his failure, however, probably explain why both Duke John and the Elector seem not to have complained of his failure to forward the appropriate payment to the university.

It is not at all clear whether Frederick also intended Karlstadt to resign as archdeacon. Karlstadt could have become a conventor without resigning.[47] The Elector's letter clearly indicated that Karlstadt must forgo "presenz" and become a conventor, but it did not specifically say that he must resign the archdeaconate.[48] It may be significant that after Karlstadt's presence at Orlamünde became problematic, the Elector never complained of any failure to resign as archdeacon.[49] On the other hand, there is one fragment of a letter available which points in the other direction.[50] Since the Elector's letter is so unclear, it is probable that Karlstadt did not think that he had been presented with the demand to resign his archdeaconate.

---

Karlstadt apparently waived his demand for compensation for his improvements (Hase, p. 112).

[47] Müller, *LuK*, p. 147. Müller, nonetheless, thinks Karlstadt was supposed to resign (*ibid.*, pp. 145-7).

[48] When the Elector wrote, "besorgen wir doch, wo er uf der pfarr sein wolt, das capitel werd ym nach vermog der statuta kain obsenz oder presenz volgen lassen, es wer dan sach, das er sein prebend zu Witenberg verlassen und dy pfarr als ein Conventor inhaben" (see above, n. 35), the word "prebend" may have connoted all Karlstadt's sources of income as archdeacon or only the "presenz" which Karlstadt did not want anyway. Köhler (*GGA*, p. 535) admits that either interpretation is possible although he is inclined to the former.

[49] Köhler (*GGA*, pp. 535-6) says the Elector did complain of such a failure, but he cites no evidence and I discovered no instance. He was criticized for not lecturing at Wittenberg (e.g. Hans von Taubenheim to the Elector, Oct. 2, 1524 [see the Appendix]), but Karlstadt believed he had permission from the Elector for this absence, for Frederick had agreed that he could leave Wittenberg (see above, n. 35).

[50] In an article of documents edited by K. Pallas from the papers left by Nic. Müller, a Jan. 1524 letter of the Elector to the university is said to contain the statement: "weil ir wist, das gedachter Karlstat das archidiaconat vorhin ubergeben hat." "Urkunden, das Allerheiligenstift zu Wittenberg betreffend, 1522-1526 II," *ARG*, XII (1915), 88, n. 4. The document was at Halle, Wittenberger Archiv V, 52. I wrote to Halle and discovered to my annoyance that already in 1913 the librarian had discovered that a batch of electoral papers, including this one, was missing (H. Schwabe to R. J. Sider, June 5, 1968). Apparently Müller never returned the letter. Hence one can only guess what data the main clause of this statement contained. It is probable, however, that one should conclude from this statement that the Elector had inferred from Karlstadt's presence in Orlamünde that he had surrendered the archdeaconry. Thus he probably intended to require that in his earlier letter. It seems, however, that it will never be possible to verify this supposition.

Since, according to the statutes, the university nominated the Orlamünde vicar, it is surprising that the Elector did not take the Duke's suggestion and explicitly recommend consultation with the university.[51] Karlstadt had no reason to bring up this issue which became important only months later. Probably assuming that he had met the demands of the Elector, Karlstadt took up residence in Orlamünde sometime in the summer of 1523.[52] To think of Karlstadt's move to Orlamünde as the act of a radical eager to defy established authority is inaccurate.

Free from Luther's supervision Karlstadt proceeded to introduce his reforms immediately instead of going slowly for the sake of the weak. Images were removed from the church.[53] Karlstadt refused to

---

[51] Müller (*LuK*, p. 146) tries to argue that the Elector in his letter of early June, 1523 (see above, n. 35), did refer to the university's *Patronsrecht*, but his only evidence is the Elector's initial statement: "Zweiveln nit e. l. wissen welcher gestalt dieselb pfarr orlamundt doctor karlstats prebend und dem archidiaconat der stiftkirchen zu Witenberg incorporirt" (Hase, p. 93). That is certainly not a clear demand that Karlstadt secure the university's approval.

[52] The exact time is not clear. The earliest date for permanent residency would be May 1, 1523 when Glitzsch had agreed to leave (Trefftz, "Karlstadt und Glitzsch," *ARG*, VII, 349-50). Thus Hertzsch ("Luther und Karlstadt," p. 87) says Karlstadt was there from May, 1523 on. Probably, however, he was not there permanently until somewhat later in the summer. In a letter to Duke John on April 19, 1524 he noted that a new conventor who would come in the summer might experience the same misfortune as he had the previous year when he lost most of his hay. What he did get cost more than it was worth (see above, n. 42). Probably Karlstadt was not there in time to have it harvested in the early summer. Furthermore, Karlstadt wrote *Fürbit Marie* at Wittenberg as late as July 27, 1523 (see *Verzeichnis*, Nos. 106-7). On the other hand, Karlstadt may very well have been at Orlamünde frequently even if not permanently from May on. In his July 29, 1523 letter Müntzer complained that Karlstadt failed to send a reply even though he had suitable letter carriers in Orlamünde (Franz, ed., *Müntzer: Schriften und Briefe*, p. 393.3-6). The letter, however, was addressed to Karlstadt at Wörlitz which was about fifteen km. west of Wittenberg (*ibid.*, n. 1). Hence Karlstadt was probably in and out of Orlamünde until August, 1523. Robert Stupperich, however, goes too far when he suggests that for nine months after Karlstadt's rejection of academic degrees on Feb. 3, 1523, "nur von Zeit zu Zeit predigte er in Orlamünde." "Karlstadts Sabbat-Traktat von 1524," *NZST*, I (1959), 368. The great devotion of the Orlamünde people for Karlstadt from April, 1524 on suggests that Karlstadt was there permanently for considerably more than five months. See Hase, pp. 97-8, 99-100, 103-4, 119-22 and Hertzsch, II, 56.3-57.10 for their repeated epistolary requests on Karlstadt's behalf.

[53] In a letter written after Luther's visit to Orlamünde, the city council commented bitterly: "Sso wir aber nuhe die verfurerische bilder bey uns aus Göttlichem bevelh, grundt der schrifft, und sunderlicher bruderlicher lieb hinweg unnd abgethan, hette uns Martinus, der halben, dem auffrurischem geist (wie woll mit heimlichen worthen) nicht durffen gleich schaczen. . . ." Orlamünde Council to Duke John, Sept. 12, 1524; Hase, p. 120.

baptize infants and interpreted the Eucharist as a memorial of Christ's death.[54] As will be seen in the next chapter, he believed that the priesthood of all believers meant that every person should be able to proclaim the word to his neighbor.[55] Perhaps it was in order to make that possible that he preached to his parishioners from the book of Acts daily and from the Gospel of John every Friday.[56] He also translated psalms into German so the laity could sing them.[57] Undoubtedly, he also implemented the other liturgical changes which he had introduced and the Elector and Luther had suppressed at Wittenberg two years earlier. For a few months in 1523 and early 1524, it seemed as if it might be possible to implement more rapid change and develop a different pattern of reformation in one small area of Saxony. But that was not to be.

---

[54] "Weiter schreibt mir der Rector zu Wittemberg doctor Caspar Glatz itzo also. ... Der Karlstat verleynt in seinen predigen die Sacrament der tauff und des heiligen Fronleichnams, jha er thuts gar ab und sagt: sie seind nichts. Er taufft die cleyen unmundige kinder nicht, gibt auch das Sacrament des heiligen Fronleichnams nyemants, Und treibt teglich alles gotlos leben, dovon ich dir ein ander mal mer schreiben will [!]." Spalatin to the Elector, early August, 1524; Hase, pp. 110-11. For Karlstadt's own statements on baptism, see below chapter VII, nn. 350-54 (especially 353-54). Glatz's statements, quoted in Spalatin's letter, to the effect that Karlstadt gave the sacrament to no one are certainly suspect. In light of Glatz's obvious exaggeration ("daily he lives an entirely godless life") and the importance Karlstadt placed on the Eucharist (see the section on the Lord's Supper in chapter VII), Glatz was clearly mistaken. Karlstadt very likely conducted the Eucharistic service according to the views given in *Priesterthum* (Dec., 1523). The bread and wine are a remembrance of Christ. "Ich bekenn für mich, und waiss, das wider Got und Christum ist, das Christus ein opffer sey, in der messe. Ich waiss das Christus, nür ein mal, durch ein opffer, in hymel gangen ist, und hat uns in ewig und unentliche erlösung und vergebung aller sünden geschenckt, und dz er nü nymmer auss der heyligen statt und hütten get, als ein priester, sunder er stet vor seynes vatters angesicht, als ein mitler, fürbitter, und versöner [Is Karlstadt quietly implying a rejection of the real presence here?]. ... Jr solt das brott und blüt des herren geniessen, zü seynem gedechtnüss, das ist, Jr solt ein hertzfreüntliche gedechtnüss des leydens, des todes, und opffers Christi haben, wie eyner eynes lieben brüders gedencken möcht, der jn vom todt, durch seinen todt, erlösst het, oder für jn gestorben were, das solt jr thün. Das brot Christi essen, und weyn trincken, in seynem namen und gedechtnüss" (*ibid.*, Dii-DiiV). Elevation was undoubtedly eliminated! There is no evidence to support M. Wähler's view that Karlstadt rebaptized adults (*Einführung*, pp. 66-7).

[55] See below, chapter VII, nn. 332-3.

[56] Karlstadt to Duke John, April 19, 1524; Hase, p. 96.

[57] "Hab auch etliche Psalmen, die er aus dem Hebreischen das Volk hat lernen deutsch singen, wie er sie verdolmetscht hat, das lahmeste Ding und losesten Fratzen, dass Wunder ist, darin ihr sehen werdet, wie er im Hebreischen geschickt ist." Caspar Glatz to Luther, January 18, 1525; Enders, *Luther's Briefwechsel*, V, 109.64-68.

## 5. RECALL TO WITTENBERG AND EXPULSION FROM SAXONY

Not until more than seven months after Karlstadt settled permanently in Orlamünde did the university take action. On March 14, 1524 Luther informed Spalatin that the university planned to summon Karlstadt away from Orlamünde where he was not called and back to Wittenberg where he was.[58] In spite of the Elector's agreement to let Karlstadt leave Wittenberg, the university of course had a legal right to demand both that its right of nominating the Orlamünde pastor be respected and also that Karlstadt fulfill the statutory obligation of the archdeacon to give lectures at the university. The delay of at least seven months, however, strongly suggests that the legal situation was not the primary consideration.[59] It is far more likely that it was Karlstadt's activity in Orlamünde and his publications in particular which prompted his recall. The first two known complaints about Karlstadt's being in Orlamünde come from Luther and both refer to his publications. On January 14, Luther told Chancellor Brück that Karlstadt had a press in Jena and was writing whatever he pleased. He requested that the princes see to it that Karlstadt either cease publication or submit his writings to censors selected by the princes.[60]

---

[58] *WABr*, III, 254.15-17.

[59] In fact, Karlstadt's lectures were already irregular by Jan., 1523 (see above, n. 8). And in Feb., 1523 he announced his intention to refuse to promote further students although that was part of his academic obligation. From at least Aug., 1523 on and quite possibly earlier, he gave no lectures at the university (see above, n. 39). Thus it is somewhat amusing when Müller (*LuK*, p. 150) attempts to explain the university's failure to act earlier with the suggestion that "die Herbstferien dazwischen gekommen waren." Actually, the fall semester began on Oct. 18, 1523 (see my "Karlstadt and Luther's Doctorate," *JTS*, XXII, 169), and Karlstadt was not summoned to Wittenberg until late March, 1524!

[60] "Verum te oro, optime vir, ut officium facias apud principes tuos, nomine et rogatu meo. Est autem huiusmodi. Carlstadius Jenae typographiam erexit illic excusurus, quod volet homo, suis infirmitatibus serviens, docere paratus, ubi non vocatur, ubi vero vocatur, semper tacendi pertinax. . . . Agant ergo principes, ut sua, quae edere volet, sub iudicium prius mittat, quorum principes voluerint, aut desistat. . . ." Luther to Brück, Jan. 14, 1524; *WABr*, III, 233.15-27. Luther noted that Karlstadt was ready to teach where not called but stubbornly silent where called. Köhler (*GGA*, p. 537) thinks the reference to "stubborn" silence indicates that Karlstadt had been asked to return privately before this time. There is no evidence for this guess, however, and it could just as well refer either to the infrequency of Karlstadt's lectures in 1523 or to their total neglect from August on. In the letter, Luther appealed to the imperial mandate of March 6, 1523 which forbade publication of books without prior censorship. Luther, himself, however, informed the Elector that he reserved the right to reply to opponents and defend evangelical truth (J. Mackinnon, *Luther and the Reformation*, III, 151-3). In August, Luther wrote a tract *Wider die Verkehrer und Fälscher käiserliches Mandats* (*WA*, XII, 58ff).

The same day he told Spalatin that Karlstadt had a new press in Jena and was publishing eighteen books "as it is reported." [61] Thus Karlstadt's publications, which certainly represented a non-Wittenberg theological stance in spite of their largely non-polemical character, probably prompted Luther and the university to think of using legal means to silence Karlstadt.

In response to a summons to appear at Wittenberg or forfeit the archdeaconry, Karlstadt met with university officials on April 4.[62] When faced with the frightening prospect of either compromising his ideals or severing all ties with established structures, Karlstadt vacillated. He obviously hesitated to lose the archdeaconry which he had held for so long. Initially he agreed to return to Wittenberg to preach and lecture provided that he would not need to have anything to do with the "Mass-holders."[63] By mid-April, however, he expressed serious second thoughts in a letter to Duke John.[64] For one thing, he demanded that the university be responsible for collecting his income from the future vicar at Orlamünde.[65] He told Duke John he would return to Wittenberg, but he obviously was hesitant about

---

[61] "Carlstadius non cessat more suo: institutis novis typis Ihenae edidit et adhuc 18 libros edet, ut dicitur." *WABr*, III, 234.5-6. Karlstadt published eight books while at Orlamünde. Luther's fear that Karlstadt was similar to the Zwickau Prophets may also have been important. In March he said of Karlstadt and others that "Claus Stork rules in these men." (Luther to Nik. Hausmann, March 14, 1524; *WABr*, III, 256.16-19). He also complained to Hausmann that Karlstadt was attacking him more atrociously than the papists (*ibid.*). If Luther referred to Karlstadt's books, then the statement is not at all accurate (see above, p. 179). This letter, however, supports the view that it was not the legal situation which prompted action. So too Wähler, *Einführung*, p. 69 and Hertzsch, "Luther und Karlstadt," p. 97.

[62] "Carlostadius adest; hodie de eius causa conveniemus." Melanchthon to Spalatin, April 4, 1524, *CR*, I, 652.

[63] Karlstadt described some aspects of the April 4 meeting in his letter of April 19, 1524 to Duke John; Hase, pp. 94-96. "Die weil sie sich sso freuntlich und trostlichen hören liessen, und alle erbothen, sie wolten mich furdern und helffen, und allsso wollt ich zcu Wittenberg seyn, lesen und predigen und nicht zcuthun haben mit den messhaltern. . . ." *Ibid.*, pp. 94-95.

[64] The letter of April 19 (see n. 63).

[65] " . . . hab ich von yhnen erbethen, das sie meinen sold alhie zcu Orlamunde von dem zcukunfftigen Vicario einnemen und sich do mit beczalen solten, sso vil ich yhnen pflichtig [Karlstadt owed the university some money]." *Ibid.*, p. 94. Karlstadt probably made this request because he knew how impoverished the Orlamünde pastorate was. It is also interesting that for a short time Karlstadt apparently agreed to accept a sinecure again. But he probably had doubts about it for a few weeks later (June 8) he informed the Elector that since God had recently assured him of the evils of holding a sinecure, he would resign as archdeacon (see below, n. 74).

doing so for he immediately adduced a long list of reasons for staying in Orlamünde for the summer.[66]

The Orlamünders' next move was politically deft and theologically sound. They elected Karlstadt pastor! None other than Luther himself had written a tract just a few months previously on a congregation's right to call its own pastor.[67] The Orlamünde council and four nearby villages informed Duke John of their action and begged him to prevent their pastor's recall to Wittenberg.[68] In reply Duke John reminded them of the legal fact that the right of nominating the Orlamünde pastor belonged to the chapter and university and suggested they direct their request to Wittenberg.[69] Accordingly, the Orlamünde council wrote and requested the chapter and university to confirm their election and nomination.[70] Instead of agreeing, however, Wittenberg turned down the request and informed the Elector of their intention to continue with legal proceedings against Karlstadt who was not legally called to Orlamünde.[71]

---

[66] Karlstadt to Duke John, April 19, 1524; Hase, pp. 94-6.

[67] *Dass eyn christliche Versammlung oder Gemeine Recht und Macht habe, alle Lehre zu urtheilen und lehrer zu berufen, ein und abzusetzen*: *LW*, XXXIX, 305ff; *WA*, XI, 401ff. See especially *LW*, XXXIX, 306, 308-10; *WA*, XI, 408.29-409.25, 411.12-413.6. "Dissen spruch las dir nicht eyn ungewissen grund seyn, der so uberflussig macht gibt der Christlichen gemeynen, das sie mag predigen, predigen lasssen und beruffen. . . . die gemeyne, die das Evangelion hatt, muge und solle unter sich selbs erwelen und beruffen, der an yhrer stad das wort lere." *WA*, XI, 413.17-23.

[68] "E. F. G. wollen sich umb solcher warheit willen den heiligen Sant Pauln, durch unser underthenig bitthen bewegen lassen sso er von der erwelung eynes pastors geschrieben und gelernet hat, das eyne iczliche gemeyne eynen pastor und hirtten, die waren reden Gottis dem volck furzulegen, der eynes guthen lebens und vol heiliges geistes ist, zcu erwelen hat. Szo kissen und erwelen wir gedachten Karlstad, welcher uns, sunst zcuvor durch Gott gegeben, . . . uns zcu eynem pastor und warhafftigen hirtten. . . . Des verhoffens e. f. g. werden gedachtem Capittell und Universitet wittenbergk mit nichts gestatten, uns eynen solchen ordentlichen erwelten hirtthen vor Goth und den menschen, hynwegk zcunehmen." Orlamünde Council (and others) to Duke John, May 3, 1524; Hase, p. 97.

[69] Duke John to Orla. Council, May 5, 1524; Hase, pp. 98-9. But he seemed to imply that he would be open to having Karlstadt nominated by the proper authorities: "Wo yhe nuhe beym Capittell ansuchung thut, und dasselbig uns Doctor Carlstadt oder eynen andern nominiren und anczeigen werdet zcu angezceigter ewrer pfarren, sso wollen wir uns darauff weitter vernemen lassen" (*ibid*.).

[70] Orla. Council to Chapter and University, May 12, 1524; Hase, pp. 99-100.

[71] Wittenberg University to the Elector, May 15, 1524; Hase, p. 101. On the 17th the Elector informed the university that he agreed with their plan to proceed according to the statutes (Hase, p. 102). See also University to Orlamünde Council, May 19, 1524; Hase, p. 103.

At this point most of the legal problems could have been cleared up had this constituted the basic problem. If the university and chapter would have officially nominated Karlstadt as vicar at Orlamünde, the new idea of congregational election could have been fused with the existing legal situation.[72] Furthermore, the university's legitimate concern that it not lose the income from Orlamünde which supplied part of the salary of a university professor could also have been satisfied. On May 22, when Karlstadt wrote a submissive letter to the Elector and placed the final decision in his hands, he indicated his willingness to administer the pastorate as a conventor and forward all income to Wittenberg.[73] The Elector, however, simply insisted that Karlstadt obey the call of the university. Unwilling to return to Wittenberg in disgrace, participate in the activities of All Saints, and accept a sinecure again, Karlstadt told the Elector that he would leave Orlamünde and resign his archdeaconry.[74] Karlstadt preferred to forsake his position of respect and prestige in the church and university rather than compromise his principles by returning to what he had formerly denounced.

Although Karlstadt intended to farm after leaving his pastoral duties at Orlamünde, he was in no hurry to give these up.[75] For one

[72] So Köhler, *GGA*, p. 538 who points out that "bei gutem Willen wäre ein anderes Arrangement wohl möglich gewesen."

[73] Karlstadt to the Elector, May 22, 1524; Hase, pp. 105-6 (see above, n. 44). Karlstadt thus would have received only 17 gulden. The Elector replied negatively on May 26; Hase, pp. 107-8.

[74] "Daz aber mich E. cf. g. nach vermog der statuten aufs archidiaconat fordern, in demselben kan ich E. cf. g. nit wilfaren noch iemand irgent einen gehorsam leisten, weil ich des in meinem gewissen treflich beswert und ein neu ergernuss des glaubens furstellen wurd, denen so nit wissen waz schades und verderbnuss aus der mess und gotzdinst kumbt. denjhenen aber, so wol verstehn, wie Got durch obvermelte greulen ungeacht und gelestert, geb' ich ursachen von Gots namen vast schimpflich zu reden. auch bin ich neulich versicheret wie es gegen Got umb die pensionen steet, derwegen ich mich abwesendes kein pension aufheben wil. darzu engstiget mich Christus leer, der sagt: es wer' deme, der den meisten gleubigen ergeret, guet daz er in tiefem mer wurd erseuft. demnach E. cf. g. ubergeb und resignier ich mein archidiaconat mit aller gerechtigkhait als ich angenomen, und wils ubergeben und resigniert haben in kraft und macht dieser meiner handschrift." Karlstadt to the Elector, June 8, 1524; W. Friedensburg, "Der Verzicht Karlstadts," *ARG*, XI, 71. On June 11, the Elector told Karlstadt to go to Wittenberg for the formal resignation; *ibid.*, p. 72. Luther breathed a sigh of relief believing that the danger from the *Schwärmer* was thereby lessened: "Der Schwärmer halben mit dem Predigen u. hoff ich, es sollt itzt der Sachen zu Orlamunde wohl geraten werden, weil Doctor Karlstadt die Pfarr ubergeben hat." Luther to Duke John Frederick, June 18, 1524; *WABr*, III, 307.66-68.

[75] The Orlamünde Council asked Duke John on Sept. 23, 1524 to give Karlstadt time to sell the lands and vineyard "welche er zu seines leybs erhaltung

thing he wanted to complete his series of sermons on Acts and John. Since he had invested considerable money on various kinds of improvements, manure and seed, he could use his demand for compensation for these as a reason for delaying his abandonment of the leadership at Orlamünde.[76] It was not until July 22 that he travelled to Wittenberg and formally resigned.[77]

While at Wittenberg, Karlstadt learned that his situation had rapidly become more serious than he had supposed. To his surprise he discovered that Duke John was very angry with him.[78] Very probably Müntzer's activity, which was rapidly increasing the danger of violent rebellion in the Saale Valley, affected the prince's attitude toward Karlstadt. Müntzer was busily preparing to destroy the evil status quo. His League of the Elect burned down a chapel in March. By June hundreds of armed people were joining Müntzer. On July 13 the fiery preacher from Allstedt preached his revolutionary sermon to the princes.[79] Karlstadt's delay in vacating his pastorate in the Saale may have led the princes to suspect that Karlstadt also favored Müntzer's revolutionary activity.

To Luther also, Karlstadt probably seemed at least semi-revolutionary. Müller has shown that by 1521 already, Luther had decided that forcing ecclesiastical reforms without the approval of the princes constituted insurgency.[80] Thus Karlstadt's insistence that every

---

erkaufft" (Hertzsch, II, 56.26-27). He also had a house at Orlamünde (Wähler, *Einführung*, p. 115). Earlier at Jena he had told Luther he would make his living with the plough (*Acta Jenensia, WA*, XV, 340.13-15).

[76] For the financial demands, see Karlstadt to Duke John, April 19, 1524; Hase, pp. 95-6. He mentioned his demand for compensation for his improvements ("pesserung") again in his letter of resignation from the archdeaconate (Karlstadt to the Elector, June 8, 1524; Friedensburg, "Der Verzicht Karlstadts," p. 71). Karlstadt officially resigned the archdeaconry on July 22 during a trip to Wittenberg (see n. 77), but the financial details were not settled until about a month later. See University to the Elector, August 22 or 23, 1524; Hase, p. 112 (see Müller, *LuK*, p. 168, n. 4 for the date of this letter).

[77] The date is now clear from Hans von Taubenheim's Oct. 2, 1524 letter to the Elector discussed in n. 39 above. Barge (*Karlstadt*, II, 121-2), Müller (*LuK*, p. 168), and Köhler (*GGA*, p. 538) wrongly dated the resignation in August because they were not aware of this letter.

[78] Karlstadt to Duke John, August 14, 1524; Hase, p. 113. Köhler, *GGA*, pp. 538-9 and Wähler, *Einführung*, p. 89 both speak of deepening seriousness in July.

[79] Eric W. Gritsch, *Reformer Without a Church* (Philadelphia, 1967), pp. 91-110.

[80] "In der 'Treuen Vermahnung' aber hatte er noch zuletzt ganz allgemein den Grundsatz ausgesprochen, dass das Recht der kirchlichen Reformen ... der weltlichen Obrigkeit vorbehalten bleiben müsse und zwar, wie er deutlich genug sagte, der Landesgewalt, nicht den landsässigen Einzelgewalten. Wer da eingreift, ohne dass es die weltliche Gewalt will, der ist Empörer" (*LuK*, p. 94).

congregation ought to remove images on its own would have appeared to verge on rebellion.[81] In a letter of July 4, 1524 Luther made no attempt to distinguish Karlstadt from the prophets who were using force.[82] Late in August in his sermon at Jena, he denounced the spirit of Allstedt which leads to rebellion and murder. He added that this spirit destroys images and removes baptism and the Eucharist. To Karlstadt's intense annoyance, Luther cleverly refused to concede a difference between Müntzer and Karlstadt even when the latter pointed out that although he did have a new conception of the Eucharist, he had nothing to do with Müntzer's revolutionary activity.[83]

That Karlstadt was not a revolutionary is quite clear. In July Müntzer wrote to both Karlstadt himself and the Orlamünders urging them to join his movement.[84] In an open letter printed at Wittenberg, the Orlamünde congregation replied that they had "nothing at all to do . . . with worldly arms" and declared their readiness to suffer rather than fight.[85] Karlstadt expressed his friend-

---

[81] See below, nn. 103-105, 110.

[82] "Satan suscitavit nobis prophetas et sectas, qui eo tandem procedunt, ut armis et vi velint tentare suarum opinionum incrementum; cum his video nobis fore negocii deinceps. Carlstadius quoque sui similis manet et illis ipsis favet." (Luther to J. Briessmann; *WABr*, III, 315.12-15). Müller suggests that a *Bildersturm* at Orlamünde during the latter part of Karlstadt's stay there made Luther class Karlstadt with Müntzer (*LuK*, pp. 166-7), but there is no evidence in the letters of 1524 that any *Bildersturm* occurred. Given Karlstadt's inclination to avoid delay, the images probably were removed in 1523.

[83] *Acta Jenensia, WA*, XV, 334.5-336.25.

[84] Apropos Karlstadt's earlier contact with Müntzer, it should be noted that his first letter to Müntzer written on Dec. 21, 1522 was both friendly and critical (Franz, ed., *Müntzer: Schriften und Briefe*, pp. 386-7). Apparently Karlstadt's invitation to Müntzer to visit him did not lead to a close acquaintance. In a letter to Luther on July 9, 1523 Müntzer asked Luther to greet Philip, Karlstadt and others *in his church*: "Philippum, Carolostadium et Jonam, Johannem—ceterosque in tua ecclesia saluta et v[ale in] domino." *Ibid.*, pp. 391.29-392.1. Three weeks later on July 29, 1523 he wrote to Karlstadt and complained of his total ignorance of Karlstadt, who had failed to write (*ibid.*, p. 393.1-6).

[85] " . . . wir darbey mit wertlicher [read: weltlicher] were [Wehren] (haben wyr anders ewer schrifften recht verstanden) gar nicht zu thun kunnen. So ist es uns zu thun nicht befohlen, die weyl Christus Petro seyn schwert eyn zu stecken gepotten hat, und ym nicht stadten vor yhn zu kemppffen. . . . Also wenn die zeyt und stund vorhanden kompt, das wir etwas von wegen Gottlicher gerechtigkeyt leyden sollen, So last uns nicht zu messern und speissen lauffen. . . . Wolt yhr aber widder ewer feynd gewapnet seyn, so kleydt euch mit dem starken stecken und unüberwindlichen harnisch des glawbens. . . ." Orlamünde Congregation to Allstedt; Hase, p. 108. The date is approximately that of Karlstadt's letter (see n. 86). See *Karlstadt* II, 115, n. 59 for the edition published at Wittenberg. On Aug. 22 at Jena, Luther acknowledged having read this letter (*Acta Jenensia, WA*, XV, 336.14-16).

ship with Müntzer but categorically refused to take part in any armed alliance. He urged Müntzer to trust in God alone.[86]

Karlstadt was trapped between the radical Müntzer and the complex Luther whose conservative fear of social disorder was at least equal to his desire for religious change. The princes decided to send Luther on a tour of the Saale valley to stem what they considered a rising tide of violence in the entire area. Luther arrived in Jena on August 21. After an early morning sermon by Luther the next day, Karlstadt and Luther confronted each other at the Black Bear in Jena. Karlstadt angrily denounced Luther for identifying him with Müntzer. He insisted that his new conception of the Eucharist did not make him a murderer or revolutionary. After an extended angry exchange Luther dared Karlstadt to attack his view of the sacrament in print and gave him a gulden as a token of his willingness to engage Karlstadt in a battle of polemics. Karlstadt indicated his eagerness to accept the challenge, and the confrontation ended.[87] After an unpleasant meeting with the people of Orlamünde, Luther finished his tour and recommended to Duke John Frederick that the princes act against Karlstadt and remove him from Orlamünde.[88] Ignoring Karlstadt's pleas for a public

---

[86] "Verum cum subtexis, quod ad Schnebergenses et 15 pagos etc. hortationis aliquid scribam, neutiquam valeo comprobare id, quod tu probas. Videntur enim mihi eiusmodi foedera cum dei voluntate vehementer pugnare. ... Optarem tibi tueque societati, ut temperavisetis vobis ab illiusmodi et litteris et conventiculis, quae hic nostratibus pepererunt metum tolerandorum malorum, quae minus ut latrones aut sediciosi fuimus tolleraturi. Ego istam procaciam quam demiror quam abhorreo atque palam fatebor nihil mihi vobiscum in tali conatu confederationeque commune futurum. Consulo idem quod Christus consuluit, quod denique nullus prophetarum non consulit: ut tu una cum fratribus nostris charissimis spem in unum Deum ponatis, qui potens est vestros adversarios confundere." Karlstadt to Müntzer, July 19, 1524; Franz, ed., *Müntzer: Schriften und Briefe*, pp. 415.18-416.8.

[87] *Acta Jenensia*, *WA*, XV, 334-41. It is certain that none of Karlstadt's tracts were published at this time. In *Against the Heavenly Prophets*, Luther said: "They have long grumbled to themselves and would not even have come out into the open unless I had lured them out through a gulden" (*LW*, XL, 144; *WA*, XVIII, 134.10-11). In a letter to Duke John on Sept. 11, Karlstadt alluded to the incident of the gulden and offered to refrain from writing against Luther for a time if a hearing could be arranged (Hase, pp. 118-9). Barge has shown that Karlstadt's Eucharistic tracts were published first at Basle in Nov., 1524. "Zur Chronologie und Drucklegung der Abendmahlstraktate Karlstadts," *Zentralblatt für Bibliothekswesen*, XXI (1904), 323-31. See also *WA*, XVIII, 37-50. On the other hand Karlstadt may very well have begun to write before this. The hypothetical tone of *Ob man ... erweysen müge* suggests that it was probably written quite early (FiiVff may have been added later).

[88] Müller (*LuK*, pp. 174-5) has examined the evidence apropos Luther's recommendation.

disputation to examine the truth of his doctrine, the princes decided not only to remove Karlstadt from the Saale valley as Luther had suggested, but also to banish him from all of Electoral Saxony. On September 18 Karlstadt was sent an official letter of banishment by the court.[89] In spite of a final attempt by the Orlamünders to secure a delay, Karlstadt had to leave Saxony promptly.[90] Driven out, as he complained, without trial or sentence, Karlstadt vented his rage by violently attacking Luther's Eucharistic doctrine and taunting him with defending the Gospel with rifles.[91]

## 6. Two Divergent Strategies

There are undoubtedly many reasons for the bitter disagreement and tragic break between these two men who for several years had worked together closely in a common cause. Certainly there were some theological differences although these were probably not as great as has often been suggested.[92] At least as important was a different sense of the proper strategy and timing for introducing change.

Luther's Eight Sermons of March 1522 and Karlstadt's retort in *On Going Slowly* published in 1524 represent a classic confrontation between a person who had become convinced that caution and delay were tactically expedient and someone whom the course of events had radicalized.[93] To Karlstadt, the slogan, "Not too fast, not too soon, consider the weak"[94] was anathema; to Luther, it represented a necessary compromise.

---

[89] Hase, pp. 123-4. For Karlstadt's requests for a theological hearing, see his letters of August 11 (*circa*) and Sept. 11 to Duke John (Hase, pp. 113 and 117-9).

[90] Orlamünde Council to Duke John and Weimar Council, Sept. 23, 1524, Hertzsch, II, 56.8-57.10.

[91] Sometime late in 1524, Karlstadt wrote a letter to the court at Weimar and informed them that he had published "alles darumb das mein wolgegründte unnd erweysslich leere, welche mir Gott geoffenbart hatt, an den hellen tag komm, unnd das man erfar, welche rechte Christen seind oder nit, Ob sye alle Christen seind, die Gottes wort mit büchsen verthedigen etc." *Ursachen . . . vertrieben,* Hertzsch, II, 58.2-6.

[92] See above, chapter IV, and below chapter VII.

[93] An English translation of Luther's Eight Sermons is available in Theodore G. Tappert, ed., *Selected Writings of Martin Luther* (4 vols.; Philadelphia, 1967), II, 234ff; the original is in *WA*, X/3, 1-64. Karlstadt's *Ob man gemach faren, und des ergernüssen der schwachen verschonen soll* (hereafter, *Gemach*) is reprinted in Hertzsch, I, 74ff.

[94] "Das sag ich, das disse geschrey: Nicht zu schnell. Nicht zu schire [=bald]. Schon, schon. Schwachen, schwachen. Krancken krancken, ein offenlicher zusatz ist zu Gottes wort." *Gemach*, Hertzsch, I, 87.32-35.

For the sake of brotherly love (and also the eventual success of his program), Luther thought it essential to delay the implementation of reforms in order not to cause offense to the weak neighbors who were not yet committed to the new ideas. By patiently bearing with the weak for a time, Luther hoped to develop a broad consensus so that, as he put it, "we do not travel heavenward alone, but bring our brethren . . . with us." [95] Overthrowing images in one small place like Wittenberg or Orlamünde would not, unfortunately, abolish them in Nürnberg and the rest of the world![96] There were many well-meaning people who would eventually join the movement if one had the patience to proceed slowly and not cause offense with precipitous haste.[97] If one preached first, the Word would bring about the desired changes by itself—and without uproar and tumult![98] Unless the hearts of all are agreed that some custom ought to be abolished, one should leave it in God's hands and wait.[99] In short, Luther thought that the call for immediate implementation was a strategic mistake.[100] Luther believed that the future of the Reformation depended on delay.[101]

Karlstadt insisted that delay constituted sinful disobedience. He mocked the suggestion that one should delay removing images and changing ecclesiastical practices until a majority agreed. "I ask whether one should not stop coveting another's goods until the others follow? May one steal until the thieves stop stealing? [102]

---

[95] Tappert, ed., *Selected Writings*, II, 236. *WA*, X/3, 6.6-10, 7.1-2.

[96] *Selected Writings*, II, 247. "Ob du schon die bilder hie umbstösst, Mainst du, du hast zü Nürmberg und in aller welt auch umb gestossen?" *WA*, X/3, 29.9-10.

[97] *Selected Writings*, II, 251. "Wenn wir aber unser freykeit on not so frech unserm nächsten zum ergernyss bräuchen wollen, so treyben wir den zurück, der nach mit der zeyt zü unserm gläuben käm." *WA*, X/3, 38.13-14, 39.1.

[98] *Selected Writings*, II, 240, 247. *WA*, X/3, 15.1-3, 28.16, 29.1-2.

[99] *Selected Writings*, II, 240. "Und wenn darnach alle gemüt und synn zusamen stympte und vereynigt wurdt, so thü man dann abe: wo aller gemüt und hertz nicht dabey ist, das lass Got walten." *WA*, X/3, 16.14, 17.1-2.

[100] This is not to deny, of course, that Luther also had theological objections to some of Karlstadt's demands. Luther repeatedly insisted in these sermons that the freedom of the Christian must be preserved. Items left to our free choice dare not be turned into "musts." See the third sermon in *Selected Writings*, II, 243-4; *WA*, X/3, 21-24.

[101] See Neuser, *Die Abendmahlslehre Melanchthons*, p. 210.

[102] "Sihe ich frag dich, ob ein son nicht ehe seine eltern eren sol, biss die schwachen hernach kommen, unnd auch verstehn unnd wollen ire eltern eeren? . . . Ich frag, ob einer nicht ehe auffhören solt ander leüthen gut zu begeren, denn biss die andere nachfolgen? Mag man so lang stelen biss die diebische auffhören zu stelen? *Gemach*, Hertzsch, I, 76.33-77.3.

Rather than have people compromise what they believe until a consensus emerged, Karlstadt preferred a decentralized approach. Every individual and every local community should proceed on its own immediately.[103] He hotly denied that the people of Orlamünde were obliged to delay until their "neighbors and the guzzlers at Wittenberg followed." [104] Scorning Luther's desire to consider the effect on "Nürnberg and the rest of the world," Karlstadt announced that "every community, whether small or large, should see for itself that it acts correctly and well and waits for no one." [105] Believers must implement God's will immediately regardless of what the disobedient masses, academic theologians or the princes may say.[106]

Karlstadt believed Luther's preoccupation with not offending the weak was misguided. In fact, Luther's gradualism was not in the best interests of the weak. Apropos images, he said:

> We should take such horrible things from the weak, and snatch them from their hands, and not consider whether they cry, call out or curse because of it. The time will come when they who now curse and damn us will thank us. . . . Therefore I ask whether, if I should see that a little innocent child holds a sharp pointed knife in his hand and wants to keep it, I would show him brotherly love if I would allow him to keep the dreadful knife as he desires with the result that he would wound or kill himself, or when I would break his will and take the knife?[107]

These words breathe the impatience of the radical.

---

[103] "Da durch ie Got klärlich anzeiget, das alle gelerten, Fürsten, unnd der gantz hauff, irren und straucheln mügen, darumb auch hat Gott allein jn gemein und sonderlich lassen sagen, das ein iglicher der gerechtigkeit für sich selberts sol nach eylen, unnd das keiner der meng volgen muss, von dem rechten, zu weichen." Ibid., pp. 74.27-75.3. Apropos images, Karlstadt said: "Ja so wir sie in unser gemein finden, ein igliche gemein in irer stadt, gleicher weyss ein igliche gemein schuldig ist die ire zu enthalten" (ibid., p. 85.26-28).

[104] "Also habet ir redliche entschüldigung, das wir alhie, wider mit der leer nach mit der that stil zuhalten schuldig gewest, Gottes gebotten zu volbrengen, biss unsere nachburn, unnd die schlemmer zu Wittenberg nachfolgten. Ein ieglich gemein, sie sey klein oder gross, sol für sich sehen, das sie recht und wol thu, und auff niemants warten." Ibid., p. 80.24-30.

[105] See n. 104.

[106] See above, n. 103. Also, ibid., pp. 75.40-76.7, 86.26-28.

[107] "Wir solten den schwachen soliche schedliche dinge nemen, und auss iren handen reyssen, unnd nicht achten, ob sie drumb weinten, schryhen, oder flüchten. Es wirt die zeit kommen, das sie uns dancken werden, die uns ietz fluchen unnd verfluchen, der auch würd den narren die rechte und beste brüderliche lieb beweysen, der iren willen mit gewalt bräch. . . . Demnach frag ich, wenn ich sehe das ein klein unmündig kindelin ein spitzig scharpff messer in seiner handt hett, und wölt es gern behalten, ob ich jm denn brüderliche lieb beweiset,

Luther's condemnation of the new innovation of permitting the communicant to take the sacrament in his own hands provides an interesting example of his and Karlstadt's different view of the legitimacy of tactical delay. Luther admitted that touching the sacrament was not a sin. But he insisted that this innovation was wrong "because it caused offense everywhere." Furthermore, "the universal custom is to receive the blessed sacrament from the hands of the priest." [108] And he demanded an end to the innovation even though it rather vividly symbolized his own doctrine of the priesthood of all believers whereas the old custom he defended was more consistent with the theory of priestly mediation of grace. This example is interesting because it shows how Luther could put his notion of not offending the weak at the service of Electoral demands. Just one month earlier, Frederick the Wise had instructed his representatives to demand an end to many of the innovations at Wittenberg. The Elector explicitly and pointedly demanded that the sacrament not be handled by the communicant.[109] Karlstadt sensed the political element in Luther's call not to offend the weak. To say that we should delay and fail to proceed with things for the sake of the weak would result, Karlstadt implied, in permitting political bodies to help determine the extent to which we will obey God.[110] To Karlstadt, tactical delay seemed to involve serving men rather than God.

wenn ich jm das schedlich messer und seinen willen liess, damitt sichs verwundet oder ertödt, oder denn, wenn ich jm seinen willen breche, und das messer näm? Du must ie sagen, wenn du dem kind nimbst, das im schaden brengt, so thustu ein vätterlich oder brüderlich Christelich werck." *Ibid.*, pp. 88.24-89.2. He also thought Luther's position was unbiblical. "Paulus in grössern sachen nit hat gemach thon, dann unsere sachen alhie gewest seind, auch nit geacht, das sich etlich ergerten, oder das sie kranck, unverstendig, und schwach waren" (*ibid.*, pp. 79.40-80.3).

[108] *Selected Writings*, II, 254. "Jr habt auch keyn güt werck gethan in dem, die weil sich dann die gantze welt daran ergert und hat es im bräuch, das sie das hochwirdig sacrament von des priesters henden empfahen." *WA*, X/3, 44.15-17.

[109] "Das [man] auch uffs aller ordenlichst unne Cristlichist mit dem Sacrament umbging, und sunderlich das das Sacrament wurd gereicht unnd nit genomen." *WB*, No. 92, p. 192. The date is about February 13, 1522.

[110] "Man sol, sprechen sie der schwachen halben verziehen, unnd nichts furt faren. Was aber ist das anders gesagt, dann das sie also sprechen, wir sollen das Concilium vor erkennen lassen, was wir thun, unnd welcher massen wir Gott dienen sollen?" *Gemach*, Hertzsch, I, 87.17-21. It is also interesting to compare a statement of Karlstadt's with Luther's comment on Karlstadt's abolition of the traditional form of the mass. Luther indicated that he approved of the abolition, but not of the "disorderly" way in which it was done: "Du sprichst: es ist recht auss der schriefft; ich bekenn es auch, aber wo bleybt die ordenung? dann es ist in eym frevel gescheen on alle ordnung, mit ergernyss des nechsten: wann man

The course of events in the Wittenberg Movement and at Orlamünde must have affected his thinking on the question of timing. The opinion which he had expressed three years earlier that one should proceed cautiously lest opponents have an opportunity for slander,[111] no longer seemed compelling. Rather than persuading him to delay in order to gain the support of "Nürnberg and the rest of the world," Karlstadt's reflection on electoral prohibitions convinced him that each small locality had a divine obligation to proceed promptly with biblically grounded reforms regardless of the consequences.

Again it must be pointed out that the emphasis here on the disagreement between Luther and Karlstadt apropos the question of the best strategy and timing for introducing change should not be taken to imply a denial of theological differences. There were some. But one cannot explain the break between Luther and Karlstadt solely, and perhaps not even primarily, in terms of theological differences. One must not either exaggerate their theological disagreement or confuse it with a difference over strategy.[112]

---

solt gar mit ernste zuvor dar umb gebetten haben und die öbersten darzü genommen haben, so wüste mann, das es auss Gott geschehen were." *WA*, X/3, 9.9-13. Cf. Karlstadt's statement: "Demnach ist dz der schluss, wo christen herschen, da sollen sie keyn oberkeit ansehen, sonder frey von sich umb hawen und nider werffen dz wider Got ist, auch on predigen" (*Gemach*, Hertzsch, I, 96.12-15).

[111] See above, chapter V, nn. 36, 37.

[112] Nor is this to say that theological factors (eg. Karlstadt's view of the binding character of the old law) had no effect on their respective positions on the question of timing.

# CHAPTER SEVEN

# KARLSTADT'S ORLAMÜNDE THEOLOGY

## (1523-early 1525)

Luther's return from the Wartburg in March, 1522, marked the end of one period of Karlstadt's theological activity. It was seen in chapter four that Karlstadt's theology was very similar to Luther's through February, 1522.[1] As late as his work on Malachi, Karlstadt clearly saw himself as one of Luther's co-workers.[2] But Luther's squelching of many of the reforms Karlstadt had helped initiate at Wittenberg ended their close cooperation and prompted Karlstadt to attempt to develop a theology distinctly different from Luther's. His writings of 1523 and 1524 reflect this attempt. At first the disagreement with Luther was only implicit; later it was explicit and violent. But it was always self-conscious.

The circumstances under which Karlstadt wrote the various pamphlets of these years varied widely. He wrote the first three before he left Wittenberg in mid 1523.[3] The next group was written at Orlamünde.[4] Karlstadt published the Eucharistic tracts in the fall of 1524 after Luther challenged him to attack him in print.[5] Finally, while living in exile from Electoral Saxony, Karlstadt published a three-fold retort in early 1525 to Luther's attack in *Against the Heavenly Prophets*.[6] In spite, however, of the widely divergent circum-

---

[1] See above, chapter four, especially the conclusion.

[2] "Paulus sagt, das ein Bischoff, soll wissen antwort tzugeben, und seine feinde nider tzelegen durch heilsame schrifft . . . Unsserre Bischoffen wissen gar nicht von heiliger schrifft. . . . Sag mir eyn Christ ab itzt eyn Bischoff versucht hab. D. M. durch. h. schrifft tzu leren oder uberwinden. . . . Sie seind nit wirdig, das wir sie botenloffer Christi schelten. Dan sie leren unss keynen gotlichen bevelh." *Malachiam* (Feb. 18, 1522), Aiv.

[3] *Sermon vom Stand* (Jan., 1523), *Von manigfeltigkeit* (March, 1523), and *Sich Gelassen* (April, 1523).

[4] *Ursachen* (Dec., 1523), *Priesterthum* (Dec., 1523), *Teuffelischen falhs* (early 1524), *Sabbat* (early 1524), *Vorstandt* (early 1524), *Zweyen höchsten gebotten* (March, 1524), *Ayn schöner Sermonn* (written Sept., 1523; published in 1524). *Fürbit Marie* was written in July, 1523 at Wittenberg, but not published until late 1523 at Jena.

[5] *Ob man . . . erweysen müge, Dialogus, Auszlegung, Wider, Missbrauch, Gemach, Gelaub, Ursachen . . . vertreyben* (all published Nov., 1524).

[6] *Erklerung* (Feb., 1525), *Testament* (March, 1525), *Anzeig* (early 1525).

stances under which these works were written, the theological conception remained essentially constant. Since Orlamünde was the locus of Karlstadt's independent reforming activity during a major portion of these hectic years, the theology of 1523-1525 can be called his Orlamünde theology.

## 1. The Usual Interpretation

In a somewhat irenic discussion of the controversy which Barge's massive biography sparked, Otto Scheel noted in 1906 that although one should not consider Luther's view normative, his evaluation of Karlstadt was actually surprisingly fair and accurate.[7] Before attempting a description of Karlstadt's Orlamünde theology, therefore, it may be valuable to note briefly the major areas in which it has been criticized by Luther, and by more recent writers who have followed Luther. One must, of course, present Karlstadt's theology in his own terms. Nevertheless, these critiques will help focus some of the right questions.

Luther charged that his sometime colleague had relapsed into works-righteousness, annulled Christian freedom, claimed special revelations and ignored the most fundamental Christian doctrine. Almost every subsequent work on Karlstadt has developed some variation on these themes.[8] Luther asserted bluntly that the devil who spoke through Karlstadt had reversed the divine order and reverted to works-righteousness by placing mortification of the flesh prior to faith.[9] Equally serious was the alleged fact that Karlstadt's prohibitions destroyed Christian liberty just as surely as the Catholic hierarchy's commands.[10] Luther's clever satire was never more effective than in his unforgettable remark that the spiritualist Karl-

---

[7] Scheel, "Individualismus und Gemeinschaftsleben in der Auseinandersetzung Luthers mit Karlstadt 1524/25," *ZTK*, XVII (1907), 354.

[8] For a more lengthy discussion of this secondary literature, see my "Karlstadt's Orlamünde Theology: A Theology of Regeneration," *Mennonite Quarterly Review*, XLV (1971), 192-195. Permission to reprint part of this article is gratefully acknowledged.

[9] *Against the Heavenly Prophets*, *LW*, XL, 149; *WA*, XVIII, 139.1-26. Walther Köhler (*GGA*, p. 549) agreed with Luther. Scheel developed a modified critique ("Individualismus," p. 365). See also Karl Holl's brief comment (*Gesammelte Aufsätze*, I, 435).

[10] *LW*, XL, 90f, 128; *WA*, XVIII, 73.11-74.14, 111.13-24. Scheel ("Individualismus," pp. 368-9) and Hayo Gerdes (*Luthers Streit mit den Schwärmern*, pp. 26ff) both agreed with Luther's charge of legalism. See also Barge's and Rupp's discussions of Karlstadt's puritanism.

stadt must have swallowed the Holy Spirit feathers and all.[11] By saying that the Spirit works directly in man without any intermediary, Karlstadt in fact removed the bridge by which the Spirit actually comes to man.[12] Finally, Luther thought Karlstadt was silent on the most fundamental aspect of Christian doctrine, namely how to obtain a good conscience before God. Karlstadt allegedly ignored that justifying faith which mediates forgiveness and reconciliation with God.[13]

One disputed issue which Luther did not raise directly must also be considered carefully. To what extent is mysticism present in Karlstadt's Orlamünde theology? Widely divergent answers to this question have been offered.[14] By determining the extent to which there was a genuine change in substance in addition to the obvious increase in mystical terminology, one will contribute to the current reexamination of the relationship between medieval mysticism and Reformation theology.

## 2. THE PROBLEM OF DEFINITION: SPIRITUALISM AND MYSTICISM

Widespread disagreement over the most useful definition of the terms spiritualism and mysticism presently exists. Gordon Rupp has volunteered the half-serious suggestion that "mysticism is perhaps

---

[11] *LW*, XL, 83; *WA*, XVIII, 66.19-20.

[12] *LW*, XL, 147; *WA*, XVIII, 137.5-19. Most writers have agreed that Karlstadt was a spiritualist in some sense. See Köhler, *GGA*, pp. 549-50; Kähler, "Karlstadts Protest," p. 299; Williams' introduction to *Spiritual and Anabaptist Writers*, ed. Williams and Mergal, p. 32; Rupp, "Word and Spirit in the First Years of the Reformation," p. 20; Wolf, "Gesetz und Evangelium in Luthers Auseinandersetzung mit den Schwärmern," p. 107; Kriechbaum, *Grundzüge*, p. 32; Gerdes, *Luthers Streit mit den Schwärmern*, pp. 28-9, 35-6. However, these different authors use the term spiritualist in different senses; hence it will be necessary to define the term carefully before using it.

[13] *LW*, XL, 222-3; *WA*, XVIII, 213.29-32. One aspect of this charge is the assertion that Karlstadt reduced the role of Christ to that of mere example; so Wolf, "Gesetz und Evangelium," p. 99. See also the more cautious statements by Kähler, "Karlstadts Protest," p. 307 and Kriechbaum, *Grundzüge*, pp. 52-3.

[14] Whereas both Barge and Hertzsch tended to deemphasize the mystical elements, Rupp and Kähler have insisted that mysticism was the dominant influence in Karlstadt's later writings (see above in the Introduction, nn. 16-20). Rupp speaks of the "long German mystical tradition from Meister Eckhart to Andrew Karlstadt." "Luther: The Contemporary Image," *Kirche, Mystik, Heiligung und das Natürliche bei Luther*, ed. I. Asheim (Göttingen, 1967), p. 14. Kähler, "Karlstadts Protest," p. 306, has argued that the mystical influence replaced the earlier Augustinian domination of Karlstadt's theology.

the most nebulous word in the whole Christian vocabulary." [15]
Since both terms will be used in the following discussion, some
indication of what the author intends to connote with them is
in order.

### (a) *Spiritualism*

An article by Walter Klaassen represents a significant attempt to
define spiritualism.[16] Agreeing with Walther Köhler against Troeltsch
that the more helpful definition is theological rather than sociological,
Klaassen argues that spiritualism is an "underlying principle that
directs itself against the externalization of religion" and asserts that
the "Holy Spirit is absolutely free and . . . does not necessarily need
media through which to work on and in the human heart." [17] Most
sixteenth century thinkers who agreed with this principle also added
that the Spirit usually uses external media. But since He is not bound
to external means, this position represents a separation of the Spirit
from the written Word.

> It must, however, be understood that this separation is not antipodal
> in the sense of a complete severance, but tensional; and that by conse-
> quence there can be only degrees of spiritualization, the tension between
> Scripture and Spirit increasing in direct proportion to the spirituali-
> zation.[18]

A spiritualist tendency can arise in two areas—in connection with
the problem of authority, and in the mediation of grace. With regard
to the first, a theologian can exhibit spiritualism either by claiming
authoritative, personal special revelations or by asserting direct
illumination from the Holy Spirit in the exegetical task. Clearly, one is
a spiritualist if one claims special revelations in the fashion of the
Zwickau Prophets.

More frequently, however, as Walther Köhler has pointed out,
spiritualism enters via the exegetical door.[19] Even Luther, of course,

---

[15] "Luther: The Contemporary Image," p. 14. At the same Third International
Congress for Luther Research, Heiko Oberman commented: "Das grösste
methodologische Hindernis ist zweifellos die Tatsache, dass die Begriffe 'Mystik'
und 'mystische Theologie' von Autor zu Autor verschiedene Bedeutung haben."
"Simul Gemitus et Raptus: Luther und die Mystik," *Kirche, Mystik, Heiligung*, ed.
Asheim, p. 21. For spiritualism, see above, n. 12.
[16] "Spiritualization in the Reformation," *MQR*, XXXVII (1963), 67-77.
[17] *Ibid.*, pp. 70-71.
[18] *Ibid.*, p. 76.
[19] *Dogmengeschichte als Geschichte des christlichen Selbstbewusstseins*. Vol. II: *Das
Zeitalter der Reformation* (Zurich, 1951), p. 101.

insisted that only the Holy Spirit could provide the proper understanding of scripture,[20] but that understanding was mediated through
scripture itself. One way of separating scripture and Spirit more than
did Luther is to assert that in the case of difficult passages, the Spirit
provides direct illumination of their meaning. As long, however, as
one insists that the directly communicated understanding has authority
only when confirmed by other written texts, scripture remains the
theological norm and the degree of spiritualism involved is small. On
the other hand, Franck's insistence that the Spirit is necessary in
exegesis because scripture itself is contradictory represents a greater
degree of spiritualism.[21]

The spiritualist can also separate word and Spirit in the mediation
of grace via the external word. Augustine believed that since the
minister can touch the ears but only God can reach the heart, the
external word is necessary but insufficient for the mediation of grace.[22]
Such a conception is only very minimally spiritualistic. To assert that
God can and does communicate grace entirely apart from any acquaintance with the external word represents a far more substantive kind of
spiritualism.[23]

Thus one can separate external word and internal Spirit in several
ways. By laying claim to normative special revelation, by introducing
direct illumination into the exegetical task and by asserting a communication of grace apart from the external word, one can move in a
spiritualist direction.[24]

(b) *Mysticism*

Christian mysticism consists essentially of preoccupation with the
soul's direct union with Absolute Reality in this life and with the
process which prepares the soul for this unification (*Einswerdung*) with
deity.[25] As Ernst Troeltsch stated in his second, technical, definition of

---

[20] *Ibid.*, p. 102.

[21] *Ibid.*, pp. 138-9.

[22] See above, chap. I, nn. 45-47.

[23] See Williams, *Radical Reformation*, p. 825 for an example.

[24] See Goeters' somewhat similar definition: "S[piritualismus] im strengeren
Sinne muss als ein Protest gegen die Kirche als rechtlich verfasste Heilsanstalt,
die ausschliessliche Gnadenvermittlung durch Wort und Sakrament und den
Gebrauch der Schrift als einziger Quelle und Norm für Glauben und Leben der
Christen verstanden werden. Dagegen setzt der S. den Geist." J. F. G. Goeters,
"Religiöse Spiritualisten," *RGG* (3rd ed.), VI, 256.

[25] L. Richter, "Begriff und Wesen der Mystik," *RGG*, IV, 1237-39. So too
Ray C. Petry, ed., *Late Medieval Mysticism* (Philadelphia, 1957), p. 18.

mysticism, "henceforward union with God, deification, self-annihilation, become the real and the only subject of religion." [26] Most mystics describe in considerable detail the process whereby the soul renounces all things especially the egocentric self in order to achieve union with God. With varying degrees of freedom most mystics employ the idea of the threefold way—purgation, illumination and union.[27] Union itself generally involves the abandonment of all discursiveness, all mental imagery and all distinctions between the ego and the non-ego.[28]

Karlstadt encountered mysticism primarily in the writings of the German mystics. The degree of Karlstadt's mysticism then, can best

---

[26] *The Social Teaching of the Christian Churches*, trans. O. Wyon (2 vols.; New York, 1960), II, 734-5.

[27] Petry, ed., *Late Medieval Mysticism*, p. 21.

[28] Joseph Maréchal, *Studies in the Psychology yf the Mystics*, trans. Algar Thorold (Albany, New York, 1964), pp. 177-85. So too Petry, ed., *Late Medieval Mysticism*, p. 44.
It is important to note one thing that mystical union is not. Christian theology has always talked about a union of every believer with Christ made possible by grace. Troeltsch apparently identified this union of the believer with the indwelling Christ with the *unio mystica*: "Further, we must also note the doctrine of mystical union with God or of the Indwelling of Christ." *Social Teaching*, II, 737. Early in this century there was an extended debate about this problem among Catholic theologians. Some argued that mystical union was merely "a prolongation of the common Christian life of sanctifying grace" whereas others insisted that it was due to a special gift of grace different from sanctifying grace. David Knowles, *The English Mystical Tradition* (New York, 1965), pp. 13-17. See Cuthbert Butler, *Western Mysticism* (2nd ed.; New York, 1966), pp. xiiiff for another discussion of this debate. The latter position seems to have prevailed. Although admitting that a Catholic may reduce mystical union to a mere quantitative increase of the infused virtues communicated by sanctifying grace at baptism, Maréchal preferred the other view: "We consider, however . . . that high contemplation implies a new element, qualitatively distinct from the normal psychological activities and from ordinary grace." Maréchal, *Psychology of the Mystics*, p. 200. Another writer stressed even more strongly the discontinuity between the mystical experience and the normal life of sanctity open to all the baptized. "A definite distinction must be drawn between the full flowering of the normal life of grace which, according to St. John of the Cross, is the full and perfect development of that union with Christ crucified into which we were brought in baptism, and the 'mystical' experience *as such*. . . . If we are to understand the mystics, . . . we must not blur the issue." Sylvia Mary, "Contemplation and Mysticism," *Church Quarterly Review*, CLXIV (1963), 85. David Knowles agrees. Knowles, *English Mystical Tradition*, pp. 17, 36-7. See also the argument (Oberman, "Simul Gemitus et Raptus," pp. 22-3) that "Hochmystik" begins not with acquired contemplation which is possible simply with the aid of sanctifying grace, but with infused contemplation. Thus, if, as I would argue, the Pauline conception of the union with Christ who dwells in the believer pertains to the regenerate, sanctified life of the ordinary Christian, it must be distinguished clearly from mystical union.

be measured by determining the extent to which he borrowed or ignored the essential ideas of German mysticism. Before beginning the analysis of his theology, therefore, it will be useful to outline some of the German mystics' characteristic concepts such as their view of sin, the preparation for union, the *unio mystica*, and the ground of the soul.[29]

Two aspects of the German mystics' view of sin should be noted. Perhaps the constant emphasis on sin as egocentrism is the most characteristic component. "The more a man follows and increases his own self-will, the farther he is from God and the true good." [30] One must abandon precisely the "I," "self," and "mine" if one wants to escape from sin.[31] A second aspect of the German mystics' view of sin was their tendency to connect sin with creation rather than with fallen creation. Eckhart could say that "there are three things that prevent us from hearing the eternal Word. The first is corporeality, the second is multiplicity, the third is temporality." [32] Clark would like to consider these words as synonyms of worldliness and self-love,[33] but it is more likely that Oberman is correct in stating that since it is precisely the three aspects of the created order, time, multiplicity and corporeality, which are the obstacles to union with God, "it seems clear to us that the Christian doctrine of creation is threatened here through a close approximation of creation and fall." [34] *Theologia Deutsch* also attributed man's inability to know God to his

---

[29] This discussion will focus primarily, although not exclusively, on Tauler since Karlstadt owned and annotated a volume of his sermons. See Kähler, "Karlstadts Protest," p. 311, n. 40.

[30] "Wan ie mehr der mensch volget und zu nympt yn seim eigen willen, sso vil er von Got und dem waren gut verrer ist." Herman Mandel, ed., *Theologia Deutsch* ("Quellenschriften zur Geschichte des Protestantismus," No. 7; Leipzig, 1908), p. 63.19-21 (chap. 32).

[31] " ... das volkumen ist allen creaturen unbegreifflich, unbekentlich und unsprechlich ynn dem als creatur. ... Die creatur als creatur mag dis nit bekennen noch begreiffen. ... Eyn Frag. Nu mocht man sprechen: seit es unbekentlich und unbegreyfflich ist von allen creaturen und die seel nu creatur ist, wie mag es den yn der seel bekant werden? Antwort: darumb spricht man: yn dem als creatur. Dass meinet als vill: die creatuer von yr creaturlicheit und geschaffenheyt; von yr icheyt und selbheyt ist es yr unmüglich. Wan yn wilcher creatur diss volkommen bekant werden soll, da muss creaturlicheyt, geschaffenheit, icheyt, selbheyt, verlören werden unde tzu nichte." *Theologia Deutsch*, chap. 1; Mandel, pp. 8.7-9.8.

[32] Sermon XX in James M. Clark, *Meister Eckhart* (Edinburgh, 1957), p. 223.

[33] *Ibid.*, p. 94.

[34] Oberman, *Harvest of Medieval Theology*, p. 329. "Everything created is, by reason of its nothingness, ugly and divided from God." Eckhart quoted in Clark, *Meister Eckhart*, p. 85.

"creaturlicheit" and "geschaffenheyt." [35] Even Tauler saw man's unfallen as well as his fallen nature as an obstacle to the return to God.[36] Sin, then, is connected with creatureliness as well as with egocentrism.

Emphasis on renunciation (*Gelassenheit*) was a hallmark of German mysticism.[37] According to Tauler, one must abandon all love of creatures.[38] It is legitimate to partake of the necessities of life, but all pleasure and delight in creatures must be forsaken.[39] The self, of course, is to be totally abandoned. To despair and despise oneself is the way to God.[40] Tauler insisted that the Holy Spirit, who has a two-fold task in the soul, could fill the soul only after it had been emptied of creatures and self via *Gelassenheit*.[41] The Holy Spirit is given to each person precisely to the extent that he abandons all things other than God.[42]

Tauler sometimes spoke of the three mystical stages. The first stage of purgation involved the forsaking of all created things and the setting aside of all unlikeness to God in the lower faculties of the soul. In the second stage man felt forsaken by God and experienced the *resignatio ad infernum*. Finally, in the third stage of the mystic union one goes beyond all human activities and becomes by grace what God is by nature.[43]

After sin has been purged away and the soul has been fully prepared by *Gelassenheit*, the *unio mystica* occurs.

---

[35] Chap. 1; Mandel, pp. 9-10 (see above, n. 31).

[36] Steven E. Ozment, *Homo Spiritualis* (Leiden, 1969) p. 27.

[37] J.-A. Bizet, "Tauler, auteur mystique?" *La Mystique Rhénane* (Paris, 1963), p. 174.

[38] Eric Colledge and M. Jane, eds., *Spiritual Conferences by John Tauler* (St. Louis, Missouri, 1961), pp. 103-4; Ferdinand Vetter, *Die Predigten Taulers* (Berlin, 1910), p. 354. 21-33. These two works will hereafter be referred to as *Sp. Conf.* and Vetter. See especially: "Wan aller der lust und minne die du zü den creaturen hast, si schine oder heisse wie heilig oder götlich oder wie si dich dunket, es müs alles von not ab, solt du iemer recht erhöhet werden oder in Got gezogen werden." Vetter, 354. 30-33.

[39] *Sp. Conf.*, 169-70; Vetter, 220.7-221.2

[40] *Sp. conf.*, 60; Vetter, 48.29-36.

[41] *Sp. Conf.*, 179-80; Vetter, 305.15-306.12.

[42] *Ibid.* Also: "Diser minneclicher heiliger geist der wurt eime ieglichen menschen also dicke und also manig werbe, also sich der mensche mit aller kraft kert von allen creaturen und keret sich zü Gotte." *Sp. Conf.*, 187; Vetter, 104.3-5.

[43] *Sp. Conf.*, 195-99; Vetter, 159.29-162.23. *Theologia Deutsch* also discusses the three stages; Mandel, p. 30 and n. 7.

The spirit loses itself in the abyss so deeply and in so groundless a way that it knows nothing of itself. It knows neither word nor way, neither taste nor feeling, neither perception nor love, for everything is one, pure sheer and simple God, one inexpressible abyss, one being, one spirit. By grace, God gives the spirit what He is by nature.[44]

What does Tauler mean? Some have argued that this union merely involved the moral transformation of man which results in a conformity of the divine and human wills.[45] At a minimum it is clear, however, as Wyser has pointed out, that mystical union involves something beyond that condition effected by sanctifying grace.[46] Thus Tauler could say that "if a man were to be rapt in God, as long as the rapture lasts he would not perform acts of virtue." [47] One can go even further, however. In the third stage of union Ozment has shown that "one is not concerned with the reacquisition of the *imago trinitatis* in its Adamic purity, nor with a fidelic, conformational union with the incarnate Christ, for one is at a stage beyond Adamic manhood and beyond historical Christology." [48]

Ozment has pointed out that those who interpret union in terms of a conformity of wills miss the fact that for Tauler "likeness to God" and "union with God" represent two different stages. When all the powers of the soul are in conformity with God's will, then man has a likeness (*gelicheit*) to God. But likeness represents only the last preparatory stage before union. Union itself, which happens in the ground of the soul, involves the abandonment of all perception, knowledge, love and self-awareness and goes beyond even moral likeness to God.[49]

---

[44] "In dem abgrunde verlúret sich der geist so tief und in so grundeloser wisen das er von ime selber nút enweis, er enweis do noch wort noch wise, noch smacken noch fuelen, bekennen noch minnen, danne es ist alles ein luter blos einvaltig Got, ein unsprechenliches abgrunde, ein wesen, ein geist; von genaden git Got dem geiste daz das er ist von naturen." Vetter, 109.20-24; translation by Ozment, *Homo Spiritualis*, p. 43.

[45] So James M. Clark, "Johann Tauler," *Spirituality Through the Centuries*, ed. James Walsh (New York, 1964), p. 218. See Ozment, *Homo Spiritualis*, p. 36 for other references.

[46] Paul Wyser, "Der Seelengrund in Taulers Predigten," *Lebendiges Mittelalter* (Freiburg, 1958), p. 248. Wyser, however, denies that Tauler taught an ontological union (*ibid.*, pp. 278-80).

[47] "Aber nu ist daz doch war, daz ein mensche von Gotte entzucket wúrde, al die wile in uebet er sich nút an werken der tugende noch an gedult noch an barmeherzikeit und vil der gelich." *Sp. Conf.*, 205; Vetter, 432.26-28.

[48] Ozment, *Homo Spiritualis*, p. 30.

[49] *Ibid.*, pp. 36-44.

The purified and clarified spirit sinks completely into the divine darkness, into a still silence and an inconceivable and inexpressible unity. In this absorption all like (gelich) and unlike (ungelich) is lost. In this abyss the spirit loses itself and knows neither God nor itself, neither like nor unlike. It knows nothing, for it is engulfed in the oneness of God and has lost all differences.[50]

This union does not involve the complete obliteration of the God-man distinction, it is true; rather, it consists of a return to the position before creation when all things existed in the divine Mind. "It is not Adamic manhood, but original uncreatedness which forms the ultimate historical goal of Tauler's order of salvation." [51]

The idea of the ground of the soul, which is the place of the mystical union, is another hallmark of German mysticism. Eckhart spoke of the spark of the soul which is accessible only to God and receives God without any medium.[52] This spark in fact is uncreated:

There is something in the soul that is so akin to God that it is one [with Him] and not united [to Him]. It is one, it has nothing in common with anything; in fact it has nothing in common with anything which is created.[53]

Perhaps because of the papal condemnation of Eckhart, Tauler spoke instead of the ground of the soul. Tauler's *Seelengrund*, however, was clearly created.[54] The ground of the soul is the most inward part, the hidden depth of the soul, and must be distinguished from the various powers of the soul such as the reason and the will. In order to achieve union with God, one must detach oneself from all images fabricated by the reason and the senses and penetrate into the pure ground of the

---

[50] "In diseme versinket der geluterte verklerte geist in daz goetteliche vinsternisse, in ein stille swigen und in ein unbegriffenlicheme und unsprechenlicheme vereinen, und in diseme insinkende wurt verlorn alles gelich und ungelich, und in diseme abegrunde verlúret der geist sich selber und enweis von Gotte noch von ime selber noch gelich noch ungelich noch von núte nút, wan er ist gesuncken in Gottes einikeit und hat verlorn alle underscheide." Vetter, 117.30-36; translation by Ozment, *Homo Spiritualis*, p. 38.

[51] *Ibid.*, p. 27.

[52] Clark, *Meister Eckhart*, p. 60.

[53] Sermon XX in Clark, *Meister Eckhart*, p. 225. Wyser ("Der Seelengrund in Taulers Predigten," pp. 253-76) rejects modern attempts to make Eckhart theologically palatable. Clark (*Meister Eckhart*, pp. 87-9) provides one not very successful attempt.

[54] Wyser, "Der Seelengrund in Taulers Predigten," pp. 276ff. Tauler's terms are "gemuete" and "grunt" which mean almost the same thing. See Claire Champollion, "La place des termes 'gemuete' et 'grunt' dans le vocabulaire de Tauler," *La Mystique Rhénane*, pp. 184-90 and Ozment, *Homo Spiritualis*, pp. 15-30.

soul.[55] Tauler cited with approval Proclus' advice to abandon all rational thought. Tauler added: "Anyone who wants to experience this [union] must turn inward, away from the activities of his faculties, both exterior and interior, away from all imaginations and all notions he has acquired from outside himself, and sink and lose himself in the depths." [56] Thus, after one has penetrated to the ground of the soul by means of *Gelassenheit*, one may experience the mystical union. That is the core of German mysticism.

## 3. A THEOLOGY OF REGENERATION

If it is correct to say that Luther's mature theology found its center, although by no means its sole emphasis, in the doctrine of justification by grace through faith in Christ's reconciling death, it is equally true to say that Karlstadt's Orlamünde theology had as its primary focus the doctrine of regeneration and sanctification. Paul's bold affirmation, "It is no longer I who live, but Christ who lives in me" (Gal. 2:20) was a favorite text.[57]

> The place where love, delight, affection and the life of our soul and all concupiscence dies . . . is the baptism in the death of Christ. That means to hang the old natural life on Christ's cross, to stab and murder it, to be buried with Christ through baptism, and to arise not with the old natural life, but rather with the new supernatural life (Romans 6) so that you may truly say, "I do not live, but Christ lives in me" (Galatians 2).[58]

---

[55] Champollion, "La place des termes 'gemuete' et 'grunt'," pp. 185-6, 190.

[56] *Sp. Conf.*, 142-4; Vetter, 300.27-301.25. Vetter, 301.22-25 has the quotation: "Der das bevinden sol, der kere sich in, verre úber alle wúrklicheit siner ussewendigen und indewendigen kreften und fantasien, und alles daz ie ingetragen wart von ussen, danne versinke und versmeltze in den grunt."

[57] "Christus sagt das alle menschen die sein flaisch essen und sein blüt trincken, in sein natur, art, leben, weyss und wesen werden verwandelt, also, das jr leben nicht mer jr leben bleybt, sonder ain leben Christi wirt, das sy warhaftigklich mögen sprechen. Ich lebe nitt, sonder Christus der lebt in mir. Gala. 3[sic]." *Sermon vom Stand*, aivV-b. So too *ibid.*, bii. "Das ist, das einer eyn getauffter Christ sey, welcher tzü dem leben Christi ist gekommen, und yn tod Christi gestorben. und synen sunden tod und erlosschen ist. und geet in einem newen leben im glauben in gerechtikeit, in warheit. und sprech, ich lebe nit. sonder Christus der lebt in mir. Ro. vi." *Von manigfeltigkeit*, F. So too *Sich Gelassen*, diiiV (see below, n. 121).

[58] "Da da müss das korn sterben und frucht bringen, da da stirbet lieb, lust, gunst und leben unser seele und alle begerung, . . . das ist, die Tauff im todt Christi, das alt natürlich leben, ans creütz Christi auffhencken durchstechen und ermörden, mit Christo durch den tauff begraben werden, und nitt mit dem allten natürlichen leben, sonder mit newem widernatürlichem leben aufferstehen Romano. 6. das du mügest in warhait sagen, Ich lebe nitt, sonder Christus lebet in mir Gala. 2." *Sich Gelassen*, eV.

His central theme was the divinely wrought supernatural rebirth of the egocentric self. The following discussion of his Orlamünde theology will illustrate the many ways in which this emphasis on regeneration shaped and molded the various parts of his entire theology.

## (a) *Sin*

Karlstadt described sin in two ways. In many places, but most extensively in the first part of *Von manigfeltigkeit*, he defined sin as an act of will contrary to God's will. "Thus it is clear that sin is nothing other than willing otherwise than, or not willing as, God wills."[59] *Theologia Deutsch* was almost certainly influential in Karlstadt's formulation of this definition of sin.[60]

His second conception of sin which also owed a great deal to German mysticism appeared even more frequently. When man takes delight in himself or other creatures rather than God Himself, he sins against the Creator. As in *Theologia Deutsch*, egocentric delight in or consideration of the "self" was denounced with particular vehemence.

> It is to be noticed that I should not seek or think of my own in any manner and way at all, if I want to please God. This word "mine" includes my honor, my dishonor, my benefit, my injury, my desire, my dislike, my reward, my pain, my life, my death, bitterness and joyfulness and all that can affect a man, whether it be external goods and bodily things or internal things such as reason, the willing power and desires. Everything in which "I" and "I-ness," "me" and "myself" may cling must depart and fall away if I am to be renounced. For renunciation presses through and flows over all that is created.[61]

---

[59] "Also ist es klar, das sund nichts anders ist, dan anders willen, ader nit willen wye Got will." *Von manigfeltigkeit*, BV.

[60] "Man sol es also versten, als ob Got sprech: wer on mich will oder nit wil als ich oder anders dan ich, der wil wider mich. Wan mein will ist, das niemant anders wollen sol dan ich oder on mich, und on meinen willen sol kein wille sein." *Theologia Deutsch*, ed. Mandel, p. 85.23-27 (chap. 42). Cf *Von manigfeltigkeit*, B: "Ehr ich das thun, wil ich etliche spruch vor mich nemen so man pflegt tzu sagen. Sunde macht der eigen will. Sunde ist nichts anders, dan nyt willen wie Got wyl. In dem wortlin nyt willen begreiff ich disse clausel. Weder Got wollen. Sintemal eyn yeder der anders oder nit wil, als Got wil, der ist wider Gots wil."

[61] "Darumb ist zumercken das ich das mein in kaynerlay weyss und weg solt süchen oder maynen wann ich Got behagen wil. Diss wort mein begreyffet, mein eere, mein uneere, meynen nutz, meinen schaden, meinen lust, meinen unlust, meinen lon, meine peen, mein leben, meinen todt, bitterkait, fröligkait, und alles das ainen menschen mag anrieren, es sey an eüsserlichen güetern, unnd leyplichen oder ynnerlichen dingen, als vernunfft, wöllende krafft und begirden. Alles darynn, ich und icheit, mich und meinhait kleben mag, das selb müss aussgeen und

Delight in one's body, reason, scholastic achievements or even one's *Gelassenheit* is sinful.[62] Sin is egocentrism.

To say that sin is delight in things other than the Highest Good is quite Augustinian; but to argue that *all* delight in created things is sinful is another matter. Sometimes Karlstadt seemed to suggest the latter. "We must give up all creatures if we want to have God as a protector and inhabitant or master." [63] Sin consists of turning away from the whole (the Creator) to the parts (creatures).[64] "He who loves something more, *or loves something along with God*, does not love God. . . . Therefore God cuts all creatures from the heart." [65] Did Karlstadt make such statements because he followed the German mystics' tendency to view creaturely existence itself as sinful? [66]

Other statements make this interpretation unlikely. Karlstadt explicitly asserted that all creation was good as it came from God.[67] Further, Karlstadt also indicated that one could legitimately love creatures for God's sake. Eve, who was created good, was intended for Adam's use as a helpmeet, but Adam unfortunately made her his

---

abfallen soll ich gelassen sein. Dann gelassenhait dringet und fleüsst durchauss, uber alles das geschaffen ist. . . ." *Sich Gelassen*, aiiiV-aiv. For the following sentences, see below n. 124. Cf. chapters 1 and 2 of *Theologia Deutsch*.

[62] *Sich Gelassen*, Ciii, eiiiV (see above, chap. VI, n. 17). "So müstu auch achtung haben, das du gelassenhait in gelassenhait habest, das ist das du dich deiner gelassenhait nit annemest, das du nit deine höchsten tugent mit lieb und lust besitzest." *Ibid.*, biiiV.

[63] "Syh gleich wie die lieb des weybes die lieb zü vater und müter ubertryfft und abschneydt. Also soll die lieb zü Got, all lieb und lust (so wir in ainiger creatur haben) abschneyden, und dem menschen nyendert wol sein dann in Gott, ja wir myessen alle creaturen gelasen wöllen wir Gott zü ainem beschützer und einwoner oder herrscher haben." *Ibid.*, aiiV. But precisely the analogy with the marriage relationship (where love for wife surpasses love for parents, and excludes a certain relationship with parents without making genuine love for parents inappropriate) suggests that Karlstadt may not have meant that any and every love for created things is sinful.

[64] "Sund ist das sich die creatur abkert von dem schopffer, oder sund ist eyn abwendung von dem gantzen tzu den teylen." *Von manigfeltigkeit*, B.

[65] "Welcher etwas mehr lieb hat, oder mit Got lieb hat, der hat Gott nyt lieb. . . . Wü ein hertz etwas gantz liebet, do magk keyn ding mehr, oder nebent Got gelibt werden. derhalben schneit Got alle creaturen vom hertzen. . . ." *Ibid.*, FiiV. See also *Sich Gelassen*, c.

[66] So Kriechbaum, *Grundzüge der Theologie Karlstadts*, p. 72.

[67] "Nü, wenn einer sagen wölt, das Got ein ursach der krefften sey, durch welche der teuffel leugt als durch sein eygenthumb. Drümb solt auch Got ein ursach sein des teufflichen falhs. Darauff sag Ich. . . . das Got nichts güts geschaffen het, wider das. Das sein götliche augen, alle ding sahen, das sie wol, gut, und recht geschaffen waren." *Teuffelischen fahls*, Aiii. See to *Von manigfeltigkeit*, E-EV.

lord by listening to her voice more than to God's.[68] It is when
we love our things and ourselves *more* than God that we act
wrongly.[69]

> We should love father and mother, wife and children and likewise
> every neighbor for God's sake and not for the sake of our own will. . . .
> All that I should love, I should love for God's sake and because that
> pleases God.[70]

The wrong use of creation, not creation itself, is sinful.

Karlstadt's frequent exhortation to forsake creatures resulted at
least in part from his reading of the German mystics. His reason for
doing so, however, differed from theirs. Creation *qua* creation does
not separate men from God. Nor is the goal of salvation original
uncreatedness as in Tauler. Nevertheless, created things can very
easily draw one away from God. Scripture says one should not try to
serve two masters. But food can very easily become one's master if
one is excessively concerned about or delighted with it.[71] "It seldom

---

[68] "Es ist nit war, das alles böss und unrecht ist, daran sich eyner zü falh brengt.
Heva wurd ye wol geschaffen, und recht, und Adam künt Got keine ursach geben
seynes falhs, drumb das yhm Got die Heva schuff, und zü gab. . . .

"Also was ye kein mangell, on der schöpffung Heve. . . . Wenn auch Adam,
seiner Heva, recht gebraucht hette, unnd wer in der ordnung, als sie Got beyde
geschaffen, bliben. So wer Adam nicht gefallen. Aber als Adam seine Heva, nit zü
eynem gehülffen, für seinen augen, datzü sie Got geschaffen hette, sondern zü
einem haubt setzt. Und sahe uber sich, do er solt unther sich oder stracks für sich
sehen. Und do Adam des dinsts Heve vergass, unnd setzet sie oben, als einen
herren, des stymm er hören wolt, . . . da missbrauchet Adam seines gehilffen, und
höret ire stymm mehr, dann Gottis stymme, unnd das yhm zü nütz und ehren
geschaffen war, das wandelt er zü seinem schaden und unehr. Drumb fiel Adam
durch das weyb, das Got wol, güt, und recht geschaffen hätt." *Teuffelischen
fahls*, AiiiV.

[69] "Nach dissen reden mocht ymant fragenn. Ich merck dat aigner will sunde
gepiret [gebürt], und wurffet von Gots augen. drumb fraig ich wie das geschicht.
Antwort das wir das unser annemen, und mehr lieben, dan Got als Christus saget,
Welcher seyn vatter oder müter meher liebet dan mich, der ist meyner niet wirdig."
*Von manigfeltigkeit*, C.

[70] "Vatter und mütter, weyb unnd kinder sollen wir lieben, des geleychen
ainen yettlichen nechsten, umb Gottes willen, und nitt umb unsers willen wegen. . . .
Alles das ich lieben soll, das soll ich umb Gottes willen lieben, und darumb, das
Gott behagt. Lieb ich umb Gottes willen, so bleybt die lieb stets, ob sich gleich
die personen bewegen und verandern." *Sich Gelassen*, eivV. See further, n. 90 below.

[71] "Nyemand kan zwayen herren dienen. . . . Wann aber wir Got mit gantzem
hertzen sollen dienen und anhangen Deu. 10. müss von nötten volgen, das ainer
Got versaumen und verlassen müss, wann er sein augen mit sorgen und vertrawen
auff narung richtet. Darauss mercke, das wir tödtlich sünden so offt wir uns narung
halben fürchten, bekümmern, befaren, oder trost, lust, und hoffnung zü gelt und
habe tragen, und das dise sund auss dem unglauben fleüsset, wiewol sy teglich in
uns ist, dz mercke wol." *Ibid.*, civV.

happens that one serves both God and one's belly." [72] Therefore one should enjoy or use all creatures as mere necessities, and be constantly aware of the fact that it is dangerous to use the least of all things with delight, for anything can very easily enslave one.[73]

Karlstadt's two basic definitions of sin were: not willing as God wills and having excessive delight and concern for the self or creatures. Thus, even though he did not adopt the German mystics' identification of sin with creation *qua* creation, his conception of sin owed a great deal to them.

(b) *Gelassenheit as preparation for regeneration*

Luther charged Karlstadt with erecting a new *mortificatio carnis* and in a sense he had a point, for Karlstadt's Orlamünde theology exhibited a self-consciously vigorous emphasis on mortification. Again and again he quoted or paraphrased Jesus' words in Luke 14:26-27:

> If anyone comes to me and does not hate his own father and mother . . . yes and even his own life, he cannot be my disciple. Whoever does not bear his cross and come after me cannot be my disciple.[74]

On the basis of Jesus' words Karlstadt declared that a surrender of self and a circumcision of delight in creatures must precede regeneration or love of God which God infuses when he performs his noble work in the heart.

> First of all, the soul must be circumcised and purified and come into its clarity and inwardness before it receives the noble work. Moses taught that clearly when he said: "God will circumcise your heart in order that you love Him with your whole heart." See, God must circumcise your heart; afterward, you can receive his high work.
> . . . . . . . . . . . . . . . . . . . . . . . . . . . . . . . . . . . . . . . . . . . . . . . . . . . . . . . . . . . .
> See how clearly God's Spirit teaches that you must first be circumcised and purified before you receive God's gifts.[75]

---

[72] "Wölt er uns fayst und dick haben, so müest er volle krippen geben, wer es uns nutz, Got wurd uns sonder zweyfel, vil für schitten. Es geschicht aber selten, das ainer Got und dem bauch diene, darumb speyset Got die seinen mit wasser und brot, und schlechter notturfft. . . ." *Ibid.*, dV.

[73] Under the heading, "Aller luste: one Gottes ist sund," Karlstadt wrote: "Es ist aller lust sünde, und ist bald geschehen, das sich ainer an essen und trincken vergreyfft und verbrennt. . . . Es ist ferlich das aller mynste ding mit lüsten zebrauchen. Denn alles das ainen gelust, das ist sein hertz unnd schatz als Christus schricht [second edition: spricht], und macht inen zü ainem knecht, und besytzet in als ain herr sein vych besitzet." *Ibid.*, aivV.

[74] E.g. *Sich Gelassen*, biii, biv, fiii; *Von manigfeltigkeit*, GiiiV-Giv; *Ursachen*, Hertzsch, I, 15.38-16.7; *Sabbat*, Hertzsch, I, 41.10-11.

[75] "Drumb muss die sele vor allem beschnitten und gefeget werden, unnd in ire klarheit und inwendigkeit kommen, eher sie das edel werck entpfaht, das hat

Thus Karlstadt agreed with Tauler's emphasis on the two-fold activity of the Holy Spirit, who first empties and then fills the soul.[76] In all the treatises the demand was that "we must give up all creatures if we want to have God as a protector and inhabitant or master." [77] *Gelassenheit* is the preparation (*berayttung*) for becoming a disciple of Christ.[78]

One must not suppose, however, that Karlstadt intended the temporal sequence of preparation for God's gifts followed by reception of regenerating grace to be taken in an absolute way. He could argue that although God's demand is that total *Gelassenheit* must precede God's gifts, nevertheless, God graciously grants righteousness before the heart is perfectly circumcised.

> If the created spirit is not sufficiently circumcised, and no man is sufficiently circumcised, then the consolation of Christ is still at hand... God the Father plants His work and fruits in our souls even when our souls are not well circumcised.[79]

Moses auch mit hellen worten geleret, so er spricht Gott wirt dir dein hertz beschneiden, uff das du in liebest, von gantzen hertzen (margin: Deut.30) Sihestu, Gott muss dein hertz beschneyden, darnach kanstu sein hoch werck an dich nemen. . . . Sihe wie klar Gottes geist leret, das du vor must beschnitten und gefeget sein, ehe du Gottes gaben entpfahest." *Zweyen höchsten gebotten*, Hertzsch, I, 61.31-37, 62.33-34. "Derhalben spricht Moses, das Got das hertz zü ersten beschneyd das ist die creaturen auss dem hertzen treybt, und das sollich beschneydung und ausstreybung der creaturen derhalben geschicht das wir Gott mit gantzem hertzen mügen lieb haben." *Sich Gelassen*, cii. Cf. also *Von manigfeltigkeit*, BivV.

[76] For Tauler, see above n. 41. It should also be noted that this great emphasis on the mortification which precedes the filling of the soul was also an important if not quite so prominent part of his theology by early 1519. Cf. *De impii justificatione*, Aiv, AivV, B where he insisted that God first frightens and mortifies before he vivifies. Cf. the section on "Justitia and Justificatio" in chapter II above.

[77] *Sich Gelassen*, aiiV (See above, n. 63).

[78] In a section entitled "Gelassenhait berait die Seele zü der Studierung Göttlicher dingen," Karlstadt wrote: "Es ist kain geringere berayttung, dann dise, das ainer ain leerjung oder discipul werd. Wann ainer ain handtwerck will lernen so bedarff er nit der aynes der sein mayster tausent behofft under allen schickligkait, ist das die mynste, wölliche leerjung haben myessen, wie wol sy gross und ettwas ist, ist sy geringschetziger dann geschickligkait des maisters. Aber Christus fordert von seynen leerjungen ain soliche geschickligkait, wölche uber alle natürliche krefften ist. Er will das wir alles gelasen sollen das wir besitzen, und das wir kain creaturisch ding in unser seele lassen eingeen, und das die seele alle ding uberwündt." *Ibid.*, biiV.

[79] "Ist aber der geschaffen geyst nit genug beschnitten, als kein mensch genugsam beschnitten ist, so ist der trost Christi dennest verhanden, das wir in Christo früchten künden, als weynreben in einem fruchtbarn weinstock, wie wol das werck oder früchte nicht voll werden, vor der endtlichen beschneydung, dannest ist es vorhanden in der sele. Aber der vatter beschneidt die weynreben und feget sye täglich, uff das sye meer unnd volkommere früchte bringen möge. Das ist

Daily God purifies those implanted in Christ so that their circumcision and therefore their love for God may constantly increase.[80] Since man is never entirely free of egocentrism in this life, *Gelassenheit* is a daily cross.[81] In his direct reply to Luther, Karlstadt explicitly reasserted this position.

> Often I accuse Christendom because many preachers do not proclaim the mortification of our life sufficiently. I also point out that some mortification precedes faith, some and that the best comes with faith and some follows.[82]

*Gelassenheit* is a constant necessity for the *viator*.

What is the precise nature of this self-denial which Karlstadt described in terms of "renunciation," "circumcision" and "crucifixion"? His concept of sin prescribed the things to be forsaken, viz. wrong delight and concern for self and creatures.

> This renunciation is an amputation of all love, desire, concern, trust and fear which we have for ourselves and our own things. In short, this renunciation is the annihilation of all that you are and a turning away from all things that you might desire.[83]

The abandonment of the self is the essential point because it really includes everything: "He who would rightly renounce his 'I' and 'I-ness,' or his 'self' and 'self-ness' would have genuinely renounced himself." [84]

Karlstadt sometimes stated his demand for the renunciation of creatures in such a way that it might seem parallel to Tauler's belief

---

ein lieblicher trost, voller freüden, und wonnreicher wort, das Gott der vatter sein werck und früchten in unsere selen pflantzet, wenn auch unsere selen nicht wol beschnitten und noch vil grobheitten und blindheyten haben." *Zweyen höchsten gebotten*, Hertzsch, I, 64.1-13.

[80] See n. 79.

[81] "Damitt leeret Christus, das solliche gelassenhait, die alle ding ubergibt, ain teglich Creütz ist, wölliches wir teglich tragen myessen." *Sich Gelassen*, biv.

[82] "Der armen Christen halben muss ich mich rümen, unnd bekennen, das ich von der tödtung des fleisch, mitt einem sollichen underscheyd geschriben hab, ... Unnd beklag die Christenheit oft, das nicht vil prediger die tödtung unsers lebens genugsam verkündigen. Zeyge auch an, das etliche tödtung vor dem glauben geet, etliche und die beste mit dem glauben kumbt, etliche aber nachvolgt." *Anzeig*, Hertzsch, II, 66.13-21.

[83] "Darumb ist dise gelassenhait ain abschneydung aller lieb, lust, sorg, vertrawen, und forcht die wie zü uns, und zü dem unnsern haben, kürtzlich diser gelass ist, vernichten alles das du bist, und ain abker von allen dingen so dich mögen gelusten." *Sich Gelassen*, ciiiV.

[84] "Darumb möcht ich wol sagen mit andern leüten, wolcher sein ich und icheit, oder sich und sein sicheit recht geliess der hett wol gelassen." *Ibid.*, diii.

that since the goal is original uncreatedness, the soul must forsake the faculties of reason and will and free the ground of all sensory and intellectual images.[85]

> He who becomes an enemy of multiplicity and forsakes all that splinters and divides his soul becomes a united whole and comes into his united inwardness and wholeness and may receive the noble work of God. If you cannot understand that, then notice that the heart must be emptied of all creaturely clothing or images, i.e. the heart must become circumcised if it wants to receive divine love.[86]

The language about the whole and part and the removing of images is clearly borrowed from the mystics. But the basic conception is very different. The return from diversity to unity or wholeness is not a return from the created manifold to the Uncreated One. Rather it is a change from a heart divided because of delight and trust in diverse things to a heart which delights and trusts solely in God. "Half-hearted" King Asa had a divided heart when he trusted in the military might of Syria rather than in Jahweh alone. All our love and work should be whole (*gantz*), i.e. from the whole heart.[87] Love and good works are in the undivided, whole heart. For Karlstadt the goal is not an ontological return to the Uncreated One, but rather the end of a heart divided by diverse affections. The "noble work" which one receives after one abandons "diversity" and "images" is precisely "divine love" which in turn leads to love of neighbor.[88] Since love of God involves the volitional faculty and love

---

[85] See above, nn 48-56. Kriechbaum (*Grundzüge* p. 88) argues that Karlstadt advocated not only an ethical *Gelassenheit* but also a physical one.

[86] "Welcher der manigfaltigkeit feynd wirt, unnd verlasset das, das sein seel zerspeltet und zerteylet, der wirt ein eynigs gantze, und kumbt in seine eynige inwendigkeit und gantzheit, und mag das edel werck Gottes an sich nemen.

"Kanstu das nit versteen, so merck darauff, das das hertz bloss muss werden von allen creaturischen kleyderen oder bildnüss, das ist, dz hertz muss werden beschnitten, wenn es götliche lieb wil entpfahen. Gott muss die verstopffungen und vorheüte des hertzens abhawen, und die seel beschneyden." *Zweyen höchsten gebotten*, Hertzsch, I, 61.4-12.

[87] "Niemant mag zweyen herren dienen. ... Du solst Gott allein dienen. Das wirt dich, das halb hertz Asaph leren, das Gott keinen glauben und vertrawen annimpt, wenn das hertz geteylt unnd ungantz ist. Gott wil gantze zuker, gantze lieb, unnd alle werck gantz haben, das ist von gantzem hertzen." *Ibid.*, p. 62.12-17. See II Chronicles 16:7-10 (so Hertzsch, *ibid.*, p. 101 who suggested that Karlstadt's marginal reference to chapter 20 was a mistake). It is possible however that Karlstadt was thinking of II Chronicles 20:14-17 where one of the sons of Asaph urged the people to trust God completely and not be afraid. In this case, the undivided heart would be one which had an unconditional trust in Jahweh.

[88] At the beginning of *Zweyen höchsten gebotten*, Karlstadt discussed "das grösest und edelst werck Gottes" (Hertzsch, I, 51.10) at length: "Nun möcht einer fragen,

of neighbor involves mental concepts, Karlstadt has obviously
borrowed a mystical phrase without intending to argue that one
must forsake one's rational and volitional faculties.[89]

That it is creatures *qua* objects of misplaced delight and concern
and not creatures *qua* created beings that man must abandon becomes explicit in the discussion of how one forsakes goods
and money.

> To have goods is to trust in goods. For as Christ himself explained, to
> have money is to have trust and consolation in money and goods.
> Mark 11. Therefore to abandon money means precisely not to have
> hope, consolation, desire or love for money. That is better than
> to forsake money physically or renounce it by one's act, but retain
> one's desires for it. Now, one is to understand renunciation in the case
> of other things in the same way that Christ explained it in the case of
> money.[90]

Since he explicitly said that one should apply Jesus' teaching about
money to other things, one should assume that Karlstadt always
intended an ethical renunciation of creatures, even when he stated the
demand in a very strong way.

Thus far we have seen that God demands the active displacement of
love and concern for self and creatures as a preparation for the reception of God's gifts. If Karlstadt had said no more, he would certainly
have been subject to Luther's charge of works-righteousness. However, Karlstadt's constant assertion that he who surrenders himself
comes to true love of God by no means implies that this active renunciation is a product of man's unaided will. Immediately after
designating total *Gelassenheit* as a necessary aptitude for becoming

---

welches ist dz höchste werck Gottes, das Gott in seinen geystern schafft? Antwort
Lieb Gottes on Kunst und on verstand ist blind und verfürisch. Glaub oder kunst
Gottes on liebe ist küle unnd todte. Drumb muss das höchste werck Gottes ein
liebreyche kunst Gottes sein, welches die schrifft zeyten lieb nennet." *Ibid.*,
p. 52.7-12.

[89] See further below, nn. 127-136.

[90] "Gütt haben, ist vertrawen in gütt, dann als sich Christus selber verklert.
gelt haben, ist vertrawen und trost in gelt und güt haben. Marci 11 [cf. 10:23-24].
Derhalben ist gelt verlassen, so vil als weder hoffnung, noch trost, noch lust oder
lieb in gellt haben, das ist besser dann gelt leyplich lassen oder mit der that gelassen, und in begirden behalten. Nu wie Christus dise gelassenhait im gelt erleüttert
hatt, also ist sy auch in andern stucken zü vernemen." *Sich Gelassen*, biii. Created
things are so dangerous precisely because men so often substitute them for God:
"Drumb müssen wir in forcht und bitter gelassenheyt stehn, der dinge aller, sso
uns tzeytlich anhangen und umbstehn, uff das wir sie yhe nit für Got annehmen,
und in creaturen, lust, trost, hülff oder radt suchen, und die ehre unserm Gotte,
damit abbrechen und enttzihen." *Sabbat*, Hertzsch, I, 43.11-16.

Christ's disciple, Karlstadt insisted that such self-surrender is entirely beyond man's powers:

> Christ demands of his disciples a kind of fitness which is beyond all natural powers. He wants us to renounce all that we possess. . . . But that is impossible for every [human] reason, as Christ confessed when he said, "What is impossible with men is possible with God." A man cannot give up his goods for God's sake unless God especially and miraculously bestows such a renunciation on him.[91]

Using the language of circumcision Karlstadt made the same point with equal force. In a chapter entitled "No One Can Circumcise Himself," he declared: "No heart can empty and free itself of creatures by its own powers; rather, it is God who circumcises." God ordained that children be circumcised by others to show that "God Himself must create and arrange in his house or temple all things that he wants to have in it." [92] In other treatises also, he underlined his view that God alone can circumcise the sinful heart. "God must cut away the obstructions and foreskin of the heart and circumcise the soul." [93] His prayer was: "Act, O God, so that I joyfully and totally surrender myself and my things to you, O Lord." [94] God creates self-renunciation.

In spite of these clear statements, however, a cursory reading might detect seemingly synergistic comments. Karlstadt suggested that God grants love and righteousness to the extent that man is circumcised. God is ready to unite Himself with man if man is free of all creatures.[95]

---

[91] See above, n. 78 for the first part of this statement. Karlstadt's next words are: "Aber das ist aller vernunfft unmüglich, als Christus bekennt, sagend. Das bey den menschen unmüglich ist, das ist müglich bey Gott. Das ain mensch sein güetter verlass umb Gottes willen, das vermag er nitt, es sey dann das ims Gott in sonderhait und wunderbarlich ain sollichen gelass verleych." *Sich Gelassen*, biiV.

[92] "Nicht das solliche lieb auss unnsern krefften wachs, Nayn. . . . Es kan sich kain hertz, der creaturen letig und bloss machen, auss aygen krefften, sonder Got der beschneydt, darumb warden die kinder von andern beschnitten, damit angezaygt würd, das sich kainer der creaturen möcht hertzlich unnd ewiglich erwegen und verzeyhen. Es vermag auch kain hertz, das es sich auss aygem vermögen zü Gott nayg oder füeg, sonder Gott müss alle ding in seinem hauss oder tempel selber schaffen und ordenen, die er darein haben will." *Ibid.*, cii.

[93] *Zweyen höchsten gebotten*, Hertzsch, I, 61 (see above, n. 86). "Gott muss dein hertz beschneyden, darnach kanstu sein hoch werck an dich nemen" (*ibid.*, p. 61.35-37). So too *Sabbat*, Hertzsch, I, 41.14-18.

[94] "Verschaff o Got, das ich, mich und das meyn dir (o herr) frolich und gentzlich ubergeeb." *Von manigfeltigkeit*, EivV.

[95] "Aber unser sunde wenden Got von uns, wie sie uns von Got keren. Er ist hewtes tages bereit sich mit dir tzu vereynen, so dw (=du) gutwillig und glewbig und in allen deinen krefften bloss, und aller creaturen ledig, und deiner werken und vermogenheit bist vertzeihen und veriehen. Er ist noch wartende, auff alle, die yne mit hertzen, in noten anruffen, yenen tzu helffen und allerley wunderbarliche wercke tzemachen." *Von manigfeltigkeit*, BivV.

"When one is ready to receive God's gifts . . ., then God gives him as much as he can receive. If his passivity is great, then God gives great gifts." [96] If these texts were read in isolation, one might assume that man can prepare himself for grace by his own powers. But the other passages exclude such an interpretation. Further the two passages cited are compatible with the view that God gives his other gifts in proportion to his gift of *Gelassenheit*. In an early section of *Zweyen höchsten gebotten*, Karlstadt asserted that God divides his talents and gifts as He wills. Man should be satisfied, and see that he does not lazily bury his talent. [97] Presumably, then, the extent of God's gift of *Gelassenheit* determines the degree of love which God will bestow. God refuses to give the *viator* total self-surrender for a very good reason. Just as the peacock's deformed legs guard against pride, so the Christian's continuing egocentrism prevents conceit. "It is for that reason that *God* does not destroy the flesh all at once but rather more and more from day to day." [98] Clearly, Karlstadt's concept of *Gelassenheit* as preparation for the new life did not involve him in works-righteousness. [99]

---

[96] "Wenn einer bereyt ist zu entpfahen Gottes gaben als glauben und lieb und andere gaben, so gibt im Gott so vil als er entpfahen mag, ist seine leydlickeit gross, so gibt Gott grosse gaben. Seytenmal Gott yegleichem gibt nach vermögenheyt des der entpfahen wil. Ist er vil und sehr und hochgeschickt zu nemen Gottes werck, so gibts im Gott vil, sehr und hoch." *Zweyen höchsten gebotten*, Hertzsch, I, 63.33-39. This statement is very similar to statements of Tauler (see above, n. 42). It will be seen, however, that whereas Tauler thought of *human* preparatory activity (Ozment, *Homo Spiritualis*, pp. 32-34), Karlstadt said only that man must be prepared. This leaves open the possibility that God effects the preparation.

[97] "Man sol aber wissen, das Gott sein höchstes werck, nit im aller besten wesen, als bald in die sele würffet, wenn er sye angreyffet eynnimpt und besitzet, denn Gott gibt erstlich pflantzen unnd anfeng seiner gaben. . . . Und das klein wesen des höchsten werck Gottes gibt Gott einem menschen höher, denn dem anderen, Gott teylet sein pfunde und güter als er wil, und wil, das jederman genügig sey an dem das er gibt, er sey nur nit faule und begrab nit sein pfund." *Zweyen höchsten gebotten*, Hertzsch, I, 51.26-52.5.

[98] "Wan wir in dieser erden unser fleisch hetten gedempfet, so mochten wir stoltz, ubermutig, unnd hochfartig werden. hette der pfaw nit ungestalte fuesse, wie solt er stoltzieren und prangen. Hette der mensche nit seyn böss wyderspenig und unlustig fleisch an sich kleben. eya wie wurd er sich erhebenn und auffblossen. . . . Drumb vertilget Got das fleisch nit mit einander, sonder von tag tzu tage meher und meher, uff das sich die grymige thyrer [i.e. pride, etc.] nyt wyder den geist versameln, unnd die sele anfallenn ynnd tzerreysenn." *Von manigfeltigkeit*, DV (my italics).

[99] One can agree with Otto Scheel ("Individualismus," p. 365) that Karlstadt's emphasis on *Gelassenheit* might encourage excessive concentration on the self (e.g. *Von manigfeltigkeit*, FiiiV) without granting that Karlstadt slipped back into medieval works-righteousness.

On the other hand Karlstadt was very concerned to avoid what he felt was a widespread tendency to belittle or ignore self-mortification.[100] Therefore he demanded zealous, daily self-denial: "This denial must not be tepid and cool, but rather heartfelt and passionate. It must last not one day but forever."[101] The fact that God grants the power for self-renunciation does not mean that man dare carelessly and lazily forget about it.[102] As the negative side of Karlstadt's central doctrine of regeneration, mortification was as important as it was unpopular.

## (c) *The new man*

As the human heart experiences *Gelassenheit*, God bestows his gifts of love, righteousness and obedience. The human will undergoes a genuine transformation. The new condition of man, of course, is a gift of God, not the result of human activity. "Everything which is good, God alone creates without us, [albeit] in us." [103] Just as the old natural life is of the earth, so the new supernatural life is of heaven.[104] An examination of the several ways Karlstadt described the regenerate state will clarify his conception of the new man.

The image of a spiritual birth followed by the emergence of a new life was very common.

> Our spiritual birth occurs with a fundamental death of our self-will. . . . For just as Christ arose with a renewed life and the mortal life was changed into an immortal one, so too the old Adam in us with all its desires and lusts, self-will and disobedience must die and lie in the grave and our life must become new in obedience and God's will.[105]

---

[100] *Anzeig*, Hertzsch, II, 66.13-21 (see above, n. 82).

[101] "Wölcher ain Christ will sein, unnd seinem herren Christo Jhesu nach volgen, der müss sich verleügnen, das ist gelassen. . . . Dise verleügnung müss nit laubig und küel sein, sonder hertzlich und hytzig, Nicht ainen tag, sonder ewig weren." *Sich Gelassen*, f iii.

[102] "Got hatt allen gleubigen, das ist Israhel, macht geben und bevolhen, das sye ir fleisch sollen dempffen und erwindten. Aber das geschicht sychtiglich und mit langer tzyt, uff das der arme unsower mensch seyner ungeschicklikeit yndechtich bleiben." *Von manigfeltigkeit*, D.

[103] "Unser vernunfft und wellende kraft, und dartzü alle unsere krefften haben nit aines klainstes steublins recht, sich gütter werck oder leydens antzünemen und erheben. Dann alles das güt ist, das schaffet Got allain, one uns, in uns, und wir thun nicht mer darbey, dann wir gethon haben, als uns Gott schüff." *Sich Gelassen*, f-fV.

[104] "Es seind zway widerwertig und spennige leben, das alt und natürlich, das new und ubernatürlich, des allten Adams leben und des newen Christi, des irdischen und des hymelischen leben." *Ibid.*, eV. See all of eV-eii.

[105] "Unsere geistliche geburt geschicht in gründlichem absterben unsers aigen willens, dann wir mussen mit Christo sterben. . . . Dann wie Christus im verneuten

Christ lives in the new-born man.[106] Therefore, he has a Christ-like life.[107] The supernatural birth results in an obedient life of conformity to Christ.

He also described the new life as a harmony between God's and man's will. The self is genuinely forsaken "when self-will is renounced, when self-will melts away and God's will obtains his work in the creature and nothing other is willed except what and as God wills."[108] Whereas the old life consists of a disobedient self-will, "the new life is the pure will of God and obedience." [109] Karlstadt could speak of the regenerate state as the will of God because he conceived of man's will as both empowered by, and in conformity with, the divine will.

A third description of the new man had a somewhat Augustinian flavor. God produces love for Himself by creating his noble work of "faith rich in love" or "love rich in faith" in the soul. "The very best and noblest work which God creates in the soul is faith rich in love and love rich in faith." [110] Love full of faith "knows and highly esteems God, just as one knows and highly esteems the thing which pleases him." [111] The description of this love of God created in man by

---

lebenn ist uff gestanden, unnd das sterblich leben, in eyn unsterblich verwandelt hat. also solt der alt Adam in unss mit allenn seynen begirden unnd lusten, aigen willen unnd ungehorsam sterben, unnd im grab lygen, unnd unser lebenn new sey, in gehorsam unnd Gottis willen." *Von manigfeltigkeit*, CiiiV. For a much earlier discussion of the burial of the old Adam, see theses 16-18, "151 Theses," Kähler, p. 14*. See also *Von manigfeltigkeit*, FivV; *Anzeig*, Hertzsch, II, 90.1-14; theses 1-4 of the Nov. 28, 1522 theses reprinted by Kolde, "Wittenberger Disputations-thesen," *ZKG*, XI (1890), 460-61; *Gelaub*, ciii: "Wenn aber der ungeschaffen windt, des menschen alt leben umbsturtzet, und gepieret eynen newen menschen, so versteht der new geborn mensch, das seyn geburt von oben herraber kumpt."

[106] "Das einer eyn getauffter Christ sey, welcher tzü dem leben Christi ist gekommen, und yn tod Christi gestorben ... und geet in einem newen leben im glauben in gerechtikeit, in warheit. und sprech, ich lebe nit. sonder Christus der lebt in mir. Ro. vi." *Von manigfeltigkeit*, F.

[107] "Jedoch hoff ich, das man jr vil mög finden, die fast hoch sein in Christiförmigen leben, unnd Christus willen haben, Gleich als wol achte ich das jr vil mer sein die begereten sterben und mitt Christo leben." *Sermon vom Stand*, bii. See also *Sich Gelassen*, diiiV (n. 121 below) and *Missbrauch* BV (n. 373 below), BivV-C (n. 151 below).

[108] *Sich Gelassen*, div (see below, n. 121).

[109] "Das alt leben ist lautter ungehorsam aygen will und liebet sein seele in allen thün und lassen. . . . Das new leben ist der rayn Gottes will und gehorsam und hasset des mennschen seele in aller thüender unnd würckender weyss." *Ibid.*, eii.

[110] "Das aller beste und edelste werck welches Gott in der seel schaffet, ist ein liebreycher glaube, oder ein glaubreyche liebe." *Zweyen höchsten gebotten*, Hertzsch, I, 53.21-23. See below under "faith" for further discussion of this concept.

[111] *Ibid.*, p. 52.17-20. See below, n. 147 for the German text. So too *Sabbat*, Hertzsch, I, 27.28-30.

divine activity is sometimes very reminiscent of Augustine's conception of *delectatio* or *amor Dei*. In a section called "What Love of God Is," Karlstadt said, "Love of God . . . is a vigorous and serious delight in God." The prophet spoke of this love when he urged: "Delight yourself in God." [112] The new man, then, is one who has been born again into a new life, who lives in conformity with the divine will and who has received the gift of loving and delighting in God.

A fourth kind of language about the union between the regenerate soul and God came from German mysticism. Karlstadt announced that the believer is to become "as God." [113] He also spoke of becoming one (*ayns werden*) with, and sinking into or melting away into, God's eternal will.[114] "Renunciation presses through and flows over all that is created and comes into its uncreated nothingness where it was uncreated and nothing, i.e. into its Source and Creator." [115] The Spirit becomes "one thing" (*ain ding*) with the soul.[116] He could even use the language of *Theologia Deutsch* and refer to the "deified" (*vergotten*) man.[117]

Did Karlstadt move beyond an ethical harmony of wills to an ontological union between God and man?[118] Was he talking à la Tauler about a mystical union in which the soul returns to its state before creation where it existed in the Divine Mind? If such is the case, then this would represent a substantial and not just a terminological influence of the mystics upon Karlstadt.

Before this view is accepted, however, these passages must be examined carefully. When Karlstadt said that man was to become "wie Gott ist," he added immediately,

---

[112] "Drumb solt ir wol mercken, das Gottes lieb (nach den gelassen werck zu reden) ein gestrackter und ernster lust ist in Gott, in welchem sich, die sele nit findet, der auch nit eyngezogen ist, von welchem der prophet redet. Gelüste dich in Gott." *Zweyen höchsten gebotten*, Hertzsch, I, 59.4-8.

[113] *Sabbat*, Hertzsch, I, 23.19 (see below, n. 119).

[114] *Sich Gelassen*, diiiV-div (see below, n. 121). Also *ibid.*, biv: "In Gottes ewigen willen verschmeltzen und zum nicht werden."

[115] *Ibid*, aiv (see below, n. 124). *Von manigfeltigkeit*, Eii speaks of "einsenckung unsers aigen willens in den abgrund auss welchem alle dyng yns wesen fallen." The passage, however, is too brief to give any significant clue to its meaning.

[116] *Sermon vom Stand*, bV (see below, n. 183).

[117] *Von manigfeltigkeit*, EiiV and FiiV; *Sich Gelassen*, fiiiV. See below, nn. 125-26. Cf. *Theologia Deutsch* which described the condition of the deified man as follows: "Da Gott und mensch eins ist und doch Gott der mensch ist". (Mandel, p. 46).

[118] So Kriechbaum, who argues that just as Karlstadt conceived of sin as both disobedience and also creaturely existence as such, and also just as he had both an ethical and a physical *Gelassenheit*, so, too, he thought of both an ethical and an ontological union with God (*Grundzüge*, pp. 88-9).

i.e. holy, still, good, righteous, wise, strong, true, kind, merciful, etc. And all God's commands demand from us a similarity to his divinity and are given to us so that we shall become God-like. As it is written: "You shall become holy and be holy for I your God and Lord am holy, says God. Keep my commands and do them." . . . God has given us his commands and counsels so that we become holy and God-like, i.e. similar to God, as God is.[119]

In this passage Karlstadt was clearly demanding a moral likeness, not an essential union.

What did Karlstadt mean when he spoke of melting away into (*verschmiltzen*) or sinking into (*einsinken*) the divine will? It will be essential to examine in detail several of the passages which appear most similar to statements of the German mystics.

> . . . a true and renounced service of God elevates the eyes of the soul into the abysmal will of God and creeps into the boundless Good which is God Himself. There, there can be no self or I. As long as a soul looks at nothing other than God's will and the eternal Good which is God, its heart rests on no creature. Indeed, through its soaring, it presses on and sinks itself in God's will and dies to itself fundamentally there. . . . Originally, man was nothing. Since he must renounce and completely surrender his anything and something or his self and "self-ness," he must surrender it to him who made him a something, anything or self.[120] He must surrender to God all that is something to-

---

[119] "Got hat alle gebot und verbot dem menschen derhalben fürgelegt, das der mensch, seines innewendiges ebenbildes gewar werd. Unnd versteh, wie yhn Got nach seynem bilde geschaffen, und das er werd, wie Got ist, das ist heylig, still, gut, gerecht, weyse, starck, warhafftig, gütig, barmhertzigk etc. Und alle gebot Gottis foddern von uns eyne gleycheit seiner gotheit, sein auch uns der ursachen halben gegeben, das wir gotformig werden sollen. Als geschrieben steht. Ir sollet heylig werden und heylig sein, dann ich, ewer Got und herr, bin heylig sagt Got, bewaret mein gebot und thut sie (margin: Levi 20 [vv. 7, 26]). Darauss ist zu leren, das uns Got seine gebot unnd rethe gegeben hat, das wir heylig und gotformigk werden, das ist Got gleich, als Got ist." *Sabbat*, Hertzsch, I, 23.16-28. Thus it is somewhat misleading for Robert Stupperich to say without additional comment that the goal of the process of renewal in Karlstadt is "glicheit seiner götheit." "Karlstadt Sabbat-Traktat von 1524," *NZST*, I (1959), 371.

[120] It is very interesting to note that Karlstadt used "icht" which was a term from Eckhart. Eckhart spoke of the "ihte in dem nihte" to refer to the uncreated, divine *Seelenfunklein* which is something in the nothingness of the creature. See Wyser, "Der Seelengrund in Taulers Predigten," pp. 254-267. Karlstadt, on the other hand, closely identified the "icht" with the "I" which must be forsaken, for he spoke of the "icht und ettwas oder sich und sicheit" (so similarly in n.181 below). There is no suggestion at all that the "icht" is uncreated. Eckhart did not recommend renouncing the "icht." In the one additional place where I have noted that Karlstadt used the term, he spoke of God's "etwas und icht" (*Sich Gelassen*, eiv). A much earlier parallel (for which I am indebted to Dr. Ulrich Bubenheimer) to the phrase "sein icht und ettwas oder sich und sicheit" is interesting: "Quam diu

gether with his self and "I-ness," and plunge into his will. If one did that, then one would be renounced in one's passivity and activity.... He who wants to be fundamentally renounced ... must freely surrender his "I-ness" or "self-ness;" then this renounced self or "self-ness" becomes a Christ-like I. ... He who desires to be renounced fundamentally and in genuine truth shall ... abandon and come out of himself and become one with the divine, eternal Will, so that he does not see, hear, taste, desire, understand or will other than God wills.... Then this renounced self or despised and forsaken I ... becomes a Christ-like I or self and a new Christian life, where one discovers and perceives that his life is not a human but a divine life. And he does not live but Christ lives in him. Gal. 2. Do not let this word self and I, "self-ness" and "I-ness" trouble you because you know that it appears many times in your *Theologia Deutsch*. ... A renounced I or "I-ness" exists when I despise myself and surrender and grant all good to Him who gave it to me, for the little stream must flow back and return to its source and its waters.... This I or self is usefully renounced when self-will is renounced, when self-will melts away and God's will obtains its work *in the creature*, and nothing other is willed except what and as God wills.... When nothing is loved except what God loves, or nothing is desired *by the creature* except what God wills, then he is renounced.[121]

---

placent homini 'ego,' 'nos,' 'nostra,' 'propria' et 'meum' [et] 'nostrum' aliquid, tam diu vicissim in homine est, quod Deo displicet." Thesis 184 of *370 Conclusiones*, Greving, p. 60. (See also theses 181-87.) "Meum [et] nostrum aliquid," which seems to be a parallel to "sein icht und ettwas," is merely an amplification of "ego, nos, nostra, propria."

[121] "Darauss ist zü mercken, was das wörtlin sich bedeüt, und wie ain warhafftiger und gelassner dienst [Barge, *Karlstadt*, II, 38 suggests "Diener," but there is no change in the second edition] Gottes, der seelen augen auff schwinget, in den abgründigen willen Gottes, und in das grundloss gütt kreücht, wölches Gott selber ist, da kain sich oder ich sein mag. Alle dieweyl ain seele auff nicht anders sicht dann auff Gotes willen, und dz ewig güt, dz Got ist, so füsset auch ir hertz an kayner creatur, Ja sy dringt auch durch jr auffschwingung und sencket sich in Gottes willen, und stirbt dar jr selber ab von grund an.... Der mensch ist anfencklich nicht gewest, weyl er sein icht und ettwas oder sich und sicheit gelassen, und ordenlich ubergeben, so müss er es dem ubergeben der in ettwas icht oder sich hatt gemacht, das ist. Er müss sich und alles das etwas in im ist, mit seinem sich und icheit, Gott auffgeben, und in seinem willen nider tauchen, wann ainer das thet, er wer in leyden und wercken gelassen. ... Wölcher von grund will gelassen sein, und der sein, der sich gelassen hat, der müss im unwidernemlich entwerden, und sein icheit oder sicheit frey aussgeben, so wirt diss gelassen sich, oder sicheit ain Christförmigs ich von wölche Christus spricht. Kurtzlich. Wölcher von grund und in rechter warhait begert gelassen werden, der soll im selbs (und allem dem seinen, das in etwas dunckel), unwidernemlich abgeen und entwerden, unnd mit dem götlichen ewigen willen ayns werden, das er nicht seh, hör, schmeck, beger, versteen, und wöll dann das Got will.... Als dann wirt, diss gelassen sich, oder veracht und verlassen ich. Sicheit oder icheit, ain Christförmigs ich oder sich, und ain newe Christlich leben, da ainer befindt unnd betzebt, das seyn leben nit ain menschlich, sonder ain götlich leben, und er nitt lebet, sonder Christus in ime Gala 2. Lasse dich dise wörtlin Sich und

Several points are significant. First, even though it might appear at the beginning as if all personal individuality is forsaken, the latter part shows that Karlstadt was talking only about a transformation of the self. It is precisely the old "I" which becomes the new Christ-like "I" after the new birth has occurred. To say that Christ lives in one is another way to say that one's self or I is forsaken. One's life is divine in the sense that it is now Christ-like. Second, whereas for Tauler sinking into the divine will in the *unio mystica* involves the abandonment of all sensory, volitional and rational powers, the union envisaged by Karlstadt does not demand the abandonment of the reason or will. The soul which plunges into and becomes one with God acts, desires, understands and wills—albeit in conformity with God's will.[122] Third, melting away into the divine will means only that God's

---

Ich, Sicheit und icheit nitt bevilhen, dann du wayst dass sy in deiner teütschen Theologien vil mals steendt. . . . Ein gelassen Ich oder Icheit ist wann ich mich veracht und ubergeb und geb dem alles das güt, der mirs geben hat, dann die flüsslin myessen in iren brunn und ir möre wider flyessen und keren, wann sy ordenlich widerkeren wöllen. Disse Ich oder Sich werden dann nützlich gelassen, wann aygner will gelassen wirt, wann aygner will verschmiltzt unnd Gottes will sein werck in der creatur bekompt, und wurd nicht anders gewolt, dann das, und wie Gott will, als dann werden Ich und sich ubergeben, und alles das dem geschaffen willen nachvolgt oder auss ime entspreüsset, dz wirt alles samptlich recht gelassen. Das ainer sein ich oder Sich also hab gelassen oder nit, das mag er dabey mörcken und abnemen, wann im nichts geliebt dann das Gott geliebt, oder von der creatur nicht begerdt denn das Gott will, so ist er gelassen." *Sich Gelassen*, diii-div. My italics.

[122] In another place, Karlstadt argued that the believer sinks into God's will precisely as he remembers Christ's sacrifice on the cross: "Demnach mag eyner täglich des gethonen opffers Christi gedencken. . . . Aber das heysst nit Christum uffs neüw opffern, sundern im dancksagen, und gedechtnüss des leydens und opffers Christi haben, und sich durch das freüntlich erkantnüss Christi, des priesters, und seynes ampts in Christum versencken, und in Christo bleyben." *Priesterthum*, DiiV. In *Sich Gelassen*, aiv, Karlstadt does say that "vernunfft, wöllende krafft und begirden" (see above, n. 61) are to be renounced, but he merely means that the reason and will dare not claim any credit for the new life in Christ. In a section on "Gelassenhait in gelassenhait," he insisted that man must not take any credit for his *Gelassenhait*. Even one's *Gelassenhait* must be renounced, even though the reason and will find this difficult. "Dann Christus spricht mitt lyechten worten, es sey dann das ayner alle ding gelass, die er besitzet, so mag er nitt mein junger sein. Syhe nu wie bitter und herb die schüel Christi ist, und ob es unnser vernunffte, willen und natur nitt ain grewlich jemerlich ding ist. . . . damit leeret Christus, das solliche gelassenhait, die alle ding ubergibt, ain teglich Creütz ist, wölliches wir teglich tragen myessen unnd nicht stillsteen, sonder Christo nachvolgen, und da sein mit willen, gedancken, lieb, lust, layd, und allem dem unserm, da Christus ist zü der gerechten Gottes in Gottes ewigen willen verschmeltzen und zü nicht werden." *Sich Gelassen*, biv. The will is still present when one sinks into God and becomes nothing. Karlstadt did not even conceive of man's faculties being transcended in heaven: "So nu der mensch in dissem sterb-

will now obtains its work in the creature. Man now hears, tastes, desires and understands as God desires. There is no ontological union of essences. Finally, although the text refers to the time before creation, speaks of returning to one's source, and demands the abandonment of one's "something," the goal envisaged is not original uncreatedness as in Tauler, but rather God's obtaining his will in an obedient *creature*. This is equally clear in an earlier passage where he said that if the soul is completely renounced, then God possesses, rules and adorns it as in the first creation.[123] There is a very sharp Creator-creature dichotomy and the goal is precisely Adamic perfection. Thus the melting away of man's will into God's will seems to connote not an ontological union but rather a moral conformity of wills effected by grace.

One other passage needs to be examined. After stating that one must renounce absolutely everything, he continued:

> Renunciation presses through and flows over all that is created and comes into its uncreated nothingness, where it was uncreated and nothing, i.e. into its Source and Creator, for when you were nothing [i.e. before creation] then you were completely at one in God's knowledge and will and there was nothing in earth or heaven which you could rightly have claimed for yourself. So too today I and everyone should do the same; I should not know or find anything of mine which delights me. I should be sunk in God's will so that I am truly dead to myself.... I should wish... that I ... would be ashamed... that I see in my soul and powers nothing other than inability for all that is good and on the other hand ability and inclination to all that is evil.... That which is good and praiseworthy, I should carry up to the Source and submit freely, entirely and completely to the judgment of Him who created and gave it.[124]

---

lichen leychnam nit mit allen krefften in Got ruhet, noch ruhen kan, und solt doch mit gantzer seelen, mit vollem hertzen, und allen krefften in Got ruhen, sso muss etwar ein volkommenheyt dem unvolkommen, und dz gantze, den teylen nachvolgen.... und der kleyn und niderig geyst, so gross werden, das er in Gotis himelreich eingehe." *Sabbat*, Hertzsch, I, 42.26-36. See also *ibid.*, p. 43.25-31.

[123] "Wöllicher also alle ding gelasset, der mag ain discipul und leerjung Christi werden, disse seele müss noch auff disen heüttigen tag form loss sein, das ist bloss unnd wüest seyn aller Creaturen, wann sy Gott soll einnemen unnd geschehen lassen, das sy Gott besytzet, herrschet unnd zyeret, als in der ersten schaffung was (hymels und erden)." *Sich Gelassen*, biv-bivV.

[124] For the preceding sentences, see above, n. 61. Karlstadt continues: "Dann gelassenhait dringet und fleüsst durch auss, uber alles das geschaffen ist, und kumpt in ir ungeschaffen nicht, da sy ungeschaffen unnd nicht gewest, das ist in iren ursprung und schöpffer, wann als du nichts gewest bist, da bistu in erkantnuss und willen Gottes gantz mit ainander gestanden, und ist auff erden und hymel nichts gewesst, des du dich hettest mögen mit recht annemen. Also soll ich und

When one looks at this total passage, it is clear that here too Karlstadt was not calling for a return to uncreatedness. He referred to the state of pre-existent unity with God before creation only to indicate that man has no claim at all to anything in creation. Man returns to his Source only in the sense that he ascribes all good things to God, the source of all things. Man can claim as his own nothing except evil. By thinking of his nothingness before creation, man is reminded that he must attribute everything to God. As the previous passage made clear, however, the goal Karlstadt envisaged was an obedient creature, not an escape from creation itself.

Karlstadt spoke of "deification" very infrequently. In one instance the usage was quite incidental.[125] In another case, being united with God and being "deified" seemed to be parallel to being infused with love by the Holy Spirit.[126] The terminology was partly mystical, but the substance was essentially Augustinian. It would seem that Karlstadt's occasional usage of the term *vergotten* did not involve any substantive borrowing from the mystics.

Karlstadt's use of the concept "ground of the soul" provides

---

menigklicher noch heütte thün, und von mir unnd von den meynen nicht wyssen oder finden, des mich gelusten möcht, und solt in Gottes willen also versuncken sein, das ich mir warhafftigklich erstorben wer. . . . Darumb solt ich wünschen . . . das ich . . . schemet . . . das ich in meiner seele und krefften nichts anders sehe, dann unvermögenhait zü allem das güt ist, und widerumb vermögenhait und züneig, zü allem dem das böss, strefflich, lesterlich und schmechlich ist, der ir ich kaines möcht und wolt annemen, sonder vil lieber verleücken, als ain böss myssethat, das aber güt und lobwirdig ist, das solt ich alles, auff in den ursprung tragen, unnd dem zü erkennen bloss und frey und gantz der es geschaffen und geben hatt." *Sich Gelassen*, aiv. An interesting text in Staupitz also contains a reference to emptying oneself of creatureliness and returning to one's origin: "Siquidem laudando deum in se immensum in nobis magnifacimus, comparatione illius et universam creaturam nihili facientes, paramus dignum deo habitaculum et efficimur templum spiritus sancti, deo plenum et omni creatura vacuum. . . . Nihil ergo creaturae felicius quam redire cum laude in suum principium, recedere a se, accedere ad deum. Neque enim potest digne laudari deus a quoquam sine sui annihilatione." *Libellus de executione aeternae praedestinationis*, chapter 2, paragraphs 4-5 (for a translation, see Oberman, *Forerunners*, p. 176). Neither Staupitz nor Karlstadt of course meant that the *viator* could return to uncreatedness. For a discussion of Staupitz' "mysticism," see Steinmetz, *Misericordia Dei*, pp. 152ff.

[125] *Von manigfeltigkeit*, EiiV.

[126] "Als dann umbgeusset der H. Geist götliche lieb yns hertze, und do wirt ein recht und gantz hertz zü Got gekert, und mit Got vereynt und vergött. Also magk es nit gescheen, das einer Got mit eynem gantzen hertzen liebe. und hab etwas nebend oder mit Got lieb" (*ibid.*, FiiV). Erich Vogelsang has pointed out that Luther also used the word deification to refer to the change affected by grace. "Luther und die Mystik," *Luther Jahrbuch*, 1937, p. 48. For a third instance, see *Sich Gelassen*, fiii-fiiiV.

another illustration of his terminological similarity to and substantive difference from the mystics. Some passages sound very much like Tauler at first. Man does not come to know God in the reason with which the doctors dispute about God, but rather, in the ground of the soul.[127] God places his noblest work in the ground of the soul where God dwells, teaches, and rules in spiritual unity. However, since the reason disapproves of God's placing this work in the soul at the beginning before he produces other works there, the ground of the soul should develop terror and bitterness toward its created reason and flee from it.[128] Is the ground of the soul uncreated? Or, is Karlstadt insisting à la Tauler that one must go beyond the rational and volitional powers of the soul into the pure ground in order to achieve union?[129]

Karlstadt's divergence from the mystics is at least three-fold. First, in contrast to Eckhart's spark, the ground of the soul is clearly created.[130] Second, Karlstadt, unlike Tauler, made no systematic attempt to distinguish the ground of the soul from the powers or faculties of the soul. It is true that the passages noted above seem to imply a distinction between the reason and the ground of the soul, although, as will be seen, Karlstadt's main point lay elsewhere. One

---

[127] "Das ewig leben steet in dem, das sy den waren Got allain erkennen, und den geschickten Jesum Christum Joan. 17. Diss erkantnuss Gotes geschicht nicht in der vernunft oder in dem falschen natürlichen liechte, als die Doctores von Got disputieren, sonder im grund der selen, in götlichem unbetrieglichem liechte, und macht den menschen ainen freünd Gottes, dann es veraynt die seele Got dem herren. . . . Also ist das ewig leben ain warhafftig erkennen Gotes und Christi, wölchs der gayst allain eingibt und leret, wann er sich mit der seele veraynt und ain ding wirdt." *Sermon vom Stand*, bV.

[128] " . . . Got leget das höchst werck vor allen in den grund der selen, in welchem grund Got wonet, leret, rästet, untherweiset, und herschet, vereyndlich, und in geistlicher eynigkeit. Weil es auch anders in der vernüfft ist dann in götlicher eindruckung, so dünckets unser vernunfft seltzam, ia nerrisch sein, das Gott sein bestes und gröstes werck zu dem aller ersten inn geschaffen geist leget, und bawhet darnach andere werck uff das selbige beste werck. Aber es sol der vernufft billich nerrisch sein, uff das sie in Gottes kunst auch zu einer nerrin werd, und der grund unserer selen einen grawhen unnd bitterkeit von irer geschaffnen vernufft fassen, und sie flihen möge. . . . So auch drucket Gott seine liebreiche kunst in ein new hertz. . . ." *Zweyen höchsten gebotten*, Hertzsch, I, 51.10-30.

[129] Cf. *ibid.*, p. 61.8-10: "Das hertz bloss muss werden von allen creaturischen kleyderen oder bildnüss." But he added immediately: "Das ist, dz hertz muss werden beschnitten." For the context, see above, n. 86. This statement must be understood in light of the following discussion.

[130] Right after stating that God creates his highest work in the ground of the soul, he restated his point in this way: "God places his best and greatest work in the created spirit." See above, n. 128. Also *ibid.*, p. 57.30-32.

other passage also suggests that he may have been aware of the distinction.[131] But here as elsewhere, Karlstadt made no use of the distinction. Generally he seemed to be oblivious to the distinction, for, as will be shown presently, he frequently interchanged "ground of the soul" with "heart" which connoted the center of man's affections. If the ground is distinct from the powers of the soul, then the affections are not in the ground.

The third and most significant divergence from the mystics is that the union with God effected in the ground of the soul does not involve the abandonment of the soul's rational and volitional faculties. The noble work which God creates in the ground where he dwells in spiritual unity is precisely knowledge which is "rich in love." [132]

> God is accustomed to descend . . . into the ground of our heart and . . . leave his work in the ground of the soul. And that very work is called faith which is a knowledge of God. And it marries the heart with God.[133]

Before partaking of the Lord's Supper, the communicant must have a passionate remembrance of Christ's death in his "ground." [134] Thus when Karlstadt castigated "created reason" in *Zweyen höchsten gebotten*, he was not urging the soul to turn inward and go beyond all distinctions of knowing and loving, for he believed that love and knowledge are in the ground of the soul. Rather he was denouncing that reason which dislikes the priority of grace. Reason objects to the fact that God must produce loving faith in the (ground of the) soul before man can love God and neighbor.[135] Similarly in the passage from *Sermon vom Stand*, it is precisely *knowledge* of God which occurs in the ground of the soul. Karlstadt insisted that this knowledge occurs in the ground of the soul rather than in that reason which conducts professional theological disputes, in order to emphasize his point that the Spirit alone inspires true (i.e. *liebreich*) knowledge of God and

---

[131] "Also zeüget er unsere krefften unnd gründ der selen an Christum." *Gelaub*, dii.

[132] See above, n. 128.

[133] "Syhe Gott pflegt durch seine krefftten in grunndt unserer hertzen absteygen, unnd sich selbs nach seyner abgeen der krafftt offenbaren, unnd aussprechen. Alles durch seynen lebendtigen mund, der eyn eynplickendt liecht ist, unnd lasset sein werck im grunde der seelen, unnd das selb werck haysset der glawb wöllicher eyn erkanndtnis Gottes ist, und verheyrattet das hertz mitt Gott, und das hertz, würdt alls bald starck." *Ayn schöner Sermonn*, BiiV. So too *Gelaub*, cii.

[134] *Ob man . . . erweysen müge*. Aiii; also *Missbrauch*, AivV, C, CV.

[135] See above, n. 128.

Christic.[136] Mere rational understanding cannot produce knowledge rich in love. In contradistinction to the German mystics, then, the union with God in the ground of the soul does not require that one go beyond the faculties of the soul.

It may be, in fact, that the term "ground of the soul" was merely a convenient, contemporary tool which Karlstadt used to underline his demand for complete sincerity and total commitment. One must know divine righteousness "in the ground" rather than in the shell or bark, i.e. superficially.[137] The proclamation of the Lord's death in the Eucharist must flow from the "ground of the heart," for God abhors those who praise him with their mouths while their hearts are far from Him.[138] Thus, one should examine oneself before going to the Lord's table.

> This examination consists of inwardness and looks right into the ground of the soul where God acts and produces his gifts. Therefore, Paul leads each person to himself, and not to another man as the papists have done [with their father confessors]. . . . When you want to take the Lord's Supper, you should go into your inwardness and not know superficially whether you have a sincere and worthy remembrance of Christ so that you may take it, but rather feel an experience, i.e. a certain knowledge of your self that you are as Christ would have you.[139]

Karlstadt constantly interchanged the word "heart" with "ground of the soul."[140] "Ground of the soul" probably had very little technical

---

[136] See above, n. 127.

[137] "Es ist nicht müglich, dz einer in dem mittel glauben selig werd. Es ist aber widerumb auch war, das keiner in diesem unglauben verthümbt wirt, denn diser glaub und unglaub sehen den kern götlicher gerechtigkeit nicht an im grund, sondern in der schelnen oder rinden." *Gelaub*, bii. So too biiV. In this treatise, Karlstadt described a middle state between genuine belief and actual unbelief.

[138] *Missbrauch*, AiiiV.

[139] "Dyse prüfung steet in der inwendigkait, und sihet gerad in den grundt der selen, in welchen Got züthün hatt, und seine gabe schaffet. Darumb füret Paul. eynen yegklichen zü sich, und nicht zü andern menschen, als die Papisten than haben. . . . In dein innwendigkait soltu geen, wenn du des herren Abentmal nemen wilt, unnd nicht oben hyn erkennen, ob du ain redlich und wirdig gedechtnuss Christi habest, dass du es nemest, sonder ain erfarung, das ist, ain gewiss erkantnuss deiner selbs, empfinden, dass du seyest, als dich Christus haben will." *Ibid.*, C (see below, n. 377 for the section omitted).

[140] E.g.: "Ich rede zeyten von der selbstendige lieb Gottes, die sich dem *hertzen* offenbar machet, zeyten von dem werck welches die selbige lieb (das ist Got selber) im *grundt der selen* lasset ligen." *Zweyen höchsten gebotten*, Hertzsch, I, 58.32-35. (My italics). So also *ibid.*, pp. 57.28-39, 58.10-14. "Und alle disse ding zerbrechen und zerstrewen die seel und verdecken den grundt, und verstopffen das hertz." *Ibid*, p. 61.26-27 (so too lines 28-40). *Ayn schöner Sermonn*, BiiV (see above, n. 133). *Missbrauch*, AiiiV. He could speak of the heart and conscience on one page and of

theological meaning for Karlstadt. Perhaps the phrase was merely a convenient way of announcing that one must experience and taste God "in the heart and not just in the head." [141] Certainly the ground of the soul was created. He did not systematically distinguish it from the soul's faculties. Accordingly, and most significantly, union with God in the ground of the soul did not involve the abandonment of the rational and volitional powers. Thus Karlstadt's use of the concept, the ground of the soul, differed greatly from that of the mystics.[142]

It is quite clear in fact that Karlstadt did not advocate the *unio mystica*. In an important passage in *Gelaub*, he spoke of God's infusion of "faith rich in love or love rich in faith" in the inward ground of the soul. This infusion, which he also called a "revelation" occurs as follows:

> The aforesaid revelation ... makes one perceive God and God's truth, and yet does not make one see God. One indeed hears God's voice, but yet does not see the eternal God. This revelation is a work inscribed in the soul as a figure of a seal is impressed in the wax. ... Just as the seal imprints its form in the wax through its figure, so also God imprints his faith in our hearts through the descending beam of his truth, *although neither God nor his divine truth are seen by us here.* ... For when God talks intimately and speaks with the soul, the heart hears God's voice, but does not see the God who speaks. ... But when the uncreated Wind transforms the man's old life and gives birth to a new man, then the new-born man understands that his birth comes from above, and he also notices who the Spirit is ..., but he cannot see the Spirit. ... [The Father] reveals Himself and the revelation is called faith which binds and glues one to the Revealer.[143]

the heart, conscience and ground of the soul on another without altering his meaning (*Testament*, BV and Biii).

[141] That, I think is a modern pietistic way of translating Karlstadt's dictum: "Der ewigen willen müss man nyt yn vernunfftiger, sonder in synlicher weiss lernen und smecken." *Von manigfeltigkeit*, F (for the preceding sentences, see above, n. 57). And that is precisely what he meant in the passage from *Sermon vom Stand*, bV discussed above.

[142] Thus it will hardly do to say, as does Kriechbaum, that in his use of the phrase, "ground of the soul," Karlstadt is solidly within the German mystical tradition (*Grundzüge*, p. 33). Another related instance of Karlstadt's significant modification of mystical concepts is provided by his use of the word "funcklin." Whereas Eckhart employed the word to refer to the uncreated ground of the soul, Karlstadt used it to speak of a divinely bestowed desire and love for God. "Gott pflantzet seine liebe oder solchen gestrengen lust (nach sich) in das hertz. Zum ersten mit kleinen füncklin ein, das ist Gott lässt zu ersten kleine füncklin seiner lieb einfliessen und uffgeen in der selen. ... Disse füncklin seind hertzliche begerungen zu dem aller besten gut." *Zweyen höchsten gebotten*, Hertzsch, I, 59. 14-23.

[143] "Das obgedachte offenbarung, wenn sie ein werck ist in der seele gelassen, Gott, und Gottes warheyt erkennen machet, und doch nicht Gott sehen machet.

The union with God experienced by the *viator* is a moral likeness to God implanted in the soul when the Spirit regenerates the old self. Faith, love and knowledge glue the soul to God:

> Through love and faith Christ dwells in ... the inner man. In and through the knowledge of the surpassing love of Christ, we have a participation [in Christ]. Ephe. 3. As it is written, "If anyone loves me, the Father and I will come to him and will dwell in him" (John 14). ... Through faith, love and knowledge of the surpassing love of Christ, we have a sharing in and participation with Christ and his fullness ... and we are filled with all gifts. ... Our participation in [Christ] consists completely and entirely of love, knowledge or faith in Christ.[144]

In a discussion of the way the participant in the Lord's Supper has a "fellowship" with Christ's body and blood, Karlstadt noted: "For participation or fellowship cannot exist without understanding [of Christ's death], just as little as can the union of the rational creature with God begin or continue without knowledge of God." [145] Such

---

Demnach höret einer Gottes stimm, und sihet doch nicht den unendtlichen Gott. Diese offenbarung ist ein werck in die selle geschriben, als ein figur eynes sigels in ein wachs gedruckt ist. ... Wie auch der sigel seine form, inss wachs durch seyn figur aussdrucket, also auch drucket Gott seynen glauben auss, in unser hertz, durch seinen abgeenden straheln seiner warheyt, wie wol weder Gott, noch seyne götliche warheyt gesehen würt von uns alhie.

"Ein ander exempel nim von dem wind den man prausen höret und dannest nit sihet. ... Also auch ist Gottes stymm dem wind vergleichet, denn wenn Gott koset oder mit der seelen redet, so höret das hertz Gottes stymm, und sihet den Gott nit der redet. Der mensch entpfindt eygentlich das züsprechen Gottes, er weiss auch für war das er etwas lernet, aber in dem ist etwan grosser zweyfel, das er nit weiss wer leret. Wenn aber der ungeschaffen windt, des menschen alt leben umbsturtzet, und gepieret eynen newen menschen, so versteht der new geborn mensch, das seyn geburt von oben herraber kumpt, und mercket also, wer der geist ist, und woher der geyst feret, er kan aber den geyst nit sehen, auch nit durchs gesicht erkennen, als durchs gehöre. So geets mit aller offenbarung des vatters, er offenbart sich ... unnd die offenbarung heysset der glaub, der an den offenbarer bindtet, und anleymet." *Gelaub*, ciiV-ciii (my italics).

[144] "Durch den glauben rayniget er die hertzen, durch lieb und glauben, wonet Christus in uns, nicht im bauch, oder im maul, sondern im geyst, in dem inwendigen menschen, In dem erkentnuss der ubertreffenlichen lieb Christi, und durchs erkentnuss haben wir gemeinschafft Ephe. 3. als geschriben, So mich jemandt liebt, zü dem wirdt der vatter und ich kommen, und werden ein wonung bey im haben, Johan. 14. Nu syhe lieber Doctor Luther, das wir durch den glauben durch lieb, durch erkenntnuss der uberschwencklichen lieb Christi gemeinschafft und gesellschafft haben mit Christo, und mit seiner fülle, und werden also durch den erkannten Christum in allerley gaben erfült. ... und unser gemeinschafft steet gar und gantz in der lieb, in erkantnuss oder im glauben Christi. ..." *Erklerung*, Ciii. So too *Zweyen höchsten gebotten*, Hertzsch, I, 53.32-38 although less explicitly.

[145] "Denn geselschafft oder gemeinschaff kan one verstand nit gesein, als wenig die vereinung der vernüfftigen creaturen mit Got one Gottes erkantnüs anfahen oder bestehen kan." *Ob man ... erweysen müge*, BivV-C.

statements leave little room for a mystical union. The only union envisaged is a moral, fiduciary one effected by sanctifying grace. Whether Karlstadt described the inner transformation of man as a new birth, a harmony of wills, a life of love for or delight in God, a sinking into God's will or a union with God in the ground of the soul, he was speaking only of an ethical change in the creature.

## (d) Faith

The great emphasis on self-denial and regeneration led to a new way of discussing genuine faith. Already in early 1523 in *Sich Gelassen*, he insisted that "it is impossible that one believes God and remains unrenounced." [146] By *Zweyen höchsten gebotten* and *Gelaub*, this emphasis had developed into Karlstadt's conception of "faith rich in love or love rich in faith."

Scripture frequently ascribes the properties of faith to love and vice versa.

> Faith without love is worthless; love without faith does not please [God]. Therefore the right work is a faith rich in love or a love rich in faith which knows and highly esteems God. . . . That the scripture allots to love the property of faith and on the other hand allots to faith the work of love is clear from the fact that only love active through faith is something before God and on the other hand only faith active through love is something before God. Faith without love is worthless (I Cor. 13), for the godless also know God.[147]

Karlstadt's subsequent work on faith and unbelief contained the same ideas. "Faith has passionate love [and] great desire for the uncreated Light; it receives the eternal Light, loves it greatly, and

---

[146] "Derwegen ist es unmüglich das ainer Gott glaub und bleyb ungelassen." *Sich Gelassen,* eiv. See too eiii. Also: "Nu geb ich dir zu erkennen ob ich unbillich geschryben, und hoff, du werdest erkennen und sprechen wa gelassenhait ist, von wölcher ich hab geredt, das da selbst der glaub, hoffnung und lieb sey zü Gott, wa ungelassenhait lebt das daselbst eyttel unglaub, aygen lieb stee" (*ibid,,* eivV-f).

[147] "Glaub on lieb taug nit. Liebe on glauben behagt nit. Drumb ist dz recht werck ein liebreicher glaub, oder glaubreiche lieb. Welche Gott erkennet und hoch schatzet als einer ein ding erkennet und hochachtet, dz im wolgefelt und lieb ist. . . . Das die schrifft der lieb die eygenschafft des glaubens, unnd widerumb den glauben die werck der liebe zu messe, ist auss dem offenbar, das die liebe allein etwas ist vor Gott, welche durch den glauben thätig ist, oder der glaub der durch die lieb geschefftig ist, der ist allein etwas vor Gott. Glaub one lieb taugt nit. I Co. 13. denn die gotlosen erkennen Gott auch." *Zweyen höchsten gebotten*, Hertzsch, I, 52.16-20, 29-34. See all of pp. 52-54. Karlstadt added: "Das hab ich alles derhalben gesagt, das man nit irr in den worten, lieb und glauben, und das ir nit ein blinde lieb habet, Oder einen bapieren und lieblosen glauben." *Ibid.*, p. 54.7-9.

delights itself in it. . . . Faith flees the works of darkness." [148] True faith is a loving knowledge of God rather than mere intellectual awareness which even the devils possess. One may of course designate the devils' knowledge faith, but "it is impossible that the devilish faith be genuine faith." "Genuine faith must receive the Light with love, delight and joy: Hence the rebirth occurs." [149] Faith is the total response and stance of the regenerate man.[150]

By defining faith as the total stance of the regenerate man, he forged a powerful weapon for attacking lax Christians. Passionate knowledge of Christ makes one Christ-like.[151] Consequently he who lacks love toward God and neighbor cannot be a believer.[152] Laziness in the performance of works of love toward the neighbor is a certain sign that one lacks a fervent remembrance of God's words.[153] In his last work against Luther he mocked Luther for supposing that his works should remain uncensured provided his doctrine was correct. Genuine faith leads to self-mortification and a new life of righteousness.[154]

---

[148] "Der glaub hat hitzige lieb, grossen lust zü dem ungeschaffnen liechte, dz ewig liecht nimbt er an, er liebets vast, und belüstet sich drinn. . . . Der glaub fleühet die werck des finsternüs mit ernster flucht. . . ." *Gelaub,* aiii-aiiiV.

[149] " . . . und des teüfels erkantnüss, mag ein glaub genent werden (fern von dem rechtem glauben zü reden) in der weiss ists auch ware, das die teufeln auch glauben. . . . Aber es ist unmöglich, das der teüfelisch glaub ein rechter glaub sey. . . . das müss seyn, und kan nit anderss sein, den das der recht glaub, das liecht, mit lieb, lust und freyden annemen müss, daher die widergeburdt kompt." *Ibid.,* dV-dii.

[150] Karlstadt's conception of faith sounds rather Thomistic, but it is not really the same. For St. Thomas, "to believe is an act of the intellect assenting to the truth." Faith must be formed by love because charity is needed to "quicken the act of faith." *Summa Theologica,* II, II, Q. 4, art. 5, and art. 3 ad. 1; in *Basic Writings of Saint Thomas Aquinas,* ed. Anton C. Pegis (2 vols.; New York, 1945), II, 1102 and 1099. Whereas Aquinas was content to define faith as an act of the intellect, Karlstadt wanted to define it as an act of the total person. Faith pertains both to the intellect and the will.

Most of Karlstadt's treatises of this period contained the concept of "faith rich in love." He used it in *Ayn schöner Sermonn,* C. In *Sabbat* he spoke of "liebereicher weisheit" (*Sabbat,* Hertzsch, I, 27.30). See also p. 31.37-32.2. In the Eucharistic tracts he talked of that faith which is a "passionate, heartfelt, liebreychen knowledge of the crucified" (*Erklerung,* Aiv). So too *Missbrauch,* BV (see below, n. 167), BivV-C.

[151] "Denn hatt er das wirdig und prünstig erkantnuss des leybs Christi, der unsere sünde mit grosser bitterkayt und verspottung getragen . . . so wirdet er Christförmig, und danckpar dem leiden, nüchtern, sittsam, weyss, vernünfftig, züchtig." *Missbrauch,* BivV-C.

[152] *Sabbat,* Hertzsch, I, 31-2 (see especially 31.37-32.4).

[153] *Gemach,* Hertzsch, I, 84.17-24.

[154] "Das leere ich, das predig ich, das schreyb ich, wenn ich nun nitt darnach thet, solt mich D. Luther straffen, der doch seyn werck ungestrafft haben will,

> I do not make external works a matter of conscience, but I convict the lying and false faith which boasts of freedom and yet is a prisoner of the devil whose he is and whose work he does. . . . He who knows Christ . . . walks in the works of Christ. But he does not become a Christian by works.[155]

Good works are a sign of that "faith rich in love" which the new birth effects.

### (e) *The mediation of grace*

During his Augustinian period Karlstadt believed the external word to be a necessary but insufficient part of the communication of grace. For a time in 1520 and 1521, it is true, he talked in a very Lutheran tone and omitted all discussion of the external word's insufficiency, but by late 1521 he again insisted that although external preaching was necessary, it could never mediate grace unless the Spirit touched the heart. It now remains to be seen whether Karlstadt in his Orlamünde theology moved beyond even his essentially Augustinian position of 1517 and late 1521 to a more spiritualist conception. Did Karlstadt come to think, as Luther charged, that the Holy Spirit requires no bridge to come to man? [156]

Some statements might seem to imply that the external word is unnecessary for the mediation of grace. God had the prophets discard various external practices of the law in order to show that "no creature can unite itself with God through external things." [157] In discussing baptism he asserted that the Spirit can accomplish his work "without physical things." [158]

---

wenn sein leere recht ist, hoff aber es werden beyde lere und werck bey mir durch Gottes gnad gespürt, das ich one rumb rede." *Anzeig,* Hertzsch, II, 93.36-94.2

[155] "Da mach ich nit gewissen [cf. p. 102.16-18, 35-38] durch die eusserliche werck, sondern ich über weyss den lugenhafftigen und falschen glauben der sich freyheit rümbt, und doch ein gefangner man ist des Teuffels, des er ist und seyn werck thut. . . . Wölcher Christum erkennt, der ist durchs erkenntnuss Christi frey worden, und geet in den wercken Christi einher, er wirdt aber nitt ein Christ durch die werck." *Ibid.,* p. 100.25-28, 35-37.

[156] Kriechbaum argues that the inward activity of the Spirit sometimes occurs quite independently of the external word in Karlstadt (Kriechbaum, *Grundzüge,* pp. 36-37).

[157] "Auch hat Got opfer und andere eusserliche geberde verwerffen lassen durch seyn propheten als Esa. 1. Psal. L. und anderen vil enden geschriben steht. und hat da mit wollen weysen und lernen, das sein ewig will, mit eusserlichenn opfern nicht wurd erfueltt. das sich auch keyn creatur mit Got durch eusserliche ding vereynen kann." *Von manigfeltigkeit,* Giii.

[158] "On leiplich dinge." *Ibid.,* GiiV (see below, n. 352 for the context).

That which must be and is unchangeable and is to remain eternally, God creates inwardly in the naked soul. For God is a Spirit; therefore the creature must join itself with God's uncreated Spirit with and through the spirit.[159]

Again with reference to the sacraments he argued that

the sacrament does not make us cry to God, "Father, Father." For it is much too coarse to touch the ground of the soul. . . . The sacrament cannot assure our spirit. . . . Assurance belongs to God's Spirit, not to any creature.[160]

It is important to remember that all these statements were made in the context of a discussion of the sacraments. Nevertheless, they seem to be stated in a general way. Further, he could also state unequivocally that many know the letter of scripture well but do not know God. "It is those who are impelled by God, not by the letter, who are God's sons." [161]

It is certainly true that Karlstadt's first concern apropos the relation between word and Spirit was to insist that mere external hearing or reading does not make one a Christian. However, if one were to conclude from this emphasis that he denied any necessary connection between word and Spirit, it would be difficult to explain why he insisted so strongly on the place of preaching. His major reason for refusing to allow each householder to select his own day for celebrating the Sabbath was that public preaching would be disrupted. If, however, the head of each household ensured the preaching and reading of God's word, then everyone could choose the most convenient day.[162] Borrowing a concept from Luther

---

[159] "Aber das seyn müss, unnd unenderlich ist, unnd ewig soll bleyben, das schüff Got inwendich in der blossen sele. Dan Got ist ein geist, derhalben müss sich die geschaffen creatur, mit unnd durch den geist, mit Gots ungeschaffen geist vereynen." *Ibid.*, GiiiV.

[160] "Das sacrament machet unns ye nit zü Got schreyen, vatter, vatter. Denn es ist vil zü grob, dass es den grundt der selen anrür. ich geschweyg, lere. . . . so kann dz sacrament unsern geist auch nit versichern, und der schwacheit unsers geists helffen. Denn solchs geschray und versicherung gehören ainem werck mayster zü. Die versicherung steet Gotss geyst, und keiner creaturn zü. . . . soll man dem gayst nach eylen, sich nach im lernen sehnen, und das durch den geyst empfahen, das dem geyst züsteet, das auch niemandts denn der gayst geben kann, nemlich, die versicherung vergebner sünden." *Missbrauch*, CiiV-Ciii.

[161] *Sich Gelassen*, bV (see below, n. 164).

[162] "Wenn auch ein ydes hauss, in eyner stadt, eynen besondern sabbat wolt halten, würd eine stadt ordnung vorruckt, und würden also die predigen auch in ein unordnung kommen. So aber dem worte Gottis oder den predigten kein abbruch geschee, oder sso man alle tage, Gottis wortt, lessen oder predigen würde, stünd es in eynes ydens haussvaters macht, einen sibenden tag, vor sich

and a line or two from Erasmus, he insisted that the priesthood
of all believers means that every Christian must proclaim the external word:

> There is God's command to all heads of households. They should
> teach their children and servants. Everyone is obliged to preach God's
> word in the house, at the table, in the morning, in the evening, in the
> field, in the barn. Whether he rests or works, he should consider
> God's word and step forward and proclaim it to those who stand
> around. . . . That is a general command to all who understand God's
> word. Through that command God has established them all as
> priests.[163]

If Karlstadt intended his dictum that the Spirit can complete his work
without anything external to apply to the external word as well as to
the sacrament, why did he both in theory, and also in practice at
Orlamünde, stress the importance of preaching?

But did he so intend that statement? Parenthetical, cursory remarks
in a number of treatises suggest that he did assume a genuine connection between external word and Spirit. In *Sich Gelassen* he condemned
those who adduce the scripture simply to appear clever, but he added
parenthetically that it is out of scripture that we should know and
love God.[164] In *Ursachen* he explained why he had remained silent from early 1523 until the end of the year. He who handles
God's word in sermon or treatise should be pure, for God's word
is pure. Accordingly, Karlstadt found himself in a dilemma for

---

und sein gesind zu erwelen, der yhm, und seinem gesinde am aller bequem-
sten sein möchte, und seiner arbeit am zutreglichsten." *Sabbat*, Hertzsch, I,
41.34-42.6.

[163] "Do steht Gottis gepott zu allen haussvettern, das sie yre kinder unnd
gesinde leren sollen, und ein yederman ist schuldig, das er Gottis wort predig ym
hauss, oder tysch, des morgens, des abendes, im acker, in der scheunen, er stee
müssig oder arbeite, so sol er Gottis wort betrachten, und erfür tretten, und
verkündigen den yenen, so umb yhn stehn oder sein. . . . Das ist ein gemein gepot
zu allen geredt, die Gottis wort verstehn, und Got hat sie alle, durch das gebot,
prister gesetzt." *Ursachen*, Hertzsch, I, 18.7-17.

[164] "Sych da wie kan ainer das gesetz Gottes handeln und halten, und Gott
weder erkennen, weder nach ime fragen. Den büchstaben erkent ainer wol oder
hatt lust in ime. Aber Gott erkennt er nit, wann er mit lieb und lust in dem büchstaben steet. Dann die Gottes süne seind die werden von Gott getryben, nit von
dem büchstaben. 20 [?] Ja es ist dise weysshait vermaledeyt und nitt ain göttliche,
sonder ain menschlich weysshait. . . . Was ist dise weysshait anders, dann ain
weysshait in menschen augen. wann wir die schrifft und andere creaturen (*auss
wölchen wir Gott solten erkennen und lieben*) zü unserm lust eintragen, und wöllen etwas
vor aynem andern wissen . . . frag dein hertz und antwurt mir. Ists nit ain ver-
flüchte weysshait?" *Sich Gelassen*, bV-bii (my italics).

he realized that he was quite unrighteous. He concluded, however, that he would preach and write, trusting that God's word would purify him:

> I know also that if I will handle God's word with a good will, it will purify me no less than faith. For Christ has made his disciples pure through his word. What should be lacking in the word which purifies those who handle it in godly fear? For God's word is like a fire which burns and purifies.[165]

A paraphrase of Romans 10:17 written a few months later underlined the importance of preaching the external word: "Faith comes from hearing the preaching, and preaching is from God's word." [166]

> The apostles and we preach the joyful message of the surrendered body and shed blood of Jesus Christ. . . . From the knowledge of Christ arises that remembrance of Christ which is not a coarse, cold, lazy remembrance but a fresh, passionate and powerful remembrance which gives joy, considers the surrendered body and shed blood of Christ as precious . . . and makes [one] Christ-like.[167]

The proclamation of Christ's death improves other people for it gives rise to that passionate remembrance from which good works flow.[168] In the dialogue on the Eucharist the priest confessed that he lacked the righteousness which the Spirit brings. The layman Peter asked in surprise: "Are you not the poor man who gives God's

---

[165] "Ich weis auch, so ich Gottis wort, mit guttem willen furen werd, das michs nicht mynder wirt reinigen, denn der glaub. Denn Christus hat seyne Jünger reyn gemacht durch sein wordt, was solt denn dem wort Gottis felen, das die reiniget, die es in götlicher furcht handeln? Weyl Gottis wort ist als ein fewr, dz brend und feget." *Ursachen*, Hertzsch, I, 19.25-30. So also p. 9.7-23 where he argued that the minister should crush each heart with God's word and then heal the broken with God's word.

[166] "Seytmal der glaub auss dem gehör der predig, das predigen aber auss den wort Gottes ist." *Missbrauch*, AiiV.

[167] "Aber die Aposteln unnd wir verkhündigen die frölice botschafft des ubergeben leibs und vergossen plüts Jesu Christi, von welchem Christus redet vor seinem todt. Auss dem erkantnuss Christi, wechset dz gedechtnuss Christi, dz nicht ain rohe, kalte, und faule gedechtnuss ist, sonder ayn frische, hitzige, und krefftige gedechtnuss ist, das frölickayt machet oder gibt, welches den ubergeben leyp, und vergossen plüt Christi tewer achtet, das hoch schatzet, das dancksaget, das Christförmig machet, und schämen machet vor allem das Christo entgegen ist." *Ibid.*, BV.

[168] "Denn, ist dz war, dz Got schlünnige straff haben wil, der doch barmhertzig ist zu vergeben, wie vil mehr ist der verflucht und ein grewel vor Gott der feüliglich [=faul] mit den wercken auss bricht, die seinem nechsten zu einer besserung geschehen. Gott wil ein frey freydigen geber haben, der schnell und williglich gibet. . . . Das alles fleüsset auss dem ewigen und einbrünstigen gedechtnüs göttlicher worter." *Gemach*, Hertzsch, I, 84.11-19.

living voice a creaturely form?" And he quickly added that if the priest sincerely desired righteousness, "the Greek scripture which you have just now read is a means bestowed for you." [169] Karlstadt concluded another Eucharistic tract by noting that just as Christ considered it important to provide his disciples with an understanding of his passion, so too "it is also necessary for us to know that. Therefore, one should preach the necessary things to us." [170] The external word would seem to be essential.

The external word may be necessary but it is certainly not sufficient. The external law can explain what things are evil, but this external revelation cannot make one turn from them.[171] Only the inner revelation given by the Holy Spirit can destroy sin.

> Neither preaching, proclamation of the law, lash nor anything else helps unless God sends into the heart of the godless his Spirit who shows him the horror of his evil and causes sin itself to begin to displease him. Man may preach whatever he likes, but the law cannot reveal the idea and understanding of a single sin in the way the revelation of evil should be, i.e. with hatred and horror for evil.[172]

This genuine revelation of sin is not of the letter. Rather, Karlstadt insisted in a genuinely Augustinian way, it happens only when "God's Spirit leads [one] into the truth and speaks in the heart what the external voice cries into the ears." [173] All scripture is a witness which

---

[169] *Dialogus*, Hertzsch, II, 17.21-26 (see below, n. 268).

[170] "Also ists auch alhie mit dieser züsag Christi, meyn leyb wirt für euch gegeben. Christus hat... gesagt, das sein leyb der sey, der für sie, und vile gegeben würd, und hat sie damit in erkantnüs seines leidens wellen füren, auff dz sie behalten würden, wie er auch züvor in den evangelien thet, wenn er von seinen leiden sagt, das uns auch von nöten ist zü wissen. Darumb solt man uns von nötlichen sachen predigen, als von dem leiden Christi." *Ob man ... erweysen müge*, Fvi.

[171] *Anzeig*, Hertzsch, II, 76.11-35.

[172] "Es hilfft weder predigen, noch des gesetzes verkündigung noch streych, noch etwas anders, wenn Gott seynen geyst ins hertz des gotlosen nicht schickt, der im den grewel seyner bossheit zeyg, und mache, das im der sünder selber anfach misshagen, Denn man predig was man wöll, so ist es dem gesetz unmöglich, den synn und verstand eyniger sünde zu offenbaren, als die offenbarung, des bösen seyn soll, Nemlich mitt hass unnd grawen wider das böss, Denn das steet dem geyst Gottes eynigklich zu." *Ibid.*, p. 75.13-21. So too p. 63.

[173] "Solt ich das nit wissen das Gottes gesetz geystlich ist, gerecht, heylig unnd gut, das es den inwendigen menschen, geystlich, gerecht, heylig und gut mache, wenn Gott seyn gesetz ins hertz schreybt, und druckt? Wenn Gottes geyst in die warheit füret, unnd das ins hertz redet, das die eusserliche stymm, in die oren schreyet?" *Ibid.*, pp. 62.37-63.2. For Augustine, see above chapter I, nn. 45-47.

points to Christ: "The law does not reveal sin any more than the scripture reveals Christ, namely as a witness." [174]

Karlstadt sharply attacked the learned who possessed mere external knowledge of God.

> [Such] understanding was like that of the highly learned people in the universities who . . . can push God's word masterfully backwards and forwards and handle it boldly, but do not know the God who has spoken it. They have their knowledge in their mouth and not in their heart. (To speak from the heart is to be sufficiently moved.) They confess and praise God with their lips . . . but their heart is far away.[175]

Karlstadt included himself. Formerly he supposed that he was a fine Christian when he culled statements from the fathers and scripture for use in debate and writing. But he discovered that one can handle God's law and yet not know God. "It is those who are impelled by God, not by the letter, who are God's sons." [176] This statement, of course, was a denial of the sufficiency, not the necessity, of the external word. He went on to quote John 6:26 and argue that just as Jesus' contemporaries followed him, not because they saw that his miraculous signs pointed to a spiritual truth, but because they desired the physical food, so he and others had occupied themselves with scripture, not because it was a sign pointing to God, but because they took delight in winning theological debates. Biblical expertise does not make one a Christian. One also needs a divinely bestowed love for that to which the scriptural sign points.[177]

In order not to misunderstand Karlstadt, it is very important to see that Karlstadt frequently spoke of the Spirit's activity in the communication of grace in terms of a "revelation," an insertion (*eindruckung*) of knowledge, or God's speaking in the heart with his living voice.

> God must write or insert his faith in our hearts through his divine truth. I understand that as follows. When God wants to make me believing and wants to pour his faith into my hungering and thirsting

---

[174] "Das gesetz offenbaret nit mer sünd, denn die geschrifft Christum offenbaret, nemlich als ein gezeügknuss." *Anzeig*, Hertzsch, II, 77. 10-11.

[175] " . . . etliche Gottes wort höreten und verstundens nicht. . . . Ir verstendtnüs war etwas, als der hochgelerten verstendtnüs ist uff den hohen schülen, die Gottes wort meysterlich hin und her setzen, und dapferlich handeln, und erkennen den Gott nicht, der es geredt hat. Sie haben ir erkantnüs im mund, und nicht im hertzen (von dem hertzen zü reden das genügsam bewegt ist). Sie bekennen und loben Gott mit lippen, zenen, unnd mund, aber ir hertz ist fern. . . . Darumb ist es oben hin in der rinden des baümes, und im eussersten büchstaben der warheit." *Gelaub*, aivV.

[176] *Sich Gelassen*, bV (see above, n. 164).

[177] *Ibid.*, bii.

powers, then God descends into my poor yearning heart with his uncreated and bright truth and reveals himself to my heart. . . . God inserts a work in our hearts through his uncreated glance and divine enlightenment. This very work is called faith which is a knowledge rich in love of God . . . or a revelation of God. . . . This work is the divine knowledge or doctrine which God inserts in the soul with his living mouth. . . .[178]

The "revelation" of the Holy Spirit, however, provides not new conceptual content, but rather the grace which effects the right relationship to what one hears preached:

Man may preach whatever he likes, but the law cannot reveal the idea and understanding of a single sin in the way the revelation of evil should be, i.e. with hatred and horror for evil. For that belongs solely to the Spirit of God. Indeed if the law could insert or pour in (that means *reveal according to Christ's way of speaking*) the understanding of sin, then the law would be a god.[179]

The Spirit's revelation provides a genuine, loving appropriation of the content of scripture.

That which God writes in the heart is the revelation of his Son. It is a knowledge or understanding of his sacrifice and shed blood which the Father alone gives. . . . It is the faith or heartfelt and lively knowledge of the death and shed blood of Christ. Thus Christ throws . . . his blood into hearts through the Holy Spirit . . . and purifies our hearts and consciences by faith.[180]

---

[178] "Demnach müss Gott seinen glauben durch sein götliche warheyt in unser hertz schreiben oder eindrucken, das verstehn ich also. Wenn mich Got wil glaubhafftig machen, und seinen glauben in mein hungerichte unnd dürstige krefften giessen. So geht Got ab, inn mein, arm, begyrigs hertz, mit seyner ungeschaffner unnd liechter warheyt, unnd offenbaret sich meinem hertzen, das er ein warhafftiger unnd getrewer Gott ist. . . . Wenn sich Got also in unserm hertzen aussredt, das er warhafftig ist u. so drucket Gott ein werck inn unser hertz, durch seine ungeschaffne blicken, und gottliches einleüchten, das selb werck heysset der glaub, welcher ein liebreiches erkäntnüss Gottes ist, und die kunst Gottes, oder ein offenbarung Gottes genent ist. . . . Aber in den creaturischen geystern, so Gott hören, heysset diese offenbarung, hören oder lernen verstehn, unnd gleich das werck ist die göttlich kunst oder leer, so Gott mit seinem lebendigem mund, unnd gleichem aussssprechen, in die seele eindruckt." *Gelaub*, cV-cii. So too ciii (see above, n. 143). See also *Ayn schöner Sermonn*, BiiV (the quotation is in n. 133 above). "Weil es auch anders in der vernufft ist dann in göttlicher eindruckung. . . . So auch drucket Gott seine liebreiche kunst in ein new hertz." *Zweyen höchsten gebotten*, Hertzsch, I, 51.17-18, 29-30 (see above, n. 128 for the full statement).

[179] For the first part of this statement, see above, n. 172. Karlstadt continued: "Ja wann das gesetz den verstand der sünden, dem hertzen kündt eintrucken oder eingiessen (das offenbaren heysst, nach der weyss der reden Christi) so wer dz gesetz ein Got." *Anzeig*, Hertzsch, II, 75.21-24. My italics.

[180] "Es seynd zwü eygenschafften, des Newen Testamentes Eine, das Got seine gesetz ins hertz wolt schreyben, Die ander das die vergebung der sünden, dem

The biblical knowledge possessed by the scholar who studies only to win debates is "cursed wisdom." "But if I could renounce my I and 'I-ness' . . . and endure my being and becoming nothing in the eyes of all men, then I might attain a genuine knowledge and love of God."[181] The content of genuine knowledge does not differ from "cursed wisdom." Genuine knowledge and love of God mean almost the same thing in this statement.[182] It is man's relationship to scripture and God which distinguishes "cursed wisdom" from "loving knowledge."

One final passage which has been used to argue that Karlstadt is a spiritualist should be examined.

> Eternal life consists in knowing the true God alone and Jesus Christ who was sent (John 17). This knowledge of God does not occur in the reason or in the false natural light as the doctors dispute about God, but in the ground of the soul, . . . and it makes man a friend of God, for it unites the soul to God. . . . Thus eternal life is a true knowledge of God and Christ which the Spirit alone inspires and teaches when he unites himself to the soul and becomes one thing [with the soul].[183]

Hayo Gerdes thought this passage meant that the spiritual understanding of the kernel or shell of scripture comes not from the activity of the reason, but rather from a direct revelation of the Spirit. Hence Karlstadt's exegesis is spiritualist.[184] Actually, the

---

selben einschreyben ins hertz, so gewiss nachfolgen solt, das Gott der sünden nichts mer will gedencken Hiere. 31. Esai. 43.

"Das Got ins hertz schreybt, das ist die offenbarung seynes Suns, ein kunst oder verstand seynes opffers und seynes vergossen blüts, wölchen verstand der vater allein gibt. Joan. 6. Math. 11. Das ist der glaub oder das hertzlich und lebendig erkanntnuss des todts und vergossen blüts Christi, Also wirft Christus als ein geystlicher priester (durch den heyligen geyst) seyn blüt in die hertzen, seelen, und gewissen, unnd, reyniget unsere hertzen unnd gewissen, durch den glauben Acto. 15. Roma.3.

"Diser offenbarung, oder dem newen gesetz volgt als bald die vergebung der sünd." *Testament*, Bii.

[181] See above, n. 164 for the first part of this discussion. Karlstadt continues: "Also suchen wir Gott auch nit, in diser weyss als angezaygt ist, darumb das er Gott ist oder uns sein wort geben hat, sonder derhalben das wir wol von der geschrifft reden künden, und werden gesehen unnd gelobt. . . . Wann aber ich, mein ich und ichait, ichts und ettwas kent [second edition: künd] zü boden und grund gelassen, unnd leyden das ich in aller menschen augen nicht wer und wurd, so möcht ich in recht erkantnuss und lieb Gottes kummen." *Sich Gelassen*, bii.

[182] Similarly in *Von manigfeltigkeit*, FiiV, Karlstadt said the Spirit "ubergeust die sele mit götlicher kunst" and then noted in the next sentence that the Spirit pours in divine *love*: "Als dann umbgeusset der H. geist götliche lieb yns hertze. . . ." Both statements mean the same thing.

[183] *Sermon vom Stand*, bV (see above, n. 127).

[184] Gerdes, *Luthers Streit mit den Schwärmern*, p. 29.

passage says nothing about the spirit or shell of the law. More importantly, Karlstadt intended only what the previous discussion has
indicated.[185] The true knowledge of God which the Holy Spirit
teaches is not some new content, but rather a right relationship with
God. Grace—or the Holy Spirit—makes one a friend of God.[186] When
Karlstadt spoke of God's revelation in the heart, God's speaking in the
soul with his living voice, and the divine insertion of genuine knowledge, he was speaking of the mediation of grace, not of a second
source of religious knowledge.

Karlstadt nowhere denied that the external word is a necessary part
of the communication of grace. Because he assumed that the Spirit
works in the heart only if the word has been proclaimed, he stressed
the importance of preaching. His own experience, however, had
taught him that reading or hearing scripture did not guarantee that the
Spirit had transformed the inner man. Therefore he emphasized the
importance of the inner activity of the Spirit who, by creating love for
Him to whom scripture points, enables men to have right knowledge
of scripture and believing love for God. Because he called this proper
relationship to God and scripture "knowledge," he could say that
God reveals himself to the soul. But this revelation is not directly
given information, but rather supernaturally bestowed grace. In
short, the external word is a necessary, albeit insufficient, part of the
mediation of grace. In that he was true to his earlier Augustinianism.

### (f) The ground of eternal salvation

It was seen in chapter one that the early Karlstadt accepted the
Augustinian view that heaven is the reward of divinely bestowed good
deeds. By 1521, however, he had adopted the more Lutheran view
that since all good deeds contain sin, eternal life depends solely on

---

[185] Namely (to give another example): "Wolcher one erkenntnuss, unnd one
erleuchtung des heyligen geystes, sünde auss vernunfft durchs gesetz allein versteet,
der versteet die sünde oder das bösse also, das er mer lust zu der sünde hat denn
vor." *Anzeig*, Hertzsch, II, 80. 9-12.

[186] There is a similar passage in *Zweyen höchsten gebotten*, Hertzsch, I, 57.28-58.1:
"Ursach und ursprung der lieb des nechsten ist disse, Gott ist die liebe selber, und
sein lieb ist ein selbstendige und ungeschaffne liebhabende krafft, die den grund
der selen, das ist das aller inwendigste anrüret. ... Gott seine ausserwelte creaturen lieb hat, Das beweyset Gott durch die sendung unnd menschwerdung
Christi. Derhalben, wenn sich die götlich lieb in eines menschen hertz *offenbaret*,
und ergeüsset, so *leret* sye auch lieb des nechsten, und machet lieb haben, alles das
Gott lieb hat" (my italics). The revelation and teaching of God do not provide
some new content; rather, this revelation or teaching is the divine grace which
enables man to follow the example of the Incarnate One.

faith in Christ's atoning death. How did his break with Luther and his new emphasis on the necessity of self-denial and inner regeneration affect his view of the ground of eternal life?

Karlstadt's first two major writings of 1523 concentrated on the absolute necessity of self-mortification and obedience to God. He underlined the importance of doing God's will in *Von manigfeltigkeit* by insisting that he who wants to stand approved before God's eyes must do God's will and live according to God's commands.[187] "The Christian's life and death, . . . blessedness and damnation depend solely on the accomplishing or abandoning of the divine will." [188]

> Evil works proceed from our will; good works from God's will. The works of our will lead to hell. . . . The works of God's will lead to blessedness. As it is written: "Not everyone who says 'Lord, Lord' will enter heaven, but rather he who does the will of my Father in heaven." . . . The more directly one pursues God's will, the nearer he is to God and the more directly he comes to the kingdom of heaven.[189]

Similarly, in *Sich Gelassen*, he said that if one does not die to self, he is condemned to hell because he does not bear fruit. Conversely, if one wants to pass the test and be received by God, one must renounce oneself.[190] If Karlstadt had said no more, one could conclude that in order to insist on the necessity of genuine moral renewal, he had returned to the Augustinian view of the ground of eternal life.

Karlstadt, however, had not forgotten what Luther had taught him about sin in good deeds. Precisely in *Sich Gelassen* he noted the way sin taints good deeds and the consequent imperfection of the *viator*. "In works toward the neighbor, self-will eats everything to the

---

[187] "Das verstehe also, welcher eyn frund Gotis sein wil, und vor götlichen ougen bestehen, der müss Gotis willen thün, und nach götlichem willen leben, wollen thun, lassen, wirken, rühen arbeiten, ader sabbatiseren." *Von manigfeltigkeit*, A ii.

[188] " . . . des Christen leben und tod, gewin und verlust, selykeyt und verdamnis in volbrengung oder nachlassung götliches willens allein stehet." *Ibid.*, A iv V-B.

[189] "Böse werck geendt uyss unserm willenn. Guthe wercke auss Gotts willenn. Werck unsers willens, furenn tzü der helle ab sye gleich am schönste glytzen unnd scheynen. Wercke götlichs willens, furen tzü der selikeit alss geschrieben ist, Nicht ein yeder der spricht, herr herre, der wirt eyn geen yns reych der hymeln. sunder der thüt den willen meynes vatters, welcher ym hymel ist. Math. vii [v.21]. Nicht dye sprechen herre herre, ader eusserliche schone werck thün, werden yns reich Gots geen. sunder die thun den willen meines vaters. . . . ye gleicher einer nach Gots willen geet ye neher ist er Got. und dest gerichter er zü den hymelreich kumpt." *Ibid.*, B ii.

[190] *Sich Gelassen*, d iv V-e.

marrow and bone and makes it totally wormy." [191] Man sins mortally as often as he puts confidence in money, property or anything other than God. Not surprisingly, this kind of unbelief "is in us daily." [192] Our spiritual life is in great danger because every consideration of self, every instance of *Ungelassenheit* is a deadly sin worthy of hell fire.[193] Since regeneration only begins in this life, the *viator* is always imperfect.[194].

How can one merit eternal life if even one's good deeds are sinful and if one is always imperfect during this life? Occasionally, especially in his early 1523 work on purgatory, Karlstadt solved this problem by pointing out that God would fully purify the soul after death before it entered heaven. Believers who die have a deficient righteousness and love for God. "They may not see God face to face while they have impurity in their eyes." Accordingly, before they enter heaven, they are purified completely in purgatory.[195] Similarly, in his work on the Sabbath, he noted that perfection is impossible here, even though God demands a perfect heart and whole soul. Therefore, "somewhere

---

[191] "In den wercken gegen dem nechsten, frist ungelassenhait auch alles marck und gepayn, unnd machet sy alle sampt wurmessig. . . . Aber weyl die gyfftig schlang, ungelassenhait oder annemligkait, so heimlich und lustigklich sich, und jr sicheit, und etwas in das verwickelt des sy sich, mitt kainem rechten anzyehen und zümessen mag, will ich noch ain exempel geben, ob sich villeicht ainer in ainen und nitt in dem andern möcht erindern, was, und wie grossen fleyss ain gottforchtsamer mensch, alle stunde, und augenblick haben müss, das er seinen schaden der ungelassenhait, Got müg bekennen und beychten, und gnügthüung Christi begeren, und glauben, das Christus der sey, der unsere sünde auff sich gelegt gebüst und gebessert hat." *Ibid.*, f.

[192] *Ibid.*, civV (see above, n. 71). See also *ibid.*, d (below, n. 223).

[193] "Es ist ain yeder gedancken und aygen will der hell wirdig, wie klain er ist wann er seiner seele zü lieb geschicht, in allerlay Gottes diensten. . . . Darbey lerne, das annemligkait unnd ungelassenhait todt sünde, und teüffelisch laster seind." *Ibid.*, eiiV.

[194] "Die wydergepurd ist alhie yn anfangen. Darumb ist disser nyderganck und absterben unsers aigen willens alhie yn anfengen nit in volbrenghung und volkommenheit." *Von manigfeltigkeit*, D. So too *Sabbat*, Hertzsch, I, 42.25-37 and *Zweyen höchsten gebotten*, Hertzsch, I, 62.33-37.

[195] "Ich fürcht das etliche selen nach dem todt mangel und gebrechen haben in irer lieb Gottes in irer gerechtigkait, in irer weysshait, das sy Got nicht mit gantzem und vollem hertzen lieben . . . und ist villeicht ir auge nicht allenthalben gerainigt. Nun mögen sy Gott nicht sehen von angesicht zü angesicht, alle dieweyl sy unraynigkait in jren auge haben." *Sermon vom Stand*, c. See all of cff. Also: "Ich halt es dafur, das sy dort studieren und leren miessen (sein sy anders versehen zur seligkait) und erkennen alle ware urtail oder sententz welche Got will haben erkandt, ee er sy in hymel nymbt." *Ibid.*, ciiV. (For an extensive analysis of this tract, see John W. Kleiner, "Andreas Bodenstein von Karlstadt's Eschatology" [Unpublished Th. M. Thesis, Harvard Divinity School, 1966].) Cf. also *Ursachen*, Hertzsch, I, 19.12-15

perfection must follow imperfection ... and the inferior spirit must become so great that it enters God's heavenly kingdom." [196] The soul cannot enter the kingdom of heaven until God has totally sanctified it. These statements still have a somewhat Augustinian flavor, for it is possible to conclude, although Karlstadt does *not* do so, that the perfection which God bestows after death is the ground of eternal life. There is a significant difference of tone, however, between saying with Augustine that divinely bestowed good deeds actually merit heaven and merely insisting, as Karlstadt does here, that the soul enters heaven only after God has perfected it.

Far more frequently, however, Karlstadt solved the problem of the Christian's constant sinfulness by pointing to the forgiveness and acceptance offered in Christ. Even *Sich Gelassen* and *Von manigfeltigkeit* contained passages in this vein. After noting that *Ungelassenheit* taints every good deed toward the neighbor, he added: "A God-fearing man must be very industrious every hour and moment so that he admits and confesses his wrong of ungelassenheit to God and desires the satisfaction of Christ and believes that it is Christ who ... atoned for our sins." [197] In *Von manigfeltigkeit* he had an opponent object to his demand for total self-denial by indicating that Paul himself admitted that his self-will was still very active (Romans 7). Karlstadt replied:

> [God] sent his beloved Son in order that we should obtain and have peace through him. As often as we sense our sin and want to atone for it, we see ... that we need a Saviour who is Jesus Christ, ... a payer and compensator of all deficiency. [198]

---

[196] *Sabbat*, Hertzsch, I, 42.26-36 (see above, n. 122).

[197] *Sich Gelassen*, f (see above, n. 191). So too eV where he argued that all concern for self is sin, and then added: "Alhie sych wider wie von grossen nötten uns Christus ist, das er alle unser sünde und gepresten trag büss und bessert, das ist das er das recht und reych der sünden unnd des todes brech. Ich wisset kainen trost, wann ich Gottes barmhertzigkait nit west."

[198] "Nu sprichestu ich muss meinem willen von grund absterben, so syhe ich das Paulo gefelt und gebresten hat der wunderbarlich bekert wart, was solt mir armen widerfaren. machestu mich nit tzweyfelhafftich.... Ich macht dich gern, an allen creaturen tzweyfelen, und an dir selber.... Auch hat er seinen lieben sone darumb geschickt, das wyr durch inen fryd sollen erlangen und haben. Als offt wyr unser sunde befynden und wollen pussen. sehen wir das unserer krefften alletzeit tzewenich ist, und das wir eynes erlosers bedurffen, der ist Jesus Christus eyn son Gots. ein erfullung des gesetzt, ein betzaler und gelder aller mangel. Gleuben wir an ynen, das er uns geschickt sy, so seynd wir sicher und gewyss, das er unser sunde auff sich leget und bezalet. der halben er vom vatter gesant ist." *Von manigfeltigkeit*, CivV-D.

Later in this treatise Karlstadt said that eternal life depends on faith:

> It is God's eternal will that we believe in the Son of God ... and receive eternal life in faith. As Christ says, "It is the will of my Father who sent me that everyone who sees the Son and believes in him has eternal life" (John 6). God's eyes look on faith.[199]

Thus even in the two works where he sometimes seemed to ground acceptance before God on a divinely transformed life, he could also say that because of the constant presence of sin, acceptance with God must depend only on faith in Christ's atonement.

The latter viewpoint was dominant in the treatises of 1524 and early 1525. "Faith through Christ makes us justified, irreproachable, and without blame and censure before God." [200] Frequently Karlstadt used Isaiah 53:11b and John 3:16 to argue that anyone who has faith in, or a passionate remembrance of, the Crucified One will have eternal life.

> When Isaiah pointed to Christ thus crucified, he said, "By his knowledge, he will make righteous"; for the Christ who was thus mocked, wounded and hanged makes righteous. That is what Christ says: The Son of Man must be glorified so that each one who sees Him hanging or believes on Him becomes blessed and does not perish.[201]

If one has a passionate remembrance of Christ's death, "then he is also certain of his redemption and has peace with God through Christ." [202]

---

[199] "Das wir in den son Gots gleuben das ist Gots ewyger will, dz wir auch das ewig leben ym glauben erlangen mögen und sollen, dz ist auch Gots ewiger will. als Christus spricht, Das ist der will meines vatters, der mich geschickt hat, dz eyn yeder dz ewig leben sol haben, der den Son sicht, und gleubet in yen. Joan. vi. Gots ougen sehen an den glauben. Hiere. v. ... Drumb wü der glaub nit ist, da wirt Got nit vereynt. und Got ist auch unbekant. ... In dem glauben zü Got, steet geistlich und götlich leben, und gerechtikeit, und alles dz Got behaget." *Ibid.*, Giv.

[200] "Also macht uns der glaub, durch Christum zü Gott, rechtfertig, unsträflich, one tadel, und one wandel." *Priesterthum*, CV. The church is eternally purified and established as blameless before God's eyes through Christ's blood; therefore, one should eternally comfort oneself with Christ's passion. *Auszlegung* (1524), diiiV, diiiiV.

[201] "Und da Esaias Christum also gekreütziget, fürgestellet hat, spricht er In seiner kunst wirt er gerecht machen [cf. Isaiah 53:11b], dass der Christus also verspot, verwundt, und auffgehenckt, machet gerecht. Das ist das Christus sagt. Der son des menschen müss erhöcht werden auff dass ain yegklicher selig werden, und nit verderb, der inen auffgehenckt ansicht, oder an in glawbet (margin: Joan.3; [cf.v.16])." *Missbrauch*, AivV-B. So too *Dialogus*, Hertzsch, II, 24.24-29.

[202] "Darumb soll ain yeglicher vorhyn ehe ers nympt, sich prüfen, ob er das gedechtnuss Christi hab oder nit. Hat ers, so ist er auch sicher seiner erlosung, und hat aynen frid zü Got durch Christon, nit durchs sacrament, und mag es frolich nemen." *Missbrauch*, CV.

In a passage that Luther could not have faulted, Karlstadt insisted that eternal life depends on faith:

> Nothing makes us blessed except faith. Nothing damns us except unbelief. Nothing leads us to eternal life and God's kingdom except faith alone. Nothing brings us to eternal death and the devil's kingdom except unbelief alone.[203]

The object of such faith is, of course, Christ on the cross: "Faith in Christ the Crucified is so rich and perfect that we should seek for forgiveness of our sins *or blessedness* nowhere else than in Christ as He died on the cross." [204] As this and the following statements indicate, forgiveness of sins through Christ *is* eternal blessedness:

> What is the righteousness of the God-fearing? Is it not faith and knowledge that he [i.e. Christ] washes away their many sins? Is the forgiveness of sins not the blessedness of believers?... God has revealed to them that one person, through the shedding of his blood, would provide certain forgiveness of sins richly, perfectly and sufficiently with complete certainty and eternal peace.[205]

Eternal peace depends on forgiveness of sins. In his defense of his activities during the Peasants' Revolt, Karlstadt declared that regardless of what earthly princes and courts might decide, God would declare him innocent at His heavenly court. But he quickly added a qualification:

> I do not say that because I am without sin. For if I sin when I do well before God, it is no wonder that I have sinned among the peasants surrounded with dangers. But this sin does not pertain to the courts of the world, but rather to the forgiveness of God who may be gracious to us all.[206]

---

[203] "Nichts seliget uns denn der glaub. Nichts verthümbt uns denn der unglaub. Nichts füret uns zü dem ewigen leben unnd reich Gottes, dann alleyn der glaub. Nichts brenget uns zü dem ewigen todt, unnd ins teufels reich, denn nür der unglaub." *Gelaub*, aii. So too with equal clarity, *ibid.*, aiii.

[204] "Finden sy nitt klärlich in meynen büchlein (wider das Sacrament geschriben) Das das erkenntnuss als Esaias, oder als Paulus sagt, der glaub an Christum den gecreützigten, so reych, unnd volkummlich ist, das wir nyendert vergebung unnser sünden, oder säligkeit, suchen sollen, Denn an Christo, Als er am Creütz gestorben." *Anzeig*, Hertzsch, II, 65.1-6 (my italics).

[205] "Was ist gerechtigkeit der gottförchtigen? ist es nicht der glaub und das erkenntnuss, das der die vile sünde abweschet. Esaie am 53. 1 Johan. 1. Ist die vergebung der sünden nicht die säligkeit, der glaubigen.... denn Gott hatts in offenbaret, das einer durch seyn blüt vergiessen wurd, sichere vergebung der sünden geben reychlich, volkomlich, und gnügsam mit volkomlicher sicherheit, und ewigen fryd Roma. 5." *Testament*, DiiV.

[206] "Das red ich nicht das ich one sund sey, denn so ich sundige, wenn ich wol thun für Gott. Ists keyn wunder das ich gesundigt hab unter den pauren mit

Since the *viator* never escapes sin, eternal life depends not on one's partially regenerate life, but rather on divine forgiveness.

It is important to see that Karlstadt could affirm this essentially Lutheran position even while vigorously maintaining the importance and necessity of genuine inner renewal and obedience. Several important passages relate this concern with the issues of continuing sin in the believer and the ground of acceptance before God. In *Priesterthum*, he insisted that those who have loving knowledge of Christ want to put away all unrighteousness.[207] They must be governed by Christ. Further, their obedience and good will is a sacrifice which they ought to offer to God. But then they see that their faith, love and holiness are so imperfect that they must flee from God's face.

> If they desire to evaluate and offer their obedience and good will (which nevertheless is a true sacrifice) to God, then they notice so much pollution that they must be ashamed of themselves. . . . They do not know where to escape because they ought to sacrifice and yet they have no sacrifice. However, through the costly, unpolluted priesthood and sacrifice of Christ, they receive courage and joyfulness to bring a sacrifice before God through Christ and from Christ. With sighs they say: My Lord and my God, thy son has given you a sacrifice as you will have and can desire one. . . . I hold myself and my sacrifice to the same [sacrifice of Christ]. And I confess to you that Christ alone is righteous before you and that before you only Christ's sacrifice is without weakness and without blame. And his sacrifice is so great in my eyes that I must consider my own as nothing. . . . Lord admit it for my sacrifice, or take mine in the same, for his sacrifice is a fullness and righteousness for my sacrifice.[208]

---

ferlikeiten umb geben. Aber disse sund steht nicht ynn dem gerichte der welt, sondern ynn der vergebung Gottis, der uns allen well gnedig seyn." *Endschuldigung* (June, 1525), Hertzsch, II, 118.8-13.

[207] *Priesterthum*, Biiff.

[208] "Wollen sie aber iren gehorsam und gütten willen gegen Got ermessen und opffern (welcher doch ein recht opffer ist) so vermercken sie so vil verfleckunge, das sie sich schemen müssen, Und müssen ire gerechtigkeit (als ein tüch eyner blütflüssigen frawen) verbergen. . . . und sie versteen und wissen nit wo sie nauss sollen. Derhalben dz sie opffern sollen, und haben doch keyn opffer. Aber durch das köstlich unbefleckt priesterampt und opffer Christi, nemen sie keckheit und freydigkeit, ein opffer für Gott, durch Christum, unnd von Christo zü bringen. Sie sagen mit seüfftzen, meyn herr und meyn Gott, deyn sün hat dir ein opffer geben, als du eyns haben wilt, und begeren kanst. . . . Zü dem selben halt ich mich, und meyn opffer. Und bekenn dir, das Christus alleyn gerecht ist, vor dir, und das Christus opffer, für dir, alleyn on gebresten oder tadel ist. Und seyn opffer, ist in meynen augen so höch dz ich meines für nichts halten müss. Das selbe nymm ich an, und halt mich dran, mit gedancken und hertzen. Herr, nyms für meyn opffer uff, oder meines in den selben, dann seyn opffer ist meynen zü eyner völle und gerechtigkeit." *Ibid.*, Biii-BiiiV. So too briefly *Testament*, CV-Cii.

Obedience and holiness are very important; but one should never suppose that they are so perfect that one's acceptance before God could depend on them.

Two other treatises contained similar passages. In *Ursachen* Karlstadt was troubled by the fact that God demanded preachers who were pure. Karlstadt knew that he was still very preoccupied with self while preaching. But God also commanded him to preach. Therefore he decided to preach in the knowledge that God was ready to forgive his sin. Failure to obey the divine command to preach would mean denying Christ "without whom no one may go before God's face."[209] In *Zweyen höchsten gebotten* where he developed his idea of believing love or loving faith, he again insisted both that God demands perfection and also that the *viator's* love is always imperfect.

> Man on earth does not accomplish any command of God, not even the smallest. However, you should not despair because of that. For it is certainly true that no one enters God's kingdom unless he believes and loves God and does his commands—as Christ also says—from his whole heart. However, the comforting Saviour Christ Jesus has nonetheless given us a consolation, [viz.] that we may believe God, love and do his commands in this wretched vale in the awareness of his fullness, although we are never totally circumcised.[210]

Since man cannot attain the perfection God's righteousness demands, man acquires acceptance before God's face only through Christ.

In his eagerness to stress the importance of self-denial and the new

---

[209] "Darumb ist es besser, ich speise meine hunrige brüder . . . und, so vil mir möglich, verkündig, denn das ich vonn Gottis angesicht verstossen wurd, oder dz mich Christus leucket, on welchen keiner für Gottis antlitz gehn darff." *Ursachen*, Hertzsch, I, 18.27-32. Cf. pp. 14.28-19.33 for the entire argument.

[210] " . . . der mensch uff erden kein gebot Gottes volbringet, auch dz kleinest nit. Du solt aber darumb nit verzweyflen, denn es ist wol war, das keiner in Gottes reich geet, er glaub dann, und lieb Gott und thu seine gebott, wie Christus auch saget von gantzem hertzen. Aber nit dester minder hat unns der trostbar heyland Christus Jesus einen trost geben, das wir in dissem jamertal Gott glauben, lieben, und sein gebott thun mögen in dem erkentnüss seiner füll, wiewol wir nit gentzlich beschnitten, auch nit in eine volle gantzheit und blossheit unsers hertzen kommen seind." *Zweyen höchsten gebotten*, Hertzsch, I, 62.37-63.6. In *Anzeig*, Karlstadt again emphasized the importance of good works without making them the basis of eternal life: "Es ist war, das die geschrifft nicht von wercken lernet, das wir unns mitt dienen, sondern den anndern, Oder das wir frumb dardurch werden, sondern das wir ein eusserlich gezeügknuss haben, der krafft unnser gerechtigkeit, wie sy sich erweysen soll, wa sy warhafftig ist, denn der freye steet nicht allein vor seynem Gott und vor seynem gewissen, Sondern auff erden, vor der gemeyn Gottes" (Hertzsch, II, 102.28-34). Works do not merit a right standing before God, but they are an important external witness of inner righteousness.

regenerate life, Karlstadt occasionally reverted to a somewhat Augustinian conception of the basis of eternal life. Even the two treatises of early 1523, however, which contained the strongest statements of this viewpoint also contained assertions which presupposed the more frequently represented viewpoint that egocentric self-will is so omnipresent and the Christian is so imperfect that the ground of eternal blessedness can only be genuine faith in the forgiveness given in Christ.

### (g) Christ's soteriological role

The preceding discussion of the ground of eternal life has already provided considerable evidence against the frequent allegation that Karlstadt reduced the role of Christ to that of example. An examination of the three major soteriological roles of Christ in Karlstadt's theology will demonstrate the inadequacy of this view.

In light of Karlstadt's primary emphasis on the regeneration of the believer, it is not surprising that a major role of Christ is his indwelling of the Christian. "I do not live, but Christ lives in me," was a favorite text.[211] He also frequently adduced Romans 6:1ff. It was not merely that Jesus' death and resurrection provided language to describe the believer's mortification and renewal. Rather, the Christ who died and arose, now transforms believers.[212] After God the Father begets and joins one to Christ, one has obedience and righteousness "from Him and through Him." [213] Karlstadt employed the Johannine terminology frequently. The believer is a branch grafted into the good vine, Jesus Christ.[214] Man obtains holiness of life only through Christ.[215]

If Christ is important as the source of the Christian's supernatural new life, he is also significant as the Christian's example. "God has sent Christ, his Son . . . especially because of this virtue, renunciation, so that we would have a true and living way . . . which we might imitate." [216] Christ's death on the cross was the culmination of a

---

[211] See above, n. 57 which lists many places where this verse was used.

[212] *Anzeig*, Hertzsch, II, 90.1-31.

[213] *Priesterthum*, Bii-BiiV (see above, n. 208).

[214] Eg.: "Felt die sele und stirbt ir selber ab von grund auff, so brengt sye götliche fruchte, die altzeyt bleyben. das ist das eyn pflantzen, in den gutigen reben stock gesetzt werd, welcher Christus ist, welchen der hymelisch vater eynpflantzet in seynen lieben son, der verleuset synen aigen willen von poden und grund. unnd nympt an sich das leben, thün und lassen, wachsen und frucht tragen nach der art unnd aigenschafft Christi." *Von manigfeltigkeit*, C.

[215] *Sabbat*, Hertzsch, I, 26.36-38, 45.16-21.

[216] "Got hat uns Christus, seinen sun, als ainen weeg, warhait und leben g.-

totally renounced (*gelassen*) and sacrificial life. He sacrificed himself constantly and in order that we might imitate (*nachvolgen*) Him by renouncing ourselves completely.[217] "We must direct and order ourselves according to Him as our model." [218] Thus the exemplary role of Christ was important in Karlstadt's Orlamünde theology.

However, quite apart from the fact that Karlstadt also had a doctrine of the atonement, his doctrine was not mere exemplarism. No one follows Christ's footsteps and bears fruit in the manner of Christ unless God through Christ has begotten him into a new supernatural life.

> He whom the Heavenly Father transplants into his dear Son forsakes his self-will completely and takes on himself the life, activity . . . and fruitbearing in the style and manner of Christ.[219]

One imitates the style of Christ only after being born into Christ. Karlstadt employed the word "Christformig" to capture both roles of Christ. In the following passage the word points to the fact that Christ is the source of power for the new life:

> Then this renounced self or despised and forsaken I . . . becomes a Christ-like (Christförmigs) I or self, and a new Christian life, where one discovers and perceives that his life is not a human, but rather a divine life. And he does not live, but Christ lives in him.[220]

On the other hand, he also used the word to connote the *Nachfolge Christi*: "We must be completely Christ-like and imitate Christ." [221] Christ is both the efficient and the formal cause of the sanctified life.

Christ also has a third important role in Karlstadt's theology. He is the propitiation of man's sins. Those who have alleged that Karlstadt virtually reduced Christ's role to that of example, have argued that his

---

sendt, in sonderhait von wegen diser tugent, gelassenhait, auff das wir ainen warhafftigen unnd lebendigen weeg hetten (der sollichs gelassen leben am höchsten und besten gefiert hatt) wölchem wir möchten dester gewysser nachfolgen, und wissen das wir unbetrogen seind, so wir ime nach schreytten, unnd geen als er gangen ist." *Sich Gelassen*, divV.

[217] *Priesterthum*, BV. So too Eii: "Demnach sollen wir versten, welcher weyse uns Christus ein exempel geben, das wir seynen füssstapffen nachvolgen, unnd leyden als er."

[218] "Denn nach im [Christus] als einen fürbild, müssen wir uns richten und stellen." *Ob man . . . erweysen müge*, Diii.

[219] *Von manigfeltigkeit*, C (see above, n. 214).

[220] *Sich Gelassen*, diiiV (see above, n. 121).

[221] "Wir müssen yhe allesampt christformig sein, und Christo nochfolgen." *Ursachen*, Hertzsch, I, 17.18-19. So too *Ob man . . . erweysen müge*, Diii.

*Von dem Priesterthum und opffer Christi,* where the doctrine of the atonement is clear, is not typical. Thus it will be essential to show that many of the major treatises other than *Priesterthum* and the Eucharistic writings contain specific references to forgiveness through Christ's atoning death.

In *Sich Gelassen* he observed that God-fearing men must confess *Ungelassenheit* every moment "and desire the satisfaction (gnügthüung) of Christ and believe that it is Christ who placed our sin upon himself and atoned for (gebüst) and corrected it." [222] Earlier, he had reminded his readers that if they took seriously Jesus' warning that he who puts his hand to the plough and then turns back is unworthy of the kingdom (Luke 9:62) they would cry out with fright: "O, we need Christ's passion every instant." [223] In *Von manigfeltigkeit* he had someone object that his demand for total self-mortification would lead to despair. After expressing his delight with this result, he added:

> [God] sent his beloved Son in order that we should obtain and have peace through him. As often as we sense our sin and want to atone for it, we see ... that we need a Saviour, who is Jesus Christ, ... a payer and compensator of all deficiency. If we believe on him, ... then we are sure and certain that he placed our sin upon himself and paid for it. The Father sent him for that purpose.[224]

In *Vorstandt des worts Pauli* Karlstadt explained that God sent his Son to the Jews "and allowed him to be born of them and to be cursed and crucified for their sin." [225] Christ truly bore "our sin, our damnation and curse." [226] At the end of the tract on the Sabbath, where Karlstadt argued that the spiritual purpose of the Sabbath is the sanctification of man, he added that "it is also not to be forgotten that the Sabbath comprehends the forgiveness of sins, for man does not become holy

---

[222] *Sich Gelassen,* f (see above, n. 191).

[223] "Setze und vergleiche die zway capittel. Das 9. und 14. Luce zesamen am end, und flichte den synn und verstand zesamen, so würdest du on zweyfel erschrecken und schreyen. O wie arme leütte seind wir. O wir bedürffen des leyden Christi alle augenblick." *Ibid.,* d.

[224] *Von manigfeltigkeit,* Civ V-D (see above, n. 198 for the original).

[225] " ... zü letzten, sandt er auch seinen sohn, Jesum von Nazareth, und liess yhn, auss yhnen geborn werden unnd umb irer sunde willen vorfluchen, creutzigen, vorspotten, und ermordten." *Vorstandt des worts Pauli,* Aiv V.

[226] " ... er unsere sunde, unsere verfluchung, und vermaledeyhung, warhafftiglich, bey Got, als vor der welt getragen hat, und nicht allein, ym schein." *Ibid.,* Bii.

before we attain forgiveness of sins and obtain reconciliation with God." [227] Finally, Karlstadt mentioned the atonement constantly in his work on the intercession of Mary:

> Paul says: There is one God and one mediator or reconciler of God and men. . . . Paul has specified the same sole mediator, saying: "The Man Jesus Christ, who gave himself as a ransom is this mediator." . . . Mary did not die for us or our sins. . . . Isaiah 53 and I Peter 2 say that Christ bore our sins and sickness and that God made him a sin and curse for us.[228]

The above quotations by no means demonstrate that Karlstadt focused on forgiveness as much as did Luther. They do prove, however, that forgiveness through Christ's atonement was an integral part of Karlstadt's Orlamünde theology, and not as Kähler said, a "foreign body" in his writings except for the very uncharacteristic *Priesterthum*.[229]

In both *Priesterthum* and the Eucharistic tracts, of course, Karlstadt made frequent statements about the atonement.

> If Christ had not died, we would all be lost; but since Christ died, we have redemption through him. For as a high priest, Christ sacrificed the best and highest sacrifice to God his Father for our sins and has merited and richly acquired forgiveness of all sins for us, and has sufficiently reconciled us to his Father from whom we were distant because of our sins.[230]

---

[227] "Es ist auch nit zuvergessen das der Sabbat vergebung der sunden begreyfft, dan der mensch wirt nit heylig ehe wir vergebung der sunden erlangen, und in Gottis versönung kommen." *Sabbat*, Hertzsch, I, 47.19-21. Cf. also *Ursachen*, Hertzsch, I, 19.22-25: "Drumb wil ich mich des trösten, das Gott zukeer fordert, und bereitt und gutwillig ist, aller sunden zuvergessen, und ir nit mer gedencken so wir armen sunder uns erkennen oder der sunde gedencken."

[228] "Das Paulus spricht, Es ist ain Got und mitler, oder versöner Gottes, und der menschen. 1 Tim. 2. . . . Darzü hat Paulus den selbigen ainigen Mitler namhafftig gemacht sagendt, der mensch Jhesus Christus, der sich selber zü ainer bezalung geben hat, ist diser mitler. 1 Tim. 2 Maria ist nicht für uns, oder unser sünde gestorben, sonder allain Christus. . . . Esa. 53. 1. Pet. 2. Sprechen, das Christus unser sünde und kranckhait hab getragen, und das Got jn in ain sünd und vermaledeyung für uns gemacht hab." *Fürbit Marie* (July, 1523), AiiV.

[229] Kähler, "Karlstadts Protest," p. 307.

[230] "Wenn Christus nit gestorben were, so weren wir alle verloren, weyl aber Christus gestorben ist, so haben wir ein erlösung durch in. Denn Christus hat, als ein höchster priester, das aller beste und höchste opffer, Gott seynen vatter geopffert, für unsere sünde, und hat uns vergebung aller sünden verdienet, und reychlich erworben, und uns seynen vatter gnügsam versönet, dem wir ferr waren durch unsere sünde, die uns von Gott weyt scheydten." *Priesterthum*, BivV-C. So too Aii, Bii, CV, Cii.

His exegesis of the words of institution of the Lord's Supper quite naturally contained numerous discussions of Christ's atoning death.

> The blessed One hanging on the cross placed our curse and damnation upon himself and became an accursed One before God and man. . . . There the Lord Christ willingly submitted to the curse of the law and blessed us, . . . when the Lord atoned for our disobedience through his obedience. . . .[231]

As Hillerbrand has noted, Karlstadt "emphasized the Cross with unsurpassable seriousness" in the Eucharistic tracts.[232] Christ's atonement was clearly a basic aspect of Karlstadt's Orlamünde theology.

One must again emphasize, however, that that does not mean that the forgiveness of sins made possible by Christ's death occupied as central a place in Karlstadt's theology as in Luther's. It did not. Karlstadt was preoccupied with self-mortification and inner regeneration. He wanted not just right doctrine, but also good works![233] One illustration of this point is the fact that, whereas in 1521 the word "righteousness" connoted primarily although not exclusively that forensic righteousness imputed to one who has faith in Christ, it now designated primarily although certainly not solely that genuine inner righteousness which produces good deeds.[234]

A second illustration of Karlstadt's different emphasis is his reminder that the Gospel includes more than forgiveness of sins.

> There are two unique characteristics of the New Testament. One is that God wants to write his law in the heart. The other is that the forgiveness of sins will so certainly follow that very inscription in the heart that God will no longer remember the sins at all. . . . That which God writes in the heart . . . is the heartfelt and lively knowledge of the death and shed blood of Christ. Thus Christ throws . . . his blood into hearts and souls and consciences through the Holy Spirit and purifies our hearts. . . . Forgiveness of sins follows this revelation or new law immediately.[235]

---

[231] "Und do der gebenedeyet unsere vermaledeiung und flüchung an den holtz hangende, uff sich legt, und ward für Got, und für den menschen, ein verflüchter. Deu 21. Do der her Christus des gesetzes verflüchung williglich underging, und uns gbenedeiet. Deu. 27. Ga. 3. Als der her durch seinen gehorsam, unseren ungehorsam büsset. Rom. 5." *Auszlegung* (1524), CiiiV-Civ. So too *ibid.*, C, Dv; *Missbrauch*, AivV-B, Bii.

[232] "Andreas Bodenstein of Carlstadt," p. 391.

[233] *Anzeig*, Hertzsch, II, 93.36-94.2 (see above, n. 154).

[234] For the latter usage, see *Von manigfeltigkeit*, Eiv, Gii-GiiV (see below, n. 348); *Dialogus*, Hertzsch, II, 47.37-49.23. But he also spoke of forensic righteousness and justification: cf. *Testament*, DiiV (see above, n. 205); *Priesterthum*, Cii. In *Missbrauch*, AivV-B, both connotations are present.

[235] *Testament*, Bii (see above, n. 180). So too *Anzeig*, Hertzsch, II, 89.26-39. One

Karlstadt clearly wanted to underline the fact that forgiveness of sins never exists apart from that inward renewal and purification effected by Christ through the Holy Spirit. He pointedly reminded Luther that "the full Gospel of Christ" does not consist only in the proclamation of Christ's grace which is the forgiveness of sins; rather, "it is richer, for there are innumerable goods and treasures in Christ, all of which Christ has acquired for us and wants to communicate to us." [236] Karlstadt's Orlamünde theology represented an attempt to focus on those additional riches, the essence of which was that inner righteousness brought by the Christ who writes his law on the heart in which he dwells. It is important, nevertheless, not to state Karlstadt's emphasis on this role of Christ in such a way that one implies that he ignored Christ's objective work on the cross. Christ is also reconciler and even example, but most of all he is sanctifier.

*(b) The problem of authority in theology*

*Sola scriptura* continued to be a frequent theme in Karlstadt's tracts of 1523 to 1525. "God has forbidden us to follow our own thoughts." Nor dare we follow the wisdom of others, whether learned or unlearned. "It follows that we are fastened to scripture, that no one may judge according to the good pleasure of his heart, and also that those who consider things other than God's word propose harlot-

---

should not take Karlstadt's statement that forgiveness follows the inner revelation (i.e. regeneration) to mean that regeneration is the ground of forgiveness. Karlstadt merely wanted to avoid any suggestion that superficial or dead faith obtains forgiveness. Genuine faith always possesses inner renewal and forgiveness but the latter does not depend on the former. One cannot agree with Barge's attempt to deemphasize the importance of the atonement in Karlstadt: "Gemäss dieser Auffassung aber beruht die Aneignung des Heils nicht auf einem einmaligen Akte der Glaubensrechtfertigung, sondern auf einem allmählichen Prozess innerer Heiligung. Für Luther bedeutet der Opfertod Christi die Gewähr, dass dem Gläubigen die Sünden vergeben sind; für Karlstadt, dass eine Erlösung möglich und die Bahn zu ihr dem Gläubigen vorgeschrieben sei" (*Karlstadt*, II, 70). For Karlstadt acceptance before God depends solely on genuine faith in Christ's sacrificial death. Such acceptance, however, is not God's sole gift to the believer.

[236] "Es steet aber das gantz Euangelium von Christo, nicht allein in verkündig der gnad Christi, wölliche zuvergebung der sünden erweysst ist, Sonder es ist reycher, Denn es seynd unmessliche gütter und schetzen in Christo, die uns Christus alle erworben, und mitteylen will, so wir an jn glauben." *Anzeig*, Hertzsch, II, 86.21-25. Nor can one agree with Scheel that Karlstadt condemned Luther's focus on forgiveness as a narrowing of the process of salvation without developing his own alternative view. The emphasis on inner renewal (God's writing on the heart in the previous quotation) is precisely the further riches and treasures of Christ which Luther allegedly overlooked. Scheel, "Individualismus," p. 366.

ry." [237] Men dare judge even the angels by means of the word proclaimed through Moses, the prophets, Christ and the apostles, for "the angels must bow before God's word and confess that they are subject, as we are, to the divine word." [238] One may not adduce the fathers' Eucharistic conception, for all fathers are subordinate to the one word of God.[239] Karlstadt devoted a lengthy section of *Von manigfeltigkeit* to God's revelation in scripture. Because of reason's inadequacy, God graciously revealed his will which man must humbly accept without murmur.[240] He vigorously denounced the Pope for hindering the study of that divine word on which the ultimate blessing or curse depends.[241] "He who wants to search out God's will should read holy scripture." [242]

Many of the various themes of the earlier *sola scriptura* emphasis reappeared. He underlined the gulf between divine and human

---

[237] "Gott nennets auch ein hurerey und hürische augen, die auff andre ding, dann auff sein richtschnur, das ist Gottes wort, sehen. Got hat uns verbotten unsern eigen gedancken noch zu volgen. . . . Nicht allein ewr eigen wissheit, lieber bruder, muss ouch zu nicht, unnd ein torheyt werden, sonder aller andern menschen weyssheit. Also, das ir euch wider gelärten nach ungelärten laset bewegen, unnd dz ir one mittel auff die blossen warheit dreffet. . . . Darauss aber volget, dz wir an die schrifft angehenckt seyn, das sich keiner nach seines hertzen gutduncken richten dörfft, das auch die jene hürerey treiben, die nach andern dingen sahen, denn nach Gottes wort. . . ." *Gemach*, Hertzsch, I, 75.3-34. One should not suppose that "one mittel" signifies a special revelation. The context shows that he was urging his readers to go directly to scripture rather than listen to learned intermediaries. A little later, he again insisted that people consider God's word directly: " . . . ir in erfarung götlicher gerechtigkeit und warheit kummen, und *gerichts* uff Gottes reden achtung geben must, unnd euch alle schrifft weisen nichts sein sollen." *Ibid.*, p. 76.16-18 (my italics). The immediate context of both passages make it certain that the polemic was against those who interpret scripture on the basis of the views of other (learned) men. One ought to go directly to scripture itself, rather than indirectly via learned interpreters.

[238] "Denn es ist war, das wir die engell urteylen mügen, wie Paulus sagt, durch götliche wort, so uns durch Mosen, Propheten, Christum und Aposteln, verkündigt, so müssen sich die engeln vor dem wort Gotis biegen, und bekennen, das sie, als wir, götlichem wort untherworffen seind." *Sabbat*, Hertzsch, I, 26.1-5. See also *ibid.*, p. 25.37ff.

[239] "Ich weyss wol ir werdet die heylige vätter erfür suchen, unnd her werffen. Ich aber weyse euch zü dem eynigen wort Gottis, dem alle vätter untherworffen seind, als ir unnd ich." *Auszlegung* (1524), dV.

[240] " . . . unnd genugigh sey, das unss Got seynen wyllen hat gnediglich lassen auffdecken, unnd wyssen, das böss unnd unrecht yst. alles das Gotis wort verbeut. ob es unser vernunfft seltzam ist, unnd unbegreyflich, das böss und unrecht seyn mocht." *Von manigfeltigkeit*, HV.

[241] *Ibid.*, J-Jiii (especially Jiii). See all of HV-Jiii.

[242] "Wölcher Gottes willen nach forschen will, der leess die hailige schrifft." *Sich Gelassen*, eivV.

thoughts: "All man's powers and thoughts are unlike God's thoughts and never can become divine."[243] He used the sufficiency of scripture argument against both Catholic and Protestant opponents.

> First Kirchner [a Catholic priest whom Karlstadt attacks] errs and makes others err if he preaches that this or that is necessary for salvation and cannot adduce any letter of scripture to prove that his little song is true. He censures the Holy Spirit and God's word for not having a sufficient doctrine. Against that is the following: "You shall add no word" (Deuteronomy 4).[244]

Frequently, as in the previous quotation, he insisted that no additions be made to scripture. If one makes doctrinal additions without a scriptural basis, one is a liar. It is a great sin to add anything to God's written word.[245] Since scripture, not the authority of learned persons, should move one, Karlstadt announced that he would call his opponents' views false "until they point out in scripture a word of their faith." When they do, then people can be "dependent solely on the truth and not on their persons." [246] Karlstadt clearly continued to affirm that scripture alone is the source and criterion of theological truth.

Gordon Rupp, however, has said that Karlstadt was led to "play up dreams and visions as a source of revelation." [247] "I said more here about visions and dreams than any other professor," [248] Karlstadt wrote to Müntzer in December, 1522, but he added no comments which might explain whether visions and dreams were a source of revelation. An examination of the 1523-1525 statements about dreams

---

[243] "Meyn gedancken seynd menschen gedanckenn gleich. . . . aller menschen krefften und gedancken, Gotis gedancken ungleich seind, unnd nymmer götlych mögen werdenn." *Von manigfeltigkeit*, Jii. So too *Wider*, iv-ivV.

[244] "Erstlich irret der Kirchner, und macht irren, so er Prediget, das diss oder jhenes sey not zur säligkayt, und vermag kainen büchstaben hayliger schrifft zübeweysen, das sein liedlein war sey, und strafft also den hayligen gayst, und Gottes wort, das ungnügsam leere hab, wider das. Du solt kain wörtlein darzü setzen. Deut.4. [v.2]" *Fürbit Marie*, Aii. So too *Dialogus*, Hertzsch, II, 32.1-7.

[245] *Dialogus*, Hertzsch, II, 37.6-9, 33-40. So too *Auszlegung* (1524), aV and *Gemach*, Hertzsch, I, 87.35-39.

[246] Karlstadt called the view that the sacrament mediates forgiveness of sins a "falschen won unnd glawben, welchen ich falsch nennen werde, so lang biss sy ain wort jres glawbens in der geschrifft anzaygen, der sy vertrawen . . . und wenn sy ain wort des rechten glawbens gepredigt und angezeygt haben, so solt jr denn der blossen warhait anhengig werden, und nicht jren personen." *Missbrauch*, AiiV. So too *Testament*, Eiii; *Dialogus*, Hertzsch, II, 7.3-30.

[247] "Word and Spirit," *ARG*, XLIX, 20.

[248] Franz, ed., *Schriften und Briefe*, p. 387 (see above, chapter V, n. 81).

and visions will help determine whether he intended to claim special revelation via dreams and visions.

The first reference to dreams and visions comes in a discussion of how man learns God's will.

> May I not answer: The word, which all believers should obey, is near you in your heart. You need not wander either up to heaven or down into the depths. God showed his will to the prophets through speech, vision and obscurities. And his eternal . . . will is announced and written in holy scripture in such unanimity through the prophets, Christ and apostles that we may study God's will sufficiently in holy scripture. . . . God has also spoken to his people from Mt. Horeb in fire, darkness and smoke with a living and miraculous voice. . . . Now I notice, says a reader of this book, that God's will is declared to men through divine commands and prohibitions, through comforting promises and frightening threats, through blessings and cursings, through visions and the like, and that his divine Mind is locked in holy scripture as a kernel in a pod. . . . [One] must seek the bark for the sake of the kernel or marrow and not break this order. But however that may be, the divine will is more clearly perceived in holy scripture than in dreams, visions and complicated figures. Jeremiah, Ezekiel, Daniel, Zechariah and other prophets, who often asked God what their perceived visions meant, confirm that. Therefore, I will make use of clear scripture.[249]

The first part of this passage intends to say that God used various media including visions to impart his original revelation to the

---

[249] "Dorfft ich nyt antwerten, das wort ist dir nahe in deinem hertzen, welchem alle gleubige sollen gefolgig seyn. du darfest wider uffgen hymel, noch tyff, unther dich reysen. Seynen willen hat Got den propheten durch tzüreden, gesichte und dunckelheiten angetzeigt. und ist syn ewiger, bestendiger und unwandelbarlicher will, in heiliger schrifft yn solcher einhellikeit durch propheten, Christum und aposteln angesagt oder tzü gheschryben, das wir Gots willen in. H. geschrifft gnugsam erstudieren mogen, unnd mogen auch durch Gots gnad eyndruckung und swynde gedancken gelernen, was Gott von uns fodert, was Got haben wil, was Got walgefelt und behagt. Auch hat Got seynem volck von dem berg oreb ym feur, ym finsternis und ym rauch, mit lebentiger und wunderbarlicher stym tzügeredt, und seyn volck geleret was eyn mensch sol thun, der in seynen gotlichen oughen wol thun wil, und alhye wil eyn langweriges leben haben Deu.iiii.v.vi. . . . Nu merck ich (spricht ein leeser disses buchlyns) das den menschen durch gotliche gebot und verbot, durch trostbare verheischung und erschreckliche betreyhung, durch benedeyhung und vermaledeyhung, durch gesichte und dergleychen Gottes will erkleert wirt. und das syn gotlich gemuth in heiliger schrifft verschlossen ist, wie eyn kern in einer schalenn, welcher den kern welt essen, der musset die schalen uffbeissen und hynwerffen, und muss die rynden von wegen des kerns oder marcks suchen, und disse ordnung nit brechen. Aber wie dem sey, so ist dannest gotlicher will in. H. geschryfft klerlicher tzümercken dan in dreymen, in gesichten, unde verwickelten geleychniss, das betzughen Hieremias, Ezechiel, Daniel, Zacharias, und andere propheten, so Got vil mals gefraget haben, was ire vorswebende gesichte bedeuten. Drumb wil ich mich der lichten schrifft behelfen. . . ." *Von manigfeltigkeit*, DiiV-DiiiV.

prophets and apostles. The commands, curses and promises are part of that original revelation which is now sufficient for us. The last three sentences, however, might appear to refer to post-scriptural visions which are somewhat authoritative albeit less so than the biblical text. It is far more likely, however, that Karlstadt meant to say that the dreams, visions and figures *of scripture*, which must be interpreted according to the spirit and not the letter if one is to decipher their kernel of truth, are less clear than other passages of scripture. In 1521 he had said that allegorical passages have no weight in theological debate unless explicitly interpreted by other scripture.[250] Dreams, like allegories, are unclear unless God explains them; hence the prophets' requests. The passage concludes with the decision to use "clear," i.e. non-allegorical, etc. passages in the following theological discussion. This interpretation is made more likely by the inclusion of "complicated figures" along with visions and dreams. He would hardly have meant to say that post-canonical figurative writings are a source of theological knowledge. If, as is very likely, the dreams, visions and figures are scriptural ones, this passage makes no claim to extra-biblical revelation via dreams.

Another passage is also important:

> Also, it was mentioned that God proclaimed and depicted his eternal will through his voice at Mount Horeb and subsequently allowed it to go into the ears of all the world through his prophets, Christ and the apostles, and allowed it to be comprehended and to be spoken to the patriarchs in visions and a living voice.[251]

If the visions and living voice were subsequent to the apostles and if the "patriarchs" were the church fathers, then the passage would refer to extra-biblical revelation. The previous passage, however, shows that Karlstadt spoke of God's "living voice" in connection with the original revelation on Mount Horeb. Further, Karlstadt's subsequent discussion makes it likely that the "altvettern" are biblical figures.[252] Another passage in *Gemach* confirms this inter-

---

[250] See above, chapter four, "Exegesis of the Word."

[251] "Auch ist berurt, das Gott seynen ewygen willenn, durch seyn stym ym bergh Oreb verkundigt, unnd beschriben, und volgend durch seyne Propheten, Christum, unnd Apostelen yn aller welt oren hat geen, unnd begreyffen lassen, und den altvettern yn gesychten unnd lebentigher stymm eynsagen" (*ibid.*, Hiv).

[252] In a section entitled "Die alte vetter fragten vor allen fleissig noch Gots willen," Karlstadt said that he would not take the time to give examples of how God's servants used the lot. At the end of the section, however, he did mention one example, and it was a biblical one: "Josue wurff des loss vor Got dem heren u.

pretation. Using Deut. 4 and referring to the revelation given to Israel through Moses, Karlstadt commented:

> God has given divine wisdom and understanding to our patriarchs in miraculous visions and stories through his lofty, noble word and to us through our ancestors. Therefore all people shall rightly say, "Surely this is an excellent people which has such high knowledge and righteous customs and laws?" And God has placed his covenant, which contains our wisdom and understanding, before us so that we . . . work, live and order things intelligently and wisely.[253]

Here the "altvettern," to whom God revealed himself in visions, are clearly biblical figures. Our understanding of God's will is mediated by these spiritual ancestors.

Although Karlstadt believed that the Spirit inwardly informs the congregation apropos the appropriate ministerial candidate, he explicitly warned against expecting dreams or visions by underlining the absence of such in the case of the selection of Paul and Barnabas.

> One should notice that it is not written, "The Spirit spoke in visions, sleep or dreams;" rather, it says without addition: "The Spirit spoke." Therefore, it is likely that God's Spirit spoke inwardly to the apostles and taught them how they should separate Paul and Barnabas.[254]

---

Josue.18. unnd teylt dye erden nach dem gluck oder lossungh, des ist das büch Josue vol" (*ibid.*, J.). See HivV-J for the entire section.

It should be noted that this entire discussion is part of a larger section in which Karlstadt advocates the casting of lots. "Das auch Gott genügsam durch heylige schryfft unss wyl gelernet habenn, tzewyssen was seynen oughen wol gefelt, oder mysshagt. Es begeben sych aber tzeytenn felh unnd sachen dye nycht in heyligher schryfft begryffen seyn" (*ibid.*, Hiv). When matters arise that are not dealt with in scripture then one should follow the example of the apostles who used to cast lots when they could not determine from scripture what action would please God (*ibid.*, Hiv-HivV). In spite of the general word "sachen," Karlstadt mentioned only one specific kind of situation in which he recommended the use of the lot. If two or three persons are equally qualified for a particular ecclesiastical office, then lots are to be cast (*ibid.*, HivV). Since the casting of lots presumably was to provide not doctrinal information but specific guidance in practical matters, the casting of lots hardly makes Karlstadt's doctrine of authority "spiritualist."

[253] "Der güttige Gott hatt etliche eüsserliche werck herfür bracht, und dar durch, sein vetterliche lieb angezeigt [cf. Deut. 4:3-4], unther den selben eins ist das, dz Got unsern altvettern in wunderbarlichen gesichten und geschichten, eine götliche wissheit und verstand [cf. v. 6], durch sein hochs, edels wort, und uns, durch unsere fürfaren gegeben hat. Der halben billich alle leüt sagen solten, wol ein treffenlich volck ist, das soliche hohe kunst und gerechte sitten und rechte hat [cf. v. 6]? Und Gott hat seinen bund, der unser weissheit und verstand inhelt, uns der halben fürgelegt, dz wir, in allen unsern wercken thun unnd lassen, klüglich und verstendiglich wirckten, lebten unnd richten." *Gemach*, Hertzsch, I, 82.32-83.4.

[254] "Man soll mercken, das nicht geschrieben steht, der geyst sprach in ge-

One can conclude that Karlstadt never thought that dreams and visions were a source of revelation.

For Karlstadt there was only one source of revelation, namely scripture. Thus far, then, he was not a spiritualist. As Köhler has suggested, however, a spiritualist tendency more frequently enters in connection with exegesis. What were Karlstadt's principles of exegesis at this time, and what was the role of the Holy Spirit? Karlstadt reaffirmed some of his earlier exegetical principles. He insisted that his own Eucharistic exegesis flowed from "the true faith and surrounding holy scripture." "From this ground of faith and the surrounding words of scripture we can and may explain these words." [255] By the "true faith," he meant the doctrine of the atonement. One's exegesis of Eucharistic texts must not be contrary to Christ's cross. Second, it must be in conformity with the text's immediate context and "all other clear and lucid texts." [256] Conformity with "the faith," conformity with the surrounding context and the priority of clear and distinct texts were three of Karlstadt's exegetical principles.

Mere external handling of the word, however, is not sufficient. The proper understanding of scripture is possible only when one is rightly related to God by means of faith rich in love. "True [i.e. liebreich] faith brings along to the heart a true understanding of the

---

sichten, im schlaff, oder im traum, sondern one tzusatz, der geyst sprach, derhalben vermutlich ist, das Gottis geyst die Aposteln innerlich angeredt, unnd gelert hat, wie sie Barnabam und Paulum absondern solten." *Ursachen*, Hertzsch, I, 12.37-13.2. Using the word dream in a somewhat different sense, Karlstadt mocked the Pope (*Von manigfeltigkeit*, Jii) and Luther (*Erklerung*, DV, Dii, Div) for following their own "dreams" rather than scripture.

255 "Itz vermeldte leüterung, dieser wort, den leyb Christi geben, und für einen geben, fleüsset auss dem warhafftigen glauben, und umbstenden heyliger geschrifft, auss welchen diese wort, das brodt welches ich geben werd, vernemlich und leicht werden, die sonst unverstendig, und schwer seynd, oder auch von den endechristen, wider Christus kreütz und herlickeyt gedeüt und aussgelegt werden.

"Auss diesem grunde des glaubens, und der umbstehnden worten der schrifften, künden und dörffen wir auch diese wort ausslegen. Der kelch, das new testament in meinem blüte, die gleich lauten, alss solt der kelch in dem blüth sein, und mögen ohne schaden sagen, das Christus nit auff diese meinung gesagt, . . . wenn gleych der text ausswendig also lautet, die weyl alle andere klare unnd helle texten verfallen müsten, so von dem geben des leibes Christi reden." *Auszlegung* (1524), bii. *Vorstandt* represents a good implementation of the second of these two exegetical principles.

256 *Auszlegung* (1524), bii (see the previous note). He stressed the importance of clear and lucid texts in several writings: e.g., *Fürbit Marie*, BiiV; *Ob man* . . . *erweysen müge*, Fiii; *Wider*, ivV; *Testament*, Dii.

righteous sayings of God." [257] The implications of this statement are especially clear in an important discussion in *Von manigfeltigkeit*.

To someone who asked how man learns God's will, Karlstadt replied:

> [God's] will is announced and written in holy scripture in such unanimity through the prophets, Christ, and apostles that we may study God's will sufficiently in holy scripture, and may also learn through God's grace, insertion and rapid thoughts what God demands from us. ... God has spoken to his people from Mount Horeb. ... God's speech consists of the ten words and articles (Deut.4). He whom God begets and implants into his Son Jesus Christ, and inspires with his divine knowledge through the Holy Spirit so that he sees precisely those ten commandments clearly with true light and accepts them with living love—that person knows what pleases God and what God hates. [258]

The ten commandments are available to everyone. But in order to have a true understanding of them, one needs God's grace or *eyndruckung*. [259] The true understanding made possible by regeneration and implantation in Christ is not some new conceptual content, but precisely loving acceptance of the ten commandments. The Holy Spirit is necessary in order that man possesses a proper, i.e. obedient relationship to scripture.

---

[257] "Seitenmal der recht glaub dem hertzen einen warhaftigen verstandt der gerechten reden Gottes mit brengt." *Gelaub*, bV.

[258] See above, n. 249 for the first part of this statement. After the reference to Deut. 4-6, Karlstadt continued: "Gottes rede stund in x worten und artickeln. Deute. iiii. Welchem Got an seinem sone Jesum Christum tzeuget, eynpflantzet, und durch den geist syner gotlicher kunst eyngibt, das er die selbe tzehen gebot mit warhafftigem licht durch syhet, und lebendiger lieb annymbt, der mais [waisst in the other edition] was Got wol gefelt, und was Got hasset. Syhe wie ein konyg seinen willen, durch seine gebot und verbot oder gesetz aussdrucket. Also offenbaret Got seynen willen auch durch seyn gesetz. Dan der will ist der geist oder sele und leben des gesetzes. wü dem willen gnug geschicht, do ist dem gesetz gnugsam bescheen. Welcher aber die pautschelen, rynden oder buchstaben eines gesetzes volbringt, unnd untherlesset doch des gesetzes meynung und gemuth, der dienet dem gesetze nicht." *Von manigfeltigkeit*, Diii. See below, n. 263 for the interpretation of "swynde gedancken."

[259] See above pp. 243-6 where it is shown that Karlstadt used the word "eindrucken" to refer not to special revelation but to the mediation of grace. Another occurrence of this word should also be interpreted in this way: "Gotlicher wil dem menschen offenbar wird ... durch die schrifft, durch indruckung oder rathe gotfruchtsamer menschen oder dergleichen" (*Von manigfeltigkeit*, Biii). In light of Karlstadt's continued emphasis on the great gulf between all human thoughts and God's thoughts, one can be certain that he did not mean to say that the advice of very godly Christians is qualitatively the same as God's revelation. Thus the parallel construction does not mean that scripture, "indruckung" and godly advice are all sources of authoritative revelation.

The Holy Spirit is also necessary in order to assure the soul that the external word is true. "When God wants to make me a believer, . . . then God descends into my poor, yearning heart . . . and assures my spirit that he is truly wise, that he is true and faithful and that all his sayings are true and righteous in themselves." [260]

> If Abraham had received the external word and promise without the inner speech and promise of God, . . . he would have been . . . full of doubt. . . . For it is entirely impossible that one becomes a friend or son of God without the inner and secret revelation [i.e. grace] of God. Just as little is it possible that one receive God's external word and hold it as a word of the Bridegroom with joy, consolation and great delight if God does not reveal himself either previously or precisely in the external hearing with his bright and clear descending beam to such an extent that he is able to hear who God is. . . . Therefore faith is full of love . . . and lifts the believer above all creaturely things as often as he hears said or sung a righteous statement of divine righteousness.[261]

One cannot recognize the external word as the word of the Bridegroom and rightly relate to it unless God works inwardly in the soul. This inner activity enables one to hear properly what the external word says. After the Spirit has transformed the heart, one responds with loving exultation whenever one hears the external word stated or sung.[262] This inner assurance from God, however, does not involve

---

[260] "Wenn mich Got wil glaubhafftig machen, und seinen glauben in mein hungerichte unnd dürstige krefften giessen. So geht Got ab, inn mein, arm, begyrigs hertz, mit seyner ungeschaffner unnd liechter warheyt, unnd offenbaret sich meinem hertzen, das er ein warhafftiger unnd getrewer Gott ist, unnd versicheret meynen geyst, das er eygentlich weiss, das Gott warhafftig unnd getrew ist, unnd das alle seyne reden, warhafftig, unnd in sich selberts gerecht seind, die Gott redet." *Gelaub*, cV-cii (see above, n. 178 for more of this statement).

[261] "Hett Abraham die eüsserliche rede unnd züsagung, one das innerlich züsprechen unnd verheyssen Gottes, angenomen, were es im unmüglich gewest, eyn frid mit Got zü haben. Er were eynes verstürtzten gemüts gewesen, voller zweyfels, gleissnerey, und glantzes.

Denn es ist ye gantz unmüglich das einer Gottes freund oder sone werd, ohne die inwendige und heimliche offenbarung Gottes, als wenig auch das geschehen mag, das einer Gottes eüsserlich wort annem, und für ein wort des preütgamss, der frölickeyt, des trostes und aussgestreckten lustes halt, wenn sich Got nit züvor, oder gleich im eüsserlichen gehör mit seinem hellen und lichten abgehenden stral offenbaret, so vil das er hören kan, wer Gott ist, was er ist, was er will, alles nach den teylen. . . . Derwegen ist der glaub voller lieb, lustes, voller freuden und wonn, unnd hebet den glaubigen auff, über alle creatürische ding, so offt er ein gerecht urteil götlicher gerechtigkeit höret singen oder sagen." *Ibid.*, ciiiV-civ.

[262] One need not conclude from the statement "if God does not reveal himself either previously or precisely in the external hearing" that Karlstadt intended to assert an activity of the Spirit prior to *all* external hearing. He may have meant only that since a divine work in the soul is necessary if one is to love divine state-

the communication of new conceptual content. Rather it enables one to accept the external word as a true message from God. That is the true understanding of scripture.

In addition to enabling man both to recognize the external word as a word from God and lovingly to obey it, the Holy Spirit can directly illuminate difficult passages.

> I should also indicate how a truly renounced man must renounce holy scripture and not know the letter, but rather enter into the power of the Lord as David says and pray without ceasing to God the Lord that he will inspire him with true understanding. That is, when one does not understand something or eagerly wants to understand a statement, then one should stand in renunciation—i.e. go out of oneself and remain still with one's reason and eagerly crave knowledge from God and listen to what God wants to tell one. Then rapid remembrance will break in upon one. One should verify and vindicate the same with the witness of holy scripture.[263]

Here Karlstadt clearly introduced a spiritualist element. God can and will provide direct revelation of the meaning of the external word. One must not overstate Karlstadt's intention, however.[264] In light of Karlstadt's previously noted advice to examine the context of scripture, one need not suppose that this passage means that one should forsake the external letter in general.[265] Rather, it is in the case

---

ments when one hears them read or sung, therefore one must either have experienced grace at some earlier time when one also heard the external word, or one must simultaneously experience inner grace and external hearing. On the other hand he may have meant that the Spirit prepares the soul prior to all external hearing. But even that need not mean, either that the external word is unnecessary or that the inner preparation involved any special revelation.

[263] "Alhie solt ich auch sagen, wie ain recht gelassner mensch die haylig schrifft müss gelasen, und nicht umb büchstaben wissen sonder eingeen in die macht des herren (als David spricht) und Gott den herren, on ablassen bitten, das er im waren verstand wölle eingeben, als wenn ainer etwas nit versteet, oder ain urtail gern wölt vernemen, so soll er in der gelassenhait stehen das ist auss im geen, und mit seyner vernunfft still halten, und gestrengklich von Got begern sein kunst, und hören was im Got will sagen, so werden ime schwinde gedechtnuss einfallen, dieselben soll er mit gezeügknuss hailiger schrifft beweren und gerechtfertigen das ich ferrer anzaygen solt, aber alhie leydet sichs nit. Lisse die Teütschen Theologiam, bistu nit züfriden, so beydt biss meyn buechlin von der schüle Gottis aussgehe." *Sich Gelassen*, dii. "Swynde gedancken" in *Von manigfeltigkeit*, Diii should probably be interpreted in light of this passage (see above, n. 249). See too *Fürbit Marie*, Biii.

[264] Kriechbaum does this when she introduces this passage with the words: "Es ist sogar das Idealbild eines gelassenen Menschen, dass er die Heilige Schrift zurücklässt und nichts von Buchstaben wissen will" (*Grundzüge*, p. 30).

[265] For instance, with reference to the meaning of discerning the Lord's body (I Cor. 11:29) he said that he who wants to discern the Lord's body must indus-

of difficult passages that one should pray for direct illumination. Furthermore, the directly communicated interpretation is authoritative only if one can verify and vindicate it in the external text. "Faith has its witness in scripture. . . . If God has impressed divine understanding upon you, you must show me a similar word in scripture." Otherwise, one would have to listen to magicians, fortunetellers and devils.[266] The spiritualist tendency is both clear and limited.[267]

If Karlstadt had said no more, his doctrine of authority would be only very minimally spiritualist. But Karlstadt, or at least one of his spokesmen, Peter the layman, did say more and that rather strikingly in an important section in his Eucharistic dialogue. The entire passage must be examined carefully for it is an important statement apropos the role of the Holy Spirit in the exegetical task.

After Gemser, the priest, had explained Karlstadt's explanation of "TOUTO," Peter the layman noted that for a long time he had believed that Christ pointed to his physical body rather than the bread when he said, "This is my body." Gemser promptly demanded who had taught him. Peter replied:

Peter: The one whose voice I heard and yet I saw him not. . . . Gemser: Who is that? Peter: Our Father in heaven. . . . Gemser: What occurred to you as an assurance so that you rest so strongly in your illusion and

triously learn what is *written* about the body of Christ, and then *from those same statements* rightly learn to know the body of Christ: "Wer des hern leyb recht untherscheiden und wol richten wil, der müss warlich in fleiss lernen, was von dem leib Christi, sonderlich geschrieben, und auss den selben urteyln, recht den leib Christi erkennen." *Auszlegung* (1524), diii.

[266] "Hastu aber Gottes wort nit, so werd ich bald sagen, der glaub hatt sein gezeugnüss in der schrifft. Ro. 10. Hat dir Got ein götlich erkantnüss eingetruckt, soltu mir ein gleychs wort in der schrifft zeygen. Denn es ist in dem gesetz begriffen, das Gott in die hertzen seiner iünger schreibet. Hie.31. Esa.8.51. Wiltu dich eines glaubens rümen, der dir sagt, das kein schrifft inhelt, bistu schon von dem rechten glauben abdrünnig. Wiltu auch so leychtfertiglich von dem glauben schwatzen, werden zauberer, warsager, und teufeln auch wol bestehn." *Ibid.*, AiiV. In light of Karlstadt's use of "eingetruckt" here, one could also legitimately interpret "eyndruckung" in *Von manigfeltigkeit* Biii and Diii in light of *Sich Gelassen*, dii.

[267] Two brief allusions to "inner hearing" should be noted. In *Sich Gelassen* Karlstadt declared that since he was so prone to take sinful delight in his public preaching, he would, but for God's command to preach, content himself with "innerlichen hören" (*Sich Gelassen*, bii). In *Ursachen*, he observed that there was a greater possibility of sin in public preaching than in "inwendigen handlung des wort Gottis, wens die sele frisch von Got höret" (Hertzsch, I, 16.30-31). Neither context provides any explanation. Both statements may refer to nothing more than quiet, private meditation. At the most, they allude to the process recommended in *Sich Gelassen*, dii for puzzling texts.

remain in it to the present? Peter: I do not have an illusion, but rather truth and certainty, and I can affix my seal that the text is true. Gemser: Therefore I ask about the assurance.[268]

After some intervening discussion in which Peter showed enthusiasm for Gemser's statements about the Greek text, Gemser asked why Peter cared about the Greek.

> Peter: The reason is that I hear an external witness whereby I may raise up and edify the fallen and silence and conquer the opponents. For myself, I would not need the external witness at all. I want to have my witness from the Spirit in my inwardness, which Christ promised. Gemser: Where? Peter: ... Christ said, the Spirit, the Comforter will witness to you and you will also witness of me [cf. John 15:26-27]. Thus it happened with the apostles who were assured inwardly through the witness of the Holy Spirit and afterward preached Christ externally and established through the scriptures that Christ had to suffer for us and that the Messiah was indeed Jesus of Nazareth the Crucified. Gemser: That was said about the apostles. Peter: Shall we not be like the apostles? ... Did Christ not promise his Spirit to us as much as to the apostles? The Spirit alone leads us into knowledge of God's statements. Therefore it follows that those who do not hear God's Spirit speak do not understand God's statements. Nor are they Christians. As Christ says, "Those who have the Spirit of Christ are of Christ." Therefore God's Spirit alone gives witness and assurance. Romans 8.[269]

---

[268] "Gems. Wer hat dichs gelert? Petr. Des stimm ich höret, und sahe in doch nit, wist auch nit, wie er zu mir, und von mir ging. Gems. Wer ist der? Pet. Unser vatter im himel. Gem. Ach hett ichs auch von jm gelernet. Pet. Hastu nit seynen geyst versprochen? Bistu nit der arm mann, der Gottes lebendiger stymm, ein creaturische form gybet. Gem. Weyland, aber itzt nicht. Pet. Hastu einen aussgestreckten lust in der gerechtigkeyt, als gerechtigkeyt, und ein brünstig hertz dartzu, so ist dir die krichisch schrifft, welche du itzt hast überlesen, eyn bescherdtes mittel. Gems. Was fiel dir für eyn versicherung ein, das du dich so festiglich auff deynen wohn legest, und drinnen biss anher bist gestanden? Pet. Ich hab nit einen wohn, sonder warheyt und gewissheyt, und kan versiegeln, das der text warhafftig ist. Gems. Darumb frag ich von der versicherung." *Dialogus*, Hertzsch, II, 17.17-31.

[269] "Gemser. Wenn du deiner sachen so erfaren bist gewesen, warumb wardestu sehr fröhlich, als ich dir sagt, wie sich die krichische sprach hielt? Pet. Drumb das ich ein eüsserlich zeugnüs höret, da durch ich die verfallen yetzt auffrichten, und erbawen, unnd die widersträber nu stillen, und überwinden mag. Meyner person halben dorfftet ich des eüsserlichen zeugnüss nicht nits. Ich wil meyn zeugnüss vom geyst, in meyner inwendigkeyt haben, das Christus verheyssen hat. Gems. Wo? Peter. Weystu abermals nit, dz Christus also saget? Der geyst, der tröster, würt euch zeugnüss geben, und ir werdet auch gezeugnüss von mir geben. Also ist es mit den Aposteln ergangen, die inwendig durch gezeugniss des geistes versichert wurden, und darnach Christum eusserlich predigten, und durch schrifften befestigten, das Christus für uns leyden must, und das der selb Christ, Jesus von Nazareth der gekreützigt war. Gems. Das ist von den Aposteln gesagt. Pet.

This passage is definitely Karlstadt's most spiritualist assertion apropos exegesis.[270]

In the passages previously examined Karlstadt said that the Holy Spirit was necessary for man to be obediently related to the external word, to recognize it as God's message and, in the case of difficult passages, to arrive at the proper exegesis which is then verified elsewhere in scripture. Here, however, Peter says that for himself he has no need of any other external, scriptural verification of the exegetical interpretation given by the Spirit. That is a far more radically spiritualist statement than the passage from *Sich Gelassen.*

In light of the rest of the treatise, not to mention Karlstadt's other words, this passage is puzzling. Earlier in the work, Victor, the other spokesman for Karlstadt, kept demanding a "clear, biblical word."[271] "I believe nothing unless you adduce the word of faith."[272] When Gemser complained impatiently that Victor was bound to the Bible, Victor retorted that scripture is a witness to the truth.[273] This, of course, could be merely clever tactics. Later, however, Peter himself demanded that Gemser prove his exegetical interpretation with a word from Christ or the apostles.[274] "Peter: Do you have a basis for that in

---

Sollen wir nit Apostel messig sein, warumb saget Petrus von Cornelio, das er den geyst entpfangen hatte wie sie? Warumb sprichet Paulus, das wir seyne nachfolger sein sollen? hat uns Christus seinen geyst nit verheyssen als den Aposteln? der geyst allein füret uns in erkäntnüss der reden Gottes, drumb folget, das die ihene Gottes reden nit verstehend, die Gottes geyst nit hören reden. Sie sind auch nit Chiisten, als Christus spricht. Die jene seind Christi, die den geyst Christi haben. Derhalben gybt Gottes geist allein gezeugnüss und versicherung. Ro.8." *Ibid.,* pp. 18.24-19.8.

[270] There is one other passage which is similar: "Dienstlich bittend [the final letter is unclear], ewer keyner wöll auff mich odei aynen andern sehen, sonder ain yegklicher auff sein ynnerlichs gezeügnuss des gaystes achtung geben. Aber so er des eüsserlichen und schrifftlichen gezeügnuss für sich oder ander bedarff, blösslich auff die schrifft sehen, die ich füren werd" (*Missbrauch*, Aii).

[271] "Ich wil ein rechts, klars, bibelischs wort haben." *Dialogus*, Hertzsch, II, 10.18.

[272] "Ich glaub doch keynes, es sey dann das du mir das wort des glaubens fürlegest." *Ibid.,* p. 12.38-39.

[273] "Zeyg mir Christus wort, oder eynen buchstaben des glaubens, auss der biblien, das Christus leib in einer kleiner hostien sey, und sihe ob ich nit glaub. Gems. Du bist an die biblien gebunden. Vict. Ich süch Got in der biblien, und nicht schrifft in den schrifften. Gem. Warzu sal dir denn schrifft? Vict. Zu eynem gezeügnuss der warheyt." *Ibid.,* p. 13.7-12.

[274] " . . . wiltu sagen. Ich rede recht, so müstu das recht mit götlicher gerechtigkeit und warheit beweisen. One das, glaub ich dir nichts. Gems. Ey wie vil hab ich gehöret, bereytet euch wirdiglich zu entpfahen, den leyb Christi. Pet. Ich glaub dirss wol. *Lege* mir aber dar ein wort Christi, oder eynes Apostels, der also redet." *Ibid.,* pp. 23.37-24.2 (my italics).

scripture? Gemser: No. Peter: Then you are a liar." [275] These statements of Peter would seem to imply the view that any exegetical
understanding must be verified in the external word.

Hillerbrand has suggested that "perhaps these words do not quite say
what they seem to say." [276] In fact, in the first discussion of the Father's
inner witness, it sounded as if he intended to talk about the divine
assurance that the written word is truly God's truth: "I can affix my
seal that the text is true." Later, however, he seemed to refer to the
verification of directly communicated exegetical insight. But then at
the end of the section, he mentioned that general "speaking" of the
Spirit which every Christian possesses. Here surely he was talking
about the inward "revelation" or grace which every believer receives.[277] And then the final comment pertained to the assurance which
the Spirit gives. One must not read too much into Peter's words.

At a minimum, one can be certain of two things. First, Karlstadt
was talking about the Spirit's role in the exegesis of canonical scripture, not an additional source of authoritative revelation. Second, he
of course assumed that the exegetical interpretation given by the
Spirit would be in conformity with scripture. Thus, near the end,
Peter affirmed his willingness to change his view if one could adduce
scripture.[278] In principle the external word remained the norm. In fact,
of course, if the Spirit's exegesis need not be verified in other scripture, the possibility of departure from the written word is clearly
present. If Karlstadt intended his statement that external verification
is unnecessary to be taken literally and applied generally, then this
exegetical principle introduced a significant spiritualist tendency into
his doctrine of authority. It is possible, however, that Peter's radical
statement should be understood more as an assertion of Karlstadt's
confidence in the validity of his Eucharistic exegesis than as a general
exegetical principle. In that case, divinely inspired exegetical insight
would presumably need scriptural verification.

---

[275] "Gems. Das ist alles war naturaliter, aber sacramentaliter und supernatura-
liter ist das ware, das Christus zu gleych an vil enden ist. Pet. Hastu des auch einen
grund in der schrifft? Gem. Nein. Pe. So bistu ein lugner." *Ibid.*, p. 37.4-8.

[276] "Carlstadt," p. 398. Rupp also minimizes the spiritualism of this passage. He
introduces it with the comment that Karlstadt's "later tracts emphasize much
more the authority of the Scriptures, with in some places an almost Methodist like
emphasis upon the witness of the Spirit." Then he quotes Peter's statement about
not needing the external witness ("Word and Spirit," p. 20).

[277] See above, pp. 243-6.

[278] "Peter. Christus ist im hymel leiblich, wenn ir schrifft zeiget, das er in ewrem
brodt ist, so wil ich anderss reden." *Dialogus*, Hertzsch, II, 43.19-21.

One final area of Karlstadt's exegetical method needs to be considered. Is it true, as it has been suggested, that his notion of the spirit of the scriptural letter led him in a spiritualist direction? Hayo Gerdes has argued that according to Karlstadt, one cannot understand the spirit of the law by means of rational insight. Rather, since God is Spirit, man grasps the inner sense of the letter only in the ground of the soul with the aid of the Spirit.[279]

How did Karlstadt arrive at the spiritual understanding of the letter? There is no evidence to support Gerdes' view that the Spirit directly reveals the spirit of the letter to the ground of the soul. Karlstadt never connected the concept of the ground of the soul with the problem of the spirit versus the letter of the law. In one passage Karlstadt implied that one obtains the spirit of the letter from the letter itself:

> Now I notice says a reader of this book, that . . . his divine mind is locked in holy scripture as a kernel in a pod. He who wants to eat the kernel must bite off the shell and throw it away. He must seek the bark for the sake of the kernel or marrow and not break this order.[280]

One should in fact go to the external bark provided that one knows that the goal is God and his will and not the external letter. In at least one instance it is clear that later scriptural revelation provided the inner sense of earlier revelation. When the Jews did not understand the figurative sayings, "God sent them prophets who revealed the concealed statements of the law so that those who stood in the knowledge of the inner kernel of scripture would enter into true freedom." [281]

In some of the places where Karlstadt actually used the mechanism of the inner sense and where it is possible to trace how he arrived at the spirit of the letter, it appears that he obtained it from other scripture. In *Vorstandt* he made a strong initial statement about the concealed nature of the inner sense:

> He who considers the intentions of the holy sayings which God's servants have given proceeds well without trouble. The intention,

---

[279] Gerdes, *Luthers Streit mit den Schwärmern,* pp. 28-9.

[280] *Von manigfeltigkeit,* DiiiV (see above, n. 249). Cf. n. 273 above where Karlstadt insists that one should seek God in the Bible rather than read scripture for its own sake.

[281] "Die Juden verstunden die gerechtigkeit nit der figurlichen reden, darumb waren sy gefangen, aber Got schickt in Propheten, wölche die verdeckten Sentenz des gesetzes offenbaren auff das sy in rechte freyheit kemen, wölche steet inn dem erkenntnuss, des innerlichen kerns der schrifft." *Anzeig,* Hertzsch, II, 101.12-16.

however, hides rather deeply under the letter and is so deep and concealed that no human eye can see it. Here, however, it is not so deep or concealed.[282]

But then he proceeded to determine the intention of the text in question by a careful, rational examination of the *context* of the passage. Similarly, he said with regard to I Thessalonians 4:13-17 that "the other, secretly understood content or understanding" of the text is that we should not grieve over those who die in Christ. The reason death is not frightening is that it frees one from the prison of the body which hinders one's sanctification during this life. But then he adduced another scripture (Romans 7:23) to support this view.[283]

In *Sabbat* he developed an argument from scripture to prove that the spirit of the Sabbath command is the divine intention that man become holy. He adduced Leviticus 20:7 and 26 to show that the purpose of all commands is inner sanctification. He also cited Isaiah's statement that God rejected their Sabbath observance but desired that evil thoughts and actions cease (Isaiah 1:13-17). His conclusion was that the spirit of the Sabbath command is man's inner sanctification.[284] Karlstadt's sometimes fanciful conception of the spiritual Sabbath is often cited as a good example of the subjective results of his notion of the spirit of the law. Actually, however, his basic interpretation depends not on a private revelation about the spirit of the command and only peripherally on his inadequate exegesis of the Hebrew; rather it depends upon this argument from Leviticus and Isaiah which he developed at some length at the very beginning of the work. Apparently Karlstadt's concept of the spirit of the letter did not lead to a spiritualist dissipation of scriptural authority.

It is also significant to note that Karlstadt sometimes used the

---

[282] "Welcher achtung hat, uff die ursachen, der heyligen reden, so Gotis knechte gesetzt haben, der geht wol, und one beschwerung. Die ursach aber, steckt etwan tieff, under dem büchstaben, und also tieff und vordeckt, das sie kein menschlich auge sehen kan. Alhie aber, ist sie nit so tieff, oder vormantelt." *Vorstandt*, AiiiV.

[283] "Der ander und haymlich begryffen inhalt, oder verstandt obbemelter Epistel ist, das wir uns von wegen der todten oder verstorben in Christo, nicht sollen bekümmern, als die jhenen so kain hofnung haben. . . . Dieweyl nun jr todt ain tewer hochschetzig und kostlich ding in den augen Gotes ist alss die schrifft sagt, sollen wir mitt nicht trawrig und betriebt sein, sonder uns höchlichen erfrewen, das sy Got von dem leyb und kercker hat erlösset, der sy gefangen hielt, unnd gefengklich ins gesetz der sünden fieret. Roma.7. [v.23]" *Sermon vom Stand*, aiiiV.

[284] *Sabbat*, Hertzsch, I, 23.16-24.26. It is also interesting to note that Karlstadt's conception of the spiritual meaning of the Sabbath command is merely an elaboration of Augustine's statements to the same effect in *De spiritu et litera*, xv (27).

language of the letter and spirit of the law to refer to a second, rather different question viz. the inadequacy of the external letter apart from grace. Some scholars deal with God's word, but do not know God.

> They have their knowledge in their mouth, but not in their heart. . . . Therefore, it is on the surface in the bark of the tree and in the most external letter of the truth.[285]

Here the question of the letter of scripture pertains not to the content of scripture, but to man's lack of inner regeneration. Similarly, after arguing in the passage discussed at length previously that man rightly knows and loves the ten commandments only after being implanted in Christ, he added: "He who fulfils the shell, bark or letter of a law and omits the meaning and heart of the law, does not serve the law." [286] Merely to fulfil the letter of the ten commandments, which of course ought to be obeyed literally, is to attempt to comply with them without the aid of grace.

Another passage should probably be interpreted in terms of this second usage. Karlstadt argued that God's eternal will was not physical circumcision, but rather circumcision of the heart or re-generation.[287]

> The eternal will of God does not consist of any external practice or physical devotion, for all that can be entirely false and deceptive. It [the eternal will] is not truly in man until God actively brings his eternal will into man, i.e. makes man will what he wills and makes him work his divine work. . . . Man wins nothing with sensory or external signs [e.g. baptism, sacrifices]. Yes, man angers God more when externals announce the inner Spirit of God which is not present, for then it lies. However, what must be and is unchanging and remains eternally, God creates inwardly in the naked soul. For God is a Spirit; therefore, the created creature must join himself to God's uncreated Spirit with and through the Spirit. Accordingly, each person can and should discover the spirit of the letter and not the skin or peel of the letter if he wants to serve God satisfactorily. You must seek the spirit of the scripture, i.e. the eternal will of God, and according to that do or forsake what the letter commands or forbids—not, of course, according to the letter, but rather according to the enclosed or concealed Spirit.[288]

---

[285] *Gelaub*, aivV (see above, n. 175). See above, chapter four ("The spirit and the letter") for a similar usage in 1521.

[286] *Von manigfeltigkeit*, Diii (see above, n. 258).

[287] *Ibid.*, GV-Gii.

[288] "Ewiger Gotis will steht in keiner eusserlicher vbung oder leiplicher andacht, dan das kan alles falsch und lugenhafftig seyn, und ist nicht warhafftig in dem menschen eher Got seynen ewigen willen ym menschen yns werck bringt. das

This passage demands the inner transformation of man's will. Since the regenerate will will live eternally, he could say that this work of God is everlasting. Any attempt to perform supposedly religious external acts without regeneration merely angers God. Such a person rests in the skin or peel of the letter and fails to discover the spirit of the letter. "The spirit of the letter, i.e. the eternal will of God" is precisely that divinely bestowed inner righteousness which enables man to do what the letter commands.[289]

Karlstadt's Orlamünde theology gave a significant role to the Spirit in the exegetical task. The Spirit enables one obediently and lovingly to relate oneself to scripture. He assures one that the text is a message from God. And he directly reveals the proper interpretation of difficult passages. The spiritualism involved in this last point is not large as long as it is asserted that one must verify the divinely bestowed exegetical insight with other scriptures. *Dialogus*, however, appeared to waive the necessity of external verification. If Karlstadt intended Peter's statement to be a general exegetical principle, then he introduced a significant spiritualist tendency. Apart from this passage,

---

ist, das er den menschen macht wellen, dz er wyl, und sein götlich werck wircken. Auch ist es alles tzeitlich und vergencklich, und klein schetzich, das Got eusserlich fodert, gepeut, und wil. man kan auch seynen wol gefelligen willen, one alle eusserheit volbrengen. Man ghewynt auch nichts mit synlicher oder eusserlicher antzeich. Ja man ertzornet Got mehr, wan eusserheit den ynnerlichenn geist Gots antzeicht, der nit vorhanden ist, dann sye leugt. Aber das seyn müss, unnd unenderlich ist, unnd ewig soll bleyben, das schüff Got inwendich in der blossen sele. Dan Got ist ein geist, derhalben müss sich die geschaffen creatur, mit unnd durch den geist, mit Gots vngeschaffen geist vereynen. Demnach magk, und sol, ein yeder den gheist des bustabs, unnd nit die rynder oder schalen des bustaben ergrunden, so er Got beheglich wil dienen. Dem geist der schrifft das ist, dem ewigen Gots willen müstu nach süchen, unnd darnach thün oder lassen, was der bustaben ghebeut oder verbeut, nit nach dem bustaben, sonder nach dem beschlosvsen oder erdeckten geist." *Ibid.*, Giii-GiiiV.

[289] It should be noted that Kriechbaum interprets this passage differently. She thinks it pertains to the first usage of letter and spirit. "Den 'gheist des bustabs' ergründen heisst: mit der ins Inwendige gelegten Erkenntnis an den Buchstaben herangehen. Im Innern ist ein Richter geschaffen, der alles Aüssere beurteilt. . . . Damit ist der schwärmerische Zirkel offenkundig" (*Grundzüge*, p. 32). But that is to overlook the fact that in this passage "eternal will of God" appears to connote not primarily the spiritual content of scripture, but rather God's inner regenerating activity. The eternal will must be *in* man, who then can live a regenerate life. Even if she were correct and the last two sentences quoted pertained to the spiritual sense of scripture (the rest clearly pertains to regeneration), the passage would not prove as much as she supposes. It would merely assert that only the regenerate man (the one whose spirit is united to God's Spirit) can discover the spirit of the law. The passage would not indicate the method for selecting the spirit from the letter of the law.

however, the spiritualist element in his exegesis was relatively limited. His notion of the spirit of the external letter did not introduce any abandonment of scriptural authority. Apropos the source and norm of theological knowledge, he continued to enunciate the earlier *sola scriptura* themes. Visions and dreams were not means of revelation. In short, although his Orlamünde theology did grant an increased role to the Holy Spirit, it was still less radically spiritualist than has often been suggested.

## (i) *Grace and law in Christian ethics*

The first thing which must be said about Karlstadt's statements about ethics is that they presuppose his central doctrine of regeneration. It is regeneration which makes possible a life of love toward neighbor. Karlstadt's full title for *Zweyen höchsten gebotten* underlined this thesis by announcing that the book would show "how true love for neighbor is not human but rather divine and how it flows from God's will." Love for neighbor is "beyond nature and beyond one's natural powers." [290]

> The cause and source of love for neighbor is this. God is love itself, and his love is a self-subsistent and uncreated loving power which touches the ground of the soul, i.e. the most inward part. . . . When divine love reveals and pours itself into a human heart, it teaches love of neighbor and makes it love all that God loves.[291]

Accordingly Karlstadt devoted the first part of this sermon on love of God and neighbor to a discussion of that noblest work of God, viz. God's infusion of faith rich in love or love rich in faith, which produces first love of God and then love of neighbor.[292] It is only after grace has regenerated the will that man can live an ethically proper life.

If grace impels the will, the law guides it. It is quite clear that Karlstadt thought divine laws and revealed commands play a very important role in the life of the Christian. After a very excellent exposition of unselfish love for neighbor, he concluded that the only

---

[290] "Weyl dann die lieb des nechsten, nach der lieb Gottes kompt, unnd göttlicher lieb gleich ist, so ist sy über natur, und übernatürliche krefften." *Zweyen höchsten gebotten*, Hertzsch, I, 57.16-18.

[291] *Ibid.*, pp. 57.28-58.1 (see above, n. 186).

[292] Cf. also *Von manigfeltigkeit*, GivV: "Wuo recht erkentnis Gots ist ym glauben, do ist recht lieb und fruntschafft Gotis. wü Gots lieb gewaltig ist, do ist auch lieb des nehsten."

concern of such love is "to fulfil the command of the great king."[293]
"It is impossible to love Christ and . . . not do what Christ commands." [294] When Paul confessed that he would not have known sin
without the law, he showed that the law preaches God's will and
shows us what is sinful. Christians should teach their children God's
law "in order that they may choose the good and flee the evil." [295]
For Karlstadt the law does not merely reveal sin and thereby drive
man to the forgiveness offered in Christ. Rather it reveals what is good
and bad so that good is done and evil avoided—by grace of course.
The category of law in the life of the Christian was a very compatible
notion for Karlstadt.[296]

Unfortunately Karlstadt stressed the role of the law without directly
stating how normative Old Testament law is in the Christian life.[297]
He could state that our well-being comes about through the keeping
of divine commands and then proceed to quote Moses' injunction to
keep all the words of the Lord.[298] He charged the Wittenbergers with
the perversion of God's word on the ground that since God in the
Old Testament assigned the act of elevation to sacrifices, one dare not
elevate the Eucharist unless one considers it a sacrifice.[299] That
Luther dared place the Mosaic law on the same level as the ancient
customs of the Germanic *Sachsenspiegel* infuriated Karlstadt.[300] Are,

---

[293] " . . . unnd du hast ein geschwinden und gestrengen ernst schlecht das
gebott des grossen königs zu volbringen." *Zweyen höchsten gebotten*, Hertzsch, I,
68.19-20. For a lengthy discussion of Karlstadt's view of the role of law in the
Christian life, see Alden L. Thompson, "*Tertius Usus Legis* in the Theology of
Andreas Bodenstein von Karlstadt" (unpublished Ph. D. dissertation, Department
of Religion, University of Southern California, 1969).

[294] "Denn die lieb, erfült Gottes gebot, und ist unmüglich das einer Christum
lieb hab, und thu wider sein gebot, oder thu nit was Christus gebut." *Gemach*,
Hertzsch, I, 78.21-24. So too *Von manigfeltigkeit*, Aii: "Das verstehe also, welcher
eyn frund Gotis sein wil, . . . der müss Gotis willen thün, und nach götlichem
willen leben, wollen, thün, lassen, wirken, rühen, arbeiten ader sabbatiseren."

[295] *Ibid.*, HV-Hii (see below, n. 301).

[296] Perhaps Bubenheimer is correct in suggesting that Karlstadt's vigorous
emphasis on *ius biblicum* is related to his earlier involvement in canon and civil law.
See "Consonantia Theologiae et Jurisprudentiae," especially pp. 240-243. If
Melanchthon is to be believed, Karlstadt urged that the Justinian code be abol-
ished and replaced by the Mosaic law. See *ibid.*, p. 241, nn. 1-3 and Guido
Kisch, *Melanchthons Rechts-und Soziallehre* (Berlin, 1967), pp. 110f., n. 18 and p. 190.

[297] Scheel pointed out this weakness in Karlstadt's theology ("Individualismus,"
pp. 368-369).

[298] *Zweyen höchsten gebotten*, Hertzsch, I, 69.32-70.5.

[299] *Wider*, iiV-iii.

[300] *Anzeig*, Hertzsch, II, 99.23-34.; cf. also p. 69.18-20. For Luther, see *LW*,
XL, 98; *WA*, XVIII, 81.4-17.

then, all the non-ceremonial Mosaic commands binding on the Christian?

Perhaps his reference to and discussion of the prohibition of images is a fair reflection of his general attitude. In this discussion Karlstadt simply assumed that passages in Deuteronomy and Exodus apply to Christians.

> Just as I dare not ask God, "Why have you created me thus and not otherwise?" just as little dare I ask God, "Why have you forbidden and made it wrong that, for instance, it should be evil for Christians to make images or keep images that are already made in houses of God?" That is beyond all reason. Nevertheless, that is evil and wrong in God's eyes. God's law teaches us that (Deuteronomy 3, 7; Exodus 20).[301]

Apparently he thought that much of the Mosaic law was normative for Christians.

He mitigated the rigidity of this stance somewhat by a partial attempt to subsume the law under the twofold command to love God and neighbor. "All commands and prohibitions consist of love of God and neighbor." [302] He even tried to subsume the Sabbath command under Christ's twofold summary. The spiritual purpose of this command is the sanctification of man, i.e. the growth of love for God. The second, "physical" purpose of the Sabbath pertains to the good of one's neighbors—namely one's maids, servants and children who need a day of rest from their tasks.[303] However, even though the

---

[301] "Also verkundigt dz gesetz, Gots willen. und leret in welchem stuck wyr wider Gottis willen thün, unnd also sundigenn. . . . alles das Gotis wort verbeut. ob es unser vernunfft seltzam ist, unnd unbegreyflich, das böss und unrecht seyn mocht. Als wenygh ich Got darff fragenn, warumb hastu mich also unnd nycht anders geschaffen, so wenyg darff ich Got fragenn, warumb hastu das verbotten, und böss gemacht als das böss seyn sal, das Christen bylder machenn, oder gemachte bilder in Gotis heuseren halten u. das ist uber alle vernunfft. dannest ist es böss unnd unrecht in Gotis ougen. Das leret unss Gotis gesetz Deute. iiii.vii. Exo.xx. . . . Drumb solten wir die kynder von jugent auff, Gots wort leren. uff das sye wisten was Got wolgefelt, was gut, und was böss. damit sie das gut erwelen, das bösse fliehen mochten." *Von manigfeltigkeit*, HV-Hii. He used another part of Deut. similarly in *Gemach*, Hertzsch, I, 82.9-29. Cf. also the use of the prohibition against kindling fires on the Sabbath (Exodus 35:3) in *Sabbat*, Hertzsch I, 29.25-29.

[302] "Damit ist auch der ander frag genug geschehen, dz, das gesetz und die propheten an zweyen geboten hangen soll, das ye war ist, Denn alle gebotten und verbotten stehn in Gottes und des nechsten lieb." *Zweyen höchsten gebotten*, Hertzsch, I, 56.9-12.

[303] *Sabbat*, Hertzsch, I, 25.1-19. See *ibid.*, pp. 23.15-24.5 for the "geystliche ursache des Sabbats."

Sabbath command is for the sake of man, it is still a command which all Christians are obliged to obey. In ordinary circumstances Christians should not allow themselves, their servants or their animals to work on the Sabbath.[304]

Similarly, he argued that since the weak were still grossly deceived by images, brotherly love required his policy of removing images before preaching had persuaded people to relinquish them gladly. The situation of Christians who clung to images was analogous, he believed, to that of a child clinging stubbornly to a dangerous knife:

> If I see that a little innocent child has a sharp, pointed knife in his hand and wants to keep it, will I show him brotherly love when I leave him with the dreadful knife and his own will . . . or when I break his will and take the knife? You must certainly say, when you take from the child what injures him, you do a fatherly or brotherly, Christ-like deed.[305]

Similarly, brotherly love required that the images be torn from the hands of those who still revered them. But Karlstadt was equally insistent that God's law necessitated the immediate removal of images.[306] If one defines legalism as that doctrinal position which prescribes considerable portions of the Old Testament law as normative for the Christian, then Luther was right in charging that Karlstadt was a legalist.[307] To the degree that the Puritan tradition also

---

[304] "Der Sabbat ist der ganzen gemeine Gottis uffgelegt." *Ibid.*, p. 25.37. For the discussion of the servants and animals, see *ibid.*, pp. 29.3-32.13.

[305] "Demnach frag ich, wenn ich sehe, das ein klein unmündig kindelin ein spitzig scharpff messer in seiner handt hett, und wölt es gern behalten, ob ich im denn brüderliche lieb beweiset, wenn ich im das schedlich messer und seinen willen liess, damitt sichs verwundet oder ertödt, oder denn, wenn ich im seinen willen breche, und das messer näm? Du must ie sagen, wenn du dem kind nimbst, das im schaden brengt, so thustu ein vätterlich oder brüderlich Christelich werck." *Gemach*, Hertzsch, I, 88.33-89.2 (see the entire argument on p. 88.1-39). So too p. 95.

[306] "Etliche gebot begriffen kein gelegenheit, zeit oder stedt, den selbigen muss man ewiglichen nachgehen unnd kein zeit darvon ablassen, oder dar wider thun, als da seynd disse gebott, du salst nicht bilder machen, haben, oder leyden, du salst nit stelen, nicht morden, nicht Eebrechen, nit falsch zeügnüs geben, nicht frembder güter begeren, und dergleichen. Solche gebott verbinden uns an alle zeit unnd in alle ende, wer ein zeit, an irgent einem ort, unnd wider eines thut, der ist ein uberschreydter, ungehorsamer, ungerechter, verachter Gottes." *Ibid.*, p. 86.16-25. See also *ibid.*, p. 85.4-26. One cannot agree with Hertzsch that "diese biblizistischen Gründe nur nebenher laufen." Hertzsch, *Karlstadt und seine Bedeutung für das Luthertum*, p. 66.

[307] Thus Scheel says that Karlstadt's legalism consists essentially in his orientation of the new life of the Christian according to the concept of law. "Nach Karlstadt besitzt das Gesetz im Leben des Christen eine massgebende Rolle" ("Individualismus," p. 368; see also p. 369).

laid great emphasis on the binding character of the Mosaic law, Rupp is quite correct in speaking of Karlstadt's Puritanism.[308]

That Karlstadt was a legalist in the sense just noted should not obscure the fact that he certainly was not entirely inflexible. As Rupp has noted, his tract on the Sabbath was not nearly as rigid as some have thought.[309] He spent considerable time arguing that some commands have priority over others.

> God has established an order in his commands. Some command great and highly esteemed things; others are of less significance. Those which command works of love, faith and mercy and the like, command the best and greatest works. Those which speak of sacrifices, sabbaths and similar ceremonies, command matters to be lightly esteemed.[310]

God has not commanded men to hold all commands at once. The best commands are those which command love and mercy toward the neighbor. The command to keep the Sabbath stands far below the command to assist one's neighbor. Furthermore, the lesser commands are not commanded when keeping them would mean breaking greater commands.[311]

The extent of freedom which Karlstadt desired is shown by the kinds of examples he suggested. He, of course, cited the instances which were obvious from Jesus' explicit teaching. One must take care of one's neighbor's sick animals and make peace on the Sabbath. Karlstadt's genuine desire for some freedom, however, becomes apparent in his declaration that since grain and hay are essential for the

---

[308] A brief aside in *Anzeig* is also indicative of a Puritan inclination. He suggested that it would be a good idea if the preachers would enumerate sins point by point—and not only the gross sins either. "Das wolt ich gern, das die prediger auss dem weytten feld und höhe des gesetzes heraber in die tal tretten, nemlich die sünd stuckweyss verzelen, und nicht allein von den groben sünden . . . .." Hertzsch, II, 84.36-39. See Rupp, "Karlstadt and Reformation Puritanism," eg. pp. 318, 326.

[309] *Ibid.*, p. 319.

[310] "Dann Gott hat ein ordnung in seynen gepotten gestelt. Ettliche gepieten gross unnd hochschetzige dinge. Ettlicher geringer. Welche die werck der liebe, des glawbens, der barmhertzickeyt gepitten, und der gleychen, die gepitten die allerbesten unnd grösssiste wercke. Die vonn opffern, unnd sabbaten, unnd der gleychen ceremonien reden, die gepiten geringschetzige sachen." *Sabbat*, Hertzsch, I, 36.12-18.

[311] "Nu hat Gott nye gepoten, das wir alle gebot, vff eynmal, halten solten. . . . Unther den besten geboten und wercken ist das gepot und werck der lieb und barmhertzickeyt tzu dem nehsten. . . . Wenn aber ein mensche die erste thut, und hat die letzte nit gethan, so zurnet Gott nit drumb, wen er nit tzeyt dartzu gehabt. Drumb seind die letzten nit gepoten in der tzeyt, wenn man die erste unterlassen müst." *Ibid.*, p. 36.19-20, 22-23, 33-36.

animals, servants should bring in their lord's crops on the Sabbath if there have been frequent storms and a great deal of wet weather.[312] Man is lord of the Sabbath: "Man has the freedom to work on the Sabbath as often   as his necessity *or benefit* demands it." [313] The freedom of the Christian man was not totally absent from Karlstadt's somewhat legalistic ethics.

More significant, however, is the fact that Karlstadt thought the proper understanding of Christian freedom pertained not primarily to the Christian's freedom apropos laws, but rather to the regenerate man's ability to obey them.

> My understanding of Christian freedom is as true, good, and certain as Doctor Luther's. . . . Freedom cannot remain for long without its own works. I do not make external works a matter of conscience, but I convict the lying and false faith which boasts of freedom and yet is a prisoner of the devil whose he is and whose work he does. . . . He who knows Christ has become free through the knowledge of Christ; and he walks in the works of Christ. But he does not become a Christian by works. . . . By the absence of such works, one would be convicted that he is imprisoned in his heart to temporal goods and the devil, and would indicate that he has not yet become free in the truth.[314]

---

[312]  *Ibid.*, pp. 36.36-37.37.

[313]  "Auff disse meynung sprach Christus, des menschen sohn ist ein herr des Sabbats, und der Sabbat ist von wegen der menschen gepotten, das ist, der mensche hat die freyheyt, das er auff den Sabbat arbeyten darff, sso offt es sein nodt oder nutz erfordert." *Ibid.*, pp. 34.36-35.2. My italics. So also *Anzeig*, Hertzsch, II, 101.12-28.

[314]  "Carolstat, Da bewget der D. Luther für, und hoffet er werd mich umb-blassen, weyss aber nitt, das mein verstand Christlicher freyheit so warhafftig, gut unnd gewiss ist, als D. Luthers ye gewest ist. . . . Wie die freyheit one werck kumbt, also wurd sy geschendt oder verradten (das sy nicht ein freyheit ist) wenn jr jre werck nit nach volgen, Darumb sagt Christus, Machet eintweder einen gutten Bawmen, und seyne früchte gutt, Oder einen bösen Bawmen, und böse früchten, Denn es ist unmöglich das einer ein rechte freyheit einer warheit hab, und ein werck bring, das lugenhafftig, böss und wider die nattur der erkanten warheit ist, Auch kan die freyheit nicht lang one jr eygen werck bleyben.

"Da mach ich nit gewissen durch die eusserliche werck, sondern ich über weyss den lugenhafftigen und falschen glauben der sich freyheit rümbt, und doch ein gefangner man ist des Teuffels, des er ist und seyn werck thut.

"Wölcher Christum erkennt, der ist durchs erkenntnuss Christi frey worden, und geet in den wercken Christi einher, er wirdt aber nitt ein Christ durch die werck, wie aber einer nit ein Christ wurd durch die diemüttige dienste, wolthat, hilff, milte stewer etc. Also wurd einer durch mangel solcher werck überweysst, das er in seynem hertzen gefangen ist, den vergengklichen güttern und dem Teuffel, und bezeügt das er noch nit frey in der warheit ist worden." *Ibid.*, pp. 100.6-101.2.

Of course, only the man born again through Christ can perform the works of Christ. Thus the doctrine of regeneration undergirds Karlstadt's notion of Christian freedom just as it provides the starting point for his entire conception of Christian ethics.

### (j) *The church of the regenerate*

Karlstadt's tracts of this period did not contain a systematic development of the doctrine of the church. The call of the minister was the only subject to which he devoted any lengthy, deliberate consideration. Perhaps this relative paucity of ecclesiological reflection suggests an individualistic emphasis. Certainly it underscores the fact that he was more concerned to inform his readers about other things such as the crucifixion of the egocentric self and the birth of the new life in Christ. In light of the primacy of this emphasis, it is not surprising that Karlstadt conceived of the church as a congregation of the regenerate.

The holy community is the body of Christ.[315] The only way a man can become a member of the people of God is by mortification and regeneration. "Only faith or circumcision of the heart gives birth to true Christians and the people of God." [316] In *Priesterthum* he described the "holy community" as a community of priests with Christ as the head.[31ʳ] His meaning becomes clear when one remembers that he had said at the beginning of the treatise that true priests are those who, because they are born of God, inwardly possess the virtues which the outer garments of the Aaronic priests signified.[318] It is only by means of "faith rich in love," which of course involves the purification of the

---

[315] "Christus thet Gottis willen im höchisten fleyss mehr dann alle creaturen, fleyssiger denn all engeln und heyligen. Reyniglicher denn seyn gantzer leyb, der seyn heylige gemeyne ist. Und der gehorsam was sein höchistes opffer, auss welchem alle andere opffere in Christo ire gerechtigkeit nemen. . . . Drumb ist Christus ein furst und haupt, nit allein der priester, sondernn ein rechtfertigung aller opffer, in hymel und erden, welche die engelen im hymell oder die heyligen menschen auff erden Gott opffern." *Priesterthum*, BV. See *ibid.*, BiiV where Karlstadt argues that all believers in Christ are priests.

[316] " . . . dann der glaub oder beschneydung des hertzen, alleyn warhafftig Christen unnd volck Gottis geperen [=gebären]. Hiere. iiii. Mar. ult. Joan. iii. Ro.ii." *Von manigfeltigkeit*, Gii.

[317] *Priesterthum*, BV (see above, n. 315).

[318] "Die, über das gesetz synd Priester gesetzt, die gen ynnwendig in den tugenden her, welche die gesetzische priester ausswendig an kleydern, durch figürliche zeychen tragen. Sie werden auch, nit von fleysch und blüt, sunder von oben herab auss Gott, in göttlicher warheit, gerechtigkeit und fryd geborn und haben ein recht göttlich wesen und leben." *Ibid.*, Aiii.

heart and the indwelling of Christ, that one is incorporated (*eingeleybt*) into the body of Christ.[319] The *Volk Gottes* or the *Leib Christi* then is the community of regenerate persons who are being sanctified through Christ their head.

Since true Christians have been truly born anew, it is possible to recognize them by the kinds of lives they live. "One Should Know God's Friends By Their Fruit" is the heading of one chapter in *Von manigfeltigkeit*.

> One recognizes a new tree by its new fruit, and an old tree by its old fruit. The man who is new and stands in God's will also blossoms forth with new works. If previously he was stingy, he now becomes generous; if previously he stole, now he works with his hands. . . . From the fruit one can judge both oneself and another man.[320]

Since genuine Christians really do live differently, one can tell by observing outward actions whether both oneself and the neighbor are true friends of God and thus genuine members of the people of God. It will be seen presently how this conception relates to the way the congregation selects its ministers.

Although Karlstadt spent little time discussing the nature and power of the local congregation, it was clear that it was to have a good deal of autonomy. The congregation chooses its own pastor and then officially designates him pastor by the laying on of hands.[321] In other matters also, "each congregation, however small or great, should see for itself that it acts rightly and properly, and waits for no one." [322] Each congregation possesses the authority, indeed the

---

[319] "Denn des Herren brot essen wir in dem gedechtnuss, Luce. 22. I. Corinthio.11. Unnd werden nicht durchs brot eingeleybt, oder des leybes Christi teylhafftig, wir seind des leybes Christi vor teylhafftig durch das erkanntnus. Esaie an dem. 53. 2. Petri.1. . . . Oder durch den liebreychen glauben, das ein ding ist, Roma.3. Gala.2. Acto.15. Durch den glauben rayniget er die hertzen, durch lieb und glauben, wonet Christus in uns, nicht im bauch, oder im maul, sondern im geyst, in dem inwendigen menschen." *Erklerung*, Ciii.

[320] "Auss newen fruchten erkent man eynen newen paumen. auss alten einen alten. Welcher mensch new ist, und in Gotis willenn steht, der grunet auch mit newen wercken. ist er vor karch gewest, so wirt er mild. hat gestolen, so arbeit er mit henden und gewynt seyn brot mit arbeyten u. Auss den fruchten magk sich einer selbert, und einen andern verstehn." *Von manigfeltigkeit*, GivV. He used the same metaphor, referred to the same scripture, and made precisely the same points two years later. We judge others by their works. Good works are also an external witness of the power of our righteousness. *Anzeig*, Hertzsch, II, 102.3-34.

[321] *Ursachen*, Hertzsch, I, 12.8-24.

[322] "Ein ieglich gemein, sie sey klein oder gross, sol für sich sehen, das sie recht und wol thu, und auff niemants warten." *Gemach*, Hertzsch, I, 80.28-30.

obligation to remove images and the mass on its own.[323] To take a council's views into consideration is to let the council decide whether and when one is to obey God.[324] Each local congregation, then, is relatively autonomous.[325]

There was little explicit reference to congregational discipline. Several remarks, however, make it clear that Karlstadt thought there were some instances under which one ought to exclude people from the Christian community and refrain from association with them. The only criterion he mentioned was right doctrine. Just as Peter demanded repentance before allowing into the Christian *Gemeinschaft* those who had killed Christ, so today true Christians should allow into the congregation only those who renounce their wicked conception of the Mass as a sacrifice. If they persist in their evil, they must stand outside the Christian community.[326]

In *Zweyen höchsten gebotten*, Karlstadt noted that Paul forbade fellowship with those who taught doctrines contrary to Christ. He then drew the astonishing conclusion that since the Bible commands Christians not to eat or associate with those who teach contrary to true doctrine, one should not consider or love them as neighbors. "Not every animal which wears a human skin and has the form of a man should be esteemed as my neighbor." [327] Karl Holl adduced this

---

That is, Orlamünde did not need to wait to remove images until "the guzzlers at Wittenberg" followed (*ibid.*, p. 80.24-27).

[323] "So auch ist es mit abthuung der gottlesterischen und Christlesterischen bildnüssen oder messen, wo wir herschen. die Gott bekennen, und götzen finden, sollen wir sie weg nemen, und mit inen geparen, als Gott gebotten. Das auch sollen wir unser leben lang thun oder alle tag. Ja so wir sie in unser gemein finden, ein igliche gemein in irer stadt, gleicher weyss ein igliche gemein schuldig ist die ire zu enthalten." *Ibid.*, p. 85.22-28.

[324] "Man sol, sprechen sie, der schwachen halben verziehen, unnd nichts furt faren. Was aber ist das anders gesagt, dann das sie also sprechen, wir sollen das Concilium vor erkennen lassen, was wir thun, unnd welcher massen wir Gott dienen sollen?" *Ibid.*, p. 87.17-21.

[325] In spite of his vigorous assertion of the rights of the individual congregation, Karlstadt apparently did not move in the direction of a separation of church and state. He repeatedly insisted that Christian rulers ought to remove images, and punish spiritual adultery (*ibid.*, pp. 82.9-29, 85.22-28 (see above, n. 323), 86.38-87.2, 96.12-15.

[326] "Aber Petrus wolt sie nit zü Christlicher gemeynschafft nemen, ee sie sich erkanten und ire missethat bereweten. Also solten die rechten Christen auch thün, Und den pfaffen sagen, das es sünd sey, Mess halten, würden sich etliche bekeren, die solten angenummen werden. Die sich aber nit wölten erkennen, die solt man ausserhalb Christlicher gemeynschafft sten las." *Priesterthum*, Div.

[327] "Nun sollen wir denen nit ein freüntlich wort mitteylen, oder grüssen noch sye zu hauss nemen, die Christu lere nit habenn, So ist unns auch verbotten, solich

argument as proof that Karlstadt had drastically narrowed the command to love neighbor. According to Holl, Karlstadt taught that
only members of one's own *Gemeinschaft* were to be numbered among
one's neighbors.[328]

Now it is true that Karlstadt said that heretics are not one's neighbors. However, it is almost certain that this remark should be understood in light of the vigorous contemporary debate about the
necessity of introducing changes slowly for the sake of the weak. All
through *Gemach* Karlstadt denounced this misplaced concern for
neighbor.

> Christ has abolished and cut off all brotherly love which is contrary
> to his commands. . . . "He who does not hate father and mother, wife
> and children cannot be my disciple." . . . It is impossible that one love
> Christ and not live according to his commands. . . . They therefore will
> not throw an apron or curtain over my eyes so that I abandon some-
> thing which God desires or do something which God forbids even if
> they would preach and write a thousand years about offenses and
> brotherly love.[329]

He devoted an entire tract to Romans 9:3 because some people were
interpreting Paul's desire to be anathema for the sake of his brethren
to mean that one should, for the sake of love of neighbor, permit
some things such as images which are contrary to God's will. Karlstadt's reply was that obedience to God stands higher than concern

---

als nechsten, zu lieben. Dessgleychen, wenn ich einen nit sol speysen oder dren-
cken, der wider Christum strebet, so müst der selbig meyn nechster nit sein. Wenn
ich auch das perlin nit darff für die sew werffen, so muss von nöten folgen, das nit
ein yegliches thier, das ein menschlich haut an sich tregt, und gestalt eines menschen hat für meynen nechsten achten sol" *Zweyen höchsten gebotten*, Hertzsch, I,
66.22-30. See also *ibid.*, p. 55.21-37.

[328] Karl Holl, "Luther und die Schwärmer," *Gesammelte Aufsätze*, I, 458-9.
Hertzsch, *Karlstadt und seine Bedeutung*, pp. 54-55 follows Holl.

[329] "Das man saget, ir solt brüderlicher lieb schonen, das laudet gar nichts,
weil es noch unentschlossen ist, ob ire brüderlich lieb nicht ein endchristischer
mantel sey, frilich so arg und schädlich, alss irgend ein fündlin des Babstes, das
aber lass ich itzt ungeurtelt und sag, das Christus alle brüderliche lieb auffgehaben
unnd abgeschnitten hat, wenn sie wider sein gebot steht, oder den aller cleinsten
von Got wendet. . . . Welcher nit vatter und mutter, weib und kinder hasset,
der kan nicht mein iunger sein etc. Nu die weils also steht, das unmüglich ist, das
einer Christum lieb, und nicht noch seinen gebotten lebe, oder stil stehe unnd
vff einen andernn sehe unnd warte ob der ander auch thun wöll, das Got gern hat,
oder nitt Dem nach werden sie mir dz schurtztüchlin oder fürhang nit für mein
augen binden, das ich etwas lass, dz Got haben wil, oder etwas thu, das Gott
verbeüt, ob sie mir tausent iar von ergernüssen und brüderlicher lieb predigten
und schreiben." *Gemach*, Hertzsch, I, 78.15-35.

for neighbor.[330] It was almost certainly because of this current dispute that he insisted in *Zweyen höchsten gebotten* that love of God takes priority over love of neighbor. If love of neighbor would require disobedience to a divine command, then one should not consider such people to be one's neighbors.

At the end of *Zweyen höchsten gebotten* Karlstadt repeated the injunction to avoid association with those who teach wrong doctrines. This time, however, he specifically recommended showing neighborly love to one's enemies. Just as God permits the sun to shine on all alike, so Christians should do good to both good and evil men. Love for neighbor entails loving one's enemies and praying for one's persecutors. Nevertheless, we should not eat with "anti-Christians" who seduce us from God.[331] Thus when Karlstadt said that the heretic is not to be considered one's neighbor, he almost certainly meant this to mean only that Christians must obey the Pauline command to refrain from eating and having fellowship with such people. He hardly intended to prohibit all human feelings for proponents of false doctrine. One should do good to good and evil alike. Holl drew too general a conclusion from this passage. Karlstadt did not think that only those in the *Gemeinschaft* were neighbors of the Christian.

Perhaps these few remarks should be viewed as part of the initial stage of the development of congregational discipline and shunning in the left wing of the Reformation. It is interesting, however, that Karlstadt advocated exclusion from the congregation only on doctrinal grounds. Neither in theory here, nor in practice at Orlamünde did he demand the exclusion of the unregenerate. The true church consists of those being sanctified, but the local visible congregation should exclude people only for doctrinal reasons.

Karlstadt used the doctrine of the priesthood of all believers to remove many barriers between the clergy and laity. Everyone who has a true understanding of God's word also has a divine command to proclaim God's word to others. Through this command God has

---

[330] *Vorstandt des worts Pauli*, Aii-AiiV and elsewhere.

[331] "Das ist auch ein lieb gegen den creaturen, wenn wir vnserm vatter Gott nachfolgen, unnd thun menschen wol, guten und bösen, als er sein sunn lässt scheynen allen in gemeyn. Unnd das ist ein werck der lieb zu dem nechsten, das eyner seinen feynden wol thut, und bitt für seine vervolger, als Christus und Steffanus than haben. Aber in disen stucken sol man nit blind und nerrisch sein das wir nit mit den widerchristischen essen, unnd uns gesellen zu denen, die vns von Gott verleyden, das sye vnns zu eynem strick werden, . . . Darauss vernympt, dz die brüderliche lieb ein fleischliche und teüffelische lieb ist, wenn sye die lieb Gottes verrücket." *Zweyen höchsten gebotten*, Hertzsch, I, 70.23-38.

established as priests each and every man to whom he has revealed himself.[332] I Corinthians 14:26-31 provided sufficient authorization for Karlstadt to insist that the layman has the right to interrupt the preacher and disclose his own understanding of the text if God has revealed something to him.[333] The unanointed can conduct the Eucharistic service even better than the tonsured ones.[334] Karlstadt's selection of Peter the layman as a major spokesman in the Eucharistic dialogue is perhaps the most striking symbol of Karlstadt's vigorous application of Luther's doctrine.

The priesthood of all believers, however, did not mean the complete abolition of the minister's role. Karlstadt believed public preachers were necessary, and he devoted a good deal of thought to the method of their selection. He proposed two basic criteria which ministerial candidates ought to meet. They must have experienced divine, regenerating grace and they must have received an inner call.

The minister who proclaims God's holy word must himself be holy. "He who wants to handle pure and holy things blamelessly should be as pure and holy as the things which he grasps and handles."[335] He denounced Luther for tolerating "poor, miserable, lousy, sinful, unbelieving pastors."[336] Karlstadt realized, of course, that no minister would ever be entirely sanctified on earth. They should preach nonetheless and take comfort in the fact that God will both forgive their sins and also purify them further through the word which they preach.[337] On the other hand, inward renewal must have begun, for the proclamation must proceed from one's heart and be a "sign or fruit of inner righteousness."[338] Before one begins to preach,

---

[332] *Ursachen*, Hertzsch, I, 18.3-18.

[333] "Das aber die Layen den Predigern dürffen einreden, und jren verstand auch offenbaren, disen gewalt gibt Paulus, sagend. Zwen oder drey mögen prophetiziern, dz ist schriften ausslegen, die andern söllen schweygen. So aber ain sitzender oder zühörer ain eröffnung hatt, soll der oberst, das ist der Redner und Prediger still schweygen, und hören was Got dem Layen offenbar gemacht hat." *Fürbit Marie*, Biii.

[334] *Dialogus*, Hertzsch, II, 33.25-30.

[335] "Gottis wort ist rein, als ein rein durchfeget silber das siebenmal ist gefegt. Wer rein und heilige dinge unschultigklich wil handeln, der sol rein und heilig sein, als die ding, so er begreyfft unnd handelt." *Ursachen*, Hertzsch, I, 15.11-15.

[336] "Denn sy wöllen mitt jrem irrtumb fürtfaren, und uns das blüt Christi nicht allein leyblich zü trincken geben, sonder darüber, arme, ellende, lausige sündige und unglaubige pfaffen setzen, als mitler des newen testamentes." *Testament*, BiiiV.

[337] See above, n. 165.

[338] "Denn die verkündigung ist eyn rede des glaubens. welche auss dem hertzen, durch den mund, aussgeht. Darumb ist das eusserlich bekentnüss oder

one must experience the inner drawing of the soul toward Christ. As Paul taught Titus, ministers must have received God's gifts and be free of vices.[339] In short, the ministerial candidate must have undergone a spiritual rebirth.

If that were all Karlstadt had said, his notion of the requirements of a minister would be related directly and solely to his doctrine of regeneration. There was a second stipulation, however, and it provided a role for the Spirit. The minister must also have a clear inner call (*innerliche beruffung*). Karlstadt adduced a number of New Testament texts to support his thesis that a merely human call was quite inadequate. Paul constantly reminded his readers that God and not man had called him. If ministers rely on a human call, God will say as he did to the false prophets that they run without being sent.[340] In some places the Holy Spirit commanded Paul to preach while in others he forbade him. The harvest is God's and he alone calls and equips the workers. When God's word is proclaimed, the wicked should be crushed and the sick healed. Only God, however, can effect such results. Accordingly man should enter God's vineyard only when the Holy Spirit inwardly and clearly compels him to do so.[341]

Karlstadt nowhere discussed the precise nature of the inner call of the minister, but his remark apropos the way the congregation inwardly learns of the prior call of the future minister probably applies to the minister's own inward call:

---

predig des todts Christi, eyn zeychen oder frucht der innerlichen gerechtigkeyt." *Dialogus*, Hertzsch, II, 28.4-8. Cf. also *Missbrauch*, Aiv.

[339] Apropos true shepherds of the flock, Karlstadt commented: "Sie müssen ye den vetterlichen tzuck, der an Christum, den warhafftigen hyrten der selen tzeucht, befinden, und das werck des geistes Christi verstehnn." *Ursachen*, Hertzsch, I, 11.14-16. See also *ibid.*, p. 13.17-26.

[340] "Das yr unnd andere meyne brüder, mich beruffen und auss schicken, ist ein menschliche und ewsserliche sendung, die yhm grund vor Got nichts werdt sein magk, ia auch wider Got. Und in der warheit, ist solche menschliche beruffung, ein ferlich und betriglich pfandt, und die nachvolgung uff menschen beruffung, ist vormessen und frevelich, so offt Gotis innerliche beruffung nit zu schewbet, und den beruffenen nit vorsichert, inwendig, als ein uffgedruckter sigill und gewiss pfandt." *Ursachen*, Hertzsch, I, 6.2-10. See all of pp. 6-7.

[341] *Ibid.*, pp. 7.32-8.6, 8.26-9.23. Also: "Die innerliche beruffung ist köstlich, sicher, und nötlich, denn sie gibet ein warhafftig getzeugknis, das der beruffen, des herrn und Gottis, ein knecht ist." *Ibid.*, p. 9.36-37. Thus Peter the layman explained that he had not disseminated his Eucharistic exegesis earlier because the Spirit had not impelled him sufficiently. "Der geyst treyb mich nit schwind genug, hett er mich genugsam getrieben, und bezwungen, ich hett jnen vil weniger gehelen, oder verborgen, denn wenn ich ein fressigs fewer, in meinen gebein ghabt." *Dialogus*, Hertzsch, II, 19.12-15.

> One should notice that it is not written, "The Spirit spoke in visions, sleep or dreams;" rather, it says without addition: "The Spirit spoke." Therefore, it is likely that God's Spirit spoke inwardly to the apostles and taught them how they should separate Barnabas and Paul.[342]

In addition to the two basic stipulations just discussed, the public minister must be selected by a congregation. The congregation selects on the basis of the two requirements just noted. God informs them outwardly and inwardly of his previous choice. They must trace God's grace and ascertain God's inward call.[343] In order to provide time for the detection of God's regenerating grace, the congregation should proceed slowly, pray earnestly and wait until the man's fruit indicates that God has bestowed his gifts.[344] The congregation should also pray that the Spirit inform them inwardly—but not through dreams and visions—of the person whom he has already called. When the congregation has prayerfully ascertained the bestowal of God's grace and the inner call, then they should lay hands upon the person and thereby announce that the man has been prepared and called by God to be a shepherd of God's sheep.[345]

It is clear from this survey of Karlstadt's observations about the church that his ecclesiology was shaped to a very great extent by his doctrine of the regeneration and sanctification of the believer.[346] It is only by inner circumcision and rebirth that men enter the body of Christ. Because God's grace produces visible results, true Christians are known by the fruit which regeneration makes possible. It is certainly true that the Spirit is important in Karlstadt's ecclesiology, for the Holy Spirit provides a direct inward call to the minister and a

---

[342] *Ursachen*, Hertzsch, I, 12.37-13.2 (see above, n. 254).

[343] "Die macht Titi ist bestrickt, durch das gebot Pauli, du solt nymant bald ufflegen. Drumb ist das die meynung Pauli. Das die Christliche gemeyn oder eintzele personen, sie seindt hoch oder nider, sich zuvor umbsehen sollen, ehe sie ire hende uff legen. Was ist aber das anders gesagt, dann das. Ir solt, vor allem die lewthe erkennen, und euch der innerlichen beruffung und Gottis heymlichen willen erkünden und Gottis gnad in dem spüren, dem ir ewre hende wolt aufflegen." *Ibid.*, p. 11.32-40.

[344] "Demnoch solt jr niemandt bald hende ufflegenn, er sey wer er woll, gelart oder ungelart, hoch oder nieder, iunck oder alt. Jr solt zu vor sehen, ab er Gotis gaben hat, oder ein menschliche weissheyt hab. Platzet nit bald tzu, der mensch kan nicht schnell in grundt sehen, lasset die wercke unnd früchten wol aussschossen." *Ibid.*, p. 13.27-32.

[345] *Ibid.*, p. 12.8-24. See also, n. 342 above.

[346] Thus when Kriechbaum (*Grundzüge*, pp. 98ff) labels Karlstadt's doctrine of the church during this period "spiritualist," she overlooks the fact that the doctrine of regeneration was probably more decisive for his ecclesiology than his doctrine of the Holy Spirit.

similar inward awareness of the same to the congregation. Nevertheless, the regeneration of the candidate and the congregation's observation of his actual righteousness are equally important. Karlstadt
joined a spiritualist element to an essentially regenerationist ecclesiology.

(k) *Baptism and the Lord's Supper as external signs of regeneration*

Rejecting the term sacrament partly because the usage was not
biblical, but even more because the word seemed indelibly stamped
with the doctrine of the sacramental mediation of grace, Karlstadt
spoke instead of external signs.[347] As mere signs they are not means
of grace. Rather, they point to that inner righteousness and union with
God effected by regeneration.

> Circumcision and baptism and other external signs make one neither
> good nor evil; nor do they unite one to God, whereas the eternal will of
> God received with the heart unites and glues one to God. Nevertheless,
> believers must receive such external signs in the proper manner and
> use them as signs of inner righteousness and union [with God].[348]

The spiritual man, of course, is not bound by the external signs, for
the Spirit can create the new life "without material things." [349] The
sacraments are external signs of the grace already received rather than
an external medium for its communication.

Thanks to the zeal of the Basle authorities who confiscated Karlstadt's tract on baptism, one must piece together his baptismal
thought from a few scattered references. "To be baptized into Christ"
means to experience the death of the old life and the emergence of a
new life.[350] Inner regeneration is the prerequisite for external baptism:
"He who wants to receive baptism properly and be baptized in the
name of Jesus must repent, forsake the old life and take up a new
life." [351] The external act is a public confession of personal faith and
inner righteousness, rather than a means of grace:

---

[347] He rejected the term "sacrament" not for himself but for the sake of the
weak who were misled. *Dialogus*, Hertzsch, II, 11.1-25.

[348] "Wie wol dye beschneydungh unnd tauff, unnd andere eusserlyche tzey-
chenn, weder frum, weder böss machenn. vereinen auch Gott nycht, als der
ewygh Gottis wyll, myt hertzen angenommen, denn menschenn Got vereynt
unnd anleymbt dannest müstenn dye gleubyghe solyche eusserlich dyng yn irer
weyss annemen, unnd als tzeychen der ynnerlichen gerechtikeit und eynikeit
gebrauchen." *Von manigfeltigkeit*, Gii-GiiV.

[349] *Ibid.*, GiiV (see below, n. 352). Karlstadt was talking about the sacraments;
hence this statement should not be applied to the question of the external word.

[350] *Anzeig*, Hertzsch, II, 90.1-28.

[351] "Wölcher die tauff recht nemen, und in dem namen Christi getaufft will

He who comes to be baptized in that name receives external baptism
because he wants to signify externally to everyone that he confesses the
triune God and holds him as his Creator . . . who can and will give
him all that is necessary and good for him. . . . Where this righteousness is not in one's spirit, the sign is false. . . . Therefore old people
cannot comfort themselves with their baptism if they do not feel the
decline of their [old] life.[352]

If the mortification of the old life and the birth of the new life have
not occurred in one, then it is quite pointless to trust in what is a
mere sign of inner righteousness.

Although just alluded to briefly, the implications Karlstadt drew
from his understanding of baptism were important. In rejecting
Luther's charge that he ignored the chief articles of the faith, he
observed that he who refuses baptism to non-believers and delays it
until the time when they have become believers promotes rather than
extinguishes the chief article of the faith.[353] Later, in the same work, he
condemned Luther for treating baptism so frivolously as to baptize
children who know nothing of their sinful inclinations, much less the
death of these through Christ.[354] Since regeneration is the prerequisite

---

werden, der müss püss thün, das alt leben verlassen, und ein newes an sich nemen
Act.2. Ro.6. Und es ist nit müglich, das einer gemeinschafft hab an der tauff, und
teyl hab mit dem teuffel zügleych, wiewol das wasserbad ein eusserlich ding ist,
und nichts mer dann wasser ist." *Erklerung*, CivV. It is divine grace, of course,
that produces this new life; it is not a product of man's will. The Spirit alone
effects inner regeneration (*Anzeig*, Hertzsch, II, 90.25-31).

[352] "Welcher sich in dem namen lesst teuffen, der nymbt die eusserlich tauff
derhalben, das ehr eusserlich vor yder menyglich wil antzeygen, das er den
dryfeltigen Got bekent, und vor seinen schepper hymels und ertrichs helt der ym
alles das geben kann und wil, das ym von nöten und gut ist. und alles das er ym
verheischt. Wü disse gerechtikeit nit ym geist ist, do ist das tzeichen falsch, und
von Got ungeacht. drumb können sich die alten ires tauffs nit getrösten, wan
sy den niderganck ires lebens nit fuelen. Derhalben ist der geistlich mensch an
eusserliche ding nit gepundten, oder von nöten, das ynnerlich eynikeit mit dem
eusserste tzeichen müst bewert und bezeucht werden, oder das der geist on
leiplich dinge sein leben und werck nit könt volbrengen." *Von manigfeltigkeit*,
GiiV. By "niderganck ires lebens," Karlstadt means the gradual death of the
egocentric self.

[353] "Wölcher die Tauff biss auff die zeytt wegert, und denen wegert so nit
glauben, biss sy glaubige seynd worden, der treybt das hauptstuck des glaubens
auf, und dempffet es nit." *Anzeig*, Hertzsch, II, 70.14-17.

[354] "Ich meyn er wiss auch nit was getaufft sey im namen Jesus. Das auch gibt
im villeycht ursach, die tauff Christi so leychtfertigklich zu handeln kinder zu
Tauffen die ire lüste nit versteen, ich geschweyg dz sy der lüsten todt, durch
Christum versteen." *Ibid.*, p. 91.2-6. These two statements probably reflect
Karlstadt's practice at Orlamünde. For Karlstadt's possible influence on the
Anabaptists, see Hillerbrand, "Origins of Sixteenth Century Anabaptism," *ARG*,

for baptism, infant baptism is not permissible. One dare baptize only those believing adults who have experienced an inner change. The doctrine of regeneration clearly shaped Karlstadt's view of baptism.

In a discussion of Karlstadt's Eucharistic doctrine, one is embarrassed by the abundance rather than the scarcity of the material. The exegetical argumentation which Karlstadt adduced to support his views is voluminous. Relative brevity as well as reasonable comprehensiveness, however, can be attained if one asks why Karlstadt adopted his new ideas rather than how he supported them. Why did Karlstadt reject first the real presence and second the sacramental mediation of grace? A third section on the proper preparation for reception of the bread and wine will show how his emphasis on inner renewal also shaped his Eucharistic theology.

An alleged tendency to belittle the historical cross, John 6, and rationalistic considerations were three of the basic factors in Karlstadt's abandonment of the real presence.[355] Karlstadt was convinced that the doctrine of the real presence had resulted in a theologically unacceptable preoccupation with the external sacrament. The Pope teaches people how to eat the host respectfully and carefully clean their teeth, but he neglects the passion of Christ. The Pope "offers us his form of the bread and elevates that so highly that we . . . forget the body and death of the Lord and consequently do not esteem at all what the Lord suffered on the cross although we should consider that the most." [356] He believed that any doctrine which affirmed the real presence would result in neglect of the cross.

---

LIII (1962), 163. One can speculate on the possibility that the Zwickau Prophets may have been the first to raise the problem of infant baptism in Karlstadt's mind (see above, chapter V, n. 66), but there is no evidence to support such speculation.

[355] For his basic exegetical arguments—e.g., that Christ pointed to himself rather than the bread, that *TOUTO* is neuter and therefore cannot refer to *ARTOS* and that since "This is my body" begins with a capital letter it is not connected with the earlier words "He took bread"—see *Ob man . . . erweysen müge*, CiiiV, F and *Dialogus*, Hertzsch, II, 14-17. One of Karlstadt's less serious, rather humorous exegetical comments is worth quoting: "Gems. Christus sprach ye, dz ist mein leyb. Pet. Christus stund gegenwertig, und saget, das ist der leib mein etc. Drumb, wenn ein pfaff spricht. Das ist mein leyb, nemet esset das brodt, und wir essen, so fressen wir einen lausichten pfaffen." *Dialogus*, Hertzsch, II, 40.23-27.

[356] "Paulus thut seinen höchsten fleiss, das er unss des todts des hern, verstendig, und indechtig mache, das stürtzet der Bapst umb, und leget unss seyne gestalt des brodts für, und hebt sie so hoch, das wir vor grosser angst, sorg und erkäntnüss seiner gestaldt, des hern leibs und todts vergessen, unnd alss dann nichts achten, was der her am kreütz erlidten hat, wenn wir allermeyste achtung druff haben solten." *Dialogus*, Hertzsch, II, 23.4-11. See also *ibid.*, p. 22.12-26, *Ob man . . . erweysen müge*, FV; *Auszlegung* (1524), dii, diiiiV; *Testament*, CV, DV.

Karlstadt was also convinced that John 6 excluded the doctrine of the real presence. He concluded from John 6:63 that the believer eats Christ's flesh and blood spiritually when he remembers the passion and believes in Christ.[357] "Those who believe have no need to dispatch teeth or stomach to eat the Lord's flesh, for their faith is useful and sufficient; the flesh is not useful."[358] Karlstadt's constant citation or allusion to John 6:63 suggests not only that it was a useful weapon, but also that it played a more basic role in his decision to reject the real presence.[359]

Rationalistic doubts were also important. Already in 1521 he had confessed that his old Adam found it difficult to believe in Christ's physical presence in the sacrament.[360] Now he argued that the Eucharistic bread is far too small for Christ to be present according to his humanity.[361] Furthermore, in the absence of scriptural proof of Christ's physical ubiquity, it is just as hard to believe that Christ's body is at many places at once as that St. Anna had five heads.[362] Christ is in heaven, not in the sacrament.

Karlstadt rejected sacramental mediation of grace as vigorously as the real presence. In the first place sacramental mediation of forgiveness detracts from the cross. "Whatever I would ascribe to the bread,

---

[357] Jn. 6:63: "It is the Spirit that quickeneth; the flesh profiteth nothing: the words that I speak unto you, they are spirit and they are life."

[358] "Dahin aber reymten sich Augustini wort, Glaub, so hast du gessen, dz Christus spricht, Mein fleisch ist nicht nütz. . . . die glauben, denen ist von unnöten das sie zene oder bauch schicken des hern fleisch zü essen, denn ir glaube ist nütz und genüg, das fleisch ist nit nütz." *Ob man . . . erweysen müge*, FiiiV-Fiiii.

[359] See in addition *Dialogus*, Hertzsch, II, 24.5, 14-21; *Auszlegung* (1524), civ-d; *Erklerung*, Aiii-AivV, Biv, DiiiV.

[360] " . . . alsso ists der natur auch unglaublich, das ein mensch Gott sein soll, und das naturlich brot der leyb Christi soll sein. Aber dem glauben seind sie beyde leicht und glaublich. Gleich wie ich weiss, das das brot weiss und rundt ist, drumb das ichs seh, sso weiss ich auch, das brot der leyb Christi ist. drumb das ichs im Evangelio seh geschrieben. Ich hab auch keynen tzweyfel, an dem wort Christi, und glaub yhm, ob mirs. und meinem adam tzusawer und wichtig ist." *Anbettung*, AivV.

[361] *Dialogus*, Hertzsch, II, 12.2-7, 40.33-41.5.

[362] "Christus würdt den hymel inn halten biss an den tag, inn welchem alle ding zum ende sollen gebracht werden. . . . Gems. Ich halt das sey dir schwer zu glauben, das Christus zu gleych an vil stedten seyn sol. Pet. Neyn. Ich glaub es gleich so liderlich, das ir jnen an vil enden brengen unnd setzen kündt inn eyner zeyt, als ich glaub, das S. Anna fünff haubt, unnd ein unschuldig kindlin eynen bart gehabt hab, zwölff elen lang." *Ibid.*, pp. 42.40-43.8. See also pp. 32.31-34, 36.40-37.8. For a sharp attack on what Karlstadt considered the foolish fideism of his opponents, see *ibid.*, p. 38.19-36.

I would take from the passion of Christ." [363] Asserting that the sacrament is a pledge of the forgiveness of sins focuses the communicant's attention just as misguidedly as the doctrine of the real presence.

> We are really anti-Christians, deniers or despisers of Christ's passion to the extent that we ascribe to our sacrament what belongs to Christ on the cross. . . . Paul says: "As often as you eat of the Lord's bread and drink of his cup, you shall proclaim the Lord's death." On the contrary, however, they teach: . . . "You shall believe that the sacrament is a sure pledge of forgiveness." [364]

Sacramental mediation not only detracts from the cross; it is also unnecessary. Paul's call for self-examination prior to the taking of communion excludes the common view that the cup is an assurance (*versicherung*) of one's forgiveness. Before partaking, one must examine oneself to ensure that one has a passionate remembrance of Christ's passion. "If one has that, then he is also certain of his redemption and has peace with God through Christ, not through the sacrament."[365] If one has loving knowledge of Christ, one already possesses certainty of forgiveness.

Third, and perhaps most important, Karlstadt did not believe that anything physical could produce assurance in the soul.

> The sacrament . . . is much too coarse to touch the ground of the soul. . . . The sacrament cannot assure our spirit and help the weakness

---

[363] "Wenn ichs gleych gestünd, das Christus leib mit dem brodt vereynt were, dannoch were es falsch und betrüglich geredt, wenn ich dem brodt eines herlinss breydt so vil macht und krafft gäbe, das es uns sünd vergeben und befriden mögt. Was ich dem brodt gäbe, dass näme ich ye dem leyden Christi." *Ibid.*, p. 30.20-25. See also *ibid.*, p. 30.29-31.6.

[364] "Wir sein warlich widerchristen, versprecher oder verachter des leidens Christi, so vil unser dem sacrament das zümessen, das Christo am Creütz angehört. . . . Paulus sagt. So offt jr von des herren prot esset, und von seinen Kelch trincket, solt jr des herren todt verkhündigen. Dar wider aber leren sy also. Jr solt glawben, dass Christus im sacrament ist. Jr solt glawben, dass euch das sacrament die sünd vergibt. Jr solt glawben, dass das sacrament ayn gewiss pfant ist, vergebung der sünden." *Missbrauch*, BiiV. See also *Testament*, Eii-EiiV.

[365] "Auss dyser red Pauli, nemlich, ayn yegklicher soll sich selbs prüfen, u volgt ain umbstürtze ayner andern rede, als mann gemaynigklich sagt. Das prot und der kelch Christi seind versicherung, unnd gewisse urkhunde, durch welche der mensch bey sich sicher unnd gewiss werden kann, das im Christus todt sein erlösung gepracht hat. Denn wo der mensch seiner erlösung das ist vergebung der sünde, durch das Abentmal sicher werden köndt oder solt, were es von unnötten, dass sich ain yegklicher, vor, ehe er des herren prot und kelch neme, prüfet Darumb soll ain yeglicher vorhyn ehe ers nympt, sich prüfen, ob er das gedechtnüss Christi hab oder not. Hat ers, so ist er auch sicher seiner erlosung, und hat aynen frid zü Got durch Christon, nit durchs sacrament." *Missbrauch*, C-CV.

of our spirit. . . . The assurance belongs to God's Spirit, not to any
creature. . . . No one other than the Spirit can give . . . the assurance of
forgiven sins.[366]

In the case of both the external word and the external sacrament,
Karlstadt insisted that the external medium is powerless apart from the
inner activity of the Spirit. In the case of the sacrament, however, he
would not even admit that it was a necessary although insufficient
means of grace. No longer would he grant as he did in 1521 that the
external sacrament strengthens faith. The notion of sacramental
communication of grace detracts from the cross, is unnecessary and
ignores the role of the Holy Spirit.

Perhaps what Karlstadt wanted to affirm provides more insight into
his theological outlook than what he denied. Whereas in 1521 Karlstadt had rejected all preparation, especially oral confession, for
taking communion, he now insisted on a prior preparatory self-
examination.[367] If one wants to partake of the Lord's table, one must
first examine oneself to determine whether one has a passionate
remembrance of Christ's death on the cross.[368]

Passionate remembrance includes both an intellectual understanding of the cross and inner regeneration. "No one should drink the
Lord's cup except he who understands why Christ shed his Blood." [369]
Mere intellectual information, of course, is quite inadequate. One's
understanding of Christ's death must be a "passionate knowledge
rich in love." [370] Mortification and inner regeneration are always a
part of such knowledge. "Knowledge and remembrance of the
blood of Christ . . . naturally bring along a surrender of our life."[371]

> Those who have genuine knowledge of Christ have righteousness in
> their ground. As Paul says, "Faith is the righteousness of the heart."

---

[366] *Missbrauch*, CiiV-Ciii (see above, n. 160).

[367] See above, chapter IV, "Confession."

[368] "Wer drincken wil, der brüfe unnd erfare sich selbs in seinem grund, ob er
ein prünstig gedechtnüs des blüts Christi hab." *Ob man . . . erweysen müge*, Aiii.

[369] " . . . niemanss des herren kelch drincken sol, denn nur der, der versteht
warumb Christus sein blut vergossen hat." *Dialogus*, Hertzsch, II, 44.33-34. So too
*Missbrauch*, Aiv.

[370] "Das gedechtnuss aber ist ain prünstige und liepreiche kunst oder erkantnuss des leybs und blüts Christi." *Ibid.*

[371] "Das erkentnüs und gedechtnüs des blüts Christi, also vergossen, brengt
natürlich mit sich ein übergebung unserss lebens, ein abwaschen der sünden. . . .
Nü welcher des herrn blüt also versteht und gedenckt . . . wirt sich nit alleyn der
volheit und trunckenheit enthalten, sonder allerley sünde flihen." *Ob man . . .
erweysen müge*, AiiiV.

> Yes, that is true if it is not a frozen or dead knowledge, but rather a passionate, burning, industrious and firm knowledge of Christ which transforms the knower into the known life and death of Christ and can do or forsake for Christ's sake all that Christ desires.[372]

"Out of the knowledge of Christ grows that remembrance of Christ which is not a coarse, cold and lazy remembrance, but rather a fresh, passionate, powerful remembrance which . . . makes one Christ-like and ashamed of all that is opposed to Christ." [373]

The inner renewal which results from knowledge of Christ is a necessary precondition for worthy reception of the sacrament. "If we are to handle it properly, we must be . . . completely devoted to Christ externally and internally . . . and forsake all that is contrary to Christ." [374] Karlstadt, of course, was demanding genuine mortification and renewal, not perfection. In another passage where he noted that self-mortification must continue throughout this life, he added: "But now, before we mortify our powers sufficiently, as often as we want to eat the Lord's bread and drink of his cup, so often we must confess the Lord's death with our heart and mind, i.e. we must also experience our death of Christ in ourselves and feel Christ's righteousness, not ours." [375] Since our inner righteousness is very imperfect, we must look to Christ's perfect righteousness. On the other hand, without the beginning of inner renewal, one dare not partake of the sacrament.[376]

Karlstadt's great concern to avoid externalization of religion can be seen in his rejection of the Catholic method of preparation for the Eucharist.

---

[372] "Welche das rechte erkantnuss Christi haben, die haben die gerechtigkayt in jrem grundt, als Paulus spricht. Der glawb ist die gerechtigkeyt des hertzens. Ja das ist war, wenns nit ain gefroren oder todte erkantnuss ist, sonder eyn inprünstige hytzige geschefftige unnd krefftige kunst Christi, die den erkenner in das erkannt leben, und todt Christi verwandelt, und umb Christus willen möcht alles thün oder lassen, das Christus haben will." *Missbrauch*, AivV.

[373] *Ibid.*, BV (see above, n. 167).

[374] "Also haben wir durchs brodt, ein gemeinschafft mit dem leyb, unnd durch den kelch eyn geselschafft mit dem blüt Christi, handeln wir recht mit, so müssen wir uns leybformig unnd blütformig fynden, unnd Christo gentzlich anhengig sein, eüsserlich unnd innerlich, im geyst, und in unserm leyb und blüt, und alles verlassen das wider Christum ist." *Ob man . . . erweysen müge*, Cii.

[375] "Aber itzt ehe wir unsern krefften genugsam absterben, so offt wir des hern brodt essen, und von seynem kelch drincken wöllen, so offt müssen wir des hern todt bekennen mit hertzen unnd muth, das ist, wir müssen auch unsern todt Christi in unss enpfinden, und die gerechtigkeyt Christi, nicht unsere fülen." *Dialogus*, Hertzsch, II, 49.17-22.

[376] An evil speaker or drunken person partakes only with injury to himself (*Ob man . . . erweysen müge*, AiiiV).

Paul leads each person to himself and not to another man as the papists have done. They direct the partakers of Christ's Supper to poor blind leaders who call themselves father confessors. But Paul was more intelligent in the matter and led each one to himself into his inwardness. For no one knows what is in a man's spirit except the spirit of each man. When you want to take the Lord's Supper, you should go into your inwardness and not know superficially whether you have a sincere and worthy remembrance of Christ.[377]

Karlstadt's renewed demand for a slightly different form of preparation for the sacrament certainly resulted from his attempt to avoid superficial, dead faith by stressing inner renewal.

Karlstadt's rejection of the real presence and the sacramental mediation of grace did not lead him to a total abandonment of the external sign. The bread and wine are a commemoration of Christ's death and, as in the case of baptism, a public sign of inner renewal. Christ himself established the external cup to be used as a remembrance of him.[378] "Those who remember the Lord and want to point out or exercise their remembrance by the cup may drink of it."[379] As the previous statements suggest, the external act is a sign to the congregation: "He who has a passionate remembrance of the surrendered body of Jesus Christ and wants to demonstrate that externally in the congregation . . . is worthy to receive the Lord's bread."[380]

---

[377] "Darumb füret Paul. eynen yegklichen zü sich, und nicht zü andern menschen, als die Papisten than haben, welche die Tischgenossen des Abentmals Christi, zü armen blinden layttern, die sich Beychtvätter haissen weiseten. Denn Paulus ist der sachen klüger gewest, und hatt yeglichen zü sich, und in seine innwendigkait gelayttet. Auss der ursach dass keyn mensch erkennt, was ins menschen gayst ist, denn ain yeglicher gayst aynes yegklichen menschen." *Missbrauch*, C (see n. 139 above for the remainder). The last two sentences make it clear why Luther would feel that Karlstadt had made the sacrament a good work by stressing man's preparation. See Jaroslav Pelikan, *Spirit Versus Structure* (New York, 1968), p. 123 and J. Pelikan, "Theology of the Means of Grace," *Accents in Luther's Theology*, ed. H. O. Kadai (St. Louis, 1967), pp. 134-6. Karlstadt would have replied that "worthy remembrance" is possible only when divine grace has regenerated man and infused "knowledge rich in love." Thus the necessary preparation is possible only *sola gratia*. On the other hand, it is clear that Karlstadt's call for self-examination to make sure one has divinely given preparation inevitably runs the danger of drawing attention to man's activity rather than God's.

[378] *Ob man . . . erweysen müge*, DiiiV.

[379] "Kürtzlich der kelch ist gestellet zü einen gedechtnüs, also, das die iene draus drincken mögen, die des hern gedencken, unnd ir gedechtnüs in den kelch anzeigen oder uben wölle." *Ibid.*, DivV.

[380] "Welcher ein inbrünstig gedechtnüss hat, des übergeben leybs Jesu Christi, und begert das eüsserlich in der gemeyn zu beweisen, in dem, dz er des hern brodt essen wil, der ist wirdig des hern brodt zü entpfahen." *Dialogus*, Hertzsch, II, 25.25-28.

Since passionate remembrance inevitably involves the beginning of inner righteousness, the external act is a public sign of inner renewal. Thus inward regeneration is both the preparation for and the thing signified by participation in the Lord's Supper.

## 4. Conclusion

At the beginning of this chapter, several basic problems in the interpretation of Karlstadt's Orlamünde theology were noted. Did Karlstadt relapse into medieval works-righteousness? Was he a spiritualist or legalist, or both? Did he ignore the objective work of Christ? To what extent did he adopt German mysticism? Some answers to these questions are now available.

It is quite clear that Karlstadt did not teach works-righteousness. He certainly wanted his readers to be active in self-mortification, but he frequently reminded them that such *Gelassenheit* was a divine gift. Only as God circumcised the heart could they hope to be active in self-denial. The new life of righteousness, likewise, is a divine gift. God infuses "love rich in faith" into the heart so that man can love God and neighbor. Only when he is miraculously born anew can he live a genuinely righteous life.

What of Karlstadt's alleged spiritualism? He did not move in a spiritualist direction by denying any role to the external word in the communication of grace. Nowhere did he teach that the Spirit would or could bestow regeneration where knowledge of the scriptural word was lacking. In fact, numerous incidental comments indicated that he continued to assume that the external word is a necessary part of the communication of grace. Without the concomitant activity of the Spirit in the soul, of course, it is quite powerless. Although insufficient by itself, the external word is nonetheless a necessary element in the communication of grace. On this issue, then, the Orlamünde theology represents a return to the Augustinian position of 1517 and 1518. Nor was his view of the source of authoritative revelation spiritualist. Dreams and visions do not supply new revelation. Scripture alone is the sole source of theological information. Even Karlstadt's view of the relationship between word and Spirit in the exegetical task was not quite as radical as has frequently been suggested. Both by example and precept, he continued to recommend the exegesis of one scripture by means of another. The Spirit's inner activity is necessary if man is to recognize the external word as a message from God. Further, inner regeneration effected by the Spirit is necessary if man is to adopt an obedient relationship to the external word. Neither activity, however, affects the content of scripture. Nor did Karlstadt's exegetical principle of the spirit of the external scriptural letter introduce a spiritualist element. Contrary to Gerdes' view that the Spirit directly communicates the spiritual understanding of the external letter, it was discovered that Karlstadt obtained the inner sense of one passage from other scriptures.

Karlstadt, however, did believe that the Spirit communicates directly with man. The Spirit provides an inner call for the future minister and he also inwardly informs the congregation of this call. The Spirit also directly communicates the proper exegetical understanding of difficult passages. As long, however, as Karlstadt insisted, as he did in *Sich Gelassen*, that this directly given understanding must be verified in other scripture, the spiritualist tendency was still relatively minimal. In *Dialogus*, however, Peter seemed to reject the need for any external witness in the case of his Eucharistic exegesis. Only the inner witness of the Spirit is necessary. Since Karlstadt continued to declare his willingness to abandon his views if confronted with clear scripture, it is quite clear that he intended scripture to be his theological norm. Nonetheless, if he intended Peter's statement as a general exegetical principle, he certainly opened the door to a substantive spiritualism. Apropos some aspects of exegesis, then, Karlstadt's Orlamünde theology granted an increased role to the Spirit. In the case of the mediation of grace via the external word and the source of religious authority, however, the spiritualist label is not really applicable.

Karlstadt was a legalist in the sense that he found congenial the notion of the normative role of Old and New Testament law in the life of the Christian. Although one can defend the Sabbath command and the prohibition of images on the basis of one's obligation to love the neighbor, both remain normative commands for the Christian. Karlstadt, however, was not entirely inflexible. His conception of a hierarchy of commands permitted a good deal of freedom. Perhaps Karlstadt stood too close to Luther to advocate an entirely wooden Puritan legalism.

The thesis that Karlstadt reduced the role of Christ either to that of example or to that of example and sanctifier was found to be mistaken. He referred to Christ's atonement, which makes forgiveness possible, not just in *Priesterthum* and the Eucharistic works but also in many of his other writings. But since he believed that the church in 1523 and

1524 was in more danger of ignoring inner renewal and good works than forgiveness of sins, he devoted more space to the consideration of mortification and the new regenerate life than to the doctrine of the atonement.

What of Karlstadt's alleged conversion to mysticism? That the mystics greatly influenced his description of sin is unquestionable. His statements about sin as not willing as God wills, as egocentric preoccupation with the self and as love of creatures could all be duplicated in Tauler and *Theologia Deutsch*. Likewise the notion of *Gelassenheit* and the constant emphasis on the importance of the renunciation of self and creatures as the preparation for grace are mystical contributions to his theology. In addition, the mystics supplied some terminology such as the "ground of the soul" and "sinking into God" which Karlstadt was able to adapt to his own purposes.

The contrast with the mystics, however, is even more important than the similarities. Karlstadt did not equate creatureliness *per se* with sin. Consequently his demand for the abandonment of creatures was a call for the cessation of misguided love for creatures, not for the renunciation of creatures because they are created. His usage of the mystical phrase "ground of the soul" typifies the way he transformed the concepts he borrowed. Certainly there is nothing uncreated in the soul. More importantly, he did not systematically distinguish the ground of the soul from the powers of the soul as did Tauler. In no case did he use this distinction. In fact it is precisely genuine love and knowledge which are in the ground of the soul. His constant interchanging of "heart" and "ground of the soul" and his frequent use of the latter term when he wanted to contrast genuine love and faith with superficial, dead faith suggests that rather than functioning as a precise technical term, "ground of the soul" was simply a convenient tool for underlining his demand for sincere faith and total commitment.

Similarly, Karlstadt used mystical language about sinking and melting into God without adopting the basic concept of the mystic union. Karlstadt never talked of any historical union with God different from that ethical harmony of wills effected by regenerating grace. Karlstadt applied the language of sinking and melting into God to the gradually emerging conformity of man's will to the divine will. Purification is never completed in this life, but to the extent that the old "I" is transformed into a Christ-like self, man possesses union with God. This union is clearly ethical rather than essential. Karlstadt never spoke, as did Tauler, of a union in which the soul abandons the rational and volitional faculties and loses all awareness of likeness and unlikeness to God. Union involves not a return to original uncreated-ness in God, but rather the moral perfection of the creature.

It is useful to think of Karlstadt's adaptation of mystical terminology in terms of what Oberman has called a late medieval democratization of mysticism.[381] "The traditional mystical terminology is adopted for the depiction of the Christian life of ordinary pious folk." [382] He suggests that Luther read "the mystics" not for their mysticism, but rather for their deep piety. Karlstadt's use of the ideas of "ground of the soul" and "sinking into the divine will" suggests that the same is true for him. Certainly Karlstadt applied the mystical terminology to every Christian and completely omitted the *unio mystica* experienced only by the few aristocrats of the spirit.

It may even be legitimate to speak of a protestantizing of mysticism. Karlstadt maintained his earlier Reformation emphasis on the omni-presence of sin in the life of the *viator*. Since even good works contain sin, perfect *Gelassenheit* is never attained. As a consequence, Karlstadt maintained the essentially Lutheran view that man's acceptance before God depends on forgiveness offered in Christ. For the mystics, on the other hand, moral perfection is the prerequisite for the *unio mystica* and, therefore, a possibility in this life. For Tauler an "inward, perfect and pure disposition to God" is the necessary and possible precondi-tion for the ultimate union.[383] During the early years of cooperation with Luther, Karlstadt had learned too much about the ever present nature of egocentrism to believe that the *viator* could attain to a perfect disposition to God. Thus Karlstadt used mystical language without abandoning this basic insight of the Reformation.

This chapter has shown that the doctrine which dominated Karl-stadt's theology in this period was that of regeneration. *Gelassenheit* was so important because it is the negative side of that inner renewal or transformation which alone makes good works possible.[384] Karlstadt

---

[381] *Harvest*, pp. 341ff and "Simul gemitus und raptus," pp. 38-9, 45, 53-4.

[382] *Ibid.*, p. 38. In *Harvest*, pp. 349-51 he points out that Gabriel Biel used the language of the birth of Christ in the soul, which Eckhart had used to connote the *unio mystica* (see Clark, *Meister Eckhart*, pp. 83-4), to describe the effect of *gratia gratum faciens* which every Christian receives. "This Christ-birth in the soul is not an exalted stage of perfection for a small privileged group, but necessary for the salvation of every Christian" (*Harvest*, p. 349).

[383] Ozment, *Homo Spiritualis*, p. 37.

[384] "Immo interioris regeneratio est exterioris mortificatio." Thesis four of the

modified his definition of faith and developed the notion of "faith rich in love" in order to emphasize the importance of actually possessing inner righteousness. The most important work of Christ is his sanctification of the believer. The new man supernaturally reborn in Christ is the presupposition of Christian ethics. Christian freedom should be understood primarily in terms of the regenerate man's new ability to obey God. The body of Christ consists of those persons who are being sanctified by the word proclaimed by the regenerate minister. Regeneration is the precondition both for baptism and the Lord's Supper, for these external acts are signs of inner righteousness rather than means of grace. Regeneration was Karlstadt's theme.

That Karlstadt returned to a central emphasis of his early Augustinianism is clear. What the Orlamünde theology described in terms of rebirth or melting into the divine will was really the same inward experience signified in the early period by the Augustinian concept of *justitia* as the divine reclothing of man by the infusion of *amor dei*. But Karlstadt returned to this important Augustinian emphasis without abandoning what he had learned from Luther about sin in good deeds and forgiveness alone as the basis of eternal life. Thus he managed—most of the time—to place inward renewal in the foreground without making it the ground of ultimate salvation.

Gordon Rupp has noted that Luther "knew, as Karlstadt did not, what it means to begin with the bruised conscience which needs peace with God." [385] It would be equally true and more illuminating to say that Karlstadt knew, as Luther did not, what it means to begin with a petty, intensely egocentric personality which badly needs God's regenerating grace. Thus his Orlamünde theology represented a response not only to Luther, but also to himself.

---

Nov. 28, 1522 theses, Kolde, "Wittenberger Disputationsthesen." *ZKG*, XI (1890), 461. See Barge, *Karlstadt*, II, 21 for the date.

[385] *Patterns of Reformation*, p. 152.

APPENDIX

Hans von Taubenheim to Frederick the Wise, October 2, 1524. The original letter is in the Staatsarchiv at Weimar: Ernestinisches Gesamtarchiv Reg O 181. The following includes Folio 1, lines 1-19, Folio 5, lines 25-31. The remainder does not pertain to Karlstadt. Dr. Carl Arthur Piepkorn kindly transcribed the letter.

[Folio 1]
Durchleuchtigster hochgebornner furst, gnedigster here, was vff E. churf. g. bevelh ich bej den beyden techenten des grosen vnd kleynen chors, der styfftungen und ander dynge halben, wie die gehalten, mich erkundet, werden E. churf. g. nachfolgent gnediglich vornemen, vnd zum ersten wie es mit den prebenden zugehee.
Der carlstat hat vff Marie Magdalene negst vorschynnen seyn prebende vfgebn vnd resigniret, vnd das corpus gelt ist jme dis jar allenthalben vmb frydens vnd aynikeit willen zufolgen nachgelassen. Aber das eynkomen diser prebend des nachfolgenden jars wirdt E. churf. g. heymfallen, E. churf. g. gefallens damit zugebaren.
gedachter carlstat hat von der pfarre zu orlamunde jerlich lxxx fl gehabt vnd jnnebehalden vnd das vorgangen jar wyder gepredigt nach gelesen, umb des willen dieselbe pension der lxxx fl zu dem archidiaconat geordenet.

[Folio 5]
datum torgau, sontags nach sant Michaelis tag, Anno domini xv$^c$xxiiij$^o$.
E. churf. g.

vnderteniger
Hans von
thawbenheym

# BIBLIOGRAPHY

## I. PRIMARY SOURCES

### A. *Karlstadt* *

*Ablas—Von vormugen des Ablas*. . . . Wittenberg, 1520. Verzeichnis, No. 29.

*Abtuhung—Von abtuhung der Bylder*. . . . Wittenberg, 1522. Reprinted by Hans Lietzmann, ed., *Andreas Karlstadt: Von Abtuhung der Bilder*. . . . ("Kleine Texte für theologische und philologische Vorlesungen und Übungen," No. 74; Bonn, 1911).

*Anbettung—Von anbettung und ererbietung der tzeychen des newen Testaments*. Wittenberg 1521. Verzeichnis, No. 68.

*Antwort . . . geweicht wasser—Antwort Andres Bo. von Carolstad geweicht wasser belangend*. . . . Wittenberg, 1521. Verzeichnis, No. 49.

*Anzeig—Anzeig etlicher Hauptartickeln Christlicher leere*. . . . [Rothenburg,] 1525. Reprinted in Hertzsch, II, 59-104.

*Appellation—Appellation Andres Bodenstein von Carolstad zu dem allerheyligisten gemeynen Concilio*. . . . Wittenberg, 1520. Verzeichnis, No. 45.

*Ausslegung* (1519)—*Ausslegung und Lewterung etzlicher heyligenn geschrifften*. . . . [Leipzig, 1519.] Verzeichnis, No. 15.

*Auszlegung* (1524)—*Auszlegung dieser wort Christi: Das ist meyn leyb*. . . . [Basel,] 1524. Verzeichnis, No. 129.

*Ayn schöner Sermonn—Ayn schöner Sermonn vonn Spalttung der gütten unnd bössen Engelischen gaystern im himel*. Strassburg, [1524]. Verzeichnis, No. 123.

*Bedingung—Bedingung Andres Bodenstein von Carolstat* . . . Wittenberg, 1520. Verzeichnis, No. 37.

*Bepstlicher heylickeit—Von Bepstlicher heylickeit*. . . . Wittenberg, 1520. Verzeichnis, No. 44.

*Berichtung—Berichtung dyesser red.: Das reich gotis leydet gewaldt*. . . . Wittenberg, 1521. Verzeichnis, No. 63.

*Beyden gestaldten—Von beyden gestaldten der heylige Messze*. . . . Wittenberg, 1521. Verzeichnis, No. 72.

*Confutatio—Confutatio Andreae Carolostadii edita adversus defensivam epistolam Joannis Eckii*. . . . Wittenberg, 1520. Verzeichnis, No. 27.

*De canonicis—De canonicis scripturis libellus*. . . . Wittenberg, 1520. Reprinted in K. A. Credner, *Zur Geschichte des Canons* (Halle, 1847), pp. 316-412.

*Defensio—Defensio Andreae Carolostadii adversus eximii D. Joannis Eckii theologiae . . . monomachiam*. . . . Wittenberg, 1518. Reprinted in V. E. Löscher, *Vollständige Reformations-Acta*, II, 108-170.

*De impii justificatione—Epitome Andree Carolostadii De impii justificatione*. . . . Leipzig, 1519. Verzeichnis, No. 13.

---

* The list is alphabetized according to the abbreviated titles used in the text. The place and date refer to the original edition. The number from the Barge-Freys Verzeichnis indicates the edition actually used in cases where there has been no modern reprint. See H. Barge and E. Freys, "Verzeichnis der gedruckten Schriften des Andreas Bodenstein von Karlstadt," *Zentralblatt für Bibliothekswesen*, XXI (1904), 153ff, 209ff, 305ff. When there has been a modern reprint, the one used is indicated.

*De intentionibus*—*De intentionibus Opusculum Magistri Andree Bodenstein Carlstadii.* . . .
Leipzig, 1507. Verzeichnis, No. 1.

*De legis litera*—*De legis litera sive carne et spiritu.* . . . Wittenberg, 1521. Verzeichnis,
No. 66.

*De sp.*—*Pro divinae gratiae defensione : Sanctissimi Augustini De spiritu et litera liber.* . . .
Wittenberg, 1518-1519. Reprinted in Ernst Kähler, *Karlstadt und Augustin*
(Halle, 1952).

*Dialogus*—*Dialogus oder ein gesprechbüchlin.* . . . [Basel,] 1524. Reprinted in Hertzsch,
II, 5-49.

*Disputatio*—*Disputatio excellentium D. doctorum Johannis Eccii & Andreae Carolostadii.*
. . . [Erfurt, 1519.] Verzeichnis, No. 22. I used Otto Seitz, *Der authentische
Text der Leipziger Disputation* (Berlin, 1903).

*Distinctiones Thomistarum*—*Distinctiones Thomistarum.* Wittenberg, 1508. Verzeichnis, No. 2.

*Empfahern*—*Von den Empfahern, zeychen und zusag des heyligenn Sacraments.* . . .
Wittenberg, 1521. Verzeichnis, No. 54.

*Endschuldigung*—*Endschuldigung D. Andres Carlstads des falschen namens der auffrür.* . . .
Wittenberg, 1525. Reprinted in Hertzsch, II, 105-118.

*Epistola*—*Epistola Andree Carolostadii adversus ineptam et ridiculam inventionem
Joannis Eckii.* . . . [Wittenberg, 1519]. Verzeichnis, No. 25.

*Erklerung*—*Erklerung des X. Capitels Cor. I.* . . . [Rothenburg,] 1525. Verzeichnis,
No. 142.

*Fürbit Marie*—*Ain frage ob auch jemant möge selig werden on die fürbit Marie.* N. p.,
[1524.] Verzeichnis, No. 108.

*Gelaub*—*Wie sich der gelaub und unglaub.* . . . [Basel,] 1524. Verzeichnis, No. 139.

*Gelubden*—*Von gelubden unterrichtung.* . . . Wittenberg, 1521. Verzeichnis, No. 50.

*Gemach*—*Ob man gemach faren und des ergernüssen der schwachen verschonen soll.* . . .
[Basel,] 1524. Reprinted in Hertzsch, I, 73-97.

*Malachiam*—*Predig oder homilien uber den propheten Malachiam gnant.* Wittenberg,
1522. Verzeichnis, No. 93.

*Missbrauch*—*Von dem wider christlichen missbrauch des hern brodt und kelch.* . . . [Basel,]
1524. Verzeichnis, No. 136.

*Missive*—*Missive vonn der aller hochste tugent gelassenheyt.* . . . Wittenberg, 1520.
Verzeichnis, No. 42.

*Ob man . . . erweysen müge*—*Ob man mit heyliger schrifft erweysen müge das Christus mit
leyb, blüt und sele im Sacrament sey.* [Basel,] 1524. Verzeichnis, No. 124.

*Ochssenfart*—*Byt und vermanung an Doctor Ochssenfart.* Wittenberg, 1522. Verzeichnis
No. 92.

*Predig* (Dec. 25, 1521)—*Predig Andresen Boden von Carolstatt.* . . . Wittenberg, 1521.
Verzeichnis, No. 78.

*Priesterthum*—*Von dem Priesterthum und opffer Christi.* Jena, 1523. Verzeichnis, No. 113.

*Sabbat*—*Von dem Sabbat und gebotten feyertagen.* Jena, 1524. Reprinted in Hertzsch,
I, 21-47.

*Sendbrief* (Jan. 5, 1522)—*Sendbrief. D. An. Boden. von Carolstat meldende seiner
Wirtschafft.* . . . Wittenberg, 1522. Verzeichnis, No. 84.

*Sendbryff* (Dec. 10, 1521)—*Sendbryff Adres Boden. von Carolstatt.* . . . Wittenberg,
1521. Verzeichnis, No. 75.

*Sermon vom Stand*—*Ein Sermon vom stand der Christ glaubigen Seelen von Abrahams
schoss.* . . . Wittenberg, 1523. Verzeichnis, No. 95.

*Sich Gelassen*—*Was gesagt ist : Sich gelassen. Unnd was das wort gelassenhait bedeüt.* . . .
N. p., 1523. Verzeichnis, No. 104.

*Super coelibatu*—*Super coelibatu monachatu et viduitate axiomata.* . . . Wittenberg, 1521.
Verzeichnis, No. 62.

*Testament—Von dem Newen und Alten Testament. Antwurt auff disen spruch: Der Kelch das New Testament in meinem blut.* . . . [Rothenburg,] 1525. Verzeichnis, No. 144.

*Teuffelischen fahls—Ap Got ein ursach sey des Teuffelischen falhs.* . . . Jena, 1524. Verzeichnis, No. 114.

*370 Concl.—CCCLXX et apologeticae conclusiones pro sacris literis.* . . . Wittenberg, 1518. Reprinted in V. E. Löscher, *Vollständige Reformations-Acta,* II, 78-104. For theses 102-213, J. Greving, ed., *Johannes Eck: Defensio* (Münster, 1919) was used.

*Ursachen—Ursachen das And. Carolstat ein zeyt still geschwigen.* . . . Jena, 1523. Reprinted in Hertzsch, I, 1-19.

*Ursachen . . . vertryben—Ursachen der halben Andres Carolstatt auss den landen zü Sachsen vertryben.* [Strassburg,] 1524. Reprinted in Hertzsch, II, 50-58.

*Verba Dei—Verba Dei, quanto candore et quam syncere praedicari, quantaque solicitudine universi debeant addiscere.* . . . Wittenberg, 1520. Verzeichnis, No. 26.

*Von manigfeltigkeit—Von manigfeltigkeit des eynfeltigen eynigen willen gottes.* . . . N. p., 1523. Verzeichnis, No. 102.

*Vorstandt—Vorstandt des worts Pauli: Ich begeret ein vorbannter seyn von Christo vor meyne brüder.* . . . Jena, 1524. Verzeichnis, No. 119.

*Wasser u. salcz—Von geweychtem Wasser und salcz.* . . . Wittenberg, 1520. Verzeichnis, No. 33.

*Welche bücher—Welche bücher Biblisch seint.* . . . Wittenberg, 1520. Verzeichnis, No. 48.

*Wider—Wider die alte und newe Papistische Messen.* [Basel,] 1524. Verzeichnis, No. 131.

*Zweyen höchsten gebotten—Von den zweyen höchsten gebotten der lieb Gottes und des nechsten.* . . . Strassburg, 1524. Reprinted in Hertzsch, I, 49-71.

B. *Other*

Bernard de Clairvaux. *Sancti Bernardi Opera.* Ed. J. Leclercq and H. M. Rochais Rome: Editiones Cistercienses, 1957-.

Bihlmeyer, Karl, ed. *Heinrich Seuse: Deutsche Schriften.* Frankfurt am Main: Minerva G. m. b. H., 1961. (Reprint of the 1907 Stuttgart ed.)

Bretschneider, Carolus Gottlieb, ed. *Corpus Reformatorum.* Halis Saxonum: C. A. Schwetschke & Sons, 1834ff.

Duns Scotus, John. *Opera omnia.* 26 vols. Paris: L. Vivès, 1891-1895.

Förstemann, Karl E., ed. *Liber decanorum facultatis theologicae academiae Vitebergensis.* Leipzig: Carolus Tauchnitius, 1838.

Friedberg, Emil. *Corpus juris canonici.* 2 vols. Leipzig: Bernhard Tauchnitz, 1879-1881.

Friedensburg, Walter. *Urkundenbuch der Universität Wittenberg, Teil I, (1502-1611).* ("Geschichtsquellen der Provinz Sachsen und des Freistaates Anhalt," Neue Reihe, No. 3.) Magdeburg: Historische Kommission der Provinz Sachsen, 1926.

Gerdes, Daniel, ed. *Scrinium Antiquarium sive Miscellanea Groningana Nova ad Historiam Reformationis Ecclesiasticam Praecipue Spectantia.* . . . 8 vols. [bound and numbered as four]. Groningen and Bremen: Hajo Spandaw and G. W. Rump, n.d. [c. 1750] - 1765.

Gerson, Jean. *Opera omnia.* 5 vols. Ed. L. E. du Pin. Antwerp, 1706.

Heckel, Johann Friedrich. *Manipulus primus epistolarum singularium, ab heroibus inclutis ac viris illustribus, celebribus ac claris ad Diversos diverso tempore scriptarum.* . . . Plaviae Variscorum: Typis Halleriaris, 1695.

Kawerau, Gustav. *Der Briefwechsel des Justus Jonas.* 2 vols. ("Geschichtsquellen der Provinz Sachsen," No. 7). Halle: Otto Hendel, 1884-1885.

Knaake, J. K. F. ed. *Johann von Staupitzens sämmtliche Werke*. Vol. I: *Deutsche Schriften*. Potsdam: A. Krausnick, 1867.

Köhler, Walther. *Dokumente zum Ablassstreit vom 1517*. ("Sammlung ausgewählter kirchen- und dogmengeschichtlicher Quellenschriften," second series, No. 3.) Tübingen and Leipzig: J. C. B. Mohr, 1902.

Kolde, Th. "Wittenberger Disputationsthesen aus den Jahren 1516 bis 1522," *Zeitschrift für Kirchengeschichte*, XI (1890), 448-471.

Löscher, Valentin Ernst. *Vollständige Reformations-Acta und Documenta*. ... 3 vols. Leipzig: Johann Grossens Erben, 1720-1729.

Luther, Martin. *Dr. Martin Luthers Briefwechsel*. Ed. Ernst Ludwig Enders. 19 vols. Frankfurt am Main, Colw & Stuttgart, 1884-1932.

——. *Dr. Martin Luthers Sämmtliche Schriften*. Ed. Joh. Georg Walch. New edition. 23 vols. in 25. St. Louis, Mo.: Concordia Publishing House, 1880-1910.

——. *D. Martin Luthers Werke*. Weimar: Hermann Böhlau, 1883ff.

——. *Luther's Works*. Ed. Helmut T. Lehmann and Jaroslav J. Pelikan. 55 vols. Philadelphia: Muhlenberg Press, 1955ff.

Mandel, Herm., ed. *Theologia Deutsch*. ("Quellenschriften zur Geschichte des Protestantismus," No. 7.) Leipzig: A. Deichert'sche Verlagsbuchhandlung, 1908.

Migne, Jacques Paul, ed. *Patrologiae cursus completus ... Series latina*. ... 222 vols. Paris: Garnier fratres, 1844-1903.

Müller, Nikolaus. *Die Wittenberger Bewegung 1521 und 1522. Die Vorgänge in und um Wittenberg während Luthers Wartburgaufenthalt. Briefe, Akten u. dgl. und Personalien*. 2nd ed. Leipzig: M. Heinsius Nachfolger, 1911.

Müntzer, Thomas. *Schriften und Briefe: Kritische Gesamtausgabe*. Ed. Günther Franz. ("Quellen und Forschungen zur Reformationsgeschichte," No. 33.) Gütersloh: Gütersloher Verlagshaus Gerd Mohn, 1968.

Pallas, K. "Urkunden, das Allerheiligenstift zu Wittenberg betreffend, 1522-1526 II," *Archiv für Reformationsgeschichte*, XII (1915), 81-131.

Seitz, Otto. *Der authentische Text der Leipziger Disputation (1519): Aus bisher unbenutzten Quellen*. Berlin: C. A. Schwetschke, 1903.

Smith, Preserved, ed. *Luther's Correspondence and Other Contemporary Letters*. 2 vols. Philadelphia: Lutheran Publication Society, 1913-1918.

Staupitz, Johannes von. *Tübinger Predigten*. Ed. Georg Buchwald and E. Wolf. ("Quellen und Forschungen zur Reformationsgeschichte," No. 8.) Leipzig: M. Heinsius Nachfolger, 1927.

Vetter, Ferdinand. *Die Predigten Taulers*. ("Deutsche Texte des Mittelalters," No. 11.) Berlin: Weidmannsche Buchhandlung, 1910.

Weissenborn, J. C. Hermann. *Acten der Erfurter Universität*. ("Geschichtsquellen der Provinz Sachsen," No. 8.) 3 vols. Halle: Otto Hendel, 1881-1899.

## II. SECONDARY SOURCES

### A. *Karlstadt*

Barge, Hermann, ed. *Aktenstücke zur Wittenberger Bewegung Anfang 1522*. Leipzig, 1912.

——. *Andreas Bodenstein von Karlstadt*. 2 vols. Leipzig: Friedrich Brandstetter, 1905.

——. "Der Streit über die Grundlagen der religiösen Erneuerung in der Kontroverse zwischen Luther und Karlstadt 1524/25." *Studium Lipsiense: Ehrengabe Karl Lamprecht*. Berlin: Weidmannsche Buchhandlung, 1909. Pp. 192-213.

——. "Die älteste evangelische Armenordnung," *Historische Vierteljahrschrift*, XI (1908), 193-225.

——. "Die Ubersiedlung Karlstadts von Wittenberg nach Orlamünde," *Zeitschrift des Vereins für thüringische Geschichte und Altertumskunde*, XXI (1913), 338-350.

——. *Frühprotestantisches Gemeindechristentum in Wittenberg und Orlamünde: Zugleich eine Abwehr gegen Karl Müllers "Luther und Karlstadt."* Leipzig: M. Heinsius Nachfolger, 1909.

——. "Luther und Karlstadt in Wittenberg: Eine Kritische Untersuchung," *Historische Zeitschrift*, XCIX (1907), 256-324.

——. "Uber eine vergessene Schrift Karlstadts," *Theologische Studien und Kritiken*, LXXIV (1901), 522-533.

——. "Zur Chronologie und Drucklegung der Abendmahlstraktate Karlstadts," *Zentralblatt für Bibliothekswesen*, XXI (1904), 323-331.

—— and E. Freys. "Verzeichnis der gedruckten Schriften des Andreas Bodenstein von Karlstadt," *Zentralblatt für Bibliothekswesen*, XXI (1904), 153-179, 209-243, 305-323.

Bauch, Gustav. "Andreas Carlstadt als Scholastiker," *Zeitschrift für Kirchengeschichte*, XVIII (1897-1898), 37-57.

Brieger, T. "Thesen Karlstadt's [sic]," *Zeitschrift für Kirchengeschichte*, XI, (1890), 479-482.

Bubenheimer, Ulrich. "Consonantia Theologiae et Jurisprudentiae: Andreas Bodenstein von Karlstadt als Theologe und Jurist auf dem Weg von der Scholastik zur Reformation 1515-1522." Unpublished doctoral dissertation, Eberhard-Karls-Universität at Tübingen, 1971.

Douglas, Crerar. "The Coherence of Andreas Bodenstein von Karlstadt's Early Evangelical Doctrine of the Lord's Supper: 1521-1525." Unpublished Ph. D. thesis, Hartford Seminary Foundation, 1973.

Friedensburg, Walter. "Der Verzicht Karlstadts auf das Wittenberger Archdiakonat und die Pfarre in Orlamünde (1524 Juni)," *Archiv für Reformationsgeschichte*, XI (1914), 69-72.

Fuchs, Gerhard. "Karlstadts radikal-reformatorisches Wirken und seine Stellung zwischen Müntzer und Luther," *Wissenschaftliche Zeitschrift der Martin-Luther-Universität Halle-Wittenberg*, III (1953-1954), 523-551.

Greving, Joseph, ed. *Johannes Eck: Defensio Contra Amarulentas D. Andreae Bodenstein Carolstatini Invectiones (1518)*. ("Corpus Catholicorum," No. 1.) Münster: Aschendorffsche Verlagsbuchhandlung, 1919.

Hase, E. "Karlstadt in Orlamünda," *Mitteilungen der Geschichts- und Altertumsforschende Gesellschaft des Osterlandes*, IV (1858), 42-125.

Hertzsch, Erich. *Karlstadt und seine Bedeutung für das Luthertum*. Gotha: Leopold Klotz, 1932.

——. ed. *Karlstadts Schriften aus den Jahren 1523-1525*. 2 vols. ("Neudrucke deutscher Literaturwerke des 16. und 17. Jahrhunderts," No. 325). Halle (Saale): Max Niemeyer, 1956-1957.

——. "Luther und Karlstadt." *Luther in Thüringen: Gabe der Thüringer Kirche an das Thüringer Volk*. Ed. Reinhold Jauernig. Berlin: Evangelische Verlagsanstalt, 1952. Pp. 87-107.

Hillerbrand, Hans J. "Andreas Bodenstein of Carlstadt," *Church History*, XXXV (1966), 379-398.

Jäger, C. J. *Andreas Bodenstein von Carlstadt: Ein Beitrag zur Geschichte der Reformationszeit aus Originalquellen gegeben*. Stuttgart: Rudolf Besser, 1856.

Kähler, Ernst. "Beobachtungen zum Problem von Schrift und Tradition in der Leipziger Disputation von 1519." *Hören und Handeln: Festschrift für Ernst Wolf zum 60. Geburtstag*. Ed. Helmut Gollwitzer and Hellmut Traub. Munich: Chr. Kaiser Verlag, 1962. Pp. 214-29.

——. "Ein übersehenes Lutherfragment," *Theologische Literaturzeitung*, LXXV (1950), 170-171.

——. *Karlstadt und Augustin: Der Kommentar des Andreas Bodenstein von Karlstadt zu Augustins Schrift De Spiritu et Litera*. ("Hallische Monographien," No. 19). Halle (Saale): Max Niemeyer, 1952.

——. "Karlstadts Protest gegen die theologische Wissenschaft." *450 Jahre Martin-Luther-Universität Halle-Wittenberg*. Vol. I: *Wittenberg 1502-1817*. Halle-Wittenberg: Martin-Luther-Universität, 1952. Pp. 299-312.

——. "Nicht Luther, sondern Karlstadt (zu WA 6, 26f.)," *Zeitschrift für Kirchengeschichte*, LXXXII (1971), 351-60.

Köhler, Walther. A review article. *Göttingische gelehrte Anzeigen*, CLXXIV (1912), 515-550.

Kriechbaum, Friedel. *Grundzüge der Theologie Karlstadts: Eine systematische Studie zur Erhellung der Theologie Andreas von Karlstadts (eigentliche Andreas Bodenstein 1480-1541), aus seinen eignen Schriften entwickelt*. ("Theologische Forschung," No. 43.) Hamburg-Bergstedt: Herbert Reich Evangelischer Verlag, 1967.

Lietzmann, Hans, ed. *Andreas Karlstadt: Von Abtuhung der Bilder und das keyn Bedtler unther den Christen seyn sollen, 1522, und Die Wittenberger Beutelordnung*. ("Kleine Texte für theologische und philologische Vorlesungen und Übungen," No. 74.) Bonn: A. Marcus & E. Weber, 1911.

Müller, Karl. *Luther und Karlstadt: Stücke aus ihrem gegenseitigen Verhältnis*. Tübingen: J. C. B. Mohr, 1907.

Oberman, Heiko A. "Wittenbergs Zweifrontenkrieg gegen Prierias und Eck: Hintergrund und Entscheidungen des Jahres 1518," *ZKG*, 80 (1969), 331-358.

Orr, Russell Stanley. "The Influence of Carlstadt upon Luther and the Reformation." Th. D. thesis, Northern Baptist Theological Seminary, 1935.

Pelikan, Jaroslav J. A review of Ernst Kähler's *Karlstadt und Augustin*. *Archiv für Reformationsgeschichte*, XLV (1954), 268.

Preus, James S. *Karlstadt's "Ordinaciones" and Luther's "Liberty": A Study of the Wittenberg Movement 1521-1522*. Cambridge: Harvard University Press, 1974.

Rupp, Gordon. "Andrew Karlstadt and Reformation Puritanism," *Journal of Theological Studies*, N. S., X (1959), 308-326.

——. *Patterns of Reformation*. Philadelphia: Fortress Press, 1969. Pp. 49-153.

Scheel, Otto. "Individualismus und Gemeinschaftsleben in der Auseinandersetzung Luthers mit Karlstadt 1524/25," *Zeitschrift für Theologie und Kirche*, XVII (1907), 352-375.

Sider, Ronald J. "Karlstadt and Luther's Doctorate," *Journal of Theological Studies*, XXII (1971), 168-69.

——. "Karlstadt's Orlamünde Theology: A Theology of Regeneration," *Mennonite Quarterly Review*, XLV (1971), 191-218, 352-376.

Stupperich, Robert, ed. "Karlstadts Sabbat-Traktat von 1524," *Neue Zeitschrift für systematische Theologie*, I, (1959), 349-375.

Thompson, Alden Lorne. "*Tertius usus legis* in the Theology of Andreas Bodenstein von Karlstadt." Unpublished Ph. D. dissertation, University of Southern California, 1969.

Trefftz, Johannes. "Karlstadt und Glitzsch," *Archiv für Reformationsgeschichte*, VII (1910), 348-350.

Wähler, Martin. *Die Einführung der Reformation in Orlamünde: Zugleich ein Beitrag zum Verständnis von Karlstadts Verhältnis zu Luther*. Erfurt: Karl Villaret, 1918.

Waltz, Otto. "Epistolae Reformatorum," *Zeitschrift für Kirchengeschichte*, II (1878), pp. 128-130.

Wolf, Ernst. "Gesetz und Evangelium in Luthers Auseinandersetzung mit den Schwärmern," *Evangelische Theologie*, V (1938), 96-109.

B. *Other*

Asheim, Ivar, ed. *Kirche, Mystik, Heiligung und das Natürliche bei Luther: Vorträge des Dritten Internationalen Congresses für Lutherforschung.* Göttingen: Vandenhoeck & Ruprecht, 1967.

Bauer, Karl. *Die Wittenberger Universitätstheologie und die Anfänge der Deutschen Reformation.* Tübingen: J. C. B. Mohr, 1928.

Bizer, Ernst. *Fides ex auditu: Eine Untersuchung über die Entdeckung der Gerechtigkeit Gottes durch Martin Luther.* 3rd. ed. Vluyn: Neukirchener Verlag, 1966.

Bizet, J. A. *Henri Suso et le Declin de la Scholastique.* Paris: Aubier, n.d.

——. "Tauler, auteur mystique?" *La Mystique Rhénane: Colloque de Strasbourg 16-19 mai 1961.* Paris: Presses universitaires de France, 1963. Pp. 169-178.

Bornkamm, Heinrich. "Zur Frage der Justitia Dei beim jungen Luther," *Archiv für Reformationsgeschichte,* LII (1962), 16-29 and LIII (1963), 1-60.

Butler, Cuthbert. *Western Mysticism.* 2nd. ed. New York: Harper Torchbooks, 1966.

Champollion, Claire. "La place des termes 'gemuete' et 'grunt' dans le vocabulaire de Tauler." *La Mystique Rhénane: Colloque de Strasbourg 16-19 mai 1961.* Paris: Presses universitaires de France, 1963. Pp 179-192.

Clark, James M. "Johann Tauler." *Spirituality Through the Centuries: Ascetics and Mystics of the Western Church.* Ed. James Walsh. New York: P. J. Kenedy & Sons, 1964. Pp. 209-219.

——. *Meister Eckhart: An Introduction to the Study of his Works with an Anthology of his Sermons.* Edinburgh: Thomas Nelson and Sons, 1957.

Colledge, Eric and M. Jane, trans. and ed. *Spiritual Conferences: John Tauler.* St. Louis, Mo.: B. Herder, 1961.

Credner, Karl August. *Zur Geschichte des Kanons.* Halle: Verlag der Buchhandlung des Waisenhauses, 1847.

Denifle, Heinrich Seuse. *Die Deutsche Mystiker des 14. Jahrhunderts: Beitrag zur Deutung ihrer Lehre.* Freiburg in der Schweiz: Paulusverlag, 1951.

Fife, Robert Herndon. *The Revolt of Martin Luther.* New York: Columbia University Press, 1957.

Filthaut, E., ed. *Johannes Tauler: Ein deutscher Mystiker.* Essen: Hans Driewer Verlag, 1961.

Fischer, E. *Zur Geschichte der evangelischen Beichte.* 2 vols. ("Studien zur Geschichte der Theologie und der Kirche," Band 8, Heft 2 and Band 9, Heft 4.) Leipzig: Dieterich'sche Verlags-Buchhandlung, 1902-1903.

Friedensburg, Walter. *Geschichte der Universität Wittenberg.* Halle a. S.: Max Niemeyer, 1917.

Garside, Charles, Jr. "Ludwig Haetzer's Pamphlet Against Images: A Critical Study," *Mennonite Quarterly Review,* XXXIV (1960), 20-36.

——. *Zwingli and the Arts.* New Haven: Yale University Press, 1966.

Gerdes, Hayo. *Luthers Streit mit den Schwärmern um das rechte Verständnis des Gesetzes Mose.* Göttingen: Göttinger Verlagsanstalt, 1955.

Gilson, Etienne. *The Christian Philosophy of St. Thomas Aquinas.* Trans. L. K. Shook. New York: Random House, 1956.

Goertz, H. J. *Innere und Äussere Ordnung in der Theologie Thomas Müntzers.* ("Studies in the History of Christian Thought," No. 2.) Leiden: E. J. Brill, 1967.

Goeters, J. F. G. "Religiöse Spiritualisten." *Die Religion in Geschichte und Gegenwart.* 3rd. ed. 6 vols. Tübingen: J. C. B. Mohr, 1957-1962. VI, 255-257.

Götze, Alfred. *Frühneuhochdeutsches Glossar.* 6 ed. ("Kleine Texte für Vorlesungen und Übungen," No. 101.) Berlin: Walter de Gruyter, 1960.

Gritsch, Eric W. *Reformer Without A Church: The Life and Thought of Thomas Muentzer.* Philadelphia: Fortress Press, 1967.

Hägglund, Bengt. "The Background of Luther's Doctrine of Justification in Late Medieval Theology," *Lutheran World*, VIII (1961), 24-46.

———. "Luther und die Mystik," *Kirche, Mystik, Heiligung und das Natürliche bei Luther*. Ed. Ivar Asheim. Göttingen: Vandenhoeck & Ruprecht, 1967. Pp. 84-94.

Hamel, Adolf. *Der junge Luther und Augustin: Ihre Beziehungen in der Rechtfertigungslehre nach Luthers ersten Vorlesungen 1509-1518 untersucht*. 2 vols. Gütersloh: C. Bertelsmann, 1934-1935.

Hillerbrand, Hans J. "The Origins of Sixteenth-Century Anabaptism: Another Look," *Archiv für Reformationsgeschichte*, LIII (1962), 152-180.

———. "Thomas Müntzer." *Reformers in Profile*. Ed. B. A. Gerrish. Philadelphia: Fortress Press, 1967. Pp. 213-229.

———. "Thomas Müntzer's Last Tract Against Martin Luther," *Mennonite Quarterly Review*, XXXVIII (1964), 20-36.

Hoernes, J. *Kurze historisch-topographische Beschreibung der Karlsburg und der Stadt Karlstadt*. Karlstadt a. M.: J. Deitz, 1898.

Holl, Karl. "Luther und die Schwärmer." *Gesammelte Aufsätze zur Kirchengeschichte*. 3 vols. 6. ed. Tübingen: J. C. B. Mohr, 1932. I, 420-467.

Kertz, Karl G. "Meister Eckhardt's Teaching on the Birth of the Divine Word in the Soul," *Traditio*, XV (1959), 327-363.

Klaassen, Walter. "Spiritualization in the Reformation," *Mennonite Quarterly Review*, XXXVII (1963), 67-77.

Knowles, David. *The English Mystical Tradition*. New York: Harper Torchbooks, 1965.

Köhler, Walther. *Dogmengeschichte als Geschichte des christlichen Selbstbewusstseins*. Vol. II: *Das Zeitalter der Reformation*. Zurich: Max Niehans Verlag, 1951.

Lohse, Bernhard. "Die Bedeutung Augustins für den jungen Luther," *Kerygma und Dogma*, XI (1965), 116-135.

———. "Die Kritik am Mönchtum bei Luther und Melanchthon." *Luther and Melanchthon: In the History and Theology of the Reformation*. Ed. Vilmos Vajta. Philadelphia: Muhlenberg Press, 1961. Pp. 129-145.

———. *Mönchtum und Reformation: Luthers Auseinandersetzung mit dem Mönchsideal des Mittelalters*. Göttingen: Vandenhoeck and Ruprecht, 1963.

Manschreck, Clyde Leonard. *Melanchthon: The Quiet Reformer*. New York: Abingdon Press, 1958.

Maréchal, Joseph. *Studies in the Psychology of the Mystics*. Trans. Algar Thorold. Albany, New York: Magi Books, Inc., 1964.

Mary, Sylvia. "Contemplation and Mysticism," *Church Quarterly Review*, CLXIV (1963), 83-93.

Moeller, Bernd. "Tauler und Luther." *La Mystique Rhénane: Colloque de Strasbourg, 16-19 mai, 1961*. Paris: Presses universitaires de France, 1963. Pp. 157-168.

Moore, Walter Lane. "Between Mani and Pelagius: Predestination and Justification in the Early Writings of John Eck." Unpublished Th. D. dissertation, Harvard University, 1967.

Müller, Johann Joachim. *Entdecktes Staatscabinet, darinnen so wohl das jus publicum, feudale, und ecclesiasticum ... illustriret wird*. Zweite Eröffnung. Jena: Christian Pohl, 1714.

Neuser, Wilhelm H. *Die Abendmahlslehre Melanchthons in ihrer geschichtlichen Entwicklung (1519-1530)*. Neukirchen-Vluyn: Neukirchener Verlag des Erziehungsvereins, 1968.

Nygren, Anders. "Simul justus et peccator bei Augustin und Luther," *Zeitschrift für systematische Theologie*, XVI (1939), 364-379.

Oberman, Heiko Augustinus. *Forerunners of the Reformation: The Shape of Late Medieval Thought*. New York: Holt, Rinehart and Winston, 1966.

——. *The Harvest of Medieval Theology: Gabriel Biel and Late Medieval Nominalism.* Cambridge: Harvard University Press, 1963.

——. "Simul Gemitus et Raptus: Luther und die Mystik." *Kirche, Mystik, Heiligung und das Natürliche bei Luther.* Ed. Ivar Asheim. Göttingen: Vandenhoeck & Ruprecht, 1967. Pp. 20-59.

Ozment, Steven E. *Homo Spiritualis: A Comparative Study of the Anthropology of Johannes Tauler, Jean Gerson and Martin Luther (1509-1516) in the Context of their Theological Thought.* ("Studies in Medieval and Reformation Thought," No. 6.) Leiden: E. J. Brill, 1969.

Pallas, K., ed. "Die Wittenberger Beutelordnung vom Jahre 1521 und ihr Verhältnis zu der Einrichtung des Gemeinen Kastens im Januar 1522. Aus dem Nachlasse des Professor D. Dr. Nik. Müller-Berlin," *Zeitschrift des Vereins für Kirchengeschichte in der Provinz Sachsen* XII (1915) 1-45 and XIII (1916), 100-137.

Pelikan, Jaroslav J. *Luther the Expositor: Introduction to the Reformer's Exegetical Writings.* St. Louis: Concordia Publishing House, 1959.

——. *Obedient Rebels: Catholic Substance and Protestant Principle in Luther's Reformation.* New York: Harper and Row, 1964.

——. *Spirit Versus Structure: Luther and the Institutions of the Church.* New York: Harper and Row, 1968.

——. "The Theology of the Means of Grace." *Accents in Luther's Theology.* Ed. Heino O. Kadai. St. Louis: Concordia Publishing House, 1967. Pp. 124-147.

Petry, Ray C. *Late Medieval Mysticism.* ("Library of Christian Classics," No. 13.) Philadelphia: Westminster Press, 1957.

Plagnieux, J. "Le Chrétien en face de la Loi d'après le *De Spiritu et Littera* de Saint Augustin." *Theologie in Geschichte und Gegenwart: Michael Schmaus zum sechzigsten Geburtstag.* Ed. Johann Auer and Hermann Volk. München: Karl Zink Verlag 1957. Pp. 364-379.

Prenter, Regin. *Spiritus Creator.* Trans. John M. Jensen. Philadelphia: Muhlenberg Press, 1953.

Riederer, Johann Bartholomäus. *Nachrichten zur Kirchen-Gelehrten-Bücher-Geschichte; gedruckten und ungedruckten Schriften.* 4 vols. Altdorf: Lorenz Schüpfel, 1764-1767.

Rupp, Gordon. "Luther: The Contemporary Image." *Kirche, Mystik, Heiligung und das Natürliche bei Luther.* Ed. Ivar Asheim. Göttingen: Vandenhoeck und Ruprecht, 1967.

——. "Word and Spirit in the First Years of the Reformation," *Archiv für Reformationsgeschichte,* XLIX (1958), 13-26.

Seeberg, Reinhold. *Die Theologie des Johannes Duns Scotus: Eine dogmengeschichtliche Untersuchung.* Leipzig: Dieterich'sche Verlags Buchhandlung, 1900.

Steinmetz, David Curtis. *Misericordia Dei: The Theology of Johannes von Staupitz in its Late Medieval Setting.* Leiden: E. J. Brill, 1968.

Stokes, Francis Griffin, trans. *On the Eve of the Reformation: "Letters of Obscure Men."* New York: Harper Torchbooks, 1964.

Tavard, George H. *Holy Writ or Holy Church: The Crisis of the Protestant Reformation.* London: Burns & Oates, 1959.

Troeltsch, Ernst. *The Social Teaching of the Christian Churches.* Trans. Olive Wyon. 2 vols. New York: Harper Torchbooks, 1960.

Uhrig, Kurt. "Der Bauer in der Publizistik der Reformation bis zum Ausgang des Bauernkrieges," *Archiv für Reformationsgeschichte,* XXXIII (1936), 70-125, 165-225.

Van der Meer, F. *Augustine the Bishop: The Life and Work of a Father of the Church.*

Trans. B. Battershaw and G. R. Lamb. London: Sheed & Ward, 1961.

Vogelsang, Erich. "Luther und die Mystik," *Luther-Jahrbuch 1937 [Jahrbuch der Luther-Gesellschaft]*, XIX (1937), 32-54.

Wappler, Paul. *Thomas Müntzer in Zwickau und die "Zwickauer Propheten."* 2nd. ed. Gütersloh: Gerd Mohn, 1966.

Williams, George Huntston. *The Radical Reformation.* Philadelphia: Westminster, 1962.

———. "Sanctification in the Testimony of Several So-Called Schwärmer." *Kirche, Mystik, Heiligung und das Natürliche bei Luther.* Ed. Ivar Asheim. Göttingen: Vandenhoeck & Ruprecht, 1967.

———. and A. M. Mergal, eds. *Spiritual and Anabaptist Writers.* ("Library of Christian Classics," No. 25.) Philadelphia: Westminster, 1957.

Wolf, Ernst. *Staupitz und Luther: Ein Beitrag zur Theologie des Johannes von Staupitz und deren Bedeutung für Luthers theologischen Werdegang.* ("Quellen und Forschungen zur Reformationsgeschichte," No. 9.) Leipzig: M. Heinsius Nachfolger Eger & Sievers, 1927.

Wyser, Paul. "Der Seelengrund in Taulers Predigten." *Lebendiges Mittelalter: Festgabe für Wolfgang Stammler.* Ed. the Philosophical Faculty of the Universität Freiburg Schweiz. Freiburg: Universitätsverlag, 1958. Pp. 203-311.

# INDEX OF NAMES

# INDEX OF SUBJECTS

## DATE DUE